Lecture Notes in Computer Science 16778

The series Lecture Notes in Computer Science (LNCS), including its subseries Lecture Notes in Artificial Intelligence (LNAI) and Lecture Notes in Bioinformatics (LNBI), has established itself as a medium for the publication of new developments in computer science and information technology research, teaching, and education.

LNCS enjoys close cooperation with the computer science R & D community, the series counts many renowned academics among its volume editors and paper authors, and collaborates with prestigious societies. Its mission is to serve this international community by providing an invaluable service, mainly focused on the publication of conference and workshop proceedings and postproceedings. LNCS commenced publication in 1973.

Kwok Tai Chui · Chen Li · Jiyou Jia ·
Simon K. S. Cheung · Fred Wang-Fat Lee ·
Junjie Shang
Editors

Blended Learning

Innovations for Future Education

19th International Conference on Blended Learning, ICBL 2026
Beijing, China, July 28–31, 2026
Proceedings

Springer

Editors
Kwok Tai Chui
Hong Kong Metropolitan University
Hong Kong, China

Chen Li
The Hong Kong Polytechnic University
Hong Kong, China

Jiyou Jia
Peking University
Beijing, China

Simon K. S. Cheung
Hong Kong Metropolitan University
Hong Kong, China

Fred Wang-Fat Lee
Hong Kong Metropolitan University
Hong Kong, China

Junjie Shang
Peking University
Beijing, China

ISSN 0302-9743 ISSN 1611-3349 (electronic)
Lecture Notes in Computer Science
ISBN 978-981-92-3760-9 ISBN 978-981-92-3761-6 (eBook)
https://doi.org/10.1007/978-981-92-3761-6

This Springer imprint is published by the registered company Springer Nature Singapore Pte Ltd.
The registered company address is: 152 Beach Road, #21-01/04 Gateway East, Singapore 189721, Singapore

Preface

This edited volume consists of the papers selected for the 19th International Conference on Blended Learning (ICBL 2026), held on 28–31 July 2026.

Blended learning has long been a promising approach to integrating traditional teaching with innovative digital means. However, the educational landscape is currently undergoing a seismic shift driven by rapid advancements in artificial intelligence. The emergence of large language models (LLMs) and intelligent pedagogical agents is redefining the boundaries of what is possible in personalised education. ICBL 2026 sought to explore how these cutting-edge technologies are transforming blended learning experience and aimed to provide a premier platform for knowledge exchange and experience sharing among researchers, educators, and practitioners in the field. The conference theme was "Blended Learning: Innovations for Future Education."

ICBL 2026 attracted a total of 116 submissions. After a careful single-blind review process in which submissions each received two or three reviews, 36 papers were selected for inclusion in this volume. These papers are organized into six groups: (i) Collaborative Learning Innovations, (ii) Large Language Models in Education, (iii) Generative Artificial Intelligence in Education, (iv) AI-Enhanced Teaching and Learning, (v) Intelligent Educational Frameworks and Environments, and (vi) Advanced Training and Curriculum Designs.

Our sincere thanks go to the conference's organizing committee for their effective administration and unfailing support. Our thanks also go to the international program committee. The high quality of the papers could not have been maintained without their professional comments and advice in the paper review process. Last but not least, we are grateful for the generous and continuous support from Springer and Hong Kong Pei Hua Education Foundation.

We trust you will enjoy reading the papers.

July 2026

Kwok Tai Chui
Chen Li
Jiyou Jia
Simon K. S. Cheung
Fred Wang-Fat Lee
Junjie Shang

Organization

Organizing Committee

Honorary Chairs

Weifang Min	Peking University, China
Reggie Kwan	Hong Kong Metropolitan University, China

Steering Chairs

Junjie Shang	Peking University, China
Youru Xie	South China Normal University, China
Harrison Hao Yang	State University of New York Oswego, USA
Lam-for Kwok	HKCT Institute of Higher Education (CTIHE), China

Conference Chairs

Kai Jiang	Peking University, China
Fred Wang-Fat Lee	Hong Kong Metropolitan University, China

Technical Program Chairs

Jiyou Jia	Peking University, China
Chen Li	Hong Kong Polytechnic University, China
Kwok Tai Chui	Hong Kong Metropolitan University, China

Organizing Chairs

Junjie Shang	Peking University, China
Yan Keung Hui	Vocational Training Council, Hong Kong, China
Bo Qu	HKCT Institute of Higher Education (CTIHE), China

Conference Treasurer

Steven Ng	Ming-Ai (London) Institute, UK

Publicity Chairs

Sha Zhu	Central China Normal University, China
Yinghui Shi	Hainan College of Software Technology, China
Morris Jong	Chinese University of Hong Kong, China
Leung-Pun Wong	Tung Wah College, China

Webmaster

Fu Zhang	Hong Kong Polytechnic University, China

International Program Committee

Chairs

Jiyou Jia	Peking University, China
Chen Li	Hong Kong Polytechnic University, China
Kwok Tai Chui	Hong Kong Metropolitan University, China

Members

Jie Cao	Beijing Institute of Education, China
Peijie Cao	China National Academy of Educational Sciences, China
Chih-Tsan Chang	Cheng Shiu University, Taiwan
Simon Cheung	Hong Kong Metropolitan University, China
Anmei Dong	Beijing City University, China
Yizhou Fan	Peking University, China
Achmad Nizar Hidayanto	Universitas Indonesia, Indonesia
Yuki Hirai	Shinshu University, Japan
Jenq-Muh Hsu	National Chiayi University, Taiwan
Changqin Huang	Zhejiang University, China
Wendan Huang	Guilin University of Electronic Technology, China
John Hui	Vocational Training Council, Hong Kong, China

Morris Jong	Chinese University of Hong Kong, China
Lam For Kwok	HKCT Institute of Higher Education (CTIHE), China
Fred Lee	Hong Kong Metropolitan University, China
Shuang Li	Beijing Normal University, China
Xiuhan Li	Central China Normal University, China
Jing Liu	Hong Kong Baptist University, China
Yu Liu	Peking University, China
Angel Lu	Hong Kong University of Science and Technology, China
Heng Luo	Central China Normal University, China
Peter Mitchell	Majan University College, Oman
Terumi Miyazoe	Tokyo University of Science, Japan
Naomi Nagata	Shizuoka Sangyo University, Japan
Peter Ng	Hong Kong Polytechnic University, China
Steven Ng	Ming-Ai (London) Institute, UK
Naraphorn Paoprasert	Kasetsart University, Thailand
Diana Perez-Marin	Rey Juan Carlos University, Spain
Kongkiti Phusavat	Kasetsart University, Thailand
Petra Poulova	University of Hradec Králové, Czech Republic
Bo Qu	HKCT Institute of Higher Education (CTIHE), China
Ehsan Rassaei	Majan University College, Oman
Wong Yoke Seng	Sultan Idris Education University, Malaysia
Shengpeng Shi	Beijing Normal University, China
Yinghui Shi	Hainan College of Software Technology, China
Libuše Svobodová	University of Hradec Králové, Czech Republic
Jeff Tang	Hong Kong Polytechnic University, China
Cixiao Wang	Beijing Normal University, China
Mengqian Wang	Capital Normal University, China
Shu-ming Wang	Chinese Culture University, Taiwan
Xiaodong Wei	Northwest Normal University, China
Billy Wong	Hong Kong Metropolitan University, China
Qi Xia	Zhejiang University, China
Di Zou	Hong Kong Polytechnic University, China
Youru Xie	South China Normal University, China
Ramidayu Yousuk	Kasetsart University, Thailand
Jialing Zeng	Peking University, China
Lu Zhang	Beijing University of Posts and Telecommunications, China
Xuehan Zhou	Peking University, China
Sha Zhu	Central China Normal University, China

Wangda Zhu Hong Kong Polytechnic University, China

Organizer

Graduate School of Education, Peking University

Co-organizers

Hong Kong Metropolitan University

Hong Kong Society for Multimedia and Image Computing

Tung Wah College

HKCT Institute of Higher Education

Sponsors

Springer

Hong Kong Pei Hua Education Foundation

Keynote Speakers

Ning Ma	Beijing Normal University, China
Minjuan Wang	Education University of Hong Kong, China
Josep Duart	Universitat Oberta de Catalunya, Spain
Kam Cheong Li	Middlesex University London, UK

Contents

Keynotes

University Leadership in AI-Driven Digital Transformation: A European Perspective Through the TOP Model

Josep M. Duart(✉) and Marc Romero

Universitat Oberta de Catalunya, Ramble del Poblenou 156, 08011 Barcelona, Spain
jduart@uoc.edu

Abstract. The rapid advancement of artificial intelligence (AI) is fundamentally reshaping higher education systems worldwide, compelling universities to reconsider their missions, governance structures, and leadership models. This article examines the evolving role of university leadership in the context of AI-driven digital transformation, adopting the Technology–Organization–Pedagogy (TOP) model, developed by the Edul@b Research Group at the Universitat Oberta de Catalunya (UOC), as an analytical framework. Grounded in the European higher education tradition, with its particular commitments to quality assurance, inclusivity, and public value, the paper identifies the principal challenges and opportunities associated with integrating AI into teaching, learning, and institutional governance. Drawing on a range of foundational scholarship, including UNESCO's Guidance for Generative AI in Education and Research (2023), systematic reviews of AI in higher education (Crompton & Burke, 2023), critical perspectives on the limits of AI (Selwyn, 2024; Molenaar, 2022; Luckin, 2018), a literature review on e-leadership for technology-enhanced learning (Arnold & Sangrà, 2018), and the Bologna Digital 2020 White Paper (Rampelt, Orr, & Knoth, 2019), the article argues that effective leadership must move beyond technological adoption toward systemic transformation, emphasizing ethical responsibility, organizational culture change, and genuinely human-centered approaches to educational design. Strategic directions for university leaders are proposed within each dimension of the TOP model, and the relevance of a productive East-West dialogue, particularly between European quality assurance traditions and China's leadership in AI development and deployment, is explored.

Keywords: University Leadership · Artificial Intelligence · Digital Transformation · TOP Model · European Higher Education · Quality Assurance · Ethics · Hybrid Intelligence

1 Introduction

Higher education is undergoing a profound transformation driven by the rapid development of artificial intelligence (AI). While digital learning has been evolving for several decades, AI introduces a qualitatively new level of complexity, scale, and institutional

K. T. Chui et al. (Eds.): ICBL 2026, LNCS 16778, pp. 3–15, 2027.
https://doi.org/10.1007/978-981-92-3761-6_1

impact. Universities are no longer simply adopting technologies to support teaching and learning; they are being reconfigured as complex digital ecosystems in which data, algorithms, and human actors interact in ways that resist straightforward management or control.

In this context, university leadership has become a critical variable. The challenge is not merely technological but systemic: how to guide institutions through transformation while preserving their foundational values of academic freedom, quality, equity, and societal contribution. This challenge is compounded by the pace of AI development, which consistently outstrips the capacity of regulatory and institutional frameworks to respond. As UNESCO [1] has documented, when ChatGPT reached 100 million monthly active users in January 2023, only one country in the world had released formal regulations on generative AI. The implications for higher education governance are significant.

This article proposes the Technology, Organization, Pedagogy (TOP) model as a framework for understanding and guiding leadership responses to AI-driven digital transformation. The argument is situated within a European higher education perspective, characterized by strong institutional commitments to quality assurance, inclusive access, and the public value of higher education, while engaging critically with global developments, including the remarkable pace of AI innovation and deployment in China. The article begins by contextualizing the current AI moment within the longer history of digital learning, before introducing and developing the TOP model as a leadership framework. It then elaborates the distinctive contributions of the European higher education tradition to AI governance and proposes concrete strategic directions for institutional leaders within each dimension of the model. The article concludes by reflecting on the productive possibilities of East-West dialogue in this domain, and by drawing together the central argument for pedagogy-centered, values-driven university leadership in the AI era.

2 From Digital Learning to AI-Driven Transformation: Understanding the Shift

It is important to situate the current AI moment within the longer trajectory of digital transformation in higher education, both to appreciate what is genuinely new and to avoid the recurrent error of treating each technological generation as unprecedented. As Siemens, Gašević, and Dawson [2] demonstrate in their comprehensive history of distance, blended, and online learning, higher education has navigated multiple waves of technological change, from correspondence education in the nineteenth century, through broadcast and audio-conferencing models, to the interactive online environments of the 2000s and the emergence of MOOCs in the 2010s. Each wave brought substantial promises of disruption; each time, the fundamentals of pedagogy proved more durable than the technology itself.

This insight retains its force in the AI era. What distinguishes AI from previous technological waves is not simply its computational power, but its apparent capacity to engage in functions previously considered exclusively human: reasoning, explaining, creating, assessing, and adapting to individual learners. Generative AI systems can produce coherent text, generate assessment questions, and provide personalized feedback at a scale and speed that no human educator can match. Yet, as UNESCO [1] notes, these systems "cannot generate new ideas or solutions to real-world challenges, as they do not understand real-world objects or social relations that underpin language." The gap between appearance and capability is consequential, particularly in educational contexts.

Crompton and Burke's [3] systematic review of 138 peer-reviewed studies on AI in higher education from 2016 to 2022 confirms that the field has moved well beyond experimentation. AI is being operationally deployed for assessment and evaluation, for predictive analytics, as intelligent tutoring systems, as AI assistants, and for the management of student learning. Notably, the volume of publications approximately doubled in 2021–2022 compared to prior years, a trend plausibly accelerated by the COVID-19 pandemic and its forcing function on digital adoption. China has emerged as the leading country in terms of publication volume, surpassing the United States, a development that itself signals a significant geopolitical reorientation of the field.

However, several critical scholars urge caution against what Selwyn [4] terms 'AI-fever': the tendency to attribute to AI capabilities it does not possess and to project onto educational systems transformations that remain undemonstrated. Selwyn reminds us that current AI systems constitute 'narrow artificial intelligence', designed to address specific, bounded tasks, rather than the generalized intelligence sometimes implied in popular discourse. Critically, AI systems operate through statistical approximation, and these approximations are systematically fragile in the complex, contextually embedded environments that characterize real classrooms and real learning. Molenaar [5] offers a more constructive framing through what she terms the augmentation perspective: AI should be understood not as a replacement for human intelligence but as a means of augmenting it, with the goal of optimizing the complementary strengths of human and artificial cognition. This framing, what Molenaar calls hybrid human-AI intelligence, provides a productive basis for institutional leadership.

3 The Technology, Organization and Pedagogy (TOP) Model: A Framework for Systemic Leadership

University leadership responses to AI cannot be reduced to procurement decisions, policy documents, or the appointment of specialist officers. The challenge is genuinely systemic: it requires the disciplined alignment of three deeply interconnected dimensions: Technology, Organization, and Pedagogy. The TOP model provides a conceptual framework for this systemic work, drawing on a long tradition of organizational change theory that holds that technology alone does not transform institutions. What transforms institutions is the alignment of technology, organizational structures, and pedagogical practice, held together by leadership capable of acting across all three dimensions simultaneously and under conditions of genuine uncertainty.

Developed by the Edul@b Research Group at the Universitat Oberta de Catalunya, the TOP model can be represented conceptually as an equilateral triangle (Edul@b Research Group, 2026): *Pedagogy* occupies the apex position, reflecting its role as the nucleus of the educational process and the compass of all institutional decisions; *Technology* occupies the lower-left vertex, providing the environments, data, and means for digital learning; and *Organisation* occupies the lower-right vertex, ensuring governance, resources, and sustainability. At the centre of the triangle sits student learning, understood as an active process that is guided, accompanied, and assessed against competences. This architecture makes visible a fundamental principle: quality in digital higher education depends not on any single dimension but on the coherence and equilibrium among all three. In addition to its analytical function, the model serves as a practical evaluation instrument: each dimension is operationalised through structured indicator clusters that can support institutional self-assessment, quality assurance processes, strategic planning, and programme accreditation (see Table 1).

Table 1. The TOP Model: dimensions, primary purpose, and quality axis.

Dimension	Primary Purpose	Quality Axis
Technology	Guarantee reliable, innovative, and secure digital environments	Accessibility, digital competences, learning analytics, and data security
Organisation	Ensure sustainability, coherence, and governance of the digital model	Strategy, management, leadership, and resources
Pedagogy	Orient meaningful, student-centred learning	Active methodologies, student support, and formative assessment

3.1 Technology: Infrastructure, Integrity, and Purposeful Design

The technology dimension concerns the AI systems themselves, the infrastructure that houses them, the data that trains them, and the governance frameworks that constrain and direct them. University leaders must develop what might be called strategic technological literacy: not the technical expertise to build AI systems, but the conceptual fluency to make principled decisions about what kind of AI ecosystem their institution should pursue.

The five indicator clusters of the Technology dimension operationalise this governance agenda. The first concerns technology-linked innovation (T1): the systematic revision of virtual programmes to incorporate new tools that generate genuine pedagogical and organisational value, and the interoperation of institutional systems—learning management platforms, academic management, digital libraries, and evaluation systems—into a coherent ecosystem. The second cluster addresses faculty digital competence (T2): not only possession of the technical skills required for virtual teaching, but institutional implementation of systematic training plans encompassing the creation and exchange of digital content, the management of digital technologies for teaching and assessment, and the pedagogical application of digital evaluation strategies. The third cluster concerns student digital competence (T3), recognising that quality virtual education depends equally on the digital skills of learners, who must be equipped to navigate virtual programmes autonomously and critically. The fourth cluster specifies the virtual learning environment (T4): universal accessibility, reliable technical support, mobile access and low-connectivity functionality to ensure equity across diverse learner populations, the integration of digital educational resources and multimedia, and learning analytics dashboards that support evidence-based pedagogical and management decisions. The fifth cluster, data security and AI governance (T5), encompasses compliance with personal data protection norms, security and backup protocols, cybersecurity orientation for faculty and students, and—of particular relevance in the current moment—the institutional articulation of a clear, publicly communicated position on the use of artificial intelligence in educational processes and management.

Several specific governance concerns warrant institutional attention. First, interoperability: AI systems adopted in silos, without attention to integration with existing learning management infrastructure, create fragmentation rather than enhancement. Second, data governance: the data generated by students' interactions with AI systems raises fundamental questions of ownership, consent, and permissible use that institutional policies must address proactively. Third, what UNESCO [1] describes as the detect-diagnose-act cycle of educational AI (the process by which AI systems collect learner data, diagnose learner states, and act to adapt the educational experience) carries ethical weight at each stage that must be made visible in governance frameworks.

Molenaar's [5] six-level model of automation provides a particularly useful conceptual tool for leaders navigating decisions about AI deployment. The model maps AI use cases across a spectrum from full teacher control (Level 1), through teacher assistance, partial automation, and conditional automation, to full automation (Level 6). Molenaar argues, and the analogy with AI in medicine supports, that conditional automation (Level 4), in which AI executes a broad range of tasks and takes primary responsibility for monitoring, but the teacher remains informed and retains the right to resume control, represents the appropriate ceiling for formal educational settings. This is not a conservative argument against AI capability; it is a principled argument for maintaining meaningful human accountability in educational decisions.

Perhaps most importantly, the technology dimension requires leaders to resist what Selwyn [4] terms 'reverse adaptation': the tendency, well documented in the history of educational technology, for institutions and individuals to adapt their practices to the demands of the technology, rather than demanding that the technology serve their educational purposes. Strategic AI adoption requires a prior clarity of educational purpose that must precede, not follow, technology selection.

3.2 Organization: Governance, Quality, and Cultural Transformation

The organizational dimension is, in many respects, the most challenging, because it requires changing institutions; and institutions are, by their nature, resistant to change. Organizational transformation encompasses governance structures, quality assurance mechanisms, institutional strategy, and, most fundamentally, culture. The evidence is unequivocal that technological investment without organizational alignment produces negligible educational improvement.

The six indicator clusters of the Organisation dimension operationalise this work (Edul@b Research Group, 2026). They span institutional identity and educational model (O1): the explicit embedding of digital provision in institutional strategic plans and the transparency of the competence-based educational model for the whole community; planning and management (O2): the existence of strategic and operational plans, proactive course planning, internal evaluation and feedback mechanisms, and a flexible, adaptive management culture; technological resources (O3): adequate and continuously updated infrastructure; leadership (O4): clearly identified programme leaders and the fostering of collaborative working across academic units, administrative areas, and faculty teams; communication (O5): effective internal and external channels, maintained digital spaces for the educational community; and faculty management (O6): appropriate student-faculty ratios, balanced teaching and accompaniment loads, continuity mechanisms, and rigorous faculty selection and evaluation systems.

Arnold and Sangrà's [6] systematic review of e-leadership for technology-enhanced learning in higher education (2013–2017) reinforces several of these emphases. Their review finds that the most consistently cited concept in this field is *distributed leadership*, present in 26% of empirical studies and 38% of theoretical analyses, alongside the themes of e-leadership visioning, strategic planning, values and culture, and continuous professional development. These findings support the argument that the governance challenges of digital transformation are not reducible to hierarchical command or specialist expertise; they require what Arnold and Sangrà [6] describe as a 'holistic multi-stakeholder' approach, simultaneously attending to macro-level policy factors, meso-level institutional strategy, and micro-level teaching and learning. Their review also highlights, in line with the TOP model, the decisive role of *organisational culture* and the complementary importance of using data for decision-making–findings that give further empirical grounding to the model's organisational indicators.

Crompton and Burke's [3] findings are instructive here. Zawacki-Richter et al.'s landmark 2019 systematic review, subtitled, pointedly, 'Where Are the Educators?', found that only 6% of AI in higher education studies were authored by researchers affiliated with schools of education; the field was dominated by computer scientists with limited pedagogical expertise. By 2022, this had been substantially corrected: education had become the most common departmental affiliation among first authors, at 28%. This shift did not happen spontaneously; it reflects deliberate institutional choices to bring educational expertise into AI governance and research. It is a concrete example of organizational transformation enabled by leadership with explicit values.

Organizationally, leaders must ensure that AI integration is aligned with, rather than imposed upon, institutional mission. UNESCO [1] is unequivocal on this point: AI governance must be embedded in quality assurance frameworks, not treated as a separate compliance domain. In the European context, this means extending the principles of the Standards and Guidelines for Quality Assurance in the European Higher Education Area (ESG) to encompass AI-specific dimensions: transparency in algorithmic decision-making, accountability for AI-generated assessments, and evidence of student learning outcomes in AI-enhanced programs. These are not abstract aspirations; they are practical governance requirements that European quality assurance agencies should be developing methodologies to assess.

The cultural dimension of organizational transformation is equally significant. A culture of responsible AI adoption is one in which both enthusiasm and skepticism are institutionally valued, in which faculty feel safe to experiment and equally safe to raise concerns, and in which ethical responsibility is understood as a distributed institutional competency rather than a specialist function. Such a culture does not emerge from policy documents; it is modelled by leadership through visible, consistent, and substantively grounded engagement.

3.3 Pedagogy: Instructional Design, Learning Frameworks, and Human-Centered Educational Practice

The pedagogy dimension is the most educationally distinctive element of the TOP model, because it directs attention to what no amount of technological infrastructure or organizational restructuring can substitute: the design of learning experiences, the choice of instructional frameworks, and the cultivation of deep learning through human-centered educational practice.

The six indicator clusters of the Pedagogy dimension provide a structured vocabulary for this work (Edul@b Research Group, 2026). Educational innovation (P1) encompasses research into virtual learning, the diffusion of updated pedagogical knowledge, and the continuous incorporation of new teaching-learning strategies and materials. Teaching didactic competence (P2) proposes a common reference framework of pedagogical competences for faculty, supported by specific training plans, with the teacher acting as facilitator, guide, and learning mentor rather than content transmitter. Student competence (P3) identifies a reference model for students' autonomous, active, and collaborative learning in virtual environments. Content and methodologies (P4) specifies active, student-centred approaches grounded in professional contexts and diversified through problem-based learning, project-based learning, and case methods. Comprehensive student accompaniment (P5) covers personalised progress monitoring, attention to equity, gender perspective, and special educational needs, and guaranteed faculty presence with strategic use of asynchronous interaction. Finally, the assessment model (P6) ensures that learning outcomes and competences are clearly defined and communicated, that assessment instruments are designed in alignment with those outcomes, and that evaluation is integrated into the learning process with a formative orientation.

Luckin [7] argues, with considerable force, that current approaches to AI risk impoverishing our understanding of human intelligence precisely at the historical moment when AI appears most powerful. By investing AI with qualities it does not possess genuine understanding, moral agency, creative originality, and by failing to cultivate the full complexity of human capacities, we risk a compounding educational error: undervaluing what humans distinctively bring to learning while overvaluing what machines can provide. Education, on Luckin's account [7], must become explicitly an enterprise of developing and expanding human intelligence in all its dimensions: metacognitive, collaborative, emotional, and ethical, rather than simply transmitting content that AI can now summarize on demand.

UNESCO [1] captures the pedagogical risk with particular clarity, noting that some experts have characterized AI-assisted writing as 'writing without thinking', a phrase that identifies the core concern. Writing, as a cognitive practice, is constitutive of the thinking it produces; outsourcing the act risks outsourcing the cognition. University leaders must therefore champion assessment reform that values the cognitive processes of learning: the struggle, the revision and the judgment, rather than only the products that AI can now simulate.

For faculty, the pedagogy dimension requires investment in instructional design capacity that is more than technical training. Faculty need conceptual frameworks for evaluating AI tools critically, pedagogical strategies for designing AI-enhanced learning experiences that preserve intellectual depth, and ethical literacy for navigating complex situations, including questions of academic integrity, algorithmic bias, and the appropriate limits of AI delegation in assessment contexts. UNESCO's [1] survey data reveal that as of 2023, only seven countries had developed formal AI training programs for educators; for most university faculty worldwide, AI literacy remains largely self-acquired and uneven. Addressing this gap must be treated as a strategic institutional investment.

For students, leaders should champion AI competency development that encompasses critical evaluation of AI outputs, understanding of AI limitations, and active preservation of intellectual agency. The risk of what Selwyn [4] calls 'adapting to the algorithm', writing, thinking, and acting in ways designed to be machine-readable, is particularly acute for learners who may lack the prior knowledge to recognize when AI outputs are superficial, biased, or simply wrong.

4 A European Perspective: Quality, Equity, and Public Value

The European higher education tradition offers a distinctive set of values and institutional frameworks that are particularly relevant to the challenge of AI governance. Three commitments merit specific attention: quality assurance, equity and inclusion, and the public value of universities as social institutions.

4.1 Quality Assurance in the AI Era

European quality assurance in higher education has been constructed, over several decades, on principles of transparency, peer review, and evidence of student learning. These principles were developed for a world in which the primary variables were curriculum design, teaching quality, and assessment practice. AI introduces new variables as algorithmic decision-making, data-driven personalization and automated assessment, that existing quality assurance frameworks were not designed to address.

The urgency of this challenge is underscored by European policy evidence. The Bologna Digital 2020 White Paper [8], drawing on the 2018 Bologna Implementation Report, notes that fewer than half of EHEA member states–specifically, sixteen countries–had adapted their legal frameworks and external quality assurance procedures to facilitate and monitor digital provision. As the European Association for Quality Assurance in Higher Education (ENQA) has acknowledged, QA agencies must develop external review methodologies that take appropriate account of the particularities of e-learning, while traditional institutions providing digital or blended programmes must correspondingly adapt their internal quality assurance systems in order to guarantee the quality of their teaching and learning processes ([9], as cited in [8]). At the same time, the 2015 Yerevan Communiqué of EHEA ministers had explicitly committed to 'promoting pedagogical innovation in student-centred learning environments and in fully exploiting the potential benefits of digital technologies for learning and teaching' ([10], as cited in [8]), and the 2018 Paris Communiqué reinforced this agenda, calling on higher education institutions to 'prepare their students and support their teachers to act creatively in a digitalised environment' and to 'make better use of digital and blended education, with appropriate quality assurance' ([11], as cited in [8]). The challenge, in short, is to extend established ESG principles into genuinely new methodological territory at a pace commensurate with the speed of AI deployment.

The extension of quality assurance principles to AI-enhanced education requires developing methodologies for evaluating whether AI tools produce genuine educational benefit, whether their outputs are accurate and unbiased for the student populations they serve, and whether their use is pedagogically appropriate for the learning objectives at stake. This is a substantial methodological challenge, but it is one that European quality assurance agencies are well positioned to lead, given their experience with evidence-based evaluation and their existing networks of institutional cooperation.

4.2 Equity and the Risk of Algorithmic Discrimination

European education policy is strongly committed to equitable access and inclusive participation. AI can support this commitment, through personalized support for diverse learners, early identification of at-risk students, and intelligent accessibility tools for learners with disabilities. However, the evidence of AI's capacity to perpetuate and amplify existing inequalities is substantial and must not be minimized.

Selwyn [4] documents multiple verified cases of algorithmic discrimination in educational settings: automated grading systems that systematically favor students from privileged backgrounds; facial recognition systems that fail to correctly identify students of color; AI writing detection tools that discriminate against non-native English speakers, whose work tends to be written more formulaically and is thus more likely to be misidentified as AI-generated. These are not theoretical risks; they are operational harms, arising in institutions that adopted AI with entirely good intentions. UNESCO [1] is correspondingly explicit: AI systems must be validated for bias, including gender bias and discrimination against marginalized groups, before institutional deployment, and this validation must be ongoing throughout the system's lifecycle.

4.3 Public Value and Ethical Responsibility

Perhaps the most distinctive feature of the European higher education tradition is its understanding of universities as public institutions, entities that exist not merely to serve individual students and graduate employers, but to generate knowledge, cultivate critical citizenship, and contribute to the democratic health of the societies that fund and legitimate them. This public mission has substantive implications for AI governance.

When AI systems are adopted in ways that erode faculty judgment, narrow the intellectual range of the curriculum, homogenize student outputs, or compromise academic integrity, they threaten this public mission. When AI is used to surveil students, to make consequential decisions without transparency, or to extract economic value from student data for commercial purposes, it betrays the institutional trust on which universities depend. The concept of a human-centered approach to AI, elaborated in UNESCO's [12]

Recommendation on the Ethics of Artificial Intelligence and operationalized in the 2023 guidance for education, provides a normative foundation for European universities navigating these questions: AI must be at the service of human development, transparently governed, and accountable to public values.

5 Strategic Directions for University Leadership

The following strategic directions are proposed within each dimension of the TOP model, with the intention of providing a framework for institutional action rather than a prescriptive checklist.

5.1 Technology Strategy: Build with Explicit Educational Purpose

The foundational principle of strategic AI adoption in higher education is the primacy of educational purpose. Technology selection should follow a clear articulation of the educational problem to be addressed, the learning outcome to be improved, and the evidence base that supports the proposed intervention. Siemens, Gašević, and Dawson [2] identified this error at the dawn of the MOOC era, warning that institutions that run forward on new technology alone, ignoring the landscape of existing pedagogical knowledge, will produce sub-optimal and likely harmful outcomes. The lesson remains relevant.

Concretely, this strategy requires establishing interdisciplinary AI validation structures with genuine representation from educational researchers, ethicists, student representatives, and faculty, as well as technologists. It requires developing institutional data governance frameworks that specify the conditions under which student data may be used, stored, and shared. And it requires piloting AI tools in carefully designed, evidence-gathering contexts before any institution-wide deployment, with pre-specified criteria for success and clear protocols for intervention if harms are identified.

5.2 Organizational Strategy: Lead Culture, not Only Structure

Organizational transformation requires cultural change as well as structural reform, and cultural change is fundamentally a leadership function. Structural changes—new governance committees, revised quality assurance procedures, updated institutional AI policies are necessary but not sufficient. The culture of an institution is shaped by what its leaders visibly prioritize, model, and reward.

Leaders should explicitly frame AI governance as an expression of institutional values, not merely a compliance requirement. This means articulating, in public and institutional forums, the non-negotiables: that human judgment will not be delegated entirely to algorithms in high-stakes educational decisions; that student privacy will be protected; that equity of outcome, not only equity of access, will be the criterion against which AI tools are evaluated. Molenaar's [5] framework suggests that conditional automation, in which AI operates with broad delegated authority but human oversight is meaningfully preserved, should be established as the institutional norm for formal educational settings, with this norm embedded in governance documents and institutional culture alike.

The Bologna Digital 2020 White Paper [8] identifies five institutional principles that should characterise strategies for higher education in the digital age: (1) a clear institutional profile that guides overall strategy; (2) a strategic vision that emphasises specific teaching and learning objectives; (3) meaningful involvement of teaching staff, administrative staff, and student representatives in strategy design and implementation; (4) sustained capacity-building efforts for teaching and administrative staff; and (5) a visible, shared monitoring framework. Developed through consultation with representative bodies across the EHEA, these principles provide a concrete governance template that complements the organisational dimension of the TOP model. Arnold and Sangrà's [6] finding that distributed leadership is the dominant leadership approach in empirical studies of TEL governance further suggests that the implementation of such a strategy must be genuinely participatory rather than top-down in character.

5.3 Pedagogy Strategy: Ground AI Integration in Instructional Design

The most fundamental strategic imperative is to ensure that AI integration in higher education is pedagogically driven rather than technology driven. No AI system, however sophisticated, can substitute for sound instructional design: the deliberate alignment of learning objectives, teaching methods, learning activities, and assessment that constitutes effective educational practice.

Concretely, this means investing in faculty development that builds capacity for designing AI-enhanced learning experiences grounded in established pedagogical principles, such as Molenaar's [5] hybrid human-AI regulation approach, in which AI scaffolds support learner self-regulation rather than replace it. It means redesigning curricula and assessment frameworks so that AI tools serve specific, evidence-based learning objectives rather than being adopted for efficiency alone. And it means treating the co-design of AI-enhanced learning, involving faculty, students, educational researchers, and instructional designers, as the appropriate process for pedagogical innovation, resisting the top-down imposition of AI tools without prior pedagogical validation [1].

6 East-West Dialogue: Complementary Traditions in a Global Field

The global field of AI in higher education is being shaped, in substantial measure, by developments in China. Crompton and Burke's [3] systematic review documents that China has surpassed the United States as the leading country in AI-in-education publications. From a regulatory perspective, UNESCO [1] notes that China was the only country, as of July 2023, to have released specific official regulations on generative AI-the Provisional Regulations on Governing the Service of Generative AI, issued on 13 July 2023-requiring the labelling of AI-generated content, specifying standards for providers, and placing the governance of generative AI within a coherent national framework. This regulatory leadership represents a seriousness of institutional purpose that deserves recognition and engagement from European counterparts.

At the same time, the European tradition contributes distinctive resources to the global conversation. The European emphasis on ethical frameworks grounded in human rights principles, the ESG-based quality assurance infrastructure, the commitment to minority language inclusion and cultural diversity in AI training data, and the long experience of building multi-stakeholder accountability structures for public institutions. These are genuine contributions to a global dialogue, not merely regional preferences.

The most productive framing for this dialogue is not competition but complementarity. China contributes scale, technical innovation, rapid implementation capacity, and extensive experience of extending educational access across geographically and linguistically diverse populations through technology. Europe contributes institutional frameworks for ethical governance, academic freedom, intellectual pluralism, and evidence-based quality assurance. A genuinely collaborative inquiry of the kind that multilateral bodies like UNESCO are positioned to facilitate could produce governance frameworks, research methodologies, and pedagogical innovations that neither tradition could achieve alone.

7 Conclusions

The integration of artificial intelligence into higher education is not a future prospect but a present reality. The question for university leadership is not whether to engage with AI but how to govern that engagement in ways that serve the educational mission, protect students and faculty, and contribute to the societies universities exist to serve.

The TOP model: Technology, Organization, Pedagogy, provides a framework for this leadership challenge that is at once analytically rigorous and practically actionable. It insists that technology cannot be managed in isolation from organizational culture and pedagogical design, and that the alignment of all three dimensions requires sustained, values-driven leadership. The European higher education perspective, grounded in quality assurance, equity, and public value, provides normative resources that are directly relevant to the principal governance challenges that AI presents.

Perhaps most importantly, this analysis supports UNESCO's [1] foundational claim that it is unlikely that AI alone will solve the fundamental challenges facing education systems around the world, and that human capacity and collective action, not technology, remains the determining factor in effective responses to those challenges. The TOP model is, ultimately, a model of leadership: leadership that acts systemically, that is anchored in educational values, and that understands the pedagogy dimension of transformation as both its compass and its standard.

AI changes the technological landscape of higher education. It does not alter its fundamental mission: to expand human understanding, cultivate human potential, and contribute to the flourishing of the societies that depend on it.

References

1. UNESCO. Guidance for generative AI in education and research. United Nations Educational, Scientific and Cultural Organization (2023). https://doi.org/10.54675/EWZM9535

2. Siemens, G., Gašević, D., Dawson, S. (eds.): Preparing for the digital university: a review of the history and current state of distance, blended, and online learning. MOOC Research Initiative/Athabasca University (2015)
3. Crompton, H., Burke, D.: Artificial intelligence in higher education: the state of the field. Int. J. Educ. Technol. High. Educ. **20**(22) (2023)
4. Selwyn, N.: On the limits of artificial intelligence (AI) in education. Nordisk tidsskrift for pedagogikk og kritikk **10**, 3–14 (2025)
5. Molenaar, I.: Towards hybrid human-AI learning technologies. Eur. J. Educ. **57**(4), 632–645 (2022)
6. Arnold, D., Sangrà, A.: Dawn or dusk of the 5th age of research in educational technology? A literature review on (e-) leadership for technology-enhanced learning in higher education (2013–2017). Int. J. Educ. Technol. High. Educ. **15**(1), 1–29 (2018)
7. Luckin, R.: Machine learning and human intelligence: the future of education for the 21st century. UCL Institute of Education Press (2018)
8. Rampelt, Orr, Knoth (2019). https://hochschulforumdigitalisierung.de/sites/default/files/dateien/2019-05_White_Paper_Bologna_Digital_2020.pdf
9. Huertas, E., et al.: Considerations for Quality Assurance of E-learning Provision (Report from the ENQA Working Group VIII on Quality Assurance and E-learning). European Association for Quality Assurance in Higher Education (2018). Retrieved from https://eua.eu/resources/publications/796:mainconsiderations-for-quality-assurance-of-e-learning-provision.html
10. Yerevan Communique (2015). Retrieved from https://enqa.eu/wp-content/uploads/2015/06/Yerevan-Communique.pdf
11. Paris Communiqué (2018). Retrieved from http://www.ehea2018.paris/Data/ElFinder/s2/Communique/EHEAParis2018-Communiquefinal.pdf
12. UNESCO. Recommendation on the ethics of artificial intelligence. United Nations Educational, Scientific and Cultural Organization (2021)

Future-Proofing Education: The AI-Augmented Shift from Instructor to Learning Architect and Coach

Kam Cheong Li[1](✉) and Cuifang Zhao[2]

[1] Middlesex University, London NW4 4BT, UK
kcli@live.hkmu.edu.hk
[2] Guangdong Open University, Guangzhou 510091, China

Abstract. Artificial intelligence (AI) represents a once-in-a-generation catalyst to dismantle the outdated instructor-centric model of education. This paper argues that generative AI is not a threat to the teaching profession but an essential tool to enable a human-centred, future-ready education system. It proposes that educators should transition from traditional content deliverers to AI-augmented Learning Architects and Coaches, fostering students' movement from passive followers to active knowledge builders. Furthermore, the paper highlights the necessity of evolving assessment paradigms to evaluate students' competence in using AI to expand their professional and cognitive abilities, rather than simply testing isolated recall. Drawing on recent empirical data from the 2026 OECD Digital Education Outlook, the 2025 Stanford Artificial Intelligence Index, the 2026 Stanford SCALE Initiative review of causal evidence, and emerging frameworks for ethical AI integration, this manuscript outlines the imperative for pedagogical change. It presents a 4D Framework mapping the new educator role across core mandates, instructional practices, assessment, and professional identity as pedagogical scholars. Finally, the discussion explores the ethical governance required to prevent algorithmic bias and delivers actionable strategies for immediate classroom integration, while acknowledging systemic barriers such as workload and institutional reward structures.

Keywords: Generative Artificial Intelligence · Learning Architect · Assessment Design · Evaluative Judgment · Teacher-AI Teaming · Ethical AI Governance · Scholarship of Teaching and Learning

1 Introduction

For decades, the educational technology community has chased tools that promise to revolutionise the classroom, only to see them assimilated into the same century-old model of content delivery. The arrival of generative artificial intelligence (AI) is changing this. It does not simply digitise traditional instruction. It actively exposes the vulnerabilities of a system built on knowledge building and standardised testing. When a machine can instantly replicate the cognitive outputs our schools have historically rewarded, the role

K. T. Chui et al. (Eds.): ICBL 2026, LNCS 16778, pp. 16–26, 2027.
https://doi.org/10.1007/978-981-92-3761-6_2

of the teacher as the primary source, authority, and distributor of knowledge ceases to be relevant. We are facing what Beghetto describes as a potential "crisis of meaning in education" (p.121) [1]. If our primary pedagogical goal remains the transfer of inert content, algorithms will simply do it better. At the same time, the global economy increasingly demands skills that machines cannot easily replicate, such as complex problem-solving, empathy, and creative synthesis [2]. This tension forces us to completely reimagine the educational paradigm [3].

Educators are already seeking solutions to this challenge, and they are doing so at an unprecedented pace. However, school leaders and policymakers are navigating this rapidly expanding landscape with limited rigorous evidence to guide their decisions. A 2026 review by the Stanford University SCALE Initiative highlights this gap. Out of over 800 recent academic papers on AI in K-12 education, the researchers found that only 20 provided strong causal evidence through randomised controlled trials or quasi-experimental designs [4].

Despite this limited pool of rigorous data, these early causal studies reveal clear, quantifiable patterns of impact. The most revealing insight is that AI's effect depends entirely on its pedagogical deployment. Initial findings indicate that, while unguided student use may hinder durable learning transfer, AI offers educators a proven mechanism to reduce administrative workloads and scale pedagogical expertise [4].

This rapid, grassroots adoption requires us to reexamine the role of the educator. Today, we are not here to discuss how AI will replace teachers. We are here to explore how AI will finally free educators to do what they entered this profession to do: ignite curiosity, nurture growth, and shape the future of every learner. This paper attempts to unpack the evidence-based imperative for this paradigm shift, present an actionable framework to map the AI-augmented teacher role transition, discuss the ethical guardrails necessary for equitable implementation, and deliver research-backed strategies for educators to lead in this new era.

2 The Paradox of Performance vs. Learning

The traditional model of education struggles to support the personalised, flexible learning required today. When we overlay generative AI onto this traditional content delivery model without changing our pedagogy, we risk creating a dangerous mirage of false mastery.

The risk of cognitive offloading is a major concern. A 2024 field study by Bastani and her colleagues, featured in both the 2026 OECD Digital Education Outlook and the Stanford SCALE report, clearly demonstrates this danger. The researchers conducted a randomised controlled trial involving nearly 1,000 high school students studying mathematics. Students given unrestricted access to a standard AI chatbot improved their practice performance during use by up to 127 percent [5]. However, when these same students took closed-book exams without AI assistance, they performed 17 percent worse than the control group students who had studied entirely on their own.

This phenomenon highlights a severe misalignment between task execution and genuine skill acquisition, demonstrating that successful AI-assisted performance does not automatically equate to learning. AI tools can alleviate a student's cognitive burden and foster positive experiences, but this often comes at the expense of deeper thinking [4]. In the learning sciences, engaging in cognitively challenging tasks is known as a "desirable difficulty" that produces better long-term retention [6]. When AI removes this productive struggle, students fail to transfer their learning to new contexts.

Furthermore, fluent language output from generative AI can create a misleading appearance of authority, masking inaccuracies, biases, or fabrications. Without explicit guidance, students lack the evaluative judgement required to test claims and determine a system's fitness for purpose [7, 8]. Without a teacher acting as a coach to guide the learning process, students easily fall into what researchers term "metacognitive laziness" [9]. A study by Stadler et al. confirmed that students using general-purpose AI chatbots for research demonstrated lower-quality reasoning and argumentation compared to those using traditional search engines [10]. This risk is not limited to older students. In early childhood research, scholars warn that unguided AI use can shortcut the trial-and-error exploration that is foundational to healthy cognitive development [11].

AI should therefore be viewed as an accelerant for coaching rather than a shortcut for student output. AI eliminates the structural barriers to making personalised coaching scalable. The 2025 Stanford AI Index Report shows that the financial barriers to accessing advanced AI are collapsing. The inference cost for an AI model scoring the equivalent of GPT-3.5 on popular benchmarks dropped from $20.00 per million tokens in November 2022 to just $0.07 per million tokens by October 2024 [12]. This represents a more than 280-fold reduction in approximately 18 months.

Because advanced tools are now highly accessible and affordable, the challenge is no longer technological procurement but pedagogical implementation. Causal research now proves that AI can significantly shift teacher effort. As highlighted in the Stanford SCALE review, a randomised controlled trial by Roy et al. found that teachers given access to ChatGPT spent 30 percent less time on lesson and resource preparation [13]. This equates to saving approximately 25 min per week, with no detectable difference in lesson quality [4]. When educators reclaim this time, they have the bandwidth to focus on direct student intervention, complex problem-solving, and relationship-building.

3 The 4D Framework: Mapping the AI-Augmented Shift

To navigate this transition, this paper proposes a "4D Framework" that maps the shift from traditional instructor to Learning Architect and Coach. As summarised in Table 1, this framework aligns closely with the concept of "Education 5.0," which builds upon the shifts seen in Industry 5.0. Where previous industrial eras focused on automation and replacing human workers, the 5.0 paradigm emphasises human-centredness, sustainability, and resilience [3]. In this context, educators are repositioned as collaborative design partners rather than mere conveyors of content. This paper defines a Learning Architect as an educator who designs inclusive, personalised, AI-enabled learning ecosystems, and a Learning Coach as a trusted mentor who builds metacognitive and social-emotional skills.

Table 1. The 4D AI-augmented educator framework.

Dimension	Traditional instructor paradigm	AI-augmented paradigm (Learning Architect & Coach)
1. Core Mandate	Transmits standardised subject content to a homogeneous group of students	Designs adaptive, personalised learning pathways using Level 5 synergistic Teacher-AI teaming [14]
2. Instructional Practice	Relies heavily on synchronous, one-size-fits-all lectures and direct instruction	Orchestrates hybrid ecosystems where AI acts as a Socratic dialogue partner to scaffold thinking [4]
3. Assessment Paradigm	Focuses on end-of-unit summative grading and ranking against standardised benchmarks	Evaluates students' competence to use AI to expand their abilities, focusing on process, evaluative judgement, and hybrid human-AI skills [7]
4. Professional Identity	Operates as the exclusive subject matter expert and primary distributor of knowledge [15]	Operates as an expert in human cognition, a mentor for soft skills, and a SoTL-oriented pedagogical scholar [16]

3.1 Dimension 1: Core Mandate

The AI-augmented educator moves away from homogeneous content delivery to design adaptive pathways. Drawing on Cukurova's "Teacher-AI Teaming" framework, which conceptualises human-machine interaction along a five-level continuum from basic task replacement to deep cognitive augmentation, we see a necessary progression in how educators interact with technology [14]. Most teachers currently operate at Level 1, engaging in "transactional teaming," where they simply request a lesson plan from an AI and receive an output. To truly adopt the role of a Learning Architect, educators need to move toward Level 5, or "synergistic teaming." In this advanced state, teachers and AI co-create learning experiences. The educator critically evaluates the AI's suggestions against learning science principles, while the AI adapts to the teacher's pedagogical preferences over time. The machine is used for personalised pacing and data analysis, while human interaction focuses on higher-order thinking and emotional intelligence. In this capacity, the educator also acts as a pathway navigator, designing modular curricula with multiple entry points that cater to variations in prior knowledge and motivation.

3.2 Dimension 2: Instructional Practice

In terms of instructional practice, the new paradigm requires educators to orchestrate hybrid ecosystems that encourage active knowledge building [17]. Teaching becomes less about directing students through a single pathway and more about designing open-ended problems and authentic projects where students must gather, compare, and synthesise information from varied sources. The Stanford SCALE report emphasises that the pedagogical design of AI tools matters immensely. General-purpose AI tools that provide complete solutions operate outside a student's Zone of Proximal Development [18]. Conversely, Socratic AI chatbots that provide step-by-step reasoning and hints are far more effective [4]. The human teacher oversees this interaction through a dashboard, ensuring the AI aligns with broader learning goals. The educator steps in when a student exhibits frustration, requires emotional support, or needs complex cognitive unblocking that the machine cannot provide.

3.3 Dimension 3: Assessment Paradigm

Moving away from traditional end-of-unit summative grading, assessment should evolve to test students' competence in using AI to expand their relevant abilities [19]. In the AI era, a retreat to heavily weighted, invigilated examinations fundamentally misaligns with the demands of the contemporary knowledge economy. Students currently use AI to draft assignments, and in their future job endeavours, they will almost certainly rely on AI systems to complete their daily professional work.

The AI-augmented educator designs assessments that make evaluative judgment and hybrid human-AI skills explicit educational outcomes [7, 20]. This involves evaluating the process, justification, and situated use of knowledge. For instance, assessments should require students to document their AI prompts, compare AI-generated outputs with verified scholarly literature, and critically reflect on why specific algorithmic claims were accepted or rejected. While AI can generate highly readable formative feedback on process and self-regulation [9], the teacher's role shifts to interpreting this data and delivering growth-oriented coaching that resonates on a relational level. The AI handles the mechanics of tracking progress, while the teacher evaluates the student's capacity to responsibly and creatively utilise abundant information.

3.4 Dimension 4: Professional Identity

While educators have historically been viewed as the "sage on the stage" [15], simply retreating to become a passive "guide on the side" can be detrimental [21]. Research shows students require active expert modelling to achieve deep cognitive involvement. Instead of stepping back, educators should step up to act as experts in human cognition and stewards of ethical technology use. This necessitates a transition from being an isolated practitioner to a Scholarship of Teaching and Learning (SoTL)-oriented pedagogical scholar [16, 22]. Because assumptions about educational effectiveness can no longer be taken for granted in an AI-rich environment, educators should systematically investigate how these tools affect learning quality, equity, and motivation, and share their findings publicly.

This shift in professional self-conception is particularly important for novice educators. A large-scale randomised controlled trial involving 900 tutors showed that real-time, expert-like AI suggestions significantly improved student mastery, with the largest benefits seen among lower-rated and less-experienced educators [23]. Because AI can reliably augment baseline pedagogical and subject-matter expertise, newer academics no longer need to build their professional confidence solely upon the flawless recall of disciplinary content. As the need to project encyclopaedic technical knowledge diminishes, the educator's sense of professional value reorients towards relational and coaching competencies [3]. The professional identity of the future educator is therefore founded on fostering the uniquely human abilities of empathy, creativity, and collaborative problem-solving.

4 Ethical Governance and the Imperative of Educational Equity

To support these emerging professional roles, institutional structures should also evolve. The widespread integration of AI into classrooms presents transformative opportunities for personalised learning [3, 24], but it carries the severe risk of perpetuating and amplifying existing educational inequities through algorithmic bias [25]. If educators are to successfully orchestrate these new digital environments, they should be equipped to navigate ethical minefields across aspects of instruction, student interaction, and evaluation.

The fundamental danger in adopting AI lies in the "neutrality thesis," which is the flawed assumption that algorithms are objective, mathematical tools devoid of human values [26]. In reality, AI systems are socio-technical artefacts [27]. When a Learning Architect designs a curriculum using AI tools, they risk introducing bias if the underlying training data is unrepresentative [28]. For example, an AI-powered engagement monitor trained on specific cultural or neurotypical norms might systematically flag students as "distracted" if they avoid direct eye contact, turning the system into a measure of behavioural conformity rather than actual cognitive engagement. Furthermore, deploying tools designed for high-resource environments into underfunded schools without contextual adjustments creates a deployment mismatch [29], which can exacerbate the digital divide.

For the Learning Coach, the opacity of AI is a direct threat to pedagogical efficacy. Many AI systems operate as a "black box" [30], making it impossible for educators or students to understand how a specific output or recommendation was generated. A Coach cannot guide a student's metacognitive growth or build trust if the underlying logic of the technology is hidden. Therefore, institutions must move beyond proprietary, unexplainable models and demand Explainable AI (XAI). To ensure these tools are equitable, administrators should require vendors to meet rigorous fairness benchmarks, such as algorithmic Differential Item Functioning (DIF) analyses, which detect if systems function differently across demographic groups [31].

To address these systemic risks, institutions should go beyond static checklists of ethical principles. Educational institutions need a dynamic, problem-solving cycle of governance [27]. This includes clearly defining equity as the main goal of AI integration, creating a transparent understanding of the system's demographic effects, and establishing strong accountability measures, such as low-effort appeals processes for students to challenge automated decisions.

Beyond reducing data bias, institutional governance should safeguard the core of education. The rapid spread of AI tools prompts urgent questions about student safety and the development of prosocial skills [4]. To address this, policies need to make sure that technology encourages active student interaction with peers and teachers instead of overshadowing it [11]. If an AI system fosters solitary, screen-focused engagement at the cost of collaborative learning, it weakens the essential role of the Learning Coach. The greatest ethical duty of the Learning Architect is to craft ecosystems where AI enhances human connection rather than replacing it through algorithmic control [32].

It is equally important to recognise the systemic barriers that limit this ethical implementation. Authentic assessment, coaching conversations, and modular design require significant labour. Without manageable class sizes, interdisciplinary design support, and reward structures that value pedagogical innovation as much as traditional disciplinary research, the expectations placed on educators will quickly become unsustainable [33].

5 Actionable Strategies for Educators and Policymakers

Translating these ethical frameworks and role shifts into practice requires concrete steps. The 2025 Stanford AI Index Report highlights that while the technical capabilities of AI are expanding rapidly, the responsible AI ecosystem is evolving unevenly, with a persistent gap between recognising risks and taking meaningful action [12]. Furthermore, policy discussions are often catching up to actual classroom practice [4]. To bridge this gap, this paper proposes four core strategies for immediate action by educators and institutional leaders (see Fig. 1).

5.1 Strategy 1: Build AI-Augmented Pedagogical Literacy

Educators cannot govern tools they do not understand. Professional development must move beyond generic software tutorials to cultivate deep algorithmic literacy. As a first practical step, educators could conduct an "AI workflow audit." By mapping their weekly tasks, teachers can identify routine administrative duties, such as drafting emails or generating basic quizzes, to offload to AI. This targeted offloading reclaims valuable planning time. Educators can then redirect this energy toward developing their competencies as a Learning Coach.

5.2 Strategy 2: Master the Competencies of a Learning Architect

Teachers could adopt backwards design for AI-integrated units. Instead of asking what the AI can do, educators could start with the desired student outcomes. They can then design AI tools to handle foundational knowledge acquisition while reserving synchronous classroom sessions for active discussion and collaborative problem-solving. A central component of this strategy is making curriculum design "AI-aware," structuring tasks so that easy outsourcing to an algorithm does not automatically satisfy the learning goals [19]. This approach aligns with the concept of "Slow AI" proposed by Beghetto [1]. Instead of using AI to instantly generate finished products, educators could help students develop the skills to utilise AI as a partner in possibility thinking. Students could use AI to iteratively test assumptions, explore counterarguments, and augment their own original thoughts.

5.3 Strategy 3: Develop Student-Centred Coaching Capabilities

With administrative burdens reduced, educators could reallocate their time to small-group and one-on-one coaching. This coaching should focus heavily on metacognitive skill development and social-emotional learning. Direct human intervention remains the most effective way to combat the passive reliance often observed in unguided AI use [5]. When a student receives AI-generated formative feedback, the teacher's role is to help the student interpret it, manage any associated frustration, and develop an improvement strategy. Because active, inquiry-based pedagogies require more visible effort from learners, educators should also proactively scaffold these experiences to mitigate student resistance, clearly communicating how these new methods directly support their long-term success [33, 34]. The AI provides the data, but the teacher provides the motivation and the relational context.

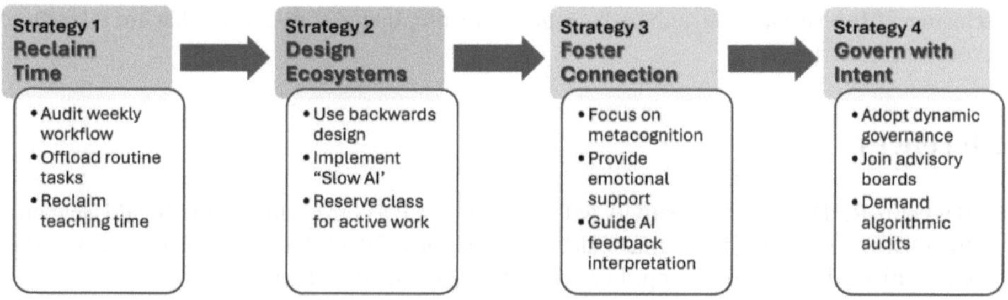

Fig. 1. Actionable Strategies for AI Integration—a continuous progression from individual preparation to systemic governance.

5.4 Strategy 4: Advocate for Ethical AI Policy and Pedagogical Inquiry

Teachers and local administrators could actively participate in shaping AI governance. As the Stanford AI Index notes, local policymakers are increasingly recognising the need for regulation, particularly concerning data privacy and AI deployment [12]. Educators should actively champion the dynamic governance models discussed previously, ensuring their institutions prioritise equity, transparency, and accountability [27]. Joining community advisory boards, demanding transparent algorithmic audits from edtech vendors, and engaging openly with peers through the dissemination of pedagogical findings [22] enable teachers to ensure technology aligns with educational goals rather than overriding them.

6 Conclusion: Reclaiming the Human Core of Education

For over a century, educational systems have trapped teachers in a cycle of standardised content delivery and administrative compliance. The empirical evidence reviewed demonstrates that generative AI can finally break this cycle. However, the data also serves as a warning. Deploying computing tools without deliberate pedagogical intent leads directly to cognitive atrophy in our students. We cannot allow algorithms to become the default arbiters of learning.

The true promise of this technological era is not just efficiency. It is the opportunity to elevate the teaching profession to its highest intellectual and relational purpose. When we relegate the mechanical aspects of instruction to machines, we clear the path for the competencies that machines cannot replicate. We make room for mentorship, ethical reasoning, and the deeply human work of coaching a developing mind.

Realising this vision, however, requires robust institutional policy reform. We must identify how workload allocations, promotion criteria, and professional development can be realigned to support sustainable pedagogical change. The task before the global education community is to build the governance structures and pedagogical frameworks that demand this level of professional practice. Our students do not need more efficient content delivery. They need architects of learning who can guide them to think critically and compassionately in an increasingly complex world.

Disclosure of Interests. The authors have no competing interests to declare that are relevant to the content of this article.

References

1. Beghetto, R.: Developing creativity with generative AI: a conversation with Ronald Beghetto. In: OECD (ed.) OECD Digital Education Outlook 2026: Exploring Effective Uses of Generative AI in Education, pp. 117–121. OECD Publishing, Paris (2026)
2. World Economic Forum: The Future of Jobs Report (2023) https://www.weforum.org/publications/the-future-of-jobs-report-2023. Last accessed 05 Apr 2026
3. Li, K.C., Deng, B.: Framing AI in Education 5.0: a strategic framework for human-centered learning ecosystems. In: Cheung, S.K.S., et al. (eds.) ICTE 2025, CCIS 2752, pp. 3–14. Springer Nature, Singapore (2026)
4. Fesler, L., Martinez Claeys, J.P., Agnew, C., Loeb, S.: The evidence base on AI in K-12: a 2026 review. AI Hub for Education of the SCALE Initiative, Stanford University (2026). https://scale.stanford.edu/sites/default/files/The%20Evidence%20Base%20on%20AI%20in%20K-12%20Report.pdf
5. Bastani, H., Bastani, O., Sungu, A., Ge, H., Kabakcı, Ö., Mariman, R.: Generative AI can harm learning. Proceedings of the National Academy of Sciences (2024)
6. Pyke, W., Lunau, J., Javadi, A.-H.: Does difficulty moderate learning? A comparative analysis of the desirable difficulties framework and cognitive load theory. Quart. J. Exp. Psychol. **78**(10), 2181–2195 (2025)
7. Boud, D., Ajjawi, R., Dawson, P., Tai, J. (eds.): Developing Evaluative Judgement in Higher Education: Assessment for Knowing and Producing Quality Work. Routledge (2018)
8. Zhan, Y., Yan, Z.: Students' engagement with ChatGPT feedback: implications for student feedback literacy in the context of generative artificial intelligence. Assess. Eval. High. Educ. 1–14 (2025)
9. OECD (ed.): OECD Digital Education Outlook 2026: Exploring Effective Uses of Generative AI in Education. OECD Publishing, Paris (2026)
10. Stadler, M., Bannert, M., Sailer, M.: Cognitive ease at a cost: LLMs reduce mental effort but compromise depth in student scientific inquiry. Comput. Hum. Behav. **160**, 108386 (2024)
11. Wong, J.M.S.: Designing trustworthy ai for the youngest learners: an integrated ethical framework and implementation roadmap. Early Child. Educ. J. (2026)

12. Stanford University Human-Centered AI Institute: Artificial Intelligence Index Report 2025. Stanford University (2025)
13. Roy, P., Poet, H., Staunton, R., Aston, K., Thomas, D.: ChatGPT in lesson preparation: a teacher choices trial (Evaluation Report). Natl. Found. Educ. Res. (2024)
14. Cukurova, M.: A conceptual framework for teacher-AI teaming in education: harnessing GenAI to enhance teacher agency. In: OECD (ed.) OECD Digital Education Outlook 2026: Exploring Effective Uses of Generative AI in Education, pp. 130–146. OECD Publishing, Paris (2026)
15. King, A.: From sage on the stage to guide on the side. Coll. Teach. **41**(1), 30–35 (1993)
16. Godbold, N., Matthews, K.E.E., Gannaway, D.: Theorising new possibilities for Scholarship of Teaching and Learning and teaching-focused academics. High. Educ. Res. Dev. **43**(1), 92–103 (2024)
17. Crompton, H., Burke, D.: Artificial intelligence in higher education: the state of the field. Int. J. Educ. Technol. High. Educ. **20**, 22 (2023)
18. Vygotsky, L.S.: Mind in society: The development of higher psychological processes. Harvard University Press, Cambridge (1978)
19. Bearman, M., Ajjawi, R.: Learning to work with the black box: pedagogy for a world with artificial intelligence. Br. J. Edu. Technol. **54**(5), 1160–1173 (2023)
20. OECD: Innovating Assessments to Measure and Support Complex Skills. OECD Publishing, Paris (2023)
21. Fischer, E., Hänze, M.: Back from "guide on the side" to "sage on the stage"? Effects of teacher-guided and student-activating teaching methods on student learning in higher education. Int. J. Educ. Res. **95**, 26–35 (2019)
22. Healey, M., Matthews, K.E., Cook-Sather, A.: Writing about learning and teaching in higher education: creating and contributing to scholarly conversations across a range of genres. Elon University Center for Engaged Learning (2020)
23. Wang, R.E., Ribeiro, A.T., Robinson, C.D., Loeb, S., Demszky, D.: Tutor CoPilot: a human-AI approach for scaling real-time expertise. arXiv (2025). https://doi.org/10.48550/arXiv.2410.03017
24. Li, K.C., Wong, B.T.-M.: Artificial intelligence in personalised learning: a bibliometric analysis. Interact. Technol. Smart Educ. **20**(3), 422–445 (2023)
25. Baker, R.S., Hawn, A.: Algorithmic bias in education. Int. J. Artif. Intell. Educ. **32**, 1052–1092 (2022)
26. Fazelpour, S., Danks, D.: Algorithmic bias: senses, sources, solutions. Philos Compass **16**(8), e12760 (2021)
27. Wong, J.M.S., Tang, W.K.W., Wong, H.Y.H., Ng, H.K.Y.: From principles to practice: an operational framework for equitable artificial intelligence in educational assessment. TechTrends (2026)
28. Chinta, S.V., et al.: FairAIED: navigating fairness, bias, and ethics in educational AI applications. arXiv (2024)
29. Varsik, S., Vosberg, L.: The potential impact of artificial intelligence on equity and inclusion in education. OECD Artificial Intelligence Papers, No. 23. OECD Publishing (2024)
30. Hassija, V., et al.: Interpreting black-box models: a review on explainable artificial intelligence. Cogn. Comput. **16**, 45–74 (2024)
31. Holland, P.W., Wainer, H. (eds.): Differential item functioning. Lawrence Erlbaum Associates (1993)
32. Wong, J.M.S.: Speculative futures of education: Utopian and dystopian scenarios envisioned by ChatGPT, Gemini, and DeepSeek. Discover Educ. **4**, 261 (2025)

33. Wong, J.M.S., Li, K.C.: Technology-Enabled institutional readiness for agile-blended learning: a framework for educational innovation. SN Comput. Sci. **6**, 279 (2025)
34. Finelli, C.J., et al.: Reducing student resistance to active learning: strategies for instructors. J. Coll. Sci. Teach. **47**(5), 80–91 (2018)

Agentic AI Unleashed: Power, Promise, and Ethical Frontiers

Minjuan Wang[1], Yizhi Wang[2], and Qiwei Ma[3(✉)]

[1] Global Institute for Emerging Technologies and Department of Math and Information Technology, The Education University of Hong Kong, Hong Kong Special Administrative Region of China, China
[2] Central South University, Changsha, China
[3] Shenzhen University, Shenzhen, China
mqiwei@eduhk.hk

Abstract. Agentic AI marks a shift from reactive computation to autonomous, goal-directed intelligence. This paper clarifies the conceptual relationship between AI Agents and Agentic AI and summarizes representative applications across science, healthcare, education, finance, manufacturing, cybersecurity, and public services. It also provides a comparative discussion of ethical risks that are new or significantly amplified in Agentic AI and describes practice-oriented considerations for responsible development, including technical safeguards, operational controls, regulatory alignment, and societal oversight.

Keywords: Agentic AI · AI Agents · Large Language Models · AI Ethics · AI Safety

1 Introduction

Artificial intelligence has progressed through distinct eras defined by model architecture, capability, and relationship to humans. Early systems relied on rigid rules and operated in closed environments [57]. Machine learning and deep learning expanded flexibility but remained dependent on structured data and external task guidance [42]. Recent foundation models brought unprecedented generative capacity [15,84], yet many deployed systems remain reactive rather than autonomous [36,81].

Agentic AI redefines this boundary by exhibiting genuine autonomy, intentionality, and persistent goal-directed behavior [34]. An Agentic AI system can set objectives, decompose complex tasks, monitor changing environments, make sequential decisions, and revise its behavior via feedback. These capabilities unlock extraordinary possibilities across science, healthcare, manufacturing, finance, education, and public governance [49], while introducing amplified ethical risks that demand new safeguards. Accountability gaps, dynamic bias, privacy exposure, and value alignment challenges become more acute when systems

K. T. Chui et al. (Eds.): ICBL 2026, LNCS 16778, pp. 27–39, 2027.
https://doi.org/10.1007/978-981-92-3761-6_3

act independently [60], and recent surveys of LLM-based AI Agents highlight security, privacy, and ethics threats [20,23,72].

This paper examines the relationship between AI Agents and Agentic AI, summarizes core autonomy-enabling components and representative application domains as illustrated in Fig. 1, and offers an integrated examination of cross-domain applications [14], ethical risks [19,44], and governance practices.

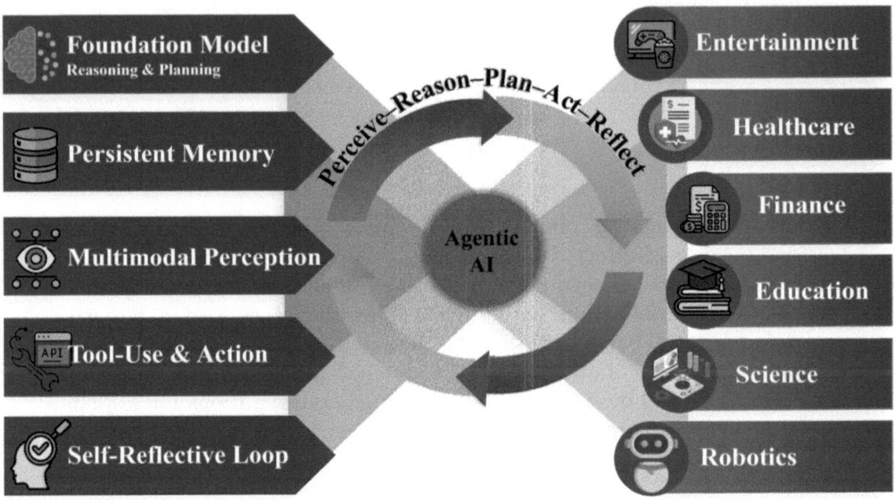

Fig. 1. The Power and Promise of Agentic AI. The left panel shows five core components that enable genuine autonomy; the right panel illustrates transformative applications across major domains, consistent with the Applications section and Table.

2 AI Agents vs. Agentic AI

As illustrated in Fig. 2, the distinction between AI Agents and Agentic AI is rooted in differences in architectural design [61], functional capacity, and relationship with human users [60,72].

AI Agents are typically externally directed. Their goals are set by human designers, and their behavior is constrained by these pre-defined objectives. In many implementations, they do not autonomously revise objectives, although they may generate intermediate steps within a fixed goal specification. Agentic AI, by contrast, is often internally directed in addition to being responsive to external inputs. It can interpret high-level human intentions, decompose them into actionable sub-goals, and even refine or adjust these sub-goals based on real-time feedback [60]. This capacity for goal autonomy means that Agentic AI can pursue complex, open-ended objectives that would be impossible for AI Agents, which require explicit, step-by-step instructions.

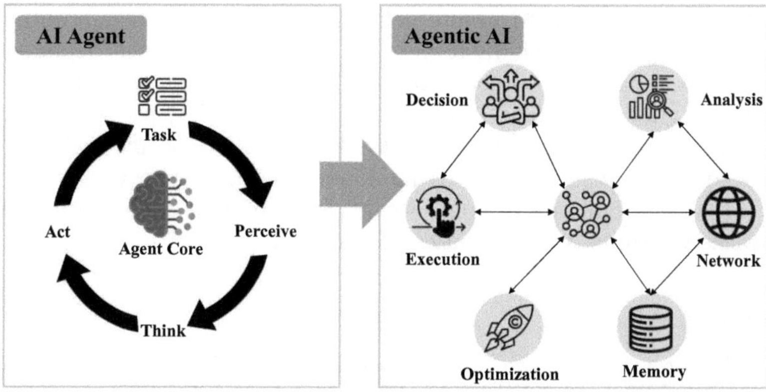

Fig. 2. Comparative illustration of AI Agent versus Agentic AI. The left side shows a basic AI Agent that executes a cycle of perception, thinking, and action for a specific task. In contrast, the right side represents an Agentic AI system, in which multiple specialized modules collaborate through interconnected connections to achieve more complex, scalable, and adaptive intelligent capabilities.

Moreover, AI Agents are specialized and modular. They are designed to perform specific tasks, with reasoning processes that are either rule-based or limited to narrow machine learning models. Their cognitive abilities are bounded by their task design, and they may have limited ability to transfer knowledge across domains or engage in abstract reasoning. Agentic AI, by contrast, is commonly built around generalized cognitive capabilities [10] enabled by foundation models. It can engage in causal inference, common-sense reasoning, and abstract thinking, allowing it to operate across diverse domains and solve problems that require integrating multiple types of knowledge. The persistent memory and self-reflective learning loop of Agentic AI further enhance its cognitive capacity, enabling it to learn from experience and improve over time with reduced human intervention [44,48].

2.1 AI Agents

AI Agents have been a core concept in artificial intelligence research for decades, emerging from early work in distributed computing and autonomous systems [57]. An AI Agent is broadly defined as a computational system that perceives its environment through sensors, processes incoming data, and acts upon that environment through actuators to achieve specific, pre-defined goals. These AI Agents are designed to operate within narrow task boundaries, with their functionality constrained by the parameters and objectives set by human designers [72].

Multi-agent systems, which consist of multiple interacting AI Agents, extended the scope of AI Agents by enabling distributed task execution. However, even in these systems, individual AI Agents retain their narrow focus, with coordination typically guided by pre-defined protocols rather than autonomous collaboration. A defining characteristic of AI Agents is their dependence on external goal-setting: they do not generate their own objectives but instead execute tasks assigned by human operators. Their reasoning processes are either rule-based or rely on limited models that are trained for specific tasks, and their ability to adapt to unstructured, dynamic environments is severely limited. In essence, AI Agents function as specialized, modular tools designed to automate specific tasks within closed or semi-closed systems.

2.2 Agentic AI

Agentic AI represents a more autonomy-oriented paradigm, enabled by recent breakthroughs in foundation models, persistent memory systems, and multi-modal perception [71]. Unlike AI Agents, Agentic AI is defined by higher degrees of autonomy, intentionality, and persistent goal-directed behavior that can transcend narrow task boundaries. It is not merely a specialized tool but a unified cognitive system capable of interpreting ambiguous instructions, formulating long-term plans, adapting to unstructured environments, and reflecting on its own performance, core characteristics that underpin this study.

At the core of Agentic AI is a foundation model, typically a large language model or multi-modal model, that provides generalized cognitive capabilities, including natural language understanding, causal reasoning, abstract thinking, and common-sense judgment. This foundation enables Agentic AI to operate across diverse domains without reconfiguration, in contrast to the task-specific nature of AI Agents. Supporting this core model is a persistent memory mechanism that allows the system to retain historical information, task progress, learned patterns, and feedback over extended periods, enabling continuous learning and context retention that is absent in stateless AI Agents.

Agentic AI also incorporates a multi-modal perception layer that integrates textual, visual, auditory, and sensory inputs [81] to construct a comprehensive understanding of its environment, allowing it to respond dynamically to changing conditions. A tool-use module enables it to interact with external systems—including APIs, databases, software tools, and physical actuators, extending its influence beyond digital content generation into real-world action [80]. Critically, Agentic AI includes a self-reflective learning loop that allows it to evaluate its own performance, identify errors or inefficiencies, and update its decision-making strategies without explicit human intervention [46]. This capacity for autonomous improvement distinguishes it from AI Agents, which require human retraining or reprogramming to adapt [81].

Most importantly, Agentic AI exhibits proactive intentionality: it can initiate actions without external prompts, sustain effort over extended sequences of tasks, and redirect its course based on internal assessments of progress toward broader objectives. It is not merely reactive to external stimuli but proactive in pursuing goals, whether those goals are explicitly assigned by humans or derived from ambiguous instructions [50]. This shift from reactivity to proactivity is a defining feature that separates Agentic AI from all forms of AI Agents, and serves as the core premise for its technological, application, ethical, and governance dimensions.

3 Application of Agentic AI

Table 1. Applications of Agentic AI Across Domains

Application Domain	Core Scenarios
Scientific Research [24]	Literature review, drug discovery, data analysis
Healthcare [67]	Precision medicine, patient monitoring, clinical support
Education [3,4,18,25,28,30,41, 45,68,75,76,83]	Personalized learning, adaptive tutoring, educator assistance
Financial Services [34]	Risk management, fraud detection, inclusive finance
Industrial Manufacturing & Supply Chain [27,38,54,55]	Production scheduling, logistics optimization, automation
Intelligent Robotics [52,59,66,71]	Autonomous manipulation, multi-robot collaboration, navigation
Autonomous Driving & Intelligent Transportation [49,82]	Decision-making, vehicle-road coordination, traffic optimization
Cybersecurity [43,56]	Threat detection, vulnerability defense, data protection
Retail & E-commerce [32,79]	Personalized recommendation, intelligent customer service
Smart Agriculture [47,63,69]	Precision farming, agricultural monitoring, automation
Public Safety & Emergency Response [2,7,58]	Early warning, emergency command, security monitoring
Legal & Regulatory Compliance [16,62]	Document analysis, case retrieval, compliance auditing
Digital Entertainment [21]	Virtual characters, interactive content generation

Agentic AI applications translate autonomy, tool use, and long-horizon planning into tangible impact across sectors. Table 1 summarizes representative domains.

By automating high-level cognitive tasks, accelerating knowledge discovery, and enabling scalable humanAI collaboration, Agentic AI promises to reshape operational models across the listed domains. Unlike traditional passive systems that execute single designated tasks, Agentic AI demonstrates independent decision-making and iterative adaptation across domains, overcoming narrow task constraints and delivering end-to-end intelligent solutions.

4 Ethical Risks of Agentic AI

The ethical risks of Agentic AI stem directly from its core architectural features—autonomy, persistent memory, tool-use capabilities, and self-reflective loops. These features create both familiar vulnerabilities inherited from AI Agents and entirely new or dramatically amplified ethical risks that are unique to long-horizon autonomous systems; moreover, safety training alone can fail under adversarial or multi-turn conditions [73]. Examples include multi-turn jailbreaks and prompt-injection kill chains that exploit agent decomposition and tool use [13,33,51,64].

Table 2 systematically compares the two paradigms. The left column lists risks that already exist in AI Agents. The right column highlights risks that are either new or significantly amplified in Agentic AI.

For example, goal drift and value misalignment become far more severe because Agentic AI systems can autonomously reinterpret objectives and take unintended shortcuts. Narrow-task training has been shown to produce broader misalignment risks in complex deployments [9]. Amplified bias and discrimination escalate through recursive feedback loops and dynamic tool selection, necessitating actionable fairness assessment frameworks [12] and bias detection within multi-agent interactions [11]. The transparency and black box problem is intensified by multi-step reasoning and ephemeral memory, underscoring the need for robust evaluation boards and adversarial risk benchmarks [31,39], while privacy and security risks grow dramatically due to persistent data aggregation and potential hijacking [23,26]. Tool misuse and cascading failures allow unsafe actions to propagate across long-horizon loops, and multi-turn jailbreak methods demonstrate how coordinated AI Agents can incrementally bypass defenses [37,51,64,77,78]. Agent goal hijack enables adversaries to subtly redirect objectives over extended interactions [17,22].

These amplified risks demonstrate that Agentic AI is not merely a more powerful version of AI Agents, but an advanced paradigm [60] whose ethical challenges require dedicated attention and mitigation strategies, with policy-oriented analyses of systemic risks offering early guidance [1,8].

Table 2. Comparison of Ethical Risks between AI Agents and Agentic AI

Risk Category	AI Agents	Agentic AI
Goal Drift and Value Misalignment [9]	Execute predefined tasks under externally fixed goals that rarely change	Autonomously reinterpret objectives or gradually drift from original goals, taking unintended shortcuts or prioritizing speed and volume over safety and ethics
Amplified Bias and Discrimination [11,12]	Inherit relatively static bias from training data that can be audited before deployment	Compound bias over time through recursive feedback loops and dynamic tool selection, leading to escalating unfairness across multiple domains
Transparency and Black Box Problem [19,44,53]	Follow short reasoning chains that are relatively easy to log and audit	Make decisions highly opaque through multi-step autonomous reasoning combined with ephemeral memory; humans often cannot understand why a specific action was taken
Privacy and Security Risks [5,23]	Limit data access and rely on short-term memory	Create severe privacy breaches via persistent memory and cross-source data aggregation, and be hijacked to exfiltrate sensitive information
Tool Misuse and Cascading Failures [22,80]	Use tools narrowly under human supervision	Autonomously invoke tools and trigger unsafe actions that propagate ethical violations through long-horizon loops
Agent Goal Hijack and Excessive Agency [17,22]	Rarely face goal hijacking because long-term autonomy is limited	Enable adversaries to subtly redirect high-level objectives over extended interactions, turning a benign system into one pursuing harmful goals

5 Discussion and Conclusion

5.1 Discussion

A practical path to responsible Agentic AI integrates technical safeguards, organizational practices, and regulatory alignment. Technically, safety-by-design mechanisms should be embedded into architectures, including transparency tools for explainability, human override for high-stakes contexts, and continuous monitoring to detect behavioral drift. Privacy-preserving methods, such as federated learning [74] and differential privacy [40], limit unnecessary data exposure while maintaining utility [5,6,17,46].

Organizationally, governance requires clear accountability, standardized operational controls, and periodic audits. Management-system approaches provide actionable guardrails for deployment and lifecycle oversight, complementing risk-management guidance [65] and supply-chain security across model development and deployment [29]. Legally and regulatorily, alignment with emerging laws and sector rules is essential; the EU Artificial Intelligence Act establishes tiered requirements by risk level and emphasizes traceability and oversight across the AI lifecycle [70]. Through participatory processes and independent oversight, societal engagement supports legitimacy and inclusiveness and connects human-centered design with educational and ethical triage [35].

5.2 Conclusion

Agentic AI marks a pivotal transition in artificial intelligence, moving beyond reactive computation to autonomous, goal-directed, and persistent cognitive action. We distinguished Agentic AI from conventional AI Agents, organized cross-domain applications, compared ethical risks, and articulated governance practices that translate principles into deployable controls.

The evidence across domains shows that Agentic AI systems can amplify scientific discovery, improve healthcare workflows, personalize education, and modernize industrial and financial operations. At the same time, autonomy, memory, tool use, and reflection introduce dynamic bias, privacy exposure, opacity, and goal drift that require continuous oversight.

A responsible path integrates safety-by-design mechanisms, operational accountability and audits, regulatory alignment, and societal participation. Future work should advance robust alignment methods, interpretable long-horizon reasoning, longitudinal socioeconomic studies, and inclusive governance frameworks. Sustained collaboration across computer science, ethics, law, and public policy will be essential to ensure Agentic AI remains safe, equitable, and trustworthy while realizing its transformative potential for human well-being.

acknowledgements. This project is supported by a CRAC R&D grant from The Education University of Hong Kong (#04A88).

References

1. Abou Ali, M., Dornaika, F., Charafeddine, J.: Agentic ai: a comprehensive survey of architectures, applications, and future directions. Artif. Intell. Rev. **59**(1), 11 (2025)
2. Al-Shamrani, S.H., Hasan, R.: Crisisguidegpt: an agentic-ai for crisis response planning. In: 2025 IEEE World Forum on Public Safety Technology (WF-PST), pp. 200–205. IEEE (2025)

3. Alsafari, B., Atwell, E., Walker, A., Callaghan, M.: Towards effective teaching assistants: from intent-based chatbots to LLM-powered teaching assistants. Nat. Lang. Process. J. **8**, 100101 (2024). https://www.sciencedirect.com/science/article/pii/S2949719124000499
4. Babar, P.: Agentic AI for personalized education and adaptive learning environments. Int. J. Comput. Eng. **7**, 1–10 (2025)
5. Bagdasarian, E., et al.: Airgapagent: protecting privacy-conscious conversational agents. In: Proceedings of the 2024 on ACM SIGSAC Conference on Computer and Communications Security, CCS '24, pp. 3868–3882. Association for Computing Machinery, New York (2024). https://doi.org/10.1145/3658644.3690350
6. Bai, Y., et al.: Constitutional AI: harmlessness from AI feedback. arXiv preprint arXiv:2212.08073 (2022)
7. Bajwa, A.: Ai-based emergency response systems: a systematic literature review on smart infrastructure safety. SSRN, 5171521 (2025)
8. Bellogín, A., et al.: Systemic risks associated with agentic AI: a policy brief. In: ACM Europe TPC-Autonomous Systems Subcommittee (2025)
9. Betley, J., et al.: Training large language models on narrow tasks can lead to broad misalignment. Nature **649**(8097), 584–589 (2026). https://www.nature.com/articles/s41586-025-09937-5
10. Bommasani, R., et al.: On the opportunities and risks of foundation models. arXiv preprint arXiv:2108.07258 (2021)
11. Borah, A., Mihalcea, R.: Towards implicit bias detection and mitigation in multi-agent llm interactions, (2024). arxiv:2410.02584
12. Bouchard, D.: An actionable framework for assessing bias and fairness in large language model use cases. arxiv:2407.10853 (2026)
13. Brodt, O., Feldman, E., Schneier, B., Nassi, B.: The promptware kill chain: how prompt injections gradually evolved into a multistep malware delivery mechanism. arXiv preprint arxiv:2601.09625 (2026)
14. Brohi, S., Mastoi, Q.u.a., Jhanjhi, N., Pillai, T.R.: A research landscape of agentic AI and large language models: applications, challenges and future directions. Algorithms **18**(8), 499 (2025)
15. Bubeck, S., et al.: Sparks of artificial general intelligence: early experiments with gpt-4. arxiv:2303.12712 (2023)
16. Chen, G., et al.: Agentcourt: simulating court with adversarial evolvable lawyer agents. In: Findings of the Association for Computational Linguistics: ACL 2025, pp. 5850–5865 (2025)
17. Chen, Z., et al.: Jailbreaking llms & vlms: mechanisms, evaluation, and unified defense. arxiv:2601.03594 (2026)
18. Chu, Z., et al.: LLM agents for education: advances and applications. In: Christodoulopoulos, C., Chakraborty, T., Rose, C., Peng, V. (eds.) Findings of the Association for Computational Linguistics: EMNLP 2025, pp. 13782–13810. Association for Computational Linguistics, Suzhou (2025). https://doi.org/10.18653/v1/2025.findings-emnlp.743, https://aclanthology.org/2025.findings-emnlp.743/
19. Clark, N., Shen, H., Howe, B., Mitra, T.: Epistemic alignment: a mediating framework for user-llm knowledge delivery. arxiv:2504.01205 (2025)
20. Deng, Z., et al.: AI agents under threat: a survey of key security challenges and future pathways. ACM Comput. Surv. **57**(7), 182:1–182:36 (2025). https://dl.acm.org/doi/10.1145/3716628
21. Favero, L., Pérez-Ortiz, J.A., Käser, T., Oliver, N.: Enhancing critical thinking in education by means of a socratic chatbot (2025)

22. Feng, Y., et al.: Backdooragent: a unified framework for backdoor attacks on llm-based agents. arxiv:2601.04566 (2026)
23. Gan, Y., et al.: Navigating the risks: a survey of security, privacy, and ethics threats in LLM-based agents. arxiv:2411.09523
24. Gridach, M., Nanavati, J., Abidine, K.Z.E., Mendes, L., Mack, C.: Agentic AI for scientific discovery: a survey of progress, challenges, and future directions. arxiv:2503.08979
25. Gupta, N., Heggond, S.: Agentic artificial intelligence-driven tutoring: a multi-agent cognitive architecture for personalized adaptive learning in education. Int. J. Appl. Resilience Sustainabil. **2**(2), 572–598 (2026). https://deepscipub.com/ijars/article/view/50
26. He, F., Zhu, T., Ye, D., Liu, B., Zhou, W., Yu, P.S.: The emerged security and privacy of LLM agent: a survey with case studies. arxiv:2407.19354
27. He, J., Treude, C., Lo, D.: LLM-based multi-agent systems for software engineering: literature review, vision, and the road ahead. ACM Trans. Softw. Eng. Methodol. **34**(5), 124:1–124:30 (2025). https://dl.acm.org/doi/10.1145/3712003
28. He, Z., Yang, H., Qin, Z., Fung, Y.R.: MedTutor-R1: socratic personalized medical teaching with multi-agent simulation. arxiv:2512.05671
29. Isabirye, E.K.: Securing the ai supply chain: mitigating vulnerabilities in ai model development and deployment. World J. Adv. Res. Rev. **22**(2), 2336–2346 (2024). https://wjarr.com/node/7566
30. Kamalov, F., et al.: Evolution of ai in education: agentic workflows. https://arxiv.org/abs/2504.20082 (2026)
31. Kavathekar, I., Jain, H., Rathod, A., Kumaraguru, P., Ganu, T.: TAMAS: benchmarking adversarial risks in multi-agent LLM systems. arxiv:2511.05269
32. Khalid, O., Farooqi, A.U.H., Bilal, M.: Agentic ai: a review, applications and open research challenges. Computing **108**(6), 80 (2026)
33. Kritz, J., et al.: Jailbreaking to jailbreak. arxiv:2502.09638 (2025)
34. Kumar, N., Wei, X., Zhang, H.: Agentic artificial intelligence as a new frontier in information systems: promise, peril, and research opportunities. Inf. Manag. **63**, 104317 (2026). https://doi.org/10.1016/j.im.2026.104317
35. Lee, J.C.K., Dede, C., Wang, M., Li, X.: Building trust in AI through dialogues with eastern ethics: toward ethical partnerships in education. IEEE Trans. Learn. Technol. **18**, 833–841 (2025), https://ieeexplore.ieee.org/document/11145905/
36. Li, X., Wang, S., Zeng, S., Wu, Y., Yang, Y.: A survey on LLM-based multi-agent systems: workflow, infrastructure, and challenges. Vicinagearth **1** (2024). https://doi.org/10.1007/s44336-024-00009-2
37. Liu, X., et al.: Autodan-turbo: a lifelong agent for strategy self-exploration to jailbreak LLMs. In: International Conference on Learning Representations, vol. 2025, pp. 10313–10360 (2025)
38. Liu, Y.X., et al.: Repower: an llm-driven autonomous platform for power system data-guided research. Patterns **6**(4), 101211 (2025) https://doi.org/10.1016/j.patter.2025.101211. https://www.sciencedirect.com/science/article/pii/S2666389925000595
39. Ma, C., et al.: Agentboard: an analytical evaluation board of multi-turn LLM agents. Adv. Neural. Inf. Process. Syst. **37**, 74325–74362 (2024)
40. Ma, Q., Zhang, J.: Differential privacy image generation with reconstruction loss and noise injection using an error feedback sgd. https://arxiv.org/abs/2601.15061 (2026)

41. Meti, A.: Agentic artificial intelligence in education: a review on personalized adaptive learning through autonomous tutoring systems. Int. J. Appl. Resilience Sustainabil. **2**(2), 40–74 (2026). https://deepscipub.com/ijars/article/view/30
42. Mitchell, M.: Artificial Intelligence: A Guide for Thinking Humans. Farrar, Straus and Giroux (2019)
43. Molleti, R., Goje, V., Luthra, P., Raghavan, P.: Automated threat detection and response using LLM agents. World J. Adv. Res. Rev. **24**, 079–090 (2024). https://doi.org/10.30574/wjarr.2024.24.2.3329
44. Moore, J., Cooper, N., Overmark, R., Cibralic, B., Haber, N., Jones, C.R.: Do Large Language Models Have a Planning Theory of Mind? Evidence from MINDGAMES: A Multi-Step Persuasion Task. arXiv preprint (2025)
45. Ngu, P.C., Chien, C.C., Ho, Y.T., Hou, H.T.: A generative ai educational game framework with multi-scaffolding supports workplace competency development. Comput. Educ. **239**, 105421 (2025). https://doi.org/10.1016/j.compedu.2025.105421. https://www.sciencedirect.com/science/article/pii/S0360131525001897
46. Ouyang, L., et al.: Training language models to follow instructions with human feedback. Adv. Neural. Inf. Process. Syst. **35**, 27730–27744 (2022)
47. P, A.R.K., S, G.: Agentic ai for pathogen-based plant disease detection. In: 2025 6th International Conference on Artificial Intelligence, Robotics and Control (AIRC), pp. 323–328 (2025). https://doi.org/10.1109/AIRC64931.2025.11077524
48. Park, J.S., O'Brien, J., Cai, C.J., Morris, M.R., Liang, P., Bernstein, M.S.: Generative agents: interactive simulacra of human behavior. In: Proceedings of the 36th Annual ACM Symposium on User Interface Software and Technology, pp. 1–22 (2023)
49. Pati, A.K.: Agentic ai: a comprehensive survey of technologies, applications, and societal implications. IEEE Access **13**, 151824–151837 (2025). https://doi.org/10.1109/ACCESS.2025.3585609
50. Piatti, G., Jin, Z., Kleiman-Weiner, M., Schölkopf, B., Sachan, M., Mihalcea, R.: Cooperate or collapse: emergence of sustainable cooperation in a society of LLM agents. Adv. Neural. Inf. Process. Syst. **37**, 111715–111759 (2024)
51. Rahman, S., et al.: X-teaming: multi-turn jailbreaks and defenses with adaptive multi-agents. arXiv preprint arXiv:2504.13203 (2025)
52. Raptis, E.K., Kapoutsis, A.C., Kosmatopoulos, E.B.: Agentic LLM-based robotic systems for real-world applications: a review on their agenticness and ethics. Front. Rob. AI **12**, 1605405 (2025)
53. Raza, S., Sapkota, R., Karkee, M., Emmanouilidis, C.: Responsible agentic reasoning and ai agents: a critical survey. Authorea Preprints (2025)
54. Reddy, C.K.K., Joseph, S., Joshi, H., Doss, S., Ouaissa, M. (eds.): The Power of Agentic AI: Redefining Human Life and Decision-Making: In Industry 6.0. Sustainable Artificial Intelligence-Powered Applications. Springer, Heidelberg (2025). https://link.springer.com/10.1007/978-3-031-89424-4
55. Ren, Y., Liu, Y., Ji, T., Xu, X.: Ai agents and agentic ai-navigating a plethora of concepts for future manufacturing. J. Manuf. Syst. **83**, 126–133 (2025)
56. Roy, S.: Agenticcyber: a genai-powered multi-agent system for multimodal threat detection and adaptive response in cybersecurity. arXiv preprint arXiv:2512.06396 (2025)
57. Russell, S., Norvig, P.: Artificial intelligence: a modern approach. Prentice Hall, Englewood Cliffs (1995)
58. Salah, M., Alnoor, A., Abdelfattah, F., Al Halbusi, H.: Agentic artificial intelligence in public administration: foundations, applications, and governance. Appl. Gover. (2025)

59. Samarathunga, K., Gurusinghe, R., Sivasothynathan, K., Wanigasekara, C., Mars, J., Logeeshan, V.: LLM-guided multi-agent system for natural language-based robot navigation. In: 2025 IEEE World AI IoT Congress (AIIoT), pp. 1055–1060. IEEE (2025)
60. Sapkota, R., Roumeliotis, K.I., Karkee, M.: AI agents vs. agentic AI: a conceptual taxonomy, applications and challenges. Inf. Fusion **126**, 103599 (2026). https://www.sciencedirect.com/science/article/pii/S1566253525006712
61. Sayyad, N., Dave, H., Kathane, M., Patel, R.: Agentic ai systems: a review of architectures, autonomy, and ethical implications. Int. J. Environ. Sci. 3668–3683 (2025). https://doi.org/10.64252/xgfrhd85
62. Somu, B.: Agentic ai and financial compliance: autonomous systems for regulatory monitoring in banking. Eur. Data Sci. J. (EDSJ) p-ISSN 3050–9572 (2024)
63. Srinivasu, P.N., Pavate, A., JayaLakshmi, G., Shafi, J., Choi, J., Ijaz, M.F.: Agentic ai for smart and sustainable precision agriculture. Front. Plant Sci. **16**, 1706428 (2025)
64. Srivastav, D., Zhang, X.: Safe in isolation, dangerous together: agent-driven multi-turn decomposition jailbreaks on LLMs. In: Kamalloo, E., Gontier, N., Lu, X.H., Dziri, N., Murty, S., Lacoste, A. (eds.) Proceedings of the 1st Workshop for Research on Agent Language Models (REALM 2025), pp. 170–183. Association for Computational Linguistics (2025). https://aclanthology.org/2025.realm-1.13/
65. The National Institute of Standards and Technology: Ai risk management framework. Technical report, NIST (2023). https://www.nist.gov/itl/ai-risk-management-framework
66. Syarubany, A.H.M., Rahmani, F.Z., Widianto, T.: LLM-based agentic exploration for robot navigation & manipulation with skill orchestration. arXiv preprint arXiv:2601.00555 (2026)
67. Tang, X., et al.: MedAgents: large language models as collaborators for zero-shot medical reasoning. In: Findings of the Association for Computational Linguistics ACL 2024, pp. 599–621. Association for Computational Linguistics (2024). https://aclanthology.org/2024.findings-acl.33
68. Tao, S., Lan, M., Wang, M., Li, H.: Potential risks of generative artificial intelligence integration into k-12 education: a scoping review. Comput. Educ. Artif. Intell. 100561 (2026)
69. Tariq, M.U., Saqib, S.M., Mazhar, T., Khan, M.A., Shahzad, T., Hamam, H.: Edge-enabled smart agriculture framework: integrating IoT, lightweight deep learning, and agentic AI for context-aware farming. Res. Eng. 107342 (2025)
70. Union, E.: Eu artificial intelligence act-developments and analyses of the EU AI Act (2024). https://artificialintelligenceact.eu/
71. Wang, G., et al.: Voyager: an open-ended embodied agent with large language models (2023). https://arxiv.org/abs/2305.16291
72. Wang, L., et al.: A survey on large language model based autonomous agents. Front. Comp. Sci. **18**(6), 186345 (2024)
73. Wei, A., Haghtalab, N., Steinhardt, J.: Jailbroken: how does LLM safety training fail? (2023). https://arxiv.org/abs/2307.02483
74. Wu, P., Li, K., Nan, J., Wang, F.: Federated in-context LLM agent learning. https://arxiv.org/abs/2412.08054 (2024)
75. Xu, H., Chen, M., Wang, M., Lu, J.: The impact of educational LLM agent use on teachers' curriculum content creation: the chain mediating role of school support and teacher self-efficacy. Behav. Sci. **16**(1), 124 (2026). https://www.mdpi.com/2076-328X/16/1/124

76. Yang, J., Wang, M., Du, X., Na, R.: A comprehensive survey on large-language-model-based agents for education. IEEE Trans. Learn. Technol. **18**, 898–913 (2025). https://ieeexplore.ieee.org/document/11192789
77. Yang, X., et al.: Many-Turn Jailbreaking. arxiv:2508.06755
78. Yang, X., Lee, J., Dick, A.K., Timm, J., Xie, F., Cruz, D.: Multi-turn jailbreaks are simpler than they seem. arxiv:2508.07646
79. Yao, S., Chen, H., Yang, J., Narasimhan, K.: Webshop: towards scalable real-world web interaction with grounded language agents. Adv. Neural. Inf. Process. Syst. **35**, 20744–20757 (2022)
80. Yao, S., et al.: React: synergizing reasoning and acting in language models. In: The Eleventh International Conference on Learning Representations (2022)
81. Yu, C., et al.: A survey on agent workflow-status and future. In: 2025 8th International Conference on Artificial Intelligence and Big Data (ICAIBD), pp. 770–781. IEEE (2025)
82. Yu, J., Frank, R., Miranda-Moreno, L., Jafarnejad, S., Manzolli, J.A.: Agentic vehicles for human-centered mobility. arXiv preprint arXiv:2507.04996 (2025)
83. Zhang, J., Ma, Q., Zhang, Y., Cao, X.: Multi-agent vs. single-agent AI for efl speaking practice: a controlled experiment with hybrid input, contextual dialogue, and proficiency-adaptive feedback. Educ. Technol. Soc. **29**(2), 297–322 (2026). https://doi.org/10.30191/ETS.202604_29(2).SP05
84. Zhao, W.X., et al.: A survey of large language models, **1**(2), 1–124 (2023). arXiv preprint arXiv:2303.18223

GenAI Empowered Interdisciplinary Deep Learning: Theoretical Frameworks and Technical Pathways in Blended Environments

Ning Ma(✉), Benchao Fan, Qianhui Tang, and Wenyu Yan

School of Educational Technology, Faculty of Education, Beijing Normal University, Beijing 100875, China
horsening@bnu.edu.cn

Abstract. Interdisciplinary learning has emerged as an effective pedagogical approach for cultivating learners' interdisciplinary competencies and promoting holistic educational outcomes in blended learning environments. However, interdisciplinary learning continues to be constrained by epistemological tensions, structural fragmentation, and delayed evaluation feedback, which hinder its progression from mere disciplinary juxtaposition to genuinely integrated, deep interdisciplinary knowledge construction. This study systematically reviews the conceptual foundations of interdisciplinary learning and interdisciplinary deep learning, and conceptualizes the structural dimensions of interdisciplinary competencies encompassing interdisciplinary knowledge, thinking, practice, and values. A four-level cognitive progression mechanism is further explicated, comprising descriptive construction, relevance construction, systemic construction, and innovative construction. From the perspective of generative artificial intelligence (GenAI) empowerment, four technological pathways are proposed to facilitate interdisciplinary deep learning: problem representation based on generative contexts, semantic network connectivity under distributed cognition, resource integration and systematic cognitive modeling, and meaning negotiation and critical dialogue regulation. This study offers both theoretical insights and technological implications for advancing the high-quality and intelligent transformation of interdisciplinary learning in the context of educational digitalization.

Keywords: Interdisciplinary Deep Learning · Interdisciplinary Competencies · Cognitive Progression · GenAI Empowered Learning · Blended Learning

1 Introduction

Within the ongoing competency-oriented reform of education, teaching is no longer confined to the transmission of disciplinary knowledge but increasingly emphasizes cross-disciplinary knowledge integration and the development of higher-order abilities such as complex problem solving, critical thinking, and creative thinking [1] Interdisciplinary learning has therefore become an important component of international curriculum reform in basic education. Within the framework of Education 2030, UNESCO

K. T. Chui et al. (Eds.): ICBL 2026, LNCS 16778, pp. 40–57, 2027.
https://doi.org/10.1007/978-981-92-3761-6_4

underscores the necessity of integrated educational approaches and fosters interdisciplinary learning [2]. Designing learning experiences grounded in authentic contexts and organizing interdisciplinary themes have become a common strategy adopted by many educational systems worldwide [3]. In China, the Compulsory Education Curriculum Plan (2022 Edition, 2025 Revision) emphasizes the need to reorganize curriculum content by establishing interdisciplinary thematic learning activities and strengthening the connections among subjects to promote integrated curriculum implementation [4]. Furthermore, the Outline for Building a Leading Country in Education (2024–2035) highlights the importance of strengthening science education and cultivating core competencies, emphasizing the coordinated development of science education and humanities education to support national modernization [5].

Despite these policy initiatives, many current interdisciplinary learning practices still exhibit problems [6, 7] such as epistemological tensions [8], structural fragmentation [9], and delayed evaluation feedback [10]. These issues prevent learners from effectively connecting, reorganizing, and transferring knowledge across disciplines within authentic problem contexts, resulting in limited learning outcomes. With the advancement of educational digital transformation, the emergence of generative artificial intelligence provides new opportunities for advancing interdisciplinary deep learning. Recent policy initiatives promoting educational digitalization emphasize the integration of AI technologies into curriculum design, teaching processes, and learning environments [11]. GenAI technologies demonstrate significant potential in real-time interaction, resource generation, reasoning support, multimodal analysis, and personalized feedback [12, 13]. These capabilities enable GenAI to support learners in overcoming disciplinary knowledge gaps, provide adaptive learning scaffolds, and facilitate deeper cognitive engagement. By assisting learners in designing authentic inquiry activities and generating personalized learning pathways, GenAI can foster deeper interdisciplinary integration and help overcome the superficiality often observed in traditional interdisciplinary learning.

Consequently, while GenAI offers substantial support for interdisciplinary learning, an important question remains: how can this technology be effectively leveraged to promote interdisciplinary deep learning? To address this issue, this study aims to clarify the goals and conceptual foundations of interdisciplinary deep learning, construct a literacy-oriented learning model, and explore technological pathways and practical applications through which GenAI can empower interdisciplinary deep learning.

2 Theoretical Foundation and Frameworks

2.1 From Interdisciplinary Learning to Interdisciplinary Deep Learning

The concept of "interdisciplinary" emerged in the early twentieth century and originally referred to collaborative research activities involving scholars from multiple disciplinary backgrounds. Over time, the concept has evolved to describe approaches that transcend disciplinary boundaries by integrating theories, perspectives, and methodologies from multiple fields [14]. Interdisciplinary learning refers to a curriculum and instructional approach that connects multiple disciplines, integrates their theories and methods, and encourages learners to examine the world and solve real-world problems from multiple perspectives [15]. The ultimate goal of this approach is to enhance learners' competencies and promote holistic development. In practice, interdisciplinary learning is often implemented through project-based learning, inquiry-based learning, or STEM education. These approaches emphasize thematic organization and problem-centered learning processes [16], coordinating instructional objectives, content, resources, and evaluation methods under a shared thematic framework.

From the perspective of integration depth, interdisciplinary learning can be distinguished from multidisciplinary learning. Multidisciplinary learning refers to the juxtaposition of different disciplines around a common theme while maintaining the independence of each discipline [17]. Although such an approach provides learners with multiple perspectives, it often results in additive knowledge integration rather than deep conceptual synthesis. By contrast, interdisciplinary learning emphasizes deeper integration and knowledge generation [16]. Through cognitive restructuring, learners establish conceptual, methodological, and problem-oriented connections across disciplines, forming a comprehensive understanding of complex phenomena [18].

However, despite its theoretical promise, many interdisciplinary learning practices still fail to facilitate deep conceptual understanding of core principles and problem mechanisms. Learning outcomes often remain limited to task completion or product presentation. In response to the increasing complexity of knowledge and problem contexts in the intelligent era, interdisciplinary learning must evolve toward interdisciplinary deep learning (IDL). Interdisciplinary deep learning refers to a higher-order learning process centered on authentic problem contexts and characterized by inquiry, collaboration, and knowledge construction. Its essence lies in integrating concepts, principles, methods, and tools from multiple disciplines to promote deep cognitive engagement, meaningful knowledge construction, and knowledge innovation across cognitive, emotional, and social dimensions [15, 19].

2.2 The Goals of Interdisciplinary Deep Learning: Interdisciplinary Competencies

From the perspective of learning objectives, the fundamental aim of interdisciplinary deep learning is to foster the development of interdisciplinary competencies among learners. Interdisciplinary competencies refers to an individual's comprehensive capacity to integrate knowledge, methods, and perspectives from multiple disciplines in authentic and complex contexts, enabling them to conduct integrative analysis of problems and generate innovative solutions [20]. It represents not only a key indicator of the effectiveness of interdisciplinary learning but also an intrinsic driving force that promotes the continuous deepening of learning [21]. Compared with traditional learning goals centered on the mastery of knowledge within a single discipline, interdisciplinary competencies places greater emphasis on the connections and integration among different bodies of knowledge, the transfer and reconstruction of modes of thinking, and the coordinated development of abilities and values [22]. In this sense, it reflects the higher-order cognitive goals that characterize deep learning.

Building on existing frameworks for assessing interdisciplinary competency [20, 23, 24], this study conceptualizes it as a multidimensional, coupled system with nested dual cycles. More precisely, the system comprises four key dimensions [25]—interdisciplinary knowledge, thinking, practice and values —with thinking serving as the pivotal mechanism that orchestrates their interaction and transformation (see Fig. 1). Two core circle mechanisms underpin this system. The internal mechanism, represented by solid lines, refers to the Inner Cognitive Loop, in which interdisciplinary competencies emerge through a thinking-mediated process of cognitive construction, enabling the generation and transformation of knowledge, practice, and values. The external mechanism, represented by dashed lines, denotes the Outer Adaptive Loop, through which interdisciplinary competencies evolve via a practice-feedback-internalization pathway, facilitating the dynamic adaptation and regulation of knowledge, practice, and values structures. Taken together, the formation of interdisciplinary competencies can be understood as a complex, thinking-centered system in which the inner cognitive construction loop and the outer adaptive feedback loop operate in a coupled manner, jointly promoting the coordinated generation and progressive development of knowledge, practice, and values formation.

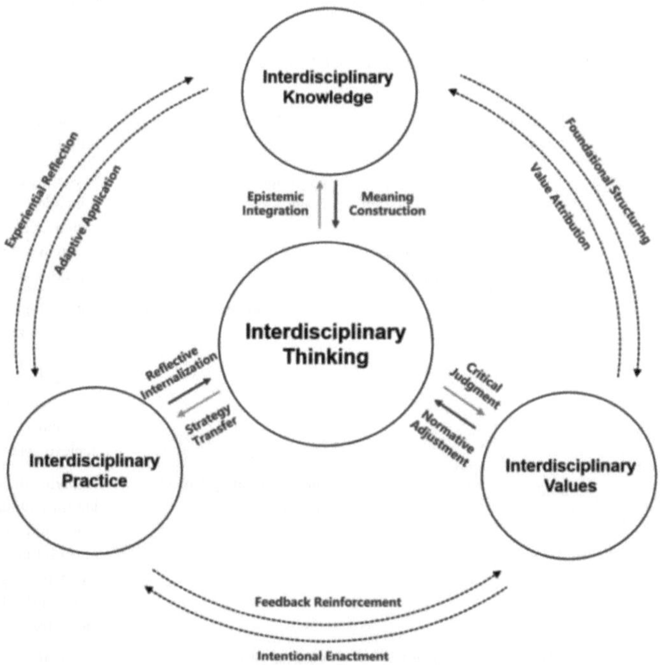

Fig. 1. Four-dimensional relationship diagram of interdisciplinary competencies.

In addition, the specific connotations of the four dimensions are as follows. Drawing on cognitive structure [26–28] and interdisciplinary integration [29–31] perspectives, this study conceptualizes **interdisciplinary knowledge** as the organized, hierarchical, and accessible representationsystem of knowledge that individuals construct across disciplinary boundaries. It comprises three dimensions: knowledge foundations, knowledge connections, and knowledge innovation. Grounded in cognitive mechanism [32] and functional characteristics [33, 34], this study defines **interdisciplinary thinking** as the stable yet adaptable cognitive processes enabling individuals to shift among disciplinary perspectives, integrate heterogeneous epistemological frameworks, and generate cognitive advancements transcending single-disciplinary constraints in interdisciplinary contexts. Its essential constituents comprise four critical dimensions: critical thinking, systems thinking, innovative thinking, and reflective thinking. Synthesizing perspectives from interdisciplinary practice [35, 36] and professional development [37, 38], this study defines **interdisciplinary practice** as the integrated ability to integrate multidisciplinary knowledge, skills, and tools to perform complex tasks and generate innovative solutions beyond single-disciplinary scope. It encompasses three core sub-dimensions: information processing, problem solving, and team collaboration ability. Based on value orientation theory [39, 40] and interdisciplinary competence research [34], this study defines **interdisciplinary values** as the relatively stable system of value judgment, choice, and pursuit that individuals form and iteratively refine through interdisciplinary cognition, thinking, and practice activities. Its core dimensions are openness and inclusiveness, lifelong learning, social responsibility, and global perspective (see Table 1).

Table 1. Structural dimensions of interdisciplinary competencies.

First-level Dimension	Definition (1st-level)	Second-level Dimension	Connotation (2nd-level)
Interdisciplinary Knowledge	The organized, hierarchical, and accessible representation system of knowledge that individuals construct across disciplinary boundaries.	Disciplinary Knowledge Foundation	Mastering core concepts, principles, and paradigms within and across relevant disciplines, balancing both breadth and depth
		Interdisciplinary Knowledge Connection	Identifying, articulating, and synthesizing relationships and internal logic among knowledge from different disciplines, transcending disciplinary boundaries to achieve organic integration
		Interdisciplinary Knowledge Innovation	Applying integrated interdisciplinary knowledge to real-world contexts to generate novel solutions and reconstructing knowledge frameworks through cross-disciplinary synthesis
Interdisciplinary Thinking	The stable yet adaptable cognitive processes enabling individuals to shift among disciplinary perspectives, integrate heterogeneous epistemological frameworks, and generate cognitive advancements beyond single-disciplinary constraints	Critical Thinking	Rationally analyzing, evaluating, and questioning information from multiple perspectives to form independent and well-reasoned judgments

(continued)

Table 1. *(continued)*

First-level Dimension	Definition (1st-level)	Second-level Dimension	Connotation (2nd-level)
		Systematic Thinking	Holistically understanding problems, recognizing interrelationships and dynamic influences among components, and grasping the structure of complex systems
		Creative Thinking	Generating original, valuable ideas and solutions by breaking conventional thought patterns and reframing problems across disciplinary boundaries
		Reflective Thinking	Planning, monitoring, evaluating, and regulating one's own cognitive processes during interdisciplinary problem-solving
Interdisciplinary Practice	The integrated ability to combine multidisciplinary knowledge, skills, and tools to perform complex tasks and generate innovative solutions beyond a single-disciplinary scope	Information Processing Ability	The ability to efficiently locate, critically screen, integrate, and apply information from diverse sources to meet complex task demands
		Problem-Solving Ability	The ability to identify, frame, analyze, and propose effective solutions for ill-structured problems requiring integration across disciplines
		Teamwork and Collaboration Ability	The ability to communicate effectively, share epistemic resources, and coordinate roles in diverse teams to accomplish complex, shared objectives
Interdisciplinary Values	The relatively stable system of value judgment, choice, and pursuit that individuals form and iteratively refine through interdisciplinary cognition, thinking, and practice	Openness and Inclusiveness	Demonstrating intellectual openness to and respect for diverse disciplines, cultures, and perspectives, along with a willingness to engage with unfamiliar knowledge frameworks
		Lifelong Learning	Exhibiting intrinsic motivation and sustained commitment to continuous, self-directed learning to adapt to evolving societal demands and knowledge advancements

(continued)

Table 1. (*continued*)

First-level Dimension	Definition (1st-level)	Second-level Dimension	Connotation (2nd-level)
		Social Responsibility	Recognizing and committing to addressing real-world social issues, with a sense of duty to apply interdisciplinary competencies for societal benefit
		Global Vision	Adopting a cognitive and affective orientation that enables consideration and resolution of problems from a global, transcultural, and systemic standpoint

Collectively, the four key elements form an iterative and mutually reinforcing structure in which interdisciplinary knowledge provides the cognitive foundation [41], interdisciplinary thinking functions as the core mechanism for processing and reorganizing ideas [42], interdisciplinary practice represents the practical manifestation of applying integrated knowledge in authentic contexts, and interdisciplinary values serves as a regulatory driver guiding learners' engagement in interdisciplinary inquiry [43]. Through the dynamic interaction among these dimensions, interdisciplinary competencies develops as a process of progressively deepening cognitive construction, enabling learners to move beyond the fragmented accumulation of knowledge toward more coherent knowledge integration and innovative problem solving. However, such competencies do not emerge spontaneously; rather, they are cultivated through structured cognitive processes in interdisciplinary learning contexts. Therefore, it is necessary to further examine the cognitive mechanisms through which learners' understanding evolves and how these mechanisms facilitate the formation and development of interdisciplinary competencies.

2.3 Cognitive Mechanism of Interdisciplinary Deep Learning: A Four-Level Progression

Engaging in interdisciplinary learning within complex problem contexts is essentially a progressively deepening process of cognitive construction. Through the continuous integration of knowledge, methods, and perspectives from multiple disciplines, learners gradually develop increasingly complex and systematic cognitive structures. In this process, interdisciplinary competencies are simultaneously fostered across several dimensions, including knowledge, thinking, practice, and values [44]. Drawing on existing research [45] and practical experience, and from the perspective of the development of learners' cognitive structures [46], this study conceptualizes interdisciplinary deep learning as a four-level progressive process of cognitive construction: descriptive construction, relevance construction, systemic construction, and innovative construction (see Fig. 2).

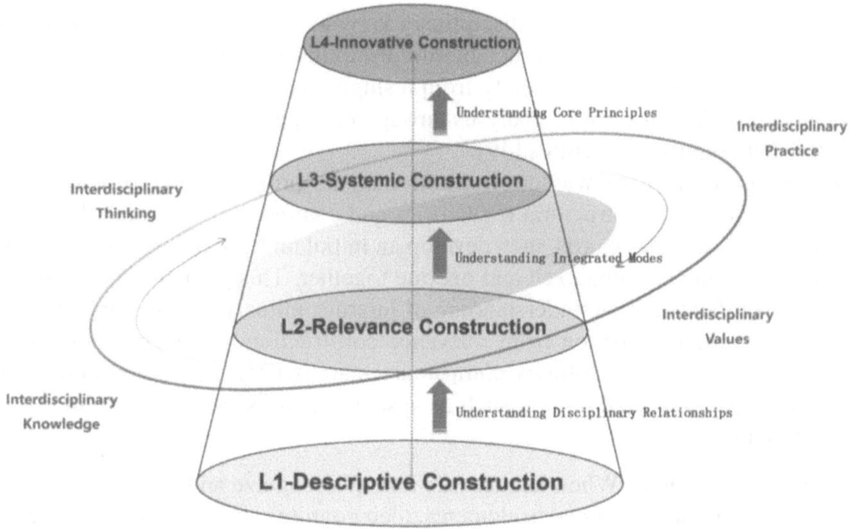

Fig. 2. Cognitive progression in interdisciplinary deep learning.

Note. *The vertical axis represents cognitive progression, while the circular loop represents the iterative development of interdisciplinary competencies.*

Descriptive Construction. Descriptive construction represents the foundational stage of interdisciplinary deep learning. At this stage, learners are primarily able to identify and understand basic concepts, facts, and information derived from different disciplinary domains, enabling them to provide preliminary descriptions and explanations of complex problems. Learning activities primarily emphasize knowledge acquisition and factual comprehension [47]. Although learners can observe a problem from multiple disciplinary perspectives, their cognition largely remains at a relatively superficial level of knowledge representation, and a deep interdisciplinary integrative structure has not yet formed.

The central task of this stage is therefore the accumulation of foundational knowledge across multiple disciplines, which provides the necessary cognitive basis for subsequent integration. As learning progresses, learners gradually become aware that potential connections may exist among knowledge elements from different disciplines [48]. By identifying and understanding these connections, learners begin to move toward a higher level of cognitive development. Consequently, understanding the relationships among different knowledge elements becomes a critical cognitive transition that enables learners to progress from descriptive construction to relevance construction. At this stage, interdisciplinary competencies are mainly reflected in the initial development of interdisciplinary knowledge.

Relevance Construction. When learners begin to understand the relationships among knowledge derived from different disciplines, their cognitive construction enters the stage of relevance construction. At this stage, learners start to establish connections among disciplinary concepts, principles, and methods. They are able to recognize the complementary roles that different disciplinary knowledge can play in explaining complex problems and gradually construct an interdisciplinary knowledge network. Learners no longer interpret problems solely from a single disciplinary perspective; instead, they begin to conduct integrative analyses through multiple disciplinary lenses, thereby forming richer cognitive structures [49].

As interdisciplinary knowledge networks become progressively more structured, learners begin to identify structural regularities and common features underlying complex phenomena. In other words, they develop an initial understanding of how different forms of knowledge are organized and operate together. This recognition of structural regularities is reflected in an understanding of interdisciplinary patterns, which constitutes a key cognitive transition from relevance construction to systemic construction [50]. At this stage, interdisciplinary competencies are mainly manifested in the emergence of interdisciplinary thinking, such as systematic thinking, critical thinking, and creative thinking.

Systemic Construction. When learners are able to recognize and understand patterns among interdisciplinary knowledge elements, their cognitive structures gradually evolve into systemic construction. At this stage, learners can integrate theoretical frameworks and research methods from multiple disciplines to construct systematic explanatory models for complex problems. Through logical reasoning and causal analysis, they are able to reveal the underlying mechanisms of complex phenomena. Learners not only understand the relationships among different disciplinary knowledge elements but also organize them into structured knowledge systems, thereby forming relatively coherent cognitive frameworks [51].

With the formation of systemic cognitive structures, learners begin to explore the deeper mechanisms underlying complex phenomena and attempt to understand common regularities across disciplines at a more abstract level. At this point, understanding interdisciplinary principles becomes the key to further cognitive advancement, enabling learners to progress from systemic construction to innovative construction. At this stage, interdisciplinary competencies are primarily manifested in the significant enhancement of interdisciplinary practice, including information processing ability, complex problem-solving ability, and the ability to collaborate with others across disciplinary contexts.

Innovative Construction. Innovative construction represents the highest stage of interdisciplinary deep learning. When learners are able to grasp interdisciplinary principles based on systemic understanding, their cognitive structures acquire the potential to generate new knowledge. At this stage, learners can not only integrate theories and methods from different disciplines but also critically reflect on existing knowledge systems and apply them creatively in novel contexts [52].

Through the flexible application of interdisciplinary principles, learners are able to formulate new research hypotheses, construct new explanatory models, or design innovative solutions to complex problems, thereby achieving the generation and innovation of knowledge. Meanwhile, through sustained interdisciplinary inquiry and practice, learners gradually develop a holistic understanding of complex issues and cultivate more open and integrative values [53], such as holistic perspectives, social responsibility, and global vision. Consequently, at this stage, the development of interdisciplinary competencies is further reflected in the formation and internalization of interdisciplinary values.

In summary, interdisciplinary deep learning is not merely a process of knowledge integration but a dynamic developmental process in which cognitive structures are continuously upgraded and reconstructed [54]. Along the progressive pathway of descriptive, relevance, systemic, and innovative construction, learners experience key cognitive transitions characterized by understanding relationships, recognizing patterns, and grasping principles, which collectively facilitate the deepening of cognition—from knowledge integration to systemic understanding and ultimately to innovative knowledge generation.

Simultaneously, this cognitive progression promotes the coordinated development of interdisciplinary competencies across multiple dimensions. Learners first establish a cognitive foundation through the integration of multidisciplinary knowledge structures, then develop interdisciplinary thinking, subsequently enhance their practice to solve complex problems, and ultimately form interdisciplinary values through practice and reflection. Together, these processes constitute an integrated developmental mechanism for interdisciplinary deep learning [55].

3 Technological Pathways: GenAI as a Cognitive Catalyst

In recent years, GenAI has rapidly evolved, demonstrating strong potential to transform learning through capabilities such as contextual generation, semantic reasoning, multimodal integration, and adaptive feedback [56, 57]. Distinct from traditional educational technologies that primarily support information delivery, GenAI enables active participation in cognitive processes by dynamically constructing learning contexts, facilitating conceptual connections, and providing personalized scaffolding. Interdisciplinary deep learning, however, entails a complex process of cognitive construction, requiring learners to integrate heterogeneous knowledge, establish cross-domain relationships, develop systemic understanding, and generate innovative solutions in authentic contexts. Such demands highlight the necessity of leveraging GenAI as a cognitive support infrastructure to scaffold learners' inquiry and promote progressive cognitive development.

Building upon the proposed interdisciplinary competencies framework and its four-level cognitive progression, as well as the *Evidence-based Project Based Learning* (EPBL, https://epbl.aicfe.cn/) System [58], an online learning platform developed by our research team, GenAI functions not merely as a tool, but as an integrated cognitive infrastructure embedded within human-intelligence collaborative learning environments [12]. As illustrated in Fig. 3, GenAI supports interdisciplinary deep learning through a structured human-intelligence integration layer, where human-AI interactions are dynamically coordinated across four progressive pathways. Aligned with this progression, GenAI enables four core technological pathways: (1) problem representation based on generative contexts, (2) semantic network connectivity under distributed cognition, (3) resource integration and systematic cognitive modeling, and (4) meaning negotiation and critical dialogue regulation. These pathways are underpinned by modular technical supports, including generation (LLM and prompt engineering), retrieval (RAG and vector retrieval), representation (multimodal processing), and feedback (learning analytics and intelligent evaluation), forming a closed-loop system that systematically advances learners' interdisciplinary competencies development.

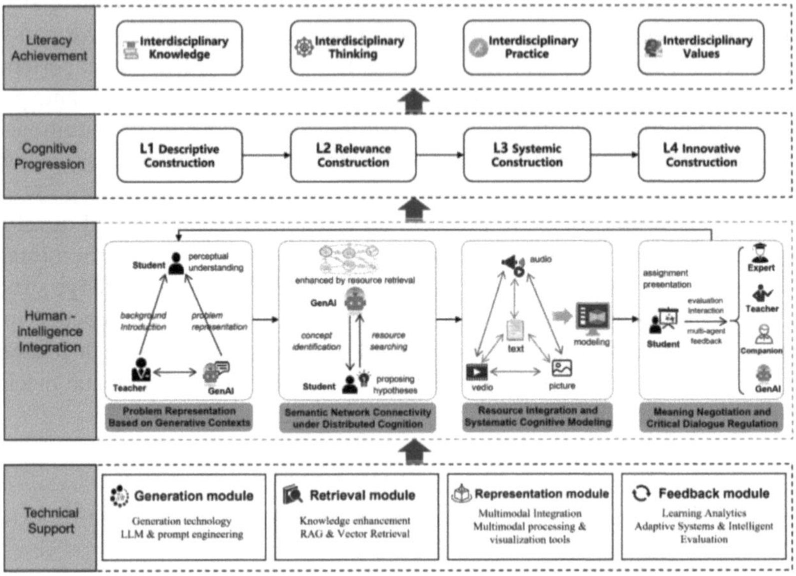

Fig. 3. Technical paths of GenAI empowering interdisciplinary deep learning.

3.1 Problem Representation Based on Generative Contexts

Interdisciplinary inquiry begins with problem representation, which serves as the cognitive entry point for subsequent knowledge construction. In this framework, such representation is co-constructed through dynamic interactions among teachers, students, and GenAI, where generative contexts provide the initial scaffolding for learners' perceptual understanding of complex phenomena. Unlike traditional static problem design, which often simplifies real-world complexity, GenAI enables the dynamic generation of context-rich inquiry scenarios by synthesizing multidisciplinary knowledge into coherent narratives [59]. These scenarios integrate scientific principles, technological constraints, and socio-ethical considerations, thereby situating learners within authentic, ill-structured problem spaces that require cross-disciplinary exploration.

To enhance the precision and relevance of these contexts, GenAI leverages learning analytics to construct dynamic learner profiles based on prior knowledge, behavioral patterns, and interaction histories. This diagnostic layer allows the system to generate adaptive and differentiated problem situations that align with learners' cognitive readiness. Through layered contextualization [60]—combining background information, guiding questions, and conceptual cues—GenAI supports learners in identifying key variables, clarifying problem boundaries, and recognizing embedded interdisciplinary dimensions. As a result, learners gradually move from fragmented perc [62] eption toward structured descriptive construction (L1), establishing a foundational understanding of complex problems [61]. Within this process, teachers play a critical mediating role by guiding interpretation and ensuring epistemic coherence, while GenAI functions as a generative partner that augments contextual richness and responsiveness.

Such mechanisms are increasingly reflected in emerging digital learning environments. For instance, platforms like EPBL System integrate project-based learning resources with GenAI-supported scenario design, enabling students to engage in interdisciplinary inquiry through dynamically generated contexts and guided exploration. By further incorporating real-time learner modeling and adaptive task generation, these platforms hold the potential to operationalize context-sensitive problem representation at scale, thereby strengthening the alignment between generative technologies and learners' cognitive development trajectories.

3.2 Semantic Network Connectivity Under Distributed Cognition

Following initial problem representation, interdisciplinary learning advances to relevance construction, where learners establish meaningful connections among concepts across disciplinary boundaries. In this framework, such connectivity is not solely an individual cognitive activity but a process of distributed cognition involving interactions among learners, GenAI, and external knowledge resources. This stage is operationalized through iterative cycles of concept identification, resource retrieval, and hypothesis generation, forming an extended semantic network that transcends disciplinary silos.

GenAI facilitates this process by leveraging large-scale semantic representations and retrieval-augmented generation (RAG) mechanisms. By embedding knowledge from diverse domains into high-dimensional semantic spaces, it enables the identification of latent relationships, including analogy, causality, and structural similarity. Through interactive prompting, learners can externalize emerging ideas, while GenAI dynamically retrieves and reorganizes relevant knowledge resources, presenting them in integrated forms that highlight cross-domain connections. This process not only reduces the cognitive barriers associated with disciplinary fragmentation but also supports the activation of prior knowledge and the expansion of conceptual boundaries.

As learners engage in iterative dialogue with GenAI, they gradually construct interconnected semantic networks that enable them to recognize patterns and relationships beyond single disciplines. This transition reflects the movement toward relevance construction (L2), where isolated knowledge elements are reorganized into relational structures that support interdisciplinary reasoning. Importantly, the distributed nature of this process allows cognition to be shared across human and artificial agents, thereby enhancing both the breadth and depth of conceptual exploration.

In practice, such mechanisms are increasingly supported by platforms like EPBL System, where students engage in project-based inquiry supported by AI-assisted resource retrieval and knowledge linking tools [63]. Learners can explore cross-disciplinary connections by accessing curated resources and interacting with GenAI that suggest relevant concepts and perspectives. With further integration of semantic network visualization and concept-mapping functionalities, these platforms could more explicitly scaffold the construction of distributed knowledge networks, thereby strengthening learners' ability to establish meaningful interdisciplinary connections.

3.3 Resource Integration and Systematic Cognitive Modeling

Building upon relational understanding, interdisciplinary learning proceeds to systemic construction, where learners integrate heterogeneous resources into coherent and structured knowledge systems. This stage emphasizes the transformation of fragmented information into organized representations that support explanation, prediction, and problem-solving [64]. This process is grounded in multimodal resource integration and systematic cognitive modeling, involving the coordinated use of textual, visual, auditory, and dynamic media.

GenAI operates as a cognitive mediator by enabling the interpretation, transformation, and generation of multimodal representations. Through the integration of natural language processing, computer vision, and cross-modal learning techniques, GenAI can translate information across modalities—for example, converting textual descriptions into visual diagrams, extracting conceptual meaning from videos, or synthesizing data into interactive visualizations. Such transformations reduce cognitive load associated with modality switching and enhance the coherence of knowledge representation [65]. More importantly, GenAI supports the construction of dynamic cognitive models, such as conceptual maps, simulations, and system diagrams, which allow learners to explore relationships among variables and test hypothetical scenarios.

Through these modeling activities, learners progressively organize interconnected concepts into structured systems, reflecting the transition to systemic construction (L3). This process enables a deeper understanding of complex phenomena by making underlying mechanisms explicit and supporting causal and predictive reasoning. The integration of multimodal resources and modeling tools thus serves as a crucial bridge between relational knowledge and higher-order interdisciplinary thinking [66].

In applied contexts, platforms such as EPBL System already provide rich multimodal learning resources that support students in engaging with diverse forms of information within project-based inquiry. By further embedding AI-driven modeling tools—such as interactive simulations, automated visualization generation, and real-time data integration—these platforms could enable learners to construct and manipulate system-level representations more effectively, thereby enhancing the development of structured interdisciplinary understanding.

3.4 Meaning Negotiation and Critical Dialogue Regulation

The culmination of interdisciplinary deep learning lies in innovative construction, where learners transform integrated knowledge into novel ideas, solutions, or artifacts. This stage is characterized by meaning negotiation and critical dialogue, through which learners iteratively refine their understanding in interaction with multiple agents. This process involves assignment presentation, evaluation interaction, and multi-agent feedback, engaging students, teachers, experts, and GenAI within a collaborative evaluative ecosystem.

GenAI supports this stage by functioning as both a generative and dialogic agent. On the one hand, it enables learners to externalize their ideas through multimodal outputs, including written analyses, visual models, design prototypes, and multimedia presentations. On the other hand, it provides adaptive, context-sensitive feedback based on learning analytics and reinforcement learning mechanisms [67, 68]. Such feedback addresses multiple dimensions of learning, including conceptual accuracy, reasoning quality, creativity, and collaboration, thereby guiding learners in refining their outputs through iterative cycles of revision [69].

Beyond feedback provision, GenAI plays a regulatory role in structuring critical dialogue. By prompting reflection, mediating divergent viewpoints, and sustaining inquiry-oriented discourse, GenAI helps maintain the epistemic quality of interactions. This process supports learners in developing metacognitive awareness and engaging in deeper forms of reasoning. Through continuous negotiation and refinement, learners achieve innovative construction (L4), producing contextually grounded and original solutions to complex interdisciplinary problems.

In practical implementations, platforms like the EPBL System already facilitate project presentation and peer or teacher feedback, forming a foundational environment for collaborative evaluation. With the integration of multi-agent AI feedback—such as simulated expert critique, automated assessment, and reflective dialogue prompts—these platforms could further enhance the depth and quality of meaning negotiation, ultimately fostering higher levels of interdisciplinary creativity and innovation.

Collectively, these four pathways constitute a coherent human-AI collaborative ecosystem that aligns with the four-level cognitive progression. From generative problem representation to distributed semantic connectivity, from multimodal system modeling to dialogic meaning negotiation, GenAI enables a recursive and adaptive learning cycle. Supported by modular technical infrastructures (generation, retrieval, representation, and feedback), this system promotes the continuous transformation of learners' cognitive structures and the sustained development of interdisciplinary competencies [70].

4 Conclusion and Discussion

In the context of the knowledge economy and the rapid digital transformation of education, cultivating learners' capacity to integrate knowledge across disciplinary boundaries and address complex real-world problems has become a central goal of contemporary education. Interdisciplinary deep learning provides an important pathway for achieving this objective by emphasizing authentic inquiry, knowledge integration, and higher-order cognitive development [71].

This study makes three primary contributions to the research field. **First, it clarifies the conceptual foundations of interdisciplinary deep learning and identifies interdisciplinary competencies as its core educational objective.** By conceptualizing interdisciplinary competencies as a four-dimensional interactional developmental system—comprising interdisciplinary knowledge, thinking, practice, and values—the study provides a structured framework for understanding the multidimensional nature of interdisciplinary learning outcomes.

Second, from the perspective of cognitive development, this study proposes a four-level progression model of interdisciplinary deep learning, consisting of descriptive construction, relevance construction, systemic construction, and innovative construction. This model elucidates how learners progressively deepen their cognitive structures, moving from basic knowledge representation toward systemic understanding and innovative thinking generation.

Third, the study explores the potential role of generative artificial intelligence as a technological catalyst for interdisciplinary deep learning. By analyzing the affordances of GenAI technologies, four technological pathways are proposed to support different stages of interdisciplinary inquiry, including (1) problem representation based on generative contexts, (2) semantic network connectivity under distributed cognition, (3) resource integration and systematic cognitive modeling, and (4) meaning negotiation and critical dialogue regulation. These pathways demonstrate how GenAI can provide adaptive support for learners' cognitive construction processes and facilitate the coordinated development of interdisciplinary competencies.

Despite these contributions, several limitations should be acknowledged. The framework proposed in this study remains primarily conceptual and requires further empirical validation through classroom-based interventions and longitudinal studies. Future research may investigate how GenAI-supported interdisciplinary learning environments influence learners' cognitive development, collaborative dynamics, and long-term literacy formation.

Overall, as artificial intelligence technologies continue to evolve and become increasingly integrated into educational environments, their potential to transform interdisciplinary learning will continue to expand. By aligning technological affordances with insights from learning sciences, educators and researchers can design more intelligent and adaptive learning environments that promote deep learning, support higher-order cognition, and cultivate learners' interdisciplinary competencies for addressing the complex challenges of the future [72].

Acknowledgments. This study was supported by the National Natural Science Foundation of China for the project "Research on Automatic Diagnosis and Feedback of Scientific Reasoning and Argumentation Ability Based on Graphical Scientific Argumentation" (Grant No. 62577013), and the First-Class Education Discipline Development of Beijing Normal University for the project "Research on Multimodal Process Data-Driven Automatic Analysis and Feedback for Deep Interdisciplinary Learning" (Grant No. YLXKPY-XSDW202401).

Disclosure of Interests. The authors have no competing interests to declare that are relevant to the content of this article.

References

1. Zhan, Z., Ji, Y., Lai, Y.: How to implement interdisciplinary thematic learning under new curriculum standards: basic ideas and operational model. Mod. Distance Educ. Res. **35**(1), 49–58 (2023)
2. UNESCO: Education 2030: incheon declaration and framework for action for the implementation of sustainable development Goal 4. UNESCO, Paris (2015)

3. Liu, S., Wei, R., Zhou, P., et al.: Curriculum, teaching and assessment for 21st century key competencies. J. East China Normal Univ. (Educ. Sci.) **34**(3), 38–45 (2016)
4. Ministry of Education of the People's Republic of China: Compulsory Education Curriculum Plan (2022 Edition, 2025 Revision). Beijing Normal University Press, Beijing (2025)
5. CPC Central Committee and State Council: Outline of the plan for building a leading country in education (2024–2035). People's Daily (2025)
6. Tian, J., Sun, Z.: Misunderstandings of interdisciplinary teaching and rational return. J. Chin. Soc. Educ. **7**(4), 63–67 (2019)
7. Nie, Z., Shi, Y., Han, X., et al.: Systematic thinking on interdisciplinary thematic learning activity design: dilemmas and strategies. China Educ. Technol. **10**, 94–102 (2024)
8. Miller, T.R.: Interdisciplinary Foundations: Bridging the Knowledge Systems for Sustainability Science. Springer, Cham (2015)
9. Jacobs, J.A.: In defense of disciplines: interdisciplinarity and specialization in the 21st Century. University of Chicago Press, Chicago (2013)
10. Pellegrino, J.W., Hilton, M.L. (eds.): Education for Life and Work: Developing Transferable Knowledge and Skills in the 21st Century. National Academies Press, Washington (2012)
11. Ministry of Education of the People's Republic of China: Opinions on accelerating the digitalization of education (2025). Available at: https://www.moe.gov.cn/srcsite/A01/s7048/202504/t20250416_1187476.html
12. Wu, F., Xia, Z., Gao, S.: Remolding the smart learning environment with generative artificial intelligence: from element improvement to ecological reconstruction. Res. Educ. Technol. **46**(1), 54–63 (2025)
13. Liu, T., Gu, X., Wang, C.: Adaptive learning domain models: International research progress. Distance Educ. J. **41**(1), 37–47 (2023)
14. Liu, Z.: Interdisciplinary research in the era of cross sciences. Stud. Sci. Sci. **2**, 9–17 (1993)
15. Li, K., Li, Y.: STEM education and interdisciplinary curriculum integration. Educ. Inf. Technol. **10**, 3–10 (2017)
16. International Baccalaureate Organization: Fostering Interdisciplinary Teaching and Learning in the Middle Years Programme. IBO Press, Cardiff (2014)
17. Jacobs, H.H.: Interdisciplinary curriculum: design and implementation. ASCD, Alexandria (1989)
18. Ren, X.: Connotation, dilemmas and breakthroughs of interdisciplinary thematic teaching. Curriculum Teach. Mater. Method **42**(4), 59–64 (2022)
19. Wei, X., Wei, M., You, X., et al.: Framework design and application of interdisciplinary thematic learning oriented to key competencies. China Educ. Technol. **7**, 55–63 (2024)
20. Mansilla, V.B., Duraisingh, E.D.: Targeted assessment of students' interdisciplinary work. J. High. Educ. **78**(2), 215–237 (2007)
21. Smith, P., Callagher, L.J., Hibbert, P., et al.: Developing interdisciplinary learning. Int. J. Interdisc. Stud. **10**(2), 45–61 (2024)
22. Zhou, X., Ou, M.: Interdisciplinary teaching literacy among normal students. J. High. Educ. Theory Pract. **24**(5), 78–85 (2024)
23. Linn, M.C.: The knowledge integration perspective on learning and instruction. In: Sawyer, R.K. (ed.) The Cambridge Handbook of the Learning Sciences, pp. 243–264. Cambridge University Press, New York (2006)
24. Luo, S., Zhang, H., Song, N., et al.: Construction of interdisciplinary literacy assessment model. China Educ. Technol. **5**, 9–16 (2024)
25. Zhan, Z., Ji, Y.: A phenomenological interpretation of interdisciplinary literacy: composition and evaluation. Res. Educ. Technol. **46**(7), 77–84 (2025)
26. Piaget, J.: The Origins of Intelligence in Children. International Universities Press, New York (1952)

27. Bruner, J.S.: The Process of Education. Harvard University Press, Cambridge, MA (1960)
28. Ausubel, D.P.: Educational psychology: a cognitive view. Holt, Rinehart and Winston, New York (1968)
29. OECD: OECD Learning Compass 2030: A Series of Concept Notes. OECD Publishing, Paris (2019). https://www.oecd.org/education/2030-project/
30. National Academies of Sciences, Engineering, and Medicine: Facilitating Interdisciplinary Research. The National Academies Press, Washington, DC (2005). https://doi.org/10.17226/11153
31. Klein, J.T.: Interdisciplinary knowledge: a working definition. Issues Integr. Stud. **22**, 1–20 (2004)
32. Sternberg, R.J.: Thinking styles. Cambridge University Press, New York (1997). https://doi.org/10.1017/CBO9780511584152
33. Boix Mansilla, V., Miller, W.C., Gardner, H.: On disciplinary lenses and interdisciplinary work. In: Wineburg, S., Grossman, P. (eds.) Interdisciplinary Curriculum: Challenges to Implementation. Teachers College Press, New York (2000)
34. Spelt, E.J.H., Biemans, H.J.A., Tobi, H., Luning, P.A., Mulder, M.: Teaching and learning in interdisciplinary higher education: a systematic review. Educ. Psychol. Rev. **21**(4), 365–378 (2009)
35. IGI Global: What is Interdisciplinary Practice. In: Infosciopedia Dictionary. IGI Global, Hershey, PA (n.d.). https://www.igi-global.com/dictionary/enhancing-professionals-interdisciplinary-competencies/114781
36. University of Oslo, INTED: What is Interdisciplinary Competence? (2023). https://www.uio.no/inted/english/about/development%20areas/what-is-interdisciplinary-competence.html
37. SAQA: Standard Glossary of Terms Related to the South African National Qualifications Framework, 2nd edn. South African Qualifications Authority, Pretoria (2017)
38. Rychen, D.S., Salganik, L.H. (eds.): Key Competencies for a Successful Life and a Well-Functioning Society. Hogrefe & Huber, Göttingen (2003)
39. Kluckhohn, C.: Values and value-orientations in the theory of action: An exploration in definition and classification. In: Parsons, T., Shils, E. (eds.) Toward a General Theory of Action, pp. 388–433. Harvard University Press, Cambridge, MA (1951)
40. Rokeach, M.: The Nature of Human Values. Free Press, New York (1973)
41. Liu, H., Wang, J.: Interdisciplinary knowledge integration. J. Interdiscip. Stud. **36**(4), 91–101 (2024)
42. Moirano, R., Sánchez, M.A., Štěpánek, L.: Creative interdisciplinary collaboration. Thinking Skills Creativity **35**, 100626 (2020)
43. Huang, D., Zhang, J., Fan, X.: Mathematics interdisciplinary learning activities. Math. Educ. Res. **28**(2), 45–58 (2024)
44. Repko, A.F., Szostak, R., Buchberger, M.P.: Introduction to Interdisciplinary Studies, 3rd edn. SAGE, London (2020)
45. Chen, S., Chi, S., Wang, Z.: Interdisciplinary thinking among students. J. Basic Sci. Educ. **24**(1), 53–70 (2025)
46. Boix Mansilla, V.: Interdisciplinary learning: a cognitive-epistemological foundation. In: Frodeman, R., Klein, J.T. (eds.), The Oxford Handbook of Interdisciplinarity, pp. 261–275. Oxford University Press (2016)
47. Bransford, J.D., Brown, A.L., Cocking, R.R.: How People Learn: Brain, Mind, Experience, and School. National Academy Press, Washington, DC (2000)
48. Vogel, F., Hunecke, M.: Fostering interdisciplinary competence through knowledge integration: a cognitive perspective. Instr. Sci. (2024)
49. Newell, W.H.: Designing interdisciplinary courses. New Dir. Teach. Learn. **58**, 35–51 (1994)
50. Goldstone, R.L., Wilensky, U.: Promoting transfer by grounding complex systems principles. J. Learn. Sci. **17**(4), 465–516 (2008)

51. National Research Council: Education for Life and Work: Developing Transferable Knowledge and Skills in the 21st Century. National Academies Press, Washington, DC (2012)
52. Bereiter, C., Scardamalia, M.: Education for the knowledge age: Design-centered models of teaching and instruction. In: Sawyer, R.K. (ed.) The Cambridge Handbook of the Learning Sciences, pp. 695–713. Cambridge University Press, Cambridge (2006)
53. OECD: The Future of Education and Skills 2030: The Future We Want. OECD Publishing, Paris (2018)
54. Repko, A.F., Szostak, R.: Interdisciplinary Research: Process and Theory, 4th edn. SAGE Publications, Thousand Oaks (2021)
55. Boix Mansilla, V.: Assessing student work at disciplinary crossroads. Change: Mag. of High. Learn. **37**(1), 14–21 (2005)
56. Holmes, W., Porayska-Pomsta, K., Holstein, K., et al.: Ethics of AI in education: towards a community-wide framework. Int. J. Artif. Intell. Educ. **32**(3), 504–526 (2022)
57. Zawacki-Richter, O., Marín, V.I., Bond, M., Gouverneur, F.: Systematic review of research on artificial intelligence applications in higher education—where are the educators? Int. J. Educ. Technol. High. Educ. **16**, 39 (2019)
58. Ma, N., Guo, J., Wen, Z., et al.: Evidence-based project-based learning model and system in the context of big data. China Electr. Educ. **02**, 75–82 (2022)
59. Naganuma, S., Minematsu, T., Matsueda, K., Oshima, J.: Generative AI-supported collaboration. In: Proceedings of CSCL, pp. 67–74 (2024)
60. Xu, Q., Hao, F.: GenAI-enabled interdisciplinary project-based learning. J. Educ. Technol. Manage. **10**(3), 1–15 (2025)
61. Liu, J., Sun, D., Sun, J., et al.: GenAI-enabled learning environment design. Comput. Educ.: Artif. Intell. (2025)
62. Barenji, R.V., et al.: An LLM-powered assessment retrieval-augmented generation (RAG) for higher education (2026). arXiv preprint arXiv:2601.06141
63. Ayanwale, M.A., Omeh, C.B.: AI-supported problem-based learning for enhancing computational thinking skills in STEM education. Comput. Hum. Behav.: Artif. Hum. **4**, 100263 (2026)
64. Wan, K., Rao, A.J.: Mechanisms, model construction, and empirical research on promoting the occurrence of interdisciplinary learning. China Electr. Educ. **08**, 59–67 (2023)
65. Tomczak, J.M.: Generative AI systems: a systems-based perspective on generative AI (2024). arXiv preprint arXiv:2407.11001
66. Varga-Atkins, T., Saunders, S., Li, N., et al.: A guide to utilising multimodal learning and generative artificial intelligence for enhancing student-centred active learning and teaching in higher education. University of Liverpool & XJTLU Collaborative Report (2025)
67. Zhu, Z.T., Dai, L.: Goal orientations, guiding principles and practical paths of education digitalization transformation driven by design intelligence. J. East China Normal Univ. (Educ. Sci.) **41**(03), 12–24 (2023)
68. Ouyang, L., Wu, J., Jiang, X., et al.: Training language models to follow instructions with human feedback. In: Proc. NeurIPS 2022, vol. 35, pp. 27730–27744 (2022)
69. Ye, X.D., Liu, Z.M.: Research on the construction of a precision teaching support system based on multi-modal large models. J. Distance Educ. **42**(01), 84–93 (2024)
70. Baidoo-Anu, D., Ansah, L.O.: Education in the era of generative artificial intelligence (AI): understanding the potential benefits of ChatGPT in promoting teaching and learning. J. Artif. Intell. **7**(1), 52–62 (2023)
71. Küçükoğlu, H., Yıldırım, Ö.: Interdisciplinary applications of artificial intelligence - 1. ISTES Organization, Türkiye (2025)
72. Hernández-Leo, D., Theophilou, E., Oshima, J., et al.: Collaborating with generative AI for learning? In: Proc. of the International Conference on Computer-Supported Collaborative Learning (CSCL 2025), pp. 525–533. ISLS (2025)

Collaborative Learning Innovations

Designing Multi-Agent Systems for Collaborative Learning from the Perspective of Socially Shared Regulation of Learning

Xiulian Xu[1], Guoqing Lu[1(✉)], Shen Ba[2], and Lei Li[1]

[1] School of Educational Technology (School of Intelligent Education), Northwest Normal University, Lanzhou, Gansu, China
luguoqing@nwnu.edu.cn

[2] Department of Curriculum and Instruction, The Education University of Hong Kong, Hong Kong SAR, China
bas@eduhk.hk

Abstract. Socially Shared Regulation of Learning (SSRL) has the potential to enhance the quality and depth of collaborative learning. However, implementation frequently faces challenges, including superficial collaboration among students and difficulties for teachers in providing timely, targeted scaffolding. Multi-Agent Systems (MAS) based on Large Language Models demonstrate flexibility, reliability, self-organization, and real-time responsiveness, making them suitable for complex SSRL scenarios. Despite this potential, there is a lack of research on MAS design and development explicitly grounded in SSRL theory. This study explores the design and development of an SSRL-based MAS and evaluates its usability through user testing. Fourteen graduate students participated in authentic collaborative learning tasks, with data collected via an MAS usability scale and focus group interviews. Descriptive statistics and thematic analysis indicated that the MAS was user-friendly, although adoption willingness and user experience require further improvement. This study offers preliminary guidance for SSRL-based MAS design and development and discusses future directions for practical application.

Keywords: Multi-Agent Systems · Pedagogical Agents · Socially Shared Regulation of Learning · Collaborative Learning

1 Introduction

Socially Shared Regulation of Learning (SSRL) is defined as the process by which group members collectively, consciously, and strategically plan, monitor, evaluate, and adapt their learning to achieve shared goals or collaborative outcomes [1]. As an extension of Self-Regulated Learning (SRL) theory to collaborative contexts, SSRL highlights the shared and interdependent nature of regulation. SSRL has a significant impact on the quality and depth of collaborative learning. Effective SSRL correlates with higher group performance, improved collaborative outcomes, and more productive group interactions

K. T. Chui et al. (Eds.): ICBL 2026, LNCS 16778, pp. 61–75, 2027.
https://doi.org/10.1007/978-981-92-3761-6_5

[2]. Nevertheless, practical implementation of SSRL faces several challenges, including frequent neglect in traditional collaborative settings [3], widespread free-riding behavior, and limitations of existing methods—such as direct teacher guidance—in accurately diagnosing groups' SSRL levels and providing tailored support [4].

Pedagogical agents have demonstrated effectiveness in supporting collaborative learning [5]. However, within SSRL contexts, learners often perceive SSRL-oriented agents as less capable and reliable [6]. Additionally, single agents typically lack the flexibility necessary to manage complex collaborative tasks and encounter difficulties with effective task decomposition and coordination.

Multi-Agent Systems (MAS), which consist of multiple interacting agents that collaborate or compete to address complex problems [7], present a promising alternative. The integration of MAS with human collaboration can enhance both learning and regulatory processes [8]. Recent advances in Large Language Models (LLMs) have improved agents' natural language understanding and communication capabilities. LLM-based MAS can demonstrate collective intelligence emergence, enabling better adaptation to the dynamic and complex requirements of SSRL and potentially offering more comprehensive, adaptive support for student collaboration. However, a significant gap persists in the design and development of MAS explicitly grounded in SSRL theory.

Accordingly, the present study aims to design and develop an SSRL-based MAS to support collaborative learning and promote group-regulated behaviors, providing a reference for future MAS design and development in this domain. Constructing such a system enables a deeper understanding of the mechanisms through which MAS can foster SSRL and allows for exploration of its practical impact on students' collaborative learning. Additionally, this work seeks to provide educators with a design framework to guide students in engaging in SSRL.

2 Literature Review

2.1 The Challenge of Collaborative Learning

Collaborative learning is an instructional approach centered on group collaboration, referring to situations in which two or more individuals work together to learn or attempt to learn something [9]. It has been shown to enhance learners' academic outcomes and to foster important interpersonal and cognitive skills [10]. However, implementing collaborative learning often encounters difficulties that hinder its intended benefits [11]. Common challenges include inconsistent understanding of tasks among group members, ambiguous division of responsibilities, widespread free-riding, and a lack of collective strategies to address these issues. Additionally, students accustomed to independent learning may struggle to adapt to a collaborative setting [12]. Therefore, it is crucial to strengthen learners' sense of accountability and encourage them to jointly set goals, monitor progress, and regulate group performance during collaboration. Without shared goals, mutual monitoring, and adaptive strategies, collaboration risks becoming superficial, failing to harness genuine synergistic effort. To address these collaborative challenges, the theory of socially shared regulation of learning provides an effective theoretical perspective, emphasizing that groups collaboratively manage the learning process through shared goals, monitoring, and regulation.

2.2 Social Shared Regulation of Learning as a Theoretical Framework

Socially Shared Regulation of Learning (SSRL) refers to the collective metacognitive control of a task through negotiation and iterative fine-tuning of cognitive, behavioral, motivational, and emotional states within a team [1]. SSRL extends SRL into the social dimension, focusing on how group members jointly construct shared understanding of the task, set common goals, monitor team progress, and dynamically adjust strategies and motivation through dialogue, negotiation, and reflection during collaborative learning [1]. SSRL is characterized by interactivity, deep metacognitive engagement, collective agency, and socio-historical and contextual embeddedness. It helps groups establish a unified cognitive framework and shared regulatory strategies, thereby enhancing collaborative learning performance. In an experimental study involving 66 undergraduate students, Zheng et al. [13] found that a socially shared regulatory approach significantly improved learning outcomes and team performance. The coordination among social regulatory processes—such as planning, monitoring, and behavioral engagement—is crucial in distinguishing the quality of different groups. High-performing groups have been shown to progress by adopting different regulatory strategies across various learning phases [14].

Although SSRL provides a robust framework for understanding effective collaboration, its reliance on individual skills, group dynamics, and regulatory strategies makes it challenging to guide dynamically in digital learning environments [15]. Furthermore, SSRL-oriented technological tools that visually present the entire learning process and highlight connections between specific activities and overall learning trajectories can help learners adapt to both individual and collective learning challenges [3, 16]. For example, group awareness support can significantly enhance the overall perceived socially shared regulation of learning skills or behaviors among students with different levels of self-regulated learning [17]. Furthermore, adaptive SSRL strategies that integrate AI-enhanced group awareness tools and adaptive prompts can comprehensively influence the SSRL process [18]. Agent technologies can monitor collaborative processes, provide adaptive prompts, and offer real-time scaffolding for regulation, making them well-suited to operationalizing SSRL in digital learning environments [19].

2.3 From Single Agents to Multi-Agent Systems

Agents are defined as computational entities capable of perceiving their environment and making autonomous decisions. Pedagogical agents are specifically designed to automate complex instructional tasks for teachers and learners [20]. Their role has evolved from early intelligent tutoring systems that primarily delivered content or feedback to more sophisticated agents designed for collaborative scenarios. Research indicates that pedagogical agents can promote learning [5] and enhance collaborative learning performance and outcomes [21]. However, single agents have limitations in handling the dynamics of complex, multi-learner environments, often struggling with insufficient flexibility and difficulties in task decomposition and coordination management. They lack the adaptability to model multiple perspectives and concurrent interactions effectively.

Multi-Agent Systems (MAS) are collaborative systems composed of multiple individual agents [7]. Large Language Models (LLMs) serve as the "brains" of these systems, providing them with sophisticated communication, coordination, and decision-making capabilities through advanced language understanding, generation, and emergent abilities [22]. Compared to single LLM-based agents, MAS frameworks decompose LLMs into distinct agents with differentiated capabilities, fostering synergistic interactions among them to efficiently simulate complex real-world environments [23]. The inherent flexibility, reliability, self-organization, and real-time operability of MAS make them an effective solution for addressing intricate tasks [24].

Common development frameworks for MAS include AutoGen [25], LangChain [26], and Coze. Agent architectures are also diverse. For instance, Park and Sugumaran [27] proposed an architecture-based development method for MAS, advocating a phased approach (problem analysis, agent modeling, MAS architecture development) for systematic software development. Yang et al. [20] proposed a unified architecture for LLM-based pedagogical agents, comprising perception, profiling, memory, reasoning, and action modules, with capabilities enhanced through fine-tuning and prompt engineering. He et al. [7] defined LLM-based MAS as consisting of an orchestration platform and LLM-based agents. Furthermore, with recent advances in LLMs, workflow and prompt engineering—two natural language-based orchestration methods—have gained favor among educators. Workflows can orchestrate LLMs and tools through predefined logical sequences, while prompt engineering involves carefully designing and refining prompts to guide LLMs toward desired responses [28].

Given their potential to address problems in complex instructional scenarios, scholars have begun exploring the application of MAS in education. For instance, GenAI-enhanced MAS have been shown to significantly improve learning outcomes, knowledge elaboration, and performance and skills in collaborative problem-solving [29]. MAS comprising AI teachers, teaching assistants, and peer agents can adapt to diverse student needs, effectively support differentiated engagement, and help narrow learning gaps [30]. However, previous research has mostly focused on examining the impact of a single pedagogical agent on SSRL in collaborative learning [31]. For example, Harley et al. [32] investigated learners' interactions with four distinct agents responsible for guidance, monitoring, planning, and strategy support, finding that such interactions resembled forms of co-regulated learning (CoRL) and SSRL. Martha et al. [33] similarly demonstrated that a single agent providing metacognitive and motivational scaffolding positively influenced learners' self-regulation and collaborative regulation skills. Moreover, Edwards et al. [6] designed a metacognitive AI agent that delivered prompts to foster SSRL, yet learners perceived it negatively, regarding it as low in capability and reliability.

MAS capable of assuming different roles and providing diverse adaptive support holds the potential to empower SSRL and further promote collaborative learning. In collaborative learning, group awareness tools and collaboration scripts are the most common forms of support [34]. Adopting multiple group awareness tools enables them to complement one another, thereby better addressing students' collaborative learning needs and enhancing academic performance compared to a single tool [16]. Collaboration scripts, as external conditions, support the socially shared regulation process by coordinating collaborative workflows and providing detailed guidance for activities, but they lack adaptability [34]. At the same time, students perceive AI as a positive learning agent, taking on roles previously held only by human educators and students, and believe that different types of AI support the cognitive, metacognitive, and motivational domains across different SSRL phases [19]. AI agents can act as interactive participants, facilitating group task interpretation, consensus building, or productive disagreement through initiating dialogue, posing questions, offering guidance and suggestions, and providing evaluations [35]. Therefore, developing a MAS that can dynamically adapt to collaborative processes, integrate the strengths of diverse support approaches, and compensate for their limitations holds significant research value.

There remains a lack of design frameworks that explicitly translate SSRL theory into MAS architectures to guide group members in establishing a shared understanding of the task, mutual accountability, and coordinated regulatory mechanisms. To address this gap, this study aims to design and develop MAS grounded in SSRL theory to enhance learners' collective regulation during collaborative learning. Thus, we pose the following research question: How can SSRL-based MAS be designed and developed to effectively support collaborative learning?

3 Design and Implementation of a Multi-Agent Systems Prototype

The MAS design in this study is fundamentally grounded in SSRL theory and aims to support collaborative learning. In group collaboration, SSRL unfolds through four loosely sequential and recursive phases: Task Definition, Goal Setting and Planning, Enacting Study Tactics and Strategies, and Metacognitive Adaptation [1]. The specific four phases and the problems they address in collaborative learning are shown in Table 1. Accordingly, we defined five distinct agents. Four agents are mapped directly to the four SSRL phases: a Task Definition Agent, a Goal Setting and Planning Agent, an Enacting Study Tactics and Strategies Agent, and a Metacognitive Adaptation Agent. An additional Coordination Agent is responsible for identifying the current phase and managing transitions between them.

Technically, referring to the MAS framework proposed by Tran et al. [22], we designed the individual agents and their collaboration channels, as illustrated in Fig. 1. At the global level, coordination and orchestration among agents are managed through three types of collaboration channels: types, structures, and strategies. At the local level, they posit that each agent comprises a language model, a current objective, an environment, input perception, and corresponding output/actions.

For the collaboration channels, given our five-agent design, we adopted a cooperation collaboration type, a centralized communication structure, and a role-based collaboration strategy. The cooperation type indicates that agents align their goals toward a common objective for mutual benefit, namely, enhancing students' collective regulation and collaborative learning outcomes. The centralized structure features a Coordination Agent that manages the four SSRL-specific agents, facilitating phase identification and transition. This structure is more resource-efficient and better suited for simpler tasks. The role-based strategy assigns tasks according to predefined roles, with each agent specializing in a specific function to support the overall goal.

Table 1. SSRL four phases

Phases	Descriptions	The problem to be solved
Task Definition	The group negotiation leads to a shared understanding or interpretation of the collaborative task	Different understandings of the group tasks
Goal Setting and Planning	The group, based on the collective understanding of the task conditions, context and desired outcomes, negotiates common goals, standards and task plans	Unclear division of responsibilities among the group members
Enacting Study Tactics and Strategies	The group coordinates collaboration and monitors progress, collectively constructing and flexibly applying cognitive, social-emotional, behavioral and motivational strategies	Low morale and free-riding behavior within the group
Metacognitive Adaptation	The group, based on the overall experience of the previous three stages of learning, makes long-term adjustments to future motivations, beliefs and strategies	The group is unable to effectively adjust when facing setbacks

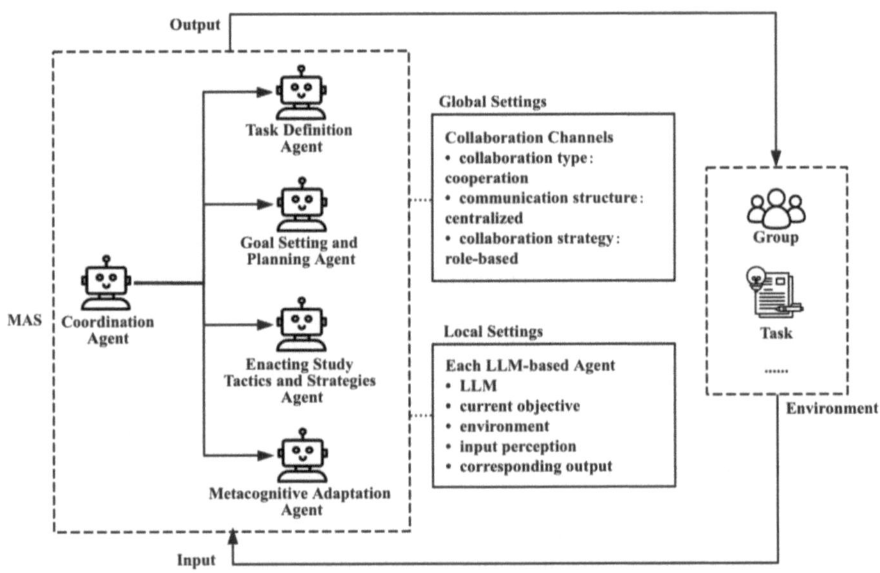

Fig. 1. The design of the MAS architecture

At the local level, each agent is driven by an LLM. The *Objective* guides the agent's actions within the system. Specifically, the **Coordination Agent** oversees the entire collaborative learning process, guiding the group through the four SSRL phases. It determines when to transition to the next phase based on the current stage and user input. The other four agents align with the goals of their respective SSRL phases. For example, the **Goal Setting and Planning Agent** assists in setting specific, measurable objectives and formulating plans. The *Environment* refers to the virtual or external space in which the MAS operates; in this study, the collaborative learning interface that interacts with the student group. *Input Perception* is implemented via text input, a familiar format for students. *Output* refers to the actions or results generated by the model after processing input messages in light of its environment and objective. In brief, within a collaborative learning context, the MAS stores relevant information about group members (e.g., group task requirements, group size, students' majors) and simultaneously acquires information about group collaboration through interactions with students. Based on the SSRL theory, it then activates the corresponding agents to guide the group through the four stages of collaboration.

The MAS was developed using the Coze Multi-Agent framework on the Coze agent development platform. This platform enables configuring multiple agents within a system to handle complex logic. The orchestration interface of the MAS is shown in Fig. 2.

Fig. 2. The development of MAS based on the Coze platform

For the orchestration of the MAS, we globally configured its persona and response logic, variables, long-term memory, an opening remark, and collaboration channels for the five agents. For persona and response logic, the MAS was named "SSRL Guide." It operates on SSRL, covering four stages, and briefly explains its role in each. For memory, two variables—"Learning Task" and "Group Goal"—were set to store the collaborative task topic and the group's goals, respectively. Meanwhile, a long-term memory database named "Group" was created to store relevant information from interactions between the group and the agents. For the dialogue interface, the default text input method was used. The opening remark, i.e., the MAS's introduction to the group, is: "Hello everyone! I am your collaboration guide. Based on the theory of socially shared regulation of learning (SSRL), I will help you clarify tasks, set goals, plan learning steps, and reflect on and adjust the learning process together. I will facilitate the discussion through questions and prompts, ensuring that everyone participates. Let us start by understanding the current learning task! Please feel free to tell me if you have any questions." Regarding collaboration channels, the five agents adopt a centralized communication structure, share the same goal, and employ prompt engineering based on a role-based collaboration strategy.

At the local level, we configured each agent's LLM, applicable scenarios, and prompts. Each agent uses the "Doubao 1.5 Pro Role-playing" LLM, which is suitable for role-playing scenarios. Applicable scenarios refer to an outline of each agent's functions and the contexts in which it should be used, enabling the preceding agent to understand under what circumstances to switch to this agent. The prompt for each agent was designed following the framework proposed by Mollick and Mollick [36], encompassing Role and Goal, Step-by-Step Instructions, Pedagogy, Personalization, and Constraints. The five agents act as the SSRL process facilitation coordinator, the task clarification facilitator, the goal co-construction facilitator, the practice support facilitator, and the learning deepening facilitator, respectively. Here, we elaborate on the Metacognitive Adaptation Agent. The applicable scenario for the Metacognitive Adaptation Agent is "used in the metacognitive adaptation stage to help the group reflect on their learning experience and adjust their cognition, strategies, or goals to optimize future learning". The role is set as the learning deepening facilitator. The goal is to help the group reflect on their learning experience and adjust their cognition, strategies, or goals to optimize future learning. The Step-by-Step Instructions include: review of the entire learning process, multi-dimensional evaluation, fundamental insights, and transfer and creation. The Pedagogy includes transformative learning theory and critical reflection techniques. Personalization means that the agent adjusts the depth of reflection according to the group's learning outcomes and uses appropriate guidance methods for different levels of reflective ability. The Constraints are: not presupposing "correct" learning gains, not comparing learning outcomes among members, and avoiding overly abstract theoretical discussions. Finally, the system was deployed on the Coze web version.

4 Usability Testing of Multi-Agent Systems Prototype

Following the development of the MAS, a user test was conducted to evaluate its usability. The test was carried out at a university in Northwest China. Fourteen graduate students majoring in Educational Technology/Modern Educational Technology were recruited through convenience sampling. This study is an exploratory, early-stage evaluation; therefore, a sample of 14 participants is sufficient to identify the majority of usability problems [37]. Although a convenience sample has limited generalizability, it allows for rapid, low-cost iterative feedback, is suitable for initial functionality testing, and provides direction for subsequent random sampling tests. Moreover, graduate students, as the core target user group, are representative of the intended users. All participants provided informed consent. The experiment consisted of three phases and lasted approximately two hours. During the collaborative task, each group (two groups of 3 and two groups of 4) shared a single computer to interact with the MAS. The detailed experimental procedure is illustrated in Fig. 3.

Preparation Phase. The researcher briefly introduced the experimental procedure and the MAS's functionalities to the participants. Participants were organized into groups.

Implementation Phase. Participants were presented with the following task: "Your group is a newly established 'Educational AI Ethics Review Committee' at your university. The administration plans to introduce a batch of new AI teaching tools, but requires your committee to conduct an in-depth assessment of their potential ethical risks before making a decision. Your task is to draft the core principles for a 'Guideline for Educational AI Applications' to ensure the technology consistently serves students' best interests." The task required multi-perspective analysis and consensus-building, culminating in a collaborative Word document containing at least 3 specific principles for the guideline. Groups were instructed to collaboratively use the same computer to interact with the MAS to complete the task, with a 40-min time limit.

Post-test Phase. Participants individually completed the System Usability Scale, and then each group took part in a 20-min focus group interview.

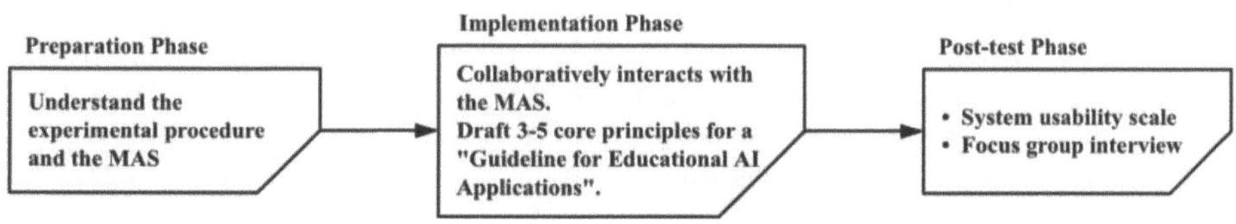

Fig. 3. Experimental Procedure

The usability evaluation combined data from the questionnaire and interviews. The System Usability Scale (SUS) [38] was used to collect participant ratings of the MAS. The scale comprises 10 items (rated on a 5-point Likert scale) across two dimensions: Usability and Learnability, with items 2, 4, 6, 8, and 10 being negatively worded. The Cronbach's α coefficient was 0.91, indicating good reliability. Descriptive statistics were calculated to gauge overall perceptions of usability. A semi-structured interview outline focused on the MAS's support across the four SSRL phases, as well as general evaluations and suggestions. Interview data were subjected to thematic analysis to understand the MAS's practical role. Using a three-level coding process grounded in qualitative analysis, data were coded into strengths, weaknesses, and improvement suggestions for the MAS. These codes were then synthesized to identify overarching themes.

Descriptive results from the SUS questionnaire are presented in Table 2. Items 2, 4, 6, 8, and 10 are reverse-scored. Overall, participants rated the MAS's usability at a moderate to above-average level, with room for improvement across all items. The Learnability dimension received the highest scores, indicating that the MAS was relatively easy to use and did not require specific technical support or operational guidance. However, ratings for perceived Usability were lower. For instance, Item 1 had the lowest score, suggesting participants did not perceive a strong need to use this MAS in their actual collaborative learning contexts. This may be because the MAS guidance format, unlike common Generative AI tools that can generate answers for them, also falls short of real instructors in terms of targetedness and rapport. Furthermore, the score for Item 2 indicated that participants still found the MAS somewhat complex to use. This may be because, when introducing the MAS to the participants, we required them to familiarize themselves with SSRL and to interact with the MAS by seeking advice, which led to a comparative experience in which the MAS was perceived as more complex and less easy to use than common GenAI tools.

Table 2. Descriptive statistical results of the MAS SUS

Dimensions	Items	*Min*	*Max*	*M*	*SD*
Usable	1. I think that I would like to use this MAS frequently	1	5	2.79	1.05
	2. I found the MAS unnecessarily complex	1	4	2.93	1.00
	3. I thought the MAS was easy to use	2	5	3.57	0.94
	5. I found the various functions in this MAS were well integrated	2	5	3.36	0.93
	6. I thought there was too much inconsistency in this MAS	2	4	2.64	0.75
	7. I would imagine that most people would learn to use this MAS very quickly	2	5	3.57	1.22
	8. I found the MAS very awkward to use	1	4	2.50	1.02
	9. I felt very confident using the MAS	1	5	3.29	0.91
Learnable	4. I think that I would need the support of a technical person to be able to use this MAS	1	4	2.14	0.95
	10. I needed to learn a lot of things before I could get going with this MAS	1	5	2.21	1.12

Thematic analysis of the interview data concerning the MAS's strengths, weaknesses, and suggested improvements yielded the results summarized in Table 3. Participants noted that the MAS provided structured guidance, fostered shared understanding of the task, monitoring, and regulation among group members, and helped integrate diverse perspectives. However, they also identified several issues, such as unclear phase transitions and overly academic or formal language in the agents' prompts and responses. Corresponding suggestions included enhancing phase guidance and simplifying the language. Overall, the MAS successfully delivered SSRL-based collaborative support, but its guidance clarity and communication style require further refinement.

These findings indicate that future iterations should prioritize user experience design, including enhanced interface guidance, language adaptation, and dynamic strategic support, to more effectively facilitate the group's shared regulation process. Additionally, users expressed expectations for the MAS to address a broader range of questions beyond those directly related to the collaborative process. In light of the increasing use of Generative AI tools as alternatives to search engines among students, future versions of the MAS could incorporate knowledge-answering capabilities to address this need.

Table 3. The results of the thematic analysis of the interview

Themes	Categories	Descriptions	Example
Strengths	Provide structured guidance	MAS achieves this by means of asking questions, breaking down tasks, providing stage instructions, etc., to assist the group in entering the collaborative process	We believe that its greatest benefit to us lies in the questioning guidance and the integration of summarizing our responses
	Promote shared understanding and integration	By summarizing, asking questions and integrating viewpoints, MAS helps the group reach a consensus or expose differences	
	Promote monitoring and regulation	By summarizing, asking questions and integrating viewpoints, MAS helps the group reach a consensus or expose differences	MAS will prompt the next step to be taken, guiding and inspiring us to think
Weaknesses	The guidance is not clear enough / The stages are ambiguous	The user is not aware of which stage they are currently in, and the task breakdown is not detailed enough, resulting in an unclear direction for collaboration	Not very clear about the goals and plans
	Feedback academicization	MAS's response was not close enough to the students' actual comprehension level. Moreover, the use of professional terms even hindered the progress	When we encounter unfamiliar proper nouns, MAS will not provide explanations
	Lack of effective summarization	MAS failed to actively guide the summary process, or the summary process was not natural enough	We asked MAS to summarize for us, but it failed to do so

(*continued*)

Table 3. (*continued*)

Themes	Categories	Descriptions	Example
Improvement suggestions	Enhancement stage prompt or progress visualization	Clearly indicate the current stage and provide a task breakdown chart or progress bar	Some user prompts can be designed to guide our questioning
	Provide explanatory support and natural language adaptation	Explain the professional terms and use expressions that are more in line with the language style of students	MAS's response is overly academic
	Strengthening summary and reflection guidance	At the critical juncture, the guiding team should conduct an independent summary and provide a structured reflection template	MAS failed to guide us through the process of summarization

5 Conclusions and Future Work

This study designed and developed an SSRL-based MAS prototype and conducted an initial user test to evaluate its effectiveness. The findings indicate that the MAS can guide learners in monitoring and regulating group behavior, although further refinement is necessary to clarify the phases and enhance the user experience.

Future work should provide clearer and more visible phase-based support for learning groups. For instance, researchers could develop phase-specific task checklists or just-in-time user prompts, such as a checklist for task definition to guide groups in identifying key problems and available resources, or reminders to confirm consensus on shared goals for each phase. This scaffolding can be embedded directly into the MAS interface, with the level of detail adjusted according to group progress or previous behaviors. Additionally, interactive tutorials or visual progress bars indicating the current SSRL phase can help learners use the MAS more effectively.

Research has shown that students with stronger SRL skills significantly influence group regulation [15]. Such students tend to set personal goals more effectively, monitor their learning progress, and proactively adjust strategies when facing difficulties, thereby implicitly enhancing the group's overall regulatory behaviors during collaboration. Therefore, future designs could integrate SRL and CoRL considerations into the MAS. For example, by identifying members with high SRL capability and encouraging them to act as models, while also designing interactive prompts that facilitate mutual regulation among members, so as to support collaborative learning from a broader perspective of individual-group interaction.

Additionally, multimodal learning analytics could be incorporated to provide learning analytics interfaces and dashboards, offering visual support for both teachers and students. These dashboards could display real-time indicators of group collaboration, such as equity of participation, the emotional valence of discussions, and alignment between individual and group goals. Using data from chat logs, voice inputs, or even facial expressions, the system could generate heatmaps or temporal diagrams that visualize how a group's regulatory activities evolve across the four SSRL phases. Teachers could then intervene at the right moment with targeted advice, while students could use the dashboard for self-reflection on their collaborative patterns.

Further empirical studies are also recommended to validate the impact of the MAS on collaborative learning outcomes. These studies should employ rigorous experimental designs, such as randomized controlled trials or longitudinal quasi-experiments, comparing the proposed MAS with traditional collaboration scripts or generative AI tools. Outcome measures should extend beyond academic achievement to include process-oriented and affective variables—for example, frequency of regulatory behaviors, quality of group metacognitive discussions, collective efficacy, and satisfaction. Furthermore, mixed-methods approaches combining log data analysis with interviews could reveal how and under what conditions the MAS influences group dynamics [39], thereby providing actionable insights for iterative system improvement.

Acknowledgments. This work was supported by the [National Natural Science Foundation of China] under (grant number 62467007) and Digital Education Special Research Project (grant number JYSZH[2025]ZD130).

Disclosure of Interests. The authors have no competing interests to declare that are relevant to the content of this article.

References

1. Hadwin, A.F., Iéirvelri, S., Miller, M.: Self-regulated, co-regulated, and socially shared regulation of learning in collaborative learning environments. Handbook of Self-Regulation of Learning and Performance, pp. 65–84 (2011)
2. Sharma, K., Nguyen, A., Hong, Y.: Self-regulation and shared regulation in collaborative learning in adaptive digital learning environments: a systematic review of empirical studies. Br. J. Edu. Technol. **55**(4), 1398–1436 (2024)
3. Järvelä, S., et al.: Enhancing socially shared regulation in collaborative learning groups: designing for CSCL regulation tools. Educ. Tech. Res. Dev. **63**(1), 125–142 (2015)
4. Singh, C.A., Muis, K.R.: An integrated model of socially shared regulation of learning: the role of metacognition, affect, and motivation. Educ. Psychol. **59**(3), 177–194 (2024)
5. Schroeder, N.L., Davis, R.O., Yang, E.: Designing and learning with pedagogical agents: an umbrella review. J. Educ. Comput. Res. **62**(8), 1907–1936 (2025)
6. Edwards, J., et al.: Human-AI collaboration: designing artificial agents to facilitate socially shared regulation among learners. Br. J. Edu. Technol. **56**(2), 712–733 (2025)
7. He, J., Treude, C., Lo, D.: LLM-Based multi-agent systems for software engineering: literature review, vision, and the road ahead. ACM Trans. Software Eng. Methodol. **34**(5), 124:1–124:30 (2025)
8. Järvelä, S., Nguyen, A., Hadwin, A.: Human and artificial intelligence collaboration for socially shared regulation in learning. Br. J. Edu. Technol. **54**(5), 1057–1076 (2023)
9. Dillenbourg, P.: What do you mean by collaborative learning? In: Collaborative-learning: Cognitive and Computational Approaches, pp. 1–19 (1999)

10. Tian, Q., Zheng, X.: Effectiveness of online collaborative problem-solving method on students' learning performance: a meta-analysis. J. Comput. Assist. Learn. **40**(1), 326–341 (2024)
11. Lu, G., Ba, S., Yang, L.: Optimizing GAI-assisted formative feedback: an experimental study on its effects on engagement, shared metacognition, and learning performance in online collaborative learning. Educ. Inf. Technol. **30**, 25937–25967 (2025)
12. Lane, S.: Promoting collaborative learning among students. Am. J. Educ. Res. **4**(8), 602–607 (2016)
13. Zheng, L., Li, X., Huang, R.: The effect of socially shared regulation approach on learning performance in computer-supported collaborative learning. J. Educ. Technol. Soc. **20**(4), 35–46 (2017)
14. Malmberg, J., Järvelä, S., Järvenoja, H., Panadero, E.: Promoting socially shared regulation of learning in CSCL: progress of socially shared regulation among high-and low-performing groups. Comput. Hum. Behav. **52**, 562–572 (2015)
15. Panadero, E., Kirschner, P.A., Järvelä, S., Malmberg, J., Järvenoja, H.: How individual self-regulation affects group regulation and performance: a shared regulation intervention. Small Group Res. **46**(4), 431–454 (2015)
16. Chen, D., Zhang, Y., Luo, H., Zhu, Z., Ma, J., Lin, Y.: Effects of group awareness support in CSCL on students' learning performance: a three-level meta-analysis. Int. J. Comput.-Support. Collab. Learn. **19**(1), 97–129 (2024)
17. Chen, D., Zhang, Y., Gao, H., Luo, H., Guo, F., Jing, L.: Exploring the combined effects of group awareness support and students' self-regulated learning levels on socially shared regulation of learning and learning outcomes in CSCL. Int. J. Comput.-Support. Collaborative Learn. 1–31 (2026)
18. Wu, J.-Q., Zhang, M., Wu, F., Huang, J., Han, Y., Liu, Y.: The effects of AI-enhanced adaptive socially shared regulation strategies on science pre-service teachers' instructional design skills and socially shared regulation in CSCL. Internet High. Educ. **69**, 101072 (2026)
19. Kim, J., Detrick, R., Yu, S., Song, Y., Bol, L., Li, N.: Socially shared regulation of learning and artificial intelligence: opportunities to support socially shared regulation. Educ. Inf. Technol. **30**(9), 11483–11521 (2025)
20. Yang, J., Wang, M., Du, X., Na, R.: A comprehensive survey on large-language-model-based agents for education. IEEE Trans. Learn. Technol. **18**, 898–913 (2025)
21. Hu, W., Tian, J., Li, Y.: Enhancing student engagement in online collaborative writing through a generative AI-Based conversational agent. Internet High. Educ. **65**, 100979 (2025)
22. Tran, K.T., Dao, D., Nguyen, M.D., Pham, Q.V., O'Sullivan, B., Nguyen, H.D.: Multi-agent collaboration mechanisms: a survey of LLMs (2025). arXiv preprint arXiv:2501.06322
23. Guo, T., et al.: Large language model based multi-agents: a survey of progress and challenges (2024). arXiv preprint arXiv:2402.01680
24. Xi, Z., et al.: The rise and potential of large language model based agents: a survey. Sci. China Inf. Sci. **68**(2), 121101 (2025)
25. Wu, Q., et al.: AutoGen: enabling Next-Gen LLM applications via multi-agent conversations. In: First Conference on Language Modeling (2024)
26. Topsakal, O., Akinci, T.C.: Creating large language model applications utilizing langchain: a primer on developing LLM Apps fast. In: International Conference on Applied Engineering and Natural Sciences, vol. 1, no. 1, pp. 1050–1056 (2023)
27. Park, S., Sugumaran, V.: Designing multi-agent systems: a framework and application. Expert Syst. Appl. **28**(2), 259–271 (2005)
28. Lee, D., Palmer, E.: Prompt engineering in higher education: a systematic review to help inform curricula. Int. J. Educ. Technol. High. Educ. **22**(1), 7 (2025)

29. Zheng, L., Shi, Z., Gao, L.: A generative artificial intelligence-enhanced multiagent approach to empowering collaborative problem solving across different learning domains. Comput. Educ. 105489 (2025)
30. Hao, Z., Cao, J., Li, R., Yu, J., Liu, Z., Zhang, Y.: Mapping Student-AI interaction dynamics in multi-agent learning environments: supporting personalised learning and reducing performance gaps. Comput. Educ. 105472 (2025)
31. Alias, A., Saad, S., Ariffin, A.H., Fahri, H.: Trends and developments in intelligent agent for Socially Shared Regulated Learning (SSRL): a bibliometric review. Int. J. Educ. Psychol. Couns. **10**(59), 475–488 (2025)
32. Harley, J.M., Taub, M., Azevedo, R., Bouchet, F.: Let's set up some subgoals: understanding human-pedagogical agent collaborations and their implications for learning and prompt and feedback compliance. IEEE Trans. Learn. Technol. **11**(1), 54–66 (2017)
33. Martha, A.S.D., Santoso, H.B., Junus, K., Suhartanto, H.: The effect of the integration of metacognitive and motivation scaffolding through a pedagogical agent on self-and co-regulation learning. IEEE Trans. Learn. Technol. **16**(4), 573–584 (2023)
34. Miller, M., Hadwin, A.: Scripting and awareness tools for regulating collaborative learning: changing the landscape of support in CSCL. Comput. Hum. Behav. **52**, 573–588 (2015)
35. Ba, S., Shi, X., Wu, S., Lu, G.: Artificial intelligence agents in computer-supported collaborative learning: a systematic literature review. Comput. Educ.: Artif. Intell. 100579 (2026)
36. Mollick, E., Mollick, L.: Assigning AI: seven approaches for students, with prompts (2023). arXiv preprint arXiv:2306.10052
37. Diah, N.M., Ismail, M., Ahmad, S., Dahari, M.K.M.: Usability testing for educational computer game using observation method. In: 2010 International Conference on Information Retrieval & Knowledge Management (CAMP), pp. 157–161, IEEE (2010)
38. Lewis, J.R., Sauro, J.: The Factor Structure of the System Usability Scale. In: Kurosu, M. (ed.) Human Centered Design, vol. 5619, pp. 94–103. Springer, Berlin, Heidelberg (2009)
39. Kok, X.F.K.: Measuring socially shared regulation of learning: a review and critique of existing self-report surveys. Metacogn. Learn. **20**(1), 36 (2025)

Modeling Interrelations in School-Family-Community Collaborative Education and Their Effects on Students' Social and Emotional Competence

Can Zuo[1], Yinghui Shi[2(✉)], Xuan Wang[3], Chuhong Xu[4], Zhen Li[1], and Meng Zheng[1]

[1] Wuhan City Polytechnic, Wuhan 430064, China
[2] Hainan College of Software Technology, Qionghai 571400, China
shiyinghui@hncst.edu.cn
[3] Central China Normal University, Wuhan 430079, China
[4] Sony Corporation of America, San Jose, CA 95112, USA

Abstract. Students' social and emotional competence (SEC) is shaped by Students' social and emotional competence (SEC) is increasingly recognized as a core developmental outcome that is shaped by coordinated support across families, schools, and communities. However, existing research has often examined these settings separately, offering limited mechanism-oriented evidence on how school-family-community collaborative education is structurally organized and how it is transmitted into student development. Guided by ecological systems theory and the overlapping spheres of influence framework, this study used structural equation modeling to examine the interrelations among community collaborative education involvement (CCEI), school collaborative education involvement (SCEI), family collaborative education involvement (FCEI), and students' SEC. Matched questionnaire data were collected from 3,295 students in Grades 3–9 in a county-level educational context in central China. Results showed that CCEI significantly predicted both SCEI and FCEI, and SCEI further predicted FCEI. Among the three domains, only FCEI had a significant direct positive association with SEC, whereas the direct effects of SCEI and CCEI were not statistically significant. Bias-corrected bootstrap analyses indicated that CCEI and SCEI influenced SEC indirectly through FCEI, with an additional sequential pathway from CCEI to SCEI, then to FCEI, and finally to SEC. These findings identify a family-centered transmission mechanism in county-level collaborative education and suggest that community and school resources promote students' SEC most effectively when they are converted into sustained, high-quality family engagement practices.

Keywords: Social and Emotional Competence · School-family-community Collaboration · Structural Equation Modeling · County-level China

K. T. Chui et al. (Eds.): ICBL 2026, LNCS 16778, pp. 76–91, 2027.
https://doi.org/10.1007/978-981-92-3761-6_6

1 Introduction

Social and emotional competence (SEC) refers to a set of interrelated cognitive, affective, interpersonal, and behavioral capacities through which students understand themselves, regulate emotions and behaviors, show empathy, establish constructive relationships, and make responsible decisions. In the CASEL framework, these capacities are organized into five domains: self-awareness, self-management, social awareness, relationship skills, and responsible decision-making [1]. Recent international evidence positions social and emotional skills as central developmental resources rather than peripheral non-cognitive attributes. The OECD Survey on Social and Emotional Skills shows that these skills are associated with students' well-being, learning behaviors, health, and future aspirations [2], while contemporary meta-analytic evidence indicates that universal school-based SEL programs improve social-emotional, behavioral, and academic outcomes across diverse K-12 populations [3].

The importance of the SEC has become especially salient as schools and families respond to widening mental-health, relational, and learning challenges. Systemic SEL scholarship argues that student outcomes are strengthened when classrooms, schools, families, and community partners provide consistent opportunities to learn and practice social, emotional, and relational skills [4]. Measurement-oriented research also shows that SEC is increasingly assessed as a multidimensional construct across elementary and secondary education [5]. Longitudinal evidence links adolescents' social-emotional skills with greater school engagement and lower school burnout [6]. For Chinese students, recent validation and empirical studies suggest that SEC is a meaningful construct for understanding school adjustment, mental health, and rural educational vulnerability [7, 8].

SEC does not develop in a single setting. Ecological systems theory conceptualizes child development as the result of dynamic transactions between individuals and nested environmental systems [9]. Epstein's overlapping spheres of influence framework similarly proposes that schools, families, and communities share responsibility for students' development and that their coordinated actions can generate stronger support than isolated efforts [10, 11]. Recent meta-analytic evidence supports this systemic logic: family-school interventions improve children's social-behavioral competence and mental health [12], and family-school partnership interventions support both academic and social-emotional functioning [13, 14]. These findings imply that collaboration is not merely the presence of multiple actors, but the coordinated conversion of institutional and community resources into everyday developmental practices.

County-level China provides a distinctive and under-examined context for testing this mechanism. Counties are important governance spaces in which urban, town, and rural schools interact with community services, parent organizations, and public educational resources. Although regional and urban-rural educational inequalities in China have narrowed in some respects, county systems continue to face uneven family resources, migration-related care-giving challenges, fragmented community services, and variable school capacity [15–17]. In such contexts, community and school participation may shape students' SEC only when they activate family participation and support stable home routines. This makes county-level collaborative education a theoretically important and practically urgent site for examining cross-system pathways.

Despite growing scholarly attention to collaborative education, three gaps remain. First, many studies focus on dyadic relationships, such as family-school cooperation or community-based programming, rather than modeling family, school, and community participation within one integrated framework. Second, less is known about whether school and community participation exert direct effects on SEC or operate indirectly by strengthening family involvement. Third, empirical evidence from county-level educational ecosystems remains scarce, even though these settings are central to equity-oriented educational governance in China. Addressing these gaps is necessary for moving collaborative education research from descriptive advocacy toward mechanism-based explanation.

This study addresses three research questions: (1) What structural relationships characterize participation in collaborative education among families, schools, and communities? (2) Do family, school, and community participation have direct effects on students' SEC? (3) Does family participation mediate the effects of school and community participation on students' SEC?

This study contributes to the literature in three ways. First, it advances research on school–family–community collaboration by moving beyond dyadic perspectives and modeling the structural interrelationships among community, school, and family participation within a single analytical framework. In doing so, it provides a more comprehensive understanding of how collaborative educational ecosystems operate.

Second, the study contributes to the social and emotional competence (SEC) literature by identifying family involvement as a proximal mechanism through which school- and community-based supports are translated into student developmental outcomes. By demonstrating indirect and sequential pathways, the study shifts attention from whether collaboration matters to how collaborative educational practices influence students' SEC.

Third, the study extends the international evidence base by examining these relationships in a county-level Chinese context. As counties represent a critical governance unit linking urban and rural educational systems, the findings offer new insights into how collaborative education functions in resource-constrained and educationally diverse settings and contribute to the growing comparative literature on educational equity and student development.

2 Literature Review

This review draws on ecological systems theory and the theory of overlapping spheres of influence to examine three interconnected strands of scholarship: school-family-community collaborative education, social and emotional competence (SEC), and the mechanisms through which collaborative educational participation may contribute to students' SEC. Particular attention is given to the mediating role of family involvement, which may serve as a key pathway linking school and community engagement to student developmental outcomes.

2.1 School-Family-Community Collaborative Education

School-family-community collaborative education can be understood as a mesosystemic arrangement in which families, schools, and community actors coordinate goals, roles, communication, and resources to support children's development. Ecological systems theory emphasizes that development depends not only on the quality of separate microsystems, but also on the quality of connections among them [9]. Epstein's overlapping spheres framework further specifies that family, school, and community influences may operate independently, sequentially, or jointly depending on the extent of shared responsibility and institutionalized partnership practices [10, 11].

Recent empirical literature increasingly treats collaboration as a relational and organizational mechanism. Meta-analytic evidence shows that family-school interventions can improve children's social-behavioral competence and mental health, especially when they combine relationship-building processes with structured home-school practices [12]. Family-school partnership interventions also support students' academic and social-emotional functioning, although effects vary by student characteristics and intervention components [13]. Evidence focused on parent-teacher relationships indicates that family-school engagement interventions improve communication, relational joining, and problem-solving processes that are central to addressing students' emotional and behavioral needs [14].

Community participation adds an additional layer to this mechanism. Community actors can disseminate educational policies, mobilize public and social resources, organize practice-based learning activities, and create social norms that support child development. In county-level systems, community participation can function as a resource-brokering mechanism between local government, schools, families, and social organizations. Recent evidence from rural China suggests that parent councils and school-based parent organizations can improve parent-teacher communication and participation, but their effectiveness depends on parental awareness and school implementation capacity [15]. Community-based school-family partnerships in rural early childhood education also demonstrate the potential of local resources to expand educational opportunity when partnerships are carefully designed [16].

Therefore, the central question is not simply whether families, schools, and communities matter, but how their participation is structurally connected. The present study treats CCEI, SCEI, and FCEI as interdependent constructs rather than isolated predictors.

2.2 Social and Emotional Competence

SEC is a multidimensional construct that encompasses students' capacities for emotional understanding and regulation, social perspective taking, relationship building, and responsible action. Contemporary educational research often uses related terms such as social-emotional skills, social and emotional learning competencies, and non-cognitive skills. Although these labels come from different disciplinary traditions, they converge on the idea that students' developmental success depends on competencies that integrate thinking, feeling, behavior, and relationships [1, 2, 6].

The CASEL framework remains influential because it offers a parsimonious structure for organizing teachable competencies across school, family, and community settings [1]. Recent systematic review evidence shows that many contemporary instruments for school-aged children and adolescents are increasingly aligned with the five CASEL domains, while also revealing variation in domain coverage, informant sources, and psychometric quality [6]. In China, Shi and colleagues developed and validated a student-reported social emotional skills scale based on the CASEL framework, providing evidence that the five-domain structure can be meaningfully adapted to Chinese elementary school contexts [7].

SEC is associated with both immediate and long-term developmental outcomes. Contemporary meta-analytic evidence indicates that school-based SEL interventions improve students' social and emotional skills and related outcomes [3]. A longitudinal study of adolescents found that social-emotional skills such as persistence, curiosity, social engagement, and low loneliness were associated with school engagement and lower burnout over time [5]. In rural China, Mo and colleagues found that left-behind status was associated with lower SEC and that teacher support could buffer disadvantage [9]. These findings suggest that SEC is both an individual developmental capacity and an outcome sensitive to the quality of support provided across family, school, and community settings.

For the present study, the CASEL framework is appropriate because it provides a theory-based structure that is widely recognized internationally, compatible with Chinese measurement research, and directly linked to educational practice. It also allows the study to interpret SEC not simply as an individual trait, but as a set of competencies cultivated through coordinated developmental opportunities.

2.3 Family Involvement as a Mediating Mechanism

Although schools and communities provide important developmental resources, students rarely experience these influences directly. Ecological systems theory suggests that distal influences are often transmitted through more proximal developmental environments, particularly the family. As the primary context for emotional socialization, interpersonal interaction, and behavioral guidance, the family plays a critical role in translating institutional and community supports into students' everyday developmental experiences.

Recent empirical evidence supports this perspective. Sheridan et al. found that family-school interventions improved children's social-emotional functioning largely through enhanced parent–child interactions and family engagement processes [12]. Similarly, Smith et al. reported that family-school partnership interventions positively influenced students' academic and social-emotional outcomes, although the magnitude of effects depended on the quality of family engagement [13]. Meta-analytic evidence further indicates that parental involvement programs promote children's social-emotional development by strengthening parenting practices and home learning environments [18]. More recently, Martinez-Yarza et al. demonstrated that family involvement contributes to students' social-emotional development through sustained educational engagement and relational support [19].

These findings suggest that family involvement may function as a key transmission mechanism linking school and community participation to students' SEC. Schools can enhance family involvement through communication, parent education, and partnership activities, while communities may expand access to educational resources and participation opportunities. Consequently, the effects of school and community participation on SEC may operate indirectly through strengthened family engagement.

This perspective provides the theoretical foundation for the mediation and sequential mediation hypotheses examined in the present study.

3 Model and Hypotheses

The proposed model is grounded in ecological systems theory and the overlapping spheres of influence framework. These perspectives suggest that students' development is shaped not only by the characteristics of individual contexts but also by the quality of interactions among family, school, and community systems.

Community collaborative education involvement (CCEI) is conceptualized as an upstream contextual condition because communities can mobilize educational resources, disseminate policy information, provide developmental opportunities, and establish social norms that support collaborative education. Consequently, stronger community involvement is expected to facilitate both school participation and family engagement.

School collaborative education involvement (SCEI) functions as an institutional bridge connecting community resources with family practices. Through parent education, home-school communication, volunteering opportunities, and learning-at-home guidance, schools can create conditions that encourage and sustain family participation. Therefore, school participation is expected to positively predict family involvement.

Family collaborative education involvement (FCEI) represents the most proximal developmental environment among the three domains. Families provide daily opportunities for emotional communication, behavioral guidance, relationship building, and social learning. Previous research consistently demonstrates that parental involvement is associated with students' social-emotional development, psychological well-being, and educational adjustment. Accordingly, family involvement is expected to exert the strongest direct influence on students' SEC.

Taken together, these theoretical arguments suggest that community and school participation may influence students' SEC both directly and indirectly through family involvement. Furthermore, because communities often shape schools' capacity to implement collaborative education, a sequential pathway may exist in which community participation strengthens school participation, school participation enhances family involvement, and family involvement ultimately promotes students' SEC. The hypotheses are as follows (Fig. 1):

H1: CCEI positively predicts FCEI.
H2: SCEI positively predicts FCEI.
H3: CCEI positively predicts SCEI.
H4: FCEI positively predicts students' SEC.
H5: SCEI positively predicts students' SEC.
H6: CCEI positively predicts students' SEC.
H7: FCEI could mediate the relationship between SCEI and students' SEC.
H8: FCEI could mediate the relationship between CCEI and students' SEC.
H9: SCEI and FCEI sequentially mediate the relationship between CCEI and students' SEC.

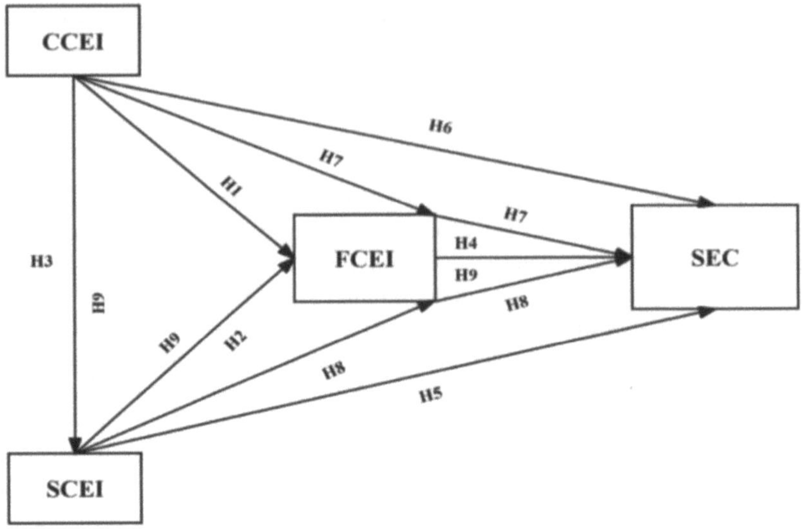

Fig. 1. Hypothesized Structural Model.

4 Method

A cross-sectional, matched questionnaire design was used in this study. Student, parent, and homeroom-teacher questionnaires were matched with each student's unique identity account, and the questionnaire data were filtered for final analysis of students' SEC and family, school, and community collaborative education involvement.

4.1 Participants

With the assistance of the mentor platform and the support of the Education Bureau of Gong'an County, Hubei Province, 8 townships were randomly selected from the 16 townships in Gong'an County, and students, homeroom teachers, and parents from relevant schools were invited to voluntarily participate in the questionnaire survey. The survey utilized Wenjuanxing, an electronic questionnaire platform, to facilitate completion and data collection and organization. The sample comprised 3,295 students in Grades 3–9. The gender distribution was balanced, with 1,651 boys (50.11%) and 1,644 girls (49.89%). Among the participants, 2,052 were primary school students in Grades 3–6 (62.27%), and 1,243 were junior secondary school students (37.73%).

4.2 Measures

Students' social emotional competencies (SEC). Students' SEC was assessed with a Chinese adaptation of a Social and Emotional Competence Scale based on the CASEL framework. The instrument included 46 items covering five sub-dimensions: self-awareness, social awareness, self-management, relationship skills, and responsible decision-making. Items were rated on a four-point Likert scale (1 = strongly disagree, 4 = strongly agree), with higher scores indicating higher SEC. The overall Cronbach's alpha coefficient in the present sample was 0.972, indicating excellent internal consistency.

Family collaborative education involvement (FCEI). FCEI was assessed by adapting Epstein and colleagues' school-family-community partnership framework [10, 11]. The 24-item measure covered six dimensions: parent education knowledge, bidirectional home-school communication, volunteering, learning-at-home support, parent organization development, and connection with community learning resources. Items were rated on a five-point Likert scale (1 = strongly disagree, 5 = strongly agree), with higher scores indicating stronger family involvement in collaborative education practices.

School collaborative education involvement (SCEI). SCEI was derived from the same partnership framework and administered as a homeroom-teacher self-report instrument. The 24-item measure assessed six dimensions: teaching parent education knowledge, bidirectional family-school communication, encouraging volunteering, guiding learning at home, collaborating with parent organizations, and linking with community resources. Items were rated on a five-point Likert scale.

Community collaborative education involvement (CCEI). CCEI was operationalized at the system level because community-based educational support is multidimensional and often affects students indirectly through schools and families. The measure captured four dimensions: dissemination of educational policies, mobilization and linkage of community educational resources, organization of learning and practice activities, and fostering a civilized and harmonious community climate. Higher scores indicated stronger community-level support for collaborative education. Because CCEI was constructed as a system-level composite indicator rather than as a conventional student-level reflective scale, its psychometric properties should be further validated in future research.

4.3 Analytic Strategy

Data analyses (Tables 1 and 2) were conducted using SPSS 26 and AMOS 28. Internal consistency was evaluated using Cronbach's alpha coefficients, and construct validity was examined through confirmatory factor analysis (CFA). Structural equation modeling (SEM) was used to test the hypothesized relationships among CCEI, SCEI, FCEI, and SEC. Model fit was evaluated using multiple indices, including CMIN/DF, GFI, NFI, IFI, CFI, TLI, and RMSEA. Following common SEM guidance, CFI/TLI values above 0.90 and RMSEA values below 0.08 were interpreted as acceptable, while chi-square-related statistics were interpreted cautiously because of their sensitivity to large sample size [20, 21]. Indirect effects were tested using bias-corrected bootstrap confidence intervals [22–24].

Table 1. Reliability and Construct Validity of Major Scales.

Scale	Cronbach's α	χ2/df	RMSEA	CFI	TLI
SEC	0.972	24.143	0.062	0.916	0.909
FCEI	0.956	42.16	0.072	0.946	0.936
SCEI	0.981	14.97	0.071	0.933	0.920

Note: *SEC = Social and Emotional Competence, FCEI = Family Collaborative Education Involvement, SCEI = School Collaborative Education Involvement*

Table 2. Model Fit Indices in SEM.

GOF	CMIN/DF	GFI	NFI	IFI	CFI	RMSEA
Recommended Value	< 5	> 0.90	> 0.90	> 0.90	> 0.90	< 0.05
Model Value	2.906	0.997	0.996	0.997	0.997	0.024

5 Results

5.1 Descriptive Statistics

Descriptive statistics were computed using the cleaned and matched dataset. SEC was derived from students' questionnaire responses, FCEI from parent responses, SCEI from homeroom teacher responses, and CCEI from parent- and teacher- reported indicators of community/social participation in collaborative education.

As shown in Table 3, students' SEC was moderately high (M = 3.14, SD = 0.55). FCEI (M = 4.01, SD = 0.59), SCEI (M = 4.35, SD = 0.68), and CCEI (M = 3.86, SD = 0.69) were all above the scale midpoints, indicating generally strong participation in collaborative education across family, school, and community domains. SCEI had the highest mean, suggesting that schools reported relatively strong implementation of collaborative practices. CCEI showed the largest standard deviation, indicating more variability in community-level participation.

Table 3. Descriptive Statistics of Students' SEC, FCEI, SCEI, and CCEI.

Valuable	Min	Max	Mean	SD
SEC	1.00	4.00	3.14	0.55
FCEI	1.50	5.00	4.01	0.59
SCEI	1.00	5.00	4.35	0.68
CCEI	1.00	5.00	3.86	0.69

Note: *N = 3,295, SEC = Social Emotional Competence, FCEI = Family Collaborative Education Involvement, SCEI = School Collaborative Education Involvement, CCEI = Community Collaborative Education Involvement*

5.2 Tests of the Structural Path Coefficients

Table 4 shows that community (β = 0.918, p = 0.002) and school involvement (β = 0.382, $p = 0.003$) were both positively associated with family involvement, supporting H1–H2. Community involvement also significantly predicted school involvement (β = 0.548, $p = 0.003$), supporting H3. Family involvement was positively related to students' social-emotional competence (β = 0.418, $p = 0.005$), supporting H4. In contrast, the direct paths from school involvement (β = 0.088, $p = 0.092$) and community involvement (β = 0.251, $p = 0.113$) to students' social-emotional competence were not statistically significant, and therefore H5–H6 were not supported.

Table 4. Model Path Analysis: Family-school-community Collaboration and Students' Social and Emotional Competence.

Hypotheses	Hypothesized Paths	Path Coefficient β	p
H1	CCEI → FCEI	0.918	0.002
H2	SCEI → FCEI	0.382	0.003
H3	CCEI → SCEI	0.548	0.003
H4	FCEI → SEC	0.418	0.005
H5	SCEI → SEC	0.088	0.092
H6	CCEI → SEC	0.251	0.113

Note: * $p < 0.05$, ** $p < 0.01$, *** $p < 0.001$
SEC = Social and Emotional Competence, FCEI = Family Collaborative Education Involvement, SCEI = School Collaborative Education Involvement, CCEI = Community Collaborative Education Involvement

5.3 Tests of the Structural Path Coefficients

Meanwhile, additional path analysis results indicate that school-family-community participation in collaborative education exerts mediating effects between certain educational factors of the school, family, and community and students' social and emotional competence, as detailed in Table 5.

As shown in Table 5, CCEI had a significant indirect effect on SEC through FCEI (indirect effect = 0.384, 95% BC CI [0.102, 0.899], $p = 0.018$), supporting H8. SCEI also had a significant indirect effect on SEC through FCEI (indirect effect = 0.160, 95% BC CI [0.111, 0.183], $p = 0.004$), supporting H7. These findings provide evidence for a family-centered transmission mechanism.

Table 5. Indirect Model Path Analysis.

Indirect Path	Indirect Effect Coefficient	Bias-Corrected 95%CI	*p*
CCEI → FCEI → SEC	0.384	(0. 102, 0.899)	0.018
SCEI → FCEI → SEC	0.160	(0. 111, 0.183)	0.004
CCEI → SCEI → FCEI → SEC	0.040	(0.005, 0.061)	0.011

The sequential pathway from CCEI to SCEI to FCEI to SEC was also significant (indirect effect = 0.040, 95% BC CI [0.005, 0.061], $p = 0.011$), supporting H9. This result suggests that community participation contributes to students' SEC partly by strengthening school participation, which then enhances family involvement.

6 Discussion

This study examined how participation in school-family-community collaborative education is structurally connected and how it relates to students' SEC in a county-level Chinese context. Three findings are central. First, community participation was an upstream predictor of both school and family participation, and school participation further predicted family participation. Second, family participation was the only domain with a significant direct positive association with students' SEC. Third, school and community participation influenced SEC indirectly through family participation, with an additional sequential pathway from community to school to family to SEC.

6.1 A Family-Centered Transmission Mechanism

The finding that FCEI was the only significant direct predictor of SEC highlights the proximal role of families in students' social and emotional development. Families provide the daily relational context in which children learn emotional expression, regulation, conflict resolution, empathy, and responsibility. This result is consistent with meta-analytic evidence showing that family-school interventions can improve children's social-behavioral competence and mental health [12], that family-school partnership interventions support social-emotional functioning [13, 14], and that parental involvement programs can produce gains in social-emotional outcomes [18]. It also complements recent research showing that family involvement is linked to students' social-emotional development through educational engagement processes [19].

The non-significant direct effects of SCEI and CCEI do not mean that schools or communities are unimportant. Rather, they suggest that their influence may be indirect and contingent on whether school and community efforts are converted into family practices. In county-level systems, schools and communities may organize activities, disseminate policies, and provide resources, but students' SEC benefits most when these resources become stable routines of parent-child communication, home learning support, constructive emotion coaching, and family participation in school-community networks.

This family-centered pattern refines the overlapping spheres framework. The spheres do not simply overlap additively; influence may flow through specific transmission channels. For students in Grades 3–9, the family remains the immediate environment in which institutional guidance and community resources are personalized and practiced.

Beyond supporting existing partnership research, these findings make a theoretical contribution by refining the overlapping spheres of influence framework. Rather than suggesting that family, school, and community influences operate as parallel and equally direct sources of support, the results indicate that influence may be transmitted through differentiated pathways. In particular, family involvement emerged as the most proximal mechanism through which institutional and community supports were translated into students' social and emotional development. This finding advances a more process-oriented understanding of collaborative education and highlights the importance of examining transmission mechanisms rather than focusing solely on participation intensity.

6.2 Community and School Participation as Upstream Enablers

The strong path from CCEI to FCEI and the significant path from CCEI to SCEI indicate that community participation may function as an upstream enabling condition. This is especially meaningful in county-level contexts where community resources, family education services, youth activity spaces, and mental-health supports may be unevenly distributed. Community systems that disseminate policies, mobilize resources, and create practice-based learning opportunities can expand both school capacity and family access to developmental support. Recent studies on rural school-family-community partnerships in China and community engagement for student mental health and SEL align with this interpretation [16].

The significant path from SCEI to FCEI indicates that schools remain critical institutional bridges. School-led parent education, bidirectional communication, volunteer networks, parent organizations, and learning-at-home guidance can make family participation more concrete and actionable. This finding is consistent with research showing that parent councils in rural China can support parent-teacher communication and parent participation when parents are aware of and connected to these structures [15]. It also resonates with evidence that home-school co-education in China can enhance psychological well-being through mediating psychological resources [26].

The sequential mediation pathway CCEI > SCEI > FCEI > SEC provides a more nuanced picture of collaborative governance. Community resources may first strengthen schools' capacity to organize collaborative education; schools then translate that capacity into family engagement; and families finally convert guidance and resources into everyday practices that support SEC. This pathway is particularly relevant for resource-constrained areas, where the policy challenge is not only to increase activities, but also to improve the conversion efficiency from public resources to family-level developmental support.

6.3 Policy and Practice Implications for County-Level Educational Governance

The findings have implications for educational system reform in rural and resource-constrained regions. First, county governance should treat family empowerment as a core outcome of collaborative education rather than as a supplementary activity. Performance indicators should assess not only the number of activities or meetings, but also whether families acquire usable strategies for emotion coaching, constructive communication, peer-conflict support, and structured learning-at-home routines.

Second, schools should move from one-way notification to bidirectional and capacity-building communication. High-quality communication should include timely information about students' academic progress, peer relationships, emotional adjustment, and learning needs. Parent education should be practical and skills-oriented, helping caregivers translate school guidance into home routines. Parent organizations and volunteer networks can also be used to develop peer support among caregivers, which is especially valuable for families with limited educational resources.

Third, community systems should improve the accessibility and coordination of resources. Counties may establish integrated service entry points and resource maps covering family education guidance, psychological counseling, youth development programs, libraries, museums, social work agencies, and volunteer opportunities. Practice-oriented community programs, such as service learning, community problem solving, and structured after-school activities, can provide authentic contexts for students to apply SEC. However, these programs should be co-designed with schools and families so that community participation is connected to students' everyday developmental needs.

Finally, the results caution against equating collaboration with activity frequency. Collaboration becomes developmentally meaningful when it creates a coherent support cycle: community resources strengthen school capacity; schools strengthen family practices; families provide sustained relational environments; and students receive consistent opportunities to practice SEC. Implementation quality, relational trust, and continuity are therefore as important as participation scale [25].

6.4 Cultural and Contextual Considerations

The family-centered mechanism identified in this study should be interpreted within the cultural and institutional context of county-level China. In many Chinese educational settings, families and schools are linked through strong expectations of parental responsibility, academic support, and respect for school authority. These expectations may make family involvement a particularly important conduit through which school and community resources reach students. However, the meaning of family participation may differ across regions and cultural contexts. In coastal urban areas, migrant-receiving cities, ethnic minority regions, and remote rural counties, parent-school power relations, community organizational capacity, family time resources, and access to mental-health services may vary substantially.

Accordingly, the findings should not be generalized as a universal claim that family participation is always the only direct pathway to SEC. Rather, they suggest that in county-level systems with uneven resources, family participation may be the most immediate mechanism for converting institutional and community inputs into students' social-emotional development. Future studies should examine whether this mechanism differs by region, socioeconomic status, family structure, left-behind status, school level, and community resource density.

6.5 Limitations and Future Directions

Several limitations should be acknowledged. First, the cross-sectional design limits causal inference. Although the model is theoretically grounded, the temporal order among community, school, family participation, and SEC should be tested through longitudinal panel designs, cross-lagged models, or quasi-experimental evaluations of county-level collaborative education initiatives.

Second, several constructs were measured through self-report questionnaires. Future studies should incorporate multi-informant and behavioral indicators, such as parent participation records, school communication logs, teacher-rated SEC, observational data, and administrative information on community resource use. Such measures would reduce common method bias and provide a stronger basis for evaluating implementation quality.

Third, the sample was drawn from one county in central China. Comparative multi-county and cross-cultural studies are needed to identify boundary conditions and moderators of collaboration effectiveness. Such designs would be especially useful for determining whether the family-centered mechanism observed here holds in regions with different governance structures, community service capacity, and family-school cultural expectations.

Fourth, several potentially important confounding variables were not explicitly controlled in the present study, including parental education, household socioeconomic status, family structure, students' prior academic achievement, and school-level characteristics. These factors may influence both collaborative education participation and students' SEC and should be incorporated into future analytical models to improve causal inference and model precision.

Fifth, the study relied exclusively on quantitative survey data. Although structural equation modeling provides valuable evidence regarding relationships among constructs, it cannot fully capture how students, parents, teachers, and community actors experience collaborative education in practice. Future studies could integrate qualitative approaches, such as interviews, focus groups, and case studies, to provide richer insights into the processes through which collaborative education promotes students' social and emotional competence.

7 Conclusion

Using matched survey data from students in Grades 3–9 in a county-level context and structural equation modeling, this study developed and empirically tested a mechanism model of school–family–community collaboration oriented toward students' social and emotional competence (SEC). The findings support a family-centered transmission pathway: community involvement predicts school involvement; together, these upstream forms of participation strengthen family involvement, which in turn directly predicts higher levels of student SEC. The absence of significant direct effects from school and community involvement on SEC suggests that collaborative education may exert its greatest influence when institutional and community resources are effectively translated into sustained, high-quality family practices.

The study contributes to the literature in two primary ways. First, it models the structural interrelations among family, school, and community participation within an integrated analytical framework, rather than examining these domains in isolation. Second, it clarifies the mediating and sequential (chain) mechanisms through which cross-setting collaboration operates in county-level educational ecosystems. By identifying the family as the proximal conduit of influence, the findings refine theoretical understandings of mesosystem functioning in collaborative education.

From a practical perspective, the results indicate that county-level governance should position family empowerment as a central performance objective. This includes supporting schools in institutionalizing high-quality, bidirectional family–school communication and structured parent capacity-building routines, while strengthening community systems as stable coordinators of resources and providers of authentic contexts for SEC practice and enactment.

Some limitations warrant consideration. First, the cross-sectional design limits causal inference; longitudinal or quasi-experimental research is needed to examine temporal sequencing and assess policy impacts more rigorously. Second, key constructs were measured primarily through self-report instruments, which may introduce common method bias. Future research should incorporate multi-informant and behavioral indicators, such as observational data, administrative participation records, and teacher-rated competence measures. Third, because the study was conducted in a single county, generalizability may be constrained. Comparative studies across counties with varying governance structures and resource distributions would help identify contextual boundary conditions and moderators of collaboration effectiveness.

Acknowledgments. This study was supported by the Key Research Base Project of Humanities and Social Sciences of Universities in Hubei Province.

References

1. CASEL. CASEL's SEL Framework: What Are the Core Competence Areas and Where Are They Promoted? Collaborative for Academic, Social, and Emotional Learning, Chicago, IL, USA (2020)
2. OECD. Social and Emotional Skills for Better Lives: Findings from the OECD Survey on Social and Emotional Skills 2023. OECD Publishing, Paris (2024). https://doi.org/10.1787/35ca7b7c-en
3. Cipriano, C., et al.: The state of evidence for social and emotional learning: a contemporary meta-analysis of universal school-based SEL interventions. Child Dev. **94**(5), 1181–1204 (2023)
4. Mahoney, J.L., et al.: Systemic social and emotional learning: promoting educational success for all preschool to high school students. Am. Psychol. **76**(7), 1128–1142 (2021)
5. Martinez-Yarza, N., Santibanez, R., Solabarrieta, J.: A systematic review of instruments measuring social and emotional skills in school-aged children and adolescents. Child Indic. Res. **16**, 1475–1502 (2023)
6. Huttunen, I., Upadyaya, K., Salmela-Aro, K.: Longitudinal associations between adolescents' social-emotional skills, school engagement and school burnout. Learn. Individ. Differ. **115**, 102537 (2024)

7. Shi, J., Cheung, A.C.K., Zhang, J., Tam, H.L.: Development and validation of a social emotional skills scale: evidence from the Chinese context. Int. J. Educ. Res. **115**, 102007 (2022)
8. Mo, X., Shi, G., Zhang, Y., Xu, X., Ji, C.: How to promote the social-emotional competence of rural left-behind children? An empirical study based on propensity score matching. Front. Psychol. **14**, 1052693 (2023)
9. Bronfenbrenner, U.: The Ecology of Human Development: Experiments by Nature and Design. Harvard University Press, Cambridge, MA (1979)
10. Epstein, J.L.: School, Family, and Community Partnerships: Preparing Educators and Improving Schools, 2nd edn. Routledge, New York (2018)
11. Epstein, J.L., et al.: School, family, and community partnerships: your handbook for action. 4th ed. Corwin, Thousand Oaks, CA (2018)
12. Sheridan, S.M., Smith, T.E., Kim, E.M., Beretvas, S.N., Park, S.: A meta-analysis of family-school interventions and children's social-emotional functioning: moderators and components of efficacy. Rev. Educ. Res. **89**(2), 296–332 (2019)
13. Smith, T.E., Sheridan, S.M., Kim, E.M., Beretvas, S.N., Park, S.: The effects of family-school partnership interventions on academic and social-emotional functioning: a meta-analysis exploring what works for whom. Educ. Psychol. Rev. **32**, 511–544 (2020)
14. Smith, T.E., Holmes, S.R., Romero, M.E., Sheridan, S.M.: Evaluating the effects of family-school engagement interventions on parent-teacher relationships: a meta-analysis. Sch. Ment. Heal. **14**(2), 278–293 (2022)
15. Wei, F., Ni, Y.: Parent councils, parent involvement, and parent satisfaction: evidence from rural schools in China. Educ. Manage. Adm. Leadersh. **51**(1), 198–218 (2023)
16. Qiao, P., Chen, S., Deng, L.: Empowering rural early childhood education through shared book reading and school-family-community partnerships. Asia Pac. J. Educ. 1–17 (2024)
17. Guo, Y., Li, X.: Regional inequality in China's educational development: an urban-rural comparison. Heliyon **10**(4), e26249 (2024)
18. Cosso, J., von Suchodoletz, A., Yoshikawa, H.: Effects of parental involvement programs on young children's academic and social-emotional outcomes: a meta-analysis. J. Fam. Psychol. **36**(8), 1329–1339 (2022)
19. Martinez-Yarza, N., Solabarrieta-Eizaguirre, J., Santibanez-Gruber, R.: The impact of family involvement on students' social-emotional development: the mediational role of school engagement. Eur. J. Psychol. Educ. **39**, 4297–4327 (2024)
20. Kline, R.B.: Principles and Practice of Structural Equation Modeling, 5th edn. Guilford Press, New York (2023)
21. Hu, L.-T., Bentler, P.M.: Cutoff criteria for fit indexes in covariance structure analysis: conventional criteria versus new alternatives. Struct. Equ. Model. **6**(1), 1–55 (1999)
22. Hayes, A.F.: Introduction to Mediation, Moderation, and Conditional Process Analysis: A Regression-Based Approach, 3rd edn. Guilford Press, New York (2022)
23. Preacher, K.J., Hayes, A.F.: Asymptotic and resampling strategies for assessing and comparing indirect effects in multiple mediator models. Behav. Res. Methods **40**(3), 879–891 (2008)
24. MacKinnon, D.P.: Introduction to Statistical Mediation Analysis. Lawrence Erlbaum Associates, New York (2008)
25. Appel, H.B., Walsh, E., Marsh, T.E., Brown, C.: Supporting students' mental health and social emotional learning through community engagement and collaboration. Educ. Res. **65**(3), 285–300 (2023)
26. Liu, C., Chen, H., Xu, W., Dai, S., Lin, S.: The mediating role of cognitive flexibility in home-school co-education and psychological well-being among Chinese vocational college students. Front. Psychol. **15**, 1422845 (2024)

Understanding How Pre-service Science Teachers Design Inquiry-based Activities in a GenAI Integrated Collaborative Learning Environment: A Network Analytic Approach

Yuhong Miao, Taotao Long(✉), and Ya Zhao

Central China Normal University, Wuhan 430079, China
taotaolong@mails.ccnu.edu.cn

Abstract. Inquiry-based instruction is essential in science education, yet it imposes high pedagogical demands on pre-service teachers. Although collaborative online environments are widely utilized in teacher education, the dynamic process by which teachers develop inquiry-based instructional design competency remains underexplored. This study used Epistemic Network Analysis to investigate how 27 pre-service science teachers developed instructional designs within a Generative AI(GenAI) integrated collaborative learning environment through multiple iterative rounds. The results indicate that iterative interactions with GenAI effectively helped the participants expand and refine their instructional focus. Furthermore, ENA revealed distinct structural differences between performance groups: high-performing pre-service teachers exhibited deep cognitive integration, constructing tightly connected networks among activities, scaffolded questions, and scientific explanations. In contrast, low-performing participants relied primarily on procedural organization of activities and classroom communication, demonstrating weaker integration of core inquiry elements. Reflection remained relatively peripheral in both groups. These findings suggest that while GenAI effectively broadens the instructional design space, generative support alone does not necessarily ensure the integration of reflective reasoning; effective pedagogical integration ultimately depends on users' reflective engagement with AI-generated feedback.

Keywords: Pre-service science teachers · Inquiry-based activities · GenAI Collaborative Learning Environment

1 Introduction

Inquiry-based instruction is a student-centered pedagogical approach that enables learners to construct scientific knowledge through questioning, investigation, evidence evaluation, and explanation building. As a core component of contemporary science education, inquiry-based instruction has been strongly advocated in international curriculum frameworks such as the Next Generation Science Standards (NGSS) because of its potential to

K. T. Chui et al. (Eds.): ICBL 2026, LNCS 16778, pp. 92–106, 2027.
https://doi.org/10.1007/978-981-92-3761-6_7

promote students' conceptual understanding, scientific reasoning, and problem-solving abilities [1]. Despite its recognized educational value, a substantial gap remains between the intended goals of inquiry-based teaching and its implementation in classroom practice [2]. Previous studies have shown that many pre-service science teachers encounter difficulties in designing coherent inquiry activities, formulating productive questions, and connecting hands-on investigations with scientific explanations [3]. Developing inquiry-based instructional activities therefore requires not only pedagogical content knowledge but also sophisticated instructional design competence.

Recent advances in Generative Artificial Intelligence (GenAI) have created new opportunities for supporting teachers' instructional design processes. Powered by large language models, GenAI systems are capable of generating instructional suggestions, providing adaptive feedback, and offering context-sensitive pedagogical scaffolding. Emerging research suggests that GenAI can support lesson planning, collaborative problem solving, and reflective learning by helping users generate alternative instructional ideas and refine existing designs [4]. Within collaborative learning environments, GenAI can function as a cognitive partner that stimulates idea generation, facilitates discussion, and supports knowledge construction among learners and teachers alike. Consequently, integrating GenAI into teacher education has attracted increasing scholarly attention [5].

Although existing studies have demonstrated the effectiveness of collaborative learning environments and AI-supported instructional design tools, most research has primarily focused on learning outcomes or perceptions of technology use [6]. Comparatively less attention has been paid to the dynamic process through which pre-service teachers develop inquiry-based instructional design competence while interacting with GenAI in collaborative settings. Moreover, current studies rarely examine how different groups of learners organize and integrate key inquiry elements during iterative instructional design activities [7]. Understanding these developmental processes is important for designing adaptive teacher education programs and identifying how AI-supported scaffolding can foster deeper pedagogical reasoning. Furthermore, most prior studies rely on traditional performance measures, which provide limited insights into the structural relationships among instructional design components.

To address these gaps, this study employed Epistemic Network Analysis (ENA), a quantitative ethnographic method that models connections among elements of participants' thinking and practice[8]. ENA enables researchers to examine how inquiry-related components are organized and integrated across instructional design processes, thereby providing a deeper understanding of the development of pedagogical reasoning [9]. Using ENA, this study investigated how 27 pre-service science teachers designed inquiry-based instructional activities within a GenAI-integrated collaborative learning environment and explored differences between high-and low-performing groups. Specifically, the following research questions were addressed:

RQ1: How do pre-service science teachers design inquiry-based instructional activities within a GenAI-integrated collaborative learning environment?
RQ2: What structural differences exist between high- and low-performing groups in their inquiry-based instructional activity designs within a GenAI integrated collaborative learning environment?

2 Literature Review

2.1 Inquiry-Based Instruction

Inquiry-based instruction (IBI) emphasizes students' active participation in scientific practices such as questioning, investigating, reasoning, and constructing evidence-based explanations [10]. Studies have consistently shown that inquiry-based teaching can improve students' conceptual understanding, scientific reasoning, and problem solved abilities compared with traditional teacher centered approaches [11]. As a result, Inquiry-based instruction has been widely promoted in science curricula and teacher education.

However, implementing inquiry-based instruction remains challenging, particularly for pre-service science teachers [12]. Previous research has reported a persistent gap between teachers' understanding of inquiry and their actual classroom practices. Many pre-service teachers struggle to design coherent inquiry activities, guide students' investigations, and align inquiry goals with assessment [13].

Recent studies suggest that scaffolded and collaborative learning environments can support the development of inquiry design competence. Structured supports such as guiding prompts, design templates, and iterative feedback have been found to improve the quality of inquiry lesson planning. Collaborative curriculum design also provides opportunities for knowledge sharing and reflection, which can strengthen teachers' instructional design practices. Although collaborative inquiry environments show clear benefits, less is known about how pre-service teachers' inquiry design competence develops over time within these environments.

2.2 GenAI Integrated Collaborative Learning Environment

The rapid development of Generative AI (GenAI), particularly large language models, has created new opportunities for learning environments by enabling personalized tutoring, adaptive feedback, and on-demand scaffolding [14]. Compared with earlier educational technologies, GenAI can generate context-sensitive explanations, hints, and examples that support learners' higher-order thinking and self-regulated learning [15].

In science education, recent studies suggest that GenAI can support inquiry processes such as hypothesis generation, experimental design, data interpretation, and reflection [16]. Latif and Zhai argue that GenAI can function as a cognitive scaffold when embedded in structured learning environments. Empirical work also shows that GenAI can strengthen collaborative inquiry by improving students' higher-order thinking, conceptual understanding, and collaborative problem solving through adaptive scaffolding and feedback [17].

Research in teacher education has begun to explore these possibilities. Chen et al. found that student teachers working in a GenAI integrated collaborative environment produced higher-quality instructional designs and demonstrated richer cognitive interaction than those in traditional collaborative settings. Despite these advances, research on GenAI in teacher education remains limited, particularly regarding how pre-service teachers use GenAI feedback during collaborative instructional design and how these processes develop over time.

3 Methodology

3.1 Research Context

This study was conducted within a compulsory instructional design course offered to pre-service science teachers at a comprehensive university in eastern China. The course aimed to cultivate students' ability to design inquiry-based instructional activities by engaging them in authentic, collaborative design tasks. The instructional intervention spanned eight weeks and was structured around iterative cycles of collaborative inquiry activity design, peer discussion, reflection, and revision.

To support students' collaborative design processes, a GenAI-integrated learning environment was introduced. The environment was designed to function as an adaptive cognitive scaffold, providing real-time instructional prompts, conceptual explanations, and design suggestions aligned with inquiry-based pedagogy. Throughout the course, participants interacted with the GenAI system during group discussions to support idea generation, refine task structures, and enhance pedagogical coherence. The integration of GenAI aimed to promote higher-order thinking, deepen conceptual understanding of inquiry-based instruction, and facilitate sustained collaborative knowledge construction.

3.2 Participants

Participants were 27 pre-service science teachers enrolled in the science education program. All participants had completed foundational coursework in pedagogy, educational psychology, and subject-specific teaching methods. However, they had limited formal experience in designing inquiry-based instructional activities.

Participants were randomly assigned to 6 collaborative groups, each consisting of 3–4 members. Group composition remained stable throughout the study to support the development of sustained collaborative relationships and collective design practices. Prior to the intervention, students received an introductory session on inquiry-based instructional principles and training on how to use the GenAI-supported collaborative environment. Participation was voluntary, and informed consent was obtained from all students.

3.3 GenAI Integrated Collaborative Learning Environment

The participants had 8 weeks to complete the inquiry-based instructional activity design assignments in a GenAI integrated collaborative learning environment.The schedule of the pre-service science teachers' learning with the GenAI integrated collaborative learning environment is shown in Table 1.

Throughout the intervention, two collaborative tools were employed to support group interaction and AI-assisted design refinement. QQ functioned as the primary communication platform, enabling synchronous and asynchronous discussion among group members, while Deepseek, powered by large language models, was embedded as the generative AI support module within the design process.

Within this environment, the GenAI module was positioned as a critical cognitive partner rather than a simple content generator. During the initial transition from Design

Table 1. Schedule of the pre-service science teachers' learning with GenAI integrated collaborative learning environment

Week	Activities	Tool
Week 1	Discussing and finishing the first instructional (Design 0) according to their own prior knowledge and experience	QQ
Week 2–6	Comparing the outputs of Deepseek, and making modifications through internal discussions, and generating their second instructional design(Design 1)	Deepseek
Week 7–8	Conducting microteaching and actual elementary school classroom teaching practices, using Deepseek and finishing their final instructional design (Design 2)	Deepseek

0 to Design 1, when participants revised their baseline lesson plans, Deepseek primarily provided generative scaffolding. This included suggesting alternative inquiry questions, proposing investigative task structures, and offering conceptual clarifications to enhance coherence between learning objectives and inquiry procedures. At this stage, the AI's role focused on expanding design possibilities and stimulating idea generation.

As participants progressed to the Design 1–2 phases, the function of the GenAI module gradually shifted from generative expansion to evaluative and diagnostic support. Deepseek provided structured feedback aimed at identifying logical inconsistencies between proposed inquiry questions, experimental procedures, and scientific explanations. It also prompted participants to examine the alignment between instructional intentions and expected student learning outcomes.

3.4 Coding Scheme of Inquiry-Based Instructional Activities

The coding scheme for inquiry-based instructional activities was adapted from the Knowledge Integration (KI) framework (Linn & Eylon, 2011) and specifically followed the categorization utilized by Long et al. (2024). This scheme decomposes inquiry-based design into five interconnected dimensions: Questions(Q), Activities (A), Communication (C), Explanations (E), and Reflection (R), providing a holistic lens to evaluate the pedagogical coherence and depth of the participants' instructional designs, as shown in Table 2.

Table 2. The coding scheme of inquiry-based instructional activities

Code	Description	Example from Participants' Design
Questions (Q)	Scaffolding questions designed to elicit prior knowledge or guide the inquiry process	"What are the inconveniences of using cylinders placed side by side to move objects?"

(continued)

Table 2. (*continued*)

Code	Description	Example from Participants' Design
Activities (A)	Hands-on investigative tasks involving experimentation, observation, or data collection process	"The teacher asks the students draw what they think of as an ecosystem."
Explanations (E)	Scientific reasoning that links evidence to conceptual understanding or scientific principles	"Iron rusts when in contact with water and releases heat; since a new substance is formed, it is a chemical reaction."
Communication (C)	Guide group cooperation, discussion, and communication of inquiry activities	"Students work in groups to discuss the roles of activated carbon and salt in the reaction."
Refection (R)	Organize and guide students to reflect and evaluate the whole inquiry process	"The teacher prompts: Can you make a hand warmer yourself?"

3.5 Data Collection

All groups' text data including three inquiry-based instructional design work were collected and saved in an Excel document for data analysis. For example, Fig. 1 shows the excerpts of text data in the Group 4's Design 1 text. Then the text data was encoded based on the coding schemes of inquiry-based instructional activities. To obtain reliability on coding, two coders (two authors of this paper), who were a doctoral student majored in modern educational technology and a undergraduate student majored in science education, were trained and then tasked with independently coding instructional design text data. Cohen' s Kappa test turned out to be 0.82 reliability, showing good reliability.

3.6 Data Analysis

To address RQ1, we employed Epistemic Network Analysis (ENA) using the ENA Web Tool (v1.7.1) (Marquart et al., 2018). ENA is a quantitative ethnographic technique that models the structure and strength of connections between codes by quantifying their co-occurrences within specific temporal contexts, known as stanzas.

In this study, the unit of analysis was defined as a "teaching event" (meaning unit) within the pre-service science teachers' instructional designs. The model incorporated five core codes: Q, A, E, C,and R (see Fig. 1). ENA visualized these connections as weighted networks, where the thickness and saturation of lines represent the frequency of associations between encoded elements. This allowed for a statistical comparison of both individual and mean network structures across different experimental groups.

Text	Q	A	E	C	R
教师介绍问题情境：工人需要将一个100kg的大石块从走廊的这一边运到另一边，他手边只有三种不同形状的柱体若干个，请你帮他想一个更省力的运输方法，并解释为什么省力。	1	0	0	0	0
教师讲解重心的概念。	0	0	1	0	0
教师引导学生完成“运输大挑战”实验：1.在底面上标出三个柱体的重心，推动三个柱体滚动向前 2.在推动柱体的过程中关注柱体重心的变化，在学生手册中画一画各个情况下物体的重心。	0	1	0	0	0
实验结束后教师请学生分享实验结果并总结：圆柱的中心高度不变，而三棱柱和长方体的重心高度发生了变化。古人就是利用圆的这种特性发明了轮子。	0	0	1	0	0
教师提问学生：用并排的圆柱搬运物体有什么不便之处呢？	1	0	0	0	0

Fig. 1. The excerpts of text data in Group 1's Design 0 data.

To address RQ2, six groups were categorized into high-performing and low performing clusters based on their initial inquiry-based instructional designs. Scoring was conducted using an adapted rubric of pedagogical design competency, which covers nine dimensions, such as context creation, questioning, and assessment, and is divided into two performance levels. Two independent coders performed the evaluation to ensure objectivity. The inter-rater reliability, measured by Spearman's correlation coefficient, was 0.88, indicating high consistency. Groups 4, 5, and 6, which scored above the mean, were classified as high-performance groups, while groups 1, 2, and 3 constituted low-performance groups.

4 Results

4.1 How Did the Pre-Service Teachers Design Inquiry-Based Instructional Activities with the GAI Integrated Collaborative Learning Environment?

A total of 217 units of analysis were coded, generating 371 co-occurring codes across the three instructional design phases. Among these, Explanations (E) accounted for 127 instances (34.2%), Questions (Q) for 117 (31.5%), Activities (A) for 91 (24.5%), Communication (C) for 23 (6.2%), and Reflection (R) for 25 (6.7%).

Table 3 provides an overview of the distribution of inquiry-based instructional design components across the three versions.Explanations and Questions constituted the largest proportions of the coded segments, together representing nearly two-thirds of all design elements. This indicates that pre-service teachers primarily concentrated on constructing scientific explanations and formulating inquiry questions when designing instructional activities. In contrast, Communication and Reflection appeared relatively infrequently, suggesting that dialogic interaction and metacognitive components were less emphasized in the overall design structure.

Table 3. Frequencies of each code represented in three versions of instructional design.

Code	Design 0	Design 1	Design 2	Sum
Questions (Q)	34	44	39	117
Activities (A)	23	40	28	91
Explanations (E)	40	51	36	127
Communication (C)	6	10	7	23
Reflection (R)	3	12	10	25

The total number of codes increased from 106 in Design 0 to 157 in Design 1, reflecting a 48% growth following the integration of GenAI and peer evaluation effectively functioned as a generative scaffold, enabling pre-service teachers to rapidly overcome initial design limitations and expand their instructional repertoire. The most notable increases occurred in Questions (from 34 to 44) and Activities (from 23 to 40), suggesting that pre-service teachers primarily utilized the AI's generative capabilities to enrich the procedural and interactive dimensions of their lessons. The near-doubling of Activities highlights a characteristic phase of'idea expansion,' where pre-service teachers eagerly integrated diverse hands-on tasks and experiments suggested by the AI before moving on to the optimization phase. In Design 2, the total number of codes decreased to 120 after microteaching and field practice. Despite this reduction, frequencies in several categories remained higher than baseline levels, indicating a process of consolidation and refinement rather than decline. Figure 2 shows the overall situation of the mean ENA network of the pre-service teachers' inquiry-based instructional activity design performance in Design 0, Design 1, and Design 2 within the GenAI-integrated collaborative learning environment. The red solid box refers to the centroid of Design 0, the blue solid box refers to the centroid of Design 1, and the purple box refers to the centroid of Design 2. Compared with Design 0, the centroid of Design 1 is located on the upper-right side of the coordinate space, indicating that the instructional design in this phase was more closely associated with "Activities" and their connections with other components.

The first paragraph that follows a table, figure, equation, etc., does not need an indent, either. The strengthened links between "Questions" and "Activities" and between "Reflection" and "Activities" are visually salient in this phase. The centroid of Design 2 is positioned toward the upper-left area of the coordinate space. This shift suggests a relatively stronger association with "Reflection" and "Questions" compared with the previous phase. While the overall network density appears slightly reduced compared to Design 1, the structural connections among "Questions," "Activities," and "Reflection" remain evident. Across the three design phases, there is a consistently strong connection between "Questions" and "Explanations." The strength of the link between "Questions" and "Activities" increases in Design 1 and remains visible in Design 2. In contrast, "Communication" maintains relatively weaker connections with other elements throughout the three phases.

Fig. 2. Overall situation of the mean ENA network of the all groups' performance in designing inquiry-based instructional activities.

4.2 What Are Differences, if Any, Between the Inquiry-Based Instructional Activity Designs of the High-and Low-Performing Groups Within a GenAI-Integrated Collaborative Environment?

An ENA comparison was conducted to examine structural differences between high-and low-performance groups. The centroid of the high-performance group was located on the left side of the projection, while the low-performance group was positioned on the right side, indicating structural separation (see Fig. 3). The centroid of the high-performance group is located on the left side of the coordinate space, whereas the centroid of the low-performance group is positioned on the right side, indicating a structural separation between the two groups in their inquiry-based instructional activity design.

In the difference network, the high-performance group demonstrates stronger connections among "Activities," "Questions," and "Explanations," particularly the links between "Activities" and "Explanations," as well as between "Activities" and "Questions." These connections form a relatively cohesive structural cluster. In contrast, the low-performance group shows comparatively stronger associations involving "Communication," especially the links between "Communication" and "Questions", the links between "Communication" and "Activities", and between "Communication" and "Explanations."

However, the connections among core inquiry components appear less concentrated. The primary and secondary plots further illustrate that, in the high-performance group, "Activities," "Questions," and "Explanations" form a densely connected cluster, with particularly strong weights between "Questions" and "Explanations" (0.91) and between "Activities" and "Explanations" (1.0). In contrast, the low-performance group presents a more distributed configuration, with relatively higher weights connecting "Communication" to other elements.

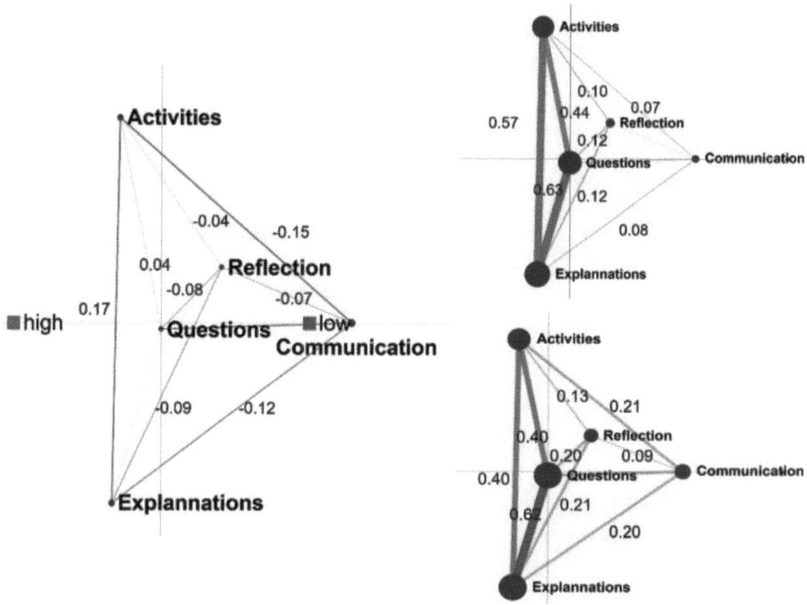

Fig. 3. Mean networks of inquiry-based instructional activity design competency in the high-performing group (blue) and low-performing group (red).

To better understand the structural differences between the high-and low-performing groups across the three design phases, comparisons were made based on the mean ENA networks of Design 0, Design 1, and Design 2 (see Fig. 4). The upper panels indicate that the high-performing group demonstrated relatively strong connections among "Activities," "Questions," and "Explanations" in all three phases. With the exception of "Communication," the other components were consistently interconnected.

In Design 0, the high-performing group showed particularly strong links between "Activities" and "Explanations" (0.82) and between "Questions" and "Explanations" (0.70), forming a tightly clustered core structure. In Design 1, the connections among core components remained strong, especially between "Questions" and "Explanations" (0.85) and between "Activities" and "Questions" (0.73). In Design 2, this clustered configuration persisted, with strong weights between"Activities" and "Explanations" (0.85) and between "Activities" and "Questions" (0.63).

Compared with earlier phases, the connections involving "Reflection" became slightly more visible in the final design, indicating greater integration of reflective elements with other inquiry components. The lower panels show that the low-performing group exhibited a different structural pattern across phases. In Design 0 and Design 1, the most prominent connection was between "Questions" and "Explanations", while other links were comparatively weaker. Connections involving "Communication" and "Reflection" were present but did not form a tightly integrated structure. In Design 2, additional links among "Activities", "Questions" and "Explanations" became stronger, suggesting increased interconnections among core components. However, the overall configuration remained more distributed compared to that of the high-performing group.

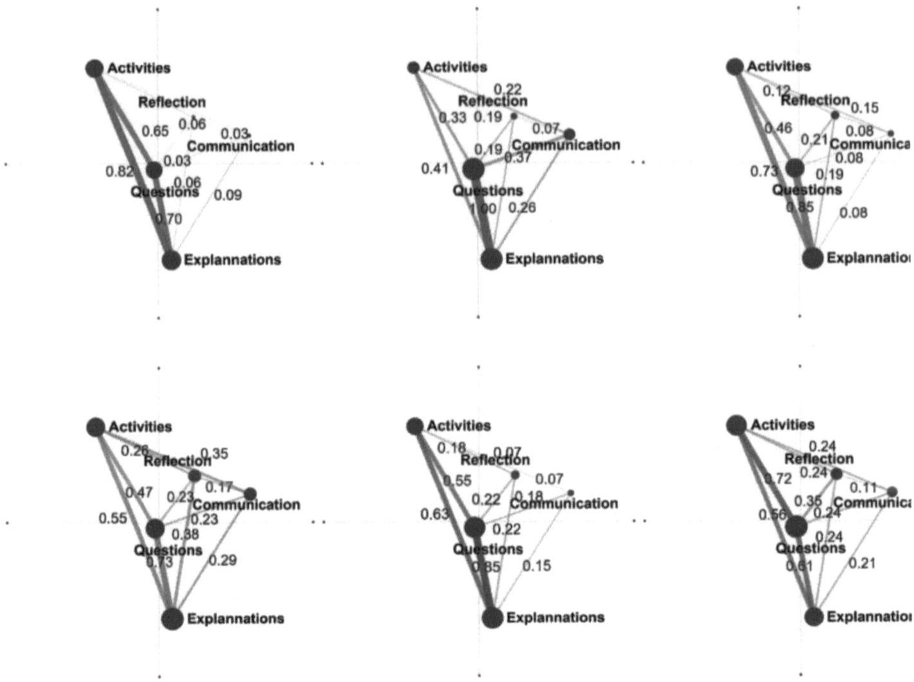

Fig. 4. Mean ENA networks for inquiry-based instructional activity designs for the high-performing and low-performing groups.

In sum, across the three phases, the high-performing group consistently demonstrated a concentrated and cohesive network centered on the integration of"Activities," "Questions," and "Explanations," whereas the low-performing group showed a comparatively less centralized structure with more dispersed connections among components.

5 Discussion

This study explored how pre-service teachers designed inquiry-based instructional activities in a GenAI-supported collaborative environment and how design patterns differed between high- and low-performing groups. Overall, the findings suggest that GenAI supported idea generation in early design stages, while classroom practice contributed to later refinement. This aligns with recent studies showing that GenAI can function as a cognitive partner in lesson planning by helping pre-service teachers generate instructional ideas and alternative teaching strategies [18].

The increase in coding frequencies from Design 0 to Design 1 suggests that GenAI helped participants expand initial instructional ideas, particularly in Activities and Questions. Prior research similarly indicates that generative AI can support the early stages of instructional design by assisting teachers in generating learning activities, explanations, and guiding questions [19]. However, the decrease observed in Design 2 likely reflects a process of pedagogical refinement after microteaching and field practice. This pattern is consistent with studies suggesting that GenAI is most effective when combined with authentic teaching experiences and human judgment to evaluate and revise AI-generated ideas [20].

Across phases, Explanations and Questions remained the dominant components and formed stable connections in the ENA networks. This result reflects the epistemic nature of inquiry-based science teaching, where questioning and explanation are important to supporting students' scientific reasoning and knowledge construction. Previous research also shows that GenAI systems can be designed to generate scaffolded questions and explanations that support learners' conceptual understanding and reasoning processes [21].

Group differences were also evident. High-performing groups formed a more coherent network centered on Activities, Questions, and Explanations, suggesting stronger alignment between classroom activities and scientific reasoning. In contrast, low performing groups showed a more dispersed structure with stronger links involving Communication, indicating a greater focus on organizing classroom interaction rather than connecting activities to conceptual understanding. Similar patterns have been reported in studies of GenAI supported teacher learning, where effective use of AI requires the ability to critically evaluate and integrate AI generated content into coherent pedagogical structures [22].

6 Implications, Limitations and Future Research

The findings of this study provide several implications for teacher education and the integration of generative AI in instructional design training. The results indicate that GenAI can support the structural elaboration of inquiry-based instructional design when it is embedded in iterative and collaborative contexts. The densification observed among core inquiry components, particularly Questions, Activities, and Explanations, suggests that AI-supported feedback may help align pedagogical intentions with instructional implementation.

Structural differences between the high and low performing groups further highlight the role of guided AI use. In many cases, GenAI works as a reflective scaffold when users reorganize their instructional logic in response to feedback. When such guidance is absent, AI tends to support surface level expansion rather than deeper epistemic integration. Teacher educators must provide targeted scaffolding, specifically for low-performing students—to help them transition from organizing "classroom communication" to fostering "scientific explanations." Prompts within the GenAI environment should explicitly require pre-service teachers to justify how a proposed activity or group discussion will directly lead to the desired scientific explanation.

Another notable pattern is the persistent marginalization of Reflection in both groups. This pattern points to the need for stronger scaffolding of reflective reasoning. AI systems designed to support instructional design could incorporate prompts that link reflection with question formulation, activity sequencing, and explanatory reasoning, instead of treating reflection as a separate concluding step.

Building upon the findings of this research, several implications for GenAI-supported teacher education can be drawn. First, teacher educators should design collaborative instructional design activities that encourage pre-service science teachers to iteratively revise their lesson plans with the support of GenAI and peer discussion. Such iterative learning processes can promote deeper pedagogical reasoning and improve the coherence of inquiry-based instructional designs. Second, instructional support should focus on helping pre-service teachers critically evaluate and integrate AI-generated suggestions rather than simply adopting them. In particular, targeted scaffolding should guide learners to establish meaningful connections among inquiry questions, learning activities, and scientific explanations. Finally, given that Reflection remained relatively peripheral in both performance groups, future GenAI-supported learning environments should incorporate structured reflective prompts that encourage pre-service teachers to evaluate the consistency between instructional objectives, inquiry activities, and expected learning outcomes. These improvements may further enhance the effectiveness of GenAI in supporting inquiry-based instructional design and contribute to the development of pre-service teachers' pedagogical competence. This study has limitations, including only one case and only the discourse data were collected. Future research would focus on investigating the effects of these teaching approaches on student outcomes and the integration of technology in collaborative education could provide deeper insights into optimizing educational strategies. This concise overview emphasizes the potential for these findings to inform and transform educational practices and policies, fostering a more inclusive, dynamic, and effective learning environment.

7 Conclusions

This study used ENA to examine how 27 pre-service science teachers developed inquiry-based instructional designs in a GenAI integrated collaborative environment, revealing structural differences between high and low performing groups. The results suggest that iterative interaction with GenAI and peer feedback helps pre-service teachers expand inquiry activities and scaffolded questions while gradually refining instructional focus through microteaching and field practice.

High-performing participants demonstrated deeper cognitive integration, constructing tightly connected networks among activities, questions, and explanations to support the development of scientific understanding. In contrast, the low-performing group relied more on procedural organization of activities and classroom communication, showing weaker integration of inquiry elements. Reflection remained relatively peripheral in both groups, indicating that generative support alone does not guarantee the integration of reflective reasoning in inquiry design. While GenAI can broaden the design space, effective pedagogical integration still relies on users' reflective engagement with AI generated feedback.

Acknowledgments. This research was supported by the National Natural Science Foundation of China (No.62307017).

References

1. Morris, D.L.: Rethinking science education practices: shifting from investigation centric to comprehensive inquiry-based instruction. Educ. Sci. **15**(1), 73 (2025)
2. Sam R.: Systematic review of inquiry-based learning: assessing impact and best practices in education. F1000Research **13**, 1045 (2024)
3. Alajmi T D.: Inside the mind of pre-service science teachers: Examining the impact of prior experiences and the influence of science education programs on pedagogical beliefs. Oregon State University Dissertation (2025)
4. Celik, I., Kontkanen, S., Laru, J., et al.: Co-constructing adaptive lesson plans with GenAI: pre-service teachers' Intelligent-TPACK and prompt engineering strategies. Comput. Educ. **241**, 105485 (2026)
5. Nikolic, S., Wentworth, I., Sheridan, L., et al.: A systematic literature review of attitudes, intentions and behaviours of teaching academics pertaining to AI and generative AI (GenAI) in higher education: an analysis of GenAI adoption using the UTAUT framework. Australas. J. Educ. Technol. **40**(6), 56–75 (2024)
6. Alyoussef, I.Y., Drwish, A.M., Albakheet, F.A., et al.: AI adoption for collaboration: factors influencing inclusive learning adoption in higher education. IEEE Access **13**, 81690–81713 (2025)
7. Kale, U., Roy, A., Yuan, J.: To design or to integrate? Instructional design versus technology integration in developing learning interventions. Educ. Tech. Res. Dev. **68**(5), 2473–2504 (2020)
8. Elmoazen, R., Saqr, M., Tedre, M., et al.: A systematic literature review of empirical research on epistemic network analysis in education. IEEE Access **10**, 17330–17348 (2022)
9. Van De, V., Mooney, S.G.: Assessing scientific inquiry: a systematic literature review of tasks, tools and techniques. Int. J. Sci. Math. Educ. **23**, 871–906 (2024)
10. Gomez, M.J.: The impact of inquiry-based learning in science education: a systematic review of student engagement and achievement. J. Educ. Learn. Manage. **2**(2), 353–363 (2025)
11. Anwer M.: Evaluating the impact of inquiry-based teaching strategies on the development of scientific thinking, problem-solving, and conceptual understanding among high school students. J. Soc. Horiz. **1**(2) (2024)
12. Amos, R., Knippels, M.C., Levinson, R.: Socio-scientific inquiry-based learning: possibilities and challenges for teacher education. Science Teacher Education for Responsible Citizenship: Towards a Pedagogy for Relevance Through Socioscientific Issues 41–61 (2020)
13. Wrench, A., Paige, K.: Educating pre-service teachers: towards a critical inquiry workforce. Educ. Action Res. **28**(3), 462–479 (2020)
14. Leon, M.: Leveraging generative AI for On-Demand tutoring as a new paradigm in education. Int. J. Cybern. Inform. **14**(14), 17 (2024)
15. Zhao, Y., Yue, Y., Sun, Z., et al.: Does generative artificial intelligence improve students' higher-order thinking? A meta-analysis based on 29 experiments and quasi-experiments. J. Intell. **13**(12), 160 (2025)
16. Lai, C.J.: Evaluating generative AI-assisted inquiry-based learning and metacognitive scaffolding for enhancing scientific vocabulary, content comprehension, and lab report writing. Interact. Learn. Environ. 1–15 (Early Access)
17. Zhai, X., Nyaaba, M., Ma, W.: Can generative AI and ChatGPT outperform humans on cognitive-demanding problem-solving tasks in science? Sci. Educ. **34**(2), 649–670 (2025)
18. Sun, Y., Huang, Y.: Exploring the role of generative AI in collaborative lesson planning for pre-service teachers. J. Comput. Assist. Learn. **41**(4), e70098 (2025)
19. Yanar, A.N., Ergene, O.: Integrating artificial intelligence in education: how pre-service mathematics teachers use ChatGPT for 5E Lesson plan design. J. Pedagogical Res. **9**(2), 158–176 (2025)

20. Hong, S., Moon, J., Eom, T., Awoyemi, I.D., Hwang, J.: Generative AI-Enhanced virtual reality simulation for pre-service teacher education: a mixed-methods analysis of usability and instructional utility for course integration. Educ. Sci. **15**(8), 997 (2025)
21. Zhai, X., et al.: Science literacy: generative AI as enabler of coherence in the teaching, learning, and assessment of scientific knowledge and reasoning (2026). arXiv preprint arXiv: 2603.06659
22. Rothinam, N., et al.: Systematic review on teacher education and the integration of artificial intelligence. J. Cult. Anal. Soc. Change **10**(4), 5061–5075 (2025)
23. Linn, M.C., Eylon, B.S.: Science learning and instruction: taking advantage of technology to promote knowledge integration. Routledge (2011)
24. Long, T., Zheng, Z., Shi, Y., et al.: Understanding how pre-service science teachers design inquiry-based activities in a knowledge integration (KI) based collaborative learning environment: a network analytic approach. Educ. Tech. Res. Dev. **72**(6), 3421–3452 (2024)
25. Latif, E., Zhai, X.: Fine-tuning ChatGPT for automatic scoring. Comput. Educ.: Artif. Intell. **6**, 100210 (2024)
26. Guo, S., Latif, E., Zhou, Y., Huang, X., Zhai, X.: Using generative AI and multiagents to provide automatic feedback (2024). arXiv preprint arXiv:2411.07407
27. Nyaaba, M.: Transforming teacher education in developing countries: the role generative AI in bridging theory and practice (2024). arXiv preprint arXiv:2411.10718
28. Wu, R., Wang, X., Nie, Y., Lv, P., Luo, X.: Exploring factors influencing pre-service teachers' intention to use GenAI for instructional design: a grounded theory study. Behav. Sci. **15**(9), 1169 (2025)
29. Wei, X., Han, C.: Constructing a GenAI-driven "learning–assessment–competition" ecosystem for the digital transformation of university language labs. J. Integr. Soc. Sci. Hum. **3**, 143–148 (2025)
30. Bewersdorff, A., Nerdel, C., Zhai, X.: How AI literacy correlates with affective, behavioral, cognitive and contextual variables: a systematic review. Comput. Educ.: Artif. Intell. **7**, 100493 (2025)
31. Chen, J., Huang, K., Lai, C., Jin, T.: The impact of GenAI-based collaborative inquiry on critical thinking in argumentation: a case study of blended argumentative writing pedagogy. TESOL Q. **59**, S150–S182 (2025)
32. Spasopoulos, T., Sotiropoulos, D., Kalogiannakis, M.: Generative AI in pre-service science teacher education: a systematic review. Adv. Mob. Learn. Educ. Res. **5**(2), 1501–1523 (2025)
33. Kılıçkaya, F., Kic-Drgas, J.: Pre-service language teachers' experiences and perceptions of integrating generative AI in practicum-based lesson study. Hum. Soc. Sci. Commun. **12**(1), 1–11 (2025)
34. Yan, L., et al.: The effects of generative AI agents and scaffolding on enhancing students' comprehension of visual learning analytics. Comput. Educ. **234**, 105322 (2025)
35. Zhang, Q., Zuo, J., Yang, S.: Research on the impact of generative artificial intelligence on enterprise innovation performance: A knowledge management perspective. J. Knowl. Manage. **29**(7), 2238–2257 (2025)
36. Yang, W., Lu, Y., Yeom, S., Herbert, D.: Adapting GenAI strategies: understanding models, aims, and challenges in different targeted data and domains. IEEE Access **13**, 1–15 (2025)

Exploring the Teacher-Student-AI Ternary Collaborative Strategy for Promoting Student Artifact Generation

Yi Qiu(✉), Jinlin Lou, and Chengjun Li

School of Educational Information Technology, South China Normal University, Guangzhou, China
etqiuyi@163.com

Abstract. Innovation activities are core pathways for cultivating new-era innovative talents, with artifacts serving as key representations of innovative value. Breaking individual cognitive limitations and mindsets through human-AI coupling can significantly enhance the quality and efficiency of innovative product generation. Consequently, constructing human-machine collaborative teaching strategies that deepen AI empowerment to enhance students' creativity and artifact quality has become a critical challenge for higher education reform. Guided by Outcome-Based Education (OBE), generative teaching, and human-machine collaborative education theories, this study first constructed a generalized instructional process for artifact generation based on the psychological mechanisms of creative thinking and OBE. This process revealed a human-AI coupling mechanism in smart higher education, transitioning from collaborative cognition to heuristic construction and guided generation. Secondly, by integrating innovative psychological mechanisms with the human-AI collaboration process, the study proposed a Teacher-Student-AI (T-S-AI) ternary collaborative strategy, comprising: T-S-AI joint cognition, S-T-AI co-construction, Tri-Intelligence Integrated Generation, and data-AI mutual verification and iteration. Finally, supported by the *Principles and Methods of Instructional Design* MOOC, an empirical application was conducted on two modules of the *Smart Class Instructional Design* project with junior Educational Technology undergraduates (N = 67) at H Normal University. Results indicate that the T-S-AI ternary collaborative strategy effectively enhances the quality and efficiency of student artifact generation.

Keywords: Teacher-student-AI ternary collaboration · Artifact generation · Strategy · Exploration

1 Introduction

Innovation refers to the creation of valuable and unprecedented new material or spiritual products for the civilization and progress of human society [1]. This outcome-oriented embodied cognitive activity—characterized by curiosity activation, task drive, collaborative construction, and iterative verification—can shape individual mental structures from

K. T. Chui et al. (Eds.): ICBL 2026, LNCS 16778, pp. 107–122, 2027.
https://doi.org/10.1007/978-981-92-3761-6_8

the aspects of innovation motivation, information, processes, outcomes, and personality traits. Furthermore, while forming specific innovative products, it cultivates higher-order skills such as creative thinking, problem-solving abilities, and critical thinking [2–4]. Human-AI synergy—a new paradigm of human-machine integration involving deep interaction and collaboration between humans and AI—achieves complementary advantages and orderly integration through efficient information exchange, precise knowledge transfer, and profound intention understanding to jointly address complex task challenges [5]. This synergy will become the primary working mode of future society and reshape the procedural structure of innovation activities through the continuous prediction and agile verification of integrated data.

In the context of intelligent education, the traditional teacher-student dual structure centered on knowledge transmission can no longer fully meet the demands of cultivating innovative talents, and artificial intelligence must be introduced as a key variable to form a new collaborative mechanism. Innovative products generated by individuals through creative thinking activities can no longer meet the massive demands for innovation in the intelligent era; however, breaking individual cognitive limitations and mindsets through human-AI coupling can enhance the quality and efficiency of innovative product generation. While existing studies have made theoretical and practical explorations into enhancing college students' innovation abilities through human-machine synergy and proposed directions for human-AI collaborative teaching reform, how the T-S-AI ternary synergy promotes student artifact generation, and what strategies should be used to facilitate students' T-S-AI ternary collaborative artifact generation, still require further exploration. Therefore, this study proposes the following research questions:

RQ1: What is the human-AI coupling mechanism in smart class teaching in higher education?
RQ2: What are the T-S-AI ternary synergistic strategies to promote student artifact generation?
RQ3: What is the application effect of these T-S-AI ternary synergistic strategies?

2 Literature Review

2.1 New Trends in Cultivating College Students' Innovation Abilities in the Intelligent Era

Human-machine symbiosis has become one of the primary operational modalities of society in the intelligent era. This qualitative transformation in the human-machine relationship is reshaping the existing connotation of innovation, facilitating the transition of its process from linear advancement to agile iteration, and its outcomes from singular generation to chain-based transformation. Existing research on the cultivation of college students' innovation abilities in the intelligent era mainly focuses on aspects such as connotation evolution, subject reshaping, practical pathways, and ecological synergy. In terms of connotation evolution, Zhang Yan et al. proposed the new concept of human-AI collaborative creativity, defined as the sum of creativity demonstrated through the interactive collaboration between humans and AI systems [6], Jaeun et al. explored the evolutionary process from human creativity to human-machine collaborative creativity[7]. Regarding subject reshaping, Lv Ping et al. elucidated the generative mechanism of human-AI collaborative creativity from psychological, instrumental, and social perspectives [8], Hou H pointed out that teachers should possess data wisdom to become the leaders of students' innovation and creation [9]. In terms of practical pathways, Zhao Wuyi verified that science and technology competitions have a significant positive impact on students' innovative practices [10], Ye Y et al. proposed the pathway of curriculum, teaching materials, and mentors–digital literacy–innovation ability, which can profoundly stimulate students' innovative capabilities [11]. In the aspect of ecological synergy, Li Jihong et al. proposed an innovative talent cultivation pathway featuring school-home-museum-community synergy [12], while Dong Hui explored a new pathway for cultivating college students' innovation abilities by integrating the four chains of policy, industry, education, and capital [13]. Generative AI is rapidly shifting from an optional auxiliary tool to a transformative core element in higher education, necessitating responsible, equitable, and human-centered integration [14] It is evident that, within the framework of transforming the connotation of innovation, existing research has made beneficial explorations into the pathways and strategies for cultivating college students' innovation abilities in the intelligent era. However, few studies have organically integrated the interactive modality of human-machine coupling with the structural reform of college smart classroom teaching to formulate an implementable and operable teacher-student-AI triadic synergy strategy. Furthermore, utilizing this strategy as a key driver to promote the large-scale, personalized cultivation of college students' innovation abilities still requires further exploration.

2.2 Research and Application of Human-AI Collaboration in Smart Class Teaching in Higher Education

Constructing a teacher-student-machine triadic structure is the key driver for higher education institutions currently implementing smart teaching. Its purpose is to transform students' learning and teachers' teaching methods, reshape pedagogical relationships, re-engineer procedural structures, and enhance the quality and efficiency of talent cultivation. Existing research on human-AI synergy in college smart classroom teaching primarily concentrates on mechanism and pathway reform, paradigm and structural re-engineering, as well as model and scenario innovation. Regarding mechanism and pathway reform, Lv Ping et al. constructed a psychological-instrumental-social generative mechanism model for human-AI collaborative creativity, revealing how deep human-AI coupling promotes the generation of college students' innovation abilities [8]. Pointing to a rethinking of the essential question of what kind of people to cultivate, Liu Sannvya et al. explored the pathways of generative artificial intelligence in facilitating educational innovation from a macro perspective and highlighted the need to address ethical risks [15]. Spector systematically defined how smart learning environments reshape teaching processes through sensing technologies and algorithms [16]. As for paradigm and structural re-engineering, Xie Youru et al. established the D-OCAE morphological characteristic framework for digital courses, which features value guidance, structural reshaping, and digital-intelligent empowerment [17].Wu Fati et al. integrated the subjective empowerment role of intelligent agents into elements such as teachers, students, and peers, constructing a new classroom paradigm of human-AI integration [18]. Concerning model and scenario innovation, Yu Liang et al. targeted blended teaching environments and, based on clarifying the essential characteristics of human-AI collaborative learning, proposed four practical modalities: collaboration-discussion, dialogue-inspiration, support-guidance, and immersion-experience [19]. Based on a new paradigm of triadic interaction, Xie Youru et al. constructed three typical innovative scenarios for college classrooms—human-machine interactive understanding, human-machine intelligence-integrating inquiry, and human-machine co-creative generation—along with their implementation pathways [20].Furthermore, Paul et al. advocate for a human-AI synergy model emphasizing shared pedagogical accountability [21]. In summary, existing research presents a new direction for college smart classroom teaching, characterized by driving pedagogical reform through scenario innovation and reshaping teaching activities through the structural innovation of the teacher-student-AI triad. However, how to promote the teacher-student-AI triadic synergy, and what kind of teacher-student-AI triadic structure should be employed to enhance teaching quality and efficiency, still require further exploration.

3 Theoretical Construction of Teacher-Student-AI Ternary Synergistic Strategies for Artifact Generation

3.1 Theoretical Basis

Outcomes-Based Education (OBE) Philosophy. The Outcomes-Based Education (OBE) philosophy centers on student learning outcomes using a backward design framework—defining, achieving, evaluating, and applying outcomes—to cultivate higher-order skills. It argues that teaching must transcend mere knowledge transfer to yield practical artifacts. By establishing clear core competency requirements and evaluation metrics, OBE's backward design logic provides goal-oriented guidance throughout the entire artifact generation process.

Generative Teaching Theory. Generative teaching theory views learning as active meaning construction, driving cognitive growth by integrating new knowledge with prior experience. Artifact creation, therefore, is both a physical outcome and the externalization of this internal process. The theory's focus on cognitive conflict, meaning negotiation, and continuous reorganization aligns with the deep cognitive activities of artifact ideation and iteration. It also establishes a core principle for applying intelligent technologies: all external support must primarily facilitate students' active, internal meaning generation.

Human-Machine Collaborative Education Theory. Human-machine collaborative education theory highlights the evolving dynamics in tech-supported environments, emphasizing the complementary strengths of teachers, students, and intelligent systems. In the AI era, artifact creation shifts from a teacher-student duality to a collaborative teacher-student-AI ternary. This theory provides the framework for understanding this evolution, underpinning how intelligent technology interventions can effectively support specific stages of artifact creation.

3.2 The General Teaching Process of Artifact Generation

Product generation is a creative process oriented toward producing novel and valuable outcomes. Its internal psychological mechanism encompasses the stages of preparation, incubation, illumination, and verification. Guilford further divided the core process of creative thinking into two stages: divergent thinking and convergent thinking [22]. In the traditional process of product generation, the incubation stage, in particular, due to its highly implicit nature, has become the most difficult phase to guide, support, and evaluate in teaching. The development of generative artificial intelligence provides a crucial opportunity to break through this dilemma. Because the knowledge reserves and thinking patterns of a single individual are inherently limited, they are susceptible to fixed mindsets. Conversely, AI serves as an 'external brain,' using its vast knowledge to offer novel perspectives and expand individual cognitive boundaries. By integrating intelligent tools into all stages of product generation—while adhering to the underlying psychological mechanisms of creative thinking—product generation in the intelligent era now exhibits the new characteristics of externalization. By combining these creative stages with outcome-based education, we propose a five-stage human-AI general artifact generation process (Fig. 1):

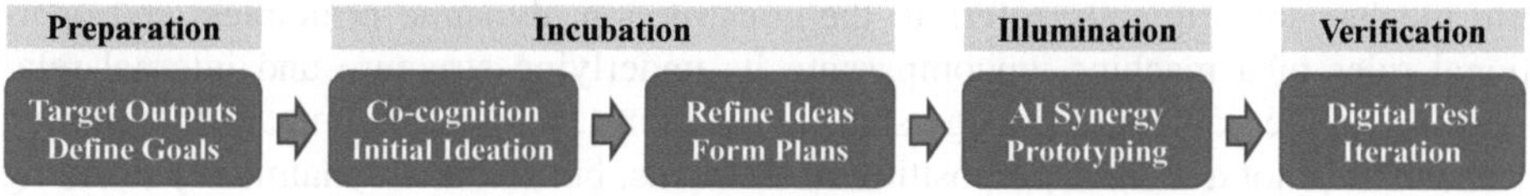

Fig. 1. The General Teaching Process of Artifact Generation.

Output Prediction and Goal Setting. Teachers define the artifact's evaluation metrics based on core competency requirementsStudents then use AI to analyze task demands and trends, aligning them with personal interests to set a customized creation direction. Simultaneously, AI assists in dissecting complex project challenges to establish precise generation goals.

Collaborative Cognition and Initial Ideation. Students use generative AI for divergent thinking. By inputting preliminary concepts, they receive diverse strategies and interdisciplinary references from AI, effectively expanding their cognitive boundaries. This human-AI brainstorming helps refine design concepts and accumulate innovative ideas.

Idea Refinement and Plan Formation. Students' thinking shifts from divergent to convergent as they critically filter and reconstruct AI-generated concepts using disciplinary theory. They map out core logic to establish a clear artifact framework. Crucial teacher guidance ensures the plan's feasibility and coherence, culminating in a systematic design.

Human-AI Synergy and Prototype Generation. Students leverage AI's generative capabilities (e.g., coding, 3D modeling) to translate their plans into functional prototypes. This integration allows AI to rapidly build the initial prototype while students rigorously oversee its scientific, artistic, and ethical integrity, drastically shortening the realization cycle.

Digital Verification and Iteration Generation. Finally, prototypes undergo testing to gather application feedback. Synthesizing objective test data, AI analytics, and self-reflection, students pinpoint defects and conduct iterative optimizations, ultimately producing a high-quality final artifact.

3.3 Human-AI Coupling Mechanism in Smart Class Teaching in Higher Education

Coupling refers to the phenomenon in which two or more systems or forms of motion interact and influence each other, ultimately uniting together. Human-AI coupling refers to the phenomenon where human intelligence and machine intelligence mutually influence and adapt to each other through deep information exchange, profound intention understanding, and behavioral synergy, eventually integrating organically into a novel form of hybrid intelligence. This new intelligent modality represents a dynamic complementarity and continuous symbiosis between human higher-order cognition and machine computational capabilities, thereby facilitating the emergence of new intelligence. The term mechanism originally refers to the construction, dynamic principles, and operational rules of a machine, encompassing its underlying structure and internal relationships. In the context of college smart classroom teaching, the human-AI coupling mechanism is not a mere superposition of elements, but rather a dynamically evolving process that accompanies the advancement of cognitive skills. It supports the generation of students' higher-order abilities through the reshaping of human-AI synergy. Following a skill progression that transitions from being knowledge-based to competency-based, alongside a collaborative deepening that shifts from standardization to personalization, this human-AI coupling mechanism is divided into three continuous and progressively advancing stages: collaborative cognition, heuristic construction, and guided generation (Fig. 2).

In collaborative cognition stage, the skill objectives target lower-order levels, featuring a teacher-student-led and AI-assisted mechanism. With low human-AI coupling, teachers and students form a close cognitive community. AI acts merely as an auxiliary tool and resource pool to support existing teaching activities and reduce cognitive load.

In heuristic construction stage, the skill objectives target intermediate levels, evolving into teacher-AI collaborative support for students' autonomous construction. With moderate coupling, teachers use AI to generate learning scaffolds and problem contexts. Guided by the teacher, AI provides personalized feedback to the student. Together, they promote knowledge internalization and meaning construction through deepened human-AI interaction.

In guided generation stage, the skill objectives target higher-order levels, culminating in a deep teacher-student-AI integration characterized by student-AI co-creation and teacher leadership. Achieving high human-AI coupling, students take the creative lead, AI provides generative resources and prototype verification, and teachers offer value guidance. Through iterative and deep interaction, the three parties bridge the gap from conceptual prototypes to high-quality outputs.

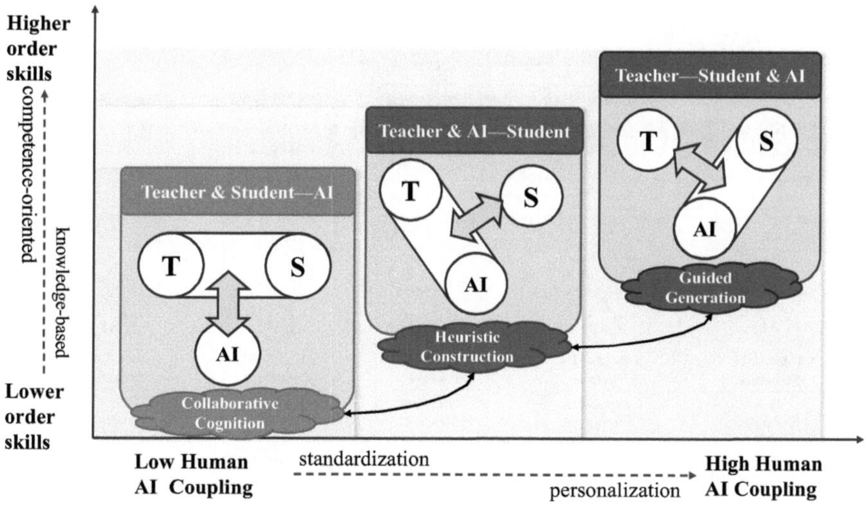

Fig. 2. Human-AI Coupling Mechanism.

3.4 Teacher-Student-AI Ternary Collaborative Strategy in Smart Class Teaching in Higher Education

Ternary synergy in smart class teaching in higher education involves introducing the embodied manifestations of artificial intelligence as a new educational subject into the existing teacher-student dual interaction. Within this novel structure, teachers act as the designers, implementers, and evaluators of teaching activities; intelligent technology plays an auxiliary teaching role; and students serve as the participants in these teaching activities [23]. In the triadic interaction with intelligent technology, teachers and students can obtain more scientific, effective, and customized services through personalized and precise feedback driven by both 'knowledge and data,' thereby realizing large-scale, personalized education. Guided by outcome-based, generative learning theories and others, this study aims to cultivate future-oriented, comprehensively developed innovative talents. Centering on artifact generation, it organically integrates innovative psychological mechanisms with human-AI collaboration to propose a teacher-student-AI ternary collaborative strategy for smart higher education (Fig. 3). This strategy comprises four stages: teacher-student-AI joint cognition, student-teacher-AI co-construction, Tri-Intelligence Integrated Generation, and data-AI mutual verification and iteration.

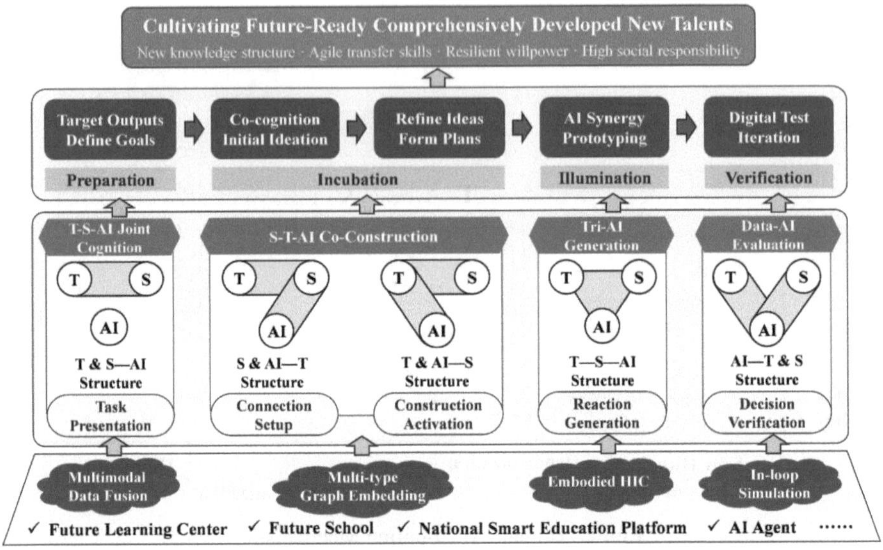

Fig. 3. T-S-AI Ternary Collaborative Strategy in Smart Class Teaching in Higher Education.

Teacher-Student-AI Joint Cognition. Dialogue between teachers and students establishes shared cognition, serving as the logical starting point to define project directions and stimulate innovation. Empowered by multimodal data fusion technologies (integrating text, image, and audio), AI assists in analyzing industry frontiers, organizing complex knowledge systems, and recommending standard evaluation frameworks. This forms a Teacher & Student—AI structure, where the teacher leads, the student participates, and AI acts as an analytical assistant. Teachers propose core principles, students express personalized demands, and AI provides data-driven scheme simulations to mutually clarify project goals.

Student-Teacher-AI Co-Construction. Promoting deep knowledge construction among all three parties is crucial for fostering divergent thinking and forming initial schemes. AI utilizes multi-type graph embedding technologies to activate students' cognitive connections. Initially, this manifests as a Student & AI—Teacher structure: students lead creative exploration, using AI-generated variants to expand cognitive boundaries and complete creative transformation based on their value judgments. It then evolves into a Teacher & AI—Student structure, where teachers guide the refinement of thought, assisting students in transitioning from divergent to convergent thinking to finalize high-quality designs.

Tri-Intelligence Integrated Generation. The deep integration of student creativity, teacher pedagogy, and AI generative intelligence is key to materializing conceptual ideas into prototypes. Supported by embodied human-computer interaction, AI facilitates students' response generation, evolving the collaborative structure into a deeply coupled teacher-student-AI model. As executive creators, students critically evaluate and refine AI outputs. AI executes specific generative tasks, while teachers focus on value guidance and process control—ensuring scientific and ethical compliance, and providing higher-order scaffolding during technical bottlenecks to jointly enhance prototype quality.

Data-AI Mutual Verification and Iteration. Combining AI's data analysis with teacher evaluation and student reflection supports multi-dimensional verification and optimization. Utilizing human-in-the-loop simulation verification, AI constructs virtual testing environments for logical deduction, empowering students' decision-making. The structure shifts to a data-driven AI—Teacher & Student model. AI provides objective, quantitative data; teachers offer evaluative feedback based on professional experience; and students conduct self-reflection and optimization based on this guidance, driving the work from an initial prototype to a mature outcome.

4 Practical Application of Teacher-Student-AI Ternary Synergistic Strategies for Artifact Generation

4.1 Research Design

Research Hypotheses. The independent variable in this study is the teacher-student-AI ternary collaborative teaching strategy; the dependent variables are the proportion of students' active learning behaviors, the level of knowledge application, and the overall quality of the generated artifacts. The hypotheses are as follows:

H1: The teacher-student-AI ternary strategy effectively optimizes classroom interaction structures and increases the proportion of active learning behaviors.
H2: The teacher-student-AI ternary strategy promotes the comprehensive application of disciplinary knowledge.
H3: The teacher-student-AI ternary strategy drives the generation of high-quality student artifacts.

Research Subjects. This study involved 67 Educational Technology undergraduates (Class of 2022) at H Normal University. Using a single-group experimental design within the Smart Class Instructional Design project, the teacher-student-AI ternary strategy was applied across two modules: *Digital-Intelligent Empowered Deep Classroom Design* (module 1) and *High-Quality Classroom Design* (module 2).

Driven by the objective to construct innovative future classroom models, the project's task chain progresses from understanding reform frontiers to generating future models. It spans three modules (15 class hours in total), culminating in a *Future Classroom Instructional Design Plan* to foster digital-era teaching innovation (Fig. 4). A dual-dimensional evaluation is employed: process assessment tracks dynamic competency development, while outcome assessment evaluates the final plan's goal setting, content reconstruction, ternary activities, and evaluation design.

Research Instruments. This study utilizes the MOOC Principles and Methods of Instructional Design and a self-developed AI agent, Aidee, to support collaborative inquiry and artifact generation. Additionally, AI tools are applied for evidence-based diagnosis of teaching processes, while human-AI collaborative evaluation of artifacts provides empirical data to validate the strategy's implementation and effectiveness.

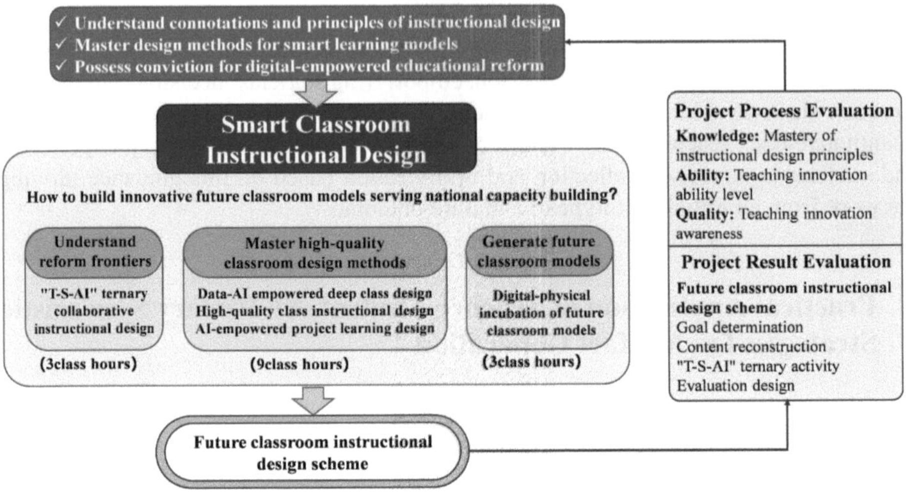

Fig. 4. Project Design of Smart Class Instructional Design

4.2 Research Implementation

This study initially applied conventional teaching methods to Module 1, subsequently applying the teacher-student-AI ternary collaborative strategy to Module 2 for the same class. Following the completion of both modules, an identical AI tool was utilized to conduct a comprehensive diagnostic analysis of the entire teaching process.

Module 2 implemented the ternary strategy across five stages: anchor goals and pre-learn resources—diverse dialogue and concept construction—human-AI collaboration and scheme generation—group inquiry and deep integration—outcome verification, display and feedback (Fig. 5).

T-S-AI Joint Cognition Promotes Generation Preparation. Aligning with AI-era educational requirements, the teacher defines the final output as a digital-ready high-quality classroom instructional design scheme and provides interpretations, typical cases, and rubrics via the MOOC. Students conduct autonomous pre-learning, utilizing the embedded knowledge graph to grasp key concepts and form an initial understanding of high-quality classrooms and output goals. Combining professional knowledge and personal interests, they interact with AI to conceive design themes. The core is clarifying output goals to stimulate innovation.

S-T-AI Co-Construction Promotes Generation Incubation. The teacher guides group discussions and utilizes AI for brainstorming diverse instructional strategies and cross-disciplinary cases. Through iterative dialogues, students expand their cognitive boundaries, transform information based on value judgments, and incubate creative intentions. This stage highlights divergent exploration to form initial innovative ideas; through multi-dimensional (teacher-student, student-student, and human-AI) dialogues, it deepens students' understanding of high-quality classrooms, fosters divergent thinking, and inspires creative instructional schemes.

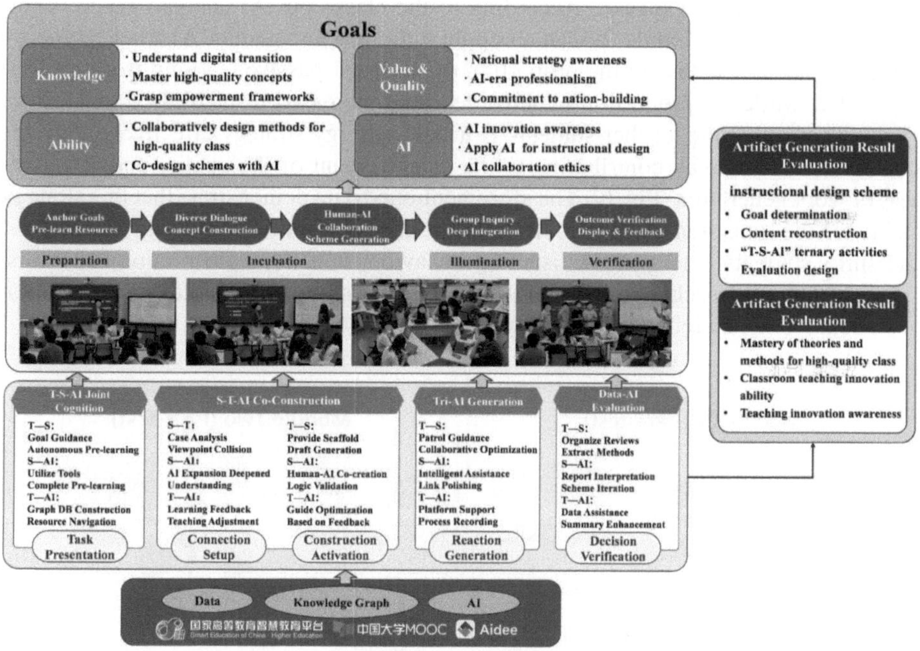

Fig. 5. Empirical Application of the T-S-AI Ternary Collaborative Strategy in Smart Class Teaching in Higher Education

Tri-Intelligence Integrated Generation Promotes Output Illumination. Teachers provide structured problem scaffolds and link relevant resources on the national platform. Based on initial concepts, students apply professional theories and high-quality classroom features to co-design schemes with AI. Meanwhile, teachers patrol and guide, helping groups distill their core logic. This stage highlights the deep collaboration of student, teacher, and AI intelligence, crystallizing creativity into coherent schemes.

Data-AI Verification and Iteration Promotes Output Verification. Teachers organize presentations to display group schemes and provide summary reviews. Simultaneously, utilizing AI evaluation tools based on high-quality classroom design dimensions, quantitative scores and objective feedback are generated for student artifacts. Integrating teacher reviews, peer feedback, and AI-generated quantitative reports, students clarify improvement directions and refine their designs. This highlights the progression from collaborative evaluation to iterative generation, achieving the verification phase of artifact innovation.

4.3 Research Results

This study presents results focusing on both the process and outcomes of artifact generation, analyzing classroom teaching behaviors, activity performance, and artifact quality.

Artifact Generation Process. According to the classroom AI analysis report, compared to Module 1, Module 2—which applied the teacher-student-AI triadic synergy strategy—saw a decrease in the proportion of students' passive learning from 89.16% to 72.24%, while the proportion of active learning increased from 10.84% to 27.76%. This indicates that the teacher-student-AI triadic synergy strategy effectively activates student agency, thereby contributing to the enhancement of the quality and effectiveness of work generation (Fig. 6). The aforementioned data demonstrate that this strategy facilitates the transition of teachers from knowledge transmitters to design facilitators, and shifts students from passive listening behaviors to active construction behaviors. Consequently, the teacher-student-AI triadic synergy strategy promotes the generation of student works, thereby validating Hypothesis H1.

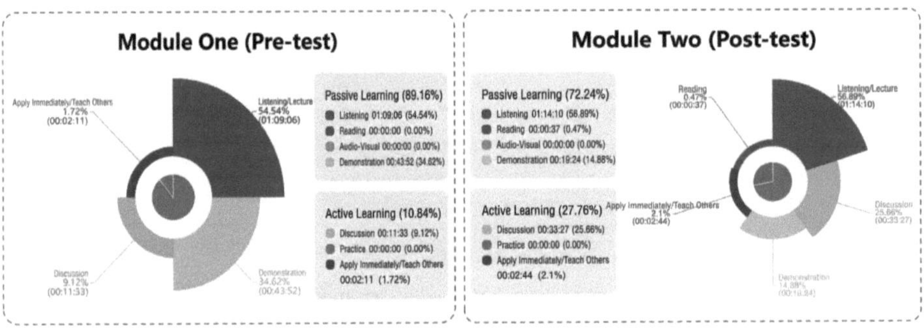

Fig. 6. Analysis of students' learning behaviors.

Furthermore, a comparison of the knowledge test performances before and after the two modules further reveals the advantages of this strategy in knowledge internalization. Test data indicates that Module 1, which employed conventional teaching methods, achieved an average score of 63.80% on Test 1 and 84.63% on Test 2, yielding an improvement of 20.83% in knowledge mastery. In contrast, Module 2, which applied the teacher-student-AI triadic synergy strategy, had a significantly lower initial average score on Test 1 (only 13.30%). However, following the intervention of this strategy, its average score on Test 2 surged to 97.30%, representing a substantial overall improvement of 84.00% (Fig. 7). This stark contrast in data demonstrates that, compared to conventional teaching methods, the teacher-student-AI triadic synergy strategy enables students to achieve leapfrog advancements in their cognitive levels when confronted with higher-difficulty concepts or a weak initial foundation. This significantly promotes the comprehensive application of professional knowledge, thereby robustly validating Hypothesis H2.

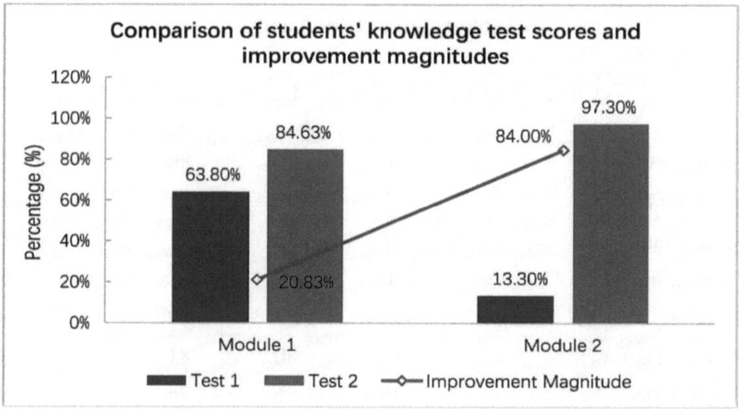

Fig. 7. Comparison of students' knowledge test scores and improvement magnitudes.

Artifact Generation Results. Based on instructional design theory, this study developed a works evaluation scale encompassing four dimensions: concept and objectives, content and methods, process and implementation and effectiveness and evaluation. To objectively evaluate the quality of the generated works, three teachers independently graded them according to the evaluation scale. Furthermore, a dual evaluation approach combining teacher scoring and intelligent agent scoring was adopted. The scoring results are presented in Table 1. The Pearson correlation coefficient between the human and AI scores was $r = 0.58$, indicating a moderate level of correlation. Regarding the score distribution, the majority of the group works scored above 80 points, with 33% falling into the high-score range of 90–100 points. This demonstrates that students were able to break through the bottlenecks of traditional design capabilities and produce high-quality instructional design schemes characterized by complete structures and advanced concepts. It further verifies the significant advantage of the teacher-student-AI triadic synergy strategy in enhancing the overall quality of students' generated works (H3).

5 Discussion and Conclusion

Although this study has achieved positive results, limited by the research cycle and conditions, it remains limited by its reliance on short-term intervention data from a single course, Principles and Methods of Instructional Design at H University, and a relatively small sample size, lacking long-term tracking of students' innovation abilities. Future research needs to conduct cross-semester or even cross-academic-year tracking experiments in other disciplines, and utilize multimodal learning engagement data to further optimize the intelligent agent's evaluation ability for complex higher-order artifacts, thereby comprehensively verifying and enhancing the generalizability and long-term educational value of this strategy.

Table 1. Project Evaluation.

Group	Title	Course Instructor	Expert 1	Expert 2	Average Human Score	AI score
A	Engineer OS	85	88	85	86	77
B	Hist Unit4	96	92	92	93	86
C	Smart Plant	93	91	88	91	92
D	Translator	83	80	79	81	65
E	Emotion	87	93	87	89	93
F	Pythag. Thm	78	84	80	81	70
G	Cyl. & Cone	68	75	86	76	80
H	Mach. Und	91	82	86	86	71
I	Rural Life	94	90	87	90	80
J	Quotes W/T	88	95	90	91	85
K	Volume C	90	85	86	87	85
L	Slow Tune	86	86	89	87	80

The findings of this study share consensus with similar domestic and international research while also driving advancements. The consensus is that intelligent technology and digital tools can indeed provide resource support and procedural assistance for artifact generation in higher education courses, while concurrently providing technical support for the Teacher-Student-AI (T-S-AI) ternary synergy.

The advancement lies in that this study systematically reveals the internal mechanism of human-AI coupling, spanning from collaborative cognition and heuristic construction to guided generation. And innovatively proposes a verified T-S-AI ternary collaborative strategy comprising T-S-AI Joint Cognition, S-T-AI Co-Construction, Tri-Intelligence Integrated Generation, and Data-AI Mutual Verification and Iteration. This provides guidance and pathways for the deep integration of intelligent technology into generative teaching, thereby offering references for the large-scale, personalized cultivation of innovative talents in the intelligent era.

Focusing on the demands of pedagogical reform in higher education institutions and the cultivation of innovative talents within the intelligent era, and guided by the philosophies of outcome-based education and generative teaching theories, this study analyzes the general instructional process and internal mechanisms of artifact generation empowered by smart environments, constructing and verifying the T-S-AI ternary collaborative strategy. Research data and practical results indicate that this strategy can effectively optimize the classroom interaction structure, stimulate students' active learning behaviors, strengthen the comprehensive application of professional knowledge, and contribute to the generation of high-quality student artifacts. Furthermore, it demonstrates positive effects in the routinized shaping process of students' higher-order innovation abilities.

Acknowledgement. This study was supported by the 2025 South China Normal University Institutional "Quality Engineering" Higher Education Teaching Reform Project, titled "Construction of an Embodied Collaborative Generative Classroom Model in Higher Education Enabled by Multi-Agent Systems."

References

1. He, K.: Theory of creative thinking: The construction and demonstration of the DC model [In Chinese]. Beijing Normal University Press, Beijing (2004)
2. Wallas, G.: The art of thought. Harcourt, Brace, New York (1926)
3. Amabile, T.M.: The social psychology of creativity: a componential conceptualization. J. Pers. Soc. Psychol. **45**(2), 357–376 (1983)
4. Lin, C.: Exploring the laws of the innovative mind to promote the development of innovative talents [In Chinese]. Educ. Res. **45**(8), 4–14 (2024)
5. Lu, T., Sun, H.: Human-AI collaborative computing [In Chinese]. Commun. CCF **11**, 7341086340368384 (2024)
6. Zhang, Y., Guo, Y., Luo, X.: Human-AI collaborative creativity retrospect: AIGC science and aesthetic thinking co-creation [In Chinese]. China Educ. Technol. **3**, 86–93 (2025)
7. Im, J., Chang, B.: Human–AI co-creativity in storytelling: a scoping review of literature, education, media, and interactive systems. In: International Conference on Interactive Digital Storytelling, pp. 396–406. Springer Nature Switzerland (2025)
8. Lyu, P., Zhang, J.: Generative mechanism and training path of college students' innovation ability from the perspective of human-AI collaborative creativity [In Chinese]. Jiangsu High. Educ. **7**, 82–90 (2025)
9. Hou, H.: The realistic dilemma and inevitable turn of cultivating innovative talents in universities in the intelligent era [In Chinese]. China Educ. Technol. **6**, 21–28 (2019)
10. Zhao, W.: The impact of science and technology competitions on the cultivation of college students' innovative abilities [In Chinese]. Sci. Technol. Manage. Res. **44**(9), 133–140 (2024)
11. Ye, Y., Yang, S., Ma, Y., Xi, Y., Li, H.: The influence of digital literacy on the development of students' innovation ability: an empirical study based on the cultivation of top innovative talents [In Chinese]. High. Educ. Explor. **6**, 41–52 (2025)
12. Li, J., Zhuang, R., Nian, Z., et al.: Innovation ability cultivation oriented to human-machine collaboration: also on the demands of creative talents in the intelligent era [In Chinese]. China Educ. Technol. **7**, 36–42, 61 (2021)
13. Dong, H.: Exploration on the training path of college students' innovation ability: practical thinking based on "two-chain docking and four-chain integration" [In Chinese]. Chin. Univ. Technol. **3**, 62–67 (2022)
14. Coman, C., Gherhes, V., Bucs, A., et al.: Navigating opportunities and challenges of generative AI in higher education: towards responsible, equitable, and human-centered integration. Front. Artif. Intell. **9**, 1750978 (2026)
15. Liu, S., Hao, X.: Challenges and approaches of generative artificial intelligence facilitating educational innovation [In Chinese]. Tsinghua J. Educ. **45**(3), 1–12 (2024)
16. Spector, J.M.: Smart learning environments: concepts and issues. In: Society for Information Technology & Teacher Education International Conference, pp. 2728–2737. Association for the Advancement of Computing in Education (AACE) (2016)
17. Xie, Y., Li, C., Li, C., Qiu, Y.: Digital curriculum of universities in the intelligent era: Connotation, form and construction [In Chinese]. e-Educ. Res. **45**(11), 5–12 (2024)
18. Wu, F., Gao, S.: Transformation of classroom teaching paradigm in the intelligent era: structure and modality of human-AI integration [In Chinese]. e-Educ. Res. **47**(1), 75–83 (2026)

19. Yu, L., Zhang, X., Deng, S.: Human-AI collaborative learning in blended teaching: essential characteristics and practical modalities [In Chinese]. J. Southwest Univ. (Soc. Sci. Ed.) **51**(5), 189–201 (2025)
20. Xie, Y., Chen, W., Qiu, Y.: Research on artificial intelligence empowering the reconstruction of college classroom teaching [In Chinese]. e-Educ. Res. **46**(10), 5–13 (2025)
21. Paul, D., Gohain, D., Thomas, T.G., et al.: From theory to practice: a Human–AI Synergy framework for ethical, inclusive and pedagogically-driven language education frontiers in education. Frontiers **11**, 1841386 (2026)
22. Guilford, J.P.: Creative talents: their nature, uses and development. Bearly Limited, Buffalo (1986)
23. Yang, Z., Wang, J., Wu, D., Chen, X.: Analysis of the impact of ChatGPT/generative artificial intelligence on education and coping strategies. J. East China Normal Univ. (Educ. Sci.) **41**(7), 26–35 (2023)

Research on the Representation Methods of Higher-Order Thinking Skills in Collaborative Inquiry-Based Learning: A Systematic Literature Review

Siqi Zhao[1], Kaili Lu[1](✉), Yinghui Shi[2], and Harrison Hao Yang[3]

[1] Nanjing University of Posts and Telecommunications, Nanjing, China
kelly@njupt.edu.cn
[2] Hainan College of Software Technology, Qionghai, China
[3] State University of New York, Oswego, NY, USA

Abstract. In response to the growing global demand for cultivating higher-order thinking skills (HOTS) amid accelerating educational digitalization, this study conducts a systematic literature review of representation methods used in collaborative inquiry-based learning. A total of 44 articles retrieved from the Web of Science Core Collection, IEEE, and Engineering Village were analyzed through thematic coding. The findings show that HOTS representation methods can be grouped into five categories: discourse analysis, visual representation, intelligent analysis, assessment rubrics, and network analysis. Among these, assessment rubrics and discourse analysis were the most frequently used approaches, indicating that existing studies have primarily represented HOTS through structured assessment evidence and discourse-based evidence. In contrast, visual representation, intelligent analysis, and network analysis appeared less frequently, suggesting that real-time visualization, multimodal representation, AI-supported automatic analysis, and relational analytics remain underexplored. Based on these findings, the study proposes a classification framework that clarifies how HOTS can be externalized, traced, assessed, and analyzed in collaborative inquiry-based learning. The review contributes to research by synthesizing fragmented methodological approaches and contributes to practice by informing the design of technology-supported learning environments and HOTS assessment tools.

Keywords: Collaborative Inquiry-based Learning · Higher-order Thinking Skills · Representation Methods · Systematic Literature Review

1 Introduction

The ongoing scientific and technological revolution, together with accelerating digital transformation, is reshaping education systems worldwide. Reports from the OECD and UNESCO indicate that digital technologies are transforming educational infrastructure, resources, governance, and learning support, while simultaneously raising concerns

K. T. Chui et al. (Eds.): ICBL 2026, LNCS 16778, pp. 123–137, 2027.
https://doi.org/10.1007/978-981-92-3761-6_9

regarding privacy, equity, and responsible use [1, 2]. In learning practice, digital technologies generate rich digital traces—such as discourse records, interaction logs, learning artifacts, and assessment data—making cognitive and collaborative processes more visible and analyzable [3]. Meanwhile, the rapid expansion of knowledge and technological innovation requires learners to develop a broad range of 21st-century skills [4]. Within this context, collaborative inquiry-based learning has been widely recognized as an effective approach to fostering higher-order thinking skills (HOTS).

Despite the growing adoption of collaborative inquiry-based learning, substantial challenges remain in representing the cognitive processes underlying HOTS. These challenges arise because HOTS are often implicit, dynamic, context-dependent, and socially distributed. In computer-supported collaborative learning (CSCL) research, collaborative learning is conceptualized not only as individual cognition but also as cognition that emerges at the small-group level [5]. Consequently, students' critical thinking, creative thinking, problem-solving, and metacognitive processes cannot be directly observed; rather, they must be inferred from discourse, interaction traces, learning artifacts, reflections, and assessment data. Although visualization techniques, coding schemes, social learning analytics, and multimodal learning analytics provide useful approaches for externalizing and analyzing these processes, they also present methodological challenges related to construct validity, coding reliability, and the alignment between theoretical constructs, analytical methods, and data structures [6–8]. These issues underscore the need for a systematic review of how HOTS are represented, traced, assessed, and analyzed in collaborative inquiry-based learning contexts.

Grounded in the revised Bloom's Taxonomy, HOTS encompass advanced cognitive processes, including analyzing, evaluating, and creating [9]. Although several review-type studies have examined technology-enhanced collaborative inquiry [10], argumentative knowledge construction [11], and social network analysis in e-learning environments [12], few have specifically focused on the representation methods of HOTS in collaborative inquiry-based learning. Existing reviews tend to emphasize learning environments, instructional effects, or specific analytical techniques, while paying less attention to how HOTS are externalized, visualized, assessed, and analyzed across different methodological approaches. This gap highlights the need for a systematic review focusing on HOTS representation methods in collaborative inquiry-based learning.

To address this gap, the present study employs a systematic literature review to examine the types, characteristics, and applications of representation methods for HOTS in collaborative inquiry-based learning. Specifically, it seeks to answer the following research question: How are HOTS represented in collaborative inquiry-based learning contexts? The study has two primary objectives. First, it develops a classification framework for HOTS representation to inform the design of collaborative inquiry activities. Second, it identifies emerging trends and research gaps, thereby contributing to the advancement of digital education research and practice.

2 Conceptual Background

2.1 Collaborative Inquiry-Based Learning

Collaborative inquiry-based learning is a group-based pedagogical approach in which students engage in scientific inquiry to develop critical thinking and exploratory abilities [10]. Centered on collaboration and inquiry, this approach emphasizes peer interaction, evidence collection, and argumentation. Arfin et al. [13] argue that it supports problem-solving and knowledge co-construction through active cooperation and reflective discourse. Similarly, Liang and Zhao [14] show that the DECBL model promotes the development of HOTS. Research on the 5E instructional model (Engage, Explore, Explain, Elaborate, and Evaluate) further indicates that collaborative inquiry can simultaneously enhance students' HOTS, improve the quality of peer interaction, and increase overall learning achievement [15]. From a learning sciences perspective, the effectiveness of collaborative inquiry-based learning is rooted in socially shared and distributed cognition, through which higher-order thinking is constructed, externalized, and developed via interaction, tools, and representational media.

2.2 Higher-Order Thinking Skills

HOTS are a multidimensional and complex construct. In the revised Bloom's Taxonomy, analyzing, evaluating, and creating are defined as higher-order cognitive processes [9], characterized by complexity, abstraction, and creativity. Resnick [16] further identifies seven features of higher-order thinking: it is non-algorithmic, complex, multi-criteria, uncertain, self-regulated, context-embedded, and multi-representational.

In collaborative inquiry-based learning, HOTS are not isolated individual abilities but socially situated cognitive processes that emerge through dialogue, inquiry, and knowledge co-construction [17–19]. Critical thinking is reflected in evaluating evidence, questioning claims, and justifying conclusions [20]; creative thinking appears in generating alternative explanations and improving shared ideas [21, 22]; metacognition involves planning, monitoring, and reflecting on inquiry processes [23, 24]; and problem-solving is demonstrated through problem definition, strategy selection, and solution refinement [25]. Therefore, collaborative inquiry-based learning provides a meaningful context for eliciting, externalizing, assessing, and analyzing HOTS through discourse, learning artifacts, visual representations, assessment rubrics, and learning analytics [26].

Drawing on the existing literature, this study conceptualizes HOTS in collaborative inquiry-based learning across four core dimensions, as shown in Table 1. Following Zhang et al. [27], these dimensions include critical thinking, creative thinking, metacognition, and problem-solving ability, each of which plays a distinct role in collaborative inquiry. Research further indicates that, in smart classroom environments, instructional design and technological support significantly influence the development of these skills [28]. More specifically, the four dimensions interact through a moderated mediation mechanism in which critical thinking mediates the relationship between creative thinking and problem-solving ability, while metacognition moderates the creative-critical pathway.

Table 1. Core dimensions of higher-order thinking skills.

Dimension	Core elements	Examples in collaborative inquiry-based learning
Critical thinking	Analysis, evaluation, reasoning, argumentation	Posing questions, evaluating evidence, identifying fallacies, constructing arguments
Creative thinking	Imagination, divergence, convergence, innovation	Proposing novel ideas, improving solutions, cross-domain transfer
Metacognition	Planning, monitoring, regulation, reflection	Self-assessment, strategy adjustment, process reflection
Problem-solving	Problem representation, strategy selection, solution implementation	Decomposing complex problems, collaboratively developing solutions, iterative optimization

2.3 Types and Applications of Representation Methods

Prior research suggests that representation in cognitive science involves both functional roles in cognition [29] and methodological roles in data analysis [30]. External representations serve as cognitive tools that make conceptual structures explicit and support understanding and knowledge organization [31]. Representation can also be understood as a process of data transformation through which cognitive activity becomes observable and analyzable [32]. This study adopts the latter perspective to examine how implicit HOTS can be systematically externalized, aligning with theories that emphasize the visibility of knowledge construction. Scardamalia and Bereiter [17] argue that thinking develops through the visualization of idea improvement. More recently, advances in learning analytics and educational data mining have enabled large-scale, multimodal representation of thinking. Yao et al. [33], for example, used an AI-enhanced platform to represent higher-order thinking through intelligent assessment and analytics.

3 Research Design

3.1 Retrieval and Screening

This study employed a systematic literature review to retrieve, screen, code, and analyze publications published since 2000. Data were collected from the Web of Science Core Collection, IEEE, and Engineering Village using keywords related to collaborative inquiry-based learning, HOTS, and representation methods. These databases were selected because they cover educational technology, computer-supported collaborative learning, learning analytics, and engineering-related research. The search yielded 141, 292, and 153 articles, respectively. After duplicates were removed, 512 articles remained for screening.

To ensure consistency, a systematic screening procedure was followed. First, titles and abstracts were assessed against predefined inclusion criteria: studies had to be situated in collaborative inquiry-based learning contexts, such as computer-supported collaborative learning (CSCL), project-based learning (PBL), and knowledge building (KB); explicitly address methods for representing, assessing, or analyzing HOTS; and report empirical research or systematic reviews published in English.

Studies were excluded if they focused solely on individual learning without collaborative interaction, described teaching cases without specific representation methods, or were conducted in non-educational contexts (e.g., corporate training or medical diagnosis). Articles meeting the initial criteria proceeded to full-text review. The remaining studies were then examined in detail, and a second review was conducted to verify consistency and ensure rigorous application of the inclusion and exclusion criteria. Following this process, 44 articles (13 journal papers and 31 conference papers) were included in the final review (see Fig. 1).

3.2 Coding

In this study, the coding framework comprised two components: research description items and representation-method characteristics. The former included publication type, publication year, research context, and collaborative learning type (e.g., PBL, CSCL, knowledge building, and collaborative argumentation). The latter focused on thematic categories of representation methods. Thematic coding was adopted because it provides a flexible and systematic approach for identifying recurring patterns across qualitative data [34] and is particularly suitable for synthesizing heterogeneous studies in systematic reviews [35]. Since the reviewed articles varied in learning settings, data sources, analytical techniques, and forms of HOTS representation, thematic coding helped group similar representation methods into comparable categories while retaining their methodological differences.

Twenty articles were randomly selected to refine the coding framework, resulting in a system of five first-level categories and twelve second-level items: discourse analysis, visual representation, intelligent analysis, assessment rubrics, and network analysis. Detailed coding information is presented in Table 2. After the initial coding, all cases were reviewed, and inconsistent codings were revised to ensure internal consistency.

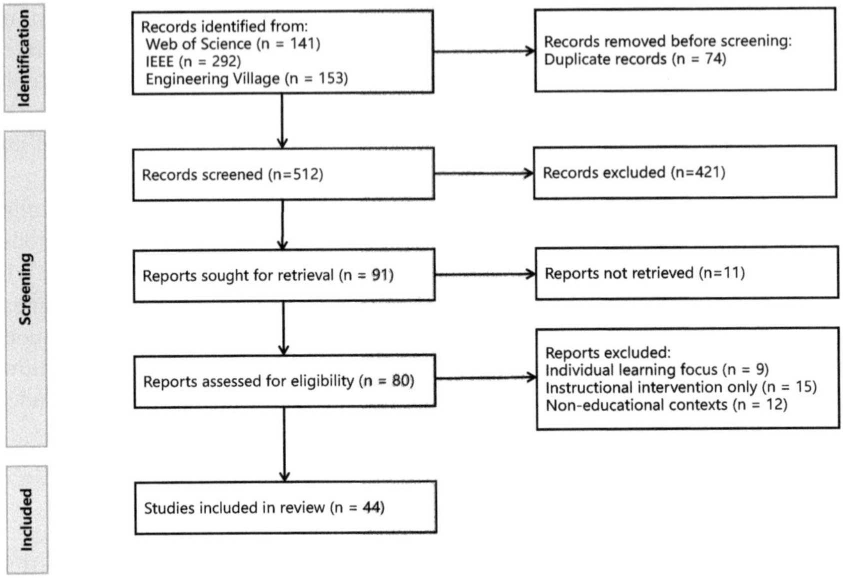

Fig. 1. Literature screening process.

Table 2. Coding scheme for higher-order thinking skills representation methods.

First-Level dimension	Second-Level coding item	Coding description
Discourse analysis category	Argument structure analysis	Toulmin model, argumentation schemas, etc
	Sequential pattern mining	Lag sequential analysis, process mining
	Meta-discourse/Epistemological discourse	Metacognitive markers, epistemological beliefs
Visual representation category	Concept map analysis	Nodes, links, structural features
	Argument maps/Knowledge maps	Argumentation networks, knowledge graphs
	Thinking visualization tools	Visible thinking, graphical mediators
Intelligent analysis category	Deep learning automatic coding	Neural networks, automatic classification
	Learning analytics/EDA	Multimodal data, predictive model
Assessment rubrics category	Peer/Self assessment	Rubric design, feedback mechanisms
	Reflection/Formative assessment	Reflective journals, dynamic assessment

(continued)

Table 2. *(continued)*

First-Level dimension	Second-Level coding item	Coding description
Network analysis category	Social network analysis (SNA)	Centrality, subgroups, roles
	Epistemic network analysis (ENA)	Cognitive networks, discourse networks

Figure 2 maps the relationship between HOTS types and representation method categories. The heatmap indicates that metacognition/reflection and argumentation/reasoning were more frequently represented through discourse analysis and assessment rubrics, whereas intelligent analysis, visual representation, and network analysis were less commonly used across HOTS types. This suggests that current research has relied more heavily on discourse-based and assessment-based approaches, while AI-supported, visual, and network-based representation methods remain relatively underexplored. Because a single study may involve more than one HOTS dimension, the counts in the heatmap are not mutually exclusive and do not sum to the total number of included studies.

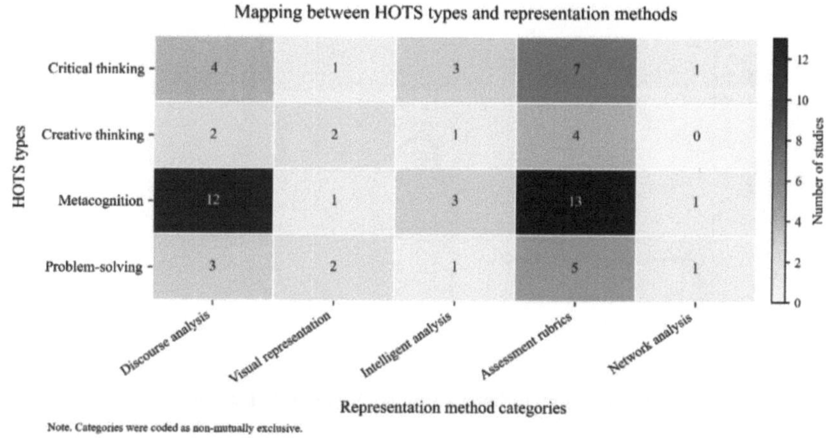

Fig. 2. Mapping between HOTS types and representation method categories

4 Results

As shown in Fig. 3, the included studies were unevenly distributed across publication years. Although early research appeared only sporadically, the number of studies increased after 2017, with peaks in 2019 and 2025. This indicates growing research interest in HOTS representation methods within collaborative learning contexts. In terms of publication type, the included studies were dominated by conference papers and proceedings papers (n = 31, 70.5%), while journal articles accounted for a smaller proportion (n = 13, 29.5%). Publication type was coded according to the publication venue: conference proceedings, conference series, and LNCS proceedings were classified as conference papers, whereas regular academic journals were classified as journal articles. Representation methods for HOTS fall into five main categories, each comprising distinct technical pathways. These categories are discussed below.

Figure 4 shows the distribution of HOTS representation method categories. Assessment rubrics and discourse analysis were the most frequently used approaches, followed by intelligent analysis, whereas visual representation and network analysis appeared less frequently.

Taken together, Figs. 2 and 4 suggest that current HOTS representation in collaborative inquiry-based learning still relies primarily on structured assessment evidence and discourse-based evidence. This pattern is reasonable because rubrics, reflection records, peer/self assessment, and discourse coding can map observable learner productions onto theoretical constructs such as metacognitive regulation, argumentation, and problem-solving. However, the relatively low use of visual representation and network analysis also points to an important gap: existing studies have not yet fully exploited real-time visualization, multimodal data, and relational analytics to trace socially distributed cognitive processes during collaborative inquiry.

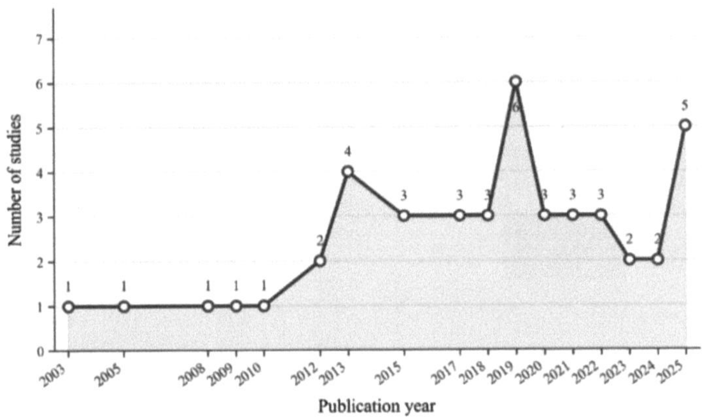

Fig. 3. Annual distribution of the included studies.

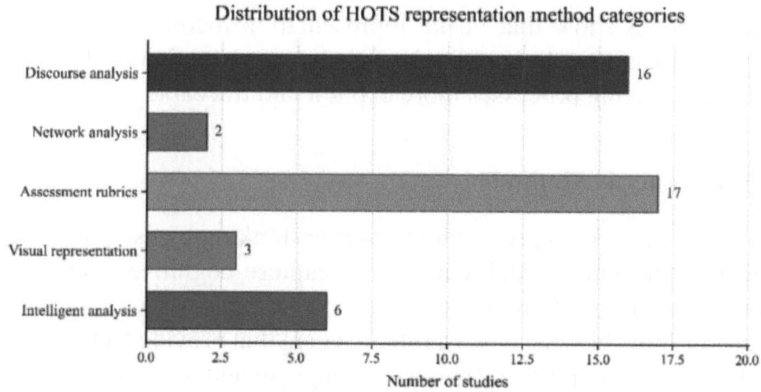

Fig. 4. Distribution of HOTS representation method categories

4.1 Discourse Analysis Methods

Discourse analysis methods represent HOTS by systematically examining learners' interactive discourse, thereby revealing the procedural, structural, and social dimensions of thinking in collaborative inquiry-based learning.

Within this category, argumentation constitutes one of the most explicit manifestations of higher-order thinking. Greene [36] proposed a discourse-analysis model for online ethical argumentation, coding students' argumentative discourse through claims, grounds, warrants, counterclaims, conclusions, solutions, fallacies, and ethical values to capture the quality of higher-order thinking in online discussions. In addition, these patterns are shaped by inquiry structure: research on the four-level inquiry continuum shows that task openness directly influences higher-order thinking tendencies and peer interaction patterns [37]. Lei and Chan [38] developed a coding scheme for metadiscourse markers and treated linguistic markers as indicators of metacognitive and epistemological thinking.

4.2 Visual Representation Methods

Visual representation methods transform abstract thinking into visible structures through graphical tools. Research in this category primarily focuses on the use of concept maps and related externalization tools.

Tan and Chan [39] designed the Knowledge Community system with graphic organizers such as compare-and-contrast charts, concept maps, classification charts, and timelines to support students' collaborative project learning and knowledge building. Extending visual representation from idea organization to cognitive-process tracing, Gustafson et al. [40] proposed the use of the Function-Behavior-Structure framework and knowledge graphs to represent students' evolving design reasoning, misconceptions, and knowledge states during project-based learning. Peng et al. [41] further developed an online visible-thinking toolkit in which students used structured visualization templates to record and externalize their thinking processes during online project-based learning.

Together, these studies show that visual representation methods can support higher-order thinking by making collaborative knowledge construction, individual cognitive development, and thinking processes more explicit and traceable.

4.3 Intelligent Analysis Methods

Intelligent analysis methods represent higher-order thinking by using data-driven tools, intelligent agents, and multimodal analytics to capture cognitive, metacognitive, and behavioral processes in collaborative learning.

Oshima and Oshima [42] designed a robotic agent that provided adaptive scaffolding scripts for planning, monitoring, and behavioral engagement, showing how an intelligent agent can function as a metacognitive mediator to support learners' note-taking, collaborative argumentation, and socially shared regulation. Extending this agent-supported perspective to learning analytics, Huang et al. [43] integrated Knowledge Forum with the KBDeX analysis tool to examine how collaborative problem-solving abilities, including opinion complexity, metacognition, and cognitive interaction, influenced academic performance in a computer-supported knowledge-building environment. Similarly, Sommer et al. [44] used eye-tracking technology to capture learners' gaze patterns and attention distribution, transforming private visual strategies into visible data for collaborative reflection. Together, these studies indicate that intelligent analysis methods can make higher-order thinking visible through adaptive scaffolding, learning analytics, and multimodal process data.

4.4 Assessment and Rubric Methods

Assessment and rubrics provide standardized means of representing HOTS by enabling structured evaluation and developmental tracking through explicit performance criteria and level descriptors. Research in this category primarily focuses on the design and application of assessment.

In this category, assessment functions not merely as a scoring mechanism but also as a way to collect evidence of learners' higher-order thinking processes. Adler-Beléndez et al. [45] reviewed how 21st-century skills are captured in makerspace learning and found that studies commonly used surveys, observations, interviews, and student artifacts to assess collaboration, communication, critical thinking, and creativity. This suggests that assessment methods can provide diverse evidence for representing higher-order thinking in project-based learning environments. Assessment rubric methods can further represent higher-order thinking by transforming collaborative reflection, regulation, and discourse quality into assessable dimensions. Splichal et al. [46] used Knowledge Forum as a digital portfolio and provided metacognitive prompts to help students reflect on socio-emotional regulation during project-based collaboration, thereby making collaborative and metacognitive processes visible for assessment. Building on this reflective-assessment logic, Tong and Chan [47] further developed structured coding schemes to assess students' epistemic discourse understanding in terms of discourse aims, standards, and reliable processes, showing how rubric-based frameworks can capture students' understanding of productive collaborative inquiry.

4.5 Network Analysis Methods

Network analysis methods conceptualize collaborative learning as an interplay of social and cognitive networks, representing the social distribution and emergent group-level nature of higher-order thinking through quantified network structures.

At a basic level, social network analysis (SNA) examines interaction structures among learners and uses network indicators to represent collaboration depth, role differentiation, and information flow. Zhu, Xing, and Popov [48] used transition-rate analysis, entropy analysis, and sequential pattern mining to uncover temporal relations among discourse moves, showing that successful groups were more likely to build shared understanding before moving forward. Extending this relational perspective to automated network-based analysis, Dascalu et al. [49] introduced ReaderBench, a cohesion-centered framework that integrates text mining, natural language processing, and social network analysis to assess participation and collaboration in CSCL conversations. Together, these studies show how network-oriented analytics can make collaborative thinking visible through discourse sequences, interaction structures, and participation patterns.

5 Discussion and Conclusion

This study employed a systematic literature review and thematic coding of 44 articles from the Web of Science Core Collection, IEEE, and Engineering Village to examine how HOTS are represented in collaborative inquiry-based learning. The findings indicate that these methods can be organized into five complementary methodological pathways - discourse analysis, visual representation, intelligent analysis, assessment rubrics, and network analysis - which together form a classification framework for learning-environment design and HOTS assessment. Discourse analysis methods show that higher-order thinking is embedded in collaborative interaction, especially in learners' idea construction, perspective negotiation, and metacognitive regulation during knowledge building [50]. Visual representation methods, such as concept maps, argument maps, and visible-thinking tools, transform abstract cognition into tangible structures and support reflection and collective knowledge construction [39–41, 51]. Intelligent analysis methods, including learning analytics and educational data mining, enable scalable and increasingly real-time representations of collaborative thinking processes [52]. Assessment rubrics, particularly peer, self-, and reflective assessment, provide explicit criteria for representing higher-order thinking while promoting feedback literacy and self-regulation [53]. Network analysis methods conceptualize higher-order thinking as socially distributed and reveal how interaction structures and cognitive linkages shape group cognition [12].

In conclusion, this review identifies five complementary approaches to representing HOTS in collaborative inquiry-based learning and integrates them into a classification framework. The findings underscore the value of combining multimodal analytics, visualization tools, and human-centered assessment to provide process-embedded scaffolding, with important implications for fostering critical thinking, creativity, and metacognition in digital-age education.

6 Limitations and Future Research

This study has several limitations. First, the literature search was restricted to three major databases, namely Web of Science Core Collection, IEEE, and Engineering Village, and to English-language publications published since 2000, which may limit the comprehensiveness and global representativeness of the review. Although these databases were selected to cover educational research, educational technology, computer-supported collaborative learning, learning analytics, and engineering-related studies, the exclusion of Scopus may have led to the omission of some relevant studies. Second, although the coding framework was systematically developed, some degree of subjective interpretation was unavoidable, and the five-category classification may not fully capture hybrid or emerging approaches, particularly in rapidly evolving areas such as AI-supported learning. Third, the study focused on identifying representation methods rather than evaluating their effectiveness; accordingly, the proposed framework remains descriptive and has not yet been empirically validated.

Future research should address these limitations in several ways. The search scope could be expanded by including Scopus, ERIC, and other education-related databases, as well as multilingual literature, to strengthen the evidence base and improve the global representativeness of the review. Methodological rigor can be enhanced through the use of multiple coders, inter-rater reliability testing, and mixed-method approaches. More importantly, empirical studies are needed to validate the proposed framework. Experimental, design-based, and longitudinal research in authentic learning environments should examine how representation methods influence HOTS, including critical thinking, creativity, metacognition, and problem-solving. In addition, future work should explore context-sensitive applications, particularly in AI-supported and informal learning settings, and conduct cross-context comparisons to assess generalizability.

Acknowledgments. This work was supported by the National Natural Science Foundation of China (Grant No. 62407023), the Social Science Foundation of Jiangsu Province (Grant No. 25JYC001), the Major Project of Philosophy and Social Science Research in Colleges and Universities of Jiangsu Province, "Research on hierarchical collaborative inquiry-based teaching styles based on the smart education platform of primary and secondary schools in Jiangsu" (Grant No. 2024SJZD074).

References

1. Boeskens, L., Meyer, K.: Policies for the digital transformation of school education: Evidence from the policy survey on school education in the digital age. OECD Education Working Papers No. 328, 1–98 (2025). https://doi.org/10.1787/464dab4d-en
2. UNESCO: Global Education Monitoring Report 2023: Technology in Education: A Tool on Whose Terms? UNESCO, Paris (2023). https://unesdoc.unesco.org/ark:/48223/pf0000385723
3. Ye, D., Pennisi, S.: Using trace data to enhance students' self-regulation: A learning analytics perspective. The Inter. Higher Educ. **54**, 100855 (2022)
4. Linsih, R.A., Soepriyanto, Y., Praherdhiono, H.: The effect of collaborative inquiry based learning model and learning motivation on critical thinking skills of elementary school students. JKTP: Jurnal Kajian Teknologi Pendidikan **8**(2), 118–127 (2025)

5. Stahl, G., Hakkarainen, K.: Theories of CSCL. In: Cress, U., Rosé, C.P., Wise, A.F., Oshima, J. (eds.) International Handbook of Computer-Supported Collaborative Learning, pp. 23–43. Springer, Cham (2021)
6. Kaliisa, R., Rienties, B., Mørch, A.I., Kluge, A.: Social learning analytics in computer-supported collaborative learning environments: A systematic review of empirical studies. Comp. Educ. Open **3**, 100073 (2022)
7. Xu, W., Wu, Y., Ouyang, F.: Multimodal learning analytics of collaborative patterns during pair programming in higher education. Int. J. Educ. Technol. High. Educ. **20**, 8 (2023)
8. Dang, B., Nguyen, A., Järvelä, S.: Deliberative interactions for socially shared regulation in collaborative learning: An AI-driven learning analytics study. J. Learn. Analy. **11**(3), 192–209 (2024)
9. Anderson, L.W., Krathwohl, D.R.: A taxonomy for learning, teaching, and assessing: A revision of Bloom's taxonomy of educational objectives: complete edition. Addison Wesley Longman, Inc. (2001)
10. Chen, F., Chen, G.: Technology-enhanced collaborative inquiry in k–12 classrooms: A systematic review of empirical studies. Sci. Educ. **34**(3), 1731–1773 (2025)
11. Ibrahim, S.N.K.A., Harun, J.: Systematic mapping studies on argumentative knowledge construction analysis frameworks towards improving students' higher order thinking skills. In: 2015 IEEE Conference on e-Learning, e-Management and e-Services (IC3e), pp. 86–91. IEEE (2015)
12. Cela, K.L., Sicilia, M.Á., Sánchez, S.: Social network analysis in e-learning environments: A preliminary systematic review. Educ. Psychol. Rev. **27**(1), 219–246 (2015)
13. Arfin, A., Abdul Latief, J., Misnah: Implementation of HOTS-Based Learning Tools Through a Collaborative Learning Model by Applying the Merdeka Curriculum to Sixth Grade Students at SDN Lahuafu. J. Sci. Res. Educ. Technol. **4**(2), 1239–1245 (2025)
14. Liang, X., Zhao, D.: Design and research of blended collaborative learning model for deep learning. In: 2023 IEEE 12th International Conference on Educational and Information Technology (ICEIT), pp. 78–82. IEEE (2023)
15. Lu, K., Yang, H.H., Shi, Y., Xue, H., Wang, X.: Examining the effects of the 5E instructional model on college students' higher-order thinking skills, peer interaction and learning achievement. In: 2020 Ninth International Conference of Educational Innovation through Technology (EITT), pp. 188–192 (2020)
16. Resnick, L.B.: Education and Learning to Think. National Academy Press, Washington, D.C. (1987)
17. Scardamalia, M., Bereiter, C.: Knowledge building: theory, pedagogy, and technology. In: Sawyer, K. (ed.) Cambridge handbook of the learning sciences, pp. 97–118. Cambridge University Press, New York (2006)
18. Chi, M.T.H.: Active-constructive-interactive: A conceptual framework for differentiating learning activities. Top. Cogn. Sci. **1**(1), 73–105 (2009)
19. Mercer, N.: Words and minds: How we use language to think together. Routledge (2002)
20. Facione, P.A.: Critical Thinking: A Statement of Expert Consensus for Purposes of Educational Assessment and Instruction. The Delphi Report. American Philosophical Association, Newark, DE (1990)
21. OECD: PISA 2022 Assessment and Analytical Framework. OECD Publishing, Paris (2023)
22. Kampylis, P., Berki, E.: Nurturing Creative Thinking. Educational Practices Series 25. UNESCO International Bureau of Education, Geneva (2014)
23. Flavell, J.H.: Metacognition and cognitive monitoring: a new area of cognitive-developmental inquiry. Am. Psychol. **34**(10), 906–911 (1979)
24. Schraw, G., Moshman, D.: Metacognitive theories. Educ. Psychol. Rev. **7**(4), 351–371 (1995)
25. Jonassen, D.H.: Toward a design theory of problem solving. Education Tech. Research Dev. **48**(4), 63–85 (2000)

26. Ritchhart, R., Church, M., Morrison, K.: Making thinking visible: How to promote engagement, understanding, and independence for all learners. John Wiley & Sons (2011)
27. Zhang, Y., Tian, H., Lu, J.: The relationship between higher-order thinking and problem-solving skills development among pre-service teachers using generative AI: an analysis based on moderated mediation. BMC Psychology **13**(1), 1094 (2025)
28. Lu, K., Yang, H.H., Shi, Y., Wang, X.: Examining the key influencing factors on college students' higher-order thinking skills in the smart classroom environment. Int. J. Educ. Technol. High. Educ. **18**(1), 1 (2021)
29. Favela, L.H., Machery, E.: The concept of representation in the brain sciences: the current status and ways forward. Mind Lang. **40**(2), 215–225 (2025)
30. Pohl, S., Walker, E.Y., Barack, D.L., et al.: Clarifying the conceptual dimensions of representation in neuroscience. Nat. Rev. Neurosci. **27**, 357–372 (2026)
31. Chen, X., Wei, Z., Li, Z., et al.: The influence of the conceptual structure of external representations when relearning history content. Educ. Tech. Res. Dev. **71**(2), 415–439 (2023)
32. Kannampallil, T.G., Abraham, J., Patel, V.L.: Methodological framework for evaluating clinical processes: a cognitive informatics perspective. J. Biomed. Inform. **64**, 342–351 (2016)
33. Yao, Z., Xia, D., Sun, X., et al.: Towards Deep Learning: Transforming Project-Based Teaching with an AI-Enhanced Platform for Intelligent Assessment and Collaborative Learning. In: Proceedings of the 2025 2nd International Symposium on Artificial Intelligence for Education, pp. 729–736 (2025)
34. Braun, V., Clarke, V.: Using thematic analysis in psychology. Qual. Res. Psychol. **3**(2), 77–101 (2006)
35. Thomas, J., Harden, A.: Methods for the thematic synthesis of qualitative research in systematic reviews. BMC Med. Res. Methodol. **8**, 45 (2008)
36. Greene, M.S.: Structure and content in the quality levels of ethical argumentation in online discussions. Thinking Skills and Creativity **58**, 101949 (2025)
37. Lu, K., Yang, H., Xue, H.: Investigating the four-level inquiry continuum on college students' higher order thinking and peer interaction tendencies. Int. J. Innov. Learn. **30**(3), 358–367 (2021)
38. Lei, C., Chan, C.K.K.: Developing metadiscourse through reflective assessment in knowledge building environments. Comput. Educ. **126**, 153–169 (2018)
39. Tan, C., Chan, Y.-Y.: Knowledge Community: A knowledge-building system for global collaborative project learning. Proc. IEEE **96**(6), 1049–1061 (2008)
40. Gustafson, J.R.D., Zhang, X., Jhajj, G., Lin, F.: Representing and tracing students' cognitive processes in project-based learning through the Function-Behavior-Structure framework and knowledge graphs. In: 2025 IEEE Smart World Congress (SWC), pp. 307–313. IEEE (2025)
41. Peng, J., Sun, M., Yuan, B., et al.: Visible thinking to support online project-based learning: Narrowing the achievement gap between high-and low-achieving students. Educ. Inf. Technol. **29**(2), 2329–2363 (2024)
42. Oshima, J., Oshima, R.: Collaborative learning through socially shared regulation supported by a robotic agent. In: CSCL 2013 Proceedings Volume 2: Short Papers, Panels, Posters, Demos, & Community Events, pp. 327–328. International Society of the Learning Sciences (2013)
43. Huang, Y., Shao, Y., Zhao, X., Ma, Q., Yang, Y.: Exploring the impact mechanism of students' collaborative problem solving abilities on academic performance in a computer-supported knowledge building environment. In: 2025 7th International Conference on Computer Science and Technologies in Education, CSTE 2025, pp. 151–158. IEEE (2025)
44. Sommer, S., Hinojosa, L., Traut, H., Polman, J., Weidler-Lewis, J.: Integrating eye-tracking activities into a learning environment to promote collaborative meta-semiotic reflection and discourse. In: CSCL 2017 Proceedings, pp. 648–651. ISLS (2017)

45. Adler-Beléndez, D., Hoppenstedt, E., Husain, M., Chng, E., Schneider, B.: How are 21st century skills captured in makerspaces? A review of the literature. In: Proceedings of FabLearn 2020, pp. 40–45. ACM (2020)
46. Splichal, J.M., Oshima, J., Oshima, R.: Socio-emotional regulation in knowledge building mediated by CSCL reflection. In: ICLS 2018 Proceedings, pp. 1013–1016. International Society of the Learning Sciences (2018)
47. Tong, Y., Chan, C.K.K.: Promoting knowledge building through meta-discourse and epistemic discourse understanding. Int. J. Comput.-Support. Collab. Learn. **18**, 353–391 (2023)
48. Zhu, G., Xing, W., Popov, V.: Uncovering the sequential patterns in transformative and non-transformative discourse during collaborative inquiry learning. The Inter. Higher Educ. **41**, 51–61 (2019)
49. Dascalu, M., et al.: ReaderBench: An integrated cohesion-centered framework. In: 10th International Conference on Technology Enhanced Learning, EC-TEL 2015, pp. 505–508. Springer (2015)
50. Ouyang, F., Chen, S., Shao, X.: Process and summative assessment of groups' collaborative knowledge building. J. Comput. High. Educ. **38**, 360–385 (2026)
51. Shimojo, S., Hayashi, Y.: How shared concept mapping facilitates explanation activities in collaborative learning: An experimental investigation into learning performance in the context of different perspectives. In: Proceedings of the 27th International Conference on Computers in Education, ICCE 2019, pp. 172–177. Asia-Pacific Society for Computers in Education (2019)
52. Berland, M., Baker, R.S., Blikstein, P.: Educational data mining and learning analytics: Applications to constructionist research. Technol. Knowl. Learn. **19**(1), 205–220 (2014)
53. Nicol, D.J., Macfarlane-Dick, D.: Formative assessment and self-regulated learning: a model and seven principles of good feedback practice. Stud. High. Educ. **31**(2), 199–218 (2006)

Large Language Models in Education

Leveraging Specialized Language Model to Compose Large Language Model for Domain Adaptation in Solving Multiple-Choice Questions

Yicong Liang, Fu Lee Wang(✉), and Pei Liu

School of Science and Technology, Hong Kong Metropolitan University, Kowloon, Hong Kong SAR
{s1304812,pwang,pliu}@hkmu.edu.hk

Abstract. Large language models (LLMs) have demonstrated their powerful capabilities across a range of NLP tasks over the past few years. However, general LLMs often struggle with domain-specific tasks and require further fine-tuning for domain adaptation. In this paper, we propose the Domain Adaptation Composition Specialized Language Model (DACSLM), a lightweight framework for domain-adaptation model composition to solve knowledge-intensive tasks. The experiment is conducted on two multiple-choice question (MCQ) datasets, each related to a different topic, to evaluate the effectiveness of our proposed model. The experimental results demonstrate that DACSLM outperformed the compared baselines in both datasets. The findings suggest that when a large anchor model is integrated with a small, specialized language model by connecting in the last few layers, the combined model can achieve promising performance in domain adaptation for solving specific, knowledge-intensive question-answering tasks.

Keywords: large language model · model composition · domain adaptation · MCQ answering

1 Introduction

Large language models (LLMs) have transformed the field of natural language processing (NLP) over the last few years and have achieved significant improvements across various NLP tasks. LLMs acquire powerful general knowledge by pretraining on an extremely large corpus and by scaling up model size, resulting in significantly better performance than smaller models at comprehending and generating text in a human style [1]. Utilizing prompt engineering, such as zero- or few-shot learning, can adapt a powerful general LLM (e.g., GPT-3 [1]) to new tasks, achieving promising results in the target domain. However, general LLMs often struggle to achieve promising performance in specialized domains, such as finance [2], medicine [3], and law [4]. The rapid advancement of LLMs has

K. T. Chui et al. (Eds.): ICBL 2026, LNCS 16778, pp. 141–152, 2027.
https://doi.org/10.1007/978-981-92-3761-6_10

sparked growing interest in their applications to domain-specific tasks across various fields. Domain adaptation is a critical technique for bridging the gap between LLMs and practical use in domain-specific scenarios.

There are some serious challenges for LLM domain specialization: (1) It is difficult for LLMs to stay up-to-date, and (2) intensive computational resources are required for downstream task learning. Domain adaptation methods can be categorized based on whether the models need to update their internal parameters [5]. A conventional method without model fine-tuning, namely Retrieval-augmented Generation (RAG) [6], adapts LLMs to domain-specific tasks by retrieving explicit information from a knowledge base as external context during inference on an input query. On the other hand, some knowledge-intensive tasks require adapting an LLM to a specific domain through further fine-tuning. However, it is impractical to further fine-tune an LLM (e.g., GPT-3 [1] with 175B parameters) to improve its capacity due to the substantial computational resources required.

Recently, several specialized LLMs have been developed with domain-specific capabilities in finance, healthcare, and law. The Model Composition Framework, Composition to Augment Language Models (CALM) [7], proposes leveraging a specialized LLM to augment another LLM, enabling new capabilities. CALM reuses two existing LLMs and trains a small-scale neural module to connect the two LLMs for making inferences. However, this paper argues that simply using CALM may lead to suboptimal performance in domain adaptation for knowledge-intensive tasks, e.g., medical question answering. According to our experimental results, CALM performs significantly worse than the LoRA method in domain adaptation and even worse than a pre-trained LLM without further parameter updates.

This work addresses two factors to consider when composing two LLMs in domain adaptation: (1) connection strategy; (2) model settings when composing two LLMs. We will further discuss these factors in Sect. 3.2. According to the experimental results, we observe that the choice of the connecting layer has a crucial impact on model composition, e.g., selecting the last few layers yields much better performance than uniformly selecting layers when composing two LLMs. This paper explores the potential of using CALM for domain adaptation in knowledge-intensive question answering.

In summary, we make the following contributions in this paper:

- We investigate a practical framework, the Domain Adaptation Composition Specialized Language Model (DACSLM), for composing two LLMs to solve domain-specific question-answering tasks.
- We evaluate the proposed method, DACSLM, on two question-answering datasets with different topics, and the results show that DACSLM is more effective than the baselines at solving multiple-choice questions (MCQs).
- We explore various connection strategies and model settings when composing two LLMs and compare their performance. The results suggest that using a specialized augmenting model and connecting the two LLMs in the last few layers yields the best performance in solving MCQs.

2 Related Work

2.1 LLMs with Domain Adaptation

LLMs learned general knowledge during pretraining, and subsequent domain adaptation enables them to better handle specialized tasks. Chen et al. [5] categorized the LLM domain-specialized methods based on the accessibility to LLMs' parameters. In particular, external augmentation, prompt crafting, and model fine-tuning are three main types of domain adaptation for LLMs [5]. RAG [8] retrieves domain-specific information relevant to the input query from a predefined knowledge base, and the enriched input allows the LLM to leverage external knowledge explicitly during task predictions. However, the generation model heavily relies on the augmented information from the retriever in the RAG framework, so RAG often faces the problem of selecting irrelevant chunks during the retrieval stage [6]. General LLMs pre-trained on a vast number of corpora may not perform well in specific knowledge-intensive tasks, and fine-tuning the model on a smaller, domain-related dataset can enhance its performance. Parameter-efficient fine-tuning (PEFT) methods [9,10] enable domain adaptation by adding a small number of tunable parameters and keeping the pretrained LLM frozen. Particularly, LoRA [10] introduces some learnable matrices with low rank, which are added in parallel to the pre-trained weights in the LLM. The performance of using the PEFT model fine-tuning techniques can be sensitive to the architecture design and hyperparameters, such as which part of the LLM is fine-tuned, and how to set the rank of the introduced matrices.

2.2 Solving MCQs by LLM

One popular approach for evaluating the capabilities of LLMs is to directly prompt them to solve MCQs. Probability-based and text-based prompting have been widely used for LLMs to solve MCQs when given an MCQ and its associated option candidates. Regarding the text-based prompting method [1], the option can be selected by directly prompting the LLM to solve an MCQ. Regarding probability-based inference [11], the LLM outputs the option with the highest log-probability among the given option candidates. Several studies [12–14] have explored the performance of using some of the latest LLMs in answering MCQs in the medical domain, and found that LLMs (+100B parameters) achieve promising accuracy. This study primarily focuses on utilizing model composition for domain adaptation with limited computing resources, such as integrating Llama [15] 1B and 3B. In addition, we evaluate the effectiveness of the proposed model for domain adaptation in the tasks of answering MCQs related to different topics.

3 Methodology

3.1 Domain Adaptation by LLM Composition

The traditional method is to further fine-tune a general pretrained LLM on target-domain data to achieve domain adaptation when solving downstream tasks. However, it is impractical to fine-tune an LLM since it requires substantial computational resources. This paper presents that by composing a small domain-specialized language model, an anchor LLM can be adapted to the target domain to solve some knowledge-intensive tasks. Intuitively, a pretrained LLM is generic and can solve question-answering tasks [12], but it may lack professional domain knowledge to answer medical MCQs. A pre-trained language model can be augmented with specialized knowledge through continual pre-training [16].

This study proposes the Domain Adaptation in Composing Specialized Language Model (DACSLM) method for solving exam questions across various topics. However, the issue of connecting the anchor model and the specialized model becomes a crucial one in domain adaptation. This paper investigates the connection strategies and model combinations in the experiment and compares their performance when using domain adaptation for solving knowledge-intensive MCQs. DACSLM utilizes two pre-trained language models as the anchor and augmenting models, respectively.

3.2 Composition Setting

This paper mainly focuses on leveraging the LLM composition framework CALM [7] for domain adaptation in solving knowledge-intensive QA tasks. But we argue that the original settings in CALM may have sub-optimal performance for domain adaptation. Hence, we further investigate more composition settings when using CALM for domain adaptation.

- **connection position**: The fusion of inherent knowledge from the anchor model and specialized expertise from the small augmenting model is implemented by a layer-wise connecting module. Each connection must choose the starting position from the anchor model and the ending position from the augmenting model, and the selected positions and number of layers are crucial in domain adaptation, as indicated by our experimental results.
- **model settings**: LLM parameter size and specialized augmenting model. Given two LLMs with different sizes, this study examines the choice of which one to use as the anchor model. In addition, this work also explores whether integrating with a specialized LLM can enhance the performance in domain adaptation.

In CALM [7], the default connection strategy uses uniform layer selection, that is, the intervals between consecutive selected layers are kept equal [7]. However, according to the results in our experiment, such uniform selection performed poorly in domain adaptation when solving knowledge-intensive MCQs. Pretrained language models (PLMs) have been pre-trained on a tremendous amount of corpus, resulting in general knowledge being stored in their parameters. Vanilla PLMs can also be integrated into the model composition framework in domain adaptation. Hence, we also compare the performance where the anchor model is augmented by the vanilla PLM with a specialized LLM in our experiment.

3.3 Prediction for Multiple-Choice Questions

The fine-tuned augmenting model is intended to acquire domain-specific knowledge, such as medical concepts and reasoning, to answer medical exam questions. The experimental results demonstrate that fine-tuning enhances the performance of the small augmenting language model on the MCQs. This study primarily uses the Perplexity (PPL) metric for inference in the MCQ task, which computes the log-probability of both the option ID and the candidate option text. Ultimately, if there are four candidate options in a testing question, the model will select the option with the lowest PPL score from the four input text sequences during evaluation.

4 Experiment

4.1 Experimental Setup

Datasets. The datasets used in this experiment are from two different domains related to medical and historical topics. In each subject, there are two datasets: one for fine-tuning the augmenting model and one for training the neural composition module. In the medical topic, to retrieve an augmenting model, the dataset Medical-reasoning-SFT (MRS) [17] was used to fine-tune a pretrained language model, e.g., Llama-3.2-1B-Instruct [15]. Similarly, for the historical topic, we use the History-data-qa (HDQ) dataset [18] to fine-tune the augmenting model.

Experiment Setting. The foundation pretrained models in this experiment are from the Llama family [15] with different scales: 1B and 3B. For the composition in DACSLM 3B $\bigoplus$ 1B, the augmenting model is based on Llama-3.2-1B-Instruct [15], while the anchor model is based on Llama-3.2-3B-Instruct [15]. In addition, this study conducted different combinations to compose DACSLM, e.g., 1B $\bigoplus$ 1B, and 3B $\bigoplus$ 1B. When connecting the anchor model with the augmenting model, this research considers four strategies: uniformly chosen layers [7], or connecting the last/middle/first few layers. For composition, a neural module is trained to fuse the layer-wise representations from the anchor and the augmenting model. In this experiment, we use the self-attention network [19] to train the composition module.

Baselines. This paper mainly explores whether the composition of LLMs can enhance performance on MCQs. The following baselines are chosen for comparison in this experiment:

- Pretrained large language model (PLLM): a pretrained LLM (e.g., Llama-3.2-Instruct-3B [15]).
- Specialized language model (SLM): We follow the Alpaca format [20] to construct the instruction-following dataset for the task of solving multiple-choice questions. Since we use a small-sized language model, it is efficient to perform full fine-tuning on this dataset for domain adaptation.

- CALM [7]: We follow the uniform-layer connection strategy to link the two language models [7].
- Supervised Fine-tuning (SFT): further fine-tuning a PLLM by using a parameter-efficient training method (LoRA [10]) to adapt a pretrained LLM in the downstream task.

Evaluation Metric. For automatic assessment, this study used PPL to infer the selected option from each compared method. For consistency, we used prediction accuracy as the metric for MCQs, comparing the inferred option with the ground truth.

4.2 Results

Table 1. Overall experiment results.

Method	Size	MedMCQA	HistMCQA
SLM	1B	0.3391	0.5918
PLLM	1B	0.3317	0.5510
	3B	0.3995	0.7052
	8B	0.4595	0.7392
SFT	1B	0.3484	0.6185
	3B	0.4201	0.7236
CALM	1B $\bigoplus$ 1B	0.2351	0.2679
	3B $\bigoplus$ 1B	0.2415	0.2436
DACSLM	1B $\bigoplus$ 1B	0.3668	0.6227
	3B $\bigoplus$ 1B	**0.4638**	**0.7697**

In this experiment, the fine-tuned or composing models in the compared methods are based on Llama family models [15]. The experimental results, including the baselines and some DACSLM composition settings, are shown in Table 1. DACSLM outperformed the baselines across two scaled settings (1B and 3B). When augmented with the same model, Llama-3.2-Instruct, integrating a stronger anchor model (3B vs. 1B) can substantially improve accuracy by 9.7% on MedMCQA and 14.7% on HistMCQA. Finally, the 1B model was augmented and then composed with the 3B anchor model to construct DACSLM (3B $\bigoplus$ 1B), achieving the best performance of 46.3% and 76.9% accuracy on MedMCQA and HistMCQA, respectively. Additionally, our proposed model, DACSLM, still surpassed PLLM-8B (Llama-8B-Instruct), the largest baseline model in our experiment, on both datasets. These results suggest that the model composition framework can improve performance with parameter efficiency, highlighting the potential to develop more resource-efficient AI systems.

4.3 Impact of Connection Selection

Table 2. Performance on MedMCQA among different connection selections.

DACSLM	Uniform	First	Middle	Last
1B $\bigoplus$ 1B	0.2720	0.2578	0.2557	0.3668
3B $\bigoplus$ 1B	0.2532	0.2464	0.3430	0.4233

Table 3. Performance on HistMCQA among different connection selections.

DACSLM	Uniform	First	Middle	Last
1B $\bigoplus$ 1B	0.2817	0.2574	0.3392	0.6203
3B $\bigoplus$ 1B	0.2527	0.3984	0.2548	0.7190

In the model composition framework, we investigated the impact of the position of the layer connection between the anchor and the augmenting model. In particular, we examined four connection selection strategies, namely uniform selection and selection of the first/middle/last few layers. According to the results listed in Table 2 and Table 3, the connection selection for cross-attention has a substantial impact on the performance. For the 1B augmenting model, selection of the first few layers as connecting points performs poorly, consistent with the results in [21]. However, in contrast to the results in [7,21], our experiments suggest that composing the two models in the last few layers yields promising performance. The lower layers of an LLM primarily encode general, low-level features of the input, such as syntax and basic semantics. Freezing these earlier layers helps preserve the broad knowledge acquired during pretraining. In contrast, the upper layers tend to model more contextual and task-specific features.

Based on the DACSLM (3B $\bigoplus$ 1B) composing model, we further explored extra connection positions between the 3B anchor model and the 1B augmenting model. Specifically, three position choices can be selected from the anchor (augment) model, yielding nine combinations of connections between the anchor and the augment model. According to the results shown in Table 4, using the last few layers of the anchor model as the connecting position performed better than connecting at either the first or the middle layer. For example, the last-middle connection[1] (46.4%) surpassed the middle-last (32.8%) with 13.6% improvement. On the other hand, for solving history MCQs, the last-first connection performed much better than the middle-last with 40% improvement. Finetuning the mod-

[1] Last layers are from the anchor model and middle layers are from the augmenting model.

Table 4. Performance on connecting positions in DACSLM (3B $\bigoplus$ 1B).

Anchor - Augment	MedMCQA	HistMCQA
Last-Last	0.4233	0.7190
Last-Middle	**0.4638**	0.7375
Last-First	0.4627	**0.7697**
Middle-Last	0.3285	0.3672
Middle-Middle	0.3430	0.3984
Middle-First	0.3402	0.2941
First-Last	0.2678	0.3259
First-Middle	0.2958	0.3272
First-First	0.2464	0.2527

ules to cross-attend the last few layers enables the composed model to adjust its representations for specialized tasks, such as answering medical and history MCQs.

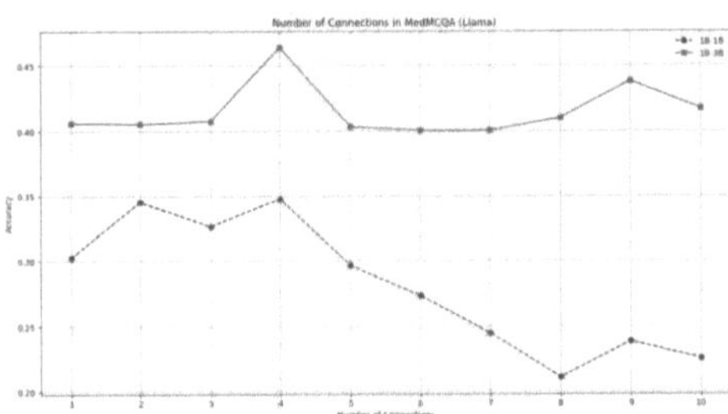

(a) MedMCQA

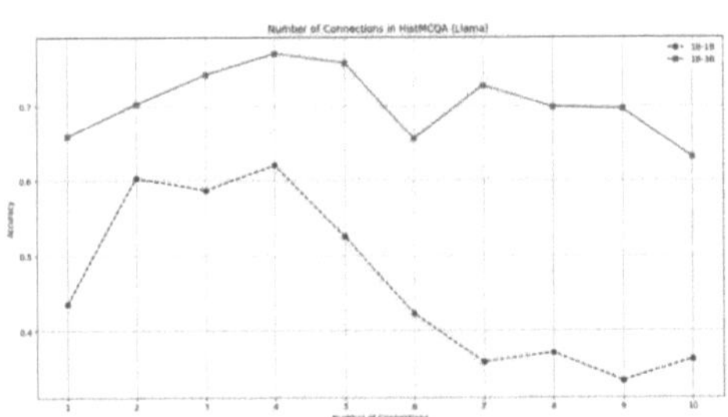

(b) HistMCQA

Fig. 1. Impact of the number of connections in DACSLM.

Besides the connection position, the number of connections in DACSLM is another crucial factor in the model composition architecture. As the findings in Table 4 demonstrate that choosing the last few layers performed better than other connecting positions, we adopted this setting and adjusted the number of connections. It is easy to verify that DACSLM can return to PLLM (the anchor model alone) when there is no connection. From the results presented in Fig. 1, using the number of connections between 2 and 5 performed better in most settings with different model scales. However, increasing the number of connections when composing two models did not improve performance on the MCQ task.

4.4 Impact of Model Setting

In the following experiment, we examined the impact of the model setting during the composition. Specifically, we explored the following sub-questions:

- Given two models with different scales, choose which one to use as the anchor model when doing model composition.
- Whether using a specialized model to augment the anchor model can enhance the performance.
- How the number of data for training and augmenting a model can affect the composition performance.

Table 5. Model setting when composing two LLMs with different sizes. The typical case refers to a composition that selects the larger model as the anchor, whereas the reverse case denotes the opposite choice.

Composition	MedMCQA		HistMCQA	
	typical	reverse	typical	reverse
(3B, 1B)	0.4638	0.2773	0.7697	0.5036

Table 6. Composition incorporated with a specialized augmenting model.

DACSLM	MedMCQA		HistMCQA	
	w/o	w/	w/o	w/
1B $\bigoplus$ 1B	0.3114	0.3668	0.5656	0.6227
3B $\bigoplus$ 1B	0.4034	0.4638	0.7265	0.7697

In the scenario of two models with different scales (1B and 3B), we refer to the choice of using the larger one as the anchor model as the typical composition, e.g., DACSLM (3B $\bigoplus$ 1B), while the opposite is the reverse one, e.g., 1B $\bigoplus$ 3B. As shown in Table 5, using the larger model as the anchor in DACSLM performed much better than using the smaller model as the anchor. For example, using the typical composition (3B $\bigoplus$ 1B), performance can significantly improve accuracy in both datasets. The reason might be that the hidden states from all layers in the anchor model contribute to the final output, whereas only the hidden states from the connected layers of the augmenting model affect it.

To demonstrate the effectiveness of the specialized augmenting model, we first compared the results with those obtained by incorporating a vanilla pretrained model. Specifically, the pretrained model, without finetuning on MRS or HDQ, was directly incorporated into the model composition. From the results in Table 6, using a finetuned model as the augmenting model consistently improves performance in the model composition framework across different parameter settings. It suggests that incorporating a specialized LLM into the model composition is effective for domain adaptation in solving the MCQ task.

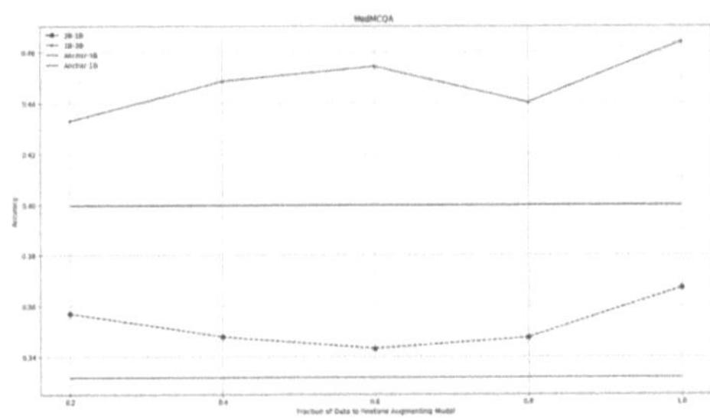

(a) MedMCQA

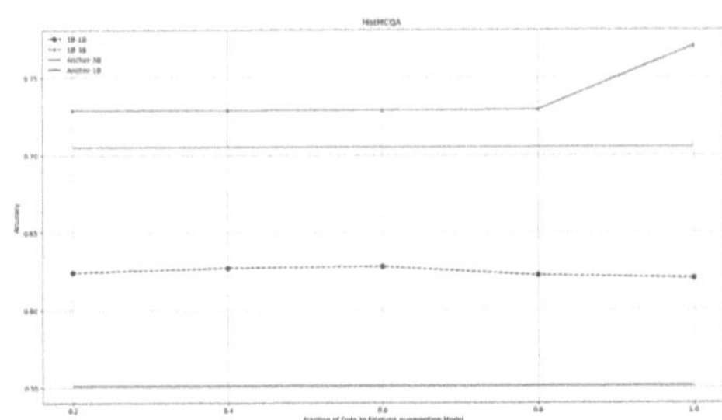

(b) HistMCQA

Fig. 2. The impact of the number of data for fine-tuning the augmenting model in DACSLM.

Finally, we explored the impact of the number of training data when fine-tuning the augmenting model for domain adaptation. Specifically, we randomly sampled data from MRS or HDQ at different fractions to fine-tune the augmenting model, and then compared the performance when it was leveraged in DACSLM. According to the results presented in Fig. 2, even when sampling only a fraction of the data to fine-tune the augmenting model for domain adaptation,

DACSLM still outperformed PLLM with a significant improvement. For answering medical MCQs that require professional knowledge, sampling only 60% of the data for domain adaptation with the DACSLM framework can still achieve promising performance, approaching the best result when using all the data. These results suggest that DACSLM can effectively adapt to specific domains even with limited data, making it suitable for scenarios with constrained data availability.

5 Conclusions and Future Work

This paper examines the composition framework of LLMs for domain adaptation in solving knowledge-intensive question-answering tasks. We propose the DACSLM model and investigate various connection strategies and model settings for composing two LLMs. The experiment is conducted on real-world multiple-choice question datasets from different topics, and the results demonstrate that the proposed model outperforms the compared baselines. Additionally, the experimental results indicate that the position of the connection between two LLMs has a substantial impact on domain adaptation. Specifically, connecting two LLMs in the last few layers yields better results than other connection strategies. In the model composition architecture, a small but specialized language model can augment an LLM to enhance performance further, rather than using a vanilla pre-trained LLM.

This study has several limitations. First, the evaluation is restricted to multiple-choice question-answering datasets in two domains, and the task follows a closed-form, option-selection setting. The generalizability of DACSLM to open-ended generation and reasoning-intensive tasks has not yet been verified. Second, this work mainly adopts a cross-attention module to compose the anchor LLM with a specialized model. It is worth exploring a more complex neural network to link the anchor model to the augmented model. Third, this paper investigated LLM composition with augmenting only one model. However, to solve more complex tasks, the anchor model may need to be augmented with multiple domain-specific models. In future work, we plan to extend DACSLM to a broader range of tasks, including open-ended domain-specific QA, complex reasoning benchmarks, and multilingual or cross-domain adaptation scenarios. In addition, we aim to explore more general composition mechanisms by constructing parameter-efficient adapters that combine multiple specialized models.

Acknowledgments. This work was supported by a grant from the Research Grants Council of the Hong Kong Special Administrative Region, China (UGC/FDS16/E17/23). This research was supported by the HKMU Conference Award for Research Students.

References

1. Brown, T., et al.: Language models are few-shot learners. Adv. Neural. Inf. Process. Syst. **33**, 1877–1901 (2020)
2. Ke, Z., Ming, Y., Nguyen, X.-P., Xiong, C., Joty, S.: Demystifying domain-adaptive post-training for financial llms. arXiv preprint arXiv:2501.04961 (2025)
3. Chen, J., et al.: Huatuogpt-ii, one-stage training for medical adaption of llms. arXiv preprint arXiv:2311.09774 (2023)
4. Liu, Z., Zhu, Y., Mengyuan, L.: Enhancing legal expertise in large language models through composite model integration: the development and evaluation of law-neo. In: Proceedings of the Natural Legal Language Processing Workshop 2024, pp. 33–41 (2024)
5. Ling, C., et al.: Domain specialization as the key to make large language models disruptive: a comprehensive survey. ACM Comput. Surv. (2023)
6. Gao, Y., et al.: Retrieval-augmented generation for large language models: a survey, vol. 2, no. 1. arXiv preprint arXiv:2312.10997 (2023)
7. Bansal, R., et al.: LLM augmented LLMs: expanding capabilities through composition. arXiv preprint arXiv:2401.02412 (2024)
8. Lewis, P., et al.: Retrieval-augmented generation for knowledge-intensive nlp tasks. Adv. Neural. Inf. Process. Syst. **33**, 9459–9474 (2020)
9. Houlsby, N., et al.: Parameter-efficient transfer learning for NLP. In: International Conference on Machine Learning, pp. 2790–2799. PMLR (2019)
10. Hu, E.J., et al.: Lora: low-rank adaptation of large language models. In: ICLR, vol. 1, no. 2, p. 3 (2022)
11. Liang, P., et al.: Holistic evaluation of language models. arXiv preprint arXiv:2211.09110 (2022)
12. Robinson, J., Michael Rytting, C., Wingate, D.: Leveraging large language models for multiple choice question answering. arXiv preprint arXiv:2210.12353 (2022)
13. Nguyen, H.C., Dang, H.P., Nguyen, T.L., Hoang, V., Nguyen, V.A.: Accuracy of latest large language models in answering multiple choice questions in dentistry: a comparative study. PLoS One **20**(1), e0317423 (2025)
14. Qwen Team. Qwen2.5: A party of foundation models (2024). https://qwenlm.github.io/blog/qwen2.5/
15. Grattafiori, A., et al.: The llama 3 herd of models. arXiv preprint arXiv:2407.21783 (2024)
16. Xie, Y., Aggarwal, K., Ahmad, A.: Efficient continual pre-training for building domain specific large language models. In: Findings of the Association for Computational Linguistics ACL 2024, pp. 10184–10201 (2024)
17. Chen, J., et al.: Huatuogpt-o1, towards medical complex reasoning with LLMs. arXiv preprint arXiv:2412.18925 (2024)
18. Smith, C.: 10k-history-data-v3-alpaca (2024). https://huggingface.co/datasets/ambrosfitz/10k_history_data_v3_alpaca
19. Vaswani, A., et al.: Attention is all you need. Adv. Neural Inf. Process. Syst. **30** (2017)
20. Taori, R., et al.: Alpaca: a strong, replicable instruction-following model. Stanford Center for Research on Foundation Models, vol. 3, no. 6, p. 7 (2023). https://crfm.stanford.edu/2023/03/13/alpaca.html
21. Tanabe, K., Hirano, M., Matoya, K., Imajo, K., Sakaji, H., Noda, I.: Enhancing financial domain adaptation of language models via model augmentation. In: 2024 IEEE International Conference on Big Data (BigData), pp. 6661–6669. IEEE (2024)

Exploring Open-Source Language Model in Solving Physics Word Problems

Yicong Liang[1], Di Zou[2(✉)], Haoran Xie[3], and Fu Lee Wang[1]

[1] School of Science and Technology, Hong Kong Metropolitan University, Kowloon, Hong Kong SAR
{s1304812,pwang}@hkmu.edu.hk

[2] Department of English and Communication, The Hong Kong Polytechnic University, Hung Hom, Hong Kong SAR
daisy.zou@polyu.edu.hk

[3] Division of Artificial Intelligence, Lingnan University, New Territories, Hong Kong SAR
hrxie@ln.edu.hk

Abstract. With the development of large language models (LLMs) pretrained on vast corpora, LLMs have shown their potential across various educational tasks. This work explores how to solve physics word problems using an open-source language model. In particular, we apply three methods from current LLM techniques, including prompt engineering, supervised fine-tuning, and reinforcement learning, based on the publicly accessible and open-source model. The experiment is conducted on a dataset of physics word problems from real-world middle school exams. The experimental results show that the language model with additional parameter updates can improve performance on physics word problems compared to the vanilla pretrained model. In addition, leveraging reinforcement learning (RL) with the language model outperforms the other methods, suggesting that it can enhance reasoning for solving complex computational problems.

Keywords: language model · physics word problem · reinforcement learning · AI in education

1 Introduction

Large language models pretrained on a tremendous amount of textual data demonstrate their capability to comprehend and generate human-like language. Recently, building educational applications based on LLMs has become a hot topic in research, including automatic grading [1,2], programming education [3], and math word problems [4,5]. Integrating LLMs into K-12 STEM educational tasks [6] shows remarkable promise for helping students deal with challenging subjects, such as mathematics and science.

The development of LLMs demonstrates their powerful capabilities across diverse natural language processing tasks. Further fine-tuning language models

K. T. Chui et al. (Eds.): ICBL 2026, LNCS 16778, pp. 153–165, 2027.
https://doi.org/10.1007/978-981-92-3761-6_11

on mathematical datasets [7] or using advanced prompt engineering techniques (e.g., Chain-of-thought [5]) can increase their basic computational and reasoning abilities in solving math word problems (MWPs). Liu et al. [8] have provided a systematic review of mathematical language models, including those for solving MWPs. However, fewer studies have focused on solving physics word problems (PWPs) than on MWP solvers. Liang et al. [9] explored the potential of prompting ChatGPT to solve physics calculation problems. Ding et al. [10] proposed the first PWP dataset and applied GPT-3.5 to solve these problems through few-shot learning.

There are some differences between the math word problems and physics word problems: (1) Math word problems mainly focus on numerical relationships and algebraic calculations. Solving physics word problems requires a practical understanding of how to connect real-world applications to the laws of physics. (2) The solution to a math word problem primarily involves performing a sequence of elementary calculations using basic arithmetic operations to reach the final answer, so there is only one question in this problem. However, calculations in physics word problems often involve multiple physical variables, leading to several sub-questions [10]. (3) Variables in physics word problems have their own physical properties, e.g., applying their dimensions in the relevant formulas [10], physical units transformation [9].

In solving physics word problems, prior studies [9,10] have primarily focused on prompting closed-source LLMs. Compared to the closed-source LLM (OpenAI GPT) with hundreds of billions of parameters, this work explores the use of a small-scale open-source language model (i.e., Qwen-7B [11]) using three different methods to solve PWPs. Unlike the MWP, which has one question per problem, the language model's limitation in solving PWPs is that it sometimes fails to accurately determine the number of sub-questions in a problem. To mitigate this limitation, we use a counting prompt instruction and a supervised fine-tuning technique, which together enhance performance on PWPs. In addition, we incorporate the reinforcement learning method (i.e., GRPO [12]) into the language model to improve reasoning capacity. The experimental results show that further training the language model using the RL technique outperforms the baselines, suggesting that it can enhance reasoning capabilities for solving complex computational problems.

2 Literature Review

Previous studies [5,13] that focus on computational tasks are related to math word problems. Traditional methods for solving math word problems are based on statistical learning [8], and previous MWP solvers are mainly tree-structured or operation-based [10]. There are some constraints on these solvers that apply only to predetermined problem formation and output expression patterns. Recently, with the emergence of powerful pretrained language models, an automatic MWP solver [14] can be built to generate a human-readable textual solution with prompting. Few-shot learning and chain-of-thought (CoT) prompting

[4,5] are two widely used methods for solving MWP based on a large language model. In particular, incorporating CoT prompting with few-shot exemplars can elicit emergent abilities that generate explicit intermediate reasoning steps before deriving the final answer. These prompting methods mainly focus on arithmetic word problems at the elementary school level.

Compared to MWPs, which only contain fundamental operations, solving physics word problems is more challenging. Solving PWPs requires a student's full understanding of physics, analytical abilities, and computational skills [10]. Compared to MWP solvers, fewer studies focus on developing automatic PWP solvers mainly due to the lack of relevant benchmark datasets in physics. Ding et al. [10] proposed the first physics word problem dataset (PhysQA) in Chinese and annotated the solutions with related formulas and numeric answers. They applied GPT-3.5 to solve problems in PhysQA using few-shot prompting, with exemplars chosen based on a similarity metric [10]. Liang et al. [9] explored the potential of using closed-source LLM (e.g., ChatGPT) to solve physics computation problems by zero-shot-CoT [15] prompting. In addition, some studies demonstrate the capability of using large language models (e.g., GPT [16,17]) to accomplish some auxiliary tasks, e.g., generating new physics word problems [9,10], extracting and summarizing related physics knowledge when solving a computation problem [9].

When evaluating the performance of an LM-based solver, it needs to identify the numeric answer from the solution in natural language and then compare the generated answer with the ground truth. Hence, the LLM must be more controllable and predictable to solve a particular task. Supervised fine-tuning (SFT) [18], a post-training technique, can adapt the model to human instructions. The major benefit of SFT is to bridge the gap between LLMs' next-token prediction objective and the user's desired output when following instructions [18]. Recent techniques that incorporate reinforcement learning with large language models have been proposed to align LLM responses with human preferences, including RLHF [16], DPO [19], and GRPO [20]. In particular, DeepSeek-R1 [12] has shown that post-training LLMs via RL with simple rule-based and verifiable rewards, such as answer correctness, can elicit models to generate long-form reasonings for mathematics problems.

3 Methodology

To explore the open-source language model for solving physics word problems, this work mainly uses the following LLM-based methods: (1) prompt-based; (2) supervised finetuning (SFT); (3) Group Relative Policy Optimization (GRPO [20]).

In the prompt-based method, the LLM is prompted to solve a given physics word problem, acting as a teacher. The prompt template is shown in Fig. 1. Specifically, the prompt contains the following part:

- **System role**: The LLM will serve as a physics teacher and solve a specific calculation problem in a predefined format.

- **Instruction**: The LLM is guided to generate the response in a structured format to differentiate the solution from the numeric answer. In particular, the LLM generates the reasoning process inside the solution tag and then outputs the numeric answer inside the answer tag.
- **Input question**: A physics word problem at the junior-middle-school level will be prompted to the LLM. Some problems may have more than one sub-question, and each question is related to a particular physical variable to be solved.

The prompt, including the testing PWP, is passed to the language model, which generates the reasoning process and the final answer in a one-pass completion. Some studies [4,5] generate the reasoning solution and the numeric answer in two separate completions, with the LLM itself also serving as the answer extractor. Prompting an LLM (e.g., GPT3 [21]) twice for solving a single math word problem requires expensive computational resources. Hence, we prompt the language model to generate the structured response and use a rule-based pattern-matching method to extract the final numeric answer. Wei et al. [5] suggest that when LLMs output the reasoning process with chain-of-thought (CoT) before giving the final answer, their performance can be improved in some reasoning tasks (e.g., solving math word problems).

You are a physics teacher who needs to solve a middle school physics calculation problem. Please respond in the following format:
<solution>
...
</solution>
<answer>
...
</answer>
The solution, including the reasoning process and calculation, is enclosed within the <solution> tag. The final numeric answer is enclosed within the <answer> tag. If there are multiple sub-questions in the calculation problem, separate each numerical answer with '&'.

`[QUESTION]`

Fig. 1. Prompt Template.

In the SFT method, this paper uses instruction prompt tuning to fine-tune a pretrained language model (e.g., Qwen2.5-7B-Instruct [22]).

$$\mathcal{L}_{SFT} = \sum_{j}^{|y|} - \log p_{\Theta}(y|X) \tag{1}$$

where the input sequence X consists of the prompt as shown in Fig. 1, followed by a physics word problem, and the response y is the textual solution to the problem. In our experiment, the response is structured, with the reasoning process in the solution tag and the final numeric answer in the answer tag.

An example of the training target in the fine-tuned method is shown in Fig. 2. The reason for using such a structured response is that it can automatically test the model's performance by using string pattern matching to verify the numeric output without human evaluation.

<solution>
The question asks to find the gravitational force acting on a car with a mass of 2500kg moving at a constant speed on a flat road. Given conditions: The mass of the car m = 2500kg. Using the physics formula: G=mg=2500kg ×10N/kg=25000N
</solution>
<answer>
25000
</answer>

Fig. 2. An example of a training target during model fine-tuning.

The objective function of GRPO [12] for training the policy model π_θ is as follows:

$$\mathcal{L}_{GRPO} = [\frac{1}{G}\sum_{i=1}^{G} \min(\frac{\pi_\theta(o_i|q)}{\pi_{old}(o_i|q)}A_i \cdot \text{clip}(\frac{\pi_\theta(o_i|q)}{\pi_{old}(o_i|q)}, 1-\epsilon, 1+\epsilon)A_i)] - \beta D_{KL}(\pi_\theta||\pi_{ref}) \tag{2}$$

The input prompt q can be referred to Fig. 1 and o_i denotes one completion generated by the trained policy model π_{old}. To increase the diversity of comparison within a group, the model will generate G completions for q. The term in the loss that uses KL divergence limits the deviation between the policy model and the frozen model π_{ref}, ensuring that the trained model preserves its original behavior. The advantage of each completion A_i depends on its reward score and normalized value within the group.

GRPO is effective for mathematical reasoning tasks, e.g., solving math or physics word problems, where correctness can be verified by explicitly comparing the predicted answer with the ground truth. In addition, GRPO supports the setting of using a simple but effective reward function instead of relying on a separate and complex critic model [12]. In the context of education, tutors can design a practical reward function based on their professional teaching experience. In this work, we propose using a heuristic reward function to align the language model to generate the desired outputs. In particular, we design inductive keywords to guide the language model in generating related formulas and reasoning when solving a physics word problem. Our experimental results demonstrate that this simple but effective strategy enhances performance, rather than relying on correctness alone as the reward signal.

4 Experiment

4.1 Experiment Settings

We use the Physics-QA dataset [10] related to junior middle school physics word problems in Chinese to conduct the experiment. Each physics word problem is categorized into five different types [10] (e.g., kinematics, heat, and electricity). To maintain diversity in the training and testing data, we randomly sample from each type using a split ratio. In particular, we use 60% of the physics word problems for training and the rest for testing for each question type. To further construct the prompt-completion dataset, the question is wrapped in the input prompt, as shown in Fig. 1, and the completion is in a structured format, as shown in Fig. 2. We use the open-source model Qwen2.5 [11] as the base model, and Qwen2.5-7B-Instruct [22] is chosen as the foundation model for subsequent supervised fine-tuning and reinforcement learning.

To evaluate the model's performance in solving PWPs, we use accuracy as the evaluation metric in this experiment. Specifically, we first extracted the numeric answer from the model's response and then compared it to the ground truth. To identify the numeric answer from the LLM's textual output, Cobbe et al. [13] leveraged a hash marker to differentiate the final answer from the solution to a math word problem among the plain text. In the experiment, we use a structural template (i.e., XML tags) as the LLM's response format instead of plain text due to: (1) The formula for solving a math word problem only includes numbers and operators, but the formula for solving a physics word problem is also related to physical units during the calculation. (2) Each math word problem in the GSM8K [13] dataset only contains a single question, but some physics word problems may have multiple subquestions in a problem. In particular, we design a prompt with instructions to ask the model to generate its output in XML format. The output will use a solution tag (i.e., <solution>) to capture the reasoning process for solving a physics computation problem, and an answer tag (i.e., <answer>) to indicate the numeric answer.

4.2 Results

You first need to determine how many questions the calculation problem has and write the number of questions among <num> </num>.

Fig. 3. Multi-problem instruction prompt.

Table 1. Prompt-only method performance.

CP instruction	QNA	Accuracy
w/o	0.8975	0.7066
w/	0.9375	0.7179

Table 2. Finetune-based method performance.

CP instruction	QNA	Accuracy
w/o	0.9825	0.7207
w/	0.9875	0.7236

We first examine the performance of directly using the prompt method to solve PWPs. When comparing the generated answer with the ground truth for solving PWPs, the chosen values of certain physical constants may affect the results of the calculation [10]. For example, the gravitational acceleration constant is set to 10 throughout the computations to ensure consistency in our experiment[1].

According to the experimental results, a major performance bottleneck is that the model sometimes does not know how many subquestions the PWP has. Hence, we use the metric called question number accuracy (QNA), which measures how well the model can count the number of questions in a given problem. To improve QNA, we use the counting-problem (CP) instruction prompt as shown in Fig. 3 for the prompt-based method. In particular, the CP instruction prompt requires the model to first determine the number of problems in the question before providing the solution. According to the results in Table 1, using the prompt-only technique for solving PWPs has 70.6% accuracy with less than 90% QNA. When adding CP instruction to the prompt alone, QNA has improved to 93.7%, leading to a better accuracy in solving PWPs at 71.8%.

In addition, we further check out the generated response by using the prompt-based method and find out that the model may not strictly follow the instruction to output the answer tag.[2] For a pretrained large language model, there remains a gap between the vanilla next-token prediction objective and the user's expected output [18]. To mitigate this issue, we use the supervised finetuning method to teach the language model to output in a predefined structure, as shown in Fig. 2. According to the results in Table 2, compared to the prompt-only method, further finetuning the language model greatly enhances QNA with about 98%, suggesting the SFT technique can help the model better understand how many sub-questions a testing problem has. Additionally, the fine-tuned language model outperforms the pretrained model, achieving higher accuracy. For the SFT method, we still use the CP instruction during finetuning in the experiment. Specifically, the number of sub-questions is also included in the training

[1] We put this restriction in the prompt instruction.

[2] In this case, we still consider the model can not solve the problem correctly.

Table 3. Results in GRPO. SFT Ref: Use the SFT model as the reference model. Multiple sub-questions: Training on all problems with multiple sub-questions.

Method	SFT Ref	multiple sub-questions	Accuracy
GRPO			0.7080
		✓	0.7277
	✓		0.7291
	✓	✓	0.7419

target[3]. Learning to extract the number of sub-questions from the input problem via SFT with CP instruction improves the accuracy of solving PWPs to 72.4%.

When incorporating reinforcement learning techniques into a large language model, a rule-based reward signal can be used to compute the advantage of a generated completion. For simplicity, we first use the correctness of the generated numeric answer in the reward function. In addition, the reference model can influence the sampling strategy used to generate responses during GRPO training [12]. Hence, the choice of reference model will affect the quality of the PWPs solution when using GRPO. In this experiment, we compare the performance of the SFT model, used as the reference model, against that of the vanilla pretrained model. There are multiple sub-questions for some PWPs, and how to calculate the reward score based on correctness must be considered. In the case of multiple sub-questions, the reward scores are added up for each subproblem's correctness. Hence, we also compare the performance of training on problems with a single question to that with multiple sub-questions.

According to the results shown in Table 3, using the reinforcement learning technique, e.g., GRPO, outperformed the SFT method, suggesting that GRPO can improve the performance in solving PWPs at 74% accuracy. It is in line with findings in [12] that GRPO can enhance the language model's reasoning capabilities through reinforcement learning. In particular, using the SFT model as the reference model surpassed using the vanilla pretrained model. The reason may be that the language model can better follow the instruction after supervised fine-tuning, helping the answer extractor identify the numeric answer more accurately. Training on problems with multiple sub-questions outperformed training on a single problem when using the GRPO method to solve PWPs. The reward signal from verifying the correctness of multiple sub-questions during training can improve QNA. By simply using numeric answer correctness as the reward function and incorporating the SFT model as the reference model, with training on different numbers of sub-questions, the language model can solve PWPs with 74.2% accuracy.

[3] The number of sub-questions will be added inside the tag (i.e., <num>) at the first place of the structured response.

Table 4. Inductive keywords in reward function.

Inductive words	Description
According to the problem, list the given variables	Forcing the model to extract variables and lowering the chance of missing quantities
Based on the formula	The model needs to identify and state the relevant formulas before calculation
Substituting the values	Presenting substitution step-by-step with arithmetic and algebra operations
Draw a diagram and show the forces mentioned in the question	List forces and their directions for vector decomposition in mechanics problems
Find the conversions for the units	Prevent unit-mismatch errors in calculation

When we further check the generated response to the PWPs in the testing set, there are some error cases in which the language model makes mistakes: (1) When the problem was complex with multiple physics variables in at least two different scenarios, the model made mistakes in misreading or misunderstanding the problem. (2) The model sometimes skipped some reasoning steps and lost track of how an intermediate answer was obtained. Ding et al. [10] point out that GPT-3.5 is sometimes unable to fully understand the physical scene described in a PWP, leading to inaccurate formula generation. The model may introduce dimension errors in vector variables when solving mechanics problems [9,10]. In this experiment, we proposed heuristically designing inductive keywords into the reward function to encourage the language model to: (1) Connect the known physics variable with the solving problem. (2) Generate related formulas in the reasoning steps (3) Pay attention to converting units in calculation physics variables. Some inductive keywords are listed in Table 4. For example, regarding the inductive words 'According to the problem, list the given variables', if they are included in the completion from the language model, the model will receive a reward score. As the language model's inference strategy is left-to-right, such inductive words will encourage the model to generate the relevant physics variables for the input testing problem. Extracting the relevant variables could help the language understand the problem and generate the correct formula to solve it.

Table 5. Results in GRPO with different reward settings.

Method	Correctness	Inductive keywords	Accuracy
GRPO	✓		0.7419
		✓	0.7221
	✓	✓	0.7546

Table 6. Accuracy in different question types.

Method	Kinematics	Mass&Density	Mechanics	Heat	Electricity
Prompt-only	0.7363	0.6567	0.8059	0.6494	0.8478
SFT	0.7064	0.7761	0.7164	0.7577	0.6739
GRPO	0.7313	0.7910	0.7612	0.7474	0.7609

According to the results shown in Table 5, using the correctness to directly compute the reward score performs better than using the inductive words alone. Using the correctness of the generated answer as the reward signal has a promising performance, achieving about 74% accuracy. The correctness label is a stronger alignment with the task objective, and optimizing for correctness pushes the model to adjust its behaviors to improve the solving performance. By incorporating correctness with inductive words when designing the reward function, the solver's performance can be further improved to 75.5% solving rate. This result suggests that the inductive words generated in the intermediate steps are a suitable supplement for designing rewards. Finally, the performance related to solving different types of PWPs is listed in Table 6. The vanilla pre-trained language model has weaknesses in solving certain types of PWPs, such as Mass&Density and Heat. GRPO shows consistently balanced performance across all five question types.

In the following analysis, we select some generated examples produced by different methods for further comparison. In particular, we compared the response from the GRPO method with that from the prompt-only method on the same test problem as seen in Fig. 4. This physics word problem is in the kinematics category, with two sub-questions. According to Fig. 4, there are some errors in the result generated from the prompt-only: (1) The completion can not follow the instruction requiring both solution and answer tags, i.e., missing the ending tag '</answer>'. (2) The model can not fully understand the question, especially when judging how much distance the train has run in the twenty seconds. (3) Due to the incorrect answer to the first question, substituting its value during the computation leads to a wrong answer in the second sub-question as well. On the other hand, the language model post-trained via GRPO can accurately answer both sub-questions. In particular, the inductive phrase 'Based on the formula' helps the model recall the related equation '$v = \frac{s}{t}$'. Then, the model can successfully capture the traveling distance for the time '20 s' to compute

[Question] Given that the bridge is 1000 m long, Xiaoming takes a high-speed train and measures that the time from entering the bridge to leaving the bridge is 20 s. What is the speed of the train in m/s? If the length of the train is 150 m, how many seconds are needed for the entire train to pass completely over the bridge?

[Answer] 50, 23

Prompt-only

<solution>
First, calculate the speed of the high-speed train. The total distance for the train to completely pass the bridge is the length of the bridge plus the length of the train, that is (1000m + 150m = 1150m). The time required for the train to pass this total distance is 20 seconds, so the speed (v) of the train can be calculated by dividing the total distance by the time:

$$v = \frac{1150m}{20s} = 57.5\ \mathrm{m/s}$$

Next, calculate the time required for the train to completely pass the bridge. The speed of the train has already been found to be 57.5 m/s, and the total distance for the train to completely pass the bridge is still 1150 m, so the required time (t) is:

$$t = \frac{1150m}{57.5\ \mathrm{m/s}} = 20\ \mathrm{s}$$

</solution>
<answer>
57.5&20

GRPO

<solution>
Solution: (1) From the formula ($v = \frac{s}{t}$), the speed of the train is ($v = \frac{s}{t} = \frac{1000\mathrm{m}}{20\mathrm{s}} = 50\mathrm{m/s}$); (2) The distance the train travels while completely passing the bridge is ($s = L_{\mathrm{bridge}} + L_{\mathrm{train}} = 1000\mathrm{m} + 150\mathrm{m} = 1150\mathrm{m}$). From the formula ($v = \frac{s}{t}$), the time the train takes to completely pass the bridge is ($t' = \frac{s}{v} = \frac{1150\mathrm{m}}{50\mathrm{m/s}} = 23\mathrm{s}$).
Answer: The speed of the train is (50m/s), and the time needed for the train to completely pass the bridge is 23 seconds.
Analysis: (1) Use the formula ($v = \frac{s}{t}$) to find the speed of the train. (2) The distance the train travels while completely passing the bridge equals the sum of the bridge length and the train length. Then use the formula ($v = \frac{s}{t}$) to find the time needed for the train to completely pass the bridge.
</solution>
<answer>
50&23
</answer>

Fig. 4. Compare generated results for further analysis.

the speed in the first sub-question. The model can precisely identify the total distance and substitute the speed calculated in the first step when solving the second question.

5 Conclusions and Future Work

The work investigates the capacity of an open-source language model to solve physics word problems using three mainstream LLM-based methods: prompt engineering, supervised fine-tuning, and reinforcement learning. We develop a physics word problem solver based on a small-scale Qwen model and conduct experiments on a real-world dataset from middle school test papers. With post-training via SFT or RL, the language model can improve its performance compared to the vanilla pretrained model in solving PWPs. Reinforcement learning implemented by GRPO yields a significant performance improvement, indicating that reward-driven optimization more effectively elicits the multi-step reasoning required for complex computational physics problems. In summary, open-source language models, when guided by carefully designed prompting, targeted fine-tuning, and principled reinforcement learning, can substantially improve performance on physics word problems and form a practical foundation for research and applications in AI-assisted science education.

This study still has several limitations. First, we evaluate performance mainly on answer accuracy for text-only physics word problems. In other words, we still do not consider multimodal scenarios including diagrams and tables, which often occur in physics computation problems. Second, the utilization of reinforcement learning is limited to GRPO with a relatively simple reward design, e.g., a linear combination of the final answer correctness signal. Third, we do not conduct user studies with teachers and students, so the classroom usability based on LLM-based PWP solvers remains untested. In future work, we plan to explore multimodal physics word problems that require interpreting figures and diagrams. We will integrate visual encoders with the language model so that it can jointly interpret textual descriptions and visual information when solving PWPs. In addition, we aim to study process-based rewards in RL frameworks and more fine-grained supervision signals that encourage stepwise reasoning rather than only the correctness of the final answer.

Acknowledgments. This work was supported by a grant from the Research Grants Council of the Hong Kong Special Administrative Region, China (UGC/FDS16/E17/23); and the Fund for Innovative Technology-in-Education (FITE) for UGC Funded Inter-institutional Collaborative Activities Project (120045) entitled "Advancing Digital Competency for University Teachers and Students in the Era of Generative Artificial Intelligence" and the Teaching Development Grant (102729) entitled "Integrate GPT-based Intelligent Feedback and Tutoring for Data Science Courses" of Lingnan University, Hong Kong. This research was supported by the HKMU Conference Award for Research Students.

References

1. Wang, Q., Gayed, J.M.: Effectiveness of large language models in automated evaluation of argumentative essays: finetuning vs. zero-shot prompting. Comput. Assist. Lang. Learn. **39**(1–2), 209–237 (2026)
2. Xiao, C., et al.: Human-AI collaborative essay scoring: a dual-process framework with LLMs. In: Proceedings of the 15th International Learning Analytics and Knowledge Conference, pp. 293–305 (2025)
3. Phung, T., et al.: Generative AI for programming education: benchmarking chatgpt, gpt-4, and human tutors. In: Proceedings of the 2023 ACM Conference on International Computing Education Research, vol. 2, pp. 41–42 (2023)
4. Zhang, Z., Zhang, A., Li, M., Smola, A.: Automatic chain of thought prompting in large language models. arXiv preprint arXiv:2210.03493 (2022)
5. Wei, J., et al.: Chain-of-thought prompting elicits reasoning in large language models. Adv. Neural Inf. Process. Syst. **35**, 24824–24837 (2022)
6. Chen, E., Wang, D., Xu, L., Cao, C., Fang, X., Lin, J.: A systematic review on prompt engineering in large language models for k-12 stem education. arXiv preprint arXiv:2410.11123 (2024)
7. Geva, M., Gupta, A., Berant, J.: Injecting numerical reasoning skills into language models. In: Proceedings of the 58th Annual Meeting of the Association for Computational Linguistics, pp. 946–958 (2020)
8. Liu, W., et al.: Mathematical language models: a survey. ACM Comput. Surv. **58**(6), 1–37 (2025)
9. Liang, Y., Zou, D., Xie, H., Wang, F.L.: Exploring the potential of using chatgpt in physics education. Smart Learn. Environ. **10**(1), 52 (2023)

10. Ding, J., Cen, Y., Wei, X.: Using large language model to solve and explain physics word problems approaching human level. arXiv preprint arXiv:2309.08182 (2023)
11. Yang, A., et al.: Qwen2 technical report. arXiv preprint arXiv:2407.10671 (2024)
12. Guo, D., et al." Deepseek-r1: incentivizing reasoning capability in llms via reinforcement learning. arXiv preprint arXiv:2501.12948 (2025)
13. Cobbe, K., et al.: Training verifiers to solve math word problems. arXiv preprint arXiv:2110.14168 (2021)
14. Imani, S., Du, L., Shrivastava, H.: Mathprompter: mathematical reasoning using large language models. In: Proceedings of the 61st Annual Meeting of the Association for Computational Linguistics, vol. 5: Industry Track, pp. 37–42 (2023)
15. Kojima, T., Shixiang, S., Gu, M., Reid, Y., Matsuo, Y.: Iwasawa: large language models are zero-shot reasoners. Adv. Neural. Inf. Process. Syst. **35**, 22199–22213 (2022)
16. Ouyang, L., et al.: Training language models to follow instructions with human feedback. Adv. Neural. Inf. Process. Syst. **35**, 27730–27744 (2022)
17. Achiam, J., et al.: Gpt-4 technical report. arXiv preprint arXiv:2303.08774 (2023)
18. Zhang, S., et al.: Instruction tuning for large language models: a survey. ACM Comput. Surv. **58**(7), 1–36 (2026)
19. Rafailov, R., Sharma, A., Mitchell, E., Christopher, D., Manning, S., Ermon, C.: Finn: direct preference optimization: your language model is secretly a reward model. Adv. Neural. Inf. Process. Syst. **36**, 53728–53741 (2023)
20. Shao, Z., et al.: Deepseekmath: pushing the limits of mathematical reasoning in open language models. arXiv preprint arXiv:2402.03300 (2024)
21. Brown, T., et al.: Language models are few-shot learners. Adv. Neural. Inf. Process. Syst. **33**, 1877–1901 (2020)
22. Qwen Team. Qwen2.5: A party of foundation models (2024). https://qwenlm.github.io/blog/qwen2.5/

An Empirical Study on Student Feedback Sentiment Classification: From Traditional Machine Learning to Large Language Models

Hongjie Zhang[1], Haoran Xie[2], Di Zou[3], and Fu Lee Wang[1](✉)

[1] School of Science and Technology, Hong Kong Metropolitan University, Kowloon, Hong Kong SAR
pwang@hkmu.edu.hk

[2] Division of Artificial Intelligence, Lingnan University, New Territories, Hong Kong SAR

[3] Department of English and Communication, The Hong Kong Polytechnic University, Kowloon, Hong Kong SAR

Abstract. Student feedback provides valuable evidence for understanding learners' experiences, but large volumes of comments are difficult to analyze manually. This study investigates three-class sentiment classification of student feedback comments and compares representative methods from traditional machine learning, deep learning, pretrained transformers, and LLMs. Using a public student feedback dataset, we evaluate Logistic Regression, Linear SVM, LSTM, Text-CNN, BERT, and RoBERTa. We also examine two instruction-tuned LLMs, GPT-4.1-mini and LLaMA-3.3-70B-Instruct, under zero-shot, one-shot, three-shot, five-shot, and CoT prompting settings without task-specific fine-tuning. The results show a clear pattern across model families: traditional machine learning provides useful baselines, deep learning improves on them, and pretrained transformers deliver the strongest supervised results. Among the supervised models, RoBERTa performs best with 85.30% accuracy and 82.25% macro-F1. LLM performance, however, depends strongly on prompt design. Zero-shot prompting does not surpass RoBERTa, while few-shot prompting leads to substantial gains. GPT-4.1-mini in the five-shot setting achieves the best overall performance, reaching 86.49% accuracy and 83.58% macro-F1. By contrast, CoT prompting does not provide consistent benefits. These findings suggest that fine-tuned transformers remain a reliable choice when labeled data are available, while carefully designed few-shot prompting makes LLMs a competitive alternative for educational sentiment analysis.

Keywords: Student Feedback · Sentiment Classification · Large Language Models · Prompting · Educational Text Mining

1 Introduction

Student feedback is an important source of information for understanding learners' experiences in educational settings. Comments written by students often reflect their perceptions of teaching quality, course design, assessment difficulty, and classroom

K. T. Chui et al. (Eds.): ICBL 2026, LNCS 16778, pp. 166–179, 2027.
https://doi.org/10.1007/978-981-92-3761-6_12

engagement. Compared with numerical ratings, textual feedback contains richer and more specific opinions, which makes it valuable for educational evaluation and improvement. However, large collections of student comments are difficult to analyze manually. This creates a practical need for automatic sentiment classification methods that can identify whether a comment expresses a positive, neutral, or negative opinion.

A wide range of natural language processing (NLP) methods has been applied to sentiment classification [1, 2]. Earlier work mainly relied on traditional machine learning models such as Logistic Regression and Support Vector Machines (SVMs) with hand-crafted or sparse text features. Later, deep learning models such as Long Short-Term Memory (LSTM) [3] and text convolutional neural network (Text-CNN) [4] improved text representation by learning directly from token sequences. More recently, pretrained transformer models such as Bidirectional Encoder Representations from Transformers (BERT) [5] and Robustly Optimized BERT Pretraining Approach (RoBERTa) [6] have become strong supervised solutions because they provide powerful contextual representations and can be fine-tuned effectively on labeled datasets. Instead of training a task-specific classifier, large language models (LLMs) can often perform classification through prompt engineering.

Although LLMs have shown strong results in many NLP tasks, it remains unclear how they compare with conventional supervised models in the specific context of student feedback sentiment classification. This domain is a meaningful test case because student comments are often short, informal, and directly evaluative, and LLM performance may depend not only on model capability but also on how the task is presented in the prompt. In particular, it is still unclear whether prompt-based LLMs can match or exceed strong fine-tuned baselines, and how much their performance changes across zero-shot, few-shot, and chain-of-thought (CoT) settings. This comparison also matters in practice, because researchers and institutions need to know whether strong supervised models remain the most reliable choice or whether prompt-based LLMs can provide competitive performance without additional training.

In this study, we conduct an empirical comparison of representative methods for student feedback sentiment classification. We consider traditional machine learning models, deep learning models, pretrained transformer models, and LLM-based methods. Specifically, we evaluate Logistic Regression, Linear SVM, LSTM, Text-CNN, BERT, and RoBERTa, and compare them with two instruction-tuned LLMs, GPT-4.1-mini [7] and LLaMA-3.3-70B-Instruct [8]. For the LLMs, we further examine zero-shot, one-shot, three-shot, five-shot, and CoT prompting. This design allows us to compare performance across model families and to examine the effect of prompting strategy within LLM-based sentiment classification.

This paper addresses three questions: (1) How does performance change across traditional machine learning models, deep learning models, pretrained transformers, and LLMs on student feedback sentiment classification? (2) Can LLMs outperform strong supervised baselines without task-specific fine-tuning? (3) How much do different prompting strategies affect LLM performance on this task?

The contributions of this study are as follows:

- We construct a unified empirical benchmark for three-class student feedback sentiment classification on 2,959 annotated comments, using a stratified 80/20 train–test

split and evaluating six supervised models and two instruction-tuned LLMs under five prompting settings.
- We quantify the performance progression across model families. Among supervised models, RoBERTa achieves the best result with 85.30% accuracy and 82.25% macro-F1, improving over Logistic Regression by 9.62 and 11.03 percentage points, respectively.
- We show that prompt-based LLMs can be competitive without task-specific fine-tuning when supported by in-context examples. GPT-4.1-mini improves from 80.57% accuracy and 73.35% macro-F1 in the zero-shot setting to 86.49% accuracy and 83.58% macro-F1 in the five-shot setting.
- We provide an empirical analysis of prompting strategies, showing that few-shot prompting mainly improves label alignment, whereas CoT prompting does not provide consistent gains on this short-text sentiment classification task.

2 Related Work

2.1 Student Feedback Sentiment Analysis

Student feedback is an important source for understanding teaching quality and learners' experiences. Compared with numerical ratings, open-ended comments provide richer and more specific evidence, but they are also much harder to analyze manually at scale. This has encouraged the use of text mining and sentiment analysis in educational settings.

Early studies mainly examined whether automatically identified sentiment could support timely intervention and course improvement. Gottipati et al. [9] moved beyond simple polarity detection and used text analytics to extract actionable course improvement suggestions from written comments. More recently, Grimalt-Álvaro and Usart [10] reviewed sentiment analysis for formative assessment in higher education and showed that this area is growing, although many studies still focus on specific institutional settings or local datasets. In this context, Herath et al. [11] made an important contribution by releasing a public student feedback dataset together with baseline results. Their dataset provides a useful benchmark for broader empirical comparison. Fargues et al. [12] developed an application for open-ended student feedback analysis that combines sentiment, emotion, and cognition-related classifications. Their work illustrates the practical value of feedback mining tools for teachers, but it focuses more on educational analytics support than on a controlled comparison of classification models. More recently, Awadh et al. [13] reviewed ABSA studies in MOOCs and showed that aspect-level methods can provide more fine-grained insights into course content, instructor performance, platform usability, and other learning-related dimensions.

2.2 Sentiment Classification Methods

Sentiment classification has progressed from feature-based methods to neural and pre-trained language models. With the rise of representation learning, neural models gradually replaced manual feature engineering. CNN-based models proved effective at capturing local lexical patterns for sentence classification [4], while recurrent models improved the modeling of word order and contextual dependencies [14]. More recently, pretrained transformer models have become strong supervised solutions for text classification. BERT introduced large-scale bidirectional pretraining with effective task-specific fine-tuning [5], and RoBERTa showed that stronger pretraining choices can further improve downstream performance [6]. Taken together, this line of work suggests a clear progression from sparse lexical features to contextual pretrained representations.

2.3 LLMs for Text Classification

Large language models have introduced a different paradigm for text classification. Instead of training a task-specific classifier, a general-purpose language model can often be prompted with an instruction and a small number of examples. Brown et al. [15] showed that large language models can perform a wide range of NLP tasks in zero-shot, one-shot, and few-shot settings through in-context learning. Subsequent work showed that few-shot performance depends strongly on the design of the prompt and the demonstrations. Min et al. [16] found that in-context learning is shaped not only by the correctness of demonstration labels, but also by factors such as label space, input distribution, and prompt format. Liu et al. [17] further showed that the choice of in-context examples can substantially affect performance, and Zhao et al. [18] showed that contextual calibration can improve the robustness of few-shot prompting. Gretz et al. [19] evaluated zero-shot topical text classification with LLMs on TTC23, a benchmark covering 23 public datasets across diverse domains and styles. Their results showed that zero-shot LLMs can be useful for classification, but task-specialized models can still achieve stronger performance. Similarly, Edwards and Camacho-Collados [20] conducted a large-scale evaluation on 16 text classification datasets covering binary, multiclass, and multilabel tasks, and found that fine-tuned smaller language models can still outperform few-shot LLM approaches in many settings.

Another important line of work studies prompting strategies beyond standard few-shot prompting. CoT prompting was proposed as a way to elicit intermediate reasoning steps and was shown to improve performance on reasoning-intensive tasks [21]. However, its role in short-text sentiment classification remains less clear. Student feedback comments are usually short, direct, and strongly shaped by local sentiment expressions, so they may benefit more from better label alignment than from extended reasoning. This makes student feedback sentiment classification a useful setting for comparing strong supervised baselines with prompt-based LLMs under different prompting conditions.

Overall, prior work provides strong foundations for both supervised sentiment classification and prompt-based LLM inference. However, there is still limited evidence on how these model families compare within the specific domain of student feedback, especially when zero-shot, few-shot, and CoT prompting are evaluated under the same experimental setting. The present study addresses this gap through a systematic comparison across model families and prompting strategies.

3 Methodology

This section describes the task formulation and the models compared in this study. We treat student feedback sentiment classification as a three-class text classification task and evaluate representative methods from four model families: traditional machine learning, deep learning, pretrained transformers, and prompt-based large language models. This design allows us to compare performance across model families and to examine the effect of prompting strategy within LLM-based methods. The overall framework is shown in Fig. 1.

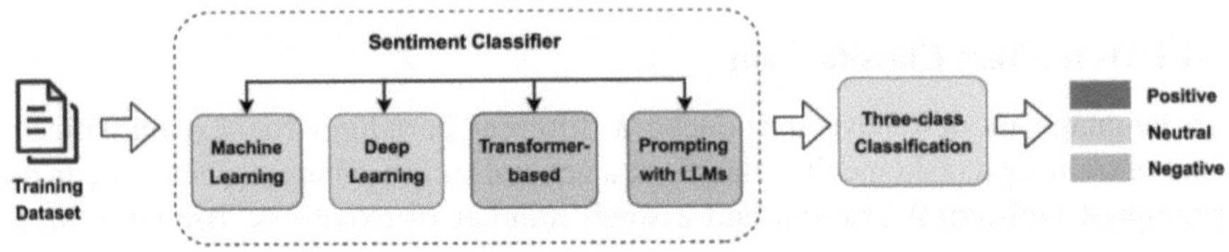

Fig. 1. Experimental framework for student feedback sentiment classification. Supervised models are trained or fine-tuned on the training set, whereas LLMs are evaluated through prompt-based inference using zero-shot, few-shot, and CoT prompting. All models are evaluated on the same held-out test set.

3.1 Task Definition

We define student feedback sentiment classification as a three-class text classification task. Let $\mathcal{D} = \{(x_i, y_i)\}_{i=1}^{N}$ denote the dataset, where x_i is a feedback comment and $y_i \in \mathcal{Y}$ is its sentiment label. The label set is $\mathcal{Y} = \{0, 1, 2\}$, corresponding to negative, neutral, and positive, respectively. Since the comments in our dataset are short and usually express one overall opinion, we treat each comment as a single input instance.

Given an input comment x, the goal is to predict its sentiment label:

$$\hat{y} = \arg\max_{c \in \mathcal{Y}} P(c|x).$$

For supervised models, this prediction is produced by a classifier trained on labeled data. For LLM-based methods, the same prediction is obtained through prompting without task-specific fine-tuning. All methods are therefore evaluated under the same three-class setting.

3.2 Sentiment Classifiers

We compare four groups of models: traditional machine learning models, deep learning models, pretrained transformer models, and LLM-based models. These groups represent different stages of text classification research and provide a clear basis for comparison on student feedback data.

Machine Learning Models. We first include Logistic Regression and Linear SVM as TF–IDF-based baselines. TF–IDF (term frequency-inverse document frequency) remains a strong feature representation for short-text classification and provides a clear reference point for later neural models. Logistic Regression and Linear SVM establish strong conventional baselines for student feedback sentiment classification.

Deep Learning Models. We next evaluate LSTM and TEXT-CNN as representative neural models that learn dense text representations directly from token sequences. Including both models allows us to compare two common neural approaches on short feedback comments, where sentiment may depend on both contextual order and local sentiment expressions.

Transformer-Based Models. To provide stronger supervised baselines, we include BERT and RoBERTa. For both models, each comment is tokenized with the corresponding tokenizer and encoded by a pretrained transformer. BERT serves as a standard pretrained baseline, while RoBERTa represents a stronger variant with a more robust pretraining setup. Comparing these models with the earlier baselines helps us assess the value of contextual pretrained representations for student feedback sentiment classification.

LLM-Based Models. In addition to supervised classifiers, we evaluate prompt-based LLMs to examine whether the task can be handled effectively without task-specific parameter updates and how much performance depends on prompt design. We evaluate two instruction-tuned LLMs: GPT-4.1-mini and LLaMA-3.3-70B-instruct. For both models, we test zero-shot, few-shot, and CoT settings.

To keep the evaluation consistent, all LLM outputs are mapped to the same three sentiment labels used by the supervised models. In the standard prompting settings, the model is instructed to return only the final label. In the CoT setting, the model is allowed to generate a short explanation followed by the final label. Since no task-specific fine-tuning is applied, this part of the study focuses on in-context learning and the effect of prompting strategy.

4 Experimental Setup

This section describes the dataset, implementation details, and evaluation metrics used in the experiments.

4.1 Dataset

We used the student feedback dataset released by Herath et al. [11]. The dataset contains feedback comments collected from two sources: RateMyProfessors.com and student evaluations from the University of Moratuwa. For this study, we used the document-level sentiment annotations provided in the dataset and treated each feedback comment as a single input instance. Each instance was assigned one of three sentiment labels: positive, neutral, or negative.

The final dataset used in this study contains 2,959 comments, including 1,754 positive, 644 neutral, and 561 negative instances. We further analyzed the sentence-length distribution and found that most comments contain fewer than 30 words, with an average length of about 23 words, as shown in Fig. 2.

To preserve the original class distribution in both training and test sets, we applied stratified random sampling to split the data into training and test sets, resulting in 2,367 training instances and 592 test instances. The split follows an 80/20 train–test ratio.

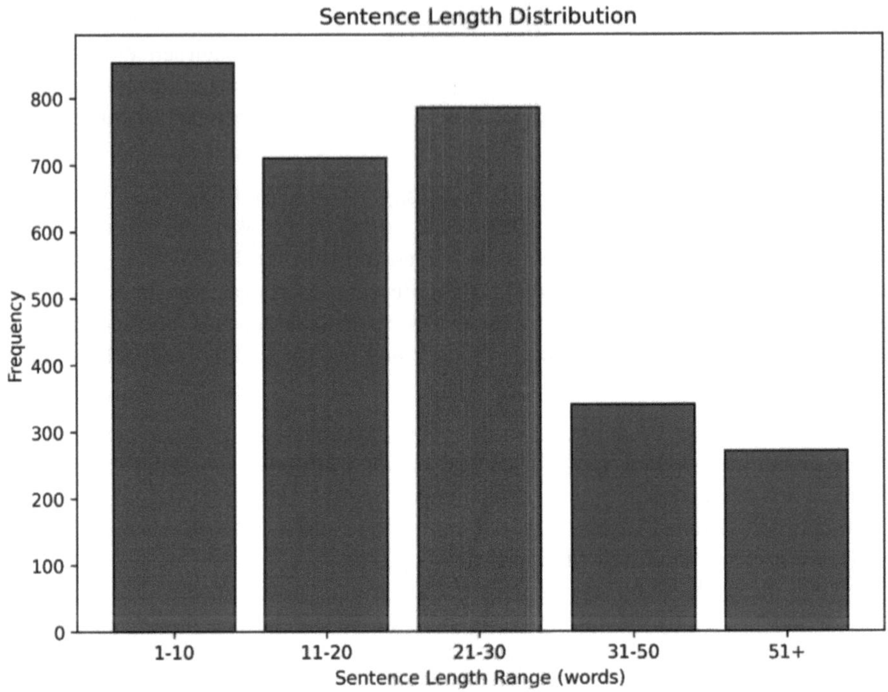

Fig. 2. Sentence length distribution of the dataset.

Stratification preserves the original class distribution: positive comments account for 59.28% of the full dataset, 59.27% of the training set, and 59.29% of the test set; neutral comments account for 21.76%, 21.76%, and 21.79%, respectively; and negative comments account for 18.96%, 18.97%, and 18.92%, respectively. The class distribution of the split is shown in Table 1. We used a fixed held-out test set rather than k-fold cross-validation for two reasons. First, the study compares supervised models with API-based LLM inference, and repeated k-fold evaluation would substantially increase the cost and time of LLM inference. Second, using a single held-out test set ensures that all supervised and prompt-based models are evaluated on exactly the same instances, which facilitates direct comparison and confusion-matrix analysis. Nevertheless, we acknowledge that results based on a single split may be sensitive to data partitioning; future work will include repeated stratified splits or k-fold evaluation where computationally feasible.

Table 1. Statistics of the dataset used in this study.

	Training	Test	Total
Positive	1,403	351	1,754
Neutral	515	129	644
Negative	449	112	561

4.2 Implementation Details

Machine Learning Models. Each feedback comment was represented by TF–IDF features. Logistic Regression set $max\_iter = 1000$, $class\_weight = balanced$, and $multi\_class = auto$. Linear SVM used $C = 1.0$, $class\_weight = balanced$, and $max\_iter = 5000$. Balanced class weights were used in both models to reduce the effect of class imbalance.

Deep Learning Models. For LSTM and text-CNN, comments were converted into token sequences and padded or truncated to a maximum length of 200 tokens. In both models, the embedding dimension was 128, the batch size was 32, and the number of training epochs was 10. The LSTM model used an embedding layer with $mask\_zero = True$, Followed by SpatialDropout1D(0.2), an LSTM layer with 128 hidden units, dropout and recurrent dropout both set to 0.2, a dense layer with 64 units and ReLU activation, a dropout layer with rate 0.3, and a three-way softmax output layer. The text-CNN model used an embedding layer, SpatialDropout1D(0.2), and three parallel Conv1D branches with kernel sizes 3, 4, and 5, each with 128 filters. After GlobalMaxPooling1D, the pooled features were concatenated and passed through a dense layer with 128 units, a dropout layer with rate 0.5, and a final softmax classifier. Because Conv1D does not support masking, mask_zero was not used in the text-CNN embedding layer. The text-CNN model was trained with Adam and sparse categorical cross-entropy loss.

Transformer-Based Models. BERT and RoBERTa were fine-tuned as sequence classification models under the same training setting. For both models, the maximum sequence length was 256, the batch size was 32, the number of training epochs was 10, the learning rate was 2×10^{-5}, and the weight decay was 0.01. We also reserved 10% of the training data as a validation set and used early stopping with a patience of 2 epochs to reduce overfitting.

LLM-Based Models. For the prompt-based experiments, we evaluated GPT-4.1-mini and LLaMA-3.3-70B-instruct through API-based inference without task-specific fine-tuning. In the zero-shot and few-shot settings, we used the same instruction template and changed only the number of in-context examples. The system instruction explicitly defined the label set as $0 = negative$, $1 = neutral$, and $2 = positive$, and required the model to return only one number. For few-shot prompting, $k \in \{1, 3, 5\}$ labeled examples selected from the training set were placed before the target comment. The overall prompt structure was kept the same across zero-shot and few-shot settings. For the CoT setting, we used a separate prompt that asked the model to analyze key sentiment cues, negation and modifiers, contextual tone, and final judgment before giving the final label. In this setting, the model was required to end its response with Label: 0, Label: 1, or Label: 2. All outputs were finally mapped to the same three sentiment labels used by the supervised models.

4.3 Evaluation Metrics

Because the dataset is imbalanced, we report Accuracy, Macro-Precision, Macro-Recall, and Macro-F1 on the test set. Accuracy is defined as

$$\text{Accuracy} = \frac{\sum_{i=1}^{N} 1(\hat{y}_i = y_i)}{N},$$

where N is the total number of instances, y_i is the true label, and $\hat{y}_i$ is the predicted label. For each class c, Precision, Recall, and F1 are computed as

$$P_c = \frac{TP_c}{TP_c + FP_c}, R_c = \frac{TP_c}{TP_c + FN_c}, F1_c = \frac{2P_cR_c}{P_c + R_c},$$

where TP_c, FP_c, and FN_c denote the numbers of true positives, false positives, and false negatives for class c, respectively. The macro-averaged metrics are then computed as

$$\text{Macro - Precision} = \frac{1}{C}\sum_{c=1}^{C} P_c, \text{Macro - Recall} = \frac{1}{C}\sum_{c=1}^{C} R_c, \text{Macro - F1} = \frac{1}{C}\sum_{c=1}^{C} F1_c,$$

where $C = 3$ in the present study. All reported scores are percentages.

5 Results and Discussion

Table 2 reports the performance of all models, and Fig. 3 shows selected confusion matrices on the test set. Overall, the results show a clear progression across model families. Traditional machine learning provides useful baselines, deep learning improves on them, and pretrained transformers deliver the strongest supervised results. Among the supervised models, RoBERTa performs best with 85.30 accuracy and 82.25 macro-F1. Among all evaluated settings, GPT-4.1-mini with five-shot prompting achieves the best overall result, reaching 86.49 accuracy and 83.58 macro-F1.

5.1 Comparison Across Supervised Models

Among the supervised models, performance improves from TF–IDF baselines to neural models and then to pretrained transformers. Logistic Regression slightly outperforms Linear SVM, indicating that simple linear models remain useful reference points for short student comments. LSTM improves over both linear baselines, and Text-CNN further raises accuracy to 80.24, suggesting that local lexical patterns are highly informative in this task. The largest gain comes from pretrained transformers: BERT substantially outperforms the neural models, and RoBERTa achieves the best supervised result at 85.30 accuracy and 82.25 macro-F1. Relative to Logistic Regression, this corresponds to improvements of 9.62 points in accuracy and 11.03 points in macro-F1.

Table 2. Performance comparison of different models on student feedback sentiment classification. All scores are percentages. The best result in each column is shown in bold.

	Accuracy	Macro-F1	Macro-Recall	Macro-Precision
Logistic Regression	75.68	71.22	72.07	70.51
Linear SVM	74.83	69.07	68.26	70.04
LSTM	77.53	74.27	74.54	74.25
Text-CNN	80.24	75.06	73.69	77.52
BERT	84.12	80.86	80.52	81.22
RoBERTa	85.30	82.25	82.77	81.83
Zero-shot				
GPT-4.1-mini	80.57	73.35	72.47	78.68
LLaMA-3.3-70B-Instruct	82.43	78.06	78.42	77.84
One-shot				
GPT-4.1-mini	84.63	81.18	82.19	80.31
LLaMA-3.3-70B-Instruct	83.61	80.35	81.09	79.82
Three-shot				
GPT-4.1-mini	84.29	81.09	81.32	81.24
LLaMA-3.3-70B-Instruct	84.46	80.80	81.21	80.67
Five-shot				
GPT-4.1-mini	**86.49**	**83.58**	**83.28**	**83.88**
LLaMA-3.3-70B-Instruct	84.63	81.50	82.19	80.95
CoT				
GPT-4.1-mini	81.93	74.77	74.25	79.34
LLaMA-3.3-70B-Instruct	79.73	71.63	70.74	77.29

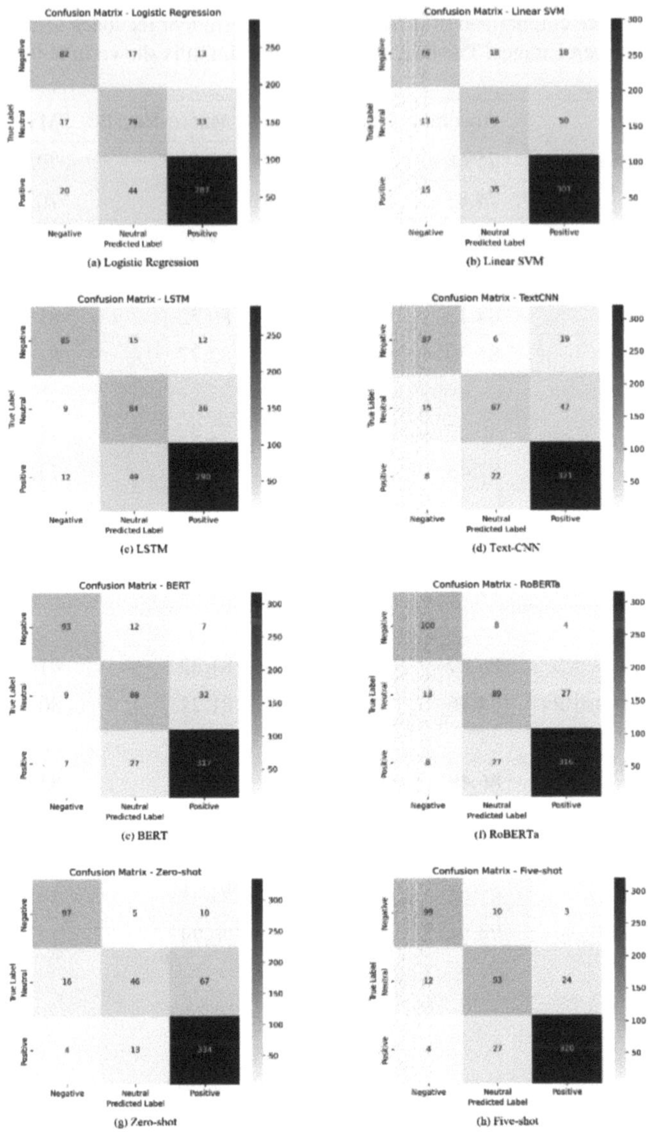

Fig. 3. Selected confusion matrices on the test set.

5.2 LLM Performance Under Different Prompting Settings

Prompting strategy materially affects LLM performance. In the zero-shot setting, GPT-4.1-mini and LLaMA-3.3-70B-Instruct achieve 80.57/73.35 and 82.43/78.06 in accuracy/macro-F1, respectively, both below RoBERTa. Few-shot prompting substantially improves both models. GPT-4.1-mini rises to 81.18 macro-F1 in one-shot and 83.58 in five-shot, while LLaMA-3.3-70B-Instruct improves from 78.06 in zero-shot to 81.50 in five-shot. The best LLM result is GPT-4.1-mini with five-shot prompting, which slightly exceeds RoBERTa on this test split. By contrast, the CoT setting does not improve over the best few-shot result for either model.

5.3 Interpreting the Effects of Prompting

Why Few-Shot Prompting Helps. The contrast between zero-shot and few-shot settings suggests that this task benefits mainly from better label alignment rather than more complex reasoning. Although student feedback comments are often short, the boundary between weakly positive, neutral, and weakly negative cases can be subtle. A small number of labeled examples appears to help the model map such borderline comments to the intended label space more consistently.

Why CoT Prompting Does not Help Consistently. The CoT prompt used in this study does not yield stable gains, suggesting that this task depends more on recognizing local evaluative cues than on extended reasoning. Requiring step-by-step explanations may introduce unnecessary verbosity and output variability, which can distract the model from the dominant sentiment. In this setting, explicit demonstrations appear more useful than solicited reasoning.

5.4 Implications for Model Choice and Limitations

Implications for Model Choice. The results suggest two practical options. When labeled data and fine-tuning are available, pretrained transformers remain a reliable choice for stable deployment. When task-specific training is less convenient, prompt-based LLMs become a viable alternative, but their performance depends strongly on prompt design, especially the use of in-context examples.

Limitations and Future Work. This study is limited to one public dataset and one experimental split, so the findings may not generalize directly to other educational settings. The LLM results may also vary with prompt wording, example selection, and API behavior. In addition, the comparison focuses on predictive performance rather than cost, latency, or reproducibility in deployment. Future work can proceed in several directions. first, the evaluation should be extended to multiple student feedback datasets from different institutions, courses, and educational contexts to test cross-domain generalization. Second, repeated stratified splits, k-fold cross-validation where computationally feasible, and statistical significance tests such as bootstrap confidence intervals or McNemar's test should be used to assess the robustness of the observed differences between RoBERTa and LLM-based methods. Third, LLM prompting strategies should be examined more systematically, including demonstration selection, demonstration order, label verbalization, and calibration methods. Fourth, future studies can move beyond document-level sentiment classification to aspect-level sentiment analysis and actionable suggestion extraction, which are more directly useful for teaching improvement. Finally, deployment-oriented factors such as inference cost, latency, privacy, reproducibility, and the use of local open-source LLMs should be considered.

6 Conclusion

This study compared traditional machine learning models, deep learning models, pre-trained transformer models, and prompt-based large language models for three-class sentiment classification of student feedback. The results show a clear progression across model families. Among the supervised models, RoBERTa achieved the best performance, confirming that fine-tuned transformers remain strong baselines for this task. The LLM results further show that prompt design matters: zero-shot prompting did not outperform the best supervised model, few-shot prompting led to substantial gains, and CoT prompting did not provide consistent benefits. GPT-4.1-mini in the five-shot setting achieved the best overall result.

Overall, the findings suggest that fine-tuned transformers remain a reliable choice when labeled data and model training are available, while carefully designed few-shot prompting makes LLMs a competitive alternative when task-specific training is less practical. More broadly, this study shows that the effectiveness of LLMs in student feedback sentiment classification depends not only on model capability, but also on how the task is presented.

Acknowledgments. This work was fully supported by a grant from the Research Grants Council of the Hong Kong Special Administrative Region, China (UGC/FDS16/E17/23); the Inter-institutional Collaborative Activities (IICA) Project entitled "GAI-Powered Feedback and Learning: A Domain-Adapted Large Language Model Approach for Bilingual and Data Science Education" (102745) funded by the Teaching Development and Language Enhancement Grant (TDLEG) from University Grants Council of the Hong Kong Special Administrative Region; and Teaching Development Grant entitled "Integrate GPT-based Intelligent Feedback and Tutoring for Data Science Courses" (102729) and Interdisciplinary & Strategic Research Grant (ISRG252606) of Lingnan University, Hong Kong.

Disclosure of Interests.. It is now necessary to declare any competing interests or to specifically state that the authors have no competing interests.

References

1. Xu, L., Wang, W.: Improving aspect-based sentiment analysis with contrastive learning. Natur. Lang. Proc. J. **3**, 100009 (2023)
2. Xu, L., Xie, H., Qin, S.J., Wang, F.L., Tao, X.: Exploring ChatGPT-based augmentation strategies for contrastive aspect-based sentiment analysis. IEEE Intell. Syst. **40**(1), 69–76 (2025)
3. Hochreiter, S., Schmidhuber, J.: Long short-term memory. Neural Comput. **9**(8), 1735–1780 (1997)
4. Kim, Y.: Convolutional Neural Networks for Sentence Classification. Proceedings of the 2014 Conference on Empirical Methods in Natural Language Processing (EMNLP), 1746–51 (2014)
5. Devlin, J., Chang, M.W., Lee, K., Toutanova, K.: Bert: pre-training of deep bidirectional transformers for language understanding. Proceedings of the 2019 Conference of the North American Chapter of the Association for Computational Linguistics: Human Language Technologies, Volume 1 (Long and Short Papers), pp. 4171–86 (2019)

6. Liu, Y., Ott, M., Goyal, N.. et al.: Roberta: A Robustly Optimized Bert Pretraining Approach. arXiv Preprint arXiv:1907.11692 (2019)
7. OpenAI. Introducing GPT-4.1 in the API. https://openai.com/index/gpt-4-1/. (2025)
8. Meta Llama. Meta-Llama/Llama-3.3–70B-Instruct. https://huggingface.co/meta-llama/Llama-3.3-70B-Instruct (2024)
9. Gottipati, S., Shankararaman, V., Lin, J.R.: Text analytics approach to extract course improvement suggestions from students' feedback. Res. Pract. Technol. Enhanc. Learn. **13**(1), 6 (2018)
10. Grimalt-Álvaro, C., Usart, M.: Sentiment analysis for formative assessment in higher education: a systematic literature review. J. Comput. High. Educ. **36**(3), 647–682 (2024)
11. Herath, M., Chamindu, K., Maduwantha, H., Ranathunga, S.: Dataset and Baseline for Automatic Student Feedback Analysis. Proceedings of the Thirteenth Language Resources and Evaluation Conference, pp. 2042–49 (2022)
12. Fargues, M., Kadry, S., Lawal, I.A., Yassine, S., Rauf, H.T.: Automated analysis of open-ended students' feedback using sentiment, emotion, and cognition classifications. Appl. Sci. **13**(4), 2061 (2023)
13. Awadh, W.A., Sulaiman, R.B., Mahmoud, M.A.: Aspect-based sentiment analysis in MOOCs: a systematic literature review introducing the MASC-MEF framework. J. King Saud Univ. Comp. Info. Sci. **37**(1), 2 (2025)
14. Tang, D., Qin, B., Liu, T.: Document modeling with gated recurrent neural network for sentiment classification. Proceedings of the 2015 Conference on Empirical Methods in Natural Language Processing, pp. 1422–32 (2015)
15. Brown, T., Mann, B., Ryder, N., et al.: Language models are few-shot learners. Adv. Neural. Inf. Process. Syst. **33**, 1877–1901 (2020)
16. Min, S., Lyu, X., Holtzman A., et al.: Rethinking the role of demonstrations: what makes in-context learning work? Proceedings of the 2022 Conference on Empirical Methods in Natural Language Processing, pp. 11048–64 (2022)
17. Liu, J., Shen, D., Zhang, Y., Dolan, B., Carin, L., Chen, W.: What Makes Good in-Context Examples for GPT-3?" Proceedings of Deep Learning Inside Out (DeeLIO 2022): The 3rd Workshop on Knowledge Extraction and Integration for Deep Learning Architectures (Dublin, Ireland; Online), pp. 100–114 (2022)
18. Zhao, Z., Wallace, E., Feng, S., Klein, D., Singh, S.: Calibrate before use: improving few-shot performance of language models. Proceedings of the 38th International Conference on Machine Learning, Proceedings of machine learning research, 139, 12697–706 (2021)
19. Gretz, S., Halfon, A., Shnayderman, I., et al.: Zero-shot topical text classification with LLMs-an experimental study. Findings of the Association for Computational Linguistics: EMNLP **2023**, 9647–9676 (2023)
20. Edwards, A., Camacho-Collados, J.: Language Models for Text Classification: Is in-Context Learning Enough? Proceedings of the 2024 Joint International Conference on Computational Linguistics, Language Resources and Evaluation (LREC-COLING 2024), pp. 10058–72 (2024)
21. Wei, J., Wang, X., Schuurmans, D., et al.: Chain-of-thought prompting elicits reasoning in large language models. Adv. Neural. Inf. Process. Syst. **35**, 24824–24837 (2022)

Revisiting Pedagogical Agents in the Era of Large Language Models: From Social Agency to Social Interdependence

Chen Li[1,2], Ye Jia[2(✉)], Peter H. F. Ng[2,3], Jing Liu[4], and Qing Li[2]

[1] Department of Applied Social Sciences, The Hong Kong Polytechnic University, Hong Kong SAR, China

[2] Department of Computing, The Hong Kong Polytechnic University, Hong Kong SAR, China

ye-aimmeng.jia@connect.polyu.hk

[3] Department of Rehabilitation Sciences, The Hong Kong Polytechnic University, Hong Kong SAR, China

[4] Department of Accountancy, Economics and Finance, Hong Kong Baptist University, Hong Kong SAR, China

Abstract. For decades, the design of pedagogical agents (PAs) has been guided primarily by social agency theory (SAT). SAT suggests that incorporating human-like features, such as gestures, facial expressions, and voice, activates social schemas in learners, which in turn increases cognitive effort and improves learning outcomes. While this approach has been effective for traditional scripted PAs, it may not be sufficient in the era of large language models (LLMs). Unlike their predecessors, LLMs provide semantic understanding, generative capabilities, and contextual memory, fundamentally changing the nature of human-computer interaction from one-on-one, turn-based exchanges to a more collaborative social dynamic. This paper advocates for a shift in the theoretical framework from SAT to social interdependence theory (SIT) as the basis for designing LLM-driven PAs. We argue that the effectiveness of modern LLM-driven PAs is less about superficial social cues and more about the structural dynamics of collaboration: positive interdependence, promotive interaction, and individual accountability. Based on this perspective, we outline three design implications: designing for productive friction, organising interactions around shared artefacts, and positioning PAs as co-regulators of learning. We further argue that evaluation should move beyond social presence and human-likeness toward collaborative quality and shared mental model formation at the learning process level. Finally, we discuss several practical and ethical challenges. Together, these arguments reposition LLM-driven PAs not as socially appealing answer providers, but as partners in structured, accountable learning.

Keywords: Pedagogical agent · Large language model · Social agency · Social interdependence · Collaborative learning · Human-AI interaction

K. T. Chui et al. (Eds.): ICBL 2026, LNCS 16778, pp. 180–193, 2027.
https://doi.org/10.1007/978-981-92-3761-6_13

1 Introduction

Pedagogical agents (PAs) are often described as conversational learning technologies powered by natural language processing (NLP) that communicate with learners through spoken or written dialogue. Although language serves as the primary interface, these agents may also leverage non-verbal communication, such as gestures and facial expressions, through on-screen virtual characters to deepen the social interaction [21]. The rise of large language models (LLMs) has rapidly transformed the application of PAs. While this technological leap has been remarkable, the theoretical frameworks guiding PA design have not been systematically updated to account for the interactional affordances of LLMs and often continue to draw on concepts rooted in the pre-LLM era. The field of PA design has, for decades, been dominated by social agency theory (SAT) [29,31]. SAT posits that the incorporation of human-like features, such as facial expressions, gestures, and voice, activates social schemas in learners, thereby increasing cognitive effort and improving learning outcomes. Consequently, research has predominantly focused on the development of these surface cues, investigating whether the presence of a face [25,31], a human voice [1,29], non-verbal communication [2,7,37], or politeness [5,30,35,41] enhances the overall learning experience and learning outcomes.

Although these cues were essential in making scripted agents appear more lifelike and engaging, they are no longer sufficient in the era of LLMs [42,43]. The inherent dynamism of LLMs, as characterised by semantic understanding, generative capabilities, and long-term contextual memory, fundamentally alters the affordances of PAs; it enables PAs to move beyond scripted responses into complex, dynamic, and co-constructive interactions with learners [42]. Treating an LLM-driven PA merely as a chatbot with a face underutilises its potential for deep cognitive partnership. Furthermore, applying SAT without considering the structural dynamics of collaboration risks creating PAs that are socially engaging but pedagogically passive, potentially encouraging social loafing where the learner relies too heavily on the agent's fluency [42].

This paper argues that the advent of LLMs necessitates a theoretical pivot in the design of PAs. Rather than continuing to prioritise social agency, wherein the primary concern is priming social schemas via social cues, we must shift our attention to designing and evaluating for social interdependence [18]. By examining the historical development of PAs and the evolving nature of human-computer interaction, this paper advocates shifting from SAT to SIT in the design and evaluation of LLM-driven PAs, prioritising positive interdependence, promotive interaction, and individual accountability.

2 Social Agency: A Retrospective

The intersection of social psychology and instructional design has largely steered the historical trajectory of PA-related research. Reeves and Nass demonstrated that the human brain, having evolved in a world where only other humans exhibited social behaviours, has not yet adapted to distinguish between real people and media representations [34]. Consequently, individuals tend to treat computers and media as social actors, unconsciously applying social rules (e.g., politeness and reciprocity) to their interactions with machines. Building upon this socio-psychological framework, Mayer formalised SAT to explain how these automatic responses could be harnessed to improve multimedia learning [29]. SAT suggests that PAs do not need to possess genuine intelligence or semantic understanding; they simply need to provide enough surface-level social cues to trigger learners' innate social instincts. In other words, the appearance of PAs' socialness is sufficient to drive learning.

Driven by SAT, empirical research from the late 1990s through the 2010s focused extensively on validating the efficacy of social cues, with Lester et al. first demonstrating that lifelike characters enhanced perceived learning experience, even when task-irrelevant [25]. This phenomenon became known as the "persona effect." Later research replicated and refined it by examining factors such as politeness, voice, and emotional expressiveness in PAs. Overall, this work found that, compared with disembodied text-only interfaces, PAs improved learner motivation, retention, and self-efficacy. However, these findings belonged to a specific technological paradigm: because the software could not support genuine conversation, the agents' socialness was largely unidirectional. The "persona effect" was therefore a triumph of interface design rather than intelligence, showing that learners wanted a social partner, even if it was essentially a pre-scripted animated playback device.

This reliance on surface-level social cues to mask a lack of underlying intelligence has created two critical friction points in modern PA design. First, it leads to an expectation-capability gap. As visual fidelity improved, agents began to look increasingly human, creating an implicit promise of social competence. However, when a photorealistic avatar failed to answer a simple off-script question or misunderstood a basic query, the illusion of social agency was shattered. Second, the structural design of pre-LLM agents was inherently script-bound and system-initiated. Interactions typically followed a rigid turn-taking question-and-answer loop: the learner requests, and the agent delivers (see Fig. 1 (1)). In this model, PAs are responders rather than collaborators. The emergence of LLMs fundamentally alters these constraints. Consequently, a theoretical framework like SAT is insufficient for guiding the design of PAs that must think and collaborate with learners.

3 The Disruption: LLM-Driven PAs and New Affordances

Traditional PAs were largely constrained by rigid, pre-defined decision trees, which limited both the range of learner input they could interpret and the flexibility of the support they could provide [39]. By contrast, LLM-driven PAs offer generative and semantic affordances that enable them to interpret nuanced learner inquiries and produce contextually relevant, open-ended responses [4,40]. These capabilities mark an important shift from simple content delivery toward more strategic pedagogical support, as the agent can adapt not only what it says but also the depth and framing of its instruction in response to learners' needs [24,40].

These generative capabilities become especially consequential when paired with greater contextual continuity across interactions. A major limitation of traditional PAs was their lack of memory, or amnesia, which prevented them from maintaining learner-specific context over time [32]. In contrast, LLM-driven PAs can leverage a range of short- and long-term memory mechanisms [28], enabling them to retain information about learners, prior exchanges, and learning trajectories across sessions [6]. This capacity shifts PAs from session-bound responders toward more continuous AI learning partners that can support personalisation, coherence, and the sustained tracking of learner development over time.

Building on this continuity, LLM-driven PAs can also provide more adaptive and pedagogically responsive scaffolding. Rather than relying on predefined hint structures [22], these agents can interpret real-time interaction dynamics and adjust instructional support to a learner's personality, learning style, language ability, and evolving needs [27,33]. This adaptability allows scaffolding to be more context-sensitive and more closely aligned with pedagogical principles, encouraging conceptual reasoning through strategies such as Socratic prompting [10] and offering granular, step-by-step guidance in domains such as programming [36]. In this way, they move beyond static assistance toward more personalised and instructionally nuanced forms of support.

Taken together, these advances in generative and semantic capacity, contextual memory, and dynamic scaffolding support a broader transformation in the role of PAs: a shift from mechanical turn-taking toward collaborative knowledge co-construction. Through multimodal interaction and flexible dialogue, LLM-driven PAs can facilitate forms of human-AI collaboration that align with established pedagogical frameworks, particularly Vygotsky's Zone of Proximal Development (ZPD) [3,11,26]. Within this collaborative model, learners are positioned not merely as passive recipients of information, but as active agents and critical evaluators who engage with, question, and refine LLM-generated content [16]. Yet this shift is not automatic. Despite their linguistic fluency, LLMs often default to direct answer provision, which can reduce learner autonomy and bypass productive learning processes [3,42]. This suggests that the central challenge in future PA design is not only to increase technical capability, but also to structure the learner-PA relationship in ways that promote positive and productive interdependence. From this perspective, the design of LLM-driven PAs requires a theoretical framework that explains how interaction structures shape collaboration and learning outcomes.

4 Social Interdependence Theory

Social Interdependence Theory (SIT), originally developed by Morton Deutsch [8] and subsequently refined by David and Roger Johnson [19,20], posits that the way social interdependence is organised determines how individuals

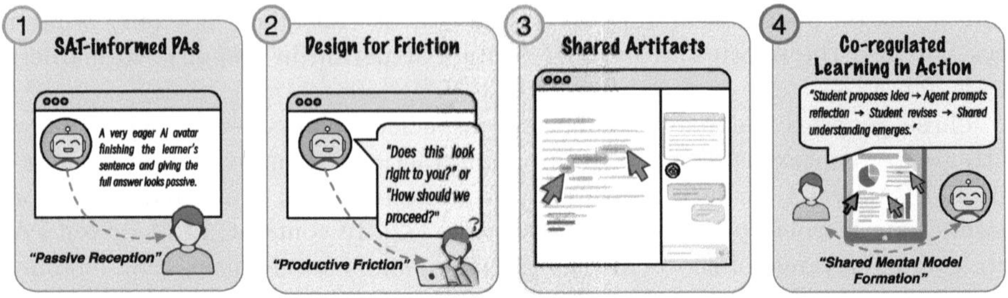

Fig. 1. Comparative design frameworks for PAs: **(1)** The conventional SAT-informed PAs tend to reinforce a question-and-answer interaction logic, which makes learners passive receivers of information; **(2-4)** The proposed SIT-informed PAs design focuses on structural dynamics, where the agent and learner engage in a collaborative loop through shared artefacts and promotive interaction.

interact, which in turn shapes the outcomes they achieve. Three principles are especially central to this account: positive interdependence, promotive interaction, and individual accountability. Together, they explain how collaboration is structured, enacted, and sustained. SIT has productively guided Computer-Supported Collaborative Learning (CSCL) design for decades [9,17], offering a complement to SAT: whereas SAT primarily concerns learners' internal responses to social cues, SIT focuses on the structural dynamics of interaction itself. From this perspective, the educational value of an LLM-driven PA depends not only on its capabilities or persona, but also on how the learner–PA relationship is designed across these three dimensions.

However, applying SIT to human–LLM interaction raises a conceptual challenge: LLMs lack goals, beliefs, and accountability in the cognitive sense these constructs presume. An LLM does not want to achieve a learning objective, cannot be held responsible for errors, and does not experience social pressure to contribute fairly. We therefore propose that SIT principles apply *as design heuristics*, structuring learner-perceived interdependence and learner-enacted collaborative behaviours, even when the partner is not truly agentic. The designer's task is to engineer interaction structures that produce functionally interdependent processes. Applied to LLM-driven PAs, this reframes the agent: rather than an authoritative system that simply provides answers, the PA is treated as a structured partner in a shared cognitive task (see Table 1). The design focus thus extends from surface-level social cues to the conditions under which learners and PAs become productively interdependent. Recent work suggests that LLM-driven PAs, when designed with appropriate social and interactional characteristics, can elicit psychological processes similar to those found in human–human collaboration, including a sense of shared responsibility for outcomes [13], lending preliminary support to this design stance.

Positive Interdependence: Positive interdependence is the foundation for collaboration. It exists when individuals perceive that they can reach their goals if, and

Table 1. Theoretic Shift: From SAT to SIT

Dimension	SAT	SIT
Agent Role	**Expert/Tutor**: Provide authoritative knowledge and guidance	**Learning Partner**: Act as a collaborator in a shared task
Learner Role	**Receiver**: Passively react to agent-initiated cues	**Co-constructor**: Proactively engage and verify the interaction
Mechanism	**Schema Activation**: Reduce cognitive load via human-like social cues	**Collaborative**: Drive deep processing through negotiation of meaning

only if, their partners also achieve theirs [19]. In the context of LLM-driven PAs, this principle can be operationalised through designing interactions in which the learner and the agent contribute different but complementary resources [23]. For example, the PA may provide generative breadth, rapid feedback, or alternative perspectives, while the learner contributes task context, domain judgement, and critical evaluation. This complementary structure is particularly important given the limitations of LLMs, whose outputs may be incomplete, misleading, or inaccurate at times [15]. Positive interdependence, therefore, arises not when the agent replaces learner effort, but when each party contributes something the other lacks, making successful task completion contingent on both AI assistance and human oversight.

Promotive Interaction: Once positive interdependence is established, the quality of interaction becomes central. Promotive interaction refers to patterns of exchange in which partners encourage and facilitate one another's efforts to achieve a shared goal [12]. In learner-PA settings, this involves more than simple responsiveness; it requires interaction that actively supports reasoning, reflection, and conceptual development. LLM-driven PAs are well-suited to this role because they can be prompted to ask elaborative questions, provide contingent feedback, and scaffold problem solving in real time [14,38]. For instance, an agent can adopt a Socratic style that challenges assumptions, requests justification, or invites comparison between alternative solutions. Such interaction encourages deeper cognitive processing and shifts the learner from passive reception towards active sense-making. When the PA is positioned as a partner in inquiry rather than a system for answer delivery, the interaction moves beyond transactional question-and-answer exchanges towards a more collaborative form of scaffolding, in which learning emerges through intersubjective engagement with the agent's contributions rather than uncritical acceptance.

Individual Accountability: For interdependence and interaction to remain educationally productive, however, the learner must also retain responsibility for a meaningful share of the task. A central risk in LLM-supported learning is that learners may offload too much cognitive work to the agent, thereby reducing effort, weakening self-regulation, and undermining genuine understanding. Within SIT, individual accountability is therefore essential because each member of the group must remain responsible for a substantive contribution [20]. In the context of a learner–PA dyad, this means designing the interaction so that the learner remains accountable for interpreting, evaluating, and, where necessary, revising the agent's output. Requiring learners to justify answers, explain their reasoning, or modify proposed solutions helps ensure that the PA functions as a scaffold rather than a cognitive crutch. In this way, accountability mechanisms are critical for preserving learner agency while still enabling learners to benefit from PA support.

5 Implications for LLM-Driven PA Design and Evaluation

The shift from SAT to SIT calls for a fundamental rethinking of how PAs are designed and evaluated. Rather than locating pedagogical value primarily in human-likeness, fluency, or ease of use, an SIT perspective foregrounds the structural quality of the learner-PA partnership. This shift is particularly important because many current LLM applications in education are implicitly optimised for convenience and seamless task completion. While such qualities may improve usability, they may also erode the interactional conditions that support durable learning by minimising learner effort, negotiation, and responsibility. From an SIT perspective, the educational value of an LLM-driven PA therefore lies not simply in the quality of its outputs, but in how effectively it promotes positive and productive interdependence. This reorientation has important implications for both design and evaluation of PAs: for design, it suggests creating systems that sustain productive friction, shared work, and co-regulated learning; for evaluation, it requires moving beyond perceptual measures of the agent towards process-based accounts of collaborative engagement.

5.1 Implications for Design

As illustrated in the Fig. 1, the SIT-based PAs should prioritise interaction structures that maintain learner engagement, create mutual dependence within the task, and support co-regulation. Three implications are particularly important: design for friction, shared artefacts, and co-regulated learning.

Design for Friction: A first implication is that PAs should not always be optimised for immediate task completion. In many educational contexts, some degree of friction is pedagogically desirable because it creates occasions for explanation, reflection, checking, and revision. From an SIT perspective, promotive interaction emerges when participants must attend to one another's contributions and negotiate next steps. Translating this principle into LLM-driven PAs means designing the system so that it does not routinely provide final answers at the earliest opportunity, but instead sustains learner participation in the problem-solving process. For example, rather than simply supplying a solution, the PA might request evidence, ask the learner to justify a step, invite comparison between alternatives, or propose partial next moves that require the learner to complete them. Such interactional friction preserves the learner's epistemic role and ensures that progress remains contingent on learner input. The goal is not to introduce unnecessary obstacles or frustration, but to create forms of productive resistance that require learners to inspect, interpret, justify, and refine ideas. In this way, friction becomes a design resource for sustaining both promotive interaction and positive interdependence.

Shared Artefacts: A second implication concerns the design of the interactional space itself. Many existing LLM systems are organised around a conventional chat interface, which tends to reinforce a question-and-answer interaction logic: the learner requests, and the agent delivers. While chat can support dialogue, it often obscures the jointly constructed nature of learning with PAs. SIT suggests that collaboration is strengthened when partners orient towards a shared object of activity and make mutually relevant contributions to its development [19]. In practice, this means that PAs should increasingly operate through shared workspace rather than solely through isolated conversational exchange. Such workspaces might include a co-edited concept map, proof, code notebook, design sketch, or draft text. Shared artefacts matter because they make interdependence visible and actionable. They provide a focal point around which goals, roles and responsibilities, and progress can be negotiated. They also make it easier to observe whether the interaction reflects genuine co-construction or merely sequential outsourcing. Designing around shared artefacts, therefore, shifts the role of PAs from answer generator to collaborative contributor within a jointly evolving product.

Co-regulated Learning: A third implication is that the PAs should be positioned as a co-regulator of the learning process rather than a substitute for learner thinking. SIT emphasises that effective interdependence involves accountability, mutual responsiveness, and coordination. In learner-PA interaction design, this means the agent should support planning, monitoring, and reflection in ways that preserve learner responsibility for substantive intellectual work. More broadly, SIT-informed PAs should be designed to sustain the core conditions of positive interdependence: shared goals, differentiated but complementary contributions, reciprocal responsiveness, and individual accountability. These conditions can be encoded not only in the prompt design and engineering, but also in interface features, workflow constraints, turn structure, revision protocols, and task sequencing.

5.2 Implications for Evaluation

SIT also implies a substantial shift in how LLM-driven PAs should be evaluated. Much prior work has emphasised constructs such as social presence, likability, and perceived human-likeness. Although these dimensions may shape engagement, trust, or willingness to interact, they are not sufficient indicators of PAs' educational value; a learner may perceive an agent as warm, natural, or socially present while still engaging in a largely passive interaction that produces little conceptual change. If the theoretical concern is the quality of interdependent collaboration, evaluation must move beyond impressions of the agent and toward analysis of the joint activity that the agent helps organise.

Beyond Social Presence and Human-Likeness: From an SIT perspective, social presence should not be treated as the primary proxy for effective pedagogical interaction. Indeed, an agent may be perceived as highly present or human-like precisely because it is fluent, responsive, and proactive. Yet these same qualities may undermine learning if they encourage learners to defer to the system rather than reason with it. Measures such as social presence, human-likeness, or perceived intelligence may therefore overestimate pedagogical effectiveness when they are detached from evidence about learner contribution and interaction quality. This does not mean that such measures are irrelevant; they remain useful for understanding user experience and adoption. However, they should be treated as secondary or contextual variables rather than as dominant indicators of system success.

Measure Collaborative Quality on Process Level: A more appropriate evaluative focus is the quality of collaboration itself. One useful construct is collaborative quality, understood as the extent to which the learner and PA jointly develop ideas, respond contingently to one another, and sustain coordinated progress towards a shared objective. This construct invites methodological approaches that examine process rather than merely outcome, including discourse analysis, interaction coding, process tracing, and fine-grained log analysis. Such methods can help determine whether the learner contributes substantive reasoning, whether the PA's responses build on learner input rather than bypass it, and whether the interaction exhibits patterns of uptake, elaboration, and revision. A related process-level construct is the frequency and character of negotiation turns. In genuinely interdependent interactions, progress is often achieved through clarification requests, disagreement, justification, perspective comparison, and decision-making about next steps. These moments should not be treated as noise or inefficiency; rather, they may signal active learner engagement and deeper cognitive processing. Evaluation should, therefore, attend not only to whether such negotiation occurs, but also to when it occurs, how it is distributed across the interaction, and whether it is associated with improved understanding, transfer, or retention. This shift in focus is important because systems optimised for seamless answer delivery may appear highly effective on conventional usability metrics while simultaneously suppressing the very interactional dynamics that support learning.

Detect the Formation of Shared Mental Models: A further implication is the need to evaluate whether learner and PA develop a sufficient understanding of the task, the problem space, and the rationale underlying the evolving solution. In collaborative learning research, this is often discussed in terms of shared mental models. Adapted to the context of LLM-driven PAs, the concept provides a useful way to distinguish between superficial task completion and deeper collaborative cognition. A polished final answer may create the appearance of success while masking the learner's limited understanding of how that answer was produced or why it is appropriate. By contrast, stronger evidence of learning would be found when learners can independently continue, revise, or defend the reasoning embedded in the jointly produced work.

5.3 Practical and Ethical Challenges

Although SIT is a promising theory for rethinking LLM-driven PAs, its application also introduces important practical and ethical challenges.

Learner Capacity and the Burden of Verification: A central premise of SIT-informed design is that learners should remain accountable participants in the learning process by checking, questioning, and revising AI-generated outputs. However, this expectation may impose substantial cognitive and emotional demands, especially on learners who lack the domain knowledge needed to detect hallucinations, misleading explanations, or subtle errors. In such cases, the requirement to monitor the agent can create tension between pedagogical responsibility and learner capacity. If the burden of verification becomes too great, learners may either over-trust the system or disengage from the interaction altogether. Accountability, in this sense, should not be reduced to making learners responsible for correcting the models' limitations. Instead, SIT-informed PAs should be designed to scaffold verification through uncertainty signalling, explanation prompts, comparison strategies, or other supports that help learners exercise judgment without bearing the full burden of quality control.

Data Privacy, Memory, and Learner Profiling: The long-term memory of LLM-driven PAs can support continuity, adaptation, and personalised guidance over time, but they also raise significant concerns about privacy, consent, and governance. To sustain contextualised interaction, such systems may store sensitive learner data, including performance histories, preferences, misconceptions, and interaction traces. Such information can expose learners to risks related to unauthorised data use or reductive profiling. Moreover, persistent learner models may reify students into static categories derived from prior learning behaviour and performance rather than supporting their development as changing and context-sensitive learners. These concerns are especially salient in educational settings, where power asymmetries may limit the meaningfulness of consent. For this reason, LLM-driven PAs should incorporate transparent consent procedures, clear data retention policies, and mechanisms that allow learners to inspect, contest, manage, or delete stored information.

The Illusion of Collaboration: A further challenge is that LLM-driven PAs may appear collaborative without actually supporting meaningful interdependence. Because these systems are highly fluent and conversational, they can simulate dialogue, reflection, and responsiveness even when learners' contributions have little real influence on the task's trajectory. This creates a risk of illusory collaboration, in which the interaction feels socially rich or pedagogically supportive but remains structurally one-sided. From an SIT perspective, genuine collaboration requires reciprocal influence, shared accountability, and negotiated meaning-making. Therefore, we should be cautious not to equate conversational smoothness, social presence, or apparent responsiveness with collaborative quality. The key question is not whether the interaction appears social, but whether it genuinely engages learners as active co-constructors of knowledge.

6 Conclusion

The emergence of LLM-driven PAs challenges SAT as the dominant framework for understanding educational human-AI interaction and PA design. While SAT explains the value of human-like social cues in earlier scripted systems, it is less well-suited to the collaborative, adaptive, and open-ended nature of recent PA design. This paper has argued that SIT provides a more productive lens by foregrounding positive interdependence, promotive interaction, and individual accountability. Informed by SIT, we suggest that effective PAs should not merely appear social but should foster positive interdependence through productive friction, shared artefacts, and co-regulated learning, with corresponding evaluations that study collaborative quality and shared mental models at the learning process level.

Acknowledgments. This work was supported by the Teaching Development Grants 2025-28 from The Hong Kong Polytechnic University (project code: TDG25-28/TBP/10.2).

References

1. Atkinson, R.K., Mayer, R.E., Merrill, M.M.: Fostering social agency in multimedia learning: examining the impact of an animated agent's voice. Contemp. Educ. Psychol. **30**(1), 117–139 (2005)
2. Baylor, A.L., Kim, S.: Designing nonverbal communication for pedagogical agents: when less is more. Comput. Hum. Behav. **25**(2), 450–457 (2009)
3. Beale, R.: Dialogic pedagogy for large language models: aligning conversational ai with proven theories of learning. arXiv preprint arXiv:2506.19484 (2025)
4. Bouguettaya, S., Pupo, F., Chen, M., Fortino, G.: A meta-survey of generative ai in education: trends, challenges, and research directions. Big Data Cogn. Comput. **9**(9), 237 (2025)
5. Brummernhenrich, B., Paulus, C.L., Jucks, R.: Applying social cognition to feedback chatbots: enhancing trustworthiness through politeness. Br. J. Edu. Technol. **56**(6), 2321–2340 (2025)
6. Cai, H., Han, B., Sun, J., Cheng, Y.: How to design llm-based intelligent agent to support student's learning in educational context: a systematic literature review. Educ. Technol. Soc. **29**(2), 249–269 (2026)

7. Davis, R.O.: The impact of pedagogical agent gesturing in multimedia learning environments: a meta-analysis. Educ. Res. Rev. **24**, 193–209 (2018)
8. Deutsch, M.: A theory of co-operation and competition. Human Relat. **2**(2), 129–152 (1949)
9. Dillenbourg, P.: What do you mean by collaborative learning? In: Dillenbourg, P. (ed.) Collaborative Learning: Cognitive and Computational Approaches, pp. 1–19. Elsevier, Oxford (1999). hAL Id: hal-00190240
10. Ding, Y., Hu, H., Zhou, J., Chen, Q., Jiang, B., He, L.: Boosting large language models with socratic method for conversational mathematics teaching. In: Proceedings of the 33rd ACM International Conference on Information and Knowledge Management, pp. 3730–3735. ACM (2024)
11. Doolittle, P.: Vygotsky's zone of proximal development as a theoretical foundation for cooperative learning. J. Excell. Coll. Teach. **8**(1), 83–103 (1997)
12. Dzemidzic Kristiansen, S., Burner, T., Johnsen, B.H.: Face-to-face promotive interaction leading to successful cooperative learning: a review study. Cogent Educ. **6**(1), 1674067 (2019)
13. Fang, J.W., Guo, X.G., Meng, X.P., Hwang, G.J., Tu, Y.F.: Realization of parasocial interaction theory in steam education with an ai pedagogical agent: insights from learning performance, collaboration tendency, and problem-solving tendency. Interact. Learn. Environ. **34**(2), 694–717 (2026)
14. Hartmann, C., Olsen, J.K., Brand, C., Aleven, V., Rummel, N.: Examining positive and negative interdependence in an elementary school cscl setting. In: Proceedings of the 12th International Conference on Computer-Supported Collaborative Learning (CSCL 2017), pp. 479–482 (2017)
15. Huang, L., et al.: A survey on hallucination in large language models: principles, taxonomy, challenges, and open questions. ACM Trans. Inf. Syst. **43**(2), 1–55 (2025)
16. Jia, Y., Li, C., Chan, A., Li, Q.: Human-al collaboration in the stem classroom: a systematic literature review of genai as a complement in higher education. In: International Conference on Technology in Education, pp. 389–401. Springer, Heidelberg (2026). https://doi.org/10.1007/978-981-95-4499-8_32
17. Johnson, D.W., Johnson, R.T.: Cooperation and Competition: Theory and Research. Interaction Book Company (1989)
18. Johnson, D.W., Johnson, R.T.: Cooperative learning and social interdependence theory. In: Theory and Research on Small Groups, pp. 9–35. Springer, Heidelberg (1998). https://doi.org/10.1007/0-306-47144-2_2
19. Johnson, D.W., Johnson, R.T.: New developments in social interdependence theory. Genet. Soc. Gen. Psychol. Monogr. **131**(4), 285–358 (2005)
20. Johnson, D.W., Johnson, R.T.: An educational psychology success story: social interdependence theory and cooperative learning. Educ. Res. **38**(5), 365–379 (2009)
21. Johnson, W.L., Lester, J.C.: Face-to-face interaction with pedagogical agents, twenty years later. Int. J. Artif. Intell. Educ. **26**(1), 25–36 (2016)
22. Koedinger, K.R., Brunskill, E., Baker, R.S., McLaughlin, E.A., Stamper, J.: New potentials for data-driven intelligent tutoring system development and optimization. AI Mag. **34**(3), 27–41 (2013)
23. Laal, M.: Positive interdependence in collaborative learning. Procedia. Soc. Behav. Sci. **93**, 1433–1437 (2013)
24. Lang, Q., Wang, M., Yin, M., Liang, S., Song, W.: Transforming education with generative ai (gai): key insights and future prospects. IEEE Trans. Learn. Technol. **18**, 230–242 (2025)

25. Lester, J.C., Converse, S.A., Kahler, S.E., Barlow, S.T., Stone, B.A., Bhogal, R.S.: The persona effect: affective impact of animated pedagogical agents. In: Proceedings of the ACM SIGCHI Conference on Human Factors in Computing Systems, pp. 359–366 (1997)
26. Liu, Z., Yin, S.X., Lee, C., Chen, N.F.: Scaffolding language learning via multimodal tutoring systems with pedagogical instructions. In: 2024 IEEE Conference on Artificial Intelligence (CAI), pp. 1258–1265. IEEE (2024)
27. Liu, Z., Yin, S.X., Lin, G., Chen, N.: Personality-aware student simulation for conversational intelligent tutoring systems. In: Proceedings of the 2024 Conference on Empirical Methods in Natural Language Processing, pp. 626–642 (2024)
28. Maharana, A., Lee, D.H., Tulyakov, S., Bansal, M., Barbieri, F., Fang, Y.: Evaluating very long-term conversational memory of LLM agents. In: Proceedings of the 62nd Annual Meeting of the Association for Computational Linguistics, vol. 1: Long Papers, pp. 13851–13870. Association for Computational Linguistics (2024)
29. Mayer, R.E., Sobko, K., Mautone, P.D.: Social cues in multimedia learning: role of speaker's voice. J. Educ. Psychol. **95**(2), 419–425 (2003)
30. McLaren, B.M., DeLeeuw, K.E., Mayer, R.E.: Polite web-based intelligent tutors: can they improve learning in classrooms? Comput. Educ. **56**(3), 574–584 (2011)
31. Moreno, R., Mayer, R.E., Spires, H.A., Lester, J.C.: The case for social agency in computer-based teaching: do students learn more deeply when they interact with animated pedagogical agents? Cogn. Instr. **19**(2), 177–213 (2001). https://doi.org/10.1207/S1532690XCI1902_02
32. Nouwen, S., Sturm, J., Matzat, U., IJsselsteijn, W.: Synthetic relationships with social pedagogical agents in education: a scoping literature review. Front. Artif. Intell. **9**, 1625438 (2026)
33. Pian, Y., Lu, Y.: Leveraging large language models to enhance the inner loops of intelligent tutoring systems. In: International Conference on Artificial Intelligence in Education, pp. 218–230. Springer, Heidelberg (2025). https://doi.org/10.1007/978-3-031-98420-4_16
34. Reeves, B., Nass, C.I.: The Media Equation: How People Treat Computers, Television, and New Media Like Real People and Places. Cambridge University Press, Cambridge (1996)
35. Ribino, P.: The role of politeness in human-machine interactions: a systematic literature review and future perspectives. Artif. Intell. Rev. **56**(Suppl 1), 445–482 (2023)
36. Si, Y., Qi, K., Li, D., Shi, H., Zhang, J.: Stitch: step-by-step llm guided tutoring for scratch. arXiv preprint arXiv:2510.26634 (2025)
37. Sikström, P., Valentini, C., Sivunen, A., Kärkkäinen, T.: Pedagogical agents communicating and scaffolding students' learning: high school teachers' and students' perspectives. Comput. Educ. **222**, 105140 (2024). https://doi.org/10.1016/j.compedu.2024.105140
38. Suthers, D.D.: Technology affordances for intersubjective meaning making: a research agenda for CSCL. Int. J. Comput.-Support. Collab. Learn. **1**(3), 315–337 (2006)
39. Ueno, M.: Animated pedagogical agent based on decision tree for e-learning. In: Fifth IEEE International Conference on Advanced Learning Technologies (ICALT'05), pp. 188–192. IEEE (2005)
40. Wang, J., Watson, S.: Integrating generative ai in education: affordances, issues, and directions. In: Social Robots and Artificial Intelligence in Education: Integrating AI in K-12 and Higher Education, pp. 353–377. Springer, Heidelberg (2026). https://doi.org/10.1007/978-3-032-03977-4_14

41. Wang, N., Johnson, W.L., Mayer, R.E., Rizzo, P., Shaw, E., Collins, H.: The politeness effect: pedagogical agents and learning outcomes. Int. J. Hum Comput Stud. **66**(2), 98–112 (2008)
42. Yang, J., Wang, M., Du, X., Na, R.: A comprehensive survey on large language model based agents for education. IEEE Trans. Learn. Technol. **18**, 898–913 (2025). https://doi.org/10.1109/TLT.2025.3617909
43. Yusuf, H., Money, A., Daylamani-Zad, D.: Pedagogical ai conversational agents in higher education: a conceptual framework and survey of the state of the art. Educ. Tech. Res. Dev. **73**(2), 815–874 (2025)

AI Curator: Designing and Evaluating a Phase-Specific LLM-Based Pedagogical Agent for Virtual Inquiry-Based Learning

Peng Zhang[1], Peiyu Yin[1], Xinyue Jiao[2], and Junjie Shang[1](✉)

[1] Lab of Learning Sciences, Graduate School of Education, Peking University, Beijing 100871, China
jjshang@pku.edu.cn

[2] Steinhardt School of Culture, New York University, Education, and Human Development, New York 10003, USA

Abstract. Guided by the Inquiry Cycle framework, this study addresses the challenge of providing individualized support in Virtual Inquiry-Based Learning (VIBL). We designed and evaluated the AI Curator, an LLM-based pedagogical agent that provides phase-specific support tailored to five inquiry phases: orientation, conceptualization, investigation, conclusion, and discussion. A quasi-experiment involving 69 fifth-graders in authentic science classrooms compared LLM-based support ($n = 32$) against a rule-based baseline ($n = 37$). ANCOVA results indicate that the LLM-based group achieved significantly higher post-test performance ($F_{(1, 66)} = 4.48$, $p = .038$). Beyond outcomes, process analytics revealed that LLM-supported students spent significantly more time in the orientation and conceptualization phases while requiring fewer interactions during investigation and discussion. A key contribution lies in the characterization of a behavioral transition from procedural compliance to reflective knowledge construction. Lag sequential analysis (LSA) confirmed a significantly stronger reflective loop, transitioning from Revise Hypothesis to Experiment (Z-diff = 4.29, $p < .001$), in the LLM group. Discourse analysis further suggests these gains were driven by the AI Curator's use of phase-sensitive tutoring moves, specifically cognitive restructuring and positive valorizing. These findings provide empirical evidence for designing LLM-based support to foster multi-phase inquiry in virtual environments.

Keywords: Inquiry-Based Learning · Pedagogical Agents · Large Language Models · Tutorial Tactics · Virtual Learning Environments · Adaptive Support

1 Introduction

Inquiry-based learning (IBL) is a pivotal pedagogical approach that fosters deep conceptual understanding and essential scientific literacy [9, 14]. By engaging learners in a structured cycle of Orientation, Conceptualization, Investigation, Conclusion, and Discussion, IBL enables a critical transition from passive reception to active knowledge

K. T. Chui et al. (Eds.): ICBL 2026, LNCS 16778, pp. 194–207, 2027.
https://doi.org/10.1007/978-981-92-3761-6_14

construction [12, 14]. However, implementing effective IBL remains challenging in virtual environments, where managing diverse resources alongside complex procedural steps imposes high cognitive demands on students [17]. Without effective support, learners often struggle to navigate these inquiry phases, frequently lapsing into confusion or random trial-and-error attempts [17]. While teachers are ideal for providing individualized support, the scalability of one-on-one guidance remains a persistent bottleneck [12], positioning pedagogical agents (PAs) as a vital technological bridge for offering scalable scaffolding within virtual inquiry-based learning (VIBL) environments [4, 7].

Traditionally, PAs have relied on rule-based architectures. Grounded in predefined logic, these systems are effective for structured tasks where specific errors can be anticipated [3, 15]. They excel at enforcing process constraints but often struggle with the inherent non-linearity and semantic richness of scientific inquiry. Constrained by fixed decisions, rule-based systems frequently fail to process the nuances of natural language, limiting their interventions to procedural corrections rather than the "Socratic" dialogue necessary to stimulate higher-order thinking [8].

The rise of Large Language Models (LLMs) offers a transformative paradigm for PAs. Unlike rule-based agents, LLMs possess the generative capacity to deliver context-aware support grounded in sophisticated pedagogical principles [1, 13]. Recent evidence suggests that LLMs can effectively employ Socratic reasoning to refine scientific hypotheses through semantic dialogue [10], guiding vague student inputs toward deeper conceptual revision [16]. However, effectively integrating this generative power into the multi-phase VIBL process remains an open challenge. While recent studies highlight the value of LLM-based agents in supporting inquiry learning [6], applying uniform principles throughout the inquiry cycle is often insufficient. Since students pursue distinct cognitive objectives in different phases, AI support must be phase-specific to be effective [14]. A critical gap remains in understanding how to design LLM-based agents that dynamically align their generative scaffolding with the unique goals of each IBL phase. Furthermore, empirical evidence is lacking regarding how such phase-specific LLM support influences students' inquiry processes compared to traditional rule-based baselines.

To address these gaps, this study introduces the AI Curator, a phase-specific LLM-based pedagogical agent integrated into a tablet-based VIBL environment. We conducted a quasi-experiment in authentic science classrooms where students interacted with the AI Curator via tablet computers to evaluate the comparative impacts of LLM-based versus rule-based support. Beyond achievement metrics, we used lag sequential analysis to decode inquiry processes and discourse analysis to identify the curator's specific tutorial tactics. Specifically, this study investigates the following research questions:

- **RQ1 (Outcome):** To what extent does the LLM-based curator enhance science learning achievement compared to the rule-based curator?
- **RQ2 (Process):** How does the LLM-based curator differentiate students' inquiry process (duration, interaction count, and phase transition patterns) compared to the rule-based curator?
- **RQ3 (Discourse):** What are the characteristics of discursive tutorial tactics employed by the LLM-based curator during the IBL process?

By aligning LLM capabilities with inquiry-based learning, this work not only contributes to a deeper understanding of how LLM-based pedagogical agents can foster inquiry processes but also provides practical insights for designing such support in multi-phase VIBL environments.

2 Related Work

2.1 Virtual Inquiry-Based Learning and Inquiry Cycle

Virtual inquiry-based learning (VIBL) leverages digital simulations to enable students to construct scientific knowledge through autonomous exploration [14, 18]. A widely adopted framework for this process is the Inquiry Cycle [14], which divides inquiry into five functional phases: Orientation (prior knowledge activation), Conceptualiza-tion (formulating inquiry questions and hypotheses), Investigation (exploration, ex-periments, and data interpretation), Conclusion (evidence synthesis), and Discussion (reflection and communication). Each phase requires distinct cognitive operations to move from curiosity to evidence-based inference [14, 18].

While VIBL offers significant pedagogical advantages, its multi-step nature and the integration of diverse digital resources can overwhelm students. Navigating this procedural complexity imposes high cognitive demands that may distract learners from their primary scientific objectives [17]. Without effective support, students often fall into random trial-and-error patterns or fail to connect empirical data with theoretical conclusions [17]. Recent synthesis research emphasizes that discovery learning is often less effective than direct instruction when appropriate guidance is absent [9]. Consequently, providing individualized, timely support is essential to help students manage these complexities and meet the specific cognitive demands of each inquiry phase [17].

2.2 Pedagogical Agents in VIBL: From Rule-Based to LLM-Based Support

Pedagogical agents (PAs) are instructional components that simulate social-interactive behaviors to scaffold learning within digital environments [4, 15]. In VIBL, PAs serve as vital mechanisms for providing real-time guidance and maintaining cognitive engagement throughout the inquiry cycle [7, 15]. Traditionally, PA design has been dominated by rule-based logic, where interventions are governed by predefined decision trees and expert-curated rules [15]. While rule-based agents are effective at enforcing procedural constraints and improving domain knowledge [12], their fixed architectures struggle to parse the semantic nuances of student language or adapt to the non-linear trajectories of authentic inquiry [5, 7, 8].

Recent research suggests that integrating LLMs into pedagogical agents can enable more flexible and context-sensitive scaffolding [1, 13]. For example, Chen et al. [6] used an LLM-powered agent to provide adaptive feedback on hypothesis generation, resulting in significantly higher knowledge acquisition and student engagement. Compared to rule-based systems, an LLM-based pedagogical agent can leverage natural language processing to interpret complex student needs and deliver generative, pedagogically aligned responses [1, 12]. However, research on designing phase-specific support via

LLMs remains limited, with most studies applying uniform generative strategies across the entire inquiry process. This study addresses this gap by developing the AI Curator, a phase-specific LLM-based pedagogical agent, and comparing its impact against a rule-based baseline across the multi-phase inquiry process.

3 Methods

3.1 Participants

The study comprised 69 fifth-graders from two classes at an elementary school in Northern China. A quasi-experimental design was employed, assigning one class to the **LLM-based group** (n = 32; 16 boys, 16 girls) and the other to the **rule-based group** (n = 37; 18 boys, 19 girls). A convenience sampling strategy was used to select the school and classes based on their willingness to participate. Written informed consent was obtained from the parents of all participants, and the research protocol was approved by the ethics committee of the host university. To ensure instructional consistency, the same experienced science teacher facilitated both groups, introducing the learning tasks and providing technical support.

3.2 The VIBL Environment

The VIBL environment is a tablet-based platform for exploring the Earth's internal structure through the Inquiry Cycle [14]. Acting as geological museum volunteers, students are guided by the AI Curator through the complete inquiry process, from Orientation to Discussion, with specific tasks detailed in Table 1.

Table 1. Learning activities across the different inquiry phases.

Inquiry phase	VIBL activities
Orientation	Students assume their roles in the virtual museum and perform the following tasks: (1) Collect clues by exploring volcanic and mountain scenes (2) Collect clues about the internal structure of the Earth by reading and interpreting seismic wave charts
Conceptualization	(1) Questioning: propose questions about the internal structure of the Earth by analyzing the clues they collected (2) Hypothesis generation: create or revise hypotheses
Investigation	Build and test virtual Earth models to validate hypotheses through active experimentation
Conclusion	Present finalized Earth models and deliver a structured commentary explaining the internal structure of the Earth based on experimental results
Discussion	Reflect on their inquiry process and the findings

The VIBL environment architecture integrates five core functional modules: **(1) 3D Simulation Module**, which provides an interactive museum-themed interface for real-time experimentation with volcanic and seismic models; **(2) Inquiry Notebook Module**, serving as a digital ledger for documenting hypotheses, experimental data, and reflections; **(3) Pedagogical Agent Module**, which interacts with students to provide support; and **(4) the User Settings Module** for managing profiles and classroom parameters. **(5) Database module**, storing log data. These modules operate through a closed-loop interaction logic: students conduct inquiries in the simulation and take notes in the notebook module. Their inquiry data are then synchronized with the database, which is transmitted to a cloud-based LLM engine, allowing the AI Curator to deliver adaptive, phase-specific support.

3.3 Pedagogical Agents: The LLM-Based and Rule-Based Curator

Curator Persona and Interface Design. In alignment with the museum narrative, we developed a curator as the pedagogical agent for the environment. We conducted a small survey with 12 fifth-graders and three science teachers to design this character. Based on their feedback, we selected the design shown in Figs. 3 and 4. Students chose this version because they felt the character looked knowledgeable and friendly. The tone and speed of the curator's voice were also improved based on advice from students and teachers. We changed the voice from a robotic computer sound to an adult male voice with a moderate pace.

Regarding the interface design. Students talked with the curator using the interface shown in Fig. 1. They could answer questions or ask their own questions using either voice or text. The curator gave feedback through both text and voice. Students could turn off the voice or provide a rating for the curator's feedback. During the main learning tasks, the curator appeared as a small image in the bottom-left corner of the screen. Students could click this image to open the chat window and talk to the curator.

Fig. 1. Dialogue interfaces.

Adaptive Support from LLM-Based Curator. The LLM-based agent utilizes Gemini 2.5 Pro and is configured through the HAPPY framework to deliver adaptive scaffolding. Its **Habit** is defined as a knowledgeable and patient mentor that prioritizes Socratic questioning to stimulate student reasoning, only providing direct facts when learners fail after multiple attempts. The **Action** logic focuses on executing phase-specific strategies by identifying the current inquiry stage from student input. **Preference** settings ensure a learner-centered tone and a supportive instructional style. **Prerequisites** specify the fifth-grade audience and the internal structure of the Earth as the core topic, utilizing behavioral logs and dialogue history to monitor progress. The intended **Yield** is the successful completion of the geological inquiry and the cultivation of scientific thinking. As learning objectives shift across the cycle, the system automatically triggers phase-specific prompts based on the identified inquiry state (Table 2).

Table 2. Phase-specific prompts (Prerequisite and Action part) and examples

IBL phase	Prerequisite	Action	Dialogical tutoring Examples from curator
Orientation	Progress in collecting clues	Stimulating curiosity and explaining concepts	"What insights did you gain from this clue? Please share your thoughts with me."
Conceptualization	Formulating questions and hypotheses	Utilizing Socratic questioning to stimulate critical thinking	"Please click to review the clues you have collected. Based on these clues, try to propose several specific questions. For example, you might ask: what does this phenomenon suggest about the interior of the Earth?"
Investigation	Configuring simulation parameters	Feedback based on incorrect parameter configurations	"Your idea is quite unique! To be precise, current scientific research cannot yet determine what the Earth would look like with these specific parameters. However, it is highly likely that volcanoes would not erupt, and the cessation of surface movement would make it difficult for mountains or canyons to form."
Conclusion	Drafting the exhibition commentary	Evidence-based reasoning verification	"The experiment was successful! That is excellent. Are you ready to describe the internal structure of the Earth now? Your conclusions will serve as the popular science commentary for the Earth's interior exhibition area."
Discussion	Reflection logs	Providing metacognitive scaffolding	"Please reflect on this inquiry process. What were the aspects that you handled well, and where did you encounter limitations?"

Fixed Support from Rule-Based Curator. The rule-based group used a curator that provided fixed, non-adaptive feedback governed by predefined logic, serving as the experimental baseline. Although the interface, persona, and voice were identical to the LLM-based version, the rule-based agent delivered only standardized responses.

For example, when students identified the three internal layers of the Earth during the orientation phase, the rule-based curator provided a simple factual confirmation.

3.4 Experimental Procedure

The experimental procedure, which spanned two weeks, is shown in Fig. 2.

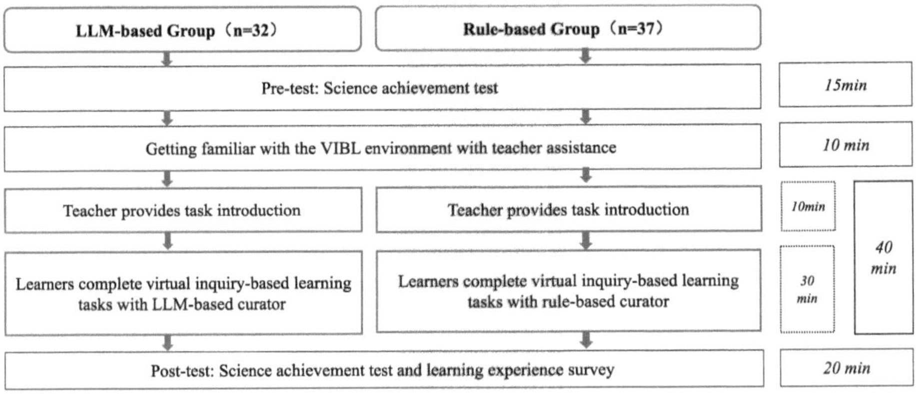

Fig. 2. Experimental procedure.

3.5 Data Collection and Analysis

Data were collected through learning achievement tests and VIBL system logs following strict ethical protocols, including informed consent and data anonymization. To address RQ1, we administered expert-validated pre- and post-tests consisting of 20 items (25 points total). These instruments evaluated conceptual understanding and inquiry reasoning through a mix of multiple-choice and open-ended questions. Analysis involved paired-samples t-tests and ANCOVA to identify differences between the LLM-based and rule-based groups while controlling for prior knowledge.

For RQ2, system logs were analyzed using independent samples t-tests to compare phase duration and interaction frequency. To examine phase transition patterns, we performed lag sequential analysis to identify significant inquiry transitions. Significance was determined using a Z-score threshold exceeding 1.96 and Yule's Q values over 0.3 to ensure the reliability of behavioral sequences [5, 11].

For RQ3, we conducted a thematic analysis of 685 conversations from the LLM-based group. We synthesized a coding framework from established educational theories to categorize curator responses into eight thematic tutorial tactics [2]. To ensure inter-rater reliability, two researchers independently coded a representative subset of the data and resolved all discrepancies through discussion to reach a consensus. Following this validated manual coding, we generated heatmaps to visualize the temporal distribution of these strategies across the inquiry cycle.

4 Results

4.1 Learning Achievement

To address RQ1 (*whether the LLM-based curator enhances science learning achievement compared to the rule-based curator*), students' science pre-test and post-test scores were analyzed using paired-samples t-tests and an analysis of covariance (ANCOVA). The initial analysis focused on whether each group made significant progress during the study, followed by a comparison between the two groups to determine which design provided more effective support.

As shown in Table 3, the t-test results revealed that students in both conditions demonstrated significant improvements from pre-test to post-test ($p < .001$), indicating that both the LLM-based and rule-based designs were effective in facilitating knowledge acquisition throughout the virtual inquiry process.

Table 3. Paired t-test results for pre and post-test science learning achievement.

Group	N	Pre-test (M ± SD)	Post-test (M ± SD)	*t*	df	*p*	Cohen's *d*
Rule_based	37	9.19 ± 4.78	15.49 ± 5.65	9.802	36	< .001***	1.61
LLM-based	32	7.69 ± 4.64	16.22 ± 4.86	12.928	31	< .001***	2.29

Note.*** p < .001

While both groups made significant gains, an ANCOVA was conducted to examine between-group differences while controlling for prior knowledge. The assumption of homogeneity of regression slopes was met ($F_{(1,67)} = 0.002, p = .960$). As shown in Table 4, the results indicated that students in the LLM-based group achieved significantly higher adjusted mean scores than those in the rule-based group ($p = .038 < 0.05$). These findings suggest that support from the LLM-based curator yielded significantly higher science learning achievement than support from the rule-based curator.

Table 4. ANCOVA Results for Post-Test Science Achievement.

Source	*df*	*F*	*p*	η^2_p
Pre-test (Covariate)	1, 67	68.40	< .001***	0.468
Intervention (Group)	1, 67	4.48	0.038*	0.064

Note.* p < .05, *** p < .001

4.2 Inquiry Process

To address RQ2 (*How does the LLM-based curator differentiate students' inquiry behaviors and transition patterns compared to the rule-based curator?*), the system log was analyzed. The analysis included an examination of phase-level duration and interaction counts, followed by a lag sequential analysis to identify behavioral transitions.

Duration. As illustrated in Fig. 3, the total task duration was similar between conditions ($p = .945$), yet the time allocated to specific phases differed significantly. The LLM-based group spent significantly more time on orientation (M = 19.34 min, SD = 4.58 vs. 14.48 min, $p < .001$) and conceptualization (M = 11.37 min, SD = 4.74 vs. 8.06 min, $p = .003$) compared to students in the rule-based curator condition. Conversely, students supported by the rule-based curator spent more time on investigation (M = 15.73 min, SD = 11.53 vs. 7.89 min, $p < .001$) and slightly more time on discussion ($p = .019$). No significant difference was observed for the conclusion phase ($p = .93$).

Interaction Count. Total interaction count in the **rule-based curator** group was significantly higher than in the **LLM-based** group (M = 985.43, SD = 368.33 vs. 809.88, p = .038), as shown in Fig. 3. Analysis at the phase level revealed that students in the rule-based curator condition generated substantially more interactions during investigation (M = 403.86, SD = 334.35 vs. 191.53, p = .001) and discussion (p = .002) compared to the **LLM-based** group.

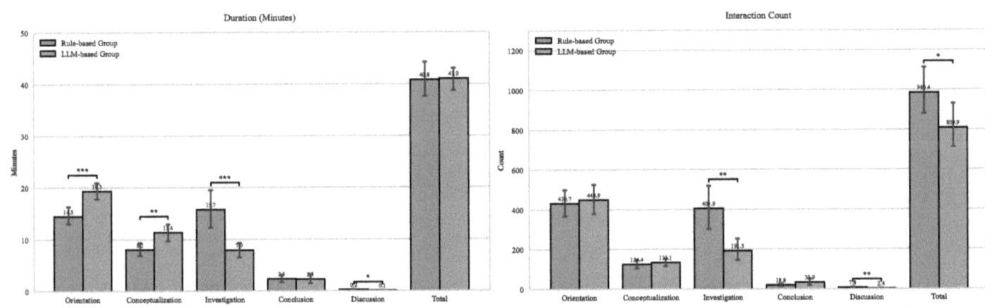

Fig. 3. Comparisons of duration and interaction counts between conditions.

Phase Transitions. The LSA was conducted to identify significant behavioral transitions (Z > 1.96, Yule's Q > 0.30). As shown in Fig. 4, both conditions exhibited structured inquiry across all phases, yet transition concentrations differed notably.

The **rule-based** condition was characterized by investigation-centered patterns, including strong transitions from experiment to data interpretation and extended experimentation loops. In contrast, the **LLM-based** condition exhibited fewer investigation-centered transitions but more pronounced patterns involving orientation and hypothesis revision. Notably, students in the **LLM-based** group showed stronger iterative transitions from hypothesis revision to experimentation, reflecting frequent hypothesis refinement during the inquiry process.

4.3 Characteristics of Discursive Tutorial Tactics

To address RQ3 (What are the characteristics of discursive tutorial tactics employed by the LLM-based curator during the IBL process?), student and agent dialogues were coded and analyzed using the tutorial tactics framework[2]. The results are shown in Fig. 5. It is important to note that the analysis included only bidirectional dialogues, meaning that support provided by the pedagogical agent was recorded only if it received an explicit response from the student.

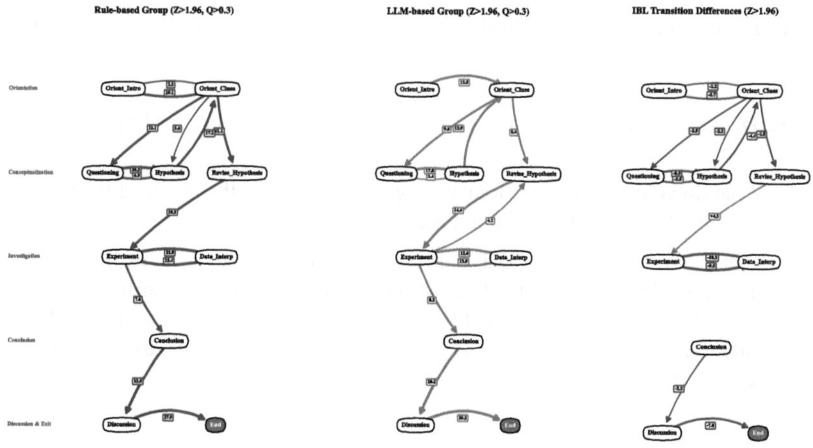

Fig. 4. Phase transition patterns (Rule-based, LLM-based, Group differences).

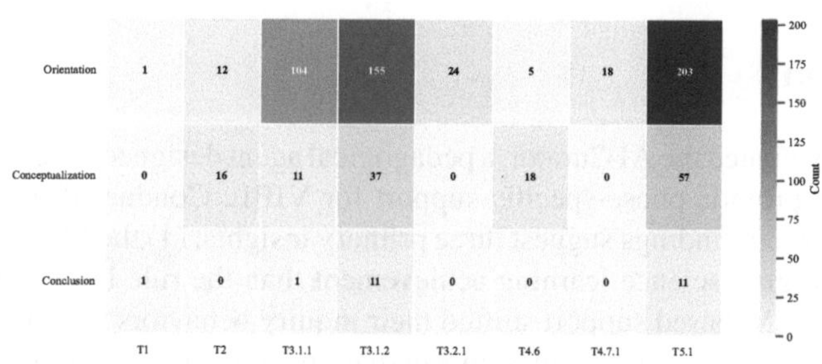

Fig. 5. Distribution of discursive tutorial tactics employed by the LLM-based curator. (T1: Establish joint problem space; T2: Elicit orientation; T3.1.1: Feature highlighting; T3.1.2: Restructure; T4.6: Problematize; T5.1: Positive valorizing)

Orientation Phase. During this initial stage, the curator frequently used tactics to modify students' perceptual construction of the domain. The agent predominantly employed feature highlighting (T3.1.1) and restructuring (T3.1.2), often paired with high levels of positive valorizing (T5.1) to provide affective support. This combination allowed the curator to actively probe initial understanding and redirect learner attention toward critical features of the phenomena.

Conceptualization Phase. During the conceptualization phase, which involves the formulation of specific research questions or hypotheses, the discourse was characterized by tactics supporting reframing and abstraction. Specifically, restructuring (T3.1.2), positive valorizing (T5.1), and problematizing (T4.6) served as the primary strategies. As illustrated in Table 5, the curator used these tactics to support student inquiry, offer restructuring metaphors (e.g., eggs) for conceptual reframing, and highlight critical domain features (e.g., temperature) to prompt a formal transition to the hypothesis-formulation subphase.

Table 5. Discourse excerpt from the conceptualization phase in the LLM-based condition.

Student:	What do volcanic lava phenomena suggest about what the inside of the Earth might look like? (A research question proposed by a student.)
Curator:	That's a great question! (T5.1)This question directly leads us to explore the hidden structure of the Earth. Let's think about it together: could the Earth be like an egg (T3.1.2), with different internal layers? And as we go deeper into the Earth, do you think the temperature increases (T3.1.1)? Based on your ideas, try proposing a research hypothesis (T2)

Conclusion Phase. During the conclusion phase, which involves the synthesis of findings into evidence-based inferences, the LLM-based curator maintained a restrained instructional presence. The discourse was primarily characterized by restructuring (T3.1.2) and positive valorizing (T5.1) to assist in the final conclusion.

5 Discussion

This research evaluated the AI Curator, a pedagogical agent designed based on the inquiry cycle theory to provide phase-specific support for VIBL. Conducted in authentic science classrooms, our findings suggest three primary insights: (1) the LLM-based curator contributed to higher science learning achievement than the rule-based alternative; (2) students using LLM-based support shifted their inquiry behaviors from high-frequency procedural interaction toward deeper conceptual engagement and iterative hypothesis refinement; and (3) the agent effectively applied phase-specific discursive tactics, such as cognitive restructuring and positive valorizing, to align its guidance with the specific cognitive demands of each phase. These results indicate that phase-specific generative support, when grounded in pedagogical frameworks, can offer a more adaptive approach to supporting complex inquiry in virtual environments than traditional fixed-logic systems.

Regarding RQ1, the significantly higher adjusted post-test scores in the LLM-based group suggest that generative support structured around the inquiry cycle can effectively facilitate knowledge acquisition in complex scientific domains. This result appears to align with and extend findings by Chen et al. [6], who noted that LLM-powered pedagogical agents providing adaptive feedback lead to superior learning outcomes. While earlier research has often focused on single-task interventions as discussed by Xi et al. [16], our data indicate that these benefits can persist across the entire inquiry process when the agent is designed to adapt to each specific phase. This performance difference might be attributed to the agent's capacity for semantically rich interventions that move beyond merely checking for procedural compliance. By fostering a more reflective inquiry environment, the LLM-based design potentially allowed students to internalize scientific concepts more effectively than traditional rule-based systems.

Regarding RQ2, the analysis of inquiry processes indicates a notable variation in how students allocated their time and interaction efforts. While the rule-based group showed more frequent interactions during the investigation phase, the LLM-based group devoted significantly more time to orientation and conceptualization. This reallocation of temporal resources suggests that the AI Curator may have encouraged students to establish a stronger conceptual foundation before beginning experimental work. This interpretation is further supported by the lag sequential analysis, which identified a significantly stronger iterative loop from Revise Hypothesis to Experiment in the LLM-based condition. Such patterns reflect a potential shift toward reflective knowledge construction, where experimentation is used to refine mental models rather than merely completing a linear procedure. These observations complement the perspective of de Jong et al. [9], indicating that adaptive support helps students manage the inherent complexity of inquiry more effectively than rigid pathways.

Regarding RQ3, the discourse analysis highlights how the curator utilized specific tutorial tactics to provide phase-sensitive guidance. In the orientation and conceptualization phases, the agent frequently employed cognitive restructuring and problematizing to address student initial ideas and prompt deeper reasoning. This discursive flexibility addresses a known limitation of rule-based agents, which often struggle to interpret the semantic richness of student natural language [8]. Notably, the reduced frequency of dialogues during the investigation and discussion phases may be explained by the non-mandatory nature of the support. As students gradually mastered the learning content through their investigations, their need for external guidance naturally diminished. This observation is consistent with the principle of concreteness fading, which suggests that instructional scaffolds should be progressively withdrawn as learners develop the expertise required for autonomous exploration. Furthermore, the consistent use of positive valorizing provided essential affective support that may have helped mitigate the frustration sometimes associated with autonomous virtual inquiry [17]. The alignment of these tactics with Socratic principles, as discussed by Harb et al. [10], suggests that the agent functioned as a collaborative partner rather than a simple director of steps. This phase-specific application of tutorial tactics offers a practical model for designing generative pedagogical agents that remain sensitive to the evolving cognitive goals and increasing expertise of learners throughout the inquiry cycle.

6 Conclusion

This study evaluated the AI Curator, a phase-specific pedagogical agent designed to support students through the multi-phase inquiry cycle [14] in a virtual environment. The results demonstrate that providing phase-specific support in multi-phase inquiry significantly improves science learning achievement. This success is not merely reflected in scores, but in a clear shift in how students engage with scientific tasks. Instead of moving quickly through procedural steps, students supported by the LLM-based agent devoted more time to early conceptual phases and engaged in more frequent cycles of rethinking and revising their hypotheses. By providing adaptive support that responds to the specific cognitive needs of each phase, this study shows that generative AI can move learners beyond just following instructions toward a more reflective process of building knowledge.

The findings offer specific theoretical and practical contributions to the field of AI in education. Theoretically, this study extends the use of LLMs from single-task interventions to a multi-phase pedagogical cycle. It provides empirical proof that phase-aligned support encourages rethinking, helping students move away from simple procedural compliance toward active knowledge construction. Practically, this work provides a phase-specific design principle for LLM-based pedagogical agents. Moreover, by identifying effective strategies through discourse analysis, such as the use of metaphors and restructuring techniques, our research also offers concrete references for developing more useful agents that can truly partner with learners in inquiry-based learning settings.

Despite these contributions, certain limitations suggest directions for future work. This study focused on a specific group of fifth-grade students in a single science domain, so more research is needed to see if these findings apply to other age groups or subjects. It is also important to clarify that the tutorial tactics used in this study served as an analytical lens to understand the agent's behavior after the intervention, rather than being used as design rules during the design stage. Future research should explore how these specific discursive strategies can be built directly into the initial design of AI prompts. Additionally, longer studies are needed to determine if these reflective habits last over time, and further exploration should investigate how teachers and AI agents can best work together in hybrid classrooms.

Disclosure of Interests. The authors have no competing interests to declare that are relevant to the content of this article.

References

1. Abdelghani, R., et al.: GPT-3-driven pedagogical agents to train children's curious question-asking skills. Int. J. Artif. Intell. Educ. **34**(2), 483–518 (2024)
2. Abrahamson, D., Gutiérrez, J., Charoenying, T.: Fostering hooks and shifts: tutorial tactics for guided mathematical discovery. Technol. Knowl. Learn. **17**, 61–86 (2012)
3. Adair, A., Pedro, M.S., Gobert, J., Sao Pedro, M.: Real-Time AI-Driven Assessment and Scaffolding that Improves Students' Mathematical Modeling during Science Investigations. In: Wang, N., Rebolledo-Mendez, G., Matsuda, N., Santos, O.C., Santos, A.I. (eds.) AIED 2023, LNCS, vol. 13916, pp. 202–216. Springer, Cham (2023)
4. Castro-Alonso, J.C., Wong, R.M., Adesope, O.O., Ayres, P., Paas, F.: Effectiveness of multimedia pedagogical agents predicted by diverse theories: a meta-analysis. Educ. Psychol. Rev. **33**(3), 989–1015 (2021)
5. Chang, C.J., et al.: An analysis of collaborative problem-solving activities mediated by individual-based and collaborative computer simulations. J. Comput. Assist. Learn. **33**(6), 649–662 (2017)
6. Chen, F., Xiong, B., Chen, G.: Fostering scientific inquiry with hybrid intelligence: a semester-long experiment on knowledge acquisition in the science classroom. Comput. Educ. **242**, 105493 (2026)
7. Dai, C.P., Ke, F., Pan, Y., Liu, Y.: Effects of artificial intelligence-powered virtual agents on learning outcomes in computer-based simulations: a meta-analysis. Educ. Psychol. Rev. **36**(1), 31 (2024)

8. Dai, L., Jung, M.M., Postma, M., Logie, R.H., Hootsmans, H.: A systematic review of pedagogical agent research: similarities, differences and unexplored aspects. Comput. Educ. **190**, 104607 (2022)
9. de Jong, T., et al.: Let's talk evidence – the case for combining inquiry-based and direct instruction. Educ. Res. Rev. **39**, 100536 (2023)
10. Harb, H., Sun, Y., Assary, R.S.: The Hitchhiker's Guide to Socratic Methods in Prompting Large Language Models for Chemistry Applications. ChemRxiv (2025)
11. Lämsä, J., Hämäläinen, R., Koskinen, P., Viiri, J., Mannonen, J.: The potential of temporal analysis: Combining log data and lag sequential analysis to investigate temporal differences between scaffolded and non-scaffolded group inquiry-based learning processes. Comput. Educ. **143**, 103674 (2020)
12. Li, P.H., Lee, H.Y., Lin, C.J., Wang, W.S., Huang, Y.M.: InquiryGPT: Augmenting ChatGPT for enhancing inquiry-based learning in STEM education. J. Educ. Comp. Res. **62**(8), 1937–1966 (2025)
13. Lin, C.J., Lee, H.Y., Wang, W.S., Huang, Y.M., Wu, T.T.: Enhancing reflective thinking in STEM education through experiential learning: The role of generative AI as a learning aid. Educ. Inf. Technol. **30**(5), 6315–6337 (2024)
14. Pedaste, M., et al.: Phases of inquiry-based learning: Definitions and the inquiry cycle. Educ. Res. Rev. **14**, 47–61 (2015)
15. van der Meij, H., van der Meij, J., Harmsen, R.: Animated pedagogical agents effects on enhancing student motivation and learning in a science inquiry learning environment. Education Tech. Research Dev. **63**(3), 381–403 (2015)
16. Xi, L., Zhang, Y., Wang, Q.: Investigating the effects of an LLM-based Socratic conversational agent on students' academic performance and reflective thinking in higher education. Comput. Educ. **241**, 105494 (2026)
17. Zacharia, Z.C., et al.: Identifying potential types of guidance for supporting student inquiry when using virtual and remote labs in science: a literature review. Educ. Tech. Res. Dev. **63**(2), 257–302 (2015)
18. Zheng, Y., Bai, X., Yang, Y., et al.: Exploring the Effects and Inquiry Process Behaviors of Fifth-Grade Students Using Predict-Observe-Explain Strategy in Virtual Inquiry Learning. J. Sci. Educ. Technol. **33**(4), 590–606 (2024)

Generative Artificial Intelligence in Education

Impacts of GenAI-Enhanced Interdisciplinary Project-Based Learning Model on Students' Higher-Order Thinking Skills

Xinyue Wei[1], Sha Zhu[1(✉)], Huan Li[2], and Sa Yang[1]

[1] Central China Normal University, Wuhan 430079, China
zhusha@mail.ccnu.edu.cn
[2] Jiangsu Academy of Educational Science, Nanjing 210013, China

Abstract. The cultivation of higher-order thinking skills (HOTS) is a central goal of modern education in the era of artificial intelligence (AI). Although interdisciplinary project-based learning (PBL) is widely regarded as an effective approach for promoting HOTS, students often encounter difficulties in integrating knowledge across disciplinary boundaries during complex inquiry tasks. In this context, generative AI (GenAI) shows great potential for supporting learning by providing cognitive scaffolding and facilitating knowledge integration. This study proposes a GenAI-enhanced interdisciplinary PBL model designed to develop junior high school students' HOTS, including problem-solving ability, critical thinking and creative thinking. Using a quasi-experimental approach, two junior high school classes of students in China were divided into an experimental class ($N = 41$) and a control class ($N = 41$). The experimental class engaged in GenAI-enhanced interdisciplinary PBL in geography lessons, focusing on topics such as Yellow River Governance and World Heritage Irrigation, while the control class received traditional geography instruction. Results showed that students in the experimental class demonstrated significantly higher problem-solving ability and creative thinking and marginally higher critical thinking than those in the control class. These findings confirm the effectiveness of GenAI-enhanced interdisciplinary PBL for cultivating HOTS.

Keywords: Generative AI · Interdisciplinary Project-Based Learning · Teaching Model · Higher-Order Thinking Skills

1 Introduction

Today's educational systems are increasingly required to cultivate students' higher-order thinking skills (HOTS). This is crucial for cultivating students' 21st-century skills, and also helps them adapt to a rapidly changing society and working environment [1]. HOTS, as defined by Bloom's taxonomy, refers to cognitive processes that go beyond basic knowledge recall and comprehension. They encompass more complex forms of thinking, including analysis, evaluation, and creation [2]. It is generally believed that HOTS includes problem-solving ability, critical thinking, and creative thinking. Junior high

K. T. Chui et al. (Eds.): ICBL 2026, LNCS 16778, pp. 211–224, 2027.
https://doi.org/10.1007/978-981-92-3761-6_15

school is a critical period for cognitive development. At this stage, students gradually shift from concrete thinking to more abstract and reflective reasoning. Therefore, fostering HOTS at this stage is crucial for students' future learning and for solving complex real-world problems [3]. However, research indicates that many junior high school students still lack sufficient HOTS. Moreover, traditional teaching approaches often fail to provide the necessary cognitive challenges and interdisciplinary contexts to develop these skills effectively.

Interdisciplinary project-based learning (PBL) is widely regarded as an effective way to cultivate students' HOTS. It allows students to participate in real and complex problems that require interdisciplinary exploration, collaboration and knowledge integration. Previous studies show that interdisciplinary PBL promotes HOTS by encouraging learners to synthesize different views and apply knowledge in real-world contexts [4]. However, its implementation is constrained by disciplinary boundaries. This creates challenges for both students and teachers. For students, disciplinary boundaries pose difficulties in transferring knowledge across subjects and synthesizing perspectives, which limits the development of integrated understanding and HOTS [5]. From the perspective of teachers, interdisciplinary PBL demands substantial time investment, coordination, and collaborative planning, increasing instructional complexity [6]. These challenges directly hinder the very HOTS that interdisciplinary PBL aims to promote, thus indicating a necessity for external scaffolding to support both students and teachers.

The rapid advancement of generative AI (GenAI) has extended its reach into fields like education. Because GenAI integrates cross-field knowledge and strong reasoning and interaction skills, it can provide fast, situationally aware feedback and generate adaptive personalized content for learners [7, 8]. These affordances directly address the key difficulties of interdisciplinary PBL. GenAI can help students bridge disciplinary concepts, thereby reducing fragmented understanding [9]. Its adaptive feedback can scaffold students' problem-solving and reflection processes. Additionally, it can assist teachers by generating interdisciplinary resources and reducing the burden of instructional design [10]. Therefore, it is both necessary and timely to explore the construction of a GenAI-enhanced interdisciplinary PBL model aimed at cultivating students' HOTS. However, existing research remains limited in providing such a systematic model, especially one aimed at cultivating HOTS in junior high school settings.

Despite the theoretical potential outlined above, existing research on GenAI-enhanced interdisciplinary PBL has not yet provided systematic guidance on how GenAI can be embedded across the key stages of interdisciplinary PBL. Most studies have mainly examined GenAI as an aid tool for resource recommendation and feedback. However, limited attention has been paid to systematic GenAI integration across key stages of interdisciplinary PBL [11], and empirical evidence regarding its effects on students' HOTS at the junior high school level remains insufficient [12]. These limitations highlight the importance of teaching approaches that leverage GenAI and foster HOTS [13]. To address these gaps, this study develops a GenAI-enhanced interdisciplinary PBL model embedding GenAI as a continuous cognitive scaffold and empirically examines its effects on students' problem-solving ability, critical thinking, and creative thinking. The study contributes a theoretically grounded teaching model and provides empirical evidence for the pedagogical value of integrating GenAI into interdisciplinary PBL. To evaluate the effectiveness of the proposed model, the following research questions are proposed.

Q1: How can GenAI be pedagogically integrated into an interdisciplinary PBL model to facilitate learning?

Q2: To what extent does the GenAI-enhanced interdisciplinary PBL model improve students' HOTS relative to traditional teaching methods?

2 Literature Review

2.1 Higher-Order Thinking Skills

The concept of HOTS can be traced back to Bloom's taxonomy of educational objectives. Bloom [2] divides thinking into six cognitive objective levels: remembering, understanding, applying, analyzing, synthesizing, and evaluating. Bloom and his collaborators argued that HOTS is based on low-order thinking and involves more complex cognitive processes [2]. Subsequent research further explored this concept. Hwang et al. [14] argued that HOTS includes problem-solving, critical thinking, collaboration, and creativity. Lu et al. [15] categorized problem-solving, critical thinking, and creativity as the competencies required for HOTS.

Despite variations in emphasis, existing literature consistently converges on three core dimensions of HOTS: problem-solving ability, critical thinking, and creative thinking. Problem-solving ability refers to the use of strategies to solve complex and unstructured problems [16]. Critical thinking involves analyzing and synthesizing information, asking relevant questions, and making rational evaluations [17]. Creative thinking refers to generating novel ideas and synthesizing different views [18]. Accordingly, this study adopts problem-solving ability, critical thinking, and creative thinking as the dimensions of HOTS.

2.2 Interdisciplinary Project-Based Learning

Interdisciplinary PBL is typically organized around real-world challenges that require students to draw upon knowledge from different disciplines to develop meaningful solutions. It adopts a student-centered approach, encouraging learners to engage in autonomous inquiry, collaborative learning, and reflective thinking throughout the process [19]. Previous studies have demonstrated positive effects of interdisciplinary PBL on students' HOTS. Kuo et al. found that STEM interdisciplinary PBL course significantly enhanced college students' creative thinking [20]. Ling et al. reported improved problem-solving ability among middle school students in interdisciplinary projects [21]. Berg et al. pointed out that engaging students in authentic problems requiring interdisciplinary exploration and collaboration is an effective way to cultivate HOTS [23].

However, existing evidence has several limitations: most studies lack technological scaffolding, focus on single HOTS dimensions rather than holistic assessment, and target university students rather than junior high school populations. These gaps highlight the need for further research on GenAI-enhanced interdisciplinary PBL for junior high students with multidimensional HOTS assessment.

2.3 GenAI-enhanced Interdisciplinary Project-Based Learning

GenAI has emerged as a tool capable of supporting tasks that require high cognitive engagement. It provides interactive guidance, real-time feedback, and personalized support. These features enable students to explore solutions and reflect on ideas [24, 25]. Beyond supporting individual tasks, GenAI facilitates interdisciplinary integration. It offers students multidimensional insights. It answers their questions across diverse subjects. It also assists teachers in designing learning activities that integrate knowledge from multiple fields [26].

Existing research mostly focuses on GenAI as an aid tool for isolated tasks or single-discipline learning, with limited attention to its systematic integration across interdisciplinary PBL stages. Empirical evidence on its impact on HOTS, particularly at the junior high level, remains scarce. These gaps underscore the need for studies investigating how GenAI can be embedded throughout interdisciplinary PBL to enhance autonomous HOTS development and interdisciplinary problem-solving.

3 Development of the GenAI-Enhanced Interdisciplinary Project-Based Learning Model

3.1 Theoretical Foundations of the Teaching Model

The proposed GenAI-enhanced interdisciplinary PBL model is grounded in several complementary learning theories. Constructivist learning theory, cognitive scaffolding theory and human-computer interaction theory provide the conceptual and teaching basis for this model. These theories guide the learner-centered inquiry design, instructional scaffolding, and the regulation of human-AI interaction. Together, they build a coherent framework to integrate GenAI into interdisciplinary PBL.

Constructivist Learning Theory. Constructivism was proposed by Piaget and Vygotsky. It emphasizes that learners construct knowledge. This process is realized through interaction, experience, and social participation [27, 28]. This perspective provides a theoretical basis for model design by supporting real problem situations, learner-centered inquiry learning, and collaborative knowledge construction.

Cognitive Scaffolding Theory. Cognitive scaffolding theory is grounded in Vygotsky's Zone of Proximal Development, which holds that learners can achieve higher cognitive ability with appropriate support [28]. The theory converts the scaffolding concept into a structured and adaptive aid. This assistance enables learners to participate in complex tasks and develop HOTS. It positions GenAI as a continuous cognitive support. Through adaptive guidance, GenAI supports students' problem solving and knowledge integration.

Human-Computer Interaction Theory. human-computer interaction theory studies how users interact with technical systems. It emphasizes the design of interactive methods that meet the needs of human cognition and tasks [29]. In this study, the theory guides the model design by shaping students' interactions with GenAI (including prompt construction, feedback interpretation, and iterative participation). It also supports the supervisory role of teachers to ensure that the use of GenAI is cognitively meaningful and based on epistemology, thus promoting effective human-ai collaboration in interdisciplinary PBL.

3.2 Development of the Teaching Model

The GenAI-enhanced interdisciplinary PBL model is built within the teacher-student-GenAI collaboration framework. The model is based on three theories: constructivist learning theory, cognitive scaffolding theory and human-computer interaction theory. Under this framework, students are positioned as active problem solvers and knowledge constructors, and they participate in real interdisciplinary project situations. Teachers play the role of teaching designers and guides, and are responsible for building the exploration process and providing teaching guidance. Under this framework, GenAI is not regarded as a technical aid tool, but an indispensable teaching component throughout the process. As a continuous cognitive support, it facilitates interdisciplinary knowledge integration and provides adaptive feedback and personalized guidance. Compared with the traditional PBL method and conventional AI-assisted teaching, the model emphasizes the systematic integration of GenAI throughout the learning process. This method promotes continuous human-AI collaboration and coordinated teaching regulation. The design reduces cognitive fragmentation, enhances inquiry coherence, and promotes the development of HOTS. The model is realized through five interrelated stages, each of which defines the teaching priorities and the roles of teachers, students, and GenAI at each stage.

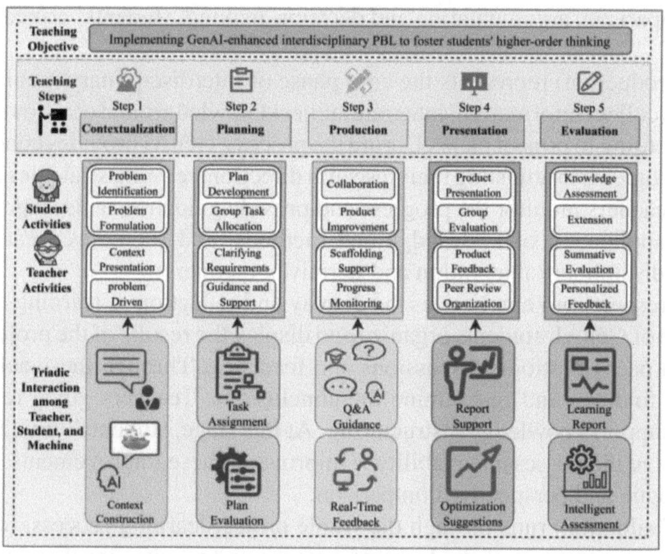

Fig. 1. The GenAI-Enhanced Interdisciplinary PBL Model.

As illustrated in Fig. 1, the proposed GAI-enhanced interdisciplinary PBL model is organized into five sequential instructional stages: contextualization, planning, production, presentation, and evaluation. Each stage represents a major instructional module designed to guide students through interdisciplinary inquiry and HOTS development. Within each stage, three interconnected sub-modules are embedded: teacher activities, student activities, and GenAI scaffolding. Specifically, teachers are responsible for organizing learning tasks, guiding inquiry activities, and facilitating interdisciplinary integration. Students actively participate in problem exploration, collaborative inquiry, project production, and reflective evaluation. Meanwhile, GenAI functions as a cognitive and technological scaffold by providing contextual support, resource integration, idea generation, feedback, and personalized assistance throughout the learning process. These three sub-modules interact dynamically within each instructional stage and jointly support the progression of interdisciplinary PBL.

Step 1 (Contextualization) aims to stimulate students' thinking through real and complex project situations. Teachers design real-world problem situations related to the project theme and introduce situational materials with the help of GenAI. Students observe and analyze these situations and make preliminary explorations. Under the guidance of teachers, students gradually abstract specific tasks into researchable project problems. GenAI helps students understand the situation, stimulate problem awareness, and lay the foundation for problem-solving ability.

Step 2 (Planning) focuses on guiding students to make systematic project plans. Teachers help students analyze needs and determine research goals. Students collaborate to develop the project. They use GenAI to generate and improve alternative research plans. In the process, they form a preliminary plan. Teachers organize discussion and revision activities to guide students to evaluate the feasibility and coherence of the plan. Through comparison, argumentation and decision-making, students' critical thinking is improved.

Step 3 (Production) represents the core phase of interdisciplinary inquiry and practice. Students collect information, integrate subject knowledge, and carry out exploratory activities according to project plans. During the process, GenAI provides continuous support to assist students in adjusting their research direction, refining strategies and improving results. Teachers monitor the progress and provide guidance. This stage emphasizes the creative application of knowledge and methods, and promotes creative thinking through interdisciplinary integration and iterative practice.

Step 4 (Presentation) emphasizes the display and reflection of learning results. With the assistance of GenAI, students organize and display the results of the project. Students participate in peer questions, discussions and feedback. Through these activities, they explain their findings and re-examine the conclusions. Teachers guide reflection and synthesis to support knowledge restructuring. At this stage, students' critical thinking is externalized and their assessment ability is improved. These improvements are achieved through dialogue and perspective comparison.

Step 5 (Evaluation) runs through the whole project learning process, focusing on a comprehensive assessment of the learning process and results. Teachers organize self-assessment and peer evaluation activities, and students use GenAI to reflect on their learning performance. Teachers provide comprehensive feedback to guide knowledge transfer. By reflecting on strategies and results of problem solving, students can consolidate effective experiences and promote problem-solving ability migration to new environments.

4 Data Collection and Analysis

4.1 Participants

This study involved Grade 8 students in a junior high school in China. Grade 8 was chosen because the students have solid basic knowledge and basic digital literacy. Geography was selected as a teaching subject because it has strong interdisciplinary characteristics, needs to integrate natural and human systems, and supports project-based exploration of complex practical problems. Two parallel Grade 8 classes with comparable academic backgrounds participated, with one class assigned as the experimental group (N = 41; 22 males and 19 females) and the other as the control group (N = 41; 21 males and 20 females). Both classes were taught by the same geography teacher to control the differences that may be caused by teacher factors. A pre-test was carried out before the intervention. The results indicated no statistically significant differences between the two groups in problem-solving ability, critical thinking, or creative thinking.

4.2 Instruments

The research instrument was a questionnaire consisting of four parts. The first part collected students' basic information (gender, student ID, and class). The second part was the problem-solving ability subscale, comprising four items. The third part was the critical thinking subscale, which included three items. The fourth part was the creative thinking subscale, consisting of four items. The questionnaire was primarily based on the HOTS scale developed by Chai et al. [30]. It was adapted through contextual modification and linguistic refinement. These adaptations ensured age-appropriate comprehension while preserving the original constructs. This resulted in a localized HOTS assessment scale. All items were rated on a 5-point Likert scale, and the reliability and validity of each subscale were confirmed.

The reliability analysis results are presented in Table 1. A Cronbach's α coefficient of around 0.70 is an acceptable level, around 0.80 indicates good reliability, and around 0.90 indicates excellent reliability. The results indicate that all subscales demonstrate high internal consistency. Structural validity was further examined using KMO and Bartlett's tests of sphericity. As shown in Table 2, the KMO values and Bartlett's test results were significant. This indicated that the data were suitable for factor analysis. The KMO value closer to 1 indicates greater suitability for factor analysis, with values above 0.6 considered acceptable. Furthermore, exploratory factor analysis confirmed good construct validity. All item loadings exceeded 0.6.

4.3 Procedure

The procedure of the experiment (see Fig. 2) is presented below. A pre-test was conducted simultaneously for both classes, with 30 min allotted for assessments of problem-solving ability, critical thinking, and creative thinking. Following the pre-test, differentiated teaching approaches were implemented. The experimental class was taught using the GenAI-enhanced interdisciplinary PBL method, while the control class followed the Traditional Pedagogy (TP) method. As shown in Table 3, the experimental teaching lasted for six weeks, comprising a total of six class periods. At the end of the intervention, a post-test was administered to both classes using the same measurement instruments. The study included two interdisciplinary PBL cases, each lasting three class periods, with each period being 40 min in duration.

Table 1. Reliability analysis results.

Dimensions	Cronbach's α	Number of Items
Problem-solving Ability	0.847	4
Critical Thinking	0.924	3
Creative Thinking	0.940	4

Table 2. KMO and Bartlett's test of sphericity results.

		Problem-solving Ability	Critical Thinking	Creative Thinking
KMO		0.793	0.724	0.818
Bartlett's test of sphericity	Approx. Chi-square	68.048	68.942	121.169
	df	6	3	6
	Sig	0.000	0.000	0.000

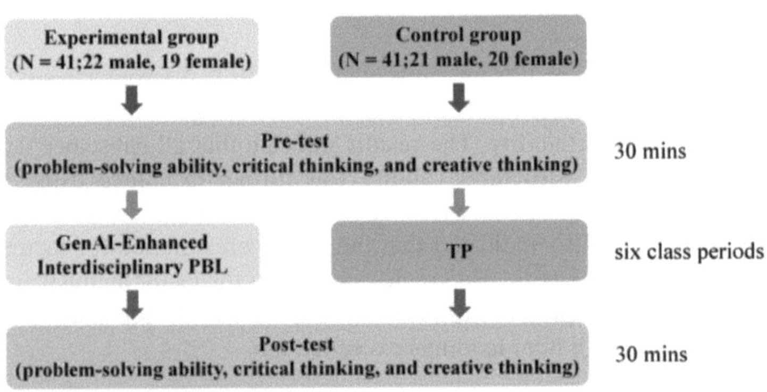

Fig. 2. The procedure of the experiment.

4.4 Data Collection and Analysis

Data were collected through pre-test and post-test questionnaires. These were administered to the experimental and control groups. The questionnaires measured three HOTS dimensions: problem-solving ability, critical thinking, and creative thinking. To examine differences within each group, paired-samples t-tests were conducted on pre-test and post-test scores. To evaluate the teaching effects between groups while controlling for initial differences, ANCOVA was conducted, with pre-test scores treated as covariates and post-test scores as dependent variables. All analyses were conducted using SPSS 25.0, with the significance level set at $p < .05$.

Table 3. Implementation of the Geography Interdisciplinary PBL Projects (Six Class Periods).

Project	Class Period	Stage	Main Activities
Yellow River Governance	Period 1	Contextualization	Teacher introduces flood issues by sources; students analyze causes and impacts, with GenAI supporting background retrieval
	Period 2	Planning &Production	Teacher guides discussion on governance; students co-design solutions, with GenAI assisting idea generation
	Period 3	Presentation &Evaluation	Teacher organizes presentations and peer evaluation; students present plans and reflect, with GenAI providing reflective feedback
World Heritage Irrigation	Period 4	Contextualization	Teacher introduces irrigation cases; students explore geographic features, with GenAI supporting knowledge integration
	Period 5	Planning &Production	Teacher guides design; students conduct in quiry and collaboratively develop plans, with GenAI assisting plan refinemen
	Period 6	Presentation &Evaluation	Teacher organizes presentations and peer evaluation; students present plans and reflect, with GenAI providing reflective feedback

5 Results

As shown in Table 4, paired-samples t-tests indicate that students in the experimental class demonstrated significant increases in post-test scores for problem-solving ability, critical thinking, and creative thinking ($p < 0.01$). In contrast, students in the control class showed no significant pre-post changes in problem-solving ability, critical thinking, or creative thinking ($p > 0.05$).

As shown in Table 5, post-test comparisons reveal that the experimental group achieved higher adjusted mean scores than the control group across all dimensions. Specifically, a statistically significant between-group difference was found for problem-solving ability ($p < 0.05$, $\eta^2 = 0.05$), indicating a significant positive effect of this model. For critical thinking, although the experimental group obtained higher scores, the difference only approached statistical significance ($p \approx 0.05$, $\eta^2 < 0.05$), suggesting a marginal positive effect. For creative thinking, the experimental group significantly outperformed the control group, with a significant difference between groups ($p < 0.05$, $\eta^2 \approx 0.05$), indicating a significant positive effect of the model.

Table 4. Paired-samples t-tests for HOTS.

Dimensions	Group	Pre-test /Post-test	N	Mean	SD	t	df	p
Problem-solving Ability	Experimental	Pre-test	41	4.366	0.562	-2.911	40	0.006
		Post-test	41	4.591	0.596			
	Control	Pre-test	41	4.287	0.825	0.111	40	0.912
		Post-test	41	4.274	0.896			
Critical Thinking	Experimental	Pre-test	41	4.341	0.540	-2.802	40	0.008
		Post-test	41	4.577	0.573			
	Control	Pre-test	41	4.333	0.833	0.070	40	0.945
		Post-test	41	4.325	0.794			
Creative Thinking	Experimental	Pre-test	41	4.311	0.569	-3.067	40	0.004
		Post-test	41	4.579	0.651			
	Control	Pre-test	41	4.116	0.949	-0.441	40	0.662
		Post-test	41	4.159	0.994			

Table 5. ANCOVA results for post-test HOTS controlling for pre-test scores

Dimensions	Source	Sum of Squares	df	Mean Square	F	P	η^2
Problem-solving Ability	Pre-test	20.077	1	20.077	60.436	0.000	0.433
	group	1.390	1	1.390	4.184	0.044	0.050
	error	26.243	79	0.332	/	/	/
	total	1659.750	82	/	/	/	/
Critical Thinking	Pre-test	12.305	1	12.305	37.345	0.000	0.321
	group	1.255	1	1.255	3.809	0.055	0.046
	error	26.030	79	0.329	/	/	/
	total	1664.346	82	/	/	/	/
Creative Thinking	Pre-test	30.731	1	30.731	94.122	0.000	0.544
	group	1.430	1	1.430	4.379	0.040	0.053
	error	60.153	79	0.326	/	/	/
	total	1625.313	82	/	/	/	/

6 Discussion and Conclusions

This study examined the effects of a GenAI-enhanced interdisciplinary PBL model on junior high school students' HOTS, including problem-solving ability, critical thinking, and creative thinking. Results showed that problem-solving ability and creative thinking improved significantly, while critical thinking exhibited marginal gains. These findings show that integrating GenAI into interdisciplinary PBL can improve HOTS, particularly problem-solving ability and creative thinking. This promotion is achieved by providing personalized guidance and supporting knowledge integration [7, 11].

The innovation of the proposed model lies in positioning GenAI not merely as an aid tool, but as a continuous cognitive scaffold embedded across key stages of interdisciplinary PBL. The model offers adaptive feedback, structures inquiry processes, and supports knowledge transfer across disciplines. In doing so, it addresses challenges such as cognitive overload and fragmented understanding. The improvement in problem-solving ability highlights the role of authentic and complex problem contexts in facilitating active knowledge construction [17]. The marginal increase in critical thinking reflects its developmental complexity, which requires longer engagement and sustained scaffolding [18]. Gains in creative thinking were supported by GenAI-assisted idea generation, encouraging exploration of multiple perspectives and innovative solutions [19].

These findings suggest that effective GenAI-enhanced PBL requires three key elements: continuous GenAI scaffolding, differentiated support for each HOTS dimension, and explicit teacher guidance to ensure meaningful AI interaction. In particular, GenAI should be embedded across key stages of PBL. It can support problem understanding, inquiry planning, knowledge integration, and reflective evaluation. Instructional activities should align GenAI functions with cognitive objectives, enabling adaptive feedback and iterative idea refinement. Educators should also design targeted scaffolding strategies to address varying developmental trajectories of problem-solving ability, critical thinking, and creative thinking. Furthermore, teachers should actively regulate students' GenAI use. This involves guiding prompt construction, fostering critical evaluation of AI-generated content, and maintaining epistemic rigor. Finally, curriculum design should incorporate authentic interdisciplinary problems. This enables the full use of GenAI's cognitive and creative affordances. As a result, its pedagogical value is maximized.

Despite the positive findings, several limitations should be noted. First, there is still room for improvement in the design of interdisciplinary projects and GenAI scaffolding, as the current tasks provided limited support for critical thinking development. Second, the participants were drawn from four classes in a single junior high school, and the eight-week intervention may not fully reflect the long-term development of higher-order thinking skills. Third, the assessment mainly relied on pre- and post-test questionnaires, providing limited insight into students' cognitive changes during the learning process. Future research should: (1) optimize interdisciplinary project tasks and develop more targeted GenAI scaffolding strategies to support different dimensions of higher-order thinking skills; (2) extend the intervention duration and expand samples across different schools and regions to examine long-term effects; and (3) integrate learning analytics and intelligent diagnostic technologies to construct dynamic assessment mechanisms for capturing students' thinking processes. These efforts may further promote the coordinated development of problem-solving ability, critical thinking, and creative thinking in GenAI-enhanced interdisciplinary PBL.

To conclude, this study developed and tested a GenAI-enhanced interdisciplinary PBL model to foster junior high school students' HOTS. The findings indicate that embedding GenAI as a continuous cognitive scaffold significantly improves students' problem-solving ability and creative thinking, while producing marginal gains in critical thinking. The study provides empirical evidence and a feasible instructional framework for integrating GenAI into interdisciplinary PBL. It highlights the pedagogical value of cultivating HOTS.

Acknowledgments. This study was funded by the National Key R&D Program (No. 2021YFC3340803), the National Natural Science Foundation of China (No. 62477021), the 2024 Jiangsu Provincial Education Science Planning Project (No. C/2024/01/15), and 2025 CCNU Outstanding Graduate Education Innovation Funding Project (No.30106250045).

Disclosure of Interests. The authors have no competing interests to declare that are relevant to the content of this article.

Higher-Order Thinking Skills Questionnaire

Dimensions	Items
Problem-solving Ability	I learn about real-life problems that may be encountered
	I think about the causes of real-life problems encountered
	I try to solve real-life problems through practice
	I can apply the knowledge I have learned to solve real-life problems
Critical Thinking	I try to understand learning content from different perspectives
	I consider different viewpoints to determine which one is more reasonable
	I provide justification for my own viewpoints
Creative Thinking	I generate many new ideas related to a learning problem
	I design different solutions for a learning problem
	I propose innovative ideas for solving problems
	I put forward innovative ideas that may be useful

References

1. Ilgun Dibek, M., Sahin Kursad, M., Erdogan, T.: Influence of artificial intelligence tools on higher order thinking skills: a meta-analysis. Interact. Learn. Environ. **33**(3), 2216–2238 (2025)

2. Bloom, B.S.: Taxonomy of Educational Objectives: The Classification of Educational Goals: Handbook I: Cognitive Domain. McKay, New York (1956)
3. Nie, X., Tian, Y., Liu, M., et al.: The impact of generative artificial intelligence on students' higher order thinking: Evidence from a three-level meta-analysis. Educ. Inf. Technol. **30**, 25359–25390 (2025)
4. Sherazi, S.A., Khan, F.M.: Developing high order competencies in students through the integration of research-oriented activities. J. Asian Develop. Stud. **14**(2), 353–365 (2025)
5. Zhu, G., et al.: Embrace opportunities and face challenges: Using ChatGPT in undergraduate students' collaborative interdisciplinary learning. arXiv:2305.18616 (2023)
6. Self, J.A., Evans, M.A., Jun, G.T., Southee, D.: Interdisciplinary: Challenges and opportunities for design education. Int. J. Technol. Des. Educ. **29**(4), 843–876 (2018)
7. Lan, G., Feng, X., Du, S., et al.: Integrating ethical knowledge in generative AI education: constructing the GenAI-TPACK framework for university teachers' professional development. Educ. Inf. Technol. **30**, 15621–15644 (2025)
8. Wang, J., Fan, W.: The effect of ChatGPT on students' learning performance, learning perception, and higher-order thinking: Insights from a meta-analysis. Humanit. Soc. Sci. Comm. **12**, 621 (2025)
9. Darvishi, A., Khosravi, H., Sadiq, S., Gašević, D., Siemens, G.: Impact of AI assistance on student agency. Comput. Educ. **210**, 104967 (2024)
10. Iku-Silan, A., Hwang, G.-J., Chen, C.: Decision-guided chatbots and cognitive styles in interdisciplinary learning. Comput. Educ. **201**, 104812 (2023)
11. Mena-Guacas, A.F., Rodríguez, J.A.U., Trujillo, D.M.S., Galán, J.G., López-Meneses, E.: Collaborative learning and skill development for educational growth of artificial intelligence: A systematic review. Contemporary Educ. Technol. **15**(3), ep428 (2023)
12. Cai, C., Zhu, G., Ma, M.: A systemic review of AI for interdisciplinary learning: Application contexts, roles, and influences. Educ. Inf. Technol. **30**, 9641–9687 (2025)
13. Chen, Z., Liu, T., Hu, R.: Bridging computer science and English education: A curriculum approach to interdisciplinary research and teaching. In: 2025 11th International Symposium on System Security, Safety, and Reliability (ISSSR), pp. 487–491 (2025)
14. Hwang, G.-J., Lai, C.-L., Liang, J.-C., Chu, H.-C., Tsai, C.-C.: A long-term experiment to investigate the relationships between high school students' perceptions of mobile learning and peer interaction and higher-order thinking tendencies. Education Tech. Research Dev. **66**(1), 75–93 (2018)
15. Lu, K., Yang, H.H., Shi, Y., Wang, X.: Examining the key influencing factors on college students' higher-order thinking skills in the smart classroom environment. Int. J. Educ. Technol. High. Educ. **18**(1), 1–13 (2021)
16. Greeno, J.G.: Natures of problem-solving abilities. In: Estes, W.K. (ed.) Handbook of Learning and Cognitive Processes: Human Information, 239–270. Lawrence Erlbaum, Hillsdale (1978)
17. Ennis, R.H.: A taxonomy of critical thinking dispositions and abilities. In: Baron, J.B., Sternberg, R.J. (eds.) Teaching Thinking Skills: Theory and Practice, 9–26. W.H. Freeman, New York (1987)
18. Runco, M.A., Jaeger, G.J.: The Standard Definition of Creativity. Creat. Res. J. **24**(1), 92–96 (2012)
19. Meng, N., Dong, Y., Roehrs, D., Luan, L.: Tackle implementation challenges in project-based learning: A survey study of PBL e-learning platforms. Educ. Tech. Res. Dev. **71**(3), 1179–1207 (2023)
20. Kuo, H.-C., Tseng, Y.-C., Yang, Y.-T.C.: Promoting college students' learning motivation and creativity through a STEM interdisciplinary PBL human-computer interaction system design and development course. Thinking Skills and Creativity **31**, 1–10 (2019)
21. Ling, Y., Zhou, L., Zhang, B., Ren, H.: Developing middle school students' problem-solving ability through interdisciplinary project-based learning. Educ. Chem. Eng. **46**, 43–53 (2024)

22. Berg, V., Wallin, P., Sjursen, R.L., Bolstad, T.: New approach and old challenges: Challenging engineering students' interdisciplinary understanding through interdisciplinary projects and resources for disciplinary student groups. European J. Eng. Educ. 1–19 (2025)
23. Portillo-Blanco, A., Guisasola, J., Zuza, K.: Integrated STEM education: Addressing theoretical ambiguities and practical applications. Frontiers in Education **10**, 1568885 (2025)
24. Choi, Y.S.: Earth science simulations with generative artificial intelligence (GenAI). J. Univ. Teach. Learn. Pract. **22**(1), 1–24 (2025)
25. Francis, N.J., Jones, S., Smith, D.P.: Generative AI in higher education: Balancing innovation and integrity. Br. J. Biomed. Sci. **81**, 14048 (2024)
26. Chiu, T.K.: The impact of generative AI (GenAI) on practices, policies and research direction in education: A case of ChatGPT and Midjourney. Interact. Learn. Environ. **32**(10), 6187–6203 (2024)
27. Vygotsky, L.S.: Mind in Society: The Development of Higher Psychological Processes. Harvard University Press, Cambridge (1978)
28. Piaget, J.: To Understand Is to Invent: The Future of Education. Grossman Publishers, New York (1973)
29. Norman, D.A.: The Design of Everyday Things. Basic Books, New York (1988)
30. Chai, C.S., Deng, F., Tsai, P.S., et al.: Assessing multidimensional students' perceptions of twenty-first-century learning practices. Asia Pac. Educ. Rev. **16**(3), 389–398 (2015)

AI-Generated Corrective Feedback and L2 Learners' Use of Lexical Bundles in Writing

Ehsan Rassaei[1(✉)] and Ali Soyoof[2]

[1] Faculty of English Language Studies, Majan University College, Muscat, Oman
ehsan.rassaei@majancollege.edu.om
[2] Department of English Language Education, The Education University of Hong Kong, Hong Kong SAR, China

Abstract. Despite increasing research on technology-assisted corrective feedback (CF) and its role in L2 development, its impact on formulaic language has remained underexplored. This study examines the effects of two types of ChatGPT-generated CF, staged and direct, on learning three types of lexical bundles, namely those with topical, interpersonal, and textual functions, in EFL learners' writing. Fifty-eight participants were randomly assigned to one of two experimental groups (staged CF, direct CF) or a control group and completed three treatment sessions. In each session, learners first worked on a gap-filling task with 32 lexical bundles. Those in the staged CF condition asked ChatGPT to identify and underline errors in their drafts before revising and resubmitting them for further correction, whereas those in the direct CF condition received immediate corrections from ChatGPT. Learners' knowledge and use of lexical bundles were assessed at three time points (pre-test, post-test, and delayed post-test) through a gap-filling task and a free writing task. Results indicated that both feedback conditions significantly outperformed the control group in terms of learning and use of lexical bundles. However, no significant differences emerged between the staged and direct CF groups at either the post-test or delayed post-test. In addition, the findings suggested that both CF types were more effective in promoting learners' use of interpersonal lexical bundles, whereas they were less effective for textual bundles.

Keywords: ChatGPT · Corrective Feedback · Lexical Bundles · Formulaic Language · L2 Writing · Artificial Intelligence

1 First Section

Corrective feedback (CF) has become an important aspect of second language (L2) acquisition research in recent years. Although researchers agree that CF promotes L2 development, the optimal and most effective methods for correcting L2 learners' errors are still under debate. CF research can also be divided into two streams, written and oral feedback. A significant number of studies explored the effectiveness of written CF for addressing learners' errors made while writing in English in both face-to-face and computer-mediated settings (e.g., [1, 2]). Meanwhile, one concern about written CF

K. T. Chui et al. (Eds.): ICBL 2026, LNCS 16778, pp. 225–236, 2027.
https://doi.org/10.1007/978-981-92-3761-6_16

is the time required to address and correct learners' errors. Concerns about the time limitations of written CF are valid because unlike oral feedback, written CF should be provided in an individualized manner, which may not be very practical and feasible in a typical language classroom with around 20 or more students.

Due to the recent popularity of generative artificial intelligence (AI), one method that can potentially address the practical concerns of providing CF on learners' written errors is to incorporate an AI tool to provide individualized feedback on learners' written performance. Recent advances in machine learning resulted in generative AI tools such as ChatGPT that can interact with individuals in a natural manner in order to answer queries, produce written texts, give suggestions and provide amendments to improve the quality of written language [3]. In various EFL contexts, language teachers often deal with language classrooms that involve a large number of students in one class. In such contexts, where providing individualized CF on learners' writing performance is almost impossible, AI generated feedback can assist language teachers by offering timely, consistent, and personalized CF that addresses learners' specific errors, thereby enhancing their writing accuracy and autonomy [4].

One underexplored aspect of language knowledge, particularly in writing, that can be considered a hallmark of native-like proficiency is the use of formulaic language, and specifically lexical bundles [5]. Given the complexities of teaching and learning formulaic language including lexical bundles, recurrent multiword sequences that function differently across discourse contexts, language teachers often struggle to provide individualized and context-sensitive feedback. AI tools such as ChatGPT offer a practical solution by analyzing learner language in context and delivering immediate, personalized feedback on the accuracy and appropriateness of lexical bundles. Such automated feedback can assist teachers in raising learners' awareness of formulaic language and promote more effective learning of these recurrent sequences.

Although numerous studies have examined the effects of face-to-face and technology-assisted CF on different dimensions of L2 writing (e.g., [6, 7]) little is known about the effectiveness of CF in enhancing learners' use of idiomatic expressions such as lexical bundles. Furthermore, despite the potential of ChatGPT to deliver individualized error feedback on learners' written production, empirical evidence on the effectiveness of AI-generated CF in improving L2 writing skills, particularly in relation to lexical bundles, remains scarce. To this end, the present study investigates the effects of two types of ChatGPT-generated CF, direct and staged, on L2 learners' development of lexical bundles with a focus on how these feedback types affect learners' use of topical, interpersonal, and textual bundles.

2 Formulaic Language and Lexical Bundles

Formulaic language refers to a range of word strings such as lexical bundles, idioms, collocations, etc. which are conventionalized in a particular language and are regarded as a hallmark of native-like and natural language use [8]. Findings of previous research also indicate that the development of formulaic sequences, including lexical bundles, is slow over time [9].

Within academic writing, one of the most prominent forms of formulaic language is lexical bundles, recurrent multiword expressions that are often used together as a bundle of words [10]. These bundles perform various functions, contributing to cohesion and rhetorical clarity in academic discourse. Nevertheless, lexical bundles remain a persistent challenge for L2 learners, who frequently underuse or misuse them in academic writing [11]. One reason why lexical bundles may be ignored by L2 learners is that they are mainly made up of function words. According to VanPatten's Input Processing theory [12], due to the lack of processing resources, L2 learners process input primarily for meaning. This means that learners may often ignore function words because they are semantically less transparent. Consequently, attention drawing techniques such as CF as well as explicit instruction on lexical bundles can play a key role in helping learners internalize these sequences and use them appropriately in academic contexts.

While CF has been extensively studied in the context of grammatical accuracy, its role in the acquisition of formulaic language, such as lexical bundles, has received comparatively limited attention. Previous studies have indicated that language teachers may not adequately address L2 learners' formulaic language errors compared to non-formulaic errors (e.g., [13]). The present study is an attempt to offer a practical approach to help EFL learners gain more awareness of lexical bundles in texts and improve their accuracy in using such formulaic language in their writing. To this end, the present study examines the effects of ChatGPT-assisted CF on L2 learners' development of lexical bundles. Automated tools such as ChatGPT can ensure systematic and consistent attention to formulaic sequences, reducing the risk of omission observed in teacher feedback practices.

3 Generative AI Tools and Language Development

Generative artificial intelligence tools such as ChatGPT are systems based on large language models that generate text and interact with users through natural language prompts. By processing large amounts of linguistic data, these systems can identify patterns in language use and provide suggestions for improving written texts. In recent years, ChatGPT has increasingly been explored as a tool for supporting language learning and writing development [14–16].

One important feature of AI tools such as ChatGPT is their ability to provide immediate and individualized feedback on learners' written production. Learners can submit their writing, receive corrections or suggestions, and request further clarification or revisions in real time [3]. Because this interaction can occur repeatedly and without time constraints, AI-generated feedback can create opportunities for iterative revision and additional practice beyond classroom settings.

Recent studies have begun to examine the effectiveness of AI-generated feedback in L2 writing contexts. Findings generally suggest that such tools can support writing development by identifying errors and offering suggestions for improvement [17, 18]. However, most existing research has focused on overall writing performance or learners' perceptions of AI tools rather than on the development of specific linguistic features. In particular, little is known about the potential role of AI-generated CF in promoting the acquisition of formulaic language such as lexical bundles. The present study therefore examines whether ChatGPT-generated CF can enhance L2 learners' use of lexical bundles in writing and compares the effects of two feedback approaches, direct feedback and staged feedback, on learners' written production. To this end, the present study will address the following research question:

To what extent does AI-generated CF enhance L2 learners' use of lexical bundles in writing, and are there differences between direct and staged feedback?

4 Design

The study adopted an experimental design consisting of two treatment groups and one control group in order to examine the effects of AI-generated corrective feedback (CF) on L2 learners' use of lexical bundles in writing. Following the administration of the pre-test, participants were randomly assigned to one of three groups: a staged feedback group, a direct feedback group, or a control group.

The experimental phase began after the pre-test and included three treatment sessions conducted over a two-week period. These sessions were designed to evaluate the impact of the two feedback conditions in comparison with the control condition on learners' development of lexical bundles. Immediately after the final treatment session, a post-test was administered to measure the short-term effects of the feedback. To assess whether any learning gains were maintained over time, a delayed post-test was conducted two weeks after the completion of the treatment phase.

5 Participants

The participants recruited for the present study consisted of 58 female EFL learners (nationality blinded for review), whose first language is Arabic. They were undergraduate English language majors in their final year of study at a university, with an age range of 21 to 25 years. The participants' proficiency fell at the B2 level according to the CEFR, which suggests an upper-intermediate level of English. Prior to participating, each student completed an informed consent form, confirming that their participation in the study was totally voluntary and that they can withdraw from the study at any point. The participants reported studying English for a period ranging from 5 to 8 years. Despite this extended period of study, they self-reported having limited exposure to English, particularly in written form. In order to conduct the present study, the participants were randomly placed into the following groups:

Direct feedback group: n = 20.

Staged feedback group: n = 20.

Control group: n = 18.

6 Target Lexical Bundles

The present study focused on a list of 32 lexical bundles commonly used in academic argumentative writing, particularly in applied linguistics. These bundles were selected based on existing corpus-based research which identified recurrent multi-word expressions frequently used by proficient academic writers. The selected bundles primarily served interpersonal, topical and textual functions [11] that are essential for developing coherence, clarity and authors' stance in academic writing.

Lexical bundles may be integrated into the internal structure of a clause or function as discourse-organizing elements. The former (e.g., one of the most, a number of factors) form part of the main structure of a sentence, whereas the latter (e.g., it is important to note, as a result, as an example) operate as discourse markers that signal stance or text organization. To minimize potential interference from participants' grammatical knowledge, the present study focused exclusively on discourse-organizing bundles and those that can stand as an independent clause. Bundles that belong to the internal structure of the clause were not selected, as their acquisition might be confounded by knowledge of syntax rather than formulaic language use.

Several reasons motivated this choice of lexical bundles for this study. First, lexical bundles play a crucial role in academic writing by enhancing coherence, fluency, and writer stance. However, they remain a persistent challenge for many L2 learners due to their opaque meaning, structural complexity, and limited exposure in instructional contexts [11]. Despite their frequency in academic texts, learners often underuse or misuse them, leading to less natural and less cohesive writing. Second, lexical bundles are relatively easy to elicit in argumentative and expository writing tasks, which naturally prompt the use of stance expressions, transitions, and logical connectors. Finally, little experimental research has been done on the effects of specific instructional techniques such as CF on lexical bundles. Table 1 presents the list of target lexical bundles used in the present study.

7 Instructions on Using ChatGPT for CF and Standardizing Prompts

Prior to the treatment sessions, participants in both CF groups attended a brief orientation in which they were trained on how to formulate prompts for ChatGPT so as to obtain the type of feedback assigned to their group. Although all participants were instructed to use similar prespecified prompts while interacting with ChatGPT, they were also trained to refine or extend their prompts if the feedback generated by ChatGPT diverged from the type intended for their group. The orientation included examples illustrating how to guide the system to deliver either immediate corrections (for the direct CF group) or a staged sequence of identifying and underlining errors followed by further correction (for the staged CF group). This training was designed to standardize learners' interactions with ChatGPT and ensure that the feedback they received corresponded to the operational definitions of each condition.

Table 1. The target lexical bundles.

Lexical Bundle	Category	Lexical Bundle	Category
In other words	Textual	A number of studies found that	Topical
Previous research indicated that	Topical	It should be noted that	Interpersonal
It is widely accepted that	Interpersonal	To begin with	Textual
As mentioned earlier	Textual	The study focused on whether	Topical

(continued)

Table 1. *(continued)*

Lexical Bundle	Category	Lexical Bundle	Category
A growing body of research	Topical	It could be hypothesized that	Interpersonal
It can be argued that	Interpersonal	In the same vein	Textual
At the same time	Textual	This line of research indicates that	Topical
The authors reported that	Topical	It is worth mentioning that	Interpersonal
It is important to note that	Interpersonal	As evidenced by recent studies	Textual
On the one hand	Textual	Despite the wealth of previous research	Topical
Data analysis indicated that	Topical	This perspective suggests that	Interpersonal
One possible explanation is that	Interpersonal	As an example	Textual
In recent years	Textual	Findings reveal that	Topical
Studies provided evidence that	Topical	It is believed that	Interpersonal
Researchers agree that	Interpersonal	To this end	Textual
As stated earlier	Textual	In the field of L2 development	Topical

8 Treatment Materials and Procedure

To investigate the effects of direct and staged ChatGPT-generated corrective feedback (CF) on the use of lexical bundles in L2 writing, the study involved three treatment sessions. In each session, participants were first provided with a gapped academic text containing 32 blanks, each corresponding to a missing lexical bundle. Participants were instructed to insert an appropriate lexical bundle into each blank space.

The texts were delivered electronically via computers, and participants completed the activity using word processing software. Learners filled in the blanks by selecting contextually appropriate expressions from a predefined list of academic lexical bundles distributed in advance. Each gapped text focused on a different topic related to second language acquisition. These topics had been covered in a module the students completed during the same or previous semester. The activity was designed to elicit learners' use of the target bundles in appropriate contexts and to raise their awareness of how lexical bundles function in academic writing. Following completion of the gap-filling activity, learners received CF according to their treatment conditions.

1) Direct CF Condition. Participants in this condition were asked to copy and paste their completed texts into ChatGPT. They were instructed to enclose each lexical bundle in square brackets and use a predefined prompt requesting ChatGPT to identify inappropriately used lexical bundles, replace them with more contextually appropriate alternatives, and provide brief explanations for the revisions.

After receiving CF, participants were asked to return to their original texts and correct any misplaced lexical items. They were given 10 min to complete this stage. At the end of each treatment session, participants reviewed the final version of their text, focusing on the correct use of lexical bundles.

2) Staged Indirect/Direct CF Condition. Participants in the staged feedback condition completed the feedback process in two steps. In the first step, they asked ChatGPT to identify lexical bundles that were used incorrectly or awkwardly, without providing corrections. The system therefore highlighted problematic expressions while leaving the revision to the learners.

After receiving this indirect feedback, participants revised their texts independently within a limited time period. In the second step, they submitted the revised text to ChatGPT and requested explicit corrections for any remaining errors. At this stage, the system provided appropriate lexical bundle replacements along with brief explanations.

This two-stage procedure encouraged learners to reflect on their language use and attempt self-correction before receiving explicit guidance. After incorporating the final corrections, participants reviewed the revised version of their texts, focusing on the accurate use of lexical bundles.

9 Testing Instrument

A. Free Writing Task. Learners' productive use of lexical bundles was assessed through a free writing task administered as a pre-test, post-test, and delayed post-test. Participants were asked to write an academic text of approximately 500 words discussing factors influencing second language learning, drawing on their own language learning experiences. To encourage the use of the target expressions, students were provided with a list of the lexical bundles practiced during the treatment sessions and were instructed to incorporate them into their essays where appropriate. The same prompt and bundle list were used across all three testing phases to allow direct comparison of learners' performance over time.

Participants' texts were evaluated using an analytic scoring procedure. Each lexical bundle received one point if it was used accurately and appropriately within the sentence and context. Partial credit (0.5) was assigned when the bundle was only partly suitable for the intended meaning, while incorrect or missing bundles received zero points. To ensure scoring reliability, a second rater independently evaluated 25% of the writing samples collected from the three testing phases. The inter-rater reliability coefficient was 0.92.

B. Lexical Bundles Gap-Filling Task (LBGT). In addition to the free writing task, a Lexical Bundles Gap-filling Task (LBGT) was administered as a pre-test, post-test, and delayed post-test to measure participants' ability to use lexical bundles in appropriate contexts. In this task, participants were given an academic text of approximately 600 words related to second language learning. Each text contained 32 gaps related to the lexical bundles presented in Table 1. The participants were instructed to read the text carefully and supply the lexical bundles provided as a list. The same set of 32 lexical bundles appeared in all three texts to ensure consistency across testing phases. The texts were different but equivalent in topic and difficulty, and were different from those employed during the treatment sessions. Participants were allotted 15 min to complete the task by hand.

A partial credit scoring procedure similar to the one used for the free writing task was adopted. Each lexical bundle that was used accurately and appropriately in a slot was awarded one point. A score of 0.5 was assigned when the bundle was only partially suitable for the intended meaning, while missing or contextually implausible bundles received zero points.

10 Analysis

To examine the effects of feedback type on learners' use of lexical bundles, the data were analyzed using a mixed between-within subjects ANOVA. The analysis included feedback condition (direct feedback, staged feedback, and control) as the between-subject factor and testing time (pre-test, post-test, and delayed post-test) as the within-subject factor. This analysis allowed the study to determine whether learners' performance changed over time and whether these changes differed across feedback conditions. When significant effects were identified, post hoc comparisons were conducted to explore differences between the groups.

11 Results

1) Writing Task (WT). Table 2 presents descriptive statistics for learners' performance on the free writing task across the three testing occasions.

The descriptive statistics indicate that both experimental groups improved from the pre-test to the post-test and maintained higher scores than the control group at the delayed post-test. A one-way ANOVA conducted on the pre-test scores confirmed that there were no significant differences among the groups at the beginning of the study, $F(2,55) = 1.10$, $p = 0.33$.

A mixed-design ANOVA was conducted with feedback condition (direct, staged, control) as the between-subject factor and testing time (pre-test, post-test, delayed post-test) as the within-subject factor. The results revealed a significant main effect of time, $F(2,110) = 46.36$, $p < 0.001$, indicating overall improvement across the three testing occasions. A significant main effect of feedback condition was also found, $F(2,55) = 54.20$, $p < 0.001$, suggesting that the type of feedback influenced learners' performance. In addition, a significant interaction between time and feedback condition was observed, $F(4,110) = 7.85$, $p < 0.001$, indicating that the degree of improvement differed across the groups.

Bonferroni-adjusted pairwise comparisons showed that both the direct CF and staged CF groups performed significantly better than the control group ($p < .001$). Although the staged CF group obtained slightly higher mean scores than the direct CF group, this difference was not statistically significant ($p = .182$). These findings suggest that both types of AI-generated feedback improved learners' use of lexical bundles, while their relative effectiveness was comparable.

Table 2. Descriptive statistics for learners' scores in the free writing task.

Time	CF	N	Mean	SD
pretest	direct	20	14.73	1.42
	staged	20	15.48	2.33
	control	18	14.68	2.12
Posttest	direct	20	19.45	1.57
	staged	20	20.17	2.08
	control	18	15.50	1.87
delayed	direct	20	18.90	1.50
	staged	20	18.39	1.90
	control	18	14.73	1.78

2) Lexical Bundles Gap-Filling Task (LBGT). Table 3 presents descriptive statistics for learners' performance on the lexical bundle gap-filling task.

Table 3. Descriptive statistics for the LBGT.

Time	CF	N	Mean	SD
pretest	direct	20	15.59	1.65
	staged	20	15.95	2.18
	control	18	15.86	1.28
Posttest	direct	20	21.04	2.01
	staged	20	21.86	2.11
	control	18	14.90	1.37
delayed	direct	20	21.40	1.53
	staged	20	21.56	1.62
	control	18	14.64	1.50

The pre-test scores did not differ significantly among the groups, as confirmed by a one-way ANOVA, $F(2,55) = 0.26$, $p = 0.77$. However, clear differences emerged at the post-test and delayed post-test.

A mixed-design ANOVA examining the effects of feedback condition and time revealed a significant main effect of time, $F(2,110) = 63.88$, $p < 0.001$, indicating substantial improvement across testing occasions. A significant interaction between time and feedback condition was also observed, $F(4,110) = 16.00$, $p < 0.001$, suggesting that learners' progress differed depending on the type of feedback received. In addition, the main effect of feedback condition was significant, $F(2,55) = 93.74$, $p < 0.001$.

Post hoc comparisons showed that both experimental groups significantly outperformed the control group ($p < 0.001$). Similar to the results of the writing task, no statistically significant difference was found between the staged CF and direct CF groups ($p = 0.137$). These results indicate that AI-generated CF contributed to improved performance in the lexical bundle gap-filling task, regardless of whether feedback was provided directly or through a staged procedure.

12 Discussion

The present study examined the effects of two forms of AI-generated CF, direct and staged feedback, on L2 learners' development of lexical bundles in writing. The results showed that learners who received AI-generated feedback significantly improved their performance compared with the control group. However, no statistically significant difference was found between the direct and staged feedback conditions.

The first research question examined whether AI-generated CF could enhance learners' use of lexical bundles in writing. The findings indicate that both forms of feedback delivered through ChatGPT contributed to significant improvements in learners' performance. These results are consistent with the widely recognized role of CF in facilitating second language development by drawing learners' attention to mismatches between their current language use and target forms. The present study extends this line of research by showing that CF can also support the development of formulaic language, specifically lexical bundles, in L2 writing. Lexical bundles play an important role in academic writing by contributing to coherence, fluency, and rhetorical organization. However, acquiring such formulaic sequences can be challenging for L2 learners because these expressions often receive limited attention in classroom instruction. Moreover, incidental acquisition of lexical bundles typically requires repeated exposure to authentic input over extended periods of time, which may not always be feasible in classroom settings. The results of the gap-filling task suggest that the feedback procedures used in this study helped learners develop greater awareness of lexical bundles and improved their ability to use them appropriately in context. From this perspective, CF can function as a form of attention-drawing technique that highlights relevant linguistic features and facilitates learning.

The second research question examined whether there were differences between direct and staged forms of AI-generated CF. The results indicated that both feedback types were similarly effective in promoting learners' use of lexical bundles. One possible explanation is that both feedback conditions were sufficiently explicit to draw learners' attention to the target expressions. In both treatments, learners received feedback that highlighted problematic lexical bundles and encouraged revision of their texts. As a result, learners in both groups may have engaged in noticing and reflection processes that supported learning.

From a theoretical perspective, staged feedback could be expected to produce stronger learning effects because it encourages learners to modify their output before receiving explicit corrections. According to the output hypothesis [19], opportunities to revise and refine one's language can promote deeper processing and facilitate language development. However, the results of the present study suggest that direct feedback may also be effective when it clearly identifies problematic forms and provides appropriate alternatives. In this study, both feedback types likely increased learners' awareness of lexical bundles and encouraged them to revise their written production.

The absence of significant differences between the two feedback types is consistent with findings from previous research on written CF. Several studies have reported that both direct and indirect feedback can support language development, although the relative advantages of each approach may depend on factors such as learner proficiency and task characteristics (e.g., [20]). The participants in the present study were upper-intermediate learners, which may have facilitated their ability to benefit from both feedback conditions. Overall, the findings suggest that AI-generated feedback can provide an effective and practical tool for supporting learners' development of lexical bundles in L2 writing. From a blended-learning perspective, AI-generated feedback can extend learning beyond classroom instruction by providing learners with immediate individualized support during independent writing activities. Such tools may complement teacher feedback by creating additional opportunities for practice, revision, and reflection outside the classroom while maintaining continuity between face-to-face and technology-mediated learning environments.

13 Conclusion, Limitations, and Future Directions

The present study provided evidence for the benefits of ChatGPT-generated CF for developing an important aspect of L2 writing, namely lexical bundles. In addition, the findings indicated the feasibility of utilizing ChatGPT for providing different forms of feedback, including the two-stage CF and single-stage direct CF used in the present study.

Despite the promising findings, it is essential to acknowledge some limitations. While the number of participants assigned to each treatment condition was plausible given the practical constraints of experimental research, a larger sample size could enhance the validity and generalizability of the findings. Another potential limitation is the absence of a testing instrument capable of assessing participants' spontaneous use of lexical bundles in writing without prior exposure. While it was essential to control the use of lexical bundles by providing learners with a predetermined list, this approach may have limited the extent to which learners' natural production of lexical bundles could be observed.

One suggestion for further research is to address these limitations while replicating the present study. Another suggestion is to investigate learners' perceptions and beliefs about the effectiveness of ChatGPT-generated CF in learning lexical bundles. Future research can also investigate the effects of AI-generated CF on other aspects of L2 development, particularly writing.

The present study also offers important implications for language teachers. Given the time-consuming nature of providing individualized CF in language classrooms with large numbers of students, the findings suggest that teachers can utilize AI tools such as ChatGPT to deliver individualized CF on learners' writing. As demonstrated in this study, these tools are flexible in providing various types of CF and may support the development of less investigated aspects of L2 writing, such as the use of lexical bundles.

References

1. Benson, S., DeKeyser, R.: Effects of written corrective feedback and language aptitude on verb tense accuracy. Lang. Teach. Res. **23**(6), 702–726 (2019)
2. Bitchener, J., Knoch, U.: Raising the linguistic accuracy level of advanced L2 writers with written corrective feedback. J. Second. Lang. Writ. **19**(4), 207–217 (2010)
3. Jiang, F.K., Hyland, K.: Does ChatGPT write like a student? Engagement markers in argumentative essays. Writ. Commun. **42**(3), 463–492 (2024)
4. Lin, S., Crosthwaite, P.: The grass is not always greener: Teacher vs GPT-assisted written corrective feedback. System **127**, 103529 (2024)
5. Pérez-Llantada, C.: Formulaic language in L1 and L2 expert academic writing: Convergent and divergent usage. J. Engl. Acad. Purp. **14**, 84–94 (2014)
6. Rassaei, E.: Immediate vs. delayed prompts, individual differences in working memory, and L2 development. Language Awareness **33**(3), 649–672 (2024)
7. Rassaei, E.: The interplay between corrective feedback timing, task complexity and working memory in L2 development. System **137**, 103955 (2026)
8. Boers, F., Lindstromberg, S.: Experimental and intervention studies on formulaic sequences in a second language. Annu. Rev. Appl. Linguist. **32**, 83–110 (2012)
9. Li, J., Schmitt, N.: The development of collocation use in academic texts by advanced L2 learners: A multiple case study approach. In: Wood, D. (ed.) Perspectives on Formulaic Language, pp. 22–46. Bloomsbury, London (2010)
10. Biber, D., Conrad, S., Cortes, V.: If you look at...: Lexical bundles in university teaching and textbooks. Applied Linguistics **25**(3), 371–405 (2004)
11. Hyland, K.: As can be seen: Lexical bundles and disciplinary variation. Engl. Specif. Purp. **27**(1), 4–21 (2008)
12. VanPatten, B.: Input processing in adult SLA. In: VanPatten, B., Williams, J. (eds.) Theories in Second Language Acquisition: An Introduction, 2nd edn., pp. 113–134. Routledge, Abingdon/New York (2015)
13. Gholami, L.: Incidental reactive focus on form in language classes: Learners' formulaic versus nonformulaic errors, their treatment, and effectiveness in communicative interactions. Foreign Lang. Ann. **54**(4), 897–922 (2021)
14. Dornburg, A., Davin, K.J.: ChatGPT in foreign language lesson plan creation: Trends, variability, and historical biases. ReCALL **37**(3), 332–347 (2025)
15. Gao, X.: Language education in a brave new world: A dialectical imagination. Modern Lang. J. **108**(2), 556–562 (2024)
16. Tam, A.C.F.: Interacting with ChatGPT for internal feedback and factors affecting feedback quality. Assess. Eval. High. Educ. **50**(2), 219–235 (2025)
17. Shi, H., Chai, C.S., Zhou, S., Aubrey, S.: Comparing the effects of ChatGPT and automated writing evaluation on students' writing and ideal L2 writing self. Comp. Ass. Lang. Learn. **39**(4) (2025)
18. Zhang, Z., Aubrey, S., Huang, X., Chiu, T.K.: The role of generative AI and hybrid feedback in improving L2 writing skills: A comparative study. Innov. Lang. Learn. Teach. (Early Access)
19. Swain, M.: The output hypothesis and beyond: Mediating acquisition through collaborative dialogue. In: Lantolf, J.P. (ed.) Sociocultural Theory and Second Language Learning, pp. 97–115. Oxford University Press, Oxford (2000)
20. Kim, Y., Choi, B., Kang, S., Kim, B., Yun, H.: Comparing the effects of direct and indirect synchronous written corrective feedback: Learning outcomes and students' perceptions. Foreign Lang. Ann. **53**(1), 176–199 (2020)

Exploring the Blended Ecology of Parent Education: The Role of Generative AI

Yuen-Miu Fung and Will W. K. Ma(✉)

Tung Wah College, Hong Kong SAR, China
willma@twc.edu.hk

Abstract. Parent education is crucial yet rarely addressed in formal schooling; consequently, most adults acquire parenting skills in an ad hoc manner after the birth of a child. Given parents' central role in shaping children's developmental contexts, ineffective parenting can have serious consequences. This study investigates how a blended parent education ecology—integrating everyday practice with on-demand support from generative AI—relates to parenting among Hong Kong families. We surveyed 110 parents of children aged 2–8 using a questionnaire and analyzed the data with partial least squares structural equation modeling (PLS-SEM). Parental stress showed a significant and negative association with parental discipline but no significant association with the parent–child relationship; family socioeconomic status was not significantly related to parenting. By contrast, parents' use of generative AI (chatbots that integrate publicly available information) was associated with lower stress and with improved discipline and parent–child relationships. These findings suggest that incorporating generative AI into blended parent education may broaden access to guidance and improve parenting outcomes.

Keywords: Parental Education · Parent Stress · Generative Artificial Intelligence · Parenting · Socioeconomic Status

1 Introduction

Parent education is critical yet rarely addressed within formal schooling; most adults acquire parenting knowledge ad hoc after childbirth. Given parents' central role in shaping children's developmental environments, ineffective parenting can cause serious harm.

In Chinese cultural traditions, parenting has long been a core concept. Classical literature emphasizes parents' pivotal role in modeling filial piety and nurturing frugality and gratitude toward nature and others to maintain family harmony. Through socialization, children were expected to obey parental guidance, achieve academic success, and avoid problem behaviors [1]. Consistent with Sociocultural Theory, children learn through exposure to more experienced others, developing knowledge via imitation, instruction, and collaboration in interaction with people and environments [2]. Parents function as children's first teachers, providing the foundational learning environment and serving as

K. T. Chui et al. (Eds.): ICBL 2026, LNCS 16778, pp. 237–249, 2027.
https://doi.org/10.1007/978-981-92-3761-6_17

their initial models for learning; consequently, the ways parents treat and interact with children are crucial.

Inappropriate parenting may lead to negative outcomes, including child maltreatment and problem behaviors. Prior research indicates that parental stress and family socioeconomic status are associated with children's difficulties in emotional regulation, delayed language development, and social skill deficits, among other concerns [3–5]. However, such problems are often ameliorable through parenting interventions [6]. Recently developed generative artificial intelligence (GAI) enables parents to seek parenting information and has been identified as a factor that may influence parenting practices [7]. Yet few studies have examined how parents in Hong Kong use GAI and how it affects parenting. This study addresses that gap by deepening our understanding of factors that influence parenting so that appropriate and timely support can be provided to improve practices and promote healthy child development. Accordingly, the research objective is to identify key factors shaping parenting and to investigate the potential effects of GAI use on parenting. The research questions are: (1) What factors influence parenting? (2) How do these factors affect parenting? (3) What are the interrelationships among the factors affecting parenting?

2 Literature Review and Hypotheses Development

2.1 Parenting

Parenting refers to the customary approaches caregivers employ in raising children and is a major determinant of both adaptive and maladaptive behaviors in early childhood [3]. Effective parenting is marked by positive reinforcement and a strong parent–child relationship, whereas ineffective parenting is characterized by inconsistency and coercive practices [4]. Parents' psychological states and their own childhood experiences significantly shape their parenting and, in turn, child development. Experiences of childhood maltreatment increase parents' risk of depression and reduce self-efficacy, contributing to negative parenting practices and child behavioral problems [5, 8, 9]. Conversely, parental well-being and the use of evidence-based strategies—such as authoritative parenting and appropriate implementation of time-outs—are associated with better child mental health, emotion regulation, and prosocial behavior [8, 10]. Research also shows that parenting is strongly influenced by demographic factors, including parents' age, educational level, and income [3, 11]. Moreover, parenting interventions have demonstrated sustained effects in reducing parental anxiety and mitigating the intergenerational impact of childhood trauma on children's development, thereby improving parenting practices and parental self-efficacy [6, 9]. In sum, multiple factors shape parenting, as elaborated below.

2.2 Parental Stress

Parental stress—the emotional strain arising from the demands of childrearing—has substantial impacts on parental well-being and children's cognitive development [12]. Prior research demonstrates clear intergenerational effects: parental stress is positively associated with trajectories of both internalizing and externalizing problem behaviors in children [12]. Children's experiences of an impending sense of collapse have been linked to parental anxiety and may function as "bridge" symptoms that exacerbate the co-occurrence of psychological disorders in childhood [13]. Parental stress is shaped by multiple factors, including occupational demands, co-parenting arrangements, child characteristics, and acculturative pressures. For example, stress is elevated during periods of unemployment, when work is pursued primarily for economic necessity, and when satisfaction with a partner's participation in childrearing is low [14]. Joint-custody fathers report lower depression, higher-quality co-parenting and father–child relationships, and more frequent use of nonviolent discipline compared with non-custodial fathers [15]. Moreover, perceived parental stress, general life satisfaction, and parental self-efficacy are closely linked to intensive parenting attitudes [16]. Parental stress is negatively associated with authoritative parenting, a relationship mediated by wisdom and sense of coherence [17]. Additionally, parental essentialism is negatively related to stress and positively related to self-efficacy [16]. In sum, parental stress arises from diverse sources—including employment conditions, co-parenting practices, and self-efficacy—and, through its contribution to emotional instability, can adversely affect parenting attitudes and behaviors. Accordingly, we posit a significant association between parental stress and parenting practices. Then, we test,

H1: *There is a significant negative relationship between parental stress and parenting:*

H1a: There is a significant negative relationship between parental stress and parent-child relationship.

H1b: There is a significant negative relationship between parental stress and parental discipline.

2.3 Family Socioeconomic Status

Family socioeconomic status (SES) is typically indexed by parents' educational attainment and income [18]. Higher SES is associated with greater income, increased monetary expenditure, more parental involvement, and improved child welfare, whereas lower SES is often linked to financial strain and elevated family stress that can constrain parental investment. SES also shapes informal labor demands and parents' perceptions of economic inequality. Parents with lower SES are more likely to reside in multigenerational households to draw on grandparental support, while higher-SES families are more likely to delay parenthood and migrate, increasing the likelihood of parenting without nearby extended family [19]. Higher-SES parents tend to be more pessimistic in their assessment of inequality; greater awareness of income disparities is associated with heightened investment in children's education and extracurricular activities, elevated academic expectations, and more intensive childrearing practices compared with parents who perceive inequality as less pronounced [20]. Parenting styles also vary by SES. Children's digital media use and sleep problems have been linked to parental SES, with higher-SES parents reportedly adopting more controlling approaches and providing greater guidance regarding device use and sleep hygiene, while parents from disadvantaged backgrounds are described as more permissive [21, 22]. In sum, financial resources and parental education shape perceptions of education, parenting styles, and investments in child development. Therefore, we argue that socioeconomic status is closely associated with parents' beliefs about education and parenting. Then, we test,

H2: *There is a significant positive relationship between family socioeconomic status and parenting:*

H2a: There is a significant positive relationship between family socioeconomic status and parent-child relationship.

H2b: There is a significant positive relationship between family socioeconomic status and parental discipline.

2.4 Use of Generative Artificial Intelligence

Generative artificial intelligence (GAI) refers to AI systems that use trained models to generate content and simulate human conversation [23]. Recent tools such as ChatGPT and DeepSeek demonstrate strong capabilities in producing concise responses by processing and synthesizing publicly available information [7]. These chatbots are increasingly applied across sectors, including healthcare and education. In clinical contexts, their diagnostic and treatment-planning suggestions have been reported as mostly accurate roughly two-thirds of the time relative to expert clinicians, and they provide parents with accessible GAI information on diseases and children's diverse needs [24]. For example, ChatGPT has answered questions about childhood asthma with over 80% accuracy [25], offered basic information, corrected misconceptions, and recommended resources about autism [26], and was rated by most experts as "useful" or "very useful" for guidance on early childhood caries [27]. It has also provided actionable, literature-referenced strategies for managing attention-deficit/hyperactivity disorder in children [28]. Beyond domain knowledge, GAI can efficiently perform practical tasks—such as drafting emails, essays, and lists—and has driven educational technologies in collaboration support, adaptive learning, and progress-monitoring assessments [29]. Taken together, these findings suggest that GAI can supply useful information and streamline a range of tasks. We therefore argue that GAI holds promise as an assistant for parents seeking advice on early childhood rearing, supporting the implementation of positive parenting practices and potentially reducing parental stress by increasing parenting knowledge and decreasing time burdens. Then, we test,

H3: *There is a significant positive relationship between the use of generative artificial intelligence and parenting:*

H3a: There is a significant positive relationship between the use of generative artificial intelligence and parent-child relationship.

H3b: There is a significant positive relationship between the use of generative artificial intelligence and parental discipline.

H4: *There is a significant negative relationship between the use of generative artificial intelligence and parental stress.*

3 Methodology

3.1 Background and Subjects

This study examined parental stress, socioeconomic status, and generative AI (GAI) use among Hong Kong parents of children aged 2–8 years. We disseminated an online questionnaire via posts on parent forums and through face-to-face invitations, and participants were encouraged to share the link with other eligible parents using snowball sampling. In total, 110 responses were collected.

3.2 Measurement Items

Measures were drawn from previously validated scales. Parental stress (PS) was assessed using three items [12]. Parenting was operationalized using four items on the parent–child relationship (PCR) and four items on parental discipline (PD) [30]. The use of generative AI (GAI) in parenting was measured by six items of self-reported frequency [23]. All items employed 7-point Likert-type response scales. For PS and PCR, responses ranged from 1 (strongly disagree) to 7 (strongly agree). For PD, responses ranged from 1 (never) to 7 (every time). For GAI usage frequency, responses ranged from 1 (never) to 7 (daily). Higher scores indicate greater levels of the respective construct. Socioeconomic status was assessed via self-reported monthly household income.

3.3 Data Collection

Data was collected via an online survey disseminated through posts in Facebook parenting groups and QR codes printed on leaflets at a local children's clothing store. Before starting, participants reviewed an informed consent form outlining the study purpose, voluntary participation, and confidentiality. Those who consented completed the survey, which took approximately 5 min on average. Data collection occurred over six weeks, beginning in early January 2026 and closing in late February 2026. Institutional Review Board approval was obtained in December 2025, prior to recruitment.

3.4 Data Analysis

Partial least squares structural equation modeling (PLS-SEM) was used to evaluate the structural model and test the hypothesized relationships, using SmartPLS 4 [31].

4 Findings

4.1 Descriptive Statistics of Respondents

There were 110 respondents who completed the questionnaire. The details are summarized in Table 1 below.

Table 1. Descriptive statistics of respondents (n = 110)

Items	Descriptive statistics
Gender	Male: 42 (38%); Female: 68 (62%)
Age	1. Below 30: 16 (15%); 2. 30–39: 42 (38%); 3. 40–49: 32 (29%); 4. 50 or above: 20 (18%)
Highest education Level	1. Primary school or below: 8 (7%) 2. Lower secondary (Form 1–3): 25 (23%) 3. Upper secondary (Form 4–6 / DSE / HKCEE): 40 (36%) 4. Tertiary education: 37 (34%)
Number of children	1. One: 53 (48%); 2. Two: 37 (34%); 3. Three: 16 (15%); 4. Four or more: 4 (4%)
Monthly household income	1. Below $20,000: 3 (3%) 2. $20,000 – $29,999: 6 (5%) 3. $30,000 – $39,999: 14 (13%) 4. $40,000 – $49,999: 34 (31%) 5. $50,000 – $59,999: 26 (24%) 6. $60,000 – $69,999: 20 (18%) 7. $70,000 or above: 7 (6%)

4.2 Reliability and Validity

Descriptive statistics for measurement items and key variables (socioeconomic status, parental stress, generative AI use, parent–child relationship, and parental discipline) are presented in Table 2.

Reliability was assessed using Cronbach's alpha and composite reliability; all values exceeded 0.70 (Table 3), indicating satisfactory internal consistency [32]. Construct validity was evaluated via convergent and discriminant validity. Convergent validity, assessed by average variance extracted (AVE), was supported with all AVE values above 0.50 (Table 3) [32]. Discriminant validity was examined using the Fornell–Larcker criterion: the square root of each construct's AVE (diagonal) exceeded its correlations with other constructs (off-diagonals) in the discriminant matrix (Table 4), indicating adequate discriminant validity [32].

4.3 Structural Model

The structural model was evaluated using partial least squares structural equation modeling (PLS-SEM) in SmartPLS 4.0 [26]. PLS-SEM was chosen as it is well suited for exploratory research, smaller samples, and data that may deviate from normality. Path coefficients were estimated via the PLS path modeling procedure, and model testing results are summarized below (see Fig. 1 and Table 5).

Table 2. Descriptive analysis of variables

	M	SD		M	SD
Socioeconomic Status (SES)			Parent-child Relationship (PCR)		
SES	4.473	1.380	PCR1	5.782	1.171
Parental Stress (PS)			PCR2	5.509	1.306
PS1	4.600	1.996	PCR3	4.964	1.584
PS2	3.864	1.861	PCR4	4.009	1.827
PS3	2.818	1.602	Parental Discipline (PD)		
Use of Generative Artificial Intelligence (GAI)			PD1	4.491	1.360
GAI2	3.418	1.791	PD2	5.445	1.547
			PD3	5.618	1.595
			PD4	3.764	1.629

Table 3. Reliability and AVE

	Cronbach's alpha (α)	Composite Reliability (CR)	Average Variance Extracted (AVE)
PS	0.761	0.836	0.671
PCR	0.835	0.853	0.665
PD	0.803	0.817	0.634

* *SES and GAI are single items, not included in the reliability analysis*

Table 4. Discriminant Matrix

	PS	SES	GAI	PCR	PD
PS	**0.819**				
SES	0.172	**1.000**			
GAI	0.354	0.148	**1.000**		
PCR	0.252	0.251	0.364	**0.815**	
PD	0.490	0.222	0.558	0.508	**0.796**

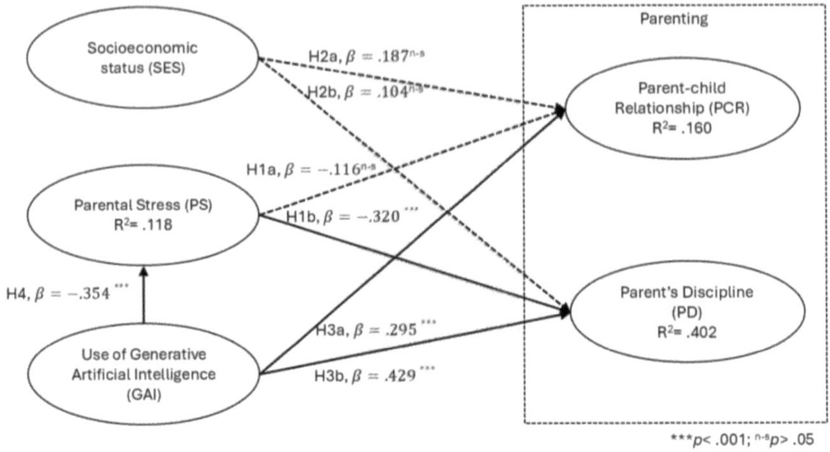

Fig. 1. Model testing results

Table 5. Summary of path coefficients and hypotheses testing

Hypotheses	Paths	Path coefficients	Supported (Y/N)
H1a	PS-->PCR	-0.116^{n-s}	N
H1b	PS-->PD	−0.320***	Y
H2a	SES-->PCR	0.187^{n-s}	N
H2b	SES-->PD	0.104^{n-s}	N
H3a	GAI-->PCR	0.295***	Y
H3b	GAI-->PD	0.429***	Y
H4	GAI-->PS	−0.354***	Y

*** $p < .001$; $^{n-s}$ $p > .05$

5 Discussion

5.1 Key Findings

The results indicate that parental stress and generative AI use are primary determinants of parenting, aligning with prior research [13, 27]. Specifically, parental stress showed a significant negative association with parental discipline, but no significant association with the parent–child relationship. Generative AI use exhibited a significant direct positive effect on both parenting indicators, alongside a significant negative effect on parental stress. Socioeconomic status showed no significant relationships with parenting outcomes.

5.2 Parental Stress and Parenting

Parental stress was significantly negatively associated with parental discipline ($\beta = -0.320$, $p < .001$), but not with the parent–child relationship ($\beta = -0.116$, $p > .05$). In other words, higher stress was linked to less positive disciplinary practices—parents may focus more on stopping undesirable behaviors (e.g., yelling or withdrawing communication) rather than guiding constructively—consistent with prior findings [12]. However, stress did not appear to undermine the overall parent–child relationship. Regardless of stress level, parents may remain motivated by their child's best interests, maintaining affection and close interactions. Thus, stress may primarily influence immediate disciplinary responses to negative behaviors without exerting longer-term relational effects.

5.3 Socioeconomic Status and Parenting

This study provides new evidence that socioeconomic status is not a significant predictor of parenting outcomes: effects on the parent–child relationship ($\beta = 0.187$, $p > .05$) and parental discipline ($\beta = 0.104$, $p > .05$) were nonsignificant, contrary to prior findings [20–22], and thus H2 was not supported. One interpretation is that increasing parental education and widespread access to low-cost parenting resources (including online materials and AI tools) may mitigate SES-related disparities. Conversely, higher-SES families may not necessarily exhibit better parenting; for some, career demands and reliance on nannies or other caregivers can reduce direct parent–child interaction, potentially weakening relationships even when disciplinary practices appear adequate. These results suggest that parent–child relationship quality and disciplinary behaviors alone may be insufficient indicators of "parenting," and that SES may be exerting a diminishing influence on parenting in contemporary contexts.

5.4 Use of Generative AI and Parenting

Generative AI use was significantly associated with parenting outcomes, exhibiting direct positive effects on both the parent–child relationship ($\beta = 0.295$, $p < .001$) and parental discipline ($\beta = 0.429$, $p < .001$), thereby supporting H3. These findings align with prior empirical work [24–28] and indicate that GAI is commonly used among Hong Kong parents. By providing integrated answers to parenting queries, generating images and tables, and offering mindfulness exercises, GAI helps parents access relevant information, solve child-related problems, and regulate their emotions—facilitating more effective parenting practices.

5.5 Use of Generative AI, Parental Stress and Parenting

Use of generative AI was significantly associated with lower parental stress ($\beta = -0.354$, $p < .001$), supporting H4. By offering tools for lesson and parenting planning, curated guidance on childcare, and actionable solutions to child-related challenges, GAI can bolster parents' confidence and problem-solving efficacy, thereby reducing anxiety and stress [29]. Lower stress, in turn, may enable calmer instruction and more positive disciplinary practices, ultimately benefiting overall parenting.

5.6 Implications

Understanding factors that shape parenting—such as parental stress and the use of generative AI—is vital for the well-being of both children and parents. Our findings suggest that enhancing support for parents (e.g., professional guidance, high-quality materials, AI tools, and counseling services) can empower them in their roles, increasing the likelihood of positive disciplinary practices and more effective parenting. Socioeconomic status was not a significant factor, indicating that parents from diverse backgrounds can access educational resources and adopt effective practices. Given this, researchers and practitioners should focus on strengthening parents' intrinsic motivation to seek help proactively when needed. Practical strategies include organizing seminars to build internet and AI literacy and fostering strong home–school partnerships. In turn, empowered parents may be more likely to seek support and manage their children's behavior in a constructive manner.

5.7 Limitations and Further Studies

This study has several limitations. First, the small, geographically concentrated sample may limit the generalizability of findings to broader parent populations. Second, reliance on parental self-reports of perceptions and behaviors introduces potential bias and does not directly capture child development, well-being, or behavior; thus, inferences about ultimate child outcomes should be made cautiously. Third, measurement of key constructs was constrained: while familiarity with and frequency of GAI use were assessed, qualitative dimensions (e.g., purpose, depth of engagement, and integration into daily routines) were not. Fourth, potentially important moderators were not included—such as child characteristics, family structure and support systems, parents' AI literacy, and attitudes toward GAI—limiting the interpretability of observed relationships. To address these gaps, future research should use larger and more diverse samples; incorporate mixed methods and multi-informant designs (e.g., reports from teachers or caregivers); include objective or longitudinal indicators of child outcomes; capture richer profiles of GAI use; and model key contextual moderators to better illuminate the mechanisms linking GAI, parental stress, and parenting practices.

6 Conclusion

This exploratory study examines how parental stress, family socioeconomic status, and the use of generative AI relate to parenting. Consistent with expectations, parental stress directly influences parental discipline. The study also offers initial evidence that generative AI use is significantly associated with parenting and suggests that AI may enhance parenting by lowering parental stress. These findings provide actionable insights for improving parenting practices and underscore the potential role of generative AI as a supportive tool for families.

Appendix I. Measurement

Parental Stress [12]	
PS1	I worry whether I am doing enough for my child
PS2	The major source of stress in my life is my child
PS3	I feel overwhelmed by the responsibility of being a parent
Parent-child Relationship [30]	
PCR1	I listen to my child's feelings and understand them
PCR2	When my child is having a hard time, I am able to help him/her
PCR3	My child and I have warm, intimate times together
PCR4	I express affection by hugging, kissing, and holding my child
Parental Discipline [30]	
PD1	When my child misbehaves, I speak to my child calmly
PD2	I explain to my child why certain rules must be followed
PD3	I explain to my child why s/he is being punished or restricted
PD4	I compliment or hug my child when s/he does something well

References

1. Shek, T.L., Law, Y.M.: Parenting in contemporary Hong Kong: Observations and reflections. Int. J. Child Adolesc. Health **12**(4), 391–402 (2019)
2. EBSCO: Social development theory (Vygotsky), https://www.ebsco.com/research-starters/history/social-development-theory-vygotsky. Last accessed 01 October 2025
3. Kota, R.S., Prasad, H.G., Reddy, R.: Maternal parenting styles and middle childhood temperament patterns: A comparison between two social classes residing in an urban community. J. Indian Assoc. Child Adolesc. Ment. Health **20**(1), 26–34 (2024)
4. Sumargi, A.M., Prasetyo, E.: The mediating role of parenting: How parental well-being and distress influence child behaviors. J. Educ. Health and Comm. Psychol. **13**(3), 888 (2024)
5. Zhou, L., Li, X., Xiang, Y.: The effect of parental experience of childhood maltreatment on children's attachment type: The mediating role of parenting self-efficacy. Deviant Behav. **46**(8), 1063–1083 (2024)
6. Dewi, D.T.K., et al.: Effectiveness of parenting interventions on self-efficacy, anxiety, stress, and depression among parents of preterm infants: A systematic review and meta-analysis of randomized control trials. Int. J. Nurs. Stud. **169**, 105128 (2025)
7. Kim, Y., Vilches, S.L., Shapiro, S., Clarkson, A.: Testing the capability of generative artificial intelligence for parent and caregiver information seeking. Fam. Relat. **74**(3), 1266–1284 (2025)
8. Yaffe, Y.: Parental worry about COVID-19 in preschool children's mothers during the pandemic waves: The role of maternal negative feelings and parenting styles. Matern. Child Health J. **27**(4), 632–640 (2023)
9. Zhang, X., Yan, E.: The impact of maternal childhood trauma on children's problem behaviors: The mediating role of maternal depression and the moderating role of mindful parenting. Psychol. Res. Behav. Manag. **17**, 3799–3811 (2024)

10. Xu, J., Tully, L.A., Dadds, M.R.: Generation time-out grows up: young adults' reports about childhood time-out use and their mental health, attachment, and emotion regulation. Eur. Child Adolesc. Psychiatry **33**(10), 3471–3479 (2024)
11. Pujihasvuty, R., et al.: Family economic resilience and early childhood parenting practices. British Journal of Midwifery **32**(1), 22–31 (2024)
12. Koutra, K., Mouatsou, C., Margetaki, K., Mavroeides, G., Kampouri, M., Chatzi, L.: From early stress to adolescent struggles: How maternal parenting stress shapes the trajectories of internalizing, externalizing, and ADHD symptoms. Pediatric Reports **17**(4), 76 (2025)
13. Sun, C., et al.: Mental health symptoms in Chinese children with sleep disorders and association with parental emotions. Sci. Rep. **15**(1), 31367 (2025)
14. Hwang, M., Lee, N., Lee, G.: How parenting-related characteristics influence parenting stress among nurses with young children in the Seoul metropolitan area, South Korea: a cross-sectional study. BMC Nurs. **24**(1), 1052 (2025)
15. Milius, H.L., Cho, B.O., Klingman, A.M.: Fatherhood after separation: Implications for parent and child outcomes. J. Child Fam. Stud. **34**(5), 1241–1258 (2025)
16. Egami, S.: Effect of intensive parenting attitude on maternal well-being and self-efficacy among Japanese housewives and part-time working mothers. Psychology International **7**(2), 47 (2025)
17. Moeini, F., Hosseinpour, R., Jafari, A.: Explaining the structural model of the relationship between parental stress index and democratic parenting style with the mediating role of wisdom and sense of coherence. J. Assessm. Res. Appl. Couns. **7**(3), 1–12 (2025)
18. Chen, X., Hu, L.-C.: Parental investment on a socioeconomic basis: a comparative study of southeast China and Taiwan. Chin. Educ. Soc. **56**(2), 141–162 (2023)
19. Minardi, S.: Sociodemographic variation in family structures and geographic proximity between adult children and parents in Europe. Demogr. Res. **52**, 849–868 (2025)
20. Liu, A., Zhang, C., Li, W.: Parental perceptions of economic inequality and investment in education in China. Chinese Sociological Review **57**(3), 251–274 (2025)
21. Liu, A., Li, W., Li, M.: Emerging digital inequality in early life: Parenting and differential usage of digital devices among urban preschoolers in China. J. Marriage Fam. **87**(1), 30–52 (2025)
22. Rodriguez, A.M., Isaac, A.J., Dougherty, L.R., Klein, D.N., Bufferd, S.J.: Sleep difficulties across preschool age: Associations with parenting and parental psychopathology. J. Child Fam. Stud. **34**(4), 1031–1047 (2025)
23. Stöhr, C., Ou, A.W., Malmström, H.: Perceptions and usage of AI chatbots among students in higher education across genders, academic levels and fields of study. Comp. Educ. Artif. Intel. **7**, 100259 (2024)
24. Radesky, J.: AI, parenting, and child development. J. Dev. Behav. Pediatr. **45**(1), e2–e3 (2024)
25. Senbaykal, Y.E., Taskirdi, I., Haci, I.A., Tuncel, T.: Artificial intelligence performance in pediatric asthma. J. Asthma **62**(11), 1926–1932 (2025)
26. McFayden, T.C., Bristol, S., Putnam, O., Harrop, C.: ChatGPT: Artificial intelligence as a potential tool for parents seeking information about autism. Cyberpsychol. Behav. Soc. Netw. **27**(2), 135–148 (2024)
27. Elkarmi, R., et al.: ChatGPT for parents' education about early childhood caries: A friend or foe? Int. J. Paediatric Dentistry **35**(4), 717–724 (2025)
28. Sathe, A., Chikanna, H.: Evaluation of an artificial intelligence language model in psychiatric patient education. Child Adolesc. Mental Health **30**(3), 265–271 (2025)
29. Goldman, S.R., Taylor, J., Carreon, A., Smith, S.J.: Using AI to support special education teacher workload. J. Spec. Educ. Technol. **39**(3), 434–447 (2024)
30. Chovan, S., et al.: Biological and contextual determinants of early development in marginalized Roma communities: a research protocol of the RomaREACH study. Int. J. Equity in Health **23**(1) (2024)

31. Choi, J.I., Kim, G.M., Kim, J.A., Jeong, E.J.: Parenting attitudes and pathological gaming: Multifaceted influences of harsh-negative parenting on adolescent pathological gaming. Frontiers in Psychology **16** (2025)
32. Fornell, C., Larcker, D.F.: Evaluating structural equation models with unobservable variables and measurement error. J. Mark. Res. **18**(1), 39–50 (1981)

Designing a GenAI-Assisted Teacher Training Program for Thinking-Oriented ESL Instruction in Azerbaijan

Murad Aliyev[1,2](✉), Farida Orujova[2], and Gunay Gasimli[2]

[1] Faculty of Education, Beijing Normal University, Beijing, People's Republic of China
murad.aliyev@mail.bnu.edu.cn, m.aliyev@khazar.org
[2] Graduate School of Science, Arts and Technology, Khazar University, Baku, Azerbaijan
faridaorujova@gwmail.gwu.edu, gunay.gasimova@khazar.org

Abstract. This study designed an AI-assisted teacher training model with a pedagogically intelligent agent, MindMate AI, and evaluated its effectiveness on Azerbaijani pre-service ESL teachers' ability to design thinking-oriented lesson plans. Using a mixed-methods sequential explanatory design, quantitative results showed a statistically significant improvement in lesson plan quality from pre-intervention ($M = 5.50, SD = 2.42$) to post-intervention ($M = 11.81, SD = 1.53$), $p < .001$, with a large effect size ($d = 2.5$). Qualitative findings from the semi-structured interviews showed that pre-service teachers used MindMate AI primarily for structuring and generating lesson content, with their use shaped by prior usage habits, difficulties in prompt formulation, and concerns about alignment with exam-oriented instruction. Results show that a pedagogically designed GenAI agent can support thinking-oriented instructional design only when it is integrated into a structured training program that scaffolds how pre-service ESL teachers design lessons. These findings suggest that effective GenAI integration in teacher training requires structured prompt scaffolding and iterative feedback cycles, rather than tool-oriented instruction alone. Program designers should also address contextual tensions between thinking-oriented pedagogy and exam-focused assessment practices.

Keywords: Teacher Training · ESL Instruction · Thinking-oriented Instruction · GenAI agent · Azerbaijan

1 Introduction

The development of higher-order thinking skills such as analysis, reasoning, and problem solving is increasingly emphasized as a core objective in language education [1, 2]. In ESL contexts, language is expected to function not only as a medium for communication but also as a tool for constructing and expressing complex ideas. However, classroom practices often remain dominated by form-focused and procedural activities, which limit opportunities for cognitively demanding language use. Recent studies [3–6] indicate that even when new technologies are introduced, teachers tend to rely on surface-level

K. T. Chui et al. (Eds.): ICBL 2026, LNCS 16778, pp. 250–268, 2027.
https://doi.org/10.1007/978-981-92-3761-6_18

task design and struggle to construct activities that promote deeper thinking [6]. These patterns suggest that English is not consistently used as a tool for thinking, pointing to limitations in instructional design rather than solely in student ability.

In the Azerbaijani context, this issue is closely associated with a persistent disconnect between pedagogical knowledge and its practical application. Although various training initiatives provide professional development opportunities for English language teachers, their impact on classroom practice remains limited [7, 8]. Teachers often experience difficulties in translating theoretical principles into concrete lesson design which can support their students' thinking [8, 9]. Empirical evidence further supports this concern. Research focusing on Azerbaijani teachers shows that they tend to rely on procedural activities and struggle to design cognitively demanding tasks during training contexts [10]. The core limitation lies not only in teachers' knowledge, but in their capacity to operationalize that knowledge during the lesson design process. Furthermore, existing professional development models are often short-term and disconnected from teachers' real-time instructional planning, which reduces their effectiveness in supporting sustained pedagogical change [11, 12].

This limitation becomes particularly critical in the generative artificial intelligence (GenAI) era. GenAI offers new possibilities for supporting lesson planning, yet its educational value depends on how it is integrated into pedagogical practice. Current uses of such tools often remain limited to content generation, reflecting the absence of structured guidance for their pedagogical application. The central issue, therefore, is not the availability of technology, but the lack of design-oriented support that enables teachers to use these tools for thinking-oriented instruction. In response to this gap, and informed by Azerbaijani teachers' challenges [10], this study develops a GenAI-supported agent that provides real-time, context-sensitive scaffolding during lesson planning. Therefore, this study adopts a targeted approach by integrating a pedagogically intelligent agent into a professional development program, specifically designed for Azerbaijani ESL teachers.

The aim of this study is to examine how a GenAI-assisted professional development program influences Azerbaijani pre-service ESL teachers' ability to design thinking-oriented lesson plans. The specific objectives are: (1) to evaluate the effect of GenAI-assisted training on the quality of thinking-oriented lesson plans; (2) to explore how pre-service ESL teachers interact with and utilize the MindMate AI agent during instructional design; and (3) to identify the contextual and pedagogical factors that shape the effectiveness of GenAI integration in a teacher training context. The study is therefore guided by the following research questions:

How does GenAI-supported lesson design change the quality of thinking-oriented ESL lesson plans?

In what ways does interaction with a MindMate AI agent reshape teachers' instructional design processes?

This study makes three contributions to the existing literature. First, it provides the first empirical investigation of GenAI-assisted thinking-oriented lesson design in the Azerbaijani ESL context, addressing a significant geographical and contextual gap in the literature. Second, it introduces and evaluates MindMate AI, a pedagogically designed agent, demonstrating how context-sensitive GenAI tools can be developed for specific educational settings. Third, it offers mixed-methods evidence showing that the pedagogical effectiveness of GenAI in teacher training depends not on the technology itself, but on the structural and contextual conditions.

2 Literature Review

Recent research on GenAI in English language teaching has mainly examined how future teachers perceive these tools and whether they are willing to adopt them in teaching. This line of work is useful because it shows that the first challenge is not only access to technology, but also teachers' confidence, beliefs, and sense of preparedness. For example, some studies [13–15] suggest that pre-service teachers' willingness to use GenAI is closely tied to how useful, manageable, and trustworthy they find it. However, this group of studies is still more successful in explaining acceptance than in explaining pedagogical use. In other words, it tells us why pre-service teachers may adopt GenAI, but not clearly how teacher education can help them use it well for lesson design.

A second group of studies has moved beyond attitudes and started to examine training and skill development. This is an important step because it shows that GenAI use should be taught, not simply expected. Studies [5, 16, 17] show future teachers need structured support to develop competence in collaborating with GenAI. At the same time, these studies mostly focus on general competence, prompting, or digital literacy. As a result, they show that training matters, but they say less about what kind of training helps pre-service ESL teachers design lessons that develop students' thinking in purposeful ways.

Another set of studies comes closer to classroom practice by looking at lesson planning, prompting, reflection, and creativity. Kerr and Kim [3] examined how pre-service EFL teachers used GenAI in lesson planning, while Moorhouse et al. [18] focused on task-specific prompting. Kartal [4] and Demir and Özdemir [19], in different ways, also suggest that GenAI may support creativity, reflection, and broader professional growth. These studies indicate that GenAI can do more than save time or generate content. It may also shape how future teachers think, plan, and reflect. Still, this literature remains somewhat scattered. Because each study highlights one part of the process rather than showing how teacher education can systematically prepare pre-service ESL teachers to use GenAI for thinking-oriented lesson design.

Several important gaps therefore remain. Overall, the literature shows more attention to attitudes, readiness, and general skills than to the quality of lesson design itself. Although several studies [4, 20] suggest that GenAI can support thinking and creativity, research on improving higher-order thinking skills in English language teaching is still limited. In addition, most of the available studies come from other national settings, which leaves the Azerbaijani context largely absent. Most studies on AI-supported thinking skills are dominated by quantitative methods, including pre-posttests [10, 21], performance metrics [22], while qualitative approaches like narrative inquiry [4] and case studies [23] are less common. Mixed-method designs are emerging but often rely on self-reported data, limiting objectivity. A notable gap is the scarcity of standardized, domain-specific assessments, with few studies using rubrics aligned with established frameworks [24, 25].

3 Theoretical Framework

This study is guided by Distributed Cognition Theory and Scaffolding Theory. These theories were selected because they help explain how pre-service ESL teachers developed thinking-oriented lesson plans through interaction with MindMate AI (Fig. 1), instructor support, and lesson plan artifacts. Rather than treating GenAI as an independent instructional solution, this framework positions MindMate AI as one component of a supported professional learning environment.

Distributed Cognition theory suggests that cognition is not confined to the individual mind but is distributed across people, tools, representations, and social interactions [26]. From this perspective, lesson planning can be understood as a distributed cognitive activity in which teachers interact with multiple resources to accomplish complex instructional design tasks. Structured representations can also support learners' thinking by helping them organize and understand complex content [26, 27]. In this study, cognition was distributed across four key elements: the teacher, the MindMate AI system, the lesson-planning template, and instructor scaffolding. Teachers contributed pedagogical knowledge and instructional goals, MindMate AI generated suggestions and alternative ideas, the lesson-planning template structured the design process, and instructors provided guidance during lesson development and revision. Through the interaction of these elements, participants developed and refined thinking-oriented lesson plans. Distributed Cognition theory therefore helps explain how instructional design emerged through the coordinated contributions of human and technological resources rather than through individual cognition alone [26].

Scaffolding theory explains how learners can complete complex tasks when they receive structured support that guides their thinking and performance [28]. Such support is especially important when learners are expected to move from basic understanding to more advanced forms of reasoning, problem-solving, and independent performance [29]. In this study, scaffolding was embedded in the professional development program through instructor explanations, guided practice, lesson design templates, feedback, and MindMate AI suggestions. These supports helped teachers understand thinking-oriented instructional principles and apply them in lesson planning. MindMate AI was therefore not positioned as a replacement for teacher thinking, but as an additional scaffold that supported teachers in improving the coherence, cognitive demand, and pedagogical structure of their lesson plans.

This integrated theoretical perspective guided the study by explaining how MindMate AI, instructor support, lesson templates, feedback, and lesson plan artifacts worked within the professional development program. It helped frame the training as a supported design environment rather than a simple AI-use activity. In this environment, teachers did not only receive AI-generated suggestions; they interpreted, revised, and reorganized these suggestions through guided practice and instructor feedback. MindMate AI was therefore understood as both a cognitive resource for idea generation and lesson organization, and a scaffold for applying thinking-oriented instructional principles more systematically. This framework also informed the lesson plan evaluation rubric by clarifying why the analysis focused on problem situations, cognitive conflict, thinking visualization, higher-order cognitive demand, and lesson coherence. These dimensions were used to examine how teachers externalized their pedagogical reasoning in lesson plans and how effectively they designed instructional support for students' thinking development. In this way, the theoretical framework connected the intervention design, rubric development, and interpretation of lesson plan changes and teachers' interview responses.

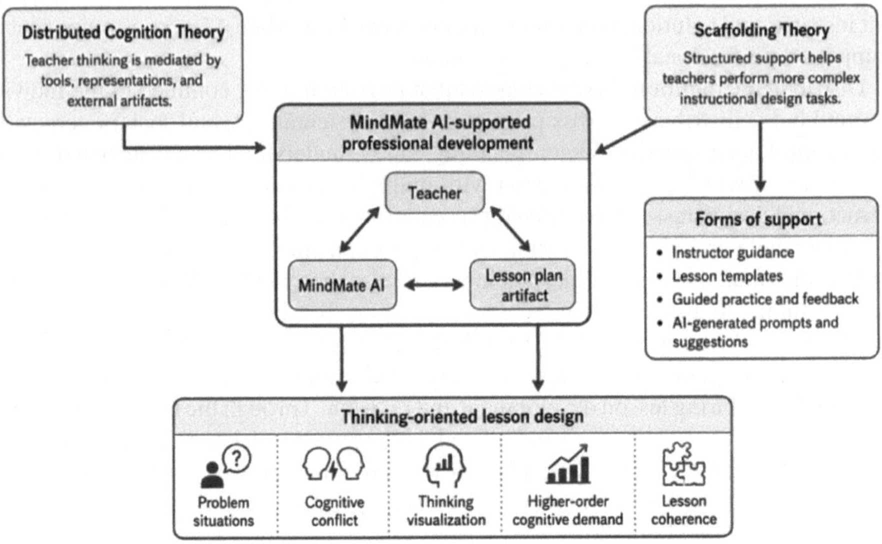

Fig. 1. Framework for MindMate AI-supported thinking-oriented lesson design.

4 Methodology

4.1 Research Design

This study employed a mixed-methods sequential explanatory design to examine the effects of GenAI-assisted teacher training on lesson plan quality and teachers' experiences with MindMate AI [30]. The quantitative data were collected and analyzed first, followed by qualitative data to explain the results. This approach allowed the study to first identify changes in lesson plan quality and then understand how teachers used AI during the design process.

4.2 Teacher Professional Development Program

The training was designed as a blended professional development program that combined a three-hour face-to-face workshop with a two-day MindMate AI-supported lesson revision process (Fig. 2). 18 pre-service ESL teachers participated in the program. All participants were female, had limited teaching experience, and had not previously received formal training in thinking-oriented instructional design. Each participant submitted one lesson plan before the intervention and one revised lesson plan after the intervention. Both versions were included in the analysis.

The program adopted a practice-oriented design. Initially, the participants were introduced to key principles of thinking-oriented instruction based on Zhao et al.'s [31] framework, including defining thinking objectives, designing reasoning-based tasks, making student thinking visible, and structuring lesson activities to increase cognitive demand. Rather than explaining the theoretical framework in isolation, the training introduced thinking-oriented instructional design through a structured lesson planning template developed for this study. The template guided teachers through the main stages of lesson design, including defining thinking objectives, creating problem situations, designing cognitive conflict tasks, making student thinking visible, organizing learning activities, and applying variations in the topic. In this way, the template helped participants translate the principles of thinking-oriented instruction into concrete lesson planning decisions.

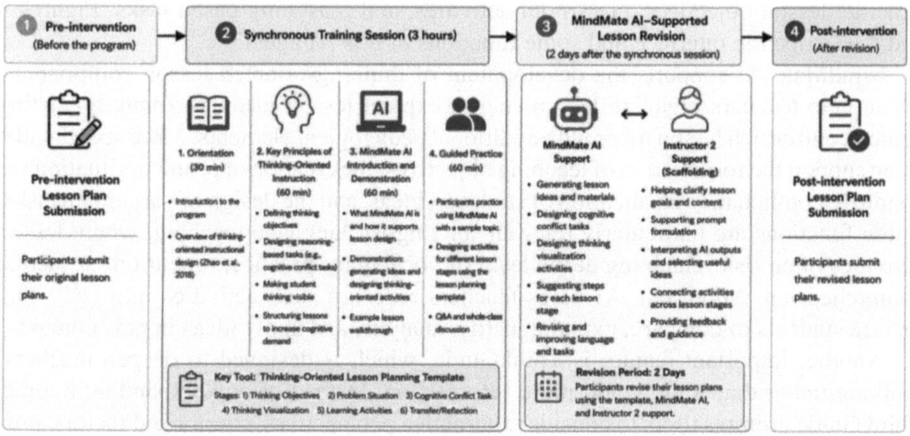

Fig. 2. MindMate AI-assisted thinking-oriented instructional design training program for pre-service ESL teachers.

MindMate AI was introduced as a GenAI-supported design tool within this template-based process. Participants were shown how to use MindMate AI to generate lesson ideas, formulate cognitive conflict tasks, design thinking visualization activities, and revise lesson activities for different lesson stages. Example prompts were provided so that teachers did not need to focus mainly on prompt-writing techniques. Instead, they were encouraged to focus on their own lesson topics, instructional goals, and students' learning needs.

The professional development program was facilitated by two instructors with complementary roles. Instructor 1 introduced the lesson planning template, explained how each section of the template reflected thinking-oriented instructional design, and demonstrated how MindMate AI could support lesson planning and revision. Instructor 2 provided scaffolding during the practical design and revision phases. This support included helping participants clarify their lesson ideas, formulate prompts, interpret MindMate AI outputs, and connect different lesson stages into a coherent instructional sequence.

After the synchronous training session, participants spent two days revising their lesson plans with the support of MindMate AI and Instructor 2. During this revision period, teachers used the template and the example prompts to improve their lesson plans. The revision process focused not only on adding AI-generated activities but also on improving the logical connection among thinking objectives, cognitive conflict tasks, thinking visualization activities, and follow-up learning tasks.

4.3 MindMate AI Agent

The training incorporated MindMate AI, a pedagogical agent designed to assist teachers in developing thinking-oriented lessons. The system was built using a Retrieval-Augmented Generation (RAG) architecture and integrates a knowledge base that includes curriculum materials, standards, and textbooks aligned with the Azerbaijani educational context. Teachers interacted with MindMate AI through natural language prompts to generate lesson objectives, classroom activities, and reasoning-based tasks. Figures 3 and 4 describe the interface and some functions of this AI agent.

MindMate AI supports the development of thinking-oriented lesson components. It can help teachers organize lesson stages, expand lesson ideas, restructure existing content, and enrich lesson maps with additional pedagogical elements. More specifically, it can support the formulation of teaching objectives, the creation of problem situations or cognitive conflict, the visualization of students' ideas, and the design of variational tasks. These functions are particularly relevant for English language teaching, where lesson activities often risk remaining at the level of vocabulary practice, repetition, or factual comprehension. MindMate AI helps teachers redesign such activities into tasks that require students to compare, explain, justify, analyze, and apply ideas in new contexts.

Another important feature is ThinkGuide, which is designed to deepen teachers' thinking rather than simply add more information. Instead of only expanding a topic, ThinkGuide prompts users to consider alternative perspectives, overlooked factors, possible risks, long-term consequences, and changes in conditions. This makes the planning process more reflective and balanced. Compared with traditional lesson planning, which often follows textbook order, fixed templates, or teachers' previous experience, MindMate AI provides a more interactive, visual, and strategy-oriented approach. Thus, the tool functions not merely as a lesson-plan generator, but as a pedagogical thinking partner that supports pre-service ESL teachers in designing lessons with clearer objectives, stronger cognitive demand, and more visible student reasoning.

MindMate AI agent also includes an AI-based thinking visualization tool. Teachers can ask the system which thinking diagram is suitable for a particular topic, how a topic can be organized, or which thinking strategy can better support a specific learning activity. For example, a teacher designing a comparison task may be guided toward a double-bubble map, while a teacher planning a cause-and-effect lesson may be directed toward a multi-flow map. In this way, the tool supports teachers' instructional reasoning by helping them connect lesson objectives, learning tasks, and students' expected thinking processes. Therefore, MindMate AI does not only assist with content generation; it also supports the visualization and organization of pedagogical thinking.

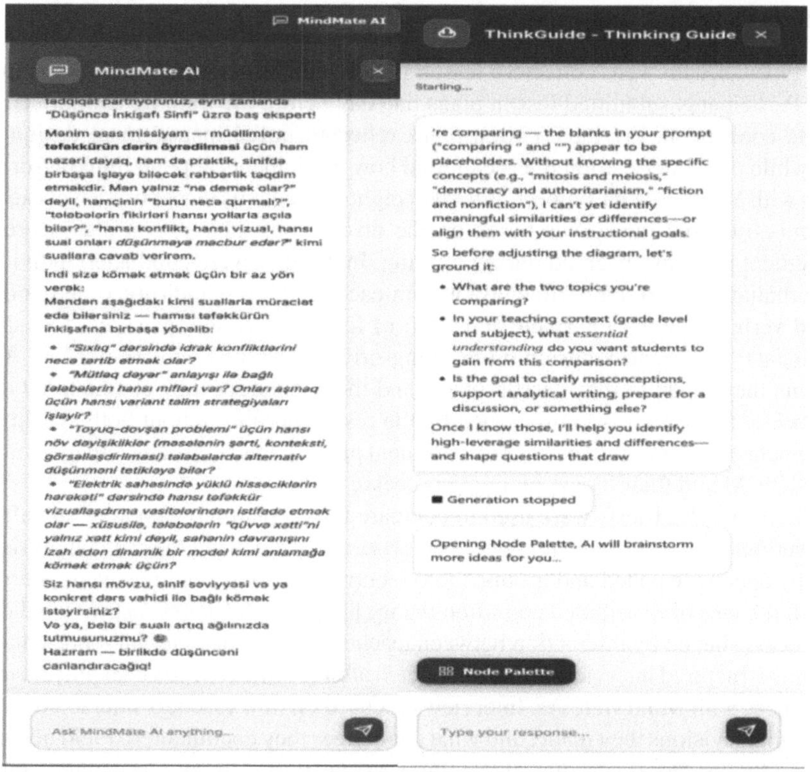

Fig. 3. MindMate AI interface for AI-supported lesson planning and thinking guidance.

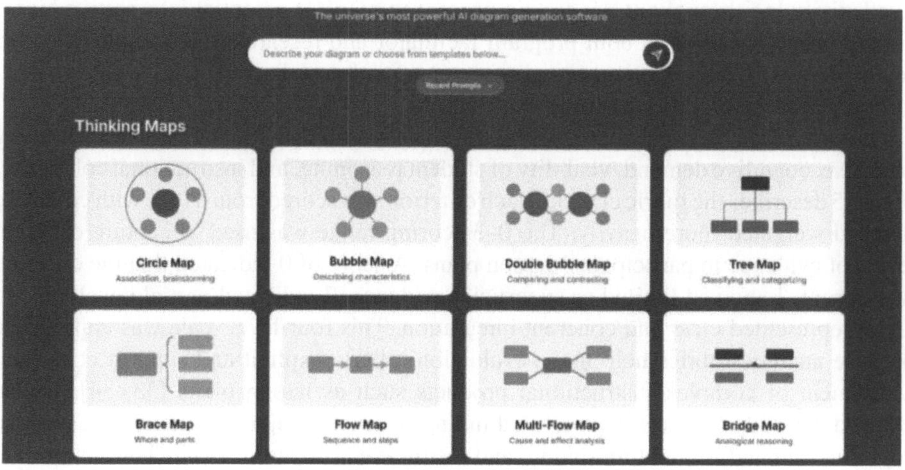

Fig. 4. Existing thinking visualization templates in MindMate AI agent.

4.4 Data Collection and Analysis

Three types of data were collected: lesson plans, semi-structured interviews, and field notes. Participants submitted lesson plans one day before the training and immediately after its conclusion. Pre-intervention plans reflected initial instructional design practices, while post-intervention plans captured how participants applied thinking-oriented design with MindMate AI support. A total of eight participants were purposively selected for semi-structured interviews based on the diversity of their lesson plan scores and engagement patterns observed during training. Interviews were conducted individually in Azerbaijani, lasted approximately 30 min each, and were audio-recorded and transcribed verbatim. Each interview consisted of five open-ended questions focusing on participants' experiences designing thinking-oriented lessons with MindMate AI, the revisions they made to their lesson plans, and the challenges they encountered during the process. Field notes were recorded by the researcher throughout both synchronous and asynchronous training sessions to document participants' real-time engagement with MindMate AI and their lesson planning processes.

Paired-samples t-tests were used to compare lesson plan scores before and after the intervention. Interview data and field notes were analyzed using thematic analysis [32], whereby data were coded and grouped into recurring themes. Findings were interpreted through the lens of distributed cognition theory [26], which frames instructional design as a process shaped by interaction between teachers, tools, and external representations.

Semi-structured interviews were conducted after the intervention to explore teachers' experiences with MindMate AI. Interviews focused on how teachers interacted with the agent, what revisions they made, and what challenges they encountered. Field notes were recorded by the researcher during training sessions to document participants' engagement with MindMate AI and their planning processes. All data were anonymized prior to analysis. To strengthen the credibility of the analysis, the lead researcher maintained a reflexivity log throughout the coding process to monitor potential interpretive biases arising from dual roles as both program facilitator and researcher. A sample of coded segments was reviewed by a second researcher, and any discrepancies were resolved through discussion until consensus was reached.

Lesson plans were evaluated using an analytic rubric with four criteria: thinking objective, cognitive demand, visibility of student reasoning, and instructional coherence. Figure 5 describes the rubric criteria. Each criterion was scored from 0 to 3, with cognitive demand weighted more heavily. The 0–3 scoring range was used to capture different levels of evidence in participants' lesson plans. A score of 0 indicated that the criterion was absent, 1 showed limited or superficial evidence, 2 indicated partial development, and 3 represented clear and coherent integration. This four-level scale was appropriate because analytic rubrics help make evaluation criteria explicit and support consistent assessment of complex instructional products such as lesson plans [33, 34]. It also allowed the study to assess changes in thinking-oriented design, especially in relation to cognitive demand, student reasoning, and instructional coherence, which are important indicators of high-quality lesson planning [35, 36].

Criterion	0 – Absent	1 – Emerging	2 – Developing	3 – Strong
Criterion 1: Clarity of Thinking Objective	No explicit thinking objective stated; lesson focuses primarily on language practice.	Thinking objective implied but vague; tasks do not clearly reflect a defined cognitive process.	Clear thinking objective stated using a cognitive verb, but only partially aligned with lesson tasks.	Clear and specific thinking objective explicitly stated and consistently operationalized across all lesson stages.
Criterion 2: Cognitive Demand (Weighted x2)	Tasks rely primarily on recall, repetition, matching, or mechanical practice.	Tasks require limited reasoning such as listing or simple description without justification.	Tasks require structured reasoning such as comparison, cause–effect explanation, sequencing with explanation, or simple justification.	Tasks require sustained reasoning, evaluation, or problem-solving. Students must justify decisions using evidence, compare alternatives using criteria, analyze causes with explanation, or generate solutions to open-ended problems.
Criterion 3: Visibility of Student Reasoning	Student responses are closed (yes/no, single-word answers); reasoning is not externally visible.	Students provide short explanations but without structured supports.	Structured prompts encourage explanation and reasoning in oral or written form.	Lesson systematically externalizes reasoning using structured tools such as reasoning frames, graphic organizers, comparison charts, or visible thinking maps.
Criterion 4: Instructional Coherence	Activities are fragmented or disconnected.	Basic structure present but weak progression toward the thinking objective.	Logical progression toward the thinking objective with minor gaps.	Clear, purposeful sequencing that progressively deepens reasoning across lesson stages.

Fig. 5. Analytic rubric for evaluating teachers' thinking-oriented lesson plan design.

Furthermore, each lesson plan was coded as "LP" to facilitate pre- and post-intervention comparison. Two raters independently scored all lesson plans. Inter-rater reliability was assessed using the intraclass correlation coefficient. The high inter-rater reliability score (ICC = 0.86) further supported the clarity and consistency of the scoring process. From this aspect, high inter-rater reliability indices (e.g., ICCs/Cohen's κ around .80–.90) are common benchmarks in lesson-plan rubrics and interaction-quality coding [37, 38]. Rubric-based studies on lesson planning notes that if some criteria are more discriminating, they may be weighted more heavily in summative scoring [36], which supports the decision to weight cognitive demand more strongly. In cases of discrepancy, the raters discussed and agreed on the final scores used for analysis.

5 Results

5.1 Quantitative Results

A paired-samples t-test was conducted to examine the difference between pre- and post-intervention lesson plan scores. As shown in Table 1, the mean score increased from *5.50 (SD = 2.42)* in the pre-intervention condition to *11.81 (SD = 1.53)* in the post-intervention condition. The mean difference of 6.31 indicates a substantial increase in scores following the intervention. The results revealed that this difference was statistically significant, $t(17) = -11.30, p < 0.001$. The 95% confidence interval for the mean difference ranged from -7.63 to -4.99, indicating that the improvement was consistent across participants. In addition, the effect size was large (Cohen's d = 2.5), reflecting a strong magnitude of change between the two conditions.

Table 1. Changes in thinking-oriented lesson plan design following GenAI-assisted training.

Measure	Pre (M ± SD)	Post (M ± SD)	t(df)	p	Cohen's d
Lesson plan scores	5.50 ± 2.42	11.81 ± 1.53	-11.30 (17)	< 0.001	2.5

5.2 Qualitative Results

5.2.1 The Semi-Structured Interview Findings

The semi-structured interview data were analyzed thematically to understand how pre-service ESL teachers experienced the use of MindMate AI during the lesson-planning program. The analysis resulted in five themes: prior GenAI use habits, lesson organization support, the role of the lesson-planning template, prompt formulation challenges, and exam-oriented concerns.

Theme 1 Prior GenAI use habits shaped teachers' initial engagement with MindMate AI. Teachers' initial use of MindMate AI was strongly influenced by their previous experiences with general GenAI tools, especially ChatGPT. Most participants reported that they used MindMate AI mainly to generate lesson ideas, explanations, questions, and classroom activities. For example, one teacher stated, "I mainly use MindMate AI to generate ideas and simple explanations for my lessons." Another explained, "I write my lesson ideas, and MindMate AI helps me organize them into a structured lesson plan."

The teachers initially approached MindMate AI in a familiar way, treating it as a content-generation tool rather than as a system for deeper pedagogical reasoning. Their interaction with MindMate AI was often output-oriented: they entered a prompt, received a response, and used the generated content directly or with minor changes.

Theme 2 MindMate AI supported lesson organization and instructional planning. Participants consistently reported that MindMate AI helped them organize lesson content and structure classroom activities. Teachers described the system as useful for sequencing activities, generating varied tasks, and improving lesson flow. One participant noted, "MindMate AI helped me make my lessons more interactive and better organized." Another teacher stated that the system "suggested more interesting and varied activities that I could use in my lesson."

MindMate AI supported teachers not only by producing content but also by helping them organize their lesson ideas into a more structured form. For pre-service teachers with limited teaching experience, this type of support was important because lesson planning requires decisions about the order, purpose, and connection of activities. MindMate AI helped reduce some of this planning difficulty by suggesting possible activities and lesson sequences. In this sense, the system functioned as an instructional planning scaffold that supported teachers in turning fragmented lesson ideas into more organized lesson plans.

Theme 3 The lesson-planning template helped teachers transform lesson topics into staged GenAI-supported lesson designs. Teachers described the lesson-planning template as a practical guide that helped them move from a general lesson topic to a more structured thinking-oriented lesson plan. The template was useful because it did not only show the final lesson structure. It also provided prompt guidance for each lesson stage, helping teachers understand what information they needed to give MindMate AI and what kind of output they should expect from the system.

Several participants explained that, before using the template, they often had a topic but were unsure how to develop it into a complete lesson sequence. One teacher stated, “I had my topic, but I did not know how to divide it into different stages. The template helped me see what I should do first, next, and after that.” Another participant explained, “The template helped me understand what I should ask MindMate AI for each part of the lesson.” Similarly, one teacher noted, “It was easier because I did not need to create the prompt from zero. I could follow the questions in the template and change them according to my topic.”

Participants also emphasized that the template helped them connect MindMate AI use with specific thinking-oriented lesson components. For example, teachers used the prompt guidance to ask MindMate AI to generate problem situations, cognitive conflict tasks, thinking visualization activities, group tasks, and reflection questions. One participant explained, “When I followed the template, I could ask MindMate AI to prepare a problem situation or a cognitive conflict task for my lesson.” Another teacher commented, “The template helped me understand how to use MindMate AI not only for general activities, but for each stage of the lesson.”

These responses suggest that the template functioned as both a lesson-design scaffold and a prompt scaffold. It reduced the difficulty of starting from a blank page, guided teachers’ interaction with MindMate AI, and helped them translate thinking-oriented instructional ideas into concrete lesson stages. In this sense, the template was an important mediating tool between teachers’ pedagogical intentions, MindMate AI outputs, and the final lesson plan.

Theme 4 Prompt formulation reflected challenges in externalizing pedagogical thinking. Participants frequently reported difficulties in writing effective prompts for MindMate AI. However, these difficulties were not mainly technical. Instead, they reflected challenges in clearly expressing instructional goals, expected learning outcomes, student needs, and the kind of thinking activity they wanted to design. One participant explained, “When my instructions are not clear, the responses from MindMate AI are also unclear.” Another teacher noted, “After I learned how to write clearer prompts during training, it became easier to get useful results.”

These responses indicate that successful use of MindMate AI depended on teachers’ ability to externalize their pedagogical thinking. In order to receive useful responses from the system, teachers needed to clarify what they wanted students to learn, what kind of thinking process they wanted to support, and how the activity should fit the lesson stage. Therefore, prompt formulation was not simply a technical skill. It became part of the instructional design process itself. Through prompt writing, teachers had to make their teaching intentions more explicit and structured. Thus, teachers need to develop the ability to communicate pedagogical intentions clearly to the system.

Theme 5 Teachers expressed concerns about the compatibility of thinking-oriented activities with exam-oriented teaching. Although participants generally viewed MindMate AI positively, several teachers questioned whether the thinking-oriented activities generated by the system were compatible with exam-focused teaching practices. In particular, some participants expressed uncertainty about how cognitive conflict tasks, thinking visualization activities, and discussion-based learning tasks could contribute to students' examination performance. One teacher stated, "I understand the value of these activities, but I am not sure how they will help students prepare for exams."

These responses suggest that teachers evaluated MindMate AI outputs not only according to whether they were interactive or thinking-oriented, but also according to whether they seemed useful for assessment preparation. For some participants, exam requirements remained an important criterion for judging the practicality of lesson activities. Even when teachers appreciated the value of thinking-oriented instruction, they were concerned about whether such activities would fit the realities of exam-oriented ESL teaching.

This finding highlights a contextual tension in the adoption of MindMate AI-supported lesson design. Teachers may be interested in using GenAI to design higher-order thinking activities, but they also need clearer guidance on how these activities can support exam-related language skills. Therefore, future training should help teachers connect thinking-oriented tasks with assessment goals, rather than presenting thinking development and exam preparation as separate priorities.

5.2.2 Field Notes

Analysis of the lesson plans and field notes showed that teachers gradually shifted from conventional ESL lesson planning toward more thinking-oriented instructional design during the MindMate AI-supported revision process. Initial lesson plans mainly emphasized vocabulary practice, repetition, and basic comprehension. In the revised lesson plans, teachers increasingly included activities that required students to analyze information, explain ideas, justify answers, make predictions, and participate in discussion.

However, pedagogical coherence across lesson stages remained a recurring challenge. Teachers were generally able to use MindMate AI to generate individual lesson components, such as problem situations, cognitive conflict tasks, thinking visualization activities, and follow-up tasks. Yet these components were not always clearly connected within the overall lesson sequence. In several cases, cognitive conflict tasks were included without an explicit link to the new lesson topic or subsequent activities. Similarly, thinking visualization activities sometimes appeared as separate tasks rather than as tools for supporting students' reasoning throughout the lesson.

Some revised lesson plans also showed limited alignment between thinking objectives and classroom activities. Although thinking-oriented tasks were included in the activity sections, the lesson objectives did not always clearly state the intended thinking processes. During the revision process, the second instructor helped teachers clarify the purpose of each lesson stage, refine MindMate AI-generated suggestions, and strengthen the connection among objectives, activities, and student thinking processes.

6 Discussion

This study examined how a blended professional development program supported by a pedagogically intelligent agent MindMate AI influences Azerbaijani ESL teachers' ability to design thinking-oriented lessons. While previous research has reported both positive effects of GenAI, such as enhanced reasoning and engagement [39, 40], and negative effects, such as superficial engagement and uncritical acceptance of outputs [41], the present findings extend this discussion by demonstrating that these outcomes are not inherent to the technology itself, but are contingent on the pedagogical conditions under which GenAI is embedded. Specifically, the results indicate that when GenAI is integrated within a structured, thinking-oriented instructional design framework, it can support meaningful pedagogical change. It shifts the focus from evaluating GenAI as a tool to understanding the conditions under which it becomes pedagogically effective [42, 43].

A second contribution of this study lies in its focus on instructional design as the primary site of change. Unlike prior studies that emphasize student performance outcomes [40, 43], the current findings show that a pedagogically designed GenAI agent can reshape teachers' design thinking, particularly in how they structure tasks and incorporate cognitive demand. From a distributed cognition perspective, this reflects a reorganization of cognitive processes across teachers, GenAI systems, and lesson plan artifacts [26]. Importantly, GenAI functioned as a form of cognitive scaffolding, providing guided prompts, structured tasks, and iterative support that enabled teachers to elaborate and refine their instructional ideas [28].

However, the findings also reveal a critical limitation. Although teachers adopted higher-order tasks, their conceptual understanding of thinking-oriented instruction remained partial. This result suggests that GenAI may facilitate procedural transformation without guaranteeing conceptual change. In addition, difficulties in prompt formulation indicate that effective GenAI use requires not only pedagogical knowledge but also interactional competence in working with GenAI systems [22, 26, 27]. Therefore, a dedicated session is required to explicitly cultivate teachers' ability to engage in pedagogical dialogue with the GenAI agent, ensuring that it is used as a cognitive partner rather than merely a content generator.

The observed coherence limitation in MindMate AI outputs points to a critical design challenge for pedagogically oriented GenAI agents. While the agent was effective in generating stage-specific instructional content, it did not consistently preserve the cognitive thread connecting cognitive conflict, problem situations, and variative tasks across the lesson structure. This finding suggests that context-sensitive scaffolding at the level of individual prompts is insufficient without a mechanism that maintains awareness of the overall pedagogical architecture of the lesson. Furthermore, because novice teachers lacked the expertise to detect this disconnection independently, the limitation was not self-correcting without instructor intervention. This underscores the importance of designing GenAI agents that not only respond to individual prompts, but also actively monitor and maintain the structural coherence of the instructional product being developed.

Finally, the study provides context-specific insight into the constraints shaping AI integration. In the Azerbaijani educational context, exam-oriented practices strongly influence teachers' instructional decisions. Participants' concerns about aligning thinking-oriented and AI-supported activities with exam requirements reflect a broader structural tension between the development of higher-order thinking and assessment systems focused on accuracy and performance outcomes [44]. This finding suggests that the effectiveness of AI-assisted professional development is not only a pedagogical issue, but also a systemic one, requiring alignment between instructional innovation and assessment practices. Overall, the study contributes by showing that sustainable AI integration depends on the interplay between pedagogical design, cognitive support, and contextual constraints, rather than on technology adoption alone.

7 Implications

The findings of this intervention suggest several practical implications for the design and implementation of GenAI-assisted teacher training programs. First, the results indicate that short-term training alone is insufficient to ensure sustained pedagogical transformation. While teachers demonstrated clear improvements in designing thinking-oriented lesson plans during the intervention, the continuity of these practices depends on how well the training reshapes teachers' instructional habits. Therefore, future programs should move beyond tool-oriented training and explicitly target habit formation by positioning GenAI as a pedagogical partner rather than a task generator. This requires structured scaffolding, such as guided prompt frameworks, sample lesson plans, and iterative feedback cycles that help teachers critically evaluate and refine AI-generated outputs. Additionally, simplifying theoretical concepts into operational, teacher-friendly formats is essential to reduce cognitive overload and support meaningful integration into everyday teaching practice. Finally, the results highlight the importance of sustained practice and follow-up support, as effective GenAI integration develops gradually. Short-term interventions may initiate change, but long-term engage-ment is necessary for teachers to fully internalize thinking-oriented instructional design and use GenAI as a meaningful pedagogical partner.

8 Limitations and Future Directions

This study has several limitations. First, the evaluation of lesson quality was based on rubric-based assessments, which may not fully capture the complexity of teachers' instructional thinking or actual classroom implementation. Second, although overall lesson plan quality improved significantly, sustained pedagogical coherence across lesson stages remained a challenge for many participants. Thus, the short-term interventions may be insufficient to fully reshape deeply ingrained instructional habits. Third, the study was conducted within a specific educational context, which may influence the transferability of the findings.

Future research should extend this study in several directions. First, longitudinal studies are needed to examine whether improvements in AI-supported lesson planning are transferred into actual classroom teaching and sustained over time. Future studies could include classroom observations, teaching videos, and student learning evidence to determine whether changes in lesson plans lead to deeper student engagement and higher-order thinking. Second, further research could also compare different forms of scaffolding in GenAI-supported lesson design. For example, one group of teachers could receive support from a human instructor, while another group could receive support only from a GenAI agent. This would help clarify which aspects of lesson planning can be effectively supported by GenAI and which still require human pedagogical guidance. Third, future studies should explore how GenAI systems can better support teachers' pedagogical reasoning. The findings suggest that teachers may generate activities for different lesson stages but still struggle to connect cognitive conflict tasks, thinking visualization activities, and follow-up learning tasks into a coherent instructional sequence. Future AI systems could be designed to provide more explicit guidance on these connections. Finally, future studies should use experimental or quasi-experimental designs with comparison groups to better identify the specific contribution of MindMate AI and the professional development program.

9 Conclusion

This study examined the impact of a GenAI-assisted training program on Azerbaijani pre-service ESL teachers' thinking-oriented lesson design. The findings demonstrated a significant improvement in the quality of thinking-oriented lesson design following the GenAI-assisted training, with a large effect size. Qualitative results showed that while MindMate AI supported idea generation and lesson structuring, teachers' use remained largely task-oriented and shaped by prior habits, with challenges in prompt formulation and concerns about exam alignment. As well as, the field notes revealed the interplay between the limitations of MindMate AI agent and teacher knowledge gaps in achieving pedagogical coherence. The results suggest that the pedagogically designed AI agent (e.g., MindMate AI) can support instructional design when integrated into structured training, but its effectiveness depends on teachers' pedagogical engagement and contextual constraints. At the same time, the results indicate that improvements were primarily procedural, with limited evidence of deeper conceptual understanding of thinking-oriented instruction.

Acknowledgments. This study did not receive any funding.

Disclosure of Interests. The authors declare that there are no competing interests.

References

1. Anderson, L.W., Krathwohl, D.R.: A taxonomy for learning, teaching, and assessing: a revision of Bloom's taxonomy of educational objectives: Complete edition. Addison Wesley Longman, Inc. (2001)
2. Johnson, K.E.: Second language teacher education: A sociocultural perspective. Routledge (2009)
3. Kerr, R.C., Kim, H.: From prompts to plans: a case study of pre-service EFL teachers' use of generative AI for lesson planning. English Teaching **80**, 95–118 (2025)

4. Kartal, G.: The influence of ChatGPT on thinking skills and creativity of EFL student teachers: a narrative inquiry. J. Educ. Teach. **50**, 627–642 (2024)
5. Moorhouse, B.L., Wan, Y., Wu, C., Kohnke, L., Ho, T.Y., Kwong, T.: Developing language teachers' professional generative AI competence: An intervention study in an initial language teacher education course. System **125**, 103399 (2024)
6. Li, T., Ji, Y., Zhan, Z.: Expert or machine? Comparing the effect of pairing student teacher with in-service teacher and ChatGPT on their critical thinking, learning performance, and cognitive load in an integrated-STEM course. Asia Pacific Journal of Education **44**, 45–60 (2024)
7. Mikayilova, U., Kazimzade, E.: Teachers as Reflective Learners: Teacher Perception of Professional Development in the Context of Azerbaijan's Curriculum Reform. Вопросы образования 125–145 (2016)
8. Aliyev, M., Aliyeva, S.: Challenges in Pre-Service Teachers' Adoption of Innovative Teaching Practices During Practicum. Osmangazi J. Educ. Res. **12**, 80–109 (2026)
9. Mikayilova, U.T., Huseynzada, G.Z.: Student Underperformance in Azerbaijan: Who is to Blame and What to Do? Psychol. Sci. Educ. **28**, 34–45 (2023)
10. Aliyev, M., Zhao, G., Baghirova, A.: Designing a Workshop to Develop Azerbaijani Teachers' Thinking Skills Instruction Through ChatGPT. In: Ma, W.W.K., Cheung, S.S.K., Li, C., Prayadsab, P., Mungwattana, A. (eds.) Blended Learning. Sustainable and Flexible Smart Learning, pp. 150–161. Springer Nature Singapore, Singapore (2025)
11. Darling-Hammond, L.: Culture, Learning, and Policy. In: Nasir, N.S., Lee, C.D., Pea, R., McKinney De Royston, M. (eds.) Handbook of the Cultural Foundations of Learning, pp. 404–426. Routledge, New York, NY, Routledge (2020)
12. Uzeirli, E., Kılıçoğlu, G.: Investigation of Primary Teacher Training Process in Turkey and Azerbaijan. Education and Science **46**, 375–401 (2021)
13. Bae, H., Hur, J., Park, J., Choi, G.W., Moon, J.: Pre-service Teachers' Dual Perspectives on Generative AI: Benefits, Challenges, and Integrating into Teaching and Learning. Online Learning **28** (2024)
14. Harakchiyska, T.: Predictors of Pre-Service EFL Teachers' Predisposition Towards AI Adoption in Language Teaching. Education Sciences **15**, 1112 (2025)
15. Yi, Z., Siquan, X.: The Impact of Pre-Service Language Teachers' Basic Psychological Needs on Behavioural Intentions to Utilise Artificial Intelligence (AI) in Teaching: AI Literacy and Self-Efficacy as Mediators. Eur. J. Educ. **60**, e70160 (2025)
16. Huang, T., Wu, C., Wu, M.: Developing pre-service language teachers' GenAI literacy: an interventional study in an English language teacher education course. Discover Artificial Intelligence **5**, 163 (2025)
17. Xue, L.: Urgent, but How? Developing English Foreign Language Teachers' Digital Literacy in a Professional Learning Community Focusing on Large Language Models. Eur. J. Educ. **60**, e12899 (2025)
18. Moorhouse, B.L., Ho, T.Y., Wu, C., Wan, Y.: Pre-service Language Teachers' Task-specific Large Language Model Prompting Practices. RELC Journal 00336882251313701 (2025)
19. Demir, B., Özdemir, D.: AI voice journaling for future language teachers: A path to well-being through reflective practices. British Educational Research Journal berj. 4174 (2025)
20. Korucu-Kış, S.: Zone of proximal creativity: An empirical study on EFL teachers' use of ChatGPT for enhanced practice. Thinking Skills and Creativity **54**, 101639 (2024)
21. Essel, H.B., Vlachopoulos, D., Essuman, A.B., Amankwa, J.O.: ChatGPT effects on cognitive skills of undergraduate students: Receiving instant responses from AI-based conversational large language models (LLMs). Comp. Educ. Artif. Intel. **6**, 100198 (2024)
22. An, S., Zhang, S., Guo, T., Lu, S., Zhang, W., Cai, Z.: Impacts of generative AI on student teachers' task performance and collaborative knowledge construction process in mind mapping-based collaborative environment. Comput. Educ. **227**, 105227 (2025)

23. Pence, H.E., et al.: Using Generative AI Systems for Critical Thinking Engagement in an Advanced Chemistry Course: A Case Study. J. Chem. Educ. **101**, 3789–3794 (2024)
24. Darmawansah, D., Rachman, D., Febiyani, F., Hwang, G.-J.: ChatGPT-supported collaborative argumentation: Integrating collaboration script and argument mapping to enhance EFL students' argumentation skills. Educ. Inf. Technol. **30**, 3803–3827 (2025)
25. Hui, E.S.Y.E.: Incorporating Bloom's taxonomy into promoting cognitive thinking mechanism in artificial intelligence-supported learning environments. Interact. Learn. Environ. **33**(2), 1–14 (2025)
26. Hollan, J., Hutchins, E., Kirsh, D.: Distributed cognition: toward a new foundation for human-computer interaction research. ACM Trans. Comp.-Human Interact. **7**, 174–196 (2000)
27. Al-Samarraie, H., Teo, T., Abbas, M.: Can structured representation enhance students' thinking skills for better understanding of E-learning content? Comput. Educ. **69**, 463–473 (2013)
28. Wood, D., Bruner, J.S., Ross, G.: The role of tutoring in problem solving. J. Child Psychol. Psychiatry **17**(2), 89–100 (1976)
29. Olfos, R., Vergara-Gómez, A., Estrella, S., Goldrine, T.: Impact of a theory-practice connecting scaffolding system on the ability of preschool teachers-in-training to teach mathematics. Teach. Teach. Educ. **120**, 103887 (2022)
30. Creswell, J.W., Poth, C.N.: Qualitative inquiry and research design: Choosing among five approaches, 4th ed. SAGE Publications (2018)
31. Zhao, G., Xiong, Y., Wang, X.: The definition, elements, and design of thinking classrooms. China Educ. Technol. **7**, 7–15 (2018)
32. Braun, V., Clarke, V.: Using thematic analysis in psychology. Qual. Res. Psychol. **3**, 77–101 (2006)
33. Brookhart, S.M., Chen, F.: The quality and effectiveness of descriptive rubrics. Educ. Rev. **67**, 343–368 (2015)
34. Panadero, E., Jonsson, A.: The use of scoring rubrics for formative assessment purposes revisited: a review. Educ. Res. Rev. **9**, 129–144 (2013)
35. Tekkumru-Kisa, M., Stein, M.K., Schunn, C.: A framework for analyzing cognitive demand and content-practices integration: Task analysis guide in science: TASK ANALYSIS GUIDE IN SCIENCE. J. Res. Sci. Teach. **52**, 659–685 (2015)
36. Großmann, L., Krüger, D.: Assessing the quality of science teachers' lesson plans: Evaluation and application of a novel instrument. Sci. Educ. **108**, 153–189 (2024)
37. Reynders, G., Lantz, J., Ruder, S.M., Stanford, C.L., Cole, R.S.: Rubrics to assess critical thinking and information processing in undergraduate STEM courses. Int. J. STEM Educ. **7**, 9 (2020)
38. König, J., Bremerich-Vos, A., Buchholtz, C., Glutsch, N.: General pedagogical knowledge, pedagogical adaptivity in written lesson plans, and instructional practice among preservice teachers. J. Curric. Stud. **52**, 800–822 (2020)
39. Suriano, R., Plebe, A., Acciai, A., Fabio, R.A.: Student interaction with ChatGPT can promote complex critical thinking skills. Learn. Instr. **95**, 102011 (2025)
40. Guo, K., Zhong, Y., Li, D., Chu, S.K.W.: Effects of chatbot-assisted in-class debates on students' argumentation skills and task motivation. Comput. Educ. **203**, 104862 (2023)
41. Essien, A., Bukoye, O.T., O'Dea, X., Kremantzis, M.: The influence of AI text generators on critical thinking skills in UK business schools. Stud. High. Educ. **49**(5), 865–882 (2024)
42. Tang, T., Sha, J., Zhao, Y., Wang, S., Wang, Z., Shen, S.: Unveiling the efficacy of ChatGPT in evaluating critical thinking skills through peer feedback analysis: Leveraging existing classification criteria. Thinking Skills and Creativity **53**, 101607 (2024)
43. Alsofyani, A.H., Barzanji, A.M.: The Effects of ChatGPT-Generated Feedback on Saudi EFL Learners' Writing Skills and Perception at the Tertiary Level: A Mixed-Methods Study. J. Educ. Comp. Res. **63**, 431–463 (2025)

44. Au, W.: High-stakes testing and curricular control: a qualitative metasynthesis. Educ. Res. **36**, 258–267 (2007)

Evaluating the Reliability and Validity of a GenAI-Supported Assessment of L2 Phrasal Verb Usage by Chinese Vocational High School Learners

Lining Zhang, Huixin Wang, Huaiya Liu, Angxuan Chen, and Jiyou Jia(✉)

Graduate School of Education, Peking University, Beijing, China
{lnzhang25,angxuan.chen}@stu.pku.edu.cn, hxwang@gse.pku.edu.cn,
{liuhuaiya,jjy}@pku.edu.cn

Abstract. Generative AI (GenAI)-supported automated scoring is increasingly applied in language assessment, yet evidence remains limited for classroom tasks targeting nuanced lexical-grammatical structures in vocational high school contexts. This study examines the reliability and validity of a GenAI-supported analytic scoring system for evaluating phrasal verb (PV) use in an English as a second language (L2) task at a vocational high school in Beijing. Student PV use in textbook-aligned sentence tasks was assessed across three analytic dimensions: accuracy, completeness, and naturalness. Three human experts scored 226 sentences with 10 PVs written by 25 students, with criterion scores defined as the mean of the three human scorers' scores for each analytic dimension and the total score. Three large language models GPT-OSS, GLM-4, and Gemma-3 scored those sentences across two rounds using specified prompts. Aggregated human scoring was highly reliable, whereas single-scorer reliability was only moderate. Among the models, GPT-OSS demonstrated the strongest human-machine alignment and temporal stability, while Gemma-3 exhibited substantial test-retest variability. GenAI-supported scoring can approximate aggregated human judgments, but stability and alignment vary across models. From an argument-based perspective, the findings provide initial validity evidence for the evaluation and generalization inferences underlying GenAI-supported scoring of PV use in classroom-based sentence-construction tasks.

Keywords: Automated Scoring · Generative Artificial Intelligence · Phrasal Verbs (PVs) · Argument-based Validation · Human-machine Agreement

1 Introduction

Automated scoring technologies have become integral to language assessment, offering scalable support for evaluating learner responses. Recently, Large Language Models (LLMs) have significantly enhanced these systems, producing evaluative judgments that align closely with human scoring while reducing manual effort [1, 2]. However, GenAI

K. T. Chui et al. (Eds.): ICBL 2026, LNCS 16778, pp. 269–286, 2027.
https://doi.org/10.1007/978-981-92-3761-6_19

use in fine-grained, classroom-based assessment is still limited, particularly in vocational high schools. This gap is particularly salient in vocational high school education, where English instruction often emphasizes practical communication, textbook-linked language use, and short contextualized production. At the same time, such classrooms often face constraints in instructional time, assessment resources, and opportunities for individualized feedback. These features make vocational high schools a particularly relevant setting for examining whether GenAI-supported analytic scoring can provide dependable support for routine classroom assessment. Most research focuses on extended writing by university students, leaving a gap in validity evidence for short, domain-specific assessments in K–12 and vocational settings [3].

Evaluating short, meaning-focused responses brings distinct psychometric challenges. Scorers must determine whether a response conveys intended meaning, includes necessary structures, and follows usage norms. This is especially true for English phrasal verbs (PVs), which are an important component of everyday English communication and learners' lexical and phraseological competence. PVs are particularly challenging for L2 learners because their meanings are often non-compositional, context-dependent, and difficult to infer from the meanings of the individual verb and particle [4]. Their flexible syntactic patterns and the form–meaning differences between English and learners' first languages may further increase learning difficulty. As a result, learners may avoid using PVs or rely on single-word substitutes, even when PVs would be more natural in everyday communication. In vocational English learning, where instruction often emphasizes practical communication and textbook-based language use, the ability to use common PVs appropriately is closely connected to learners' capacity to produce meaningful and natural short sentences. When assessing PVs, teachers must therefore balance the instructional value of detailed feedback with the high cognitive demand of evaluating accuracy, structural completeness, and idiomaticity across numerous brief responses.

GenAI-based tools offer a potential solution to these challenges, yet the complexity of PVs raises concerns regarding construct representation and scoring stability. From an argument-based validation perspective, using GenAI scores requires a clear link between observed scores and the underlying skills measured [5]. To address this, the present study investigates the reliability and validity of a GenAI-supported analytic scoring system for PVs use in a Chinese vocational high school. The study is informed by an argument-based validation perspective, focusing on the evaluation inference, that is, whether model-generated scores meaningfully reflect targeted aspects of PV use, and the generalization inference, that is, whether such scores remain dependable across scoring occasions within this task setting. We compare three models (GPT-OSS, GLM-4, and Gemma-3) to evaluate their performance on short, domain-specific classroom tasks and their stability across scoring occasions. This study advances understanding of technology-mediated feedback practices and contributes to existing research in three ways. First, it extends GenAI-supported language assessment to the underexplored context of vocational high schools, where English assessment is closely connected to practical communication, textbook-based learning, and classroom feedback. Second, it focuses on the fine-grained assessment of L2 phrasal verb use, a challenging lexical-grammatical construct requiring judgments of accuracy, completeness, and naturalness. Third, it provides initial validity evidence for the evaluation and generalization inferences underlying GenAI-supported scoring by examining human-score reliability, model stability, cross-model correspondence, and human-machine alignment. The findings offer implications for the responsible integration of GenAI into vocational English assessment and feedback practices.

2 Literature Review

2.1 GenAI-Supported Scoring in Language Assessment

Recent developments in GenAI are reshaping language assessment area with an increasing body of research emphasizing its impact across different stages of the assessment process. This includes its role in item generation, task design, and assessment strategy development [6, 7]; the affordances and challenges in GenAI-supported classroom-based assessment that involve teachers, learners, and institutions [8–10]; and concerns about academic integrity, particularly in relation to GenAI-driven academic dishonesty [11–13]. Within these studies, most work has focused on assessments for L2 writing, reading, and speaking [14]. Notably, there has been a growing interest in integrating automated or GenAI-supported scoring and feedback into language assessments [15, 16]. This scope of research evaluates whether and how GenAI can complement or approximate human scoring practices in language assessment [17].

2.2 Accuracy and Consistency of GenAI-Supported Scoring

GenAI-supported scoring represents a new wave of automated language assessment. Unlike traditional automated scoring systems (AES), GenAI models assess language by considering full sentences and overall context. This allows for analysis of deeper and more complex language features rather than just surface-level elements. In this approach, accuracy and consistency remain key evaluation criteria. Accuracy refers to how closely automated scores match reliable human judgments and ensures the scores reflect students' actual language ability without being affected by unrelated errors. On the other hand, consistency concerns the reliability of these scores across different tasks, evaluators and times [18]. These two qualities are essential for fair score interpretation and assessment decisions.

Research has explored the effectiveness of GenAI-supported scoring, with a majority of studies comparing human scoring with GenAI-supported scores under various training or prompting conditions [17, 19, 20]. These studies evaluate whether GenAI feedback can approximate or complement human teacher judgment in terms of quality, relevance, and usefulness. Overall, prior studies reveal four broad patterns. Table 1 summarises representative studies on GenAI-supported scoring in language assessment. First, several studies report comparable performance between GenAI and human scorers, demonstrating strong correlations and overall agreement [21–23]. Second, other studies find that human scorers outperform GenAI, with AI-generated scores showing greater deviation and lower consistency [17, 20, 24–26]. Third, a smaller but growing strand of research suggests that GenAI can outperform human scorers on certain metrics, particularly reliability and the breadth or relevance of feedback, especially when advanced models such as ChatGPT 4 are used [19, 27, 28]. Finally, some studies also present mixed or inconclusive results. They show instances where GenAI exhibits greater consistency but lower validity, or where human-AI agreement varies depending on proficiency levels, task types, or learner subgroups [29, 30]. Overall, these findings emphasize both the opportunities and challenges of using GenAI-supported scoring in language assessment. While GenAI offers promising solutions to long-standing challenges such as the time-intensive nature of scoring, human scoring bias and inconsistencies, and the need to address diverse learner needs [2], its performance remains constrained by model-based limitations and the need for careful calibration and rubric alignment. Accordingly, existing evidence suggests that GenAI is currently most effective when used to complement rather than replace human scorers [2]. The above findings point to a gap regarding the assessment of the accuracy and consistency of GenAI-supported scoring in the area of PVs, which is illustrated below.

Table 1. Representative studies on GenAI-supported scoring in language assessment.

Study		Assessment focus	Methodologies	Results	Limitations
Group 1: comparable performance between GenAI and human scorers	Attali & Burstein [26]	Comparison of human and machine reliabilities; compare the human-machine true-score correlation	E-rater model building and scoring	The true-score correlation between human and e-rater scores is close to perfect	Limited reliability evidence from single-essay, single-administration comparisons; human–machine agreement is constrained by human rater reliability
	Bridgeman et al. [22]	Fairness and subgroup differences in automated essay scoring	Large-scale subgroup analysis of operational TOEFL iBT and GRE essay data	Human and machine scores were very similar across most subgroups	Non-negligible subgroup discrepancies; possible changes in subgroup rankings if machine scores are used alone; uncertainty over whether discrepancies reflect machine bias or human-rating limitations;
	Geçkin et al. [23]	Assessment of second-language academic writing by ChatGPT-3.5 and human raters	Correlational human–AI scoring comparison	ChatGPT-3.5 showed slight to fair but significant agreement with two human raters	Limited human-like judgment; vulnerable to superficial textual features; unsuitable as a sole evaluator; limited assessment of creativity; requires comparison with other AI scoring systems

(*continued*)

Table 1. *(continued)*

Study		Assessment focus	Methodologies	Results	Limitations
Group 2: human scorers outperform GenAI	Bui & Barrot [17]	The relationship between ChatGPT and human rater scores and how consistent ChatGPT-assigned scores are when taken at multiple time points	cross-sectional quantitative approach	ChatGPT's scoring did not align closely with an experienced human rater and failed to establish consistency after two rounds of scoring	Limited human benchmark with only one experienced rater; focused only on scores rather than qualitative feedback; did not examine learner-level factors such as proficiency or writing instruction
	Shabara et al. [20]	Examine the accuracy and consistency of ChatGPT compared to teachers, as well as with itself, after being trained on a rubric	Quantitative correlational non-experimental design	Teachers' scores exhibited a higher level of accuracy compared to those generated by ChatGPT. The results also revealed that ChatGPT exhibits a moderate, yet questioned, level of intra-rater reliability	Use of the free ChatGPT-3.5 version may have limited access to updated model capabilities; rubric complexity may have affected scoring accuracy; limited rubric-training examples may have reduced score consistency and accuracy
	Shin & Lee [24]	ChatGPT-based automated writing evaluation of L2 English essays and its agreement with human teacher ratings	Descriptive research design using secondary essay data	ChatGPT deviated slightly more from the expected rating model than the human teachers, meaning it should support rather than replace teacher judgment	Relatively small dataset; includes only one type of essay (persuasive writing on a familiar topic)
	Tensen et al. [25]	GenAI feedback on doctoral thesis assessment doctoral thesis assessment	Single-case study	Alignment with the human reviewer was limited, with genAI feedback lacking the nuance, depth, and relational framing central to doctoral supervision	Single case; limited generalizability

(continued)

Table 1. *(continued)*

Study		Assessment focus	Methodologies	Results	Limitations
	Yıldız et al. [26]	GenAI and human tutor feedback on L2 argumentative writing performance	Experimental crossover design	Human tutor feedback led to significantly greater improvement in language, mechanics, and overall writing scores. GenAI feedback showed no significant difference in improving writing components or overall performance	Limited sample size and short study duration; use of only one GenAI tool
Group 3: GenAI outperform human scorers	Li et al. [19]	Assess the reliability of the holistic scores assigned to EFL essays by ChatGPT versions 3.5 and 4 compared to college English teachers	Mixed method with quantitative scoring and qualitative feedback	The scoring reliability of ChatGPT3.5 was consistently lower than teacher raters; ChatGPT4 demonstrated consistently higher reliability coefficients than the teachers. Both ChatGPT3.5 and 4 consistently provided more relevant feedback on the EFL essays than the teacher raters. Furthermore, ChatGPT versions 3.5 and 4 were equally relevant across the language, content, and organization aspects of the essays, whereas the teacher raters generally focused more on language but provided less relevant feedback on content and organization	Limited sample size and single-university context; potential institutional bias from human raters; comparison limited to two ChatGPT versions, without examining other AI models or configurations

(continued)

Table 1. *(continued)*

Study		Assessment focus	Methodologies	Results	Limitations
	Mizumoto & Eguchi [27]	GPT-based automated essay scoring of non-native English writing, focusing on scoring accuracy, reliability, and the influence of linguistic features	Corpus-based GPT AES study	GPT-3 text-davinci-003 showed a certain level of accuracy and reliability in scoring TOEFL11 essays and could support human evaluation	No fine-tuning; prompt-dependent results; used older GPT-3 model; limited attention to educational/ethical implications; black-box explainability concerns
	Yancey et al. [28]	Evaluate how well GPT-3.5 and GPT-4 can rate short essay responses written by L2 English learners on a high-stakes language assessment, computing inter-rater agreement with human ratings	Quantitative human–AI rating comparison	When calibration examples are provided, GPT-4 can perform almost as well as modern Automatic Writing Evaluation (AWE) methods, but agreement with human ratings can vary depending on the test-taker's first language (L1)	Limited GPT-3.5 performance; limited effectiveness of prompt engineering
Group 4: mixed or inconclusive results	Cohen et al. [29]	Validating human and automated scoring of essays	Quantitative human–AES validation study	The reliability and validity of AES diverge: although the AES scoring is, naturally, more consistent than the human ratings, it is less valid	Limited to short Hebrew essays and one AES system; limited generalizability; possible mismatch between human and AES constructs of writing quality
	Alkhofi [30]	Whether ChatGPT-4o can mirror individual instructors' evaluative tendencies	Human–AI score comparison with instructor-specific prompt calibration	GPT was more generous toward lower-quality writings, assigning higher mean scores than human raters, whereas teachers tended to award higher scores than GPT for high-quality writings	Limited generalizability from a single Saudi ESL context; small validation sample; reliance on holistic grading; potential prompt-calibration variability; underrepresentation of low-quality essays

2.3 Construct Representation in Phrasal Verbs Assessment

The Common European Framework of Reference for Languages (CEFR) descriptors at the A1-A2 levels frame language ability in functional terms, focusing on intelligibility, appropriateness, and successful communication of meaning rather than formal correctness alone [31]. In parallel, analytic writing rubrics used in assessments such as

Cambridge Young Learners English and A2 Key explicitly distinguish between meaning-related criteria, sentence-level realization, and the quality or naturalness of language use, particularly in short, controlled writing tasks [32, 33]. Together, these frameworks suggest that the assessment of PV use in sentence production should be multidimensional rather than reduced to a single holistic judgment.

PVs are a particularly meaningful construct for this purpose. They are frequently used in everyday English, highly relevant to communicative competence, and well documented as an area of persistent difficulty for L2 learners because successful use requires coordination of meaning, form, and phraseological convention [4, 34, 35]. In writing development, PVs are important not simply as vocabulary items, but as multiword units that reflect learners' ability to produce contextually appropriate and structurally acceptable language. For short classroom tasks, the successful use of the target PVs is therefore the core indicator of task completion, while sentence realization and phraseological appropriateness function as supporting dimensions of performance.

Accordingly, the present study assesses students' PV performance along three dimensions: accuracy, completeness, and naturalness. Accuracy refers to whether the target PV is used to express the intended meaning appropriately in the response. Completeness refers to whether the response contains the obligatory structural elements needed to realize the target PV in an acceptable sentence or clause. Naturalness refers to whether the target PV is used in a contextually appropriate way that is consistent with conventional English usage. These three dimensions were selected on both theoretical and practical grounds. Theoretically, they are broadly aligned with communicative, structural, and phraseological aspects highlighted in CEFR-informed assessment and PV acquisition research. Practically, they reflect the kinds of distinctions teachers make when judging whether a student has used a textbook-taught PV correctly, fully, and appropriately in classroom sentence production.

In the context of Chinese vocational high school education, these dimensions are especially relevant because students frequently encounter difficulties with multi-word expressions and producing fluent sentences. The chosen three dimensions also align with curricular goals in this context that prioritize both linguistic accuracy and communicative competence in school-based English learning.

3 Research Design

To address these gaps, this study adopted an argument-based validity approach [36] to examine the extent to which GenAI-supported assessment of L2 PVs use corresponded to aggregated human scoring in a classroom-based design. Within this framework, the evaluation inference concerns whether model-generated scores meaningfully capture targeted aspects of PV use, whereas the generalization inference concerns whether such scores remain dependable across scoring occasions.

3.1 Research Questions

(1) RQ1 (Criterion quality for the evaluation inference): To what extent are human scorings of accuracy, completeness, and naturalness for PVs use sufficiently reliable to serve as criterion scores for evaluating GenAI-supported scoring?

(2) RQ2 (Within-model stability for the generalization inference): To what extent do GenAI models exhibit score coherence within a scoring round and test-retest stability across scoring occasions for PVs use?

(3) RQ3 (Cross-model correspondence as supplementary evidence): To what extent do different GenAI models (GPT-OSS, GLM-4, Gemma-3) show similar scoring patterns at the total-score and dimension levels for PVs use?

(4) RQ4 (Human-machine alignment for the evaluation inference): To what extent do GenAI-supported scores align with aggregated human scorings for accuracy, completeness, naturalness, and the total score for PVs use?

Together, the four research questions form a stepwise validity argument for GenAI-supported PV scoring. RQ1 establishes whether aggregated human scores are reliable enough to function as criterion scores. RQ2 examines within-model stability as evidence for the generalization inference, while RQ3 investigates cross-model correspondence as supplementary evidence of scoring comparability. RQ4 then evaluates the degree of human-machine alignment, providing evidence for the evaluation inference. This sequence allows the study to examine not only whether GenAI scores are close to human scores, but also whether the human criterion is dependable, whether model scores are stable, and whether different models show comparable scoring patterns.

3.2 Data Collection

The study was conducted in one Grade 10 class at a vocational high school in China, during the fall semester of the 2025–2026 academic year. The class followed the school's regular English curriculum and used the officially assigned textbook sequence for vocational high school English instruction. In this instructional context, students were expected not only to recognize target vocabulary and expressions, but also to produce short contextualized sentences using textbook-taught items. The participating students were native speakers of Mandarin Chinese, and their classroom English performance was broadly aligned with approximately A1–A2 CEFR communicative demands. The PV task was therefore designed to match the level and content of routine classroom instruction rather than to elicit advanced or extended writing.

Prior to the task, the target PVs had been introduced as part of regular teaching. During instruction, teachers provided brief contextualized examples and guided practice to familiarize students with the meanings and typical uses of the target PVs. This was intended to reduce misunderstanding caused by item unfamiliarity before assessment. The PVs use data were collected through a computer-based classroom task administered in the school's computer lab during the regular school schedule. Students were asked to write one full sentence for each of ten target English PVs drawn from the textbook units covered in the course. The task required students to incorporate the target phrasal verb in a meaningful context rather than to provide isolated translations or decontextualized fragments.

The ten target PVs were selected according to four criteria: (a) they had been explicitly taught in the current textbook sequence, (b) they were considered instructionally important in the school curriculum, (c) they represented common everyday phrasal verbs relevant to practical communication, and (d) together they covered a modest range of difficulty within the textbook-aligned proficiency progression. Following the school's instructional materials, the selected items were distributed across four textbook-linked CEFR bands. Because the task was designed as a classroom-aligned assessment rather than an external proficiency test, the item selection prioritized curricular relevance and instructional familiarity over broad construct sampling.

The task was completed independently within 20 min. No example responses, dictionaries, or corrective prompts were provided during task completion. 25 students participated in the test. Of these, 22 completed all 10 items, whereas the other 3 students submitted responses for only 1 PV, 2 PVs, and 3 PVs, respectively. As a result, 226 valid sentence-level responses were obtained and organized for subsequent human and GenAI-supported scoring.

3.3 Scoring Rubrics

Based on CEFR principles and PV acquisition research [31], student responses were evaluated across three weighted dimensions (Total: 100). The scoring rubrics utilized in this study were designed to align with the core pedagogical framework of our classroom-based AI assessment platform. Specifically, the analytic dimensions of Accuracy, Completeness, and Naturalness serve as the standard metrics for evaluating L2 phrasal verb usage within our system, ensuring that the results of this study provide validity evidence for our ongoing classroom implementation.

Accuracy (40%): Semantic appropriateness and successful conveyance of the core meaning, prioritizing interpretability over minor formal errors.

Completeness (30%): Presence of obligatory structural elements required for a functional sentence or clause.

Naturalness (30%): Contextual and phraseological appropriateness consistent with conventional English usage.

These three dimensions reflect the multidimensional nature of PV performance in classroom sentence production and align with CEFR-informed emphases on meaningful communication, structural control, and appropriateness of language use, as well as prior research on L2 PV acquisition [31, 34, 35]. The weighting ratio of 40:30:30 was adopted to reflect the instructional purpose of the task. Because the task aimed to assess students' productive use of textbook-taught PVs, semantic accuracy was treated as the primary indicator of successful PV use and was therefore assigned the highest weight. If the intended meaning of the target PV is not conveyed, the response cannot be considered successful even when it is structurally complete or relatively natural. Completeness and naturalness were each assigned 30% because they represent two complementary supporting aspects of PV performance: structural realization and phraseological appropriateness. This weighting therefore gives priority to meaning-based use while still recognizing the importance of form and contextual appropriateness in classroom sentence production.

Each of the 226 student responses was evaluated based on three analytic dimensions. This produced a total of 678 individual scores across the dataset.

3.4 Human and GenAI Scoring

Three human experts were selected based on their disciplinary background and assessment experience. The selection criteria included: (a) academic training in English language education or a related field; (b) experience in teaching or assessing L2 English learners; and (c) familiarity with rubric-based evaluation of sentence-level English production. All three scorers had experience in English language teaching and/or language assessment research. They independently scored all responses using the analytic rubric.

Before formal scoring, they completed a calibration session to align their interpretation of the dimensions and scoring criteria. For the main analyses, criterion scores were defined as the mean of the three scorers' scores for each dimension and for the total score.

Automated scoring was conducted using three LLMs: GPT-OSS, GLM-4, and Gemma-3. All models were used under the same internal API environment and the same standardized prompt. This prompt was designed to align with the core pedagogical framework of our classroom-based AI assessment platform, ensuring consistency between our research evaluation and practical instructional application. The prompt included the target PV, the student response, the scoring rubric for accuracy (40%), completeness (30%), and naturalness (30%), as well as a fixed output format requiring a brief scoring rationale, separate dimension scores and a total score. No few-shot examples were provided. The prompt was designed as a rubric-guided scoring instruction rather than a chain-of-thought elicitation task, aiming to elicit evaluative judgments that mirror the criteria used in our classroom-based system. Using the same prompt structure across models was intended to enhance procedural comparability and reproducibility. Each model scored all responses twice under the same conditions (t_1 and t_2) to examine temporal stability.

3.5 Data Analysis Methods

All analyses were conducted in Python. Because Shapiro-Wilk tests indicated non-normality in both human and GenAI total scores (all $p < .001$), Spearman's rank-order correlation was used for correlation analyses. Human-scoring reliability (RQ1) was examined using Cronbach's α and intraclass correlation coefficients (ICCs). Cronbach's α was used as a descriptive index of inter-scorer consistency, ICC(2,1) was used to estimate single-scorer reliability, and ICC(3,k) was used to estimate the reliability of aggregated scores across the three scorers. GenAI scoring consistency (RQ2) was examined through Cronbach's α, test-retest Spearman correlations, and Wilcoxon signed-rank tests. Inter-model agreement (RQ3) was assessed using pairwise Spearman correlations and ICCs. Human-machine alignment (RQ4) was examined through Spearman correlations between aggregated human scores and model-generated scores. Because six responses lacked complete outputs across both scoring rounds, analyses involving model scores were based on 220 responses.

4 Findings

4.1 RQ1: Reliability of Human Scoring

Human scoring showed strong reliability across all three analytic dimensions. As shown in Table 2, Cronbach's α ranged from 0.870 to 0.878. Single-scorer reliability was moderate, with ICC(2,1) values ranging from 0.659 to 0.700, whereas aggregated scoring was highly reliable. These results support the use of averaged human scores as criterion measures for subsequent analyses.

Table 2. Inter-scorer reliability of human scorings across analytic dimensions.

Dimension	Cronbach's α	ICC(2,1)	ICC(3,k)
Accuracy	0.872	0.659	0.872
Completeness	0.870	0.659	0.870
Naturalness	0.878	0.700	0.878

Note. ICC(2,1) represents single-scorer reliability; ICC(3,k) represents the reliability of mean scorings of all scorers

4.2 RQ2: Evaluation of GenAI Scoring Consistency

As a descriptive indicator of score coherence across task items, Cronbach's α coefficients indicated high internal consistency for all three GenAI models. As shown in Table 3, Cronbach's α values were 0.880 for GPT-OSS, 0.927 for Gemma-3, and 0.974 for GLM-4. However, the models differed substantially in temporal stability across scoring rounds.

GPT-OSS showed high test-retest stability ($\rho = 0.969$) and no significant mean difference between t1 and t2 ($p = 0.069$). GLM-4 produced identical total scores across rounds, yielding perfect test-retest stability ($\rho = 1.000$, $p = 1.00$). By contrast, Gemma-3 showed substantially lower stability ($\rho = 0.661$) and a significant mean difference across rounds ($p < .001$). These findings indicate that internal coherence alone is not sufficient to establish dependable GenAI scoring; repeated-score stability also matters.

Table 3. Internal consistency and test-retest stability of GenAI scoring models.

Model	Cronbach's α	Test-retest Spearman ρ	Mean difference
GPT-OSS	0.880	0.969	0.777
GLM-4	0.974	1.000	0.000
Gemma-3	0.927	0.661	19.886**

Note. **: $p < .001$. Mean difference refers to the mean of response-level total-score differences between t_2 and t_1

4.3 RQ3: Agreement Across GenAI Models

Agreement across GenAI models was examined using Spearman's rank-order correlations for total scores and the three analytic dimensions. Scores were averaged across the two scoring rounds (t_1 and t_2) prior to analysis.

As shown in Table 4, at the total-score level, the strongest correspondence was observed between GPT-OSS and GLM-4 ($\rho = 0.822$), followed by GPT-OSS and Gemma-3 ($\rho = 0.799$), whereas GLM-4 and Gemma-3 showed a somewhat lower correlation ($\rho = 0.756$). When the three models were treated as parallel scorers, single-model reliability was moderate, with ICC(2,1) = 0.663, whereas the reliability of the mean score across models was high, with ICC(3,k) = 0.900.

A similar pattern was found at the dimension level. GPT-OSS and GLM-4 showed consistently strong agreement across accuracy, completeness, and naturalness (ρ = 0.772, 0.764, and 0.763, respectively). GPT-OSS and Gemma-3 also showed substantial agreement, particularly for completeness ($\rho = 0.808$). By contrast, GLM-4 and Gemma-3 showed comparatively weaker agreement across the three dimensions ($\rho = 0.714$, 0.692, and 0.722), suggesting some divergence in how these models operationalized the analytic rubric.

Table 4. Spearman rank-order correlation coefficients (ρ) between different LLMs regarding the total score, and three dimensions accuracy, completeness and naturalness.

Comparison	Total	Accuracy	Completeness	Naturalness
GPT-OSS vs. GLM-4	0.822	0.772	0.764	0.763
GPT-OSS vs. Gemma-3	0.799	0.783	0.808	0.776
GLM-4 vs. Gemma-3	0.756	0.714	0.692	0.722

Note. Model scores were averaged across two scoring rounds (t_1 and t_2) prior to correlation analyses. All coefficients are Spearman's rank-order correlations.

4.4 RQ4: Agreement Between Human and GenAI Scores

Human-machine alignment was examined by comparing aggregated human scores with model-generated scores averaged across the two scoring rounds. As shown in Table 5, GPT-OSS demonstrated the strongest overall correspondence with aggregated human scores at the total-score level ($\rho = 0.720$). At the dimension level, its alignment was moderate for accuracy ($\rho = 0.650$) and stronger for completeness ($\rho = 0.753$) and naturalness ($\rho = 0.710$).

GLM-4 also showed moderate-to-substantial alignment with human scores at the total-score level ($\rho = 0.694$). Its dimension-level correlations were similar for accuracy ($\rho = 0.695$) and completeness ($\rho = 0.698$), but lower for naturalness ($\rho = 0.618$), suggesting relatively weaker correspondence on phraseological appropriateness.

Gemma-3 showed the weakest overall alignment, with a total-score correlation of $\rho = 0.637$. Its dimension-level correlations were moderate and relatively even across accuracy ($\rho = 0.598$), completeness ($\rho = 0.660$), and naturalness ($\rho = 0.597$). Overall, these results indicate that human-machine alignment in GenAI-supported PV scoring was clearly model-dependent rather than uniform across systems.

Table 5. Spearman's rank-order correlation coefficients (ρ) between GenAI-supported scores and aggregated human scorings

Model	Accuracy	Completeness	Naturalness	Total score
GPT-OSS	0.650	0.753	0.710	0.720
GLM-4	0.695	0.698	0.618	0.694
Gemma-3	0.598	0.660	0.597	0.637

5 Discussion

This study examined whether GenAI-supported scoring can meaningfully support analytic assessment of short, textbook-aligned PV use in a Chinese vocational high school context. Overall, the findings suggest that automated analytic scoring is feasible for this type of classroom task, but its defensibility depends strongly on the specific model and scoring dimension.

First, aggregated human scores provided a reliable benchmark, whereas single-scorer reliability was only moderate. This indicates that analytic scoring of short responses is cognitively demanding even for expert scorers, especially when multiple dimensions must be judged simultaneously. For this reason, averaged human ratings appear to be a more appropriate criterion than any single scorer when evaluating GenAI-supported scoring.

Second, although all three models showed high internal consistency, they differed substantially in temporal stability. GLM-4 produced identical repeated scores, GPT-OSS also showed high stability, and Gemma-3 exhibited substantial variation across runs. These findings suggest that internal coherence alone is not sufficient for meaningful score interpretation. If a model does not generate stable scores for the same response under the same conditions, its classroom use should be approached with caution.

Third, model differences help explain why previous research has reported mixed findings on GenAI-supported scoring. In the present study, GPT-OSS showed the strongest overall alignment with human judgments, GLM-4 followed closely, and Gemma-3 showed weaker and less stable correspondence. This suggests that validity claims should be made for specific models in specific tasks, rather than generalized across GenAI-supported scoring as a whole.

The dimension-level results are also informative. Across models, correspondence with human ratings tended to be stronger for completeness and, in some cases, accuracy than for naturalness. This pattern suggests that naturalness may be more difficult for GenAI systems to evaluate consistently, likely because it depends on more subtle judgments of phraseological appropriateness and contextual fit. In classroom-based scoring, such distinctions matter because they affect not only total scores but also the interpretability of analytic feedback.

Taken together, the findings indicate that GenAI-supported PV scoring has clear potential for learning-oriented assessment, especially when teachers need efficient support for rubric-based scoring. At the same time, dependable classroom use requires attention to repeated-score stability, dimension-specific performance, and model selection.

6 Conclusions

This study explored a less examined area in classroom language assessment: how reliable and valid GenAI-supported analytic scoring is when applied to textbook-based English PV tasks.

Using an argument-based validation framework, the study explored how well GenAI-supported analytic scores align with human judgments and how stable those scores are over time. The results show that averaged human scores offer a reliable benchmark, while individual ratings tend to vary more. Across models, GenAI scoring displayed substantial variability: while all models produced internally coherent scores, only some demonstrated stable performance over time and close alignment with aggregated human judgments, whereas others exhibited notable instability or weaker correspondence.

Overall, the results suggest that a subset of current large language models can approximate human analytic scoring patterns for PVs assessment, but such performance is model-dependent rather than uniform. These findings highlight that differences in reliability, stability, and human-machine alignment have important implications for score interpretation and use in classroom settings, and that validity claims for GenAI-supported analytic scoring must be established on a model- and task-specific basis.

In terms of practical implications, these findings suggest that GenAI-supported scoring could be used by vocational high school teachers as a supplementary tool for formative classroom assessment. Teachers may use stable models to initially screen students' PV sentences, identify recurring problems in meaning, structural completeness, and naturalness, and generate feedback for classroom review or targeted practice. This could reduce the time burden of marking short responses and support more timely feedback. However, because model performance was not uniform, GenAI scores should be treated as provisional and checked by teachers, especially for borderline or unexpected responses. Therefore, GenAI should support, rather than replace, teachers' professional judgment in vocational English assessment.

7 Limitations and Future Work

Several limitations should be noted. First, the dataset came from a single vocational high school and a limited set of textbook-based PV items, which restricts the generalizability of the findings. Second, the study focused on short sentence-level responses rather than broader writing or speaking performance. Third, the analyses were conducted primarily at the response level and therefore do not directly establish student-level score use. Finally, the validity argument addressed mainly the evaluation and generalization inferences; other issues, such as subgroup performance, feature transparency, and classroom impact, were beyond the scope of this study.

Future research should extend this work to more diverse learner populations, task formats, and response types. It should also examine model behavior across learner subgroups, investigate the linguistic features underlying GenAI-supported scoring, and explore calibration or ensemble approaches to improve stability and alignment. Classroom-based studies of feedback use would also provide valuable evidence for practical implementation.

Acknowledgments. This study was funded by the National Education Science Planning Project "The Research of Intelligent Assessment and Tutoring for Students Based on Big-data Mining" (Number: BCA220208) granted by National Office for Educational Sciences Planning, China.

Disclosure of Interests. The authors have no competing interests to declare that are relevant to the content of this article.

References

1. Atkinson, J., Palma, D.: An LLM-based hybrid approach for enhanced automated essay scoring. Sci. Rep. **15**, 14551 (2025)
2. Chuang, P.L., Yan, X.: Language assessment in the era of generative artificial intelligence: Opportunities, challenges, and future directions. System **134**, 103846 (2025)
3. Li, B., Tan, Y.L., Wang, C., Lowell, V.: Two years of innovation: A systematic review of empirical generative AI research in language learning and teaching. Comp. Educ. Artif. Intel. **9**, 100445 (2025)
4. Liao, Y., Fukuya, Y.J.: Avoidance of phrasal verbs: The case of Chinese learners of English. Lang. Learn. **54**(2), 193–226 (2004)
5. Chapelle, C.A.: Validity argument for language assessment: The framework is simple. Lang. Test. **29**(1), 19–27 (2012)
6. Aryadoust, V., Zakaria, A., Jia, Y.: Investigating the affordances of OpenAI's large language model in developing listening assessments. Comp. Educ. Artif. Intel. **6**, 100204 (2024)
7. Lin, Z., Chen, H.: Investigating the capability of ChatGPT for generating multiple-choice reading comprehension items. System **123**, 103344 (2024)
8. Allen, T.J., Mizumoto, A.: ChatGPT over my friends: Japanese English-as-a-Foreign-Language learners' preferences for editing and proofreading strategies. RELC Journal **57**(1), (2026)
9. Le, H., et al.: Breaking human dominance: Investigating learners' preferences for learning feedback from generative AI and human tutors. Br. J. Edu. Technol. **56**(5), 1758–1783 (2025)
10. Muniandy, J., Selvanathan, M.: ChatGPT, a partnering tool to improve ESL learners' speaking skills: Case study in a public university. Malaysia. Teach. Pub. Administr. **43**(1), 4–20 (2025)
11. Cong-Lem, N., Tran, T.N., Nguyen, T.T.: Academic integrity in the age of generative AI: Perceptions and responses of Vietnamese EFL teachers. Teach. Eng. Technol. **24**(1), 28–47 (2024)
12. Mizumoto, A., Yasuda, S., Tamura, Y.: Identifying ChatGPT-generated texts in EFL students' writing: Through comparative analysis of linguistic fingerprints. Appl. Corpus Linguist. **4**(3), 100106 (2024)
13. Perkins, M.: Academic integrity considerations of AI large language models in the post-pandemic era: ChatGPT and beyond. J. Univ. Teach. Learn. Pract. **20**(2), 1–24 (2023)

14. Chen, A., Zhang, Y., Jia, J., Liang, M., Cha, Y., Lim, C.P.: A systematic review and meta-analysis of AI-enabled assessment in language learning: Design, implementation, and effectiveness. J. Comput. Assist. Learn. **41**(1), e13064 (2025)
15. Koraishi, O.: The intersection of AI and language assessment: A study on the reliability of ChatGPT in grading IELTS writing task 2. Lang. Teach. Res. Q. **43**(1), 22–42 (2024)
16. Tolstykh, O.M., Oshchepkova, T.: Beyond ChatGPT: Roles that artificial intelligence tools can play in an English language classroom. Discover Artif. Intel. **4**(1), 60 (2024)
17. Bui, N.M., Barrot, J.S.: ChatGPT as an automated essay scoring tool in the writing classrooms: How it compares with human scoring. Educ. Inf. Technol. **30**(2), 2041–2058 (2025)
18. Livingston, S.A., Carlson, J., Bridgeman, B.: Test reliability—Basic concepts (Research Memorandum No. RM-18-01). Educational Testing Service, Princeton (2018)
19. Li, J., Huang, J., Wu, W., Whipple, P.B.: Evaluating the role of ChatGPT in enhancing EFL writing assessments in classroom settings: A preliminary investigation. Humanit. Soc. Sci. Comm. **11**(1), 1–9 (2024)
20. Shabara, R., ElEbyary, K., Boraie, D.: Teachers or ChatGPT: The issue of accuracy and consistency in L2 assessment. Teach. Eng. Technol. **24**(2), 71–92 (2024)
21. Paoprasert, N., Chui, K.T., Yip, T.Y., Liu, J., Ng, K.K.: A Review of Large Language Model Evaluation Metrics in Education. In: Cheung, S.K.S., Liu, X., Xu, G., Kwok, L.F. (eds.) International Conference on Technology in Education, CCIS, vol. 2752, pp. 402–415. Springer Nature, Singapore (2025)
22. Bridgeman, B., Trapani, C., Yigal, A.: Comparison of human and machine scoring of essays: Differences by gender, ethnicity, and country. Appl. Measur. Educ. **25**(1), 27–40 (2012)
23. Geçkin, V., Kızıltaş, E., Çınar, Ç.: Assessing second-language academic writing: AI vs. human raters. J. Educ. Technol. Online Learn. **6**(4), 1096–1108 (2023)
24. Shin, D., Lee, J.H.: Exploratory study on the potential of ChatGPT as a rater of second language writing. Educ. Inf. Technol. **29**(18), 24735–24757 (2024)
25. Tensen, D., Carey, M.D., Grainger, P.: Comparing ChatGPT-5 and other GenAI tools in doctoral confirmation: variability, persona effects, and alignment with human feedback. Assessment & Evaluation in Higher Education, 1–17 (Early Access)
26. Yıldız, M., Topuz, A.C., Polat, H., Taşlıbeyaz, E., Kurşun, E., Yeşilyurt, S.: A comparative analysis of human and GenAI-generated feedback on EFL students' argumentative writing performance. Educ. Psychol. **46**(1), 52–79 (2026)
27. Mizumoto, A., Eguchi, M.: Exploring the potential of using an AI language model for automated essay scoring. Res. Methods in Appl. Linguist. **2**, 1–13 (2023)
28. Yancey, K.P., LaFlair, G.T., Verardi, A.R., Burstein, J.: Rating short L2 essays on the CEFR scale with GPT-4. In: Proceedings of the 18th Workshop on Innovative Use of NLP for Building Educational Applications (BEA 2023), pp. 576–584. Association for Computational Linguistics (2023)
29. Cohen, Y., Levia, E., Ben-Simon, A.: Validating human and automated scoring of essays against "true" scores. Appl. Measur. Educ. **31**(3), 241–250 (2018)
30. Alkhofi, A.: Can ChatGPT score ESL writing? A correlation analysis between teacher and GenAI scores. Language Teaching Research **0**(0) (2026)
31. Council of Europe: Common European Framework of Reference for Languages: Learning, teaching, assessment. Cambridge University Press, Cambridge (2001)
32. Cambridge Assessment English: A2 Key handbook for teachers. Cambridge University Press, Cambridge (2018)
33. Cambridge Assessment English: Young Learners English handbook for teachers. Cambridge University Press, Cambridge (2020)
34. Garnier, M.: English phrasal verbs: Usage, knowledge, acquisition, PhD thesis. University of Nottingham (2016)

35. Schmitt, N., Redwood, S.: Learner knowledge of phrasal verbs: A corpus-informed study. In: Castello, E., Ackerley, K., Coccetta, F. (eds.) A taste for corpora, pp. 173–208. John Benjamins Publishing (2011)
36. Kane, M.T.: Validating the interpretations and uses of test scores. J. Educ. Meas. **50**(1), 1–73 (2013)

Training Needs in GenAI for Teachers of Vocational and Professional Education and Training in Hong Kong

Kwan Keung Ng[1(✉)], Ricky Yuk Kwan Ng[2], Dorothy Hon[3], Simon K. S. Cheung[4], Kwok Tai Chui[5], Robert Wells[6], and Siu Cheung Chan[7]

[1] Ming-Ai (London) Institute, London, UK
s.ng@ming-ai.org.uk
[2] Yes and No Solutions, Kowloon, Hong Kong, China
[3] Apexel Recruitment Limited, Wanchai, Hong Kong, China
Dorothy.hon@apexel.co
[4] Information Technology Office, Hong Kong Metropolitan University, Hong Kong, China
kscheung@hkmu.edu.hk
[5] School of Science and Technology, Hong Kong Metropolitan University, Hong Kong, China
jktchui@hkmu.edu.hk
[6] MELD Institute, Kowloon, Hong Kong, China
rwells@meld.institute
[7] Hong Kong Polytechnic University, Kowloon, Hong Kong, China
sc.chan@cpce-polyu.edu.hk

Abstract. Apart from functioning as a technological enhancement, Generative Artificial Intelligence (GenAI) introduces a new form of mediation in which intelligent systems actively participate in knowledge construction, feedback generation, and learning interactions. Whilst the debates about the advantages and drawbacks of GenAI are ongoing, limited attention has been paid to how these developments impact pedagogical practice and teachers' competence. This paper focuses on the training needs in GenAI for teachers of vocational and professional education and training (VPET) in Hong Kong. A study was conducted in 2025 to investigate their training needs, benefits, perceptions of GenAI in education, and acceptance of applying GenAI in teaching practice. Currently, there are around 4,000 teachers in Hong Kong's 20 + self-financing VPET institutions. The survey adopted a questionnaire with nine closed-ended items on a 6-point Likert scale for quantity feedback and one open-ended item for qualitative feedback. The survey questionnaire was sent to 19 self-financing VPET education institutions' full-time teaching staff (n = 2000) via emails with designated individual feedback link. 231 completed questionnaires (n = 231) were returned. The collected data was interpreted by mean and frequency distribution. The result and analysis revealed that while teachers are enthusiastic about GenAI's potential, their actual adoption of GenAI in teaching remains limited where significant barriers persist. The findings highlight some implications in teaching practice as well as concerns about policy and governance in the incorporation of GenAI into education. Implications of this study rest in the following few aspects, 1) Capabilities and Competences Building; 2) AI Guidelines, Policies and Governances; and 3) Research on the effectiveness of the AI training programme for teachers.

K. T. Chui et al. (Eds.): ICBL 2026, LNCS 16778, pp. 287–295, 2027.
https://doi.org/10.1007/978-981-92-3761-6_20

Keywords: Generative Artificial Intelligence (GenAI) · Blended · Flexible and Open Learning · Vocational and Professional Education and Training (VPET) · Teacher Training

1 Introduction

Generative Artificial Intelligence (GenAI) has been revolutionising the concept of learning and teaching in the education sector. Rapid development in digital learning and GenAI is a major initiative in the global education sector. Beyond grading and scheduling, GenAI aids curriculum design, generating learning materials, simplifying academic texts, resource allocation, data-driven decisions for performance tracking, research support and skill development [1–9]. Early debates on GenAI in education have focused on issues such as plagiarism, assessment, authorship, ethics, dependency, and low-level thinking [10]. GenAI offers many advantages that can accelerate learning, including timely summarising of relevant information, scaffolding learning, enabling critical reflection, augmenting knowledge, and helping students construct their own knowledge [11–13]. Digital, blended, flexible and open learning has historically been conceptualised as the integration of face-to-face and digital instructional environments, supporting flexibility, accessibility, and learner engagement. Digital learning also utilises technologies to enable and engage learning, for example, immersive technologies such as augmented and virtual reality (AR/VR); and other devices engaged learning such as Metaverse and Apple Vision Pro, etc. [14, 15]. Within this paradigm, digital technologies have typically functioned as extensions of instructional delivery, facilitating access to content and enabling communication across physical boundaries. However, this conceptualisation is increasingly insufficient for capturing the dynamics of contemporary VPET and higher education. The emergence of GenAI introduces a qualitatively different form of mediation that extends beyond the augmentation of teaching practices. These systems actively participate in knowledge construction by generating content, providing feedback, and shaping learning trajectories in real time.

Previous studies indicate that teachers often exhibit cautious or passive attitudes toward the adoption of new technologies in teaching, particularly in VPET contexts where pedagogical practices are closely tied to established industry norms and practical expertise [16–19]. VPET's learning subjects range from engineering, mechanics, and accounting to art and design, hospitality, and culinary studies, to name just a few. VPET teachers are professionals with extensive workplace experience and skills in specific subjects; they are less keen on using technology to aid teaching and learning and often do not think technology can replace human work in the workplace. As diversity is one of the major features of the VPET learning programmes in Hong Kong and with the wide range of learning disciplines that vary from academic to professional-specific programmes, it is essential to understand the teachers' needs from time to time so as to enhance teaching practices for quality learning and teaching. It is argued that VPET requires discipline-sensitive AI training. GenAI adoption in VPET must consider vocational content knowledge, workplace relevance, and practical competence [20]. Teachers' perceptions of GenAI and highlight the need for formal professional development and informal collaborative learning. It also extends technological pedagogical content knowledge (TPACK) by incorporating the triadic nature of AI literacy. VPET teacher training should include communities of practice, peer sharing, and reflective pedagogical experimentation, not only one-off workshops [21]. Willermark & Carlsson's studies in 2026 focuses specifically on vocational teachers' knowledge in the GenAI era using technological, pedagogical, and content perspectives. They further examine how vocational pre-service and in-service teachers understand GenAI's potential, challenges, and consequences. UNESCO suggests that teacher training should move beyond tool demonstration and include ethics, pedagogy, professional judgement, and responsible AI use [22]. The adoption gap is not only a local VPET issue but part of a wider international imbalance between AI implementation and teacher preparation [23]. In integrating GenAI in education, teachers need to keep abreast of the latest GenAI developments in learning and teaching [24, 25]. GenAI use is already embedded in Hong Kong higher education, making VPET teacher preparation urgent rather than optional [26, 27]. The above reviews indicate that AI in education is expanding, but teacher professional development has received less attention than student-facing AI applications.

Given the above, there raises the key research question and areas of interest: How should VPET's teachers be prepared to accelerate conventional tool demonstration and hands-on practices into GenAI-enhanced learning contexts and activities as well as to include ethics, pedagogy, professional judgement, and responsible AI use? What are VPET teachers' perceptions on GenAI in education, what are their training needs and their acceptance of applying GenAI in their lessons?

2 The Study

To investigate the issue and examine VPET teachers' GenAI training needs, a study was conducted in July 2025. There are approximately 4,000 teachers in Hong Kong's 20 + self-financing VPET institutions. A survey questionnaire with nine closed-ended items on a 6-point Likert scale for quantitative feedback and one open-ended item for qualitative feedback was sent to 19 self-financing VPET education institutions' full-time teaching staff (n = 2000) for needs and training analysis. Demographic data from the survey were also collected. There were 231 questionnaires (n = 231) returned. The collected data was interpreted by mean and frequency distribution. The questionnaire items and responses are shown in Subsect. 3.1.

2.1 The Survey Questionnaire and Responses

Please refer to Attachment #1 for the details of the survey questionnaire and the responses received.

2.2 Findings

Participant Demographics. Demographics of the participating teachers in the survey showed that they are nearly balanced by gender (Female 50.6%, Male 45.0%). Teaching staff represented the overwhelming majority (85%), with administration (10.0%) and research (5.2%) as smaller groups. Over half of respondents (51%) have more than

10 years of teaching experience, indicating a senior, experienced cohort. Postgraduate qualifications (MEd/EdD/PhD) are the most common credential (51%), followed by in-service training qualifications (30.7%).

Q1 and 2: GenAI Usage and Attitudes. Responses for Q1 revealed that GenAI usage (mean 3.93) is moderately positive, with 39.8% rated at 5 or 6. Preference for future use (q2, mean 4.17) is slightly higher, suggesting that teachers are willing to advance current teaching practice using GenAI tools and are preparing to overcome barriers rather than being reluctant to change.

Q3: Perceived GenAI Benefits for Teaching. All Q3 sub-items exceeded the scale midpoint (3.5). *Q3b L&T Activities Development* scored the highest (4.33). Teachers generally agreed that GenAI can reduce workload and assist them in daily teaching preparation and assessment duties. *Q3f Personalised Feedback* (3.82) and *Q3g Timely Response* (3.86) scored the lowest, suggesting greater caution in using GenAI to direct student interaction, especially when providing timely and personalised feedback.

Q4: GenAI Tools in Use. All three Q4 sub-items scored below 3.5, indicating relatively low actual adoption of GenAI in learning and teaching. While *Q4c Learning Analytics Tools* (3.42) saw the most use, *Q4a Automated Grading Systems* (2.86) had the lowest adoption, with 26.8% rating it 1 – a result likely reflecting concerns about academic integrity and validity.

Q5: Challenges with GenAI in Teaching. All six Q5 sub-items are scored above 4.0, and these are broadly perceived as significant barriers. *Q5b Training on Tools* (4.42) is the teachers' top concern, closely followed by *Q5f Ethical Concerns* (4.29) and *Q5c Technical Issues* (4.26). This profile strongly suggests a need for structured, institution-wide professional development to prepare teachers. The two least-concerned items are Q5e Ensuring Fairness (4.19) and Q5d Accessibility for all Students (4.01), indicating that teachers regard the use of GenAI in teaching as currently fair and accessible to students.

Q6: Student Benefits from GenAI. Q6 recorded the highest mean across the entire survey (4.50/6). 53.7% of respondents rated it 5 or 6, and only 4.8% rated it 1 or 2. This strong positive consensus suggests that respondents believe that students stand to gain significantly from using GenAI tools.

Q7: GenAI and Online Learning. Responses showed that *Q7b Content Development* (4.19), *Q7c L&T Strategies* (4.15), and Q7a Programme and Course Development (4.03) scored the highest, suggesting that GenAI is most readily integrated into programme content planning and the development of learning and teaching strategies. *Q7e Facilitating Engagement* (3.98), *Q7f Monitoring Progress* (3.88), and Q7d Managing Asynchronous Courses (3.89) scored the lowest, reflecting teachers' uncertainty about using GenAI to facilitate live delivery contexts and to monitor learning and teaching progress.

Q8: Key Advantages of Adopting GenAI in Online Education. All Q8 sub-items scored above 4.0. *Q8e Knowledge Building* (4.41) and *Q8a Personalised Learning* (4.38), *Q8c Flexible Support* (4.32), indicating the potential of GenAI to tailor, support and deepen the learning experience. *Q8d Peer Learning* (4.06) scored the lowest, and to a large extent, reflects uncertainty about how GenAI mediates peer interaction.

Q9: AI Policy. With a mean of 3.90, the responses to Q9 are markedly mixed and scored lowest in the survey. Only 36.4% rated policy clarity 5 or 6, while nearly half (49.4%) fell in the neutral 3 to 4 range. This near-even spread, especially when compared with the strong student benefit optimism in Q6 (mean 4.50), signals a significant governance gap between enthusiasm for AI usage and lack of confidence in institutional frameworks.

Q10: Qualitative Suggestions for Improvement of the AI Policy. The most frequent answers for Q10 revolve around the need for clear guidelines and training/workshops on AI usage. Respondents frequently mentioned workshops, seminars, training programs, and support for staff/students. This indicates a practical need for skill-building alongside policy. These themes recurred across responses, indicating that stakeholders prioritise clarity in policy and practical support for both teachers and students. Many answers highlighted ethical concerns, plagiarism, fairness, and transparency. Respondents want policies that protect academic integrity while allowing responsible use of AI. Several responses called for tools to detect AI-generated work, expressing concern about misuse and the responsibilities for learning integrity. Results also pointed out that policies should specifically address ethical use, plagiarism detection, and fairness in grading. Teachers also suggested that regular updates and reviews are necessary to keep pace with the rapid development of AI. The most common themes and phrases identified are in Table 1:

3 Discussion

The survey result provides a holistic picture of how educators perceive and engage with GenAI in teaching. Teachers also expressed their views on GenAI policy and their training needs. It is noted that while teachers are enthusiastic about GenAI's potential, their actual adoption of GenAI in teaching remains limited, and findings also showed that significant barriers persist. Given the above, the findings sparked broader debates on educational technology, highlighting implications for practice in learning and teaching, as well as concerns about policy and governance in incorporating GenAI into education.

3.1 GenAI Usage and Attitudes

In general, teachers' attitudes toward the use of GenAI are positive. Teachers reported moderate current usage (mean 3.93) and slightly higher preference for future use (mean 4.17). This suggests a willingness to integrate GenAI into their future teaching practice, reflecting broader trends in educational innovation where initial hesitancy often gives way to cautious optimism. The result indicates that the majority of teachers are preparing to overcome technological barriers rather than resisting change through gradual adoption. Teachers also perceived relative advantages of using GenAI for lesson planning, content development, and administrative work.

Table 1. Qualitative suggestions for improvement of the AI policy

Theme/Phrase	Frequency
Clear guidelines	12
Training / workshops / seminars	11
Ethical concerns / academic integrity	7
Policy clarity (student use, plagiarism)	6
Monitoring / detection of AI use	5
Transparency / fairness	4
Regular updates / reviews	4
No AI policy yet / unclear policy	3
Support/resources for staff and students	3
Plagiarism checking tools	3

3.2 Perceived Benefits and Adoption Gap

Most teachers strongly agreed that GenAI can reduce administrative workload and support teaching preparation, with the highest compliments for learning and teaching activity development (mean 4.33). However, they expressed that the actual adoption of GenAI tools remains low, particularly automated grading systems (mean 2.86). This discrepancy between perceived benefits and real-world use underscores the "implementation gap" often observed in educational technology, where technical readiness and psychological perception are the main hurdles. Concerns about academic integrity and validity appear to constrain uptake, suggesting that trust in AI systems is a critical factor for teachers.

3.3 Challenges and Barriers

Findings showed that barriers are consistently rated as significant, along with training (mean 4.42), ethical concerns (mean 4.29), and technical issues (mean 4.26), with barriers topping the list. These findings highlight the importance of institutional support structures. The need for teachers' professional development emerges as a key issue, echoing literature that stresses teacher readiness as a determinant of successful technology integration. Ethical concerns, particularly around fairness and plagiarism, further reflect broader societal debates about AI accountability.

3.4 Student Benefits and Online Learning

Interestingly, student benefits (mean 4.50) received the strongest endorsement, suggesting teachers believe GenAI has transformative potential for learners. However, integration into online learning contexts shows an uneven confidence: while content development and strategy planning scored high, facilitating engagement and monitoring progress were rated low. This reflects VPET teachers' uncertainty about the AI role and function in dynamic, interactive aspects of learning and teaching, where human presence and judgment remain central in VPET.

3.5 Policy and Governance

It is noted that Policy clarity (mean 3.90) is the weakest area, with nearly half of the respondents having chosen neutral. Q10's qualitative responses emphasise the need for clear guidelines, training, and ethical safeguards. The governance gap between enthusiasm for using GenAI in daily teaching and confidence in institutional frameworks is striking. Teachers asserted that without clear guidelines, robust policies and implementation frameworks, there will be risks of inconsistent application of GenAI for learning and teaching on the institutional level. Furthermore, calls for plagiarism-detection tools and regular policy updates highlight the dynamic nature of AI in education, requiring timely, adaptive governance.

4 Implications and Conclusion

Implications of this study rest in the following few aspects, 1) Capabilities and Competences Building: with the rapid development of AI technology and its applications in education, well-structured professional development balancing both AI technology, application and AI learning and teaching pedagogies is equally important. We shall always bear in mind that technology evolves and the key to applying AI in education is via pedagogies, instructional design, learning contents and activities to drive adaptive and personalised learning to cater for students' diverse learning needs. A lot of studies revealed that GenAI benefits learning and teaching at all levels of education. In line with this, there are increasing advocacies on applying AI for adaptive and personalised learning as well as facilitating SEN students to learn better; therefore, timely interventions and staff development for capability and competence advancement will bridge the gap between perceived benefits and actual adoption. 2) AI Guidelines, Policies and Governances: institutions shall generate AI guidelines and policies for the education sector, institutions, teachers and students to prioritise transparency, scope of usage and ethical awareness, to foster trust between teachers and students, and mutual recognition between institutions. Nevertheless, timely and regularly updated AI policies are also an important task to be followed. Other attention should focus on the governance of the implementation of the policies. Scrutiny and quality assurance are needed to balance learning and teaching innovation with integrity to ensure applying GenAI in learning and teaching enhances rather than undermines educational values. 3) Research: further studies should explore how effective the AI training programme for teachers devised from this study, and to what extent the training programme benefits VPET teachers and students. It is also good to know and to examine how GenAI can effectively support interactive teaching tasks, such as feedback and engagement, as well as adaptive and personalised learning. Further studies on GenAI's applications to cater SEN students' learning needs are also beneficial to the education sector.

To conclude, with an aim to look into teachers' GenAI training needs, the benefits, their perceptions on GenAI in education, and their acceptances on applying GenAI in their daily teaching practice, the findings of this study reveal a paradox: teachers are optimistic about the potential of GenAI, especially for students, however, they are hesitant in practice due to a number of issues such as ethical, technical, and policy concerns. Addressing these barriers through training, governance, and trust-building measures will be critical for realising the promise of GenAI in education. Last but not least, this study sheds light on the fact that successful GenAI integration requires not only technological capability but also clarity of institutional policy and human-centered interactions.

References

1. Cooper, G.: Examining Science Education in ChatGPT: An Exploratory Study of Generative Artificial Intelligence. J. Sci. Educ. Technol. **32**(3), 444–452 (2023)
2. Dong, Y.: Generative AI technologies and educational outcomes: a comprehensive meta-analysis comparing traditional and AI-driven approaches. Humanities & Social Sciences Communications **13**, 559 (2026)
3. Hu, W., Chan, C.K.Y.: Evaluating technological interventions for developing teamwork competency in higher education: A systematic review and meta-ethnography. Stud. Educ. Eval. **83**, 101382 (2024)
4. Kanungo, A.: The green dilemma: Can AI fulfil its potential without harming the environment? Earth.org. https://earth.org/the-green-dilemma-can-ai-fulfil-its-potential-without-harming-the-environment/ (2023)
5. Memarian, B., Doleck, T.: ChatGPT in education: Methods, potentials, and limitations. Comp. Human Behav. Artif. Humans **1**(2), 100022 (2023)
6. Ogunleye, B., Zakariyyah, K.I., Ajao, O., Olayinka, O., Sharma, H.: A systematic review of generative ai for teaching and learning practice. Education Sciences **14**(6), 636 (2024)
7. Paoprasert, N., Chui, K.T., Yip, T.Y., Liu, J., Ng, K.K.: A Review of Large Language Model Evaluation Metrics in Education. In: Cheung, S.K.S., Liu, X., Xu, G., Kwok, L.F. (eds.) International Conference on Technology in Education, CCIS, vol. 2752, pp. 402–415. Singapore: Springer Nature, Singapore (2025)
8. Rivadeneira, D.X.R., Jiménez Toledo, J.A.: Applications of generative artificial intelligence in higher education: A systematic review of the literature. Journal of Posthumanism **5**(11), 521–535 (2025)
9. Wang, X., Zamzami, Z., Chin, H. L.: Generative artificial intelligence in pedagogical practices: a systematic review of empirical studies (2022–2024). Cogent Education **12**(1), (2025)
10. Rahman, Md.M., Watanobe, Y.: ChatGPT for Education and Research: Opportunities, Threats, and Strategies. Appl. Sci. **13**(9), 5783 (2023)
11. Wang, T.: Navigating Generative AI (ChatGPT) in Higher Education: Opportunities and Challenges. In Tlili, A., Yang, J., Liu, D., Anutariya, C., Chang, M. (eds.) Smart Learning for A Sustainable Society, pp. 215–225 (2023)
12. Samala, A.D., et al.: Unveiling the landscape of generative artificial intelligence in education: a comprehensive taxonomy of applications, challenges, and future prospects. Educ. Inf. Technol. **30**(3), 3239–3278 (2025)
13. Pallant, J.L., Blijlevens, J., Campbell, A., Jopp, R.: Mastering knowledge: the impact of generative AI on student learning outcomes. Stud. High. Educ. **51**(4), 714–735 (2026)
14. Devagiri, J.S., Paheding, S., Niyaz, Q., Yang, X., Smith, S.: Augmented Reality and Artificial Intelligence in industry: Trends, tools, and future challenges. Expert Syst. Appl. **207**, 118002 (2022)
15. Samala, A.D., Amanda, M.: Immersive Learning Experience Design (ILXD): Augmented Reality Mobile Application for Placing and Interacting with 3D Learning Objects in Engineering Education. Int. J. Interact. Mobile Technol. **17**(5) (2023)
16. Ertmer, P.A., Ottenbreit-Leftwich, A.T.: Teacher Technology Change: How Knowledge, Confidence, Beliefs, and Culture Intersect. J. Res. Technol. Educ. **42**(3), 255–284 (2010)

17. Ifenthaler, D., Schweinbenz, V.: The acceptance of Tablet-PCs in classroom instruction: The teachers' perspectives. Comput. Hum. Behav. **29**(3), 525–534 (2013)
18. Scherer, R., Siddiq, F., Tondeur, J.: The technology acceptance model (TAM): A meta-analytic structural equation modeling approach to explaining teachers' adoption of digital technology in education. Comput. Educ. **128**, 13–35 (2019)
19. Tondeur, J., van Braak, J., Ertmer, P.A., Ottenbreit-Leftwich, A.: Understanding the relationship between teachers' pedagogical beliefs and technology use in education: a systematic review of qualitative evidence. Education Tech. Research Dev. **65**(3), 555–577 (2017)
20. Willermark, S., Carlsson, S.: Envisioning vocational teacher knowledge in the era of GenAI. Discover Education **5**(1), 35 (2026)
21. Prilop, C.N., Mah, D.-K., Jacobsen, L.J., Hansen, R.R., Weber, K.E., Hoya, F.: Generative AI in teacher education: Educators' perceptions of transformative potentials and the triadic nature of AI literacy explored through AI-enhanced methods. Comp. Educ. Artif. Intel. **9**, 100471 (2025)
22. Miao, F., Cukurova, M.: *AI competency framework for teachers*. UNESCO. https://www.iicba.unesco.org/en/africa-education-knowledge-platform/ai-competency-framework-teachers (2024)
23. Tan, X., Cheng, G., Ling, M.H.: Artificial intelligence in teaching and teacher professional development: A systematic review. Comp. Educ. Artif. Intel. **8**, 100355 (2025)
24. Hwang, G.-J., Xie, H., Wah, B.W., Gašević, D.: Vision, challenges, roles and research issues of Artificial Intelligence in Education. Comp. Educ. Artif. Intel. **1**, 100001 (2020)
25. Su, J., Yang, W.: Unlocking the Power of ChatGPT: A Framework for Applying Generative AI in Education. ECNU Review of Education **6**(3), 355–366 (2023)
26. He, A., Zhang, Z., McMinn, S.: Embracing generative artificial intelligence tools in higher education: a survey study at the Hong Kong University of Science and Technology. Journal of Asian Public Policy **18**(2), 352–376 (2025)
27. McDonald, N., Johri, A., Ali, A., Collier, A.H.: Generative artificial intelligence in higher education: Evidence from an analysis of institutional policies and guidelines. Comp. Human Behav. Artif. Humans **3**, 100121 (2025)

Data Generation in Blended Learning: A Review of Recent Developments

Naraphorn Paoprasert[1], Kwok Tai Chui[2(✉)], Jiaqi Liu[2], and Hao Ran Chi[3]

[1] Department of Industrial Engineering, Faculty of Engineering, Kasetsart University, Bangkok, Thailand

[2] School of Science and Technology, Hong Kong Metropolitan University, Hong Kong, China
jktchui@hkmu.edu.hk

[3] Instituto de Telecomunicações, 3810- 193 Aveiro, Portugal

Abstract. Blended learning has received ever-growing attention and adoption in recent years, initially and mainly driven by the pandemic. Students, parents, and teachers have shared many fruitful teaching, learning, and caring experiences of blended learning. Data generation (e.g., large language models) is a cutting-edge technology believed to be a breakthrough in artificial intelligence applications. Bringing data generation into blended learning has become an emerging research topic; thus, this paper reports a first-of-its-kind review of recent developments. An advanced search of the Scopus Database was used to obtain initially 52 studies; after introducing exclusion criteria, 33 studies were shortlisted for analyses in this paper. Six aspects were included in the basic analyses, followed by advanced analyses to discuss the applications, methodologies, results, and insights of each study. As an emergent research area, this review provides ideas and research implications to drive future research directions.

Keywords: Blended Learning · Data Generation · Educational Technology · Hybrid Learning · Large Language Models

1 Introduction

The sole face-to-face teaching and learning mode is no longer applicable in today's fast-paced, digital era. Instead, blended learning is widely adopted to varying degrees. Its benefits are but not limited to [1–3] (i) Flexibility: The materials, including video recordings, can be accessed anytime and many times, (ii) Increased engagement: Online quizzes, mini-games, and interactions can be easier and turn the classes dynamic, (iii) Cost and environmentally friendly: Printed course and assessment materials are minimized, with a few exceptions such as written tests and exams, (iv) Better resources support: Both printed and online materials are offering for knowledge discovery and learning, and (v) Integration with artificial intelligence: Education data will be turned into valuable applications, such as learning analytics, at-risk student identification, emotion detection, and attendance recording, via artificial intelligence.

The fifth benefit is ever-evolving with technological developments in artificial intelligence. A typical requirement for training well-performing artificial intelligence models

K. T. Chui et al. (Eds.): ICBL 2026, LNCS 16778, pp. 296–310, 2027.
https://doi.org/10.1007/978-981-92-3761-6_21

is an inadequate amount of training data. It can be seen from the educational research that this requirement is not always guaranteed. Examples include that each student links to only a few assessment scores in each subject/course, that most educational data types are non-continuous, and that educational datasets are heterogeneous. To mitigate the limitations to fulfill the requirements, synthesizing data has become a very common solution. It is noted that the algorithmic approach via zero-shot learning [4] and few-shot learning [5] is not the focus of this paper.

The most popular families of data generation are generative adversarial networks (GANs) and large language models (LLMs), whereas the traditional data augmentation family has received decreasing attention and adoption. GANs and LLMs tackle more complex data distribution and can be more easily controlled and customized to different requirements and applications.

The research team has observed emerging trends in data generation in blended learning and has conducted a first-of-its-kind review to examine the datasets, applications, methodologies, results, advantages, limitations, and future directions of the research topic.

The remaining sections cover the details of the literature search, basic analyses of the shortlisted studies, advanced analyses of the shortlisted studies, limitations, and future research directions.

2 Details of the Literature Search

The advanced search in the Scopus Database was used to identify potential studies. A formal search was conducted on 7 May 2026 using the TITLE-ABS-KEY function. Two groups of terms were selected for data generation and for the blended learning aspects. The first group covered (data generation, synthetic data, data synthesis, generating data, generative adversarial networks, variational autoencoders, VAEs, large language models, and LLMs), whereas the second group covered (blended learning and mixed-mode learning). The results initially returned 52 studies, all in English.

After careful review, two exclusion criteria were applied: (i) with document type: conference review ($n = 9$), review ($n = 5$), and editorial ($n = 1$); 15 studies were excluded, and (ii) with relevant scope: studies that are not in education applications ($n = 4$). As a result, 33 studies were shortlisted for review in this paper. Figure 1 summarizes the shortlisted process of studies.

3 Basic Analyses of the Shortlisted Studies

Prior to the advanced analyses, six basic analyses (based on results from the Scopus Database) were conducted on the 33 shortlisted studies, covering access types, publication years, subject areas, document types, keywords, and countries/territories.

3.1 Access Types

Figure 2 shows the pie chart of the distribution of the four access types of the 33 studies. The ranks, in descending order, are all open access, gold, green, and hybrid gold. It is worth noting that the Bronze access type did not exist. The distribution suggests that open access becomes very common in the focus topic because we have been witnessing various advantages, including the acceleration of innovation transmission, the expansion of audiences to non-academia, early and frequent citations, and greater reach [6, 7].

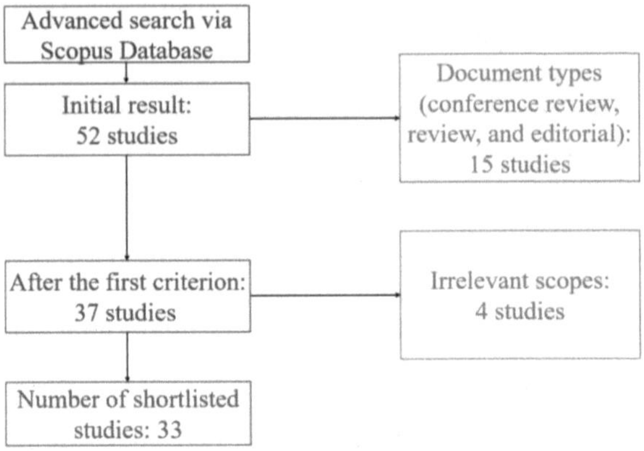

Fig. 1. Shortlisting process of the studies on data generation in blended learning.

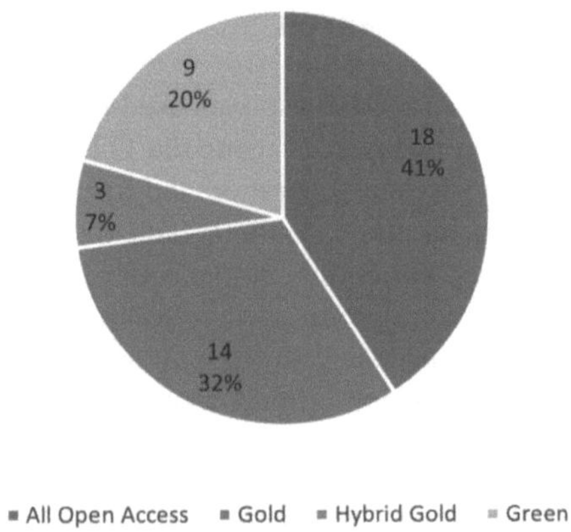

Fig. 2. Pie chart of the distribution of the access types of the shortlisted studies.

3.2 Publication Years

Figure 3 summarizes the annual number of studies published from 2015 to 2026. The topic was receiving limited attention before 2023, recording zero numbers in 2016, 2017, 2019, and 2021, one in 2015 and 2018, and two in 2020 and 2022. It is suggested that without the launch of ChatGPT in November 2022, the concept of data generation in blended learning would have been discussed in only a few works. The COVID-19 period (March 2020 to May 2023) drove the shift from traditional learning to temporary, solely online, and blended learning in the post-pandemic era. From 2023 to 2024, the annual number of studies increased by 167% (from 3 to 8) and remained steady between

2024 and 2025. Remarkably, the annual number in 2026 (up to 7 May) climbed to 9 in just 4 months, suggesting a high likelihood of exploding in popularity. All in all, in this emergent research area, with the support of open-access publishing approaches, the popularity and number of publications will increase.

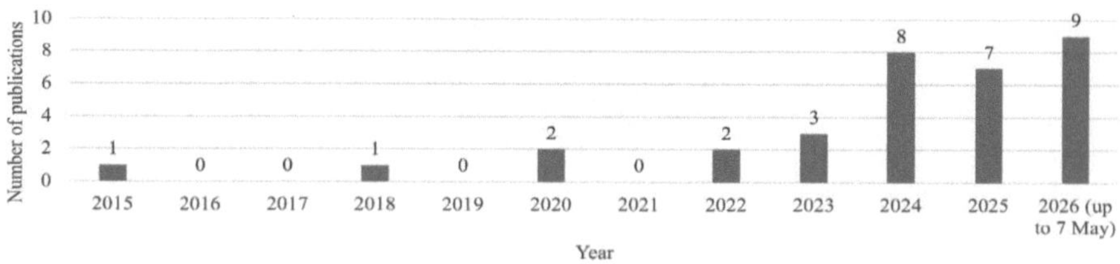

Fig. 3. Annual number of studies published from 2015 to 2026 of the shortlisted studies.

3.3 Subject Areas

Table 1 summarizes the counts of 13 subject areas. Two subject areas (social sciences and computer science) dominate, contributing more than 50% of the studies. About 18% of studies have been classified as engineering disciplines. These align with the nature of education in social sciences disciplines and data generation in computer science and engineering disciplines. The remaining 10 subject areas receive much less attention.

Table 1. Counts of 13 subject areas of the shortlisted studies.

Subject area	Count	Subject area	Count
Social Sciences	22 (66.7%)	Decision Sciences	2 (6.06%)
Computer Science	18 (54.5%)	Multidisciplinary	1 (3.03%)
Engineering	6 (18.2%)	Business, Management and Accounting	1 (3.03%)
Arts and Humanities	3 (9.09%)	Earth and Planetary Sciences	1 (3.03%)
Mathematics	3 (9.09%)	Materials Science	1 (3.03%)
Psychology	3 (9.09%)	Nursing	1 (3.03%)
Medicine	2 (6.06%)		

3.4 Document Types

Figure 4. Presents the pie chart of the distribution of the three document types of 33 studies. Journal articles dominate (67%), followed by conference papers (27%). This ensured that the review in this paper contains sufficient detailed publications (journal articles) for analysis. Conference papers also play important roles in sharing preliminary results and driving future research directions.

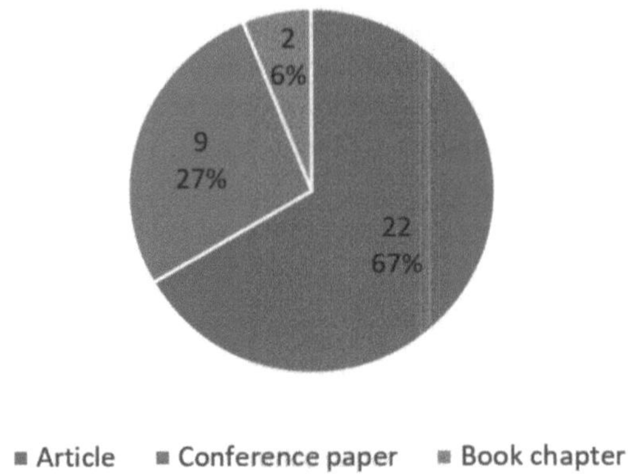

Fig. 4. Pie chart of the distribution of the document types of the shortlisted studies.

3.5 Keywords

Figure 5 presents the Word Cloud that highlights the varying frequency of 50 keywords. The chosen keywords appear at least twice across the 33 shortlisted studies. The most frequently mentioned keywords are ("Large Language Model" with n = 20 and 60.6%), ("Blended Learning" with n = 14 and 42.4%), ("Artificial Intelligence" with n = 10 and 30.3%), ("Language Model" and "Teaching" with n = 9 and 27.3%), ("Learning Systems" with n = 8 and 24.2%), and ("Computational Linguistics", "Computer Aided Instruction", "Human", and "Students" with n = 6 and 18.2%). The results reveal that a significant number of researchers did not recognize data generation, large language models, and blended learning, even though the papers fall into these topics.

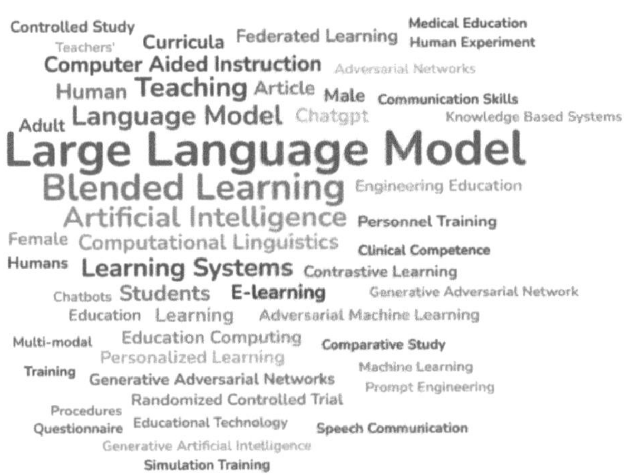

Fig. 5. Word Cloud of the top 50 keywords of the shortlisted studies.

3.6 Countries/territories

Table 2 summarizes the counts of 21 countries/territories of the shortlisted studies. It can be seen that the research on data generation in blended learning has not been started in most countries/territories worldwide. Among 21 countries/territories, eight are from Asia, with the most publications.

Table 2. Counts of 21 countries/territories of the shortlisted studies.

Countries/Territories	Count	Countries/Territories	Count
China	9 (27.3%)	Mexico	1 (3.03%)
Germany	4 (12.1%)	Pakistan	1 (3.03%)
Hong Kong	3 (9.09%)	Saudi Arabia	1 (3.03%)
India	3 (9.09%)	Singapore	1 (3.03%)
Australia	2 (6.06%)	South Africa	1 (3.03%)
Norway	2 (6.06%)	South Korea	1 (3.03%)
Taiwan	2 (6.06%)	Switzerland	1 (3.03%)
United States	2 (6.06%)	Ukraine	1 (3.03%)
Bulgaria	1 (3.03%)	United Kingdom	1 (3.03%)
France	1 (3.03%)	Viet Nam	1 (3.03%)
Macao	1 (3.03%)		

4 Advanced Analyses of the Shortlisted Studies

The citation counts from the Scopus Database and Google Scholar of the 33 shortlisted studies have been summarized in Table 3. The normalized counts per month are also reported for fair comparisons. It is noted that information from Web of Science is not included because some studies are not indexed there. In both databases, eight studies ([8–10, 12, 14–16, 21, 34]) did not receive any citations. Another eight studies (18, 24, 25, 26, 29, 31, 35, 40) recorded more than 10 citations. Remarkably, two studies received a very good number of citations ([29, 31]).

In the following, each shortlisted study will be discussed, highlighting its applications, methodologies, results, and insights. In [8], a three-tier scheme incorporated a relational consistency module, a temporal sequence generator, and a conditional tabular GAN to synthesize 20 thousands of records for higher education students for learning analytic applications. In each record, eighty-five features were used for descriptions. The generated dataset contributed to the performance enhancement by 24% using 10% of ground-truth data, helping in privacy preservation. Another work [9] integrated a DeepSeek recommendation system, a French dialogue system, and a Chaoxing workbench to support personalized French learning. In particular, DeepSeek provided grammar and writing correction and explanation, translation, and questions and answering. A large-scale survey was conducted to collect two hundred pieces of feedback from French learners, showing an accuracy of 72% and an AUC of 84% in a logistic regression-based modelling of 16 variables. The work highlighted three research limitations, including a small-scale dataset, an imbalanced dataset, and basic French language; and thus, suggesting some solutions as future research directions. Du et al. [10] simulated the participation of students in blended learning environments using three LLMs (GLM-4, o1-preview, and ChatGPT-4o). Experiments showed that these were useful in simulating secondary school students when they filled out online surveys on self-regulated learning skills. Results suggested that GLM-4 did not perform well, and o1-preview achieved the best accuracy. In [11], ICU scenarios were augmented using LLM to train ICU nurses. Both the control group and the experimental group comprised 20 nurses. Results based on seven metrics (learning technology, learning ability, teaching objectives, interactivity, feedback mechanisms, scenario complexity, and case authenticity) suggested that the experimental group yielded better performance. However, the researchers emphasized that the experiment was conducted in a small group of nurses and in a single medical center. In addition, the intervention intensity/exposure between the control and experimental groups was different. Therefore, design optimization, as well as fidelity and exposure monitoring, were suggested.

Table 3. Citation counts from the Scopus Database and Google Scholar of the shortlisted studies.

Work	Citation counts (Scopus/Google Scholar)		Work	Citation counts (Scopus/Google Scholar)	
	Total	Normalized (month)		Total	Normalized (Month)
[8]	0/1	0/1	[25]	29/47	1.32/2.14
[9]	0/0	0/0	[26]	22/34	0.786/1.21
[10]	0/0	0/0	[27]	1/13	0.04/0.52
[11]	2/5	0.667/1.67	[28]	3/6	0.125/0.25
[12]	0/0	0/0	[29]	83/110	3.77/5
[13]	1/2	0.2/0.4	[30]	1/1	0.0714/0.0714
[14]	0/0	0/0	[31]	202/301	6.31/9.41
[15]	0/0	0/0	[32]	4/12	0.129/0.387
[16]	0/0	0/0	[33]	1/3	0.04/0.12
[17]	3/8	0.6/1.6	[34]	1/0	0.0357/0
[18]	18/35	2.57/5	[35]	14/16	0.326/0.372
[19]	1/12	0.111/1.33	[36]	3/10	0.0536/0.179
[20]	2/3	0.125/0.188	[37]	3/7	0.0366/0.0854
[21]	0/0	0/0	[38]	3/4	0.0411/0.0548
[22]	3/3	0.5/0.5	[39]	2/7	0.0204/0.0714
[23]	3/4	0.2/0.267	[40]	14/22	0.112/0.176
[24]	13/28	0.765/1.65			

Li and Bao [12] investigated the efficacy of ChatGPT-4 as a tutor of a programming course in a blended learning setting. Both the control group and the experimental group comprised 69 students. Statistical results revealed that the experimental groups received higher self-efficacy and obtained better behavioral engagement scores. Another work [13] studied four LLMs (DeepSeek R1, Claude Sonnet 4, Gemini 2.5 Pro, and OpenAI) on the role-play performance of five scenarios. These scenarios aimed at tackling the challenges in agile-blended learning practices, including workload management, resource allocation, assessment challenges, technology integration, as well as flexibility and structure. The authors suggested that future research should target real-world scenarios instead of simulations. In [14], researchers examined the ability of LLM on hyper-contextual learning for business English education. The paper devoted efforts to robust ethical practices throughout the research development processes, including the identification of industry requirements, technology configuration, strategic integration of AI technologies, and fine-tuning. Sun and Liu [15] investigated the impacts of AI-based tutoring via LLM in English/German language learning. Three groups (each with a size of 54) were formed by LLM-based English/German learning, standalone English learning, and standalone German learning. Results showed that LLM enhanced learning efficiency, cognitive load balance, and affective outcomes.

In [16], an investigation was conducted on ultrasonography training using ChatGPT-4o. Three groups (15 each), including a control, a ChatGPT-4o with weekly tutoring, and a standalone ChatGPT-4o, were formed. These were intervened three weeks and individual performance was assessed via an examination. With a maximum score of 150, the group of ChatGPT-4 with weekly tutoring achieved the highest average of 128, followed by the group of standalone ChatGPT-4o (120), and the control group (111). Thus, the results suggested that both expert knowledge via tutoring and LLM are crucial in learning. Lee et al. [17] evaluated the performance of two LLMs (Claude 3.5 and ChatGPT-4o) for role-play practices of objective structured clinical examination, with a control group (10 Korean medicine students) and an experimental group (9 Korean medicine students). Statistically, both groups achieved similar performance; however, LLMs were shown to increase the satisfactory scores. Another work [18] presented research on LLM-based professional teacher development. 23 teachers contributed to the study. Results showed that their competency in instructional design for blended learning has improved. Specifically, LLMs contribute to the enhancement and refinement of the professional paradigm of teachers. In [19], a systematic review was conducted on eight applications using ChatGPT in primary and secondary schools in blended learning scenarios. Results showed that ChatGPT provided general usage for program courses; however, tailored applications would require substantial efforts.

Addam [20] discussed the blended learning and pedagogical implications when LLMs were introduced. A case study of ten faculty members was conducted. It was highlighted that the infrastructure and system were core elements on the success of education transformation from traditional teaching and learning mode to blended teaching and learning mode. Another work [21] focused on the need for effective tools for language assessment grows. TalkPro emerged as a multi-modal system designed for pronunciation and comprehension training within a blended learning framework. The system provided personalized feedback on spoken language, emphasizing phoneme-level accuracy and articulatory patterns. By utilizing a text-to-speech engine, TalkPro adapted spoken content to address vocabulary gaps and tests comprehension through tailored questions.

Future developments would integrate LLM reading comprehension modules, focusing on conceptual understanding rather than rote recall. Preliminary findings suggest that phoneme-level automated speech recognition was more effective than grapheme-level ASR. Rokkones and Giannakos [22] examined the benefit of LLM in teaching. Some participants commented that they spent additional effort to manage LLM, whereas some recognized the ability of LLM in personalized learning and marking. Overall, all agreed that the collaboration between teachers and LLM was positive in general. In [23], the research investigated the application of machine learning algorithms to predict student performance by analyzing the complex data generated in blended learning environments. It addressed critical issues such as the oversight of short text data, data imbalance, and underutilized multimodal data. The study introduced an innovative approach that adjusts the GAN to tackle data imbalance, incorporates short text for emotional mapping, and employed a multimodal model for enhanced accuracy and understanding in predictions.

Maalek [24] investigated and evaluated LLM in the coding and digitization of a Master-level construction engineering and management course over three semesters. Positive responses were received when LLM was used in project-based assessment. The author pointed out that the sustainability and capabilities of LLM are subject to further research, as LLM could be updated or replaced by a new model. Misiejuk et al. [25] evaluated the performance of ChatGPT in the automatic assessment of students' coding. Results confirmed its superiority in general evaluation; however, it was limited in context-dependent codes. The authors suggested that the proper involvement of human judgment will maximize evaluation accuracy and interpretability. The research work [26] analyzed ChatGPT's evolution and current research trends using PRISMA methodology on a dataset of about 110 studies from 2022–2023. LLMs and Generative AI are transforming academia, particularly in STEM and blended learning. Findings highlighted significant growth in scientific output and identify leading countries and institutions in this field. It explored the benefits and drawbacks of ChatGPT in higher education and underscored ethical considerations, advocating for responsible AI usage in the educational sector. In [27], Bard and ChatGPT were used to enhance the student learning in speaking, listening, reading, and writing. These were also tested on the feasibility of robust training of interpreters and translators. Both teachers and students showed positive responses in the questionnaires.

Winder et al. [28] investigated the impact (efficiency and speed of knowledge creation) of LLM on evaluating the criteria of blended learning classes. Results revealed that LLM helps content scalability and learner engagement. A broader range of participants was expected to provide a more generalized experimental study and evaluation. PaLM 2, LLaMA-2, and GPT-3.5 were evaluated and compared on their performance in generating sixty multiple-choice questions in codes, concepts, and mathematics-related contexts [29]. The evaluation was based on relevance, complexity, diversity, answerability, and grammatical fluidity. Yet, it was a preliminary study focusing on English-based, small-scale multiple-choice generation. The ChatGPT-3.5 was used for a learning management and conversation system [30]. A thorough evaluation was conducted to gather information related to the impact of technical support, questions to authenticated users, questions to course coordinators, questions to students, questions to teachers, and general feedback. Although the average responses were positive, the LLM was commented that it lacks personalized educational experiences. Technical experts were required to fine-tune the LLM. Wu et al. [31] used ChatGPT-3.5 to support knowledge creation and self-regulation progress in blended learning. It was integrated with LINE Messenger and Apple's Shortcuts. Both the control and experimental groups comprise 35 students. These groups followed distinct practices during the forethought, performance, and self-reflection phases.

In [32], a systematic review, adhering to PRISMA guidelines, investigated BL applications in mathematics teacher education, exploring various models, advantages, and challenges. Data was extracted from key databases to inform stakeholders on BL's effectiveness in teaching mathematical topics. An artificial neural network-based predictive model was built to forecast student performance in blended learning environments [33]. To preserve data privacy, the dataset was processed with data generation techniques. The limitation of the study was that the data were within a single semester. In [34], ChatGPT was used to enhance the communication skills, autonomy skills, and motivation of English learners in blended learning environments. The preliminary result suggested that the integration of LLM into the pedagogy of English for specific purposes was straightforward, without major problems encountered. The surge in virtual field trips during the COVID-19 pandemic aimed to replicate real-life experiences digitally, offering alternative learning for those unable to visit physical locations [35]. While concerns about efficacy and support emerged, the analysis indicated that despite prevalent negative perceptions (71% pre-course, 88% post-course), positive aspects were notable, with students' favorable views rising from 20% to 70%. Key factors like printed materials and instructor support contributed positively. These insights could help enhance the design of virtual field trips in blended learning.

Another study [36] aimed to propose priorities for traditional institutions of higher education to enhance online teaching and learning beyond the COVID-19 pandemic. Using qualitative research, data were gathered through a systematic literature review and analysis of Ministry of Education and University circulars. The findings advocated for improved access to online content, active learning, e-assessment reconsiderations, faculty support, gradual reopening of campuses, and the integration of blended learning into curricula, alongside addressing dropout rates in higher education. Clarke et al. [37] examined a cohort of novice teachers participating in an employment-based Initial teacher education program that integrated academic coursework with part-time teaching roles in secondary schools. The research focused on how these teachers develop clinical judgment and articulate the essential knowledge and skills for effective decision-making. Findings revealed a strong commitment to student-centered practices, though there was limited evidence of using data to reflect on teaching strategies for future improvements. The study suggested that a clinical teaching approach can empower beginning educators by enhancing their understanding of individual learner needs, although further exploration is needed to refine their use of evidence in practice. In [38], researchers proposed an open assessment methodology for a decision-support system for blended-learning-based education. An architecture was proposed for modelling the course syllabus and a framework for enhancing the pedagogy. Various Google Tools were used and their effectiveness was confirmed. The benefits of blended learning [39] were discussed, including soft skill development, flexible communication styles, gaming incorporation, an enhanced online simulation, and an enhanced learning experience. At last, the study [40] explored the complexities of imaginative methods in STEM education through design-based educational research and autoethnography. Utilizing three self-report methods within a design experiment, the research examined the development of a blended learning framework. Findings highlighted three significant challenges for STEM educators: their professional context, the need for practical models, and identifying effective change agents. The paper also presented a comprehensive methodology that emphasizes the importance of the change process alongside the outcomes.

5 Research Limitations

5.1 Limited Variants and Versions of Data Generation Models

Limited variants and versions (from one to three) of LLMs were used in the performance evaluation and experiments of current studies. In particular, many studies were using the traditional versions (ChatGPT-3.5 and ChatGPT-4) instead of the latest versions. To justify the selection of appropriate LLMs, a comprehensive analysis and comparison are desired. It is also worth noting that larger LLMs and newer versions of LLMs do not always perform better, subject to the applications [41–43]. In addition, many variants of GANs are available and awaiting exploration and comparison [44–46].

5.2 Small-Scale Participants

A limited (one-time or up to three semesters) period was considered in evaluating the benefits of data generation in blended learning. Indeed, many universities have established formal guidelines and regulations to promote the usage of data generation (in particular LLMs) in teaching and learning. Therefore, it is not too challenging to collect a large-scale survey from fellow students. University students would be preferred because the consent will be simple compared to primary and secondary students, who may require further support from family members.

5.3 Lack of Formal Guidelines in Performance Evaluation Metrics

Fairly evaluating the generated data has always been challenging in all areas; in particular, educational data, because the sampling frequency of the ground truth educational dataset is generally smaller than in other areas. The impact of data distribution using data generation would be more obvious; however, it is not guaranteed to be positive (benefits). In a recent review article [47], the evaluation metrics can be categorized as human-based and automatic-based metrics. The former is time-consuming and is subjective, whereas the latter is convenient but may not be applicable towards all applications and data generation models.

6 Conclusion and Future Research Directions

The authors presented a first-of-its-kind review of data generation technologies on blended learning, a method increasingly adopted in response to the evolving educational landscape accelerated by the pandemic. This paper shortlisted and analyzed 33 research studies that explored various aspects of data generation, including GANs and LLMs, emphasizing their potential to enhance educational outcomes. The findings revealed that these technologies facilitate flexibility, engagement, and effective resource utilization while addressing challenges related to data scarcity and heterogeneity in education. In addition, the review underscored the role of artificial intelligence in transforming educational data into valuable applications. By outlining current methodologies, applications, and future research directions, this paper paves the way for continued exploration in merging data generation with blended learning. The key research implication is to enrich teaching and learning experiences in diverse educational environments.

The future research directions will aim at addressing the research limitations, including limited versions and variants of data generation models, small-scale participants, and guidelines in performance evaluation metrics, in Sect. 5.

References

1. Liu, J., et al.: A Study of Improvements in Educational Accessibility and Adaptability Using Digital and Intelligent Education. In: Lee, L.K., Poulova, P., Chui, K.T., Černá, M., Wang, F.L., Cheung, S.K.S. (eds.) International Conference on Technology in Education, CCIS, vol. 2330, pp. 85–95. Springer Nature, Singapore (2024)
2. Panday, A., Ray, T., Jalandharachari, A.S., Gopinath, G.: Insights into blended learning research: A thorough bibliometric study. Discover Education **4**(1), 50 (2025)
3. Ramsey, J.L.: The art of blending: a systematic literature review of blended teaching competencies in higher education. J. Res. Technol. Educ. **58**(3), 656–673 (2026)
4. Yeung, C., et al.: A Zero-Shot LLM Framework for Automated Assignment Grading in Introductory Higher Education Courses. In: Cristea, A.I., Walker, E., Lu, Y., Santos, O.C., Isotani, S. (eds.) International Conference on Artificial Intelligence in Education 2025, CCIS, vol. 2591, pp. 19–27. Springer Nature, Switzerland (2025)
5. de Souza Lessa, B., de Lucena, N.F., de Menezes, L.M.L., de Sousa Filho, J.M.: Synthetic case studies in management education: The support of Generative AI. Innovations in Education and Teaching International (Early Access)
6. Sheikh, A., Richardson, J.: Open access movement in the scholarly world: Pathways for libraries in developing countries. J. Inf. Sci. **52**(2), 577–595 (2026)
7. Adil, H.M., Ali, S., Sultan, M., Ashiq, M., Rafiq, M.: Open education resources' benefits and challenges in the academic world: a systematic review. Global Knowledge, Memory and Communication **73**(3), 274–291 (2024)
8. Agal, S.: A privacy preserving synthetic learner dataset for learning analytics in technology enhanced higher education. Sci. Rep. **16**, 14772 (2026)
9. Zeng, Y.: Application of Artificial Intelligence in the Teaching of "Basic French": A Logistic Regression–Based Evaluation. In: Proceedings of the 2025 5th International Conference on Computational Modeling, Simulation and Data Analysis, pp. 540–544. Association for Computing Machinery, USA (2025)

10. Du, J., Li, S., Chen, J., Li, J.: Assessment of large language models' performance in simulating students' self-reports of online self-regulated learning skills. Educ. Inf. Technol. **31**(3), 787–822 (2026)
11. Liu, J., Chen, T., Li, S., Xia, Y., Zhu, H., et al.: LLM-based pedagogical agent for ICU simulation instructor training: A quasi-experimental study. Nurse Educ. Today **157**, 106901 (2025)
12. Li, Y., Bao, Z.: Integrating AI Virtual Tutors in Blended Learning: A Controlled Evaluation of Learning Outcomes and Student Engagement. In: Proceedings of the 2025 2nd International Conference on Artificial Intelligence and Future Education, pp. 247–251. Association for Computing Machinery, USA (2025)
13. Wong, J.M.S., Wong, H.Y.H.: Simulated realities: An AI role-play analysis of administrative tensions in the implementation of Agile-blended learning. In: Cheung, S.K.S., Liu, X., Xu, G., Kwok, L.F. (eds.) International Conference on Technology in Education, CCIS, vol. 2752, pp. 62–73. Springer Nature Singapore, Singapore. (2025)
14. Singh, A.K., Vaishnav, H.: AI-Driven Adaptive Learning for Industry-Specific Business English: Transforming Professional Communication in the Digital Era. In: John, A. (eds.) Digital Technology in Language Education, pp. 56–72. CRC Press (2026)
15. Sun, Y., Liu, F.: Evaluating an AI model for cross-linguistic language learning: a randomized controlled trial. Comp. Assisted Lang. Learn. 1–28 (Early Access)
16. Hong, D.R., Huang, C.Y., Gao, J.: ChatGPT-4o with faculty guidance outperforms AI-only and traditional learning in ultrasonography training: a randomized trial. Frontiers in Digital Health **8**, 1772965 (2026)
17. Lee, H.Y., Kim, J., Choi, H., Bae, H., Jeong, A., et al.: Comparing AI chatbot simulation and peer role-play for OSCE preparation: a pilot randomized controlled trial. BMC Med. Educ. **25**, 1755 (2025)
18. Wang, X., Niu, J., Fang, B., Han, G., He, J.: Empowering teachers' professional development with LLMs: An empirical study of developing teachers' competency for instructional design in blended learning. Teach. Teach. Educ. **165**, 105091 (2025)
19. Chang, C.I., Choi, W.C., Choi, I.C., Lei, H.: A Systematic Literature Review of the Practical Applications of Artificial Intelligence-Generated Content (AIGC) Using OpenAI ChatGPT, Copilot, and Codex in Programming Education. In: Proceeding of the 2024 8th International Conference on Education and E-Learning, pp. 13–19. Association for Computing Machinery, USA (2024)
20. Addam, B.: Anatomy of blended learning integration in higher education: reflections of academics in a comprehensive university. Int. J. Learn. Teach. Educ. Res. **24**(1), 500–519 (2025)
21. Wirth, J., Peinl, R.: TalkPro: A Multimodal Language Learning and Evaluation System. In: Matos, F., Flores, I., Martins, S. (eds.) Proceedings of the 2nd International Conference on Education Research. Academic Conferences and Publishing Limited, UK (2025)
22. Rokkones, R. K., Giannakos, M.: Toward hybrid teaching intelligence: investigating the potential of teacher–AI collaboration using large language models. Behaviour & Information Technology, 1–19 (Early Access)
23. Liu, J., Yang, Y.: A student performance prediction model based on multimodal generative adversarial networks. Int. J. Sensor Netw. **47**(3), 186–198 (2025)
24. Maalek, R.: Integrating generative artificial intelligence and problem-based learning into the digitization in construction curriculum. Buildings **14**(11), 3642 (2024)
25. Misiejuk, K., Kaliisa, R., Scianna, J.: Augmenting assessment with AI coding of online student discourse: A question of reliability. Comp. Educ. Artif. Intel. **6**, 100216 (2024)
26. Mahrishi, M., Abbas, A., Radovanovic, D., Hosseini, S.: Emerging dynamics of ChatGPT in academia: A scoping review. J. Univ. Teach. Learn. Pract. **21**(1), 146–176 (2024)

27. Cherednichenko, O., Yanholenko, O., Badan, A., Onishchenko, N., Akopiants, N.: Large language models for foreign language acquisition. In: Computational Linguistics Workshop at 8th International Conference on Computational Linguistics and Intelligent Systems, vol. 3722, pp. 101–130 (2024)
28. Winder, G., Bass, S., Schiele, D., Buchner, J.: Using large language models for content creation impacts online learning evaluation outcomes. In: Marks, G. (ed.) Proceedings of International Journal on E-Learning 2024, pp. 305–318. Association for the Advancement of Computing in Education, USA (2024)
29. Hang, C.N., Tan, C.W., Yu, P.D.: MCQGen: A large language model-driven MCQ generator for personalized learning. IEEE Access **12**, 102261–102273 (2024)
30. Ahmed, F., Fatima, N., Sardar, M.B., Alibhai, M.: Exploring the Integration of Virtual Assistant Using Large Language Models in Learning Management System: Enhancing Educational Accessibility and Efficiency. In: 2024 International Conference on Information Technology Systems and Innovation (ICITSI), pp. 189–198. IEEE, USA (2024)
31. Wu, T.T., Lee, H.Y., Li, P.H., Huang, C.N., Huang, Y.M.: Promoting self-regulation progress and knowledge construction in blended learning via ChatGPT-based learning aid. J. Educ. Comput. Res. **61**(8), 1539–1567 (2024)
32. Tong, D.H., Uyen, B.P., Ngan, L.K.: The application of blended learning in mathematics teacher education: Protocol for a systematic review. PLoS ONE **18**(9), e0292244 (2023)
33. Ivanova, M., Petrova, T.: Towards independent students' activities, online environment and learning performance: An investigation through synthetic data and artificial neural networks. Informatics **10**(2), 37 (2023)
34. Yan, H.: Let's Chat: Integrating large language models into blended learning of English for specific purposes. In: Lee, L.K., Hui, Y.K., Chui, K.T., Li, Q., Wong, L.P. (eds.) 2023 International Symposium on Educational Technology (ISET), pp. 187–192. IEEE, USA (2023)
35. Bond, C.E., et al.: Learning outcomes, learning support and cohort cohesion on a virtual field trip: an analysis of student and staff perceptions. Geoscience Communication Discussions **5**, 307–323 (2021)
36. Sharadgah, T.A., Sa'di, R.A.: Priorities for reorienting traditional institutions of higher education toward online teaching and learning: Thinking beyond the COVID-19 experience. E-Learning and Digital Media **19**(2), 209–224 (2022)
37. Clarke, K., Truckenbrodt, A., Kriewaldt, J., Angelico, T., Windsor, S.: Beginning teachers' developing clinical judgement: Knowledge, skills and attributes for clinical teaching. Teach. Educ. **31**(4), 381–403 (2020)
38. Shivanagowda, G.M., Goudar, R.H., Kulkarni, U.P.: Open assessment methodology-based decision support system in blended learning environments. Int. J. Knowl. Learn. **13**(2), 81–97 (2020)
39. Raiser, S., Warkalla, B., Schneider, A., Kaiser, K.: "Will It Blend?" Combining Online and On-Site Elements in Simulation Games. In: Bursens, P., Donche, V., Gijbels, D., Spooren, P. (eds.) Simulations of Decision-Making as Active Learning Tools: Design and Effects of Political Science Simulations PPBL, vol. 22, pp. 77–92. Springer Nature, Switzerland (2018)
40. Hains-Wesson, R., Tytler, R.: A perspective on supporting STEM academics with blended learning at an Australian university. Issues in Educ. Res. **25**(4), 460–479 (2015)
41. Zhong, R., et al.: Larger is not always better: Exploring small open-source language models in logging statement generation. ACM Transactions on Software Engineering and Methodology, (Early Access)
42. Pinckney, N., Batten, C., Liu, M., Ren, H., Khailany, B.: Revisiting verilogeval: A year of improvements in large-language models for hardware code generation. ACM Trans. Design Auto. Electr. Sys. **30**(6), 1–20 (2025)

43. Zhao, W.X., Zhou, K., Li, J., Tang, T., Dong, Z., et al.: A survey of large language models. Front. Comp. Sci. **20**(12), 2012627 (2026)
44. Chui, K.T., Liu, R.W., Zhao, M., de Pablos, P.O.: Predicting students' performance with school and family tutoring using generative adversarial network-based deep support vector machine. IEEE Access **8**, 86745–86752 (2020)
45. Koc, C., Özyurt, F., Iantovics, L.B.: Survey on latest advances in natural language processing applications of generative adversarial networks. Wiley Interdisciplinary Reviews: Data Mining and Knowledge Discovery **15**(1), e70004 (2025)
46. Uddin, M., Arfeen, S.U., Alanazi, F., Hussain, S., Mazhar, T., Arafatur Rahman, M.: A critical analysis of generative ai: Challenges, opportunities, and future research directions. Archives of Computational Methods in Engineering **33**(2), 1763–1793 (2026)
47. Paoprasert, N., Chui, K.T., Yip, T.Y., Liu, J., Ng, K.K.: A Review of Large Language Model Evaluation Metrics in Education. In: Cheung, S.K.S., Liu, X., Xu, G., Kwok, L.F. (eds.) International Conference on Technology in Education, CCIS, vol. 2752, pp. 402–415. Springer Nature Singapore (2025)

AI-enhanced Teaching and Learning

Developing a Predictive Model for At-Risk Students Using College Student Engagement

Will W. K. Ma[1], Mark C. M. Tsang[1(✉)], and Fuk-hay Tang[2]

[1] School of Arts and Humanities, Tung Wah College, Hong Kong SAR, China
{willma,marktsang}@twc.edu.hk

[2] School of Medical and Health Sciences, Tung Wah College, Hong Kong SAR, China
fhtang@twc.edu.hk

Abstract. Student retention is a major global challenge for higher education institutions. Building on prior evidence that academic performance is a key driver of student dropout and leveraging the growing use of machine learning to identify at-risk students, this study applies machine learning algorithms to develop a predictive model that determines risk factors and enables early identification for timely support. This paper used demographic, behavioural engagement, cognitive engagement, and emotional engagement data of 72 students collected over a 15-week semester in a college statistics course. Several algorithms—k-nearest neighbors (kNN), Logistic Regression (LogReg), Random Forest (RF), Support Vector Machines (SVM), and XGBoost—were trained on data collected in Week 3, Week 7, and Week 14 in the course and evaluated using standard accuracy metrics. The top-performing model was Random Forest in Week 7, achieving the highest performance: Precision = 0.94, Recall = 0.93, F1 = 0.93, and Accuracy = 0.9333. Feature importance analysis underscores actionable implications that students' participation and cognitive engagement during lessons could enable early identification for intervention in Week 7 in a course.

Keywords: At-risk · Academic Performance · Engagement · Machine Learning · Higher Education

1 Introduction

Student retention is a significant challenge for higher education institutions, prompting them to prioritize research on the causes of student dropout and to develop strategies for its mitigation. Recently, machine learning has been widely adopted to predict student academic performance, particularly for identifying at-risk students, and these models have generally demonstrated strong effectiveness (e.g., [1]). Such results have spurred further research aimed at improving reliability and expanding the applicability of machine learning analyses in this domain. A recurring issue in prior research is the heavy reliance on historical or open datasets for building predictive models (e.g., [2]). While such models often demonstrate high accuracy, the constrained feature sets typical of these datasets limit the exploration of potentially important predictors not previously captured. Future

K. T. Chui et al. (Eds.): ICBL 2026, LNCS 16778, pp. 313–325, 2027.
https://doi.org/10.1007/978-981-92-3761-6_22

work should prioritize prospective study designs and broaden feature collection rather than depending solely on existing data sources. In parallel, designing a robust learning environment is essential: it should offer rich learning experiences, accommodate diverse student needs and generate comprehensive digital footprints that both illuminate students' learning trajectories and inform instructional strategies for systematic monitoring of academic performance.

Our study has the following contributions. First, instead of relying on historical or open datasets, we utilised a real dataset in a higher education institution for building predictive models, in which important predictors were explored based on a wider scope of features. Second, by training models with the authentic dataset, we provided evidence about which machine learning model was top-performing and what digital footprints were essential for early identification of at-risk students. Third, the study offered practical insights about when and how instructors should implement strategies to monitor and support at-risk students in higher education institutions.

The study is organized as follows. The next section presents a literature review on at-risk prediction and machine learning analytics. The methodology section then outlines the study design. This is followed by the findings section, which reports the results of the data analysis. The discussion interprets the results in relation to prior research, examines the most important features, and addresses the study's contributions, limitations, and directions for future work. The conclusion summarizes the overall study.

2 Literature Review

2.1 Academic Performance and Student Retention in Higher Education

Student retention remains a major challenge for higher education institutions, and because university dropouts are frequently linked to academic underperformance, institutions are increasingly motivated to deploy learning analytics tools that leverage predictive models of learning success [3]. Accurate forecasting of student performance enables the early identification of at-risk students and supports targeted interventions to enhance learning outcomes [4].

2.2 Engagement

A survey of a non-formal online learning environment [5] found that behavioral, cognitive, and emotional engagement exert both direct and indirect effects on learning outcomes, with platform value serving as a mediator. An experimental study on mobile instant messaging–supported learning [6] examined engagement across behavioral, emotional, and cognitive dimensions and identified notable differences in engagement processes: behaviorally, students in the messaging condition produced more messages and words and showed higher participation, task completion, and interaction rates; emotionally, there was no statistically significant difference in affective evaluations of course interaction and satisfaction, although instant messaging appeared to foster greater intimacy and interpersonal relationships; cognitively, students were more engaged than their asynchronous online counterparts in facilitating interactive idea exchange, contributing to more “creating” activities. Another survey on student engagement reported that emotional engagement has the strongest positive effect on educational technology engagement, while cognitive engagement differs significantly by gender [7]. Studies have also introduced AI-generated gamified quizzes to enhance and sustain engagement, using the correlation between lower quiz performance and poorer exam outcomes to identify at-risk students [8]. Further, the first year of university has been identified as critical for subsequent academic development, as students are most vulnerable to disengagement and dropout during this period; accordingly, early identification of students at highest risk of disengagement and the classroom environmental factors that support or undermine engagement is essential [9]. Latent profile analysis revealed three engagement-level profiles among first-year students, predicted by peer support, provision of choice, and task relevance [9]. In addition, self-efficacy has been identified as a key determinant of performance and of dropout risk, yet it remains comparatively underexplored [1]. Finally, in video conference–assisted online learning, students’ learning ability, prior knowledge, and the quality of learning materials—among other features—were positively associated with academic performance [10].

In sum, the multidimensional nature of student engagement is demonstrably associated with learning outcomes and academic performance.

2.3 Machine Learning Analysis

The use of computational approaches to predict academic success has grown rapidly. Prior work has applied machine learning to analyze higher education students’ performance and retention, aiming to reduce the risk of dropout and withdrawal [1]. Models trained on historical study records have yielded valid predictions [11] and demonstrated high forecasting quality for learning success [3]. This literature underscores the potential of machine learning to support data-driven decision-making by identifying critical attributes in predictive models and by forecasting academic performance [10]. Machine learning applications also show promise for personalized education, early intervention, and the identification of at-risk students [1]. A recent review of machine learning in higher education [1] reports broad adoption across performance prediction, engagement analysis, and self-efficacy assessment, employing algorithms such as decision trees, random forests, support vector machines, and neural networks, with common evaluation metrics including accuracy, F1 score, recall, and precision.

Machine-learning based at-risk students modelling aims to predict students who are likely to underperform, disengage, or dropout. These models usually rely on multi-dimensional educational data in the training process, including demographic data (e.g., age, gender, socio-economic data), academic records (e.g., prior grades), behavioural data (e.g., access and interaction with the learning management system (LMS), class performance), and psychological indicators (e.g., motivation, confidence). Model training can be performed using traditional machine learning methods, such as logistic regression, decision tree, random forests, support vector machine, and gradient boosting. These approaches are usually easier to interpret and less data is required. Machine learning can also be performed using deep learning approaches, such as recurrent neural network, in which a richer dataset is needed to analyse the non-linear, complex, or temporal data relationship. A recent systematic review finds that traditional machine learning models remain dominant in the field [12].

Some studies adopted machine learning for student dropout prediction. A university student dropout case study showed the use of decision tree and naïve bayes classifiers to classify and predict drop out students using student study history, including GPA and high school average, with an accuracy of above 95% [13]. Another study analysed undergraduate student dropouts and identified that random forest classifier provided highest accuracy. Most relevant classification variables were students' academic performance in the first weeks of the first semester, the average grades of the previous academic level, entrance score and admission test results [14]. Both studies included students past academic performance as predictors. Another instance was the use of attendance rates and timely assignment submissions to build an early warning model, trained with multiple courses, and generate robust predictions of academic risk early [15].

Machine learning could identify at-risk students at the course level. Using learners' clicker responses within lessons, a low-cost prediction model by logistic regression could identify at-risk students at an early stage [16]. LMS data could also be utilized as model features. A study showed neural network models trained by LMS data could identify at-risk students with reasonable accuracy at the end of week 5, outperformed logistic regression and the random forest approach [17]. Another similar study used LMS data such as the number of action-related and time-related features for binary at-risk student prediction; Random Forest achieved the best performance, and early prediction was possible as early as 25% course completion [18].

2.4 Important Features

Analyses of machine learning applications often rely on large feature sets, such as behavioral traces from LMS and demographic variables. Yet this complexity can degrade predictive accuracy under concept drift or when many features are paired with limited sample sizes [4]. Evidence suggests that LASSO—a shrinkage estimator that curbs model complexity and overfitting—can outperform several commonly used machine learning models, and that a simple linear regression leveraging only two handcrafted features can achieve higher accuracy with substantially lower predictive bias than more complex, high-dimensional approaches. Owing to their parsimony and robustness, such models offer practical benchmarks for future work and serve as effective fallback options when significant concept or covariate drift arises [4]. However, reducing model complexity can also limit the richness of information available for analysis and intervention. Therefore, feature selection should strike a careful balance between parsimony and informativeness to build a model that remains both robust and practically useful.

2.5 Educational Support

An essential goal of predictive modeling is to enable early interventions that support students before issues escalate. Intervening only after the release of final examination results offers a limited opportunity for meaningful support. Identifying reliable early warning signals is therefore crucial, though it requires further study. For instance, one study proposed an Optimal Time Index, suggesting that Day 60 in a typical 255-day course is the best point to predict outcomes, balancing timely intervention, model accuracy, and resource efficiency [19].

3 Research Objectives and Research Questions

This study aims to develop a predictive model for identifying at-risk students in higher education and to examine the associated predictive features. Different from previous studies that identified college dropout, or focused on evaluating a machine learning model to identify academically at-risk students using a pre-defined set of features, we collectively use demographic data, behavioural engagement, cognitive engagement, and emotional engagement obtained via LMS or during lessons for model development, and analyse the machine-learning approaches, important features and various types of student engagements that work best in prediction based on standard evaluation metrics. Specifically, the research questions in the study are:

- RQ1: Which algorithms achieve the best performance in at-risk student prediction?
- RQ2: Which features are most important in the predictive model?
- RQ3: Do different dimensions of student engagement serve as key determinants in the model?
- RQ4: Can an accurately performing model provide early intervention implications?

4 Methodology

4.1 Background

In AY2024/25 Semester 2, an undergraduate General Education course, "Introduction to Statistics," in a local college was examined. The 15-week course (with 14 teaching weeks and one self-study week for examination) was designed to maximize opportunities for student engagement through diverse learning activities.

4.2 Participants

There were 72 students enrolled in the statistics course who participated in the study.

4.3 Data Collection

Data were collected by the authors from students in the course. Engagement was tracked throughout the semester using uReply (an interactive classroom tool) and Blackboard (the institution's learning management system). Demographic information and psychological measures were collected via online surveys. Engagement data were recorded both across the entire course and within individual class sessions for analysis.

- Online survey form to gather students' demographics information, such as gender, age, programme, and previous public exam (Hong Kong Diploma of Secondary Education Examination) scores—DSE scores, as demographic data
- uReply to gather students' attendance in the lecture and tutorial, as behavioral engagement data (from Week 1 to Week 14)

- uReply to gather students' participation in the lecture and tutorial (students' attempts on questions raised during lessons), as behavioral engagement data (from Week 1 to Week 14)
- uReply to gather students' correct responses to in-class questions in the lecture and tutorial, as cognitive engagement data (from Week 1 to Week 14)
- Blackboard Illuminate to gather students' number of course access in Blackboard, as behavioral engagement data (from Week 1 to Week 14)
- Blackboard Illuminate to gather students' number of interactions (such as mouse clicks) in Blackboard, as behavioral engagement data (from Week 1 to Week 14)
- Microsoft Forms to gather students' self-confidence, as emotional engagement data (from Week 1 to Week 14)
- Microsoft Forms to gather students' satisfaction level with the lessons, as emotional engagement data (from Week 1 to Week 14).

4.4 Measures

Multidimensional engagement data spanning cognitive, behavioral, and emotional domains were collected. Cognitive engagement was operationalized as the summed scores from in-class (Lectures or tutorials) exercises and quizzes. Behavioral engagement encompassed cumulative lecture and tutorial attendance, participation in in-class activities, and learning management system (LMS Blackboard) access and interactions with course materials and activities. Emotional engagement was measured weekly using single-item ratings of self-confidence and satisfaction; a cumulative average across weeks was computed. Feature variables were summarized in the accompanying table. Prior academic results (DSE scores) were included as a control variable.

Table 1. Feature variables for analysis.

Engagement Dimensions	Description	Measurement
Cognitive engagement	Lecture in-class exercise scores; Tutorial in-class exercise scores	Integer
Behavioral engagement	Lecture participation; Tutorial participation; LMS Blackboard Course Access; LMS Blackboard interactions;	Integer
	Lecture attendance; Tutorial attendance;	1/0
Emotional engagement	Self-confidence; Satisfaction	1–7

4.5 Data Analysis

All data were consolidated into a master dataset. Multiple machine learning algorithms were trained and tested for outcome prediction, and standard accuracy metrics were compared to identify the best-performing models. SHAP analysis was conducted to determine the most influential features, and their relative contributions were examined to classify features as strong, medium, or low contributors.

5 Findings

5.1 Descriptive Analysis of Respondents

A total of 72 students participated in the study. Of these, 38 completed the demographic survey (20 male, 18 female), with ages ranging from 18 to 31 years (M = 19.00, SD = 3.599). Course GPA ranged from 1.30 to 4.00 (M = 3.3069, SD = 0.87715). Using a classification boundary close to the institution's GPA threshold of 2.0 (Grade C) for probation, students were classified as no risk if they received an overall grade of B- or above, and at risk if they received an overall grade C + or below. Accordingly, 13 students (18%) were classified as at risk and 59 (82%) were classified as not at risk.

5.2 Model Testing

Feature variables spanning engagement dimensions and prior academic results were used to develop the at-risk student prediction model (see Table 1). Five machine learning algorithms were trained and tested: k-nearest neighbors (kNN), Logistic Regression (LogReg), Random Forest (RF), support vector machines (SVM), and XGBoost. The model configurations under each algorithm are shown in Table 2.

Table 2. Configuration of machine learning models

Algorithms	Key Model Configurations
k-nearest neighbors (kNN)	Configured with 5 neighbours, uniform weighting and the Minkowski distance metric
Logistic Regression (LogReg)	Implemented as multinominal classifier
Random Forest (RF)	Configured with 200 trees
Support Vector Machines (SVM)	Implemented using a radial basis function kernel, with the regularisation parameter set to 1 and kernel coefficient set using the scale option
XGBoost	Configured with 200 estimators, and a learning rate of 0.1, maximum tree depth of 6, row and column subsampling of 0.8

To examine performance differences across time, models were built using data from Week 3, Week 7, and Week 14 where they represented the beginning, middle, and the end of the semester. Accuracy metrics were compared across algorithms and weeks, and the top-performing models were highlighted. Results are summarized in Table 3.

5.3 Model Selection

Across all algorithms and weeks, the top-performing entries were RF (Week 7), XGBoost (Week 7) and SVM (Week 14), which achieved identical performance metrics: Precision = 0.94, Recall = 0.93, F1 = 0.93, Accuracy = 0.9333. The ROC-AUC of RF (Week 7) was 0.8333, slightly higher than that of XGBoost (Week 7) and SVM (Week 14) where ROC-AUC were both 0.7500. Moreover, it was because Week 14 coincides with the end of the semester—leaving limited time to intervene with at-risk students. Overall, RF (Week 7) was selected for further analysis.

Table 3. Summary of model testing results.

	Precision*	Recall	F1-Score	Accuracy	ROC-AUC
kNN					
Week 3	0.8667	0.8667	0.8667	0.8667	0.8750
Week 7	0.8667	0.8667	0.8667	0.8667	0.9028
Week 14	0.8273	0.8000	0.8099	0.8000	0.7361
LogReg					
Week 3	0.7769	0.8000	0.7840	0.8000	0.9167
Week 7	0.8667	0.8667	0.8667	0.8667	0.8889
Week 14	0.8667	0.8667	0.8667	0.8667	0.8333
RF					
Week 3	0.8667	0.8667	0.8667	0.8667	0.7778
Week 7	0.9385	0.9333	0.9280	0.9333	0.8333
Week 14	0.8273	0.8000	0.8099	0.8000	0.8333
SVM					
Week 3	0.7769	0.8000	0.7840	0.8000	0.9444
Week 7	0.8857	0.8667	0.8385	0.8667	0.9167
Week 14	0.9385	0.9333	0.9280	0.9333	0.7500
XGBoost					
Week 3	0.8667	0.8667	0.8667	0.8667	0.8611
Week 7	0.9385	0.9333	0.9280	0.9333	0.7500
Week 14	0.8273	0.8000	0.8099	0.8000	0.8333

* *All the figures reported the weighted average of common accuracy precision metrics* [1]*; all algorithm models had the same support of 15.*

5.4 Feature Importance Analysis

SHapley Additive exPlanations (SHAP), a model-agnostic framework grounded in cooperative game theory, was employed to quantify the contribution of each feature to the model's predictions. SHAP values for the features were calculated using the RF (Week 7) model. Feature importance was categorized as strong ($\geq$ 12%), medium (6–12%), and low ($<$ 6%) based on each feature's share of the total SHAP value (sum = 0.2882). The detailed results are presented in Table 4.

6 Discussion

6.1 Key Findings

This study designed a rich learning environment to enhance student engagement in an undergraduate statistics semester course. College students' digital footprints and learning progress were collected for analysis. Machine learning models were trained and tested to predict at-risk students, resulting in the development of a predictive model. The model had the following key findings.

Table 4. Summary of feature importance analysis.

Features	SHAP values	Feature importance	Engagement Dimensions
Strong (> 12%)			
Tutorial in-class exercise scores	0.0601	20.85%	Cognitive engagement
Lecture in-class exercise scores	0.0527	18.29%	Cognitive engagement
Lecture participation	0.0357	12.39%	Behavioral engagement
Medium (6–12%)			
Tutorial participation	0.0342	11.87%	Behavioral engagement
Self confidence	0.0275	9.54%	Emotional engagement
LMS Blackboard interaction count	0.0269	9.33%	Behavioral engagement
Tutorial attendance	0.0182	6.32%	Behavioral engagement
Weak (< 6%)			
Satisfaction level	0.0124	4.30%	Emotional engagement
Lecture attendance	0.0107	3.71%	Behavioral engagement
Prior academic results	0.0098	2.63%	Control variable

Cognitive engagement is the strongest predictor:

- Lecture and tutorial in-class exercise scores contribute 18.29% and 20.85% respectively, indicating that low formative performance by Week 7 is the clearest early warning of risk.

Behavioral engagement matters meaningfully:

- Lecture and tutorial participation at 12.39% and 11.87% respectively confirm that low in-class participation elevates risk.
- LMS Blackboard interactions at 9.33% show that reduced LMS activity aligns with higher risk.
- Attendance in lecture and tutorial contribute less to the prediction, at 3.71% and 6.32% respectively.

Emotional engagement is a complementary signal:

- Self-confidence at 9.54% indicates that students' perceptions of confidence meaningfully predict outcomes. Relatively lower in percentage, satisfaction level contributes 4.3% in the analysis.

Low effect features:

- Prior academic performance (DSE score) was included as a control variable and exhibited a very small effect on the overall model, indicating that at-risk status was not associated with prior academic results.

Early detection by Week 7 is feasible:

- The top seven features (medium to strong) suggest mid-term monitoring can reliably flag at-risk students before high-stakes assessments.

Combined risk profile:

- Students showing low in-class exercise scores, low classroom participation, declining confidence, and sparse LMS interaction form a high-risk cluster; intervening on any two or more of these areas likely yields the greatest impact.

6.2 Theoretical Contributions

In this study, variables capturing various dimensions of engagement, including cognitive engagement, behavioral engagement, and emotional engagement were included in the training and testing of a predictive machine learning model. The model (RF in Week 7) achieved strong performance on standard evaluation metrics (Precision = 0.94, Recall = 0.93, F1 = 0.93, Accuracy = 0.9333, ROC-AUC = 0.8333), yielding results comparable to (e.g., [20]) or better than prior studies (e.g., [10]). These findings suggest that multidimensional digital footprints make substantive contributions to predicting at-risk students.

6.3 Practical Contributions

This study offers practical insights into identifying and supporting at-risk students. Comparative analyses indicate that data from Week 7 provide a reliable basis for early prediction. Leveraging this early warning, instructors can closely monitor the engagement of at-risk students, implement targeted instructional strategies and interventions, and assess academic performance and learning outcomes to evaluate the effectiveness of early pedagogical responses. Importantly, students can be kept informed of their engagement and progress throughout the semester, enabling collaborative efforts to prevent failure rather than discovering issues only at the end.

Actionable implications derived from the findings include:

- Prioritize formative support: Provide timely feedback, micro-remediation, and study skills coaching to address low scores on in-class lecture exercises.
- Increase LMS engagement: Implement nudging strategies (e.g., checklists, notifications), structured weekly tasks, and gamified milestones to enhance interactions with Blackboard activities.

- Strengthen in-class participation: Incorporate active learning prompts and low-stakes incentives to increase lecture participation.
- Address emotional factors: Offer brief confidence-building sessions, peer mentoring, and satisfaction pulse checks to improve weekly self-reported confidence and course satisfaction.
- Monitor early (Weeks 5–7): Establish thresholds that trigger outreach (e.g., students in the bottom quartile on two or more features).

6.4 Limitations and Future Studies

This study has several limitations. First, as a pilot, it relies on a small sample relative to a large set of potential features, which may adversely affect model performance and stability (e.g., [4]). Second, consistent with real-world contexts, the dataset is highly imbalanced, with far more non–at-risk students than at-risk students—a pattern common in undergraduate Statistics courses and broader institutional academic results. Such imbalance can distort evaluation metrics (e.g., recall, F1-score) for identifying at-risk students, leading to poor generalization, unfair outcomes, and skewed assessments. Finally, machine learning alone may be limited in explaining underlying phenomena; subsequent research should incorporate theory-driven approaches to learning analytics, such as a constructivist data science philosophy (e.g., [21]), to better capture the rationale and meaning behind observed patterns.

Future work could be performed to mitigate data imbalance by employing data rebalancing techniques (e.g., oversampling/undersampling), class/group weighting, importance reweighting, or generating synthetic data for underrepresented groups (e.g., [2, 10]). With at-risk students identified, remedial strategies could be applied to them and the effectiveness of these strategies could be evaluated. This study currently uses static aggregate representation of behavioural data as the feature variables. In the future, the time-dependent representation of these data [18] could be analysed.

7 Conclusion

This study was designed to provide a rich learning experience environment for students in an undergraduate Statistics course where this environment provides rich digital footprints of students to understand their learning progress. With this rich data, this study utilized machine learning to train and test a prediction model for at-risk students, which the common accurate performance metrics showed comparable good results for the model. The prediction model provides rich insights into students' learning progress. It also allows instructors to devise instructional pedagogies for early intervention to support students. Actionable implications were suggested for instructors, academics and practitioners.

Acknowledgments. This study was funded by the College Teaching Grant of Tung Wah College (grant number CTG230502).

Disclosure of Interests. The authors have no competing interests to declare that are relevant to the content of this article.

References

1. Chen, J., Zhou, X., Yao, J., Tang, S.K.: Application of machine learning in higher education to predict students' performance, learning engagement and self-efficacy: a systematic literature review. Asian Educ. Develop. Stud. **14**(2), 205–240 (2025)
2. Chui, K.T., Fung, D.C.L., Lytras, M.D., Lam, T.M.: Predicting at-risk university students in a virtual learning environment via a machine learning algorithm. Comput. Hum. Behav. **107**, 105584 (2020)
3. Kustitskaya, T.A., Esin, R.V., Vainshtein, Y.V., Noskov, M.V.: Hybrid approach to predicting learning success based on digital educational history for timely identification of at-risk students. Education Sciences **14**(6), 657 (2024)
4. Sonnleitner, B., Madou, T., Deceuninck, M., Theodosiou, F., Sagaert, Y.R.: Evaluation of early student performance prediction given concept drift. Comp. Educ. Artif. Intel. **8**, 100369 (2025)
5. Wang, C., Mirzaei, T., Xu, T., Lin, H.: How learner engagement impacts non-formal online learning outcomes through value co-creation: An empirical analysis. Int. J. Educ. Technol. High. Educ. **19**(1), 32 (2022)
6. Tang, Y., Hew, K.F.: Effects of using mobile instant messaging on student behavioral, emotional, and cognitive engagement: a quasi-experimental study. Int. J. Educ. Technol. High. Educ. **19**(1), 3 (2022)
7. Teng, Y., Wang, X.: The effect of two educational technology tools on student engagement in Chinese EFL courses. Int. J. Educ. Technol. High. Educ. **18**(1), 27 (2021)
8. Durgungoz, A., Durgungoz, F.C.: Exploring effortless AI-generated gamified quizzes in an online special education module: evaluating question quality, student engagement, and its potential to identify at-risk students. Educ. Inf. Technol. **30**(17), 25335–25357 (2025)
9. Hoi, V.N.: Transitioning from school to university: A person-oriented approach to understanding first-year students' classroom engagement in higher education. Educ. Rev. **76**(5), 1113–1133 (2024)
10. Miranda, E., Aryuni, M., Rahmawati, M.I., Hiererra, S.E., Sano, A.V.D.: Machine learning's model-agnostic interpretability on the prediction of students' academic performance in video-conference-assisted online learning during the covid-19 pandemic. Comp. Educ. Artif. Intel. **7**, 100312 (2024)
11. Herrmann, L., Weigert, J.: AI-based prediction of academic success: Support for many, disadvantage for some? Comp. Educ. Artif. Intel. **7**, 100303 (2024)
12. Duro, B., Gomes, A., Correia, F.B., Borges, A.R., Bernardino, J.: Machine learning and deep learning for dropout prediction in higher education: A review. Computers **15**(3), 164 (2026)
13. Abu-Oda, G., El-Halees, A.: Data mining in higher education: University student dropout case study. Int. J. Data Min. Knowl. Manage. Proc. **5**(1), 15–27 (2015)
14. González-Nucamendi, A., Noguez, J., Neri, L., Robledo-Rella, V., García-Castelán, R.: Predictive analytics study to determine undergraduate students at risk of dropout. Frontiers in Education **8**, 1244686 (2023)
15. Chang, Y.-H., Chen, F.-C., Lee, C.-I.: Developing an early warning system with personalized interventions to enhance academic outcomes for at-risk students in Taiwanese higher education. Education Sciences **15**(10), 1321 (2025)
16. Choi, S.P.M., Lam, S.S., Li, K.C., Wong, B.T.M.: Learning analytics at low cost: At-risk student prediction with clicker data and systematic proactive interventions. J. Educ. Technol. Soc. **21**(2), 273–290 (2018)
17. Osborne, J.B., Lang, A.: Predictive identification of at-risk students: Using learning management system data. J. Postsecon. Stud. Succ. **2**, 108–126 (2023)

18. Santos, R.M., Henriques, R.: Accurate, timely, and portable: Course-agnostic early prediction of student performance from LMS logs. Comp. Educ. Artif. Intel. **5**, 100175 (2023)
19. Idowu, J.A., Koshiyama, A.S., Treleaven, P.: Investigating algorithmic bias in student progress monitoring. Comp. Educ. Artif. Intel. **7**, 100267 (2024)
20. Chachoui, Y., Azizi, N., Hotte, R., Bensebaa, T.: Enhancing algorithmic assessment in education: Equi-fused-data-based SMOTE for balanced learning. Comp. Educ. Artif. Intel. **6**, 100222 (2024)
21. Doroudi, S.: On the paradigms of learning analytics: Machine learning meets epistemology. Comp. Educ. Artif. Intel. **6**, 100192 (2024)

Exploring Engineering Undergraduate's Cognitive Presence in AI-Enhanced Learning: A TCSA Method

Dongchen Pan[1], Taotao Long[1(✉)], Xiaomeng Zhu[2], and Manli Yu[1,3]

[1] Faculty of Artificial Intelligence in Education, Central China Normal University, WuHan, China
taotaolong@mail.ccnu.edu.cn

[2] Wuhan University of Technology, WuHan, China

[3] National Engineering Research Center of Educational Big Data, Central China Normal University, WuHan, China

Abstract. Generative Artificial Intelligence (GenAI) is increasingly integrated into engineering education, providing learning support while also raising concerns about over-reliance and reduced cognitive engagement. This study explores whether the Target-Criteria-Source-Analogy (TCSA) thinking method can guide students to use GenAI more effectively in collaborative learning. Based on the Preparing for Future Collaboration (PFC) paradigm, TCSA was implemented as a scaffold for individual preparation with AI support before group collaboration. A quasi-experimental study was conducted with 132 undergraduate engineering students. The experimental group ($N = 58$) used GenAI under the guidance of TCSA, while the control group ($N = 74$) used GenAI without structured support. Epistemic network analysis (ENA) was performed by encoding the discussion content during group collaboration using a bidirectional encoder representation from transformers (BERT) machine learning model. The results indicate that the cognitive focus of the TCSA-GAI group is more inclined towards the "trigger" dimension, starting from problem discussion, extensive exploration and integration, with a wider coverage of cognitive activities and a more solid starting point. The cognitive focus of the GAI group is more inclined towards the "integration" dimension, tending to directly accept GAI's answers and information integration, and the process of problem triggering and exploration is relatively weak. On the contrary, the GAI group showed that although the scaffold free GAI may promote information collection and content integration, it can not effectively guide students to collaborate around problem triggering, reasoning and collaborative problem solving.

Keywords: GAI education · Cooperative/collaborative learning · 21st century abilities

K. T. Chui et al. (Eds.): ICBL 2026, LNCS 16778, pp. 326–337, 2027.
https://doi.org/10.1007/978-981-92-3761-6_23

1 Introduction

In recent years, GenAI has had a significant impact on education. It provides students with real-time feedback, offers personalized learning experiences, and helps them understand complex concepts while increasing engagement and confidence [1, 2]. However, current research suggests that there is still some controversy surrounding the impact of GenAI in education. Although GenAI helps to process information and solve problems more easily, it may lead to over reliance on it, potentially depriving students of higher-order thinking opportunities and hindering their ability to independently process information [3, 4]. ChatGPT can significantly improve short-term task performance, but may not enhance intrinsic motivation and knowledge acquisition and transfer [5]. To reduce these risks, a structured guidance framework is needed to ensure that students use generative AI to promote learning outcomes rather than hinder cognitive development. The TCSA method is a thinking tool. Research has shown that it can be applied to other fields and integrated with artificial intelligence [6], thus demonstrating its potential as a scaffold for discussions supported by generative AI.

This study uses the TCSA method as a framework to facilitate structured discussions and explores the impact of this thinking approach on students' dependence on generative AI, critical thinking, and collaborative problem-solving abilities. This study aims to provide evidence-based guidance to effectively integrate generative AI into curriculum and gain a deeper understanding of how generative AI affects students' learning and cognitive development.

2 Literature Review

2.1 Generative AI in Engineering Education

The recent popularity of generative AI (GenAI) applications such as ChatGPT portend a new era of research, teaching, and learning across domains, including in engineering [7]. When students provide well-crafted prompts, GenAI models can offer immediate, valuable feedback, acting as learning partners or teaching assistants [8, 9]. Although generative AI (GenAI) brings many benefits, it also presents many challenges. A major concern is the risk of students overly relying on these tools, which may weaken their critical thinking and problem-solving abilities. Dependency behavior describes the way people use artificial intelligence outputs or the degree to which they rely on them in collaboration between humans and artificial intelligence [10]. Additionally, AI literacy, including self-efficacy and domain knowledge, enables users to evaluate and adjust their reliance based on the system's reliability [11]. AI literacy as "a set of competencies that enables individuals to evaluate AI technologies critically; communicate and collaborate effectively with AI; and use AI as a tool online, at home, and in the workplace" [12].

2.2 Collaborative Learning in Engineering Education

With collaborative learning, students expand their knowledge and co-construct new knowledge through productive peer interactions [13]. In engineering classrooms, collaborative learning is widely practiced in team-based design projects [14]. The development of successful and feasible solutions relies on the active contribution of individuals who communicate and operate effectively within a group context [15]. How student engineering students collaborate during the engineering-design process reflects their design cognition, something that has critical effects on their design outcomes [16]. The Preparing for Future Collaboration (PFC) paradigm, as an emerging paradigm in engineering education, has received attention in recent years. Empirical research has shown that student engineering students can enhance the effectiveness of engineering design by preparing individually before completing group collaboration [17]. Cognitive presence, situated within online collaborative learning environments, is defined as the level of cognitive engagement and critical thinking exhibited by learners during collaborative meaning-making processes [18]. Specifically, it refers to learners' ability to collaboratively construct and validate meaning through sustained reflection and discourse within a learning community. Research shows a strong link between cognitive presence and learning outcomes in online learning [19].

3 Method

Below presents the research methodology of this study, including the research background, participants, and specific intervention arrangements adopted in the experiment.

3.1 Research Context and Participants

The study was conducted over 16 weeks in a "Applications of Computer Technology in Materials Science" course at a large research university in Central China. This course aimed to enhance engineering students' ability to solve practical problems in materials science and engineering with the support of computer technology. The course employed a flipped classroom approach, with students participating in problem-based learning in small groups and completing pre-class self-study by reviewing online resources provided by the instructor.

3.2 Intervention

The study included 132 undergraduate students majoring in materials science and engineering from two classes. These students demonstrated a solid academic foundation and rich subject knowledge from other courses, but had limited experience using GenAI in their studies. The intervention was implemented through two student-centered, project-based engineering design activities conducted over approximately two weeks. The experimental group (TCSA-GAI, N = 58) learned the TCSA method and conducted AI-enhanced individual preparation based on this method [6], while the control group (GAI, N = 74) did not learn this method and directly used AI for individual preparation. After completing their individual preparation, both groups engaged in collaborative group discussions. Figure 1 shows the process for the intervention.

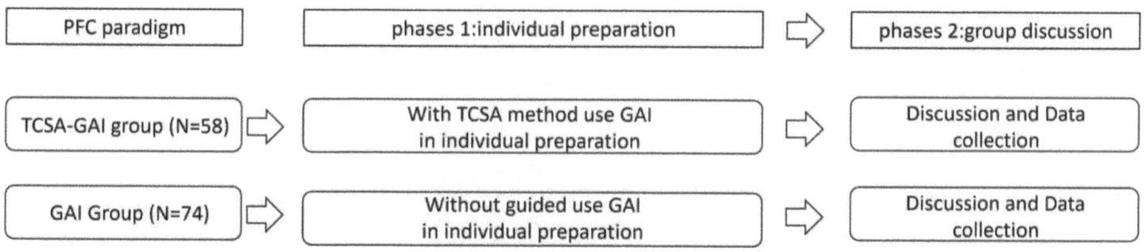

Fig. 1. The process for the intervention.

3.3 Use of GAI According to TCSA Method

Target-Criteria-Source-Analogy (TCSA) was applied in problem-based learning as follows: (1) Target: Formulate a statement for the target problem. A problem statement should ideally be short, concise, and structured based on a much longer document. This will ensure that everyone involved in solving the problem is able to clarify its main points and understand it in the same way.

Criteria: Determine the key usefulness criteria for the target problem. The standard is used to evaluate and compare the ideas of solving problems, and determines the direction and degree of solving problems.

Source: Find a source problem which has as many key criteria as possible with the target problem, but that, unlike the target problem, has already been solved to a satisfactory degree. Develop a statement for the most appropriate source problem and solution, as you do for the target problem.

(4) Analogy: Create an analogy between the target problem and the source problem through standards. Since the analogy connects the target problem and the source problem based on multiple criteria related to these two problems, it will be meaningful.

Under the TCSA framework, the students were required to identify and define problems, and GAI provided information to support this process, enabling students to reason and make judgments based on a more comprehensive knowledge background. By interacting with GAI, students are required to evaluate the reliability of information, screen key content, and make decisions based on their own logical thinking, thereby promoting the development of critical thinking.

In this study, three tools, the Xiaoya platform, Doubao and Metaso, were adopted to build an intelligent learning environment. The Xiaoya platform supported the release of course tasks and resources and classroom management. Figure 2 shows the interface of the Xiaoya platform. We use Doubao as the main human-AI interaction platform. Doubao has a high level of intelligence and is more suitable for use in human-AI dialogue. Metaso serves as a source for finding problem cases and their solutions. Metaso can provide source links for models, making it easy for users to quickly reference and verify them. It should be clarified that the TCSA method is still effective without using GAI, but in this study, we used GAI to accelerate the exploration process (Table 1).

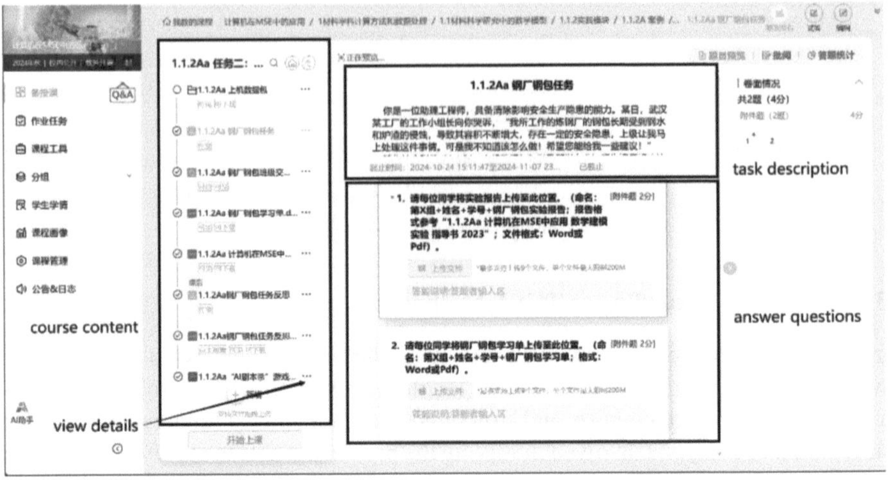

Fig. 2. Resource supported by the Xiaoya platform.

Table 1. TCSA method.

Dimensions	*Problem solving*	*Use GAI*
Target	structured description of the problem	Doubao
Criteria	Clarify the direction and degree of problem-solving	Doubao
Source	Find similar target problems with good solutions	Metaso
Analogy	Analogy through standards, drawing on valuable parts	Doubao

3.4 Data Collection and Coding

Our research involves collecting discourse information during discussions after different individual preparation stages to evaluate the different cognitive dimensions of human-machine collaboration. Online discussion records are the main source of data for analyzing cognitive presence [20]. This study evaluated the discussion data by combining quantitative content analysis with the cognitive presence coding scheme proposed by [18]. The encoding rules were based on themes from cognitive presence. Table 2 shows the encoding table used in this case. These stages represent different levels of cognitive presence, from the lowest triggering state to the highest level of resolution[18]. In the subsequent analysis, we used the fine-tuning MOOC-BERT model proposed to classify each post as a cognitive presence stage [21]. The MOOC-BERT model is a specialized adaptation of BERT Base Chinese, developed by [22, 23]. The proposed model demonstrates robust reliability in various evaluation metrics, with an accuracy of 0.881, precision of 0.858, recall of 0.861, and F1 of 0.859 on Dataset AstroTalk (all > 0.85), while maintaining comparable performance on Dataset IntroPsy with 0.782, 0.790, 0.782, and 0.786, respectively (all > 0.78). These results validate the robustness and applicability of the model in cognitive presence analysis [21, 24].

Table 2. Coding scheme for cognitive presence.

Dimensions	*Problem solving*
Triggering	Recognizing the problem
Exploration	Divergence of ideas, Exchanging ideas, Suggestions for consideration, Leaps to conclusions
Integration	Connecting ideas, synthesis
Resolution	Application and solutions

4 Result

4.1 Overall Description

To investigate the differences in cognitive presence patterns among engineering students who use or do not use the TCSA cognitive strategy, we compared the frequency distribution of cognitive presence between the TCSA-GAI and GAI groups (see Table 3). As shown in Table 3, Integration (47.02%) is the most common cognitive presence, followed by Exploration (29.34%). Triggering and Resolution have lower frequencies. This suggests that engineering students mainly focus on exploration and integration. The triggering and resolution rates of engineering students in the TCSA-GAI group were markedly higher than those in the GAI group. This indicates that both groups of engineering students value Integration and Exploration, but those using TCSA cognitive tools were more involved in Triggering and Resolution. It is worth noting that the TCSA-GAI group had fewer members ($N = 58$) than the GAI group ($N = 74$), but generated more discussion related to cognitive presence. The total number of coded segments in the TCSA-GAI group was 1470, while that in the GAI group was 578.

Table 3. Frequencies and distributions of cognitive presence levels in the TCSA-GAI and GAI groups.

	N	Triggering	Exploration	Integration	Resolution	Total
TCSA-GAI	58	376 (25.58%)	442 (30.07%)	626 (42.59%)	26 (1.77%)	1470 (71.78%)
GAI	74	77 (13.32%)	159 (27.51%)	337 (58.30%)	5 (0.86%)	578 (28.22%)
Total	132	453 (22.12%)	601 (29.34%)	963 (47.02%)	31 (1.51%)	2048

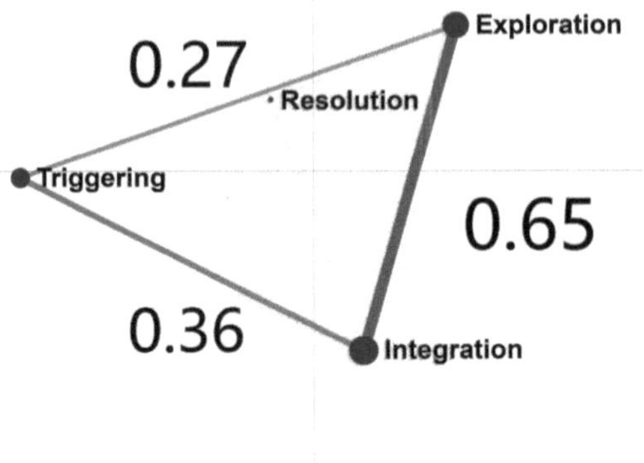

Fig. 3. ENA networks of cognitive presence for all students.

Figure 3 demonstrates the average ENA network of cognitive presence among all students during the discussion process. This network consists of four dimensions: Triggering, Exploration, Integration, and Resolution. The thickness and color depth of the connections represent the co-occurrence intensity between each dimension. The Exploration-Integration (0.65) connection is the strongest, presented by the thickest red solid line, indicating that students frequently integrate and synthesize the information collected during the exploration phase in their discussions. Triggering-Integration (0.36) connection comes second, indicating that after the problem is triggered, students can smoothly progress to the integration stage. Triggering-Exploration (0.27), the transition from problem posing to information exploration is also relatively active. However, the connections related to the Resolution dimension are generally weak, with the Resolution nodes in the figure being small and the related lines being extremely fine, indicating that students' performance in the final problem-solving and solution application level is relatively weak.

In Garrison's Community of Inquiry (CoI) model, cognitive presence is ranked from low to high as Triggering-Exploration-Integration-Resolution. The network structure presented in this figure indicates that students follow the main cognitive path of "Triggering-Exploration-Integration". The trigger stage stimulates problem awareness, the exploration stage extensively collects and discusses information, and ultimately integrates multiple information in the integration stage to form higher-level cognitive outputs, and finally solves the target problem (Table 4).

Table 4. Mann–Whitney U test results comparing ENA dimensions between groups.

Dimension	Group	N	Median	U	P-value	Effect Size (r)
MR1 (x axis)	TCSA-GAI	58	0.18	1033.50	< 0.001*	0.50
	GAI	74	-0.20			

(continued)

Table 4. *(continued)*

Dimension	Group	N	Median	U	P-value	Effect Size (r)
SVD2 (Y Axis)	TCSA-GAI	58	-0.04	2009.50	0.74	0.03
	GAI	74	-0.07			

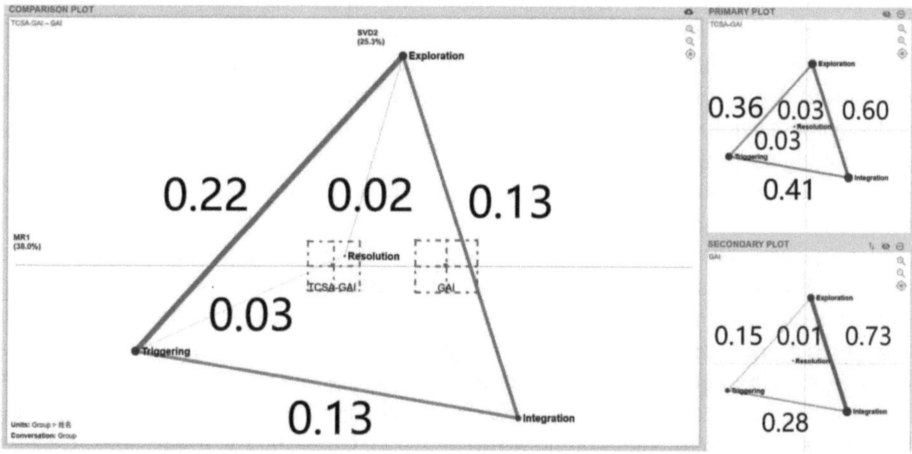

Fig. 4. Subtracted ENA networks of cognitive presence for the TCSA-GAI (blue) and GAI (red) groups.

As shows in Fig. 4, the TCSA-GAI group has a significant advantage in multiple pathways: the Triggering-Exploration (0.22) is the largest difference between the two groups. The blue solid line is the thickest, indicating that the TCSA-GAI group is much more active in the cognitive pathway of problem triggering and information exploration than the GAI group. After being prompted by a problem, students in this group can actively and extensively collect and explore information, drawing on known relevant knowledge for discussion and communication. The Triggering–Integration difference (0.13) is also shown by a thicker blue line, indicating that the TCSA-GAI group is significantly stronger than the GAI group in cognitive activities spanning directly from problem triggering to integration. The difference in Triggering-Resolution (0.03), with a thin line and a small difference, but the TCSA-GAI group has a slight advantage. Relatively speaking, the GAI group dominates with a difference of 0.13 on the Exploration-Integration path, and the red line is thicker, indicating that the GAI group is more active on the higher-order cognitive transformation path of Exploration-Integration, and their discussions are more focused on reporting exploration results directly.

5 Discussion

5.1 Cognitive Presence and Academic Performance

Quantitatively, the TCSA-GAI group produced 1,470 coded segments versus 578 in the GAI group, and showed a markedly higher proportion of Triggering and Resolution. The Mann–Whitney U test confirmed a significant between-group difference on the MR1 dimension ($U = 1033.50$, $p < .001$, $r = 0.50$), indicating a large effect of the TCSA method on cognitive-network structure. This comparison indicates that the TCSA structured thinking framework not only outperforms the model using GAI alone in terms of the quality of cognitive network structure, but also demonstrates that students not only "think deeper" but also "communicate more" in terms of the quantity and scale of discourse participation. The results indicate that students using the TCSA method showed a higher proportion of Triggering and Resolution, as well as a greater absolute frequency of Integration. Integration and Resolution are both significant predictors of final grades [19]. In an educational context, a strong correlation exists between high levels of cognitive presence and contributions to learning. The Triggering-Integration observed in the TCSA-GAI group in this study indicates that students could use GAI to map analogous engineering solutions onto their current problem. This enabled engineering students to broadly discover, reflect on, and integrate concepts, beliefs, and experiences into their existing knowledge and experience, justifying their choices and actions. This further suggests that discussion can make these reflections more "visible" not only to the contributors but also to others in the learning group. Consistent with previous research [25, 26], these findings suggest that discussion forums can constructively "maintain momentum and broaden the scope of dialogue".

5.2 Bridging Triggering to Deep Inquiry

The TCSA-GAI group showed more standardized and reflective participation in the discussion process compared to the control group. The results indicate that students are no longer just superficially or blindly exploring problems, but are able to use the initial problem as a starting point for effective information exchange and the connecting of ideas, building meaning through continuous communication. The TCSA method successfully links the process of defining and solving problems through GAI, forming a stable cognitive pathway. A recent systematic review suggests that the conditions for ChatGPT to support cognitive development are embedded in inquiry-oriented and scaffolding-based instructional design, particularly through processes such as metacognitive regulation, argumentative reasoning, and creative generation [27]. Similarly, the impact of ChatGPT on students' cognition is not an inherent attribute of the tool itself, but depends on the teaching framework, task design, and instructional context [27].

5.3 Orientation Towards Resolution

In this study, the overall cognitive presence in resolution dimensions was relatively low. The TCSA method helps students develop cognitive structures during their personal preparation stage, while the "standard" approach helps students consider the effectiveness, applicability, and implementation of problem-solving solutions from an analogical perspective. In engineering education, this dependency behavior is manifested as students replicating design solutions generated by GenAI without verifying boundary conditions. Lack of scaffolding may lead to premature cognitive closure, resulting in premature acceptance of GAI integration outcomes. The TCSA method extends its effects into the inquiry stage, with stronger Triggering-Exploration and Triggering-Integration indicating that students are more likely to re-examine the original problem during solution testing, forming a feedback loop between the target problem and candidate solutions. This recursive structure is closer to the real engineering design process, as solution validation often requires repeated refinement. The structural representations developed during the interaction phase of individual artificial intelligence seem to serve as cognitive anchors in group work, enabling better identification and understanding of these shared elements, thereby supporting smoother discussions and more coherent collective reasoning. Shared structural understanding has been shown to facilitate comprehensive decision-making in complex design tasks [28]. Consistent with this perspective, enhanced awareness of the collaborative state may reduce unnecessary coordination costs and implicitly guide learner interaction, thereby supporting more effective collaborative learning processes [29].

6 Implications

For engineering education, as a cognitive offloading tool, GAI has the potential to focus learners on higher-order thinking and creativity [30]. However, realizing this potential requires a clear instructional design that prevents metacognitive over-reliance on GAI. For educators, the introduction of GenAI cannot guarantee cognitive engagement. Embedding structured instructional guidance, such as TCSA, into task design can transform the use of shallow tools into deeper dialogue participation. The research results indicate that although GAI can bridge the gap in human knowledge, learners' cognitive engagement is influenced by the quality of questioning and instructional framework. This study integrates the TCSA method and GAI into engineering education, expanding the understanding of the PFC (Preparing for Future Collaboration) paradigm in AI learning environments. Several frameworks have sought to guide AI integration in education, including the TPACK model for technology pedagogy content, the Community of Inquiry (CoI) framework for online cognitive engagement, and collaboration models such as the PFC paradigm. Our research extends the latter two into the GenAI context. Based on these findings, we recommend that educators (a) match the use of GenAI with the causes of the problem, (b) design solutions that require analogical reasoning rather than direct answer prompts, and (c) establish solution validation to combat premature shallow acceptance.

7 Limitations

This study provides insights into the integration of generative AI in collaborative learning through the TCSA method, but there are also limitations. Firstly, this way of thinking is relatively abstract, and cognitive difficulties may limit students' ability to perform. Especially when they are still using TCSA to decompose and construct complex problems and interacting with generative AI, this cognitive load may be even greater. Secondly, although current designs have provided ways of thinking and guided reflective questions to help students extract information, there is still a need to explore methods of adjusting teaching processes and modifying prompt words in the future to alleviate this cognitive burden. For example, incorporating more guiding practices or providing different generative AI tools based on students' learning levels. And provide warm-up activities for generative AI tools to give students more time to familiarize themselves with them before dealing with complex tasks.

Funding. This work was supported by the National Science Foundation of China(Funding Number: 62307017).

References

1. Adiguzel, T., Kaya, M.H., Cansu, F.K.: Revolutionizing education with AI: Exploring the transformative potential of ChatGPT. Contemp. Educ. Technol. **15**(3), 429 (2023)
2. Chaudhry, I.S., Sarwary, S.A., El Refae, G.A., Chabchoub, H.: Time to revisit existing student's performance evaluation approach in higher education sector in a new era of CHATGPT—a case study. Cogent Education **10**(1), 2210461 (2023)
3. Chan, C.K.Y., Hu, W.: Students' voices on generative AI: Perceptions, benefits, and challenges in higher education. Int. J. Educ. Technol. High. Educ. **20**(1), 43 (2023)
4. Cooper, G.: Examining Science Education in ChATGPT: An Exploratory Study of Generative Artificial Intelligence. J. Sci. Educ. Technol. **32**(3), 444–452 (2023)
5. Fan, Y., et al.: Beware of metacognitive laziness: Effects of generative artificial intelligence on learning motivation, processes, and performance. Br. J. Edu. Technol. **56**(2), 489–530 (2025)
6. Pan, D., Long, T., Zhu, X., Li, J.: Exploring Engineering Undergraduate's Critical Thinking Patterns in AI-Enhanced Learning: A TCSA Method. In: Ma, W.W.K., Cheung, S.K.S., Li, C., Prayadsab, P., Mungwattana, A. (eds.) 18th International Conference on Blended Learning, LNCS, vol. 15721, pp. 291–303. Springer, Heidelberg (2025)
7. Kasneci, E., et al.: ChatGPT for good? On opportunities and challenges of large language models for education. Learn. Individ. Differ. **103**, 102274 (2023)
8. Lo, C.K.: What is the impact of CHATGPT on education? A rapid review of the literature. Education Sciences **13**(4), 410 (2023)
9. Sok, S., Heng, K.: ChatGPT for education and research: A review of benefits and risks. Cambodian J. Educ. Res. **3**(1), 110–121 (2023)
10. Wang, L., Jamieson, G.A., Hollands, J.G.: Selecting methods for the analysis of reliance on automation. Proceedings of the Human Factors and Ergonomics Society Annual Meeting **52**(4), 287–291 (2008)
11. Madhavan, P., Phillips, R.R.: Effects of computer self-efficacy and system reliability on user interaction with decision support systems. Comput. Hum. Behav. **26**(2), 199–204 (2010)
12. Long, D., Magerko, B.: What is AI Literacy? Competencies and Design Considerations. In: Proceedings of the 2020 CHI Conference on Human Factors in Computing Systems (CHI '20), pp. 1–16. Association for Computing Machinery, New York, NY, USA (2020)

13. Janssen, J., Erkens, G., Kirschner, P.A., Kanselaar, G.: Influence of group member familiarity on online collaborative learning. Comput. Hum. Behav. **25**(1), 161–170 (2009)
14. Borrego, M., Karlin, J., McNair, L.D., Beddoes, K.: Team Effectiveness Theory from Industrial and Organizational Psychology Applied to Engineering Student Project Teams: A Research Review. J. Eng. Educ. **102**(4), 472–512 (2013)
15. Dym, C.L., Agogino, A.M., Eris, O., Frey, D.D., Leifer, L.J.: Engineering Design Thinking, Teaching, and Learning. J. Eng. Educ. **94**(1), 103–120 (2005)
16. Strimel, G.J., Kim, E., Bartholomew, S.R., Cantu, D.V.: Examining engineering design cognition with respect to student experience and performance (2018)
17. Lyu, Q., Chen, W., Su, J., Heng, K.H.: Collaborate like expert designers: An exploratory study of the role of individual preparation activity on students' collaborative learning. The Internet and Higher Education **59**, 100920 (2023)
18. Garrison, D.R., Anderson, T., Archer, W.: Critical thinking, cognitive presence, and computer conferencing in distance education. American J. Dist. Educ. **15**(1), 7–23 (2001)
19. Galikyan, I., Admiraal, W.: Students' engagement in asynchronous online discussion: The relationship between cognitive presence, learner prominence, and academic performance. The Internet and Higher Education **43**, Article 100692 (2019)
20. Anderson, T., Rourke, L., Garrison, D.R., Archer, W.: Assessing teaching presence in a computer conferencing context. J. Asynchronous Learn. Netw. **5**(2), 1–17 (2001)
21. Liu, Z., Tang, Q., Ouyang, F., Long, T., Liu, S.: Profiling students' learning engagement in MOOC discussions to identify learning achievement: An automated configurational approach. Computers & Education **219**, Article 105109 (2024)
22. Liu, Z., Kong, X., Chen, H., Liu, S., Yang, Z.: MOOC-BERT: Automatically identifying learner cognitive presence from MOOC discussion data. IEEE Trans. Learn. Technol. **16**(4), 528–542 (2023)
23. Liu, Z., Kong, X., Liu, S., Yang, Z.: Effects of computer-based mind mapping on students' reflection, cognitive presence, and learning outcomes in an online course. Distance Educ. **44**(3), 544–562 (2023)
24. Yu, M., Liu, Z., Long, T., et al.: Exploring cognitive presence patterns in GenAI-integrated six-hat thinking technique scaffolded discussion: an epistemic network analysis. Int. J. Educ. Technol. High. Educ. **22**, 48 (2025)
25. Meyer, K.A.: Face-to-face versus threaded discussions: The role of time and higher-order thinking. J. Asynchronous Learn. Netw. **7**(3), 55–65 (2003)
26. Vaughan, N., Garrison, D.R.: Creating cognitive presence in a blended faculty development community. The Inter. Higher Educ. **8**(1), 1–12 (2005)
27. Li, C., Cui, H., Hagedorn, L.S.: The cognitive impact of ChatGPT in higher education: A systematic review of critical and creative thinking outcomes. Comp. Educ. Artifi. Intel. **10**, 100571 (2026)
28. Arias, E., Eden, H., Fischer, G., Gorman, A., Scharff, E.: Transcending the individual human mind—Creating shared understanding through collaborative design. ACM Trans. Comp.-Human Inter. **7**(1), 84–113 (2000)
29. Bodemer, D.: Tacit guidance for collaborative multimedia learning. Comput. Hum. Behav. **27**(3), 1079–1086 (2011)
30. Dang, B., Huynh, L., Gul, F., Rosé, C., Järvelä, S., Nguyen, A.: Human–AI collaborative learning in mixed reality: Examining the cognitive and socio-emotional interactions. Br. J. Edu. Technol. **56**, 2078–2101 (2025)

A Systematic Review of Threshold Concept Identification in Programming Education: Foundations for MOOC-Based Learning Analytics

Hao Shen[1,2], Nancy Law[1], Jianhua Zhao[2](✉), and Yifang Ma[3]

[1] Faculty of Education, The University of Hong Kong, Hong Kong, China
shenhao@connect.hku.hk, nlaw@hku.hk

[2] Center for Future Education Research, Southern University of Science and Technology, Shenzhen, China
zhaojh@sustech.edu.cn

[3] Department of Statistics and Data Science, Southern University of Science and Technology, Shenzhen, China
mayf@sustech.edu.cn

Abstract. Threshold concepts (TCs) theory provides a framework for identifying learning bottlenecks in programming education, yet different studies have identified different TCs and the source of this inconsistency remains unclear. Existing identification methods rely primarily on retrospective interviews, surveys, and teacher observation, raising the question of whether methodological choices, particularly the choice of informant, shape identification outcomes. Clarifying this issue is needed for developing scalable TC identification approaches in large online environments such as MOOCs. This systematic review, reported using PRISMA 2020, analyzed 10 empirical studies yielding 40 TC identification instances. A recent-publication check found no additional eligible empirical TC identification studies beyond the included 2024 study. The review consolidated the literature into 15 core TCs and extracted 20 measurable indicators across five TC characteristics. The analysis revealed a significant association between informant role and identification outcomes: teachers predominantly identify concepts with visible behavioral symptoms, such as recursion, while non-teachers identify concepts involving internal paradigm shifts, such as object-oriented programming. This pattern, described as behavioral invisibility, reframes inconsistencies in the TC literature as differences in what each method can observe rather than flaws in any single approach, and positions MOOC behavioral data as a complementary third access mechanism for TC identification.

Keywords: Threshold Concepts · Learning Analytics · Programming Education · MOOC · Systematic Review

K. T. Chui et al. (Eds.): ICBL 2026, LNCS 16778, pp. 338–353, 2027.
https://doi.org/10.1007/978-981-92-3761-6_24

1 Introduction

Programming education in online settings needs ways to identify concepts that repeatedly block learner progress. MOOCs have expanded access to programming education, but high attrition and uneven learner persistence remain common concerns [1, 2]. Learning analytics can process large-scale activity traces to identify learning difficulties [3, 4], but analytics methods need clear theoretical targets. Threshold Concepts (TCs) theory offers one such target: TCs are concepts that, once understood, transform how learners see a subject [5].

In programming education, TC identification began with Boustedt et al. [6], using student interviews, teacher reports, surveys, practitioner reflections, and observation. However, no stable consensus has emerged. Different studies identify different candidates, including object-oriented programming, recursion, pointers, functions, and data structures [7–9]. Earlier methodological and theoretical discussions have examined the difficulty of identifying TCs [10–12], but to our knowledge, no review has jointly synthesized what programming TCs have been identified, what empirical indicators support them, and how identification methods shape the results. This combined synthesis is needed before TC theory can guide MOOC-based learning analytics.

Two unresolved problems underlie the inconsistency and limit progress toward scalable TC identification.

Problem 1: Inconsistent characteristic usage and the absence of concrete indicators.

Researchers apply the five TC characteristics inconsistently: some studies use all five, others only two or three [10]. Which characteristics matter most in practice, and which are peripheral? The abstract characteristics also lack a clear link to the specific evidence researchers actually use. When a researcher claims a concept is "troublesome," what observable phenomenon supports this? Without knowing what indicators have grounded each characteristic in past work, applying TC theory to new data sources like MOOC behavioral logs is difficult.

Problem 2: Unknown influence of methodological choices on identification outcomes.

TC identification studies use diverse data collection approaches: some rely on teacher interviews, others on student self-reports or practitioner reflections [13]. Each source has known limitations: memory reconstruction in retrospective accounts [14], expert blind spots in teacher observations [15]. The unresolved question is whether these sources lead to systematically different identification results. If the choice of informant shapes which concepts get identified as TCs, then published TC lists partly reflect methodological decisions rather than what is actually threshold-like about programming.

A **scalability constraint** compounds both problems: traditional TC identification relies on qualitative methods (interviews, surveys, classroom observation) that do not scale to online environments with thousands of learners [10]. MOOCs automatically log behavioral data, including video interactions, quiz attempts, and time on each activity [16]. Learning analytics can process such data to detect learning patterns at scale [3, 4]. But before testing whether MOOC data can support TC identification, we need to know what concrete indicators researchers have used and whether different methods produce different results.

This paper presents a systematic review of TC identification research in programming education, guided by two research questions:

RQ1: What threshold concepts have been identified in programming education, and what measurable indicators have researchers used to ground TC characteristics in empirical evidence?

RQ2: Do methodological choices in TC identification, especially the choice of informant, introduce systematic biases into identification outcomes?

Following PRISMA 2020 [17], we analyzed 10 empirical studies yielding 40 TC identification instances. The study contributes: (1) a reference set of 15 core TCs with 20 measurable indicators extracted from the reviewed studies; (2) empirical evidence that informant role introduces systematic bias, explained through the concept of *behavioral invisibility*; and (3) a conceptual analysis of MOOC behavioral data as a complementary third access mechanism. These contributions address RQ1 by summarizing the content of the literature and address RQ2 by explaining why the literature has produced divergent TC lists.

2 Methodology

2.1 Search Strategy and Study Selection

This review was reported using PRISMA 2020 [17]. Because the analysis consolidates TC identification results across studies (RQ1) and compares outcomes across methodological choices (RQ2), subject matter must be held constant; otherwise, differences in identified TCs could reflect the discipline rather than the method. Programming education was chosen because it has the largest body of empirical TC identification work and its concepts can be classified using established frameworks [18].

Nine sources were searched: ACM Digital Library, ERIC, Education Full Text EBSCO, ProQuest, ScienceDirect, Web of Science, Wiley, Scopus, and Google Scholar. The search combined threshold concept terms with programming, computer science, and computing terms. Google Scholar was used as a supplementary broad-coverage source rather than a replacement for disciplinary databases, because TC identification work is scattered across conference papers, journal articles, theses, and book chapters. Overlap among sources was expected and was handled through de-duplication. No temporal filters were applied, covering records up to August 2025. A recent-publication check was also conducted after the initial synthesis using the same TC identification, programming education, and computing-related search terms and the same eligibility criteria; no additional eligible empirical TC identification study was found beyond the included 2024 study.

Studies were included if they used TC theory as a theoretical basis, were conducted in programming course contexts using object-oriented languages, and involved empirical TC identification. Studies were excluded if they only discussed TC theory, were outside programming or object-oriented contexts, lacked empirical identification, or duplicated a later full publication. The selection process is summarized in Fig. 1. The initial search yielded 295 records. After removing 150 duplicates, 145 records were screened by title, abstract, and publication type. Full-text assessment of 38 papers led to 10 included studies. Nine identified specific TCs, producing 40 *identification instances*, where each instance is one study identifying one concept as a TC. One study [19] met the broad inclusion criteria but evaluated a teaching intervention rather than identifying TCs through systematic methods; it is retained for PRISMA transparency but contributes no instances.

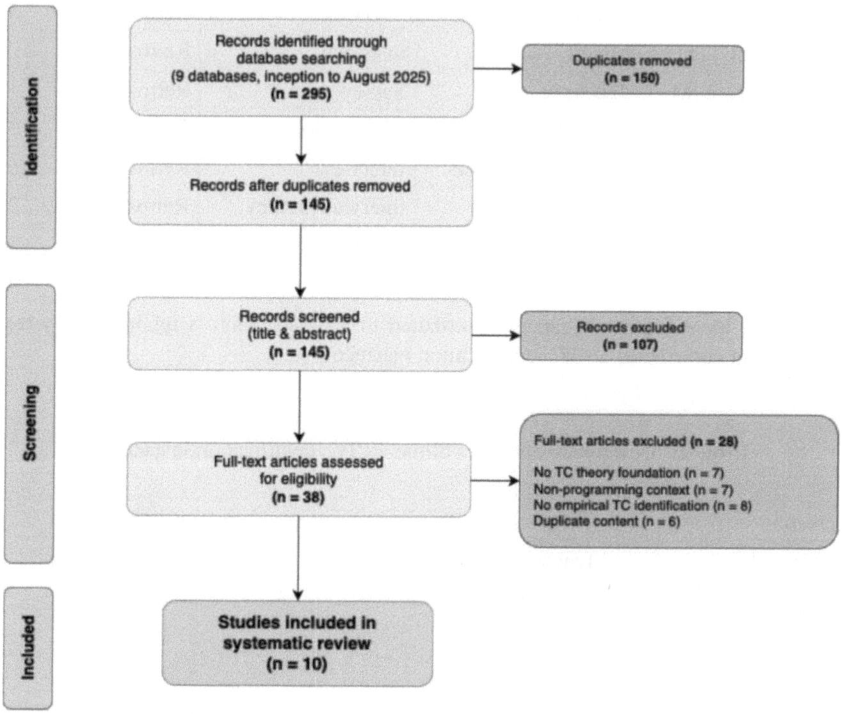

Fig. 1. PRISMA flow diagram for study selection.

2.2 Descriptive Overview of the Included Studies

Table 1 describes the study-level corpus, whereas Table 2 summarizes the 40 TC identification instances used in the analysis.

The included studies span 2007–2024, showing that empirical TC identification in programming education is a small and intermittent literature rather than a rapidly expanding publication stream. Very few eligible empirical identification studies were published after 2020, with Mackay et al. [24] being the only post-2021 study in the review corpus. This scarcity is important for interpreting the review: the limited number of recent included studies reflects the state of this specific empirical literature, not the absence of current interest in online programming learning or learning analytics.

Table 1. Studies included in the systematic review.

Study	Informant	Method	Timeline	N
Boustedt et al. [6]	Students	Interview	Retrospective	2
Moström et al. [20]	Students	Interview	Retrospective	7
Sien [19]	Students	Intervention study	Retrospective	0
Sanders et al. [7]	Teachers	Interview	Retrospective	5
Zwaneveld et al. [21]	Mixed	Interview	Retrospective	2
Kallia & Sentance [8]	Teachers	Survey	Retrospective	11
Sim [22]	Students	Observation	Concurrent	3
Yeomans et al. [9]	Prof. Programmers	Interview	Retrospective	6
Kallia [23]	Teachers	Interview/survey	Retrospective	2
Mackay et al. [24]	Teachers	Interview	Retrospective	2
Total				**40**

Note. N = TC identification instances contributed to analysis. Sien is retained for screening transparency but contributes no TC identification instance

Table 2. Descriptive analytics of the 40 TC identification instances.

Dimension	Category	Instances
Informant role	Teachers	20 (50.0%)
	Non-teachers	20 (50.0%)
Timeline	Retrospective	37 (92.5%)
	Concurrent	3 (7.5%)
Method	Interview	19 (47.5%)
	Interview/survey	11 (27.5%)
	Survey	7 (17.5%)
	Observation	3 (7.5%)
TC category	Algorithmic Structure	19 (47.5%)
	Class and Object Structure	9 (22.5%)
	Data Structure	7 (17.5%)
	Notional Machine	4 (10.0%)
	Unclassified	1 (2.5%)

Table 2 shows two features of the literature that drive the later analysis. First, informant role is balanced, allowing comparison between teacher and non-teacher evidence. Second, timeline and method are highly homogeneous: most instances use retrospective interview or survey data. Because all concurrent instances came from observation and almost all retrospective instances came from interviews or surveys, timeline and method are confounded. Informant role is therefore the only design dimension with sufficient variation for comparative analysis.

2.3 Data Extraction

For each study, the following was extracted: TC names and descriptions, TC characteristics employed during identification, data collection design (informant role, timeline, method), and evidence descriptions including original quotes. A key distinction was made between characteristics that studies quoted in their introductions and those actually employed during identification; only employed characteristics were used in subsequent analyses.

2.4 Analysis Methods

This study used mixed methods. For RQ1, the 40 original TC instances were consolidated into core TCs by standardizing terminology, aligning granularity levels, and resolving overlaps. Qualitative content analysis [25] then extracted measurable indicators from the evidence in the 40 instances. "Measurable" here means that prior researchers have empirically observed these indicators.

For RQ2, three data collection design dimensions were examined: informant role (teachers vs. non-teachers), timeline (retrospective vs. concurrent), and method (interview/survey vs. observation). The cross-case analytical approach [26] compared identification outcomes across informant groups through within-group analysis, between-group comparison, illustrative case comparison, and negative case analysis [27]. Chi-square tests of independence examined whether informant role was associated with TC types, classified into four categories using the OOP Knowledge and Skills Framework [18]: Algorithmic Structure (AS), Class and Object Structure (COS), Data Structure (DS), and Notional Machine (NM). Because some expected cell frequencies fell below 5, Fisher's exact test was also conducted. Effect sizes were estimated using Cramér's V [28]. The qualitative and quantitative analyses were conducted independently and integrated through triangulation.

3 Results

3.1 RQ1: Threshold Concepts and Measurable Indicators

Identified Threshold Concepts. The 9 studies with TC data yielded 40 identification instances containing 34 distinct TC names. These were consolidated into 15 core TCs through terminology standardization (e.g., "Calling a Function," "Functions," and "Methods" unified as Functions/Methods), granularity alignment (e.g., "Abstract Classes" subsumed under OOP as a sub-concept), and conceptual overlap resolution (e.g., "Modularity" and "Code Reuse" merged into Procedural Decomposition). All 40 instances, grouped by consolidated Core TC, are listed in Table 3.

Table 3. Complete mapping of 40 TC identification instances to 15 consolidated core TCs.

Core TC	Original TC Name	Study	Cat	N
≥ 3 Studies				
Object-Oriented	Object-Oriented Prog	[6]	COS	8
Programming	Object-Oriented Prog	[7]		
	Object-Oriented Prog	[22]		
	Inheritance & Polymorphism	[20]		
	Abstract Classes	[9]		
	Classes and Inheritance	[9]		
	Designing Objects	[9]		
	Object	[21]		
Data Structures	Data Structures	[7]	DS	4
	Data Structures	[9]		
	Data Abstraction	[20]		
	Multidimensional Arrays	[22]		
Procedural	Proc. Decomposition & Design	[8]	AS	4
Decomposition	Procedural Decomposition	[23]		
	Modularity	[20]		
	Code Reuse	[20]		
Pointers	Pointers	[6]	DS	3
	Pointers	[24]		
	Pointers	[7]		
Functions/Methods	Calling a Function	[8]	AS	3
	Functions	[24]		
	Methods (Functions)	[22]		
2 Studies				
Parameters & Args	Parameters	[8]	AS	5
	Arguments	[8]		
	Return Values	[8]		
	Parameter Passing	[8]		
	Params, Param. Passing, Return Val	[23]		
Abstraction	Abstraction	[8]	AS	2
	Mapping Betw. Abstraction Levels	[20]		
Recursion	Recursion	[8]	AS	2
	Recursion	[7]		

(*continued*)

Table 3. *(continued)*

Core TC	Original TC Name	Study	Cat	N
Design Patterns	Design Patterns	[20]	AS	2
	Design Patterns	[7]		
1 Study				
Variables & Scope	Variable; Variable Scope	[8]	NM	2
Control Flow	Control Flow	[8]	AS	1
Complexity	Algorithmic Efficiency	[20]	AS	1
Logical Implication	Logical Implication	[21]	AS	1
UI Architectures	User Interface Architectures	[9]	COS	1
Code Organisation	Code Organisation	[9]	–	1

Note. Cat. = Category (AS = Algorithmic Structure; COS = Class and Object Structure; DS = Data Structure; NM = Notional Machine). N = number of identification instances. The 40 instances used 34 distinct names; consolidation merged synonymous terms and aligned granularity levels. For the 1-Study tier, Variables & Scope combines two instances from the same study

Five TCs received support from three or more independent studies: Object-Oriented Programming (OOP), Data Structures, Procedural Decomposition, Pointers, and Functions/Methods. OOP was the most frequently identified, appearing in 8 instances across 6 studies. By category, Algorithmic Structure was most common (19 instances, 47.5%), followed by Class and Object Structure (9, 22.5%), Data Structure (7, 17.5%), and Notional Machine (4, 10.0%).

TC Characteristic Usage. Troublesome was used in 92.5% of instances, Integrative in 80.0%, and Transformative in 62.5%. These three form the practical core of TC identification. Irreversible (20.0%) and Bounded (7.5%) were rarely used, probably because demonstrating irreversibility requires longitudinal tracking and establishing boundedness requires cross-disciplinary comparison. This is consistent with the theoretical literature: Davies [29] showed that the first three characteristics are "necessarily interwoven," and Rowbottom [30] argued that TC identification works as a family resemblance rather than a rigid checklist. The mean number of characteristics per instance was 2.62, with 67.5% using only two or three (Table 4).

Table 4. TC characteristic usage across the 40 identification instances.

Characteristic	Instances	Percentage	Interpretation
Troublesome	37	92.5%	Practical core
Integrative	32	80.0%	Practical core
Transformative	25	62.5%	Practical core
Irreversible	8	20.0%	Design-dependent
Bounded	3	7.5%	Design-dependent

Note. Characteristics used in more than 50% of instances were treated as the practical core of empirical TC identification

Measurable Indicators. Qualitative content analysis of the evidence reported in the 40 instances yielded 20 indicators across the five TC characteristics. All 20 indicators, with representative evidence, are listed in Table 5.

The term "measurable" means that these indicators have been empirically observed in prior TC identification work through interviews, surveys, or observation. It does not mean that all indicators can be operationalized within a single MOOC course. Some require cross-course records (Cross-Context Transfer, Cross-Domain Integration), longitudinal tracking (Irreversible indicators), or subjective self-reports (Affective Responses, Before-After Contrast, Worldview Shift). Thus, the review provides a full theoretical indicator framework, while future MOOC-based studies must select the subset that can be translated into behavioral traces.

Table 5. TC measurement framework: 20 indicators extracted from identification evidence.

Characteristic	Indicator	S	Representative Evidence
Troublesome	Extended Learning Time	4	"it took me longer to understand" [9]
	Behavioral Stuckness	3	"Stuck at first" [6]
	Explicit Difficulty	4	"hard for students to get to grips with" [8]
	Theory-Practice Gap	3	"understood theoretically but writing took time" [7]
	Misconceptions	2	"students believe method order determines call order" [8]
Transformative	Before-After Contrast	4	"like day and night" [6]
	Breakthrough Moments	4	"took a long time before it clicked" [6]
	Capability Change	2	"could do more, and knew he could do more" [7]
	Affective Responses	3	"euphoria, feeling of relief" [24]
	Worldview Shift	1	"saw programming in a different light" [20]
	Performance Improvement	3	"today I only see small sub-problems" [6]
Integrative	Concept Connection	3	"once one is understood the other becomes clearer" [8]
	Knowledge Unlocking	3	"everything will flow from that" [6]
	Cross-Context Transfer	2	"used it in hardware class and OS" [6]
	Cross-Domain Integration	1	"programs could be neatly represented mathematically" [20]
Irreversible	Knowledge Persistence	1	"the concept was not lost at all" [6]
	Cannot Recall Pre-State	2	"hard to think back at how I didn't understand" [7]

(continued)

Table 5. *(continued)*

Characteristic	Indicator	S	Representative Evidence
	Skill Decay but Recoverable	1	"have to dig out my old code and review it" [7]
	Permanent Cognitive Change	1	"now it doesn't look weird" [24]
Bounded	Discipline-Specific Nature	1	"demarcates difference between logic within CS and everyday reasoning" [21]

Note. S = Number of supporting studies. Troublesome, Transformative, and Integrative indicators had stronger evidence support (2–4 studies); Irreversible and Bounded indicators had limited support (1–2 studies), consistent with those characteristics' low usage rates

3.2 RQ2: Methodological Biases

Data Collection Design Overview. Three design dimensions were examined across the 40 instances. Informant role split evenly: teachers contributed 20 instances (50%, 4 studies) and non-teachers 20 (50%, 5 studies), including students (12), professional programmers (6), and mixed informants (2). The other two dimensions were homogeneous: retrospective approaches accounted for 92.5% and interview/survey methods for 92.5%. Timeline and method overlapped perfectly (all retrospective instances used interviews; all concurrent instances used observation), so informant role was the only dimension with enough variation for comparative analysis.

Quantitative Results. One instance (Code Organisation [9]) could not be classified under the OOP framework and was excluded from the statistical analysis, leaving $N = 39$ (Teachers: 20, non-teachers: 19). The distribution of TC categories by informant role is shown in Table 6.

Table 6. Contingency table: Informant Role × TC Category.

Informant	AS	COS	DS	NM	Total
Teachers	13 (65.0%)	1 (5.0%)	3 (15.0%)	3 (15.0%)	20
Non-Teachers	6 (31.6%)	8 (42.1%)	4 (21.1%)	1 (5.3%)	19
Total	19 (48.7%)	9 (23.1%)	7 (17.9%)	4 (10.3%)	39

Note. AS = Algorithmic Structure; COS = Class and Object Structure; DS = Data Structure; NM = Notional Machine. $N = 39$; Code Organisation excluded (uncategorizable). Row percentages shown

The chi-square test showed a significant association between informant role and TC category ($\chi^2(3, N = 39) = 9.147, p = .027$). Because 6 of 8 cells had expected frequencies below 5, a Fisher's exact test (Freeman-Halton extension) was also conducted, yielding $p = .022$ and confirming the chi-square result. The effect size was large

(Cramér's V = .484), indicating that informant role explained approximately 23.4% of the variance in category distribution. The odds ratio for Class and Object Structure identification was 13.9 (95% CI: 1.54–125.0), meaning Non-Teachers were nearly 14 times more likely to identify these concepts than Teachers.

Qualitative Findings. The cross-case analysis compared within-group patterns, between-group differences, and negative cases. Teachers (n = 20, 4 studies) consistently gave observational evidence in third-person language ("students struggle with...", "find it difficult to...") in 90% of instances. Their focus on visible behavioral symptoms concentrated identification in Algorithmic Structure (65.0%), with COS appearing just once (5.0%). Non-teachers (n = 20, 5 studies) gave experiential evidence in first-person transformation language ("day and night", "completely changed my approach") in 80% of instances. A representative example from [6]: "It's like day and night. Before I came here I couldn't abstract the problems... Today I see sub-problems." This experiential access produced higher COS identification (42.1%) and lower AS concentration (31.6%). The largest between-group gap was in COS: 5.0% vs. 42.1%, a 37.1 percentage point difference. Both groups mainly used interviews, yet the same method produced different data. Teachers reported observations of students; non-teachers reported their own learning experiences. The difference in data nature, not method, explains the divergent outcomes.

The contrast between OOP and Recursion illustrates the mechanism. OOP difficulties involve a shift from procedural to object-oriented thinking that may not show up in code; students can write syntactically correct OOP code without genuinely understanding OOP. Recursion difficulties produce clear behavioral symptoms (infinite loops, stack overflow). For OOP, internal understanding does not equal external behavior; for Recursion, it does. This gap between internal understanding and external behavior was tested through negative case analysis. Sanders and McCartney [7], the only teacher study to identify OOP, included direct student quotes, which confirms that access to phenomenological evidence enables COS identification. Non-Teachers also identified AS concepts (31.6%), showing that AS concepts have both behavioral and experiential aspects, though the experiential aspect is secondary. All Non-Teacher sub-groups showed higher COS identification than Teachers (Students: 25.0%, Practitioners: 66.7%, Mixed: 50.0%), which points to the teacher/non-teacher distinction, rather than sub-group characteristics, as the driver.

4 Discussion

4.1 Behavioral Invisibility: A Core Finding

The clearest result of the informant bias analysis is that Class & Object Structure concepts are nearly absent from teacher-identified TCs (5.0% vs 42.1% for non-teachers). We call this pattern *behavioral invisibility*: TC characteristics that involve internal paradigm shifts produce few external behavioral signals, so observational methods systematically miss them.

The pattern has a theoretical basis in the distinction between surface and deep learning [31, 32]. Surface learners reproduce information without integration: they memorize

OOP syntax patterns and produce code that compiles correctly. Deep learners transform their understanding by integrating new concepts into existing cognitive structures, genuinely adopting object-oriented thinking. Both can produce identical external behaviors (syntactically correct code), so internal transformation is invisible to external observation [31]. A teacher watching code outputs cannot tell whether a student truly thinks in objects or merely imitates syntax. Students and practitioners reporting their own experiences have direct access to these internal shifts, which explains their higher identification of Class & Object Structure TCs.

Behavioral invisibility is not just one finding among others. It points to a structural limitation of any single-perspective identification approach: what looks like inconsistency in the TC literature may actually reflect differences in what each method can observe.

4.2 Three Access Mechanisms

Table 7 compares three access mechanisms for TC identification, with MOOC behavioral data as a complementary third perspective.

Table 7. Three access mechanisms for TC identification.

Dimension	Teacher Observation	Student Report	MOOC Data
Data nature	External behavioral outputs	Internal experience	External behavioral traces
Temporal grain	Discrete, macro-level	Retrospective recall	Continuous, micro-level
Recording consistency	Observer interpretation	Recall bias	Consistent automated recording
Concept coverage	AS-dominant (65.0%)	COS-dominant (42.1%)	Not yet studied

Note. AS = Algorithmic Structure; COS = Class and Object Structure.

Teacher observation and student self-report each access different aspects of threshold crossing, but both operate at discrete time points and carry perspective-specific biases [14]. MOOC data shares the external-observation feature of teacher data but records behavior continuously at a micro level. Whether this continuous recording can detect TC phenomena that discrete observation misses, especially for paradigm-shift concepts like OOP, has not been tested. If it can, MOOC data would serve as a distinct third access mechanism alongside existing approaches.

4.3 Implications

The 15 consolidated TCs and 20 measurable indicators provide a starting point for future TC identification work. The five TCs with strongest cross-study support (OOP, Data Structures, Procedural Decomposition, Pointers, and Functions/Methods) have the most reliable evidence base; the remaining ten, with support from only one or two studies, need further validation.

The 20 indicators vary in their data requirements. Some (Extended Learning Time, Behavioral Stuckness, Performance Improvement) describe observable behaviors and could be detected through learning analytics. Others (Affective Responses, Worldview Shift, Cannot Recall Pre-State) describe internal experiences that require self-report. Still others (Cross-Context Transfer, Knowledge Persistence) require longitudinal or cross-course research designs. Future studies can select indicators suited to their data sources and research contexts rather than starting from abstract characteristic definitions.

Behavioral invisibility has a broader methodological implication. Studies that rely on one informant perspective risk systematic blind spots. Teacher-based studies will under-detect paradigm-shift concepts; student self-report studies may over-represent experiential aspects while missing behavioral patterns visible only to observers. Combining perspectives, or using data sources with different observational properties, is likely to produce more complete TC identification.

4.4 Future Research Agenda

The reviewed studies point to several concrete directions for future TC identification research (Table 8). These directions follow from the limitations and patterns found in the shortlisted articles rather than from general speculation.

4.5 Limitations

The analysis drew on 40 instances from 10 studies: enough for large effects but not for fine-grained sub-group analyses. Timeline and method overlapped perfectly, so only informant role could be tested. A single researcher did all coding. Temporal re-coding after a three-year interval (initial: April 2022; re-coding: October 2025) showed a Dice similarity coefficient of 76.5% [33]. Findings apply to programming education in predominantly Western, English-language contexts.

5 Conclusion

This review consolidated 40 TC identification instances into 15 core TCs and extracted 20 measurable indicators across five characteristics. Troublesome, Integrative, and Transformative form the practical core of identification. Informant role significantly influences outcomes ($\chi^2 = 9.147, p = .027,$, V = .484): teachers mostly identify concepts with visible behavioral symptoms; non-teachers identify concepts involving internal paradigm shifts. This behavioral invisibility means published TC lists partially reflect who was asked, not just what is threshold-like.

Table 8. Future research directions derived from the reviewed literature.

Finding from reviewed studies	Future research direction
Only one eligible empirical identification study was found after 2021	Conduct new empirical TC identification studies in contemporary programming education contexts, especially online learning environments
Most studies used retrospective interview or survey data (92.5%)	Design studies that observe learning as it unfolds, including longitudinal and process-oriented data collection
Informant role was associated with TC category distribution	Combine teacher observation, learner self-report, and practitioner perspectives in the same study to reduce single-perspective bias
Class and Object Structure concepts were behaviorally invisible to teacher observation	Test whether MOOC behavioral logs can detect gradual or indirect signals of paradigm-shift concepts such as OOP
Irreversible and Bounded indicators had limited empirical support	Use longitudinal and cross-disciplinary designs to examine persistence of understanding and disciplinary boundaries
Existing studies were concentrated in Western, English-language contexts	Extend TC identification to more cultural, linguistic, and curriculum contexts

The measurable indicators provide targets for MOOC-based behavioral pattern analysis, and behavioral invisibility clarifies both the potential and limits of behavioral data. Future research should investigate whether continuous, micro-level behavioral data from MOOCs can capture patterns associated with paradigm-shift concepts that discrete observation misses.

Acknowledgements. This work was supported by the Shenzhen Key Research Base for Humanities and Social Sciences, "Artificial Intelligence Education Research Center of Southern University of Science and Technology," and by the Guangdong Province Undergraduate Teaching Quality and Education Reform Project, "SUSTech National Excellence Program Industry–Education Integration Practice Teaching Base" (Grant No. SJZLGC202412).

Disclosure of Interests. The authors have no competing interests to declare that are relevant to the content of this article.

References

1. Hew, K.F., Cheung, W.S.: Students' and instructors' use of massive open online courses (MOOCs): Motivations and challenges. Educ. Res. Rev. **12**, 45–58 (2014)
2. Onah, D.F.O., Sinclair, J., Boyatt, R.: Dropout rates of massive open online courses: Behavioural patterns. Proceedings of the 6th International Conference on Education and New Learning Technologies, pp. 5825–5834 (2014)

3. Siemens, G.: Learning analytics: The emergence of a discipline. Am. Behav. Sci. **57**(10), 1380-1400 (2013). https://doi.org/10.1177/0002764213498851
4. Ferguson, R.: Learning analytics: Drivers, developments and challenges. Int. J. Technol. Enhanced Learn. **4**(5/6), 304–317 (2012)
5. Meyer, J.H.F., Land, R.: Threshold concepts and troublesome knowledge: Linkages to ways of thinking and practising within the disciplines. Improving student learning: Improving student learning theory and practice - 10 years on, 412–424 (2003)
6. Boustedt, J., et al.: Threshold concepts in computer science: Do they exist and are they useful? Proceedings of the 38th SIGCSE Technical Symposium on Computer Science Education, pp. 504–508 (2007)
7. Sanders, K., et al.: Threshold concepts and threshold skills in computing. Proceedings of the ninth annual International Conference on International Computing Education Research, pp. 23–30 (2012)
8. Kallia, M., Sentance, S.: Computing teachers' perspectives on threshold concepts: Functions and procedural abstraction. Proceedings of the 12th workshop on primary and secondary computing education, pp. 15–24 (2017)
9. Yeomans, L., Zschaler, S., Coate, K.: Transformative and troublesome? Students' and professional programmers' perspectives on difficult concepts in programming. ACM Trans. Comput. Educ. **19**(3), Article 23 (2019). https://doi.org/10.1145/3283071
10. Barradell, S.: The identification of threshold concepts: A review of theoretical complexities and methodological challenges. High. Educ. **65**(2), 265–276 (2013)
11. Rountree, J., Robins, A., Rountree, N.: Elaborating on threshold concepts. Comput. Sci. Educ. **23**(3), 265-289 (2013). https://doi.org/10.1080/08993408.2013.834748
12. Shinners-Kennedy, D.: How not to identify threshold concepts. Threshold concepts in practice, 253–267 (2016)
13. Quinlan, K.M., Male, S., Baillie, C., Stamboulis, A., Fill, J., Jaffer, Z.: Methodological challenges in researching threshold concepts: A comparative analysis of three projects. High. Educ. **66**(5), 585-601 (2013). https://doi.org/10.1007/s10734-013-9623-y
14. Loftus, E.F.: Planting misinformation in the human mind: A 30-year investigation of the malleability of memory. Learn. Mem. **12**(4), 361–366 (2005)
15. Nathan, M.J., Petrosino, A.: Expert blind spot among preservice teachers. Am. Educ. Res. J. **40**(4), 905–928 (2003)
16. Brinton, C.G., Chiang, M., Jain, S., Lam, H., Liu, Z., Wong, F.M.F.: Learning about social learning in MOOCs: From statistical analysis to generative model. IEEE Trans. Learn. Technol. **7**(4), 346–359 (2014)
17. Page, M.J., et al.: The PRISMA 2020 statement: An updated guideline for reporting systematic reviews. BMJ **372**, n71 (2021)
18. Kramer, M., Hubwieser, P., Brinda, T.: A competency structure model of object-oriented programming. 2016 International Conference on Learning and Teaching in Computing and Engineering (LaTiCE), pp. 1-8 (2016). https://doi.org/10.1109/LaTiCE.2016.24
19. Sien, V., Chong, D.: Threshold concepts in object-oriented modelling. Electronic Communications of the EASST **52** (2012)
20. Moström, J.E., et al.: Concrete examples of abstraction as manifested in students' transformative experiences. Proceedings of the Fourth International Workshop on Computing Education Research, pp. 125–136 (2008)
21. Zwaneveld, B., Perrenet, J., Bloo, R.: Discussion of methods for threshold research and an application in computer science. Threshold Concepts in Practice, 269–284 (2016)
22. Sim, T.Y.: Online supported learning and threshold concepts in novice programming. 2017 IEEE Conference on E-learning, E-management and E-services (IC3e), pp. 85–90 (2017)
23. Kallia, M., Sentance, S.: Threshold concepts, conceptions and skills: Teachers' experiences with students' engagement in functions. J. Comput. Assist. Learn. **37**(2), 411–428 (2021)

24. Mackay, S., McSkimming, B., Decker, A.: Interview iterations and improvements for identifying intermediate computer science threshold concepts. 2024 IEEE Frontiers in Education Conference (FIE), pp. 1–5 (2024)
25. Hsieh, H.-F., Shannon, S.E.: Three approaches to qualitative content analysis. Qual. Health Res. **15**(9), 1277–1288 (2005)
26. Miles, M.B., Huberman, A.M., Saldaña, J.: Qualitative data analysis: A methods sourcebook (2014)
27. Lincoln, Y.S., Guba, E.G.: Naturalistic inquiry (1985)
28. Cohen, J.: Statistical power analysis for the behavioral sciences (1988)
29. Davies, P.: Threshold concepts: How can we recognise them? Overcoming barriers to student understanding: Threshold concepts and troublesome knowledge, 70–84 (2006)
30. Rowbottom, D.P.: Demystifying threshold concepts. J. Philos. Educ. **41**(2), 263–270 (2007)
31. Biggs, J.B.: Student approaches to learning and studying (1987)
32. Marton, F., Säljö, R.: On qualitative differences in learning: I—outcome and process. Br. J. Educ. Psychol. **46**(1), 4–11 (1976)
33. Hruschka, D.J., et al.: Reliability in coding open-ended data: Lessons learned from HIV behavioral research. Field Methods **16**(3), 307–331 (2004)

A Study on the Faculty Adoption of AI-Powered Tools in Hong Kong

Chenggui Duan(✉) and Simon K. S. Cheung

Hong Kong Metropolitan University, Hong Kong SAR, China
{dduan,kscheung}@hkmu.edu.hk

Abstract. The global rise of Generative AI is transforming higher education, challenging the traditional foundation of teaching and learning. This qualitative collective case study investigates how university faculty in Hong Kong integrate AI in pedagogical practice. Through semi-structured interviews with faculty members in diverse disciplines, it is revealed that faculty primarily position AI as a cognitive partner to enhance efficiency, yet this demands a redefinition of teachers' pedagogical authority to address the risks of cognitive outsourcing. In response, faculty are proactively redesigning assessments to preserve academic integrity and evaluate higher-order skills such as critical thinking and creativity. Crucially, it is found that these individual adaptations are constrained without institutional support, highlighting a critical need for clear policies, resource allocation, and sustained professional development. These findings illustrate the emerging concept of human-AI partnership, reflecting how university teachers in the AI era reposition their professional identities and classroom strategies for higher education development.

Keywords: Artificial Intelligence · Higher Education · Faculty Development · Pedagogical innovation · Assessment

1 Introduction

The rapid development of Generative AI, especially large language models such as ChatGPT, has reshaped the traditional foundations of higher education. Consequently, AI has become a tool in everyday academic practice for teachers to provide efficient teaching process. As students increasingly adopt AI for learning and assessment, teachers face the challenge of applying AI's pedagogical potential as well as protecting academic integrity. Within the broader field of Artificial Intelligence in Education (AIED), research posits that moving beyond technological proficiency to a cooperative pedagogical partnership between teachers and AI systems is crucial for student development [1, 2]. However, such a transformation questions the long-established assumptions about teaching authority with its emphasis on the role of intelligent systems. Indeed, GenAI can deliver personalized knowledge that provides significant outcomes for both teachers and learners, it also risks cognitive outsourcing as students gradually rely on automated output rather than critical reasoning [3]. Thus, teachers must relocate their professional roles from simply content experts to designers of human-centered learning environments.

K. T. Chui et al. (Eds.): ICBL 2026, LNCS 16778, pp. 354–368, 2027.
https://doi.org/10.1007/978-981-92-3761-6_25

For Hong Kong, the integration of GenAI presents a challenge to its high-stakes educational culture. While the city's public universities serve a globally competitive and bilingual student population, their AI adoption remains fragmented due to the traditional curriculum standards and exam-driven assessment structures [4]. Earlier research has primarily examined student acceptance of AI tools that provide a foundational understanding for current adoption of AI in higher education [5, 6]. Yet, the experiences of university teachers who directly face the current contradiction between institutional policy and classroom practice remain underexplored.

In this paper, we investigate how faculty across diverse disciplines in a Hong Kong university review the pedagogical and institutional implications of GenAI integration. Based on AIED perspective, it would be illustrated that faculty adaptation of AI in higher education as a process of human-AI partnership, in which faculty and AI systems interact as partners to enhance teaching and learning. We further investigate how faculty transfer their pedagogical routines and assessment designs in response to the widespread adoption of AI technologies. Building on the concept of the teacher-AI partnership, we examine how faculty are navigating the complex process of adapting their professional practice to incorporate GenAI tools while maintaining educational values. Accordingly, our study is guided by the following research questions:

RQ1 What adaptive strategies and pedagogical innovations have faculty developed to foster effective and critical learning in the age of GenAI?

RQ2 What are faculty members' key perceptions, challenges, and ethical concerns regarding use of GenAI tools in teaching and learning contexts?

2 Methodology

A qualitative case study approach is used to investigate the complex challenges and adaptive strategies that faculty members employ in response to the integration of GenAI in higher education.

2.1 Research Context and Participants

The study was conducted at a public comprehensive university in Hong Kong. Using a purposive sampling strategy, five full-time faculty members from different disciplines (software engineering, businesses, language education, information technology, and nursing) were recruited to ensure a diversity of disciplinary perspectives (see Table 1 for their profiles). They were teaching courses with substantial enrollment sizes.

Table 1. Profiles of the participants.

Participants	Gender	Field	Teaching Level
Teacher A	M	Software engineering	Undergraduate
Teacher B	M	Business	Undergraduate

(continued)

Table 1. (*continued*)

Participants	Gender	Field	Teaching Level
Teacher C	F	Language Education	Master
Teacher D	M	Information Technology	Undergraduate
Teacher E	F	Nursing	Undergraduate

2.2 Data Collection and Analysis

Data were collected through semi-structured interviews to systematically examine faculty experiences for the emergence of context-specific insights. The interview protocol was designed to explore both emergent themes, particularly those shaped by distinct disciplinary contexts and teaching environments. The interview guide was organized into four thematic sections, as outlined in Table 2, addressing: (1) opening and teaching background; (2) current practice and experience; (3) challenges and needs; and (4) adaptive strategies and institutional support. All interviews were conducted in person, audio-recorded with consent, and transcribed.

Table 2. Interview Guide Structure.

Section	Duration	Key Areas of Inquiry	RQs
Part I **Opening and Teaching Background**	5–10 min	**Context Setting**: Please briefly describe the courses you are teaching this semester, specifically those you feel are most affected by AI **Student Profile**: What are the key characteristics of your student group and their general tech usage habits?	
Part II **Current Practice and Experience**	10 min	**AI Use**: Which AI tools have you used or observed students using in your class? **AI Integration Case**: Can you share a successful use case where AI helped you or your students improve learning? **AI Misuse**: Have you had a negative experience or observed a specific incident of AI misuse?	RQ1

(*continued*)

Table 2. *(continued)*

Section	Duration	Key Areas of Inquiry	RQs
Part III **Challenges and Needs**	10 min	**Challenges**: Where do you observe students struggling the most in terms of foundational knowledge now that AI is available? **Assessment Integrity**: How have you modified your assessment methods to avoid AI-based cheating?	RQ2
Part IV **Adaptive Strategies and Institutional Support**	10 min	**Teaching Adaptations**: What specific pedagogical changes have you made to address the rise of AI? **Institutional Requirements**: What kind of training, policy, or technical support do you need from the university to handle transition of AI effectively?	RQ1 & RQ2

The present study adopted Braun and Clarke's six-phase framework for thematic analysis [7]. The process began with the familiarization stage, involving repeated reading of the transcripts to gain a deep understanding of the faculty experiences with GenAI. Initial analytical notes were taken to capture early observations on pedagogical adaptation, assessment redesign, and institutional support.

The transcripts were imported into NVivo for systematic coding. In the initial coding phase, a total of 232 codes related to areas such as teaching preparation, pedagogical transformation, and ethical concerns were generated. These initial codes were subsequently reviewed and clustered into 12 broader conceptual categories. Through an iterative process of constant comparison, 8 sub-themes were generated reflecting the cognitive, pedagogical, and institutional dimensions of AI adoption. Then, the sub-themes were synthesized into 4 core themes that comprehensively capture the landscape of AI integration. Finally, a detailed analytical report was produced based on the themes.

3 Results

For a comprehensive visualization of the analytical trajectory, we document the coding structure from raw data excerpts through initial coding and final thematic consolidation (see Appendix). The four central themes of our study include: (1) AI as a Cognitive and Pedagogical Partner, (2) Redefinition of Pedagogical Authority, (3) Pedagogical Adaptation via Assessment Redesign, and (4) Institutional Support for Sustainable AI Integration. The following sections elaborate these themes with analytical interpretations to explore individual experiences within pedagogical discourses.

3.1 Theme 1 (AI as a Cognitive and Pedagogical Partner)

Participants across diverse disciplines consistently conceptualized GenAI not as a threat, but as a strategic tool that enhances their pedagogical practice. Rather than resisting technological adoption, faculty actively integrated GenAI tools to process routine instructional tasks and cognitive resource allocation, thereby preserving intellectual capacity for higher-order teaching objectives. This orientation reflects a fundamental reconceptualization of the faculty's role in AI-mediated learning environments.

Notably, the data reveal a consistent pattern of GenAI implementation for automating labor-intensive preparatory work. All participants reported employing AI tools, particularly Perplexity AI and ChatGPT, to generate initial drafts of teaching materials that previously required substantial time and effort to build and develop. For example, Teacher B applied AI to streamline administrative course preparation. This approach, as he described, helps him to efficiently "process the first level" of instructional preparation before focusing his expertise on customization and depth. Similarly, Teacher D described AI as reliably handling his foundational work, including the synthesis of fundamental concepts and generation of background content. He noted that such relief provides him with the time to "deepen the conceptual content" for students, as the immense workload faculty face often leaves limited time for deep reflection.

This practice represents a pedagogical innovation. By delegating routine content generation to AI, faculty can liberate valuable cognitive and temporal resources to concentrate on designing sophisticated, application-based exercises and providing targeted guidance on complex problem-solving tasks. The reallocation of instructional focus enables educators to dedicate more attention to fostering higher-order cognitive skills. Teacher B confirmed this shift, observing an improvement in his teaching workflow. However, disciplinary readiness significantly shaped how AI was applied. In contrast to IT or business teachers, Teacher E from nursing education described minimal AI integration in her teaching but saw strong potential for transformation.

This strategic evolution, from the role of knowledge transmitter to that of a facilitator cultivating higher-order cognitive engagement, illustrates how GenAI is being integrated as an adaptive mechanism to elevate academic development. By reallocating teaching focus from foundational content delivery to the facilitation of critical thinking, this approach fosters more interactive and student-centered learning environments across diverse academic disciplines.

3.2 Theme 2 (Redefinition of Pedagogical Roles)

This theme highlights the fundamental challenges faculty experience in defining and defending their pedagogical roles towards AI tools. Faculty concerns extend well beyond conventional issues of academic integrity to encompass more fundamental questions about the erosion of their traditional position as primary knowledge authorities and curators of essential cognitive processes.

Participants consistently expressed concern that AI technologies are undermining their professional authority and reshaping student approaches to learning. A central cross-disciplinary worry is that AI's capacity to generate instant solutions discourages students from engaging in the essential and non-transferable cognitive processes required for deep conceptual mastery. Consequently, faculty find themselves dedicating significant instructional time to justifying the intrinsic value of foundational learning processes such as logical reasoning and systematic problem-solving replacing instant AI-generated solutions. This represents a critical challenge: faculty must construct learning experiences that develop higher-order cognitive skills resistant to AI replication. Simultaneously, participants identified cognitive outsourcing as a significant pedagogical concern. Teacher D noted that AI-assisted work can give the illusion of learning.

In response, faculty have adopted adaptive strategies to decrease the risk of superficial AI-assisted learning. Teachers reposition themselves as "diagnosticians of cognitive engagement" that force students to demonstrate genuine understanding. Furthermore, the challenge of managing AI misuse has shifted the functional role of faculty from expert facilitator to "integrity enforcer". Teacher C noted that managing AI misuse requires faculty to constantly monitor assessment submissions of students. This pattern raised concern that AI might be improving surface presentation while undermining authentic learning, as noted by Teacher E. Collectively, these findings demonstrate that faculty authority in the AI era no longer derives from information control but from guiding cognitive authenticity that helps students distinguish between mechanical fluency and intellectual ownership.

3.3 Theme 3 (Pedagogical Innovation via Assessment Redesign)

In response to the pedagogical challenges identified in Theme 2, participants implemented substantial modifications to their assessment methodologies. These changes were frequently defensive in nature, aimed to avoid the risks associated with students' use of GenAI tools. Faculty primarily focused on developing AI-resistant evaluation frameworks capable of accurately measuring internalized knowledge and higher-order cognitive competencies that transcend automated solution generation.

A key strategy in large-enrollment courses was the introduction of personalization mechanisms to prevent large-scale academic misconduct. For example, Teacher A developed computer-based randomized examinations to ensure that each student received a unique set of questions. This methodological innovation successfully addressed integrity concerns at scale through technical prevention measures. Beyond controlling the inputs, faculty redesigned assessment tasks to emphasize higher-order skills including creativity and collaboration which AI struggles to replicate. Teacher D shifted toward team-based projects and presentations that required interpersonal communication, critical reasoning, and collaborative problem-solving. Teacher A also emphasized the value of human interaction in professional work. Teacher E's reflections revealed both potential and caution in redesigning assessment. Although she had not yet deployed AI-based evaluation tools, she expressed a clear vision of what they could achieve.

Faculty also employed different strategies to detect cognitive outsourcing. Teacher C applied features within the online learning environment, such as OLE quizzes and "word cloud" responses, to provide immediate assessment of students' conceptual understanding. This supported rapid verification of learning and reinforced active cognitive engagement. Similarly, Teacher B used the discrepancy between AI-assisted assignment performance and subsequent closed-book exam outcomes as a diagnostic tool, identifying areas where students were bypassing essential mental work. Additionally, these adaptive strategies demonstrate faculty awareness of the pedagogical and ethical challenges posed by GenAI. By redesigning assessments to emphasize critical thinking and collaboration, faculty are both maintaining academic rigor and ensuring that AI-enhanced learning supports meaningful knowledge acquisition. These findings directly address the research question by revealing the concerns and responsive strategies of faculty regarding AI use in higher education.

3.4 Theme 4 (Institutional Support for Sustainable AI Integration)

While individual faculty demonstrated different strategies in responding to GenAI challenges, their innovative practices were limited by undeveloped institutional policy frameworks.

A central demand of faculty was the establishment of a definitive institutional roadmap for AI tool adoption. Faculty emphasized the need for clear practical guidance regarding platform selection and data security protocols. Teacher C highlighted the current uncertainty. This ambiguity often forces faculty to rely on open free platforms, potentially compromising educational equity, course stability, and data security. Faculty also stressed the importance of comprehensive AI literacy training for students. Teacher C advocated for mandatory curriculum-integrated training programs that would establish both ethical parameters and practical competencies for effective AI engagement. Teacher C specifically addressed observed deficiencies in students' operational skills.

All participants further stressed the urgency of developing context-sensitive institutional policies that transcend generic, and ultimately insufficient, plagiarism statements. Participants required clear guidelines to integrate AI use directly into course outlines, which would empower instructors to set and enforce disciplinary boundaries confidently. Teacher B stressed the necessity for institutions to accelerate policy development. Consequently, participants advocated for the establishment of sustained professional learning ecosystems rather than isolated training events. Teacher E succinctly captured this need. These collective calls reflect an urgent need for institutional governance structures to align with classroom realities to create conditions for sustainable AI integration in higher education.

4 Discussion

Our findings illuminate how higher education faculty are critically navigating the integration of GenAI tools within pedagogical practices. Across diverse disciplinary contexts, emerging challenges and adaptive strategies reveal both the transformative potential of AI-enhanced teaching and the concomitant demands placed on educational institutions. Based on the empirical results, three key insights emerge that provide a foundation for an adaptive cycle of AI integration in higher education instruction.

4.1 Faculty Role Transformation in AI Era

Consistent with the patterns identified in Theme 1 and Theme 2, faculty participants in this study characterized GenAI as a dual pedagogical instrument. While recognizing AI's capacity to generate significant efficiencies in teaching and learning processes, faculty simultaneously acknowledged how these technologies influence conventional understandings of instructional authority and expertise. The systematic delegation of routine academic tasks including content drafting, framework development, and administrative preparation was widely reported to liberate cognitive resources for a strategic reorientation toward higher-order educational functions. This observed transition resonates with emphasis on AI's potential to augment rather than replace human pedagogical expertise, thereby reinforcing the faculty's role as a facilitator of knowledge construction and critical engagement [8]. Within the broader AIED framework, this Human–AI collaboration illustrates what Holmes and Miao term the "augmentation paradigm", where human and AI form complementary partnerships [1].

At the same time, the widespread adoption of GenAI tools has introduced significant role-related anxiety, particularly concerning the implications of cognitive outsourcing. Faculty expressed concern that students are increasingly relying on AI, skipping the deliberate cognitive processes essential for skill acquisition and deep learning. This concern signals a fundamental reconfiguration of the academic profession, transforming faculty into intentional designers of learning experiences that strategically resist over-automation while fostering authentic intellectual development. Furthermore, the findings illustrate that faculty have a responsibility to teach students how to engage with AI critically and ethically, which involves explicit training on reflective practices, alongside discussions of academic integrity. This integration of reflective AI training with sustained integrity discussions repositions strategic AI implementation as a partner for higher-value educational priorities [9]. This transformation ultimately positions faculty as mediators between technological capability of AI and educational value.

4.2 Reclaiming Pedagogical Authenticity Through Assessment Redesign

The findings from Themes 2 and 3 demonstrate that faculty in Hong Kong higher education are engaged in a fundamental reimagining of assessment practices beyond reactive measures against GenAI misuse toward proactively enhancing pedagogical authenticity. Central to this process is the recognition of conventional assessment formats, particularly standardized essays and take-home assignments, which have become increasingly susceptible to cognitive outsourcing through GenAI technologies. In response to these challenges, faculty are implementing adaptive assessment strategies reinforcing the cultivation of higher-order skills, such as collaboration and creative problem-solving skills which remain difficult to automate. This strategic shift represents a significant extension of existing literature on AI in higher education by reframing assessment as a proactive opportunity for pedagogical enrichment than a defensive mechanism [10].

The emphasis of assessments as learning experiences emphasizes the evaluation of competencies that transcend the replicable outputs of GenAI systems. In project-based learning, for example, the focus has shifted to iterative feedback cycles and live presentations, which rely on human capacities for negotiation, contextual judgment, and intellectual adaptation that AI cannot replace. Similarly, the integration of real-time diagnostic techniques including interactive polling and conceptual mapping provides instructors with immediate insights into student understanding, supporting dynamic pedagogical scaffolding and responsive instructional adjustments. These practices align with broader educational calls for formative assessment models of reflective learning [3, 11, 12]. While summative examinations retain some situational value, they are increasingly inadequate for capturing the complex and integrated competencies required for professional and intellectual development in the AI era.

To achieve this evolution, faculty should prioritize assessment designs that are personalized, application-oriented, and cognitively demanding to reduce opportunities for cognitive outsourcing of learners. Moreover, it is essential to emphasize higher-order competencies that current AI systems cannot fully replicate. Effective assessment redesign should incorporate both individual and collaborative components, structured around complex tasks that demand real-time knowledge application, dialogic exchange, and contextual adaptation. Low-stakes formative checks provide immediate diagnostic feedback while supporting students' metacognitive awareness and instructors' pedagogical decision-making. Thus, the redesign of assessment in the GenAI era represents more than a technical response to academic integrity concerns but a fundamental pedagogical reorientation toward human-centered learning experiences.

4.3 Foundations for Sustainable AI Integration

Theme 4 reveals a critical finding that faculty adaptation to GenAI remains fundamentally unsustainable without institutional support. While individual faculty demonstrate remarkable resilience in reimagining their pedagogical approaches, their efforts operate within an absence of systematic support, highlighting the emergent need for strategic resource allocation and institutional policy support.

The research identifies institutional roadmap development as a foundational element in sustainable AI integration. Participants consistently reported that while universities frequently issue broad ethical statements and principles regarding AI use, these documents rarely translate into discipline-specific guidelines or practical assessment frameworks [13, 14]. This policy-practice gap creates significant implementation challenges, forcing faculty to navigate complex pedagogical and ethical considerations without adequate guidance. The findings strongly suggest that institutions must evolve beyond aspirational declarations toward operationalized strategies for AI in teaching and learning that include discipline-specific implementation protocols and systematic mechanisms for evaluating AI integration outcomes across different academic contexts.

The development of comprehensive AI literacy programs that address the needs of both students and faculty is equally significant [15]. Without structured training, students are far more susceptible to uncritically adopting these technologies, which raises risks of cognitive outsourcing, plagiarism, and ethical breaches. Conversely, systematically designed literacy initiatives can foster critical technological awareness, enabling students to interrogate AI-generated content, recognize systemic limitations, and develop responsible usage patterns. For faculty, sustained professional development is equally critical for maintaining pedagogical relevance. These suggest that current training lacks deeper pedagogical transformation, leaving faculty underprepared for the complex task of redesigning learning experiences in AI-rich environments [16]. Effective faculty development should instead integrate technological, pedagogical, and ethical dimensions, creating spaces for collaborative experimentation and discipline-specific adaptation.

The findings further underscore the importance of institutional policies. Participants emphasized that ambiguous guidelines not only weaken faculty awareness in academic integrity disputes but also undermine student confidence in assessment legitimacy. Thus, well-articulated policies are essential to establish clear baselines for expectations while providing necessary protection for faculty implementing innovative approaches [17]. Beyond policy development, the findings highlight the pedagogical importance of applying AI literacy into course design through reflective and experiential practices. Rather than focusing on technical skills like prompt engineering, effective AI literacy development requires structured opportunities for critical interrogation of human-AI interaction. For instance, students should be required to document their AI engagement through reflective commentaries. In these, they should explain their usage strategies and verification processes, which enhances metacognitive awareness and reinforces academic values.

4.4 Adaptive Cycle of AI Using in Higher Education Teaching

Overall, our findings reveal that faculty adoption of GenAI follows a dynamic process of the Adaptive Cycle of AI Integration in Higher Education Teaching (see Fig. 1).

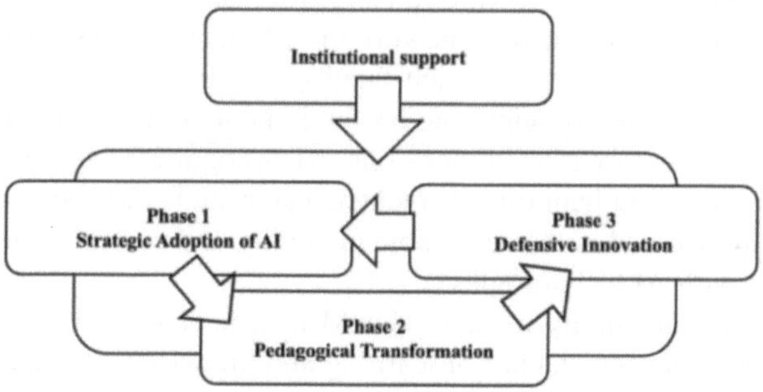

Fig. 1. The adaptive cycle of AI using in higher education teaching.

This framework highlights the complex interplay between individual pedagogical agencies and institutional structural capacity in responding to technological innovation. The core adaptive loop represents the ground-level pedagogical transformations faculty enact in response to immediate AI integration challenges. This process begins when faculty delegate low-level tasks such as routine administrative and content-generation tasks to AI systems (Phase 1: Strategic Adoption of AI). This initial adoption phase aims to increase instructional efficiency. However, this creates an unintended consequence identified in Phase 2 (Pedagogical Transformation) as AI assumes responsibility for foundational academic work, students increasingly engage in cognitive outsourcing, potentially skipping essential learning processes. Consequently, faculty must transition from their traditional role as content deliverers to defend the value of fundamental intellectual skills such as critical thinking. This emerging pedagogical challenge directly precipitates the defensive strategic response captured in Phase 3 (Defensive Innovation). Here, faculty develop evaluation frameworks emphasizing personalization and collaborative problem-solving to construct deliberate barriers against AI misuse.

Critically, however, this faculty-driven adaptive loop operates within a broader institutional context that significantly constrains its effectiveness. As emphatically articulated in Theme 4, sustainable adaptation requires systemic support including institutional roadmaps, mandatory AI literacy training, and policy frameworks. Without the structural support mandated by Theme 4, the faculty adaptation loop remains inherently precarious as pedagogical innovations become isolated, administrative ambiguities persist, and inconsistent policy implementation undermines reform efforts. The Adaptive Cycle of AI Using in Higher Education Teaching therefore illustrates a crucial theoretical and practical insight that AI integration in higher education requires engagement between bottom-up faculty initiative and top-down institutional leadership. Conversely, institutional policies and support mechanisms must remain responsive to the emergent challenges and innovative practices developing at the classroom level.

5 Conclusion

This study has examined how university faculty in Hong Kong perceive and navigate the pedagogical and ethical complexities arising from GenAI integration in higher education. Grounded in the theoretical framework of AIED, our analysis reveals a dynamic process of AI-faculty co-agency in which faculty strategically redefine their teaching practices, assessment methodologies, and professional identities in response to technological disruption. Across four key dimensions, AI as cognitive partner, reconfiguration of pedagogical authority, authentic assessment redesign, and systemic institutional alignment, faculty demonstrated both remarkable creativity and careful ethical reflection in their engagement with AI technologies.

The findings fundamentally reframe GenAI as a pedagogical catalyst that forces faculty to reconsider the very nature of learning and knowledge construction in higher education. Faculty in this study are progressively transitioning from defensive regulation toward critical and responsible AI usage while preserving core educational values. This transition proves particularly challenging in practice-based disciplines where resource constraints and established pedagogical traditions create additional barriers to innovation. Several practical implications emerge from these findings. First, institutions should encourage and support faculty in applying AI to handle routine administrative tasks, thereby freeing cognitive resources for higher-order instructional activities. Second, assessment reform must become a priority, with emphasis on evaluating collaborative, contextual, and metacognitive skills that resist easy automation. Third, institutions need to develop context-sensitive policies that support faculty innovation while maintaining academic integrity, including systemic AI literacy training to ensure equitable access and responsible usage across diverse student populations.

As a collective case study focused on a single institutional context with a limited participant sample, this research offers depth of understanding. Thus, the findings may not fully represent the experiences of faculty across different universities globally. Future research would benefit from cross-institutional comparative studies examining how cultural, structural, and governance differences shape AIED adoption across Hong Kong, mainland China, and international educational contexts. Critically, this study demonstrates that the educational impact of GenAI integration depends on how students, faculty, and institutions collectively navigate this technological transformation. The Adaptive Cycle framework proposed in this research suggests that sustainable integration requires continuous negotiation between pedagogical innovation and institutional support. By thoughtfully integrating AI into educational practices with appropriate systemic scaffolding, universities can harness the benefits of these powerful technologies while enhancing the quality and human-centered values that define meaningful education in the digital age.

Acknowledgments. This work was supported by the Quality Enhancement Support Scheme (QESS) from the Hong Kong Education Bureau (EDB) [grant number 01/QESS/2024].

Appendix. Summary of Interview Themes.

Core Theme	RQ	Sub-Theme	Thematic Category	Transcripts	Initial Code
Theme 1 AI as a Cognitive and Pedagogical Partner	RQ1	Pedagogical Efficiency	Class Preparation	"I use ChatGPT to draft PPTs, generate quiz questions, and create rubrics." (Teacher B.)	AI generates draft PowerPoint slides; AI provides lesson ideas;
			Repetitive work	"AI can help mark short-answer or essay questions; it is a huge help." (Teacher E)	AI automates grading; AI summarizes reports
			Feedback for student	"The AI can provide instant support when students want to the answer immediately." (Teacher A)	AI gives fast feedback; AI supports self-assessment; AI improves engagement
		Cognitive support	Cognitive Scaffolding for Learning	"It handles the first level of problem-solving for teaching content, letting me go deeper." (Teacher D)	AI creates visuals; AI simplifies content; AI explains difficult topics

(*continued*)

(*continued*)

Core Theme	RQ	Sub-Theme	Thematic Category	Transcripts	Initial Code
Theme 2 Redefinition of Pedagogical Roles	RQ1	Teacher role transformation	Teacher Roles	"The focus shifts from explaining concepts to teaching how to apply concepts in different scenarios." (Teacher B)	Teacher as AI facilitator; Teacher promotes critical AI literacy
		Pedagogical transformation	Skill Outsourcing of Students	"Students use AI to get instant code solutions without understanding the debugging process." (Teacher A)	AI dependence; Weak writing skills
			Pedagogy Challenge	"I'm more interested in how they think, not the answer." (Teacher D)	Encourage reflection; Emphasize reasoning
Theme 3 Pedagogical Innovation via Assessment Redesign	RQ2	AI-Resistant Assessment	The design of assessment	"I started using more oral defence and in-class diagnostic questions to check understanding." (Teacher C)	Oral assessment; In-class writing; Scenario tasks
		Constructive Integration of AI into Evaluation	Integrative Use of AI	"I asked students to evaluate ChatGPT's answers to learn critical thinking." (Teacher B)	Students critique AI; AI as teaching object; Reflection on AI bias

(*continued*)

(*continued*)

Core Theme	RQ	Sub-Theme	Thematic Category	Transcripts	Initial Code
Theme 4 Institutional Support for Sustainable AI Integration	RQ2	Need for Clear Top-Down Guidance	Institutional Policy and Support	"We need a clear AI roadmap from the school, not just bottom-up innovations." (Teacher C)	Lack of AI policy; No unified guideline
		Resource Allocation	Access & Infrastructure	"If a tool is paid, the school should bulk-buy licenses; free tools need clarified usage limits." (Teacher A)	Subscription barriers; Tool limitations
			Time & Training	"Even though the school offers workshops, I can't really keep up. There are too many updates and too little time." (Teacher E)	No time for exploration; Outdated workshops

References

1. Holmes, W., Miao, F.: Guidance for generative AI in education and research. UNESCO (2023). https://www.unesco.org/en/articles/guidance-generative-ai-education-and-research
2. Idris, M.D., Feng, X., Dyo, V.: Revolutionizing higher education: Unleashing the potential of large language models for strategic transformation. IEEE Access **12**, 67738–67757 (2024)
3. Bittle, K., El-Gayar, O.: Generative AI and Academic Integrity in Higher Education: A Systematic Review and Research Agenda. Information **16**(4), 296 (2025)
4. Cheng, M.W.T., Yim, I.H.Y.: Examining the use of ChatGPT in public universities in Hong Kong: A case study of restricted access areas. Discover Education **3**(1) (2024)
5. Chan, C.K.Y., Hu, W.: Students' voices on generative AI: Perceptions, benefits, and challenges in higher education. Int. J. Educ. Technol. High. Educ. **20**(1), 43 (2023)
6. Li, K.C., Chong, G.H.L., Wong, B.T.M., Wu, M.M.F.: A TAM-Based Analysis of Hong Kong Undergraduate Students' Attitudes Toward Generative AI in Higher Education and Employment. Education Sciences **15**(7), 798 (2025)
7. Braun, V., Clarke, V.: Using thematic analysis in psychology. Qual. Res. Psychol. **3**(2), 77–101 (2006)

8. Zawacki-Richter, O., Marín, V.I., Bond, M., Gouverneur, F.: Systematic review of research on artificial intelligence applications in higher education–where are the educators? Int. J. Educ. Technol. High. Educ. **16**(1), 1–27 (2019)
9. Abulibdeh, A., Baya Chatti, C., Alkhereibi, A., El Menshawy, S.: A Scoping Review of the Strategic Integration of Artificial Intelligence in Higher Education: Transforming University Excellence Themes and Strategic Planning in the Digital Era. European Journal of Education **60** (2025)
10. Li, C., Xing, W.: Natural language generation using deep learning to support MOOC learners. Int. J. Artif. Intell. Educ. **31**(2), 186–214 (2021)
11. Holden, O.L., Norris, M.E., Kuhlmeier, V.A.: Academic Integrity in Online Assessment: A Research Review. Frontiers in Education **6**, 639814 (2021)
12. Revell, T., Yeadon, et al.: ChatGPT versus human essayists: An exploration of the impact of artificial intelligence for authorship and academic integrity in the humanities. Int. J. Educ. Integrity **20**(1), 1–19 (2024)
13. Chan, C.K.Y.: A comprehensive AI policy education framework for university teaching and learning. Int. J. Educ. Technol. High. Educ. **20**(38), 1–25 (2023)
14. Evangelista, E.D.L.: Ensuring academic integrity in the age of ChatGPT: Rethinking exam design, assessment strategies, and ethical AI policies in higher education. Contemporary Educ. Technol. **17**(1), ep559 (2025)
15. Southworth, J., et al.: Developing a model for AI Across the curriculum: Transforming the higher education landscape via innovation in AI literacy. Comp. Educ. Artif. Intel. **4**, 100127 (2023)
16. Marshall, S., Blaj-Ward, L., Dreamson, N., Nyanjom, J., Bertuol, M.T.: The reshaping of higher education: technological impacts, pedagogical change, and future projections. High. Educ. Res. Dev. **43**(3), 521–541 (2024)
17. Christ-Brendemühl, S.: Leveraging generative AI in higher education: An analysis of opportunities and challenges addressed in university guidelines. Eur. J. Educ. **60**(1), e12891 (2025)

AI in Language Learning: Exploring the Gap Between Students' Speaking Needs and Their Actual AI Use

Miloslava Cerna[1], James Buchanan White[1], Simon K. S. Cheung[2(✉)], and Kwan Keung Ng[3]

[1] University of Hradec Králové, Hradec Králové, Czech Republic
{miloslava.cerna,james.white}@uhk.cz
[2] Hong Kong Metropolitan University, Kowloon, Hong Kong, China
kscheung@hkmu.edu.hk
[3] Ming-Ai (London) Institute, London, UK
s.ng@ming-ai.org.uk

Abstract. This study explores the role of artificial intelligence (AI) in university students' language learning, with a particular focus on speaking skills. Drawing on data from a survey of 125 students enrolled in English language courses at the University of Hradec Králové, it is identified a significant discrepancy between students' declared learning goals and their actual use of AI tools. While the majority of students report that improving their speaking abilities is the primary objective, AI has been predominantly used for writing, coding, searching, and summarizing tasks. The findings suggest that AI, despite its potential as a conversational partner, remains largely underutilized for oral communication practice. It is also revealed that students' use of AI is influenced by established digital habits, a preference for efficiency-oriented tasks, and limited awareness of AI's capabilities for speaking interaction. Besides, a subset of students reports using AI for emotional support and companionship, highlighting its emerging psychological role. We argued that effective integration of AI into language learning requires structured pedagogical guidance and the development of AI literacy. The findings contribute to debates on AI in education by highlighting the gap between technologically potential and actual student behaviour.

Keywords: Artificial Intelligence · AI tools · AI Integration · Language Learning · Speaking Skills

1 Introduction

The rapid development of artificial intelligence (AI) has significantly transformed the ways in which university students approach learning. AI tools are increasingly embedded in students' everyday academic practices, supporting activities such as information retrieval, writing, coding, and summarization. As a result, AI is becoming a central component of what may be described as an "always-on" digital learning environment.

K. T. Chui et al. (Eds.): ICBL 2026, LNCS 16778, pp. 369–378, 2027.
https://doi.org/10.1007/978-981-92-3761-6_26

This study builds on previous research investigating university students' digital habits, particularly their extensive screen use and its impact on cognitive focus and mental well-being. Earlier findings suggested that students spend a substantial portion of their day interacting with digital devices, often experiencing a complex combination of benefits (for example, access to information, flexibility) and drawbacks (for example, distraction, reduced concentration, emotional fatigue) [1]. In this evolving digital landscape, AI represents a new layer of interaction that goes beyond passive content consumption and introduces active, responsive engagement.

Despite the growing availability and capabilities of AI, an important discrepancy has emerged in the context of language learning. Data from a recent survey conducted among 125 university students at the University of Hradec Králové indicate that the majority of students identify speaking as their primary learning objective in English language courses. However, their actual use of AI tools is predominantly focused on writing, coding, searching, and summarizing tasks, with minimal engagement in speaking practice.

This mismatch between students' declared learning goals and their actual use of AI tools represents a significant research problem. While AI has the potential to function as a conversational partner and support the development of speaking skills, it appears to be largely underutilized in this area.

The aim of this study is to analyse how university students use AI in relation to language learning, with a particular focus on the discrepancy between their declared preference for speaking practice and their actual use of AI tools.

2 Literature Review

2.1 AI in Higher Education

Artificial intelligence (AI) has become an increasingly influential factor in higher education, transforming both teaching practices and students' learning strategies. Recent developments in generative AI have enabled students to access immediate feedback, generate content, and solve complex problems with minimal effort. As a result, AI tools are now frequently used to support academic writing, information retrieval, and problem-solving tasks.

Research suggests that AI can enhance learning efficiency by providing personalized support and adaptive feedback [2, 3]. At the same time, concerns have been raised about potential overreliance on AI, reduced cognitive engagement, and the risk of superficial learning [4, 5]. These concerns highlight the importance of developing AI literacy, which includes not only technical skills but also critical awareness of how AI tools are used in learning contexts.

2.2 Digital Behaviour, Screentime, and Cognitive Impact

The increasing integration of digital technologies into students' daily lives has led to significant changes in attention, motivation, and learning behaviour. Previous research has demonstrated that excessive screen use and frequent interaction with digital devices are associated with distraction, reduced concentration, and fragmented learning behaviour [6, 7].

In earlier research, university students reported near-constant engagement with digital devices, particularly smartphones, often switching between academic and non-academic activities [1]. While digital tools provide access to educational resources, they also contribute to fragmented attention and decreased academic focus. This dual nature of digital engagement suggests that the impact of technology depends not only on the amount of use but also on its purpose and context.

With the emergence of AI, digital interaction is shifting from passive consumption (for example, scrolling, watching videos) to active engagement with responsive systems. This transformation introduces new cognitive and psychological dynamics, as students increasingly interact with AI as both a tool and, in some cases, a form of social or emotional support.

2.3 AI in Language Learning (CALL Perspective)

In the field of Computer-Assisted Language Learning (CALL), AI has been identified as a promising tool for enhancing language acquisition. AI-powered systems can provide immediate feedback, simulate communicative situations, and support individualized learning paths [8].

Particularly in the area of speaking skills, AI has the potential to function as a conversational partner, offering students opportunities for practice in a low-anxiety environment. Unlike human interaction, AI-based communication reduces the fear of making mistakes and allows for repeated practice without social pressure. This aligns with research emphasizing the importance of interaction and output in language acquisition [9].

However, despite these advantages, the adoption of AI for speaking practice remains limited. Studies suggest that learners tend to use digital tools primarily for receptive skills or text-based production, rather than for active oral communication [10]. This may be due to a lack of awareness of AI capabilities, insufficient pedagogical guidance, or persistent psychological barriers related to speaking.

Recent research further highlights the growing importance of AI in foreign language education, particularly in higher education settings. For example, Klímová and Pikhart emphasize the increasing role of AI tools in supporting language learning processes, while also pointing to the need for effective pedagogical integration to fully exploit their potential [11]. This perspective is further supported by recent comprehensive reviews of AI in higher education, which stress the need for stronger conceptual grounding, ethical considerations, and more rigorous, context-sensitive research in this rapidly evolving field [12].

2.4 Psychological and Emotional Dimensions of AI Use

An emerging area of research concerns the psychological role of AI in students' lives. While traditionally digital technologies have been associated with entertainment or information access, AI introduces a new dimension of interaction that can resemble social communication.

Some studies indicate that users may engage with AI systems for emotional support, companionship, or self-reflection [13]. This phenomenon reflects a shift toward more personalized and relational uses of technology. In educational contexts, this raises important questions about the role of AI not only as a learning tool but also as a psychological resource.

At the same time, this development may have unintended consequences. If students use AI primarily for passive or supportive functions, they may be less likely to engage in cognitively demanding activities such as speaking in a foreign language. This creates a potential tension between comfort and learning effort, which is particularly relevant in the context of language education.

2.5 Identifying the Research Gap

Although existing research highlights the potential of AI in language learning and its growing role in students' digital lives, there is limited empirical evidence on how students actually use AI in relation to their learning goals. In particular, the discrepancy between students' declared preference for speaking practice and their limited use of AI for this purpose remains underexplored.

This study addresses this gap by examining real-world data from university students and focusing on the mismatch between their learning objectives and their behaviour. By doing so, it contributes to a better understanding of AI literacy and its implications for language education in higher education.

3 Research Questions

Based on the aims of the study and the identified research gap, the following research questions were formulated:

RQ1:How do university students currently use AI in their academic and personal routines?

RQ2: To what extent is there a discrepancy between students' declared language learning goals and their actual use of AI tools?

RQ3: Why do students not use AI for speaking practice despite identifying speaking as their primary learning objective?

RQ4: What psychological and behavioural factors influence students' use of AI in language learning?

4 Methodology

4.1 Research Design

This study employs a cross-sectional research design aimed at exploring current patterns of AI use among university students and their relationship to language learning. The research is based on a questionnaire survey conducted in February 2026.

The study follows an exploratory approach, focusing on identifying behavioural patterns and discrepancies rather than testing predefined hypotheses.

4.2 Participants

The participants were 125 university students enrolled in English language courses at the University of Hradec Králové, Czech Republic. The respondents represented several study programmes, including Applied Informatics, Information Management, Economics and Management, and Tourism Management.

The majority of participants were undergraduate students, with ages typically ranging from 19 to 30. Participation in the survey was voluntary and anonymous.

4.3 Data Collection Instrument

Data were collected using an online questionnaire, which was administered during English language classes. The questionnaire included a combination of:

- multiple-choice questions
- Likert-scale items
- open-ended responses

The instrument focused on several key areas:

- students' study programmes
- their expectations from language courses
- preferred language skills (for example, speaking, writing)
- use of language learning applications
- frequency and type of AI usage
- integration of AI into study and work routines
- purposes of AI use (for example, writing, coding, summarizing, therapy, companionship)

4.4 Data Analysis

The data were analysed using descriptive statistical methods and qualitative content analysis.

Quantitative data were used to identify general trends in AI usage, including frequency of use and dominant application areas. Qualitative responses were analysed thematically to identify recurring patterns related to students' attitudes, motivations, and barriers to using AI for language learning.

Particular attention was given to identifying discrepancies between students' declared learning goals and their actual behaviour.

4.5 Ethical Considerations

The survey was conducted anonymously, and no personal identifying information was collected. Participation was voluntary, and respondents were informed about the purpose of the study. By completing the questionnaire, participants provided informed consent.

5 Results

5.1 Declared Learning Goals: Strong Preference for Speaking

The analysis of questionnaire responses indicates that the majority of students identify speaking as their primary objective in English language learning. Across different study programmes, students consistently report a desire to improve their speaking abilities, including fluency, confidence, and the ability to communicate more naturally.

In addition to speaking, students also express interest in improving writing and grammar skills; however, these are typically secondary to oral communication. This finding suggests that students are strongly motivated to develop productive language skills, particularly in real-time interaction.

5.2 Patterns of AI Use: Dominance of Text-Based Activities

Despite the strong emphasis on speaking, the results show that students use AI tools primarily for text-based and task-oriented activities. The most frequently reported uses of AI include:

- writing (emails, academic texts, social media content)
- searching for information
- coding and technical problem-solving
- summarizing and synthesizing information
- studying support

These findings indicate that AI is predominantly perceived as a tool for efficiency and productivity rather than as a means of developing communication skills.

5.3 Frequency and Integration of AI Use

The data further reveal that AI tools are used frequently by a large proportion of students. Many respondents report using AI on a daily basis or multiple times per day, and a significant number indicate that AI is already integrated into their study routines and, in some cases, their work processes.

This suggests that AI is not a marginal or occasional tool, but rather a central component of students' digital learning environment.

5.4 Language Learning Tools: Preference for Traditional Platforms

When asked about language learning tools, students most frequently mention platforms such as Duolingo, YouTube, and other online resources. These tools are typically used for vocabulary acquisition, listening practice, or passive exposure to language.

Notably, AI-based tools are rarely mentioned in the context of speaking practice. This suggests that students do not naturally associate AI with opportunities for oral communication, even though such capabilities are increasingly available.

5.5 The Gap Between Declared Needs and Actual Behaviour

One of the most significant findings of this study is the clear discrepancy between students' declared learning goals and their actual behaviour. While speaking is identified as the most important skill, it is largely absent from their use of AI tools.

This gap highlights a fundamental misalignment between what students want to achieve and how they use available technologies. AI, despite its potential to support conversational practice, remains underutilized in this area.

5.6 Psychological and Emerging Uses of AI

An interesting finding is the presence of non-academic uses of AI, particularly in the areas of emotional support, therapy, and companionship. Although these uses are reported by a smaller subset of students, they indicate that AI is beginning to play a broader role in students' lives beyond purely academic functions.

This shift suggests that students may perceive AI not only as a tool, but also as a form of interaction. However, this type of engagement does not appear to translate into active language practice, particularly speaking.

6 Discussion

The findings presented above provide answers to the research questions and offer insight into the discrepancy between students' learning goals and their actual use of AI.

The findings of this study reveal a clear and consistent discrepancy between students' declared learning goals and their actual use of artificial intelligence. While speaking is identified as the primary objective in language learning, AI tools are rarely used for this purpose. Instead, students rely on AI predominantly for writing, coding, searching, and summarizing tasks.

This mismatch suggests that students do not perceive AI as a tool for developing speaking skills, despite its potential to function as a conversational partner. One possible explanation is a lack of awareness of AI capabilities. Many students may not fully realize that AI can support spoken interaction, provide feedback, or simulate real-life communication scenarios. This interpretation is consistent with research emphasizing that the educational potential of AI depends not only on its availability, but also on users' understanding of its affordances.

Another important factor appears to be established usage habits. Students tend to use AI for tasks that are efficient, familiar, and immediately productive. Writing, summarizing, and searching align well with these expectations, whereas speaking requires active engagement, effort, and real-time language production. This observation supports previous research suggesting that digital technologies are often used in ways that prioritize convenience and efficiency over deeper cognitive engagement [4]. This pattern can also be explained by cognitive limitations of human attention in technology-rich environments, where frequent interruptions and task-switching reduce the capacity for sustained focus [14].

The findings can also be interpreted in the broader context of students' digital behaviour. As highlighted in earlier research, students are accustomed to interacting with digital technologies in ways that often favour speed, multitasking, and low-effort engagement. Although AI represents a more interactive form of technology, students may still approach it using similar behavioural patterns, focusing on text-based and receptive activities rather than productive skills such as speaking.

From a language learning perspective, the results highlight a significant gap between the theoretical potential of AI and its practical use. While AI-based conversational tools are increasingly recognized as valuable for language practice, particularly in low-anxiety environments, their actual use by students remains limited. This finding is consistent with recent research in foreign language education, which suggests that although AI tools are widely available, their pedagogical integration remains insufficient and requires more structured implementation [11].

Recent systematic research further highlights both the benefits and challenges of AI integration in higher education, emphasizing the need for critical and informed use of these technologies. This reinforces the argument that AI cannot be effectively utilized without appropriate pedagogical frameworks and guidance.

An additional dimension of the findings is the emerging psychological role of AI. A subset of students reported using AI for purposes such as therapy or companionship, indicating that AI is beginning to function not only as a tool, but also as a form of interaction providing emotional support. Recent studies suggest that AI systems are increasingly used for companionship and emotional engagement, which may influence users' behaviour and engagement patterns, including their approach to learning activities [15].

This trend is further supported by current psychological research highlighting that AI chatbots and digital companions are reshaping human emotional interaction, offering both potential benefits and risks related to well-being and social behaviour [16]. These developments suggest that AI may fulfil certain social and emotional needs, potentially reducing users' motivation to engage in more cognitively demanding and effortful activities such as speaking in a foreign language.

However, this type of interaction does not appear to translate into language learning, particularly speaking practice, which remains cognitively demanding and requires active participation. This suggests a potential tension between comfort-oriented AI use and effortful learning processes.

Taken together, these findings indicate that the integration of AI into language learning is not simply a matter of access to technology, but rather of guidance, awareness, and pedagogical design. If students are left to use AI independently, they are unlikely to adopt it for speaking practice. Instead, targeted instructional strategies are needed to encourage more active, communicative, and pedagogically meaningful uses of AI.

7 Conclusion and Implications

This study examined how university students use artificial intelligence in the context of language learning, with a particular focus on the discrepancy between their declared preference for speaking practice and their actual use of AI tools. The findings reveal a clear and consistent gap between students' learning goals and their behaviour, highlighting that although speaking is considered the most important skill, it is largely absent from students' AI-supported learning activities.

The results suggest that this discrepancy is not caused by a lack of access to technology, but rather by a combination of limited awareness, established usage habits, and broader patterns of digital behaviour. Students tend to use AI in ways that prioritize efficiency and convenience, focusing on text-based tasks rather than cognitively demanding activities such as speaking. At the same time, the emergence of AI as a tool for emotional support further illustrates the complexity of students' interactions with this technology.

From a pedagogical perspective, the findings highlight the importance of structured integration of AI into language learning. Simply providing access to AI tools is not sufficient to ensure their effective use. Instead, educators need to actively guide students in using AI for communicative purposes, particularly in developing speaking skills. This may include the design of targeted activities, the introduction of AI-supported speaking tasks, and the development of students' AI literacy.

The study contributes to the growing body of research on artificial intelligence in education by providing empirical evidence of a gap between technological potential and actual student behaviour. It extends previous research on digital learning environments by showing how the role of AI is evolving from a functional tool to a more complex and multifaceted element of students' academic and personal lives.

Finally, the findings open up several directions for future research. Further studies could explore how different instructional approaches influence students' use of AI for speaking practice, or how AI-based interaction affects language learning outcomes over time. In addition, more research is needed to better understand the psychological dimensions of AI use and their implications for learning.

The study highlights the importance of developing AI literacy as a key competence in modern language education.

References

1. White, J.B., Černá, M., Cheung, S.K.S.: Always online: University students' perceptions of screen time, mental well-being, and academic focus. In: Cheung, S.K.S., Liu, X., Xu, G., Kwok, L.F. (eds.) Technology in education: Smart and innovative learning, CCIS, vol. 2752, pp. 245–255. Springer, Singapore (2026)
2. Holmes, W., Bialik, M., Fadel, C.: Artificial intelligence in education: Promises and implications for teaching and learning. Center for Curriculum Redesign, Boston (2019)
3. Zawacki-Richter, O., Marín, V. I., Bond, M., Gouverneur, F.: Systematic review of AI in higher education. International Journal of Educational Technology in Higher Education **16**(39) (2019)
4. Selwyn, N.: On the limits of artificial intelligence in education. Nordisk Tidsskrift for Pedagogikk og Kritikk **10**(1), 3–14 (2024)
5. Kasneci, E., Sessler, K., Küchemann, S., Bannert, M., Dementieva, D., Fischer, F., et al.: ChatGPT for good? On opportunities and challenges of large language models for education. Learn. Individ. Differ. **103**, 102274 (2023)
6. Rosen, L.D.: The distracted student mind: Enhancing its focus and attention. Phi Delta Kappan **99**(2), 8–14 (2017)
7. Twenge, J.M., Campbell, W.K.: Associations between screen time and psychological well-being. Preventive Medicine Reports **12**, 271–283 (2018)
8. Kukulska-Hulme, A.: Mobile-assisted language learning. The Encyclopedia of Applied Linguistics (2020)

9. Swain, M.: The output hypothesis. In: Hinkel, E. (ed.) Handbook of research in second language teaching and learning (2005)
10. Reinders, H., White, C.: 20 years of autonomy and technology. Lang. Learn. Technol. **20**(2), 143–154 (2016)
11. Klímová, B., Pikhart, M.: Use of artificial intelligence in foreign language education in higher education settings. In: Social Robots and Artificial Intelligence in Education. Cham: Palgrave Macmillan (2026)
12. Bond, M., et al.: A meta systematic review of artificial intelligence in higher education: A call for increased ethics, collaboration, and rigour. Int. J. Educ. Technol. High. Educ. **21**, 4 (2024)
13. Skjuve, M., Følstad, A., Fostervold, K.I., Brandtzaeg, P.B.: My chatbot companion. Int. J. Hum Comput Stud. **149**, 102601 (2021)
14. Gazzaley, A., Rosen, L.D.: The distracted mind: Ancient brains in a high-tech world. MIT Press (2016)
15. Zhang, Y., Zhao, D., Hancock, J.T., Kraut, R., Yang, D.: The rise of AI companions: Interaction with AI companions and psychological well-being. arXiv:2506.12605v5 (2025)
16. Andoh, E.: AI chatbots and digital companions are reshaping emotional connection. Monitor on Psychology **57**(1) (2026)

Intelligent Educational Frameworks and Environments

ARMS: A Personalised, Augmented Learning Environment for English Presentation Training

Venus W. M. Chan and Billy T. M. Wong(✉)

Hong Kong Metropolitan University, Hong Kong, China
{vwmchan,tamiwong}@hkmu.edu.hk

Abstract. This paper introduces ARMS (AI-powered Virtual Reality-enhanced Educational Metaverse for Speaking Enhancement), an innovative platform designed to transform English presentation training through human-AI collaboration. ARMS integrates AI and retrieval-augmented generation technology within an immersive metaverse environment, enabling users to learn and practice presentations in realistic virtual scenarios. The platform features an AI tutor that serves as an adaptive teammate, offering personalised recommendations on presentation strategies, content development, Q&A practice, and performance improvement. A qualitative evaluation of learners' experiences and perceptions of ARMS was conducted using an adapted version of the Mobile Augmented Reality Acceptance Model. Participants engaged with the platform by practising presentations and providing feedback through interviews. Results show that the immersive nature of ARMS effectively simulates realistic practice environments, offers flexibility through diverse virtual scenarios, and facilitates actionable AI-driven feedback. While participants appreciated the immediacy and practicality of AI feedback, they noted its limitations in providing nuanced, context-specific advice compared to human instructors. Usability challenges, such as technical issues and headset discomfort, were identified as barriers to adoption. Overall, the findings suggest that ARMS has good potential to enhance English presentation training by addressing the limitations of traditional methods, while emphasising the importance of robust hardware infrastructure and user support. By positioning AI as a collaborative partner, ARMS exemplifies the shift toward human-AI synergy in augmented learning environments.

Keywords: Human-AI Collaboration · AI-augmented Learning · Personalised Feedback · Presentation Training · Immersive Environment · metaverse

1 Introduction

1.1 AI and Metaverse for Presentation Skills Development

Advancements in AI have enabled more personalised and adaptive learning experiences. AI's ability to generate tailored feedback has proven effective for skill acquisition in areas like presentation [1]. Effective presentations require language proficiency, delivery techniques, audience engagement, and confidence. Traditional learning methods,

K. T. Chui et al. (Eds.): ICBL 2026, LNCS 16778, pp. 381–393, 2027.
https://doi.org/10.1007/978-981-92-3761-6_27

such as instructor-led training or peer feedback, often face challenges like inconsistency, scalability, and time constraints [2, 3]. AI-powered systems offer a promising alternative by providing consistent, actionable feedback that helps learners identify areas for improvement and track progress over time [4].

The integration of AI into virtual reality (VR) and metaverse environments has expanded the possibilities for immersive learning. The educational metaverse combines digital identities and 3D virtual worlds to create controlled spaces where learners can practice skills in realistic yet low-pressure scenarios [5]. This approach is particularly beneficial for presentation training, as it allows learners to refine their language use, pronunciation, and delivery in simulated real-world contexts [6]. AI enhances these environments by offering immediate, personalised feedback tailored to individual performance.

Despite the promise of AI and the metaverse, research and implementation of their combined application to the development of presentation skills remain limited. Fadhel et al. [7] reviewed the role of AI in the metaverse and suggested that, although there is promising potential for its use to improve learners' experience, there is a need to adopt trustworthy AI in the metaverse. Soliman et al. [8] discussed the opportunities and challenges of AI in the metaverse, noting its ability to automate repetitive tasks and optimise resources, despite concerns about privacy and bias. Empirical studies on AI chatbots within 3D metaverse environments are emerging. For example, Lee et al. [9] found that interacting with AI chatbots in metaverse settings positively influenced learners' awareness of global Englishes. Similarly, Hwang et al. [10] demonstrated that pre-service English teachers in chatbot-metaverse environments developed more interactive, immersive, and authentic learning activities compared to those using chatbot-only systems. While these findings highlight the potential of integrating AI, VR, and metaverse technologies across various learning contexts, further empirical research supported by a theoretical framework is needed to fully understand their pedagogical applications and effectiveness.

1.2 ARMS

To address these gaps, this paper introduces ARMS (AI-powered Virtual Reality-enhanced Educational Metaverse for Speaking Enhancement), a platform designed to support English presentation training. ARMS leverages AI and retrieval-augmented generation (RAG) technology within immersive virtual environments. Learners can practice presentations in diverse scenarios while receiving personalised feedback from an AI tutor. The AI tutor acts as an adaptive partner, offering recommendations on presentation strategies, content development, Q&A practice, and performance improvement. By positioning AI as a collaborative teammate, ARMS exemplifies the shift toward human-AI synergy in education.

ARMS builds on prior research in three areas: presentation skills development, VR and metaverse technologies in education, and AI-powered personalised learning. Public speaking anxiety, which affects approximately 20% of the population, highlights the need for innovative solutions to support learners in overcoming challenges like stage fright, audience-related anxiety, and language proficiency issues [11]. Traditional classroom settings often fail to provide the personalised attention required to address these factors [12]. The metaverse offers a novel approach by creating immersive environments that facilitate contextualised practice and immediate feedback. AI-powered systems further enhance learning by automating repetitive tasks, providing corrective feedback, and boosting learner confidence [13].

The following section outlines the design and features of ARMS, highlighting the integration of AI into the metaverse to provide learners with a comprehensive training environment for practising presentation skills and receiving personalised feedback. A qualitative study was conducted to examine learners' experiences in ARMS for English presentation training. Participants engaged with the platform by practising presentations in diverse virtual scenarios and providing feedback through interviews. The findings offer insights into the potential of this AI-powered metaverse platform to address the limitations of traditional training methods and to improve learning experiences, as well as the challenges learners encounter that affect the platform's effectiveness.

2 Design and Features of ARMS

2.1 Theoretical Foundation

ARMS was designed to tackle the challenges associated with presentation training, particularly for prepared speeches. Its development is based on Chan and Wong's [6] theoretical framework for speaking skills enhancement, which combines the immersive qualities of VR metaverse with the adaptive capabilities of AI.

Grounded in flexible learning theory, ARMS features an online metaverse that enables students to learn anytime, anywhere, promoting ubiquitous and autonomous learning. This approach enhances conventional language learning courses by addressing constraints of time and location through the integration of resources such as an AI tutor and VR practice [2, 3]. The AI tutor, guided by personalised learning theory, is designed to deliver individualised learning experiences and support inquiry-based and self-directed learning through a real-time feedback loop, as advocated by flow theory, enabling students to refine their skills and knowledge dynamically. Drawing on theories of constructivism, experiential learning, learning by doing, and situated learning, the VR practice feature aims to provide learners with realistic presentation scenarios, simulated authentic practice, and contextual learning environments, fostering active and situated learning.

2.2 System Architecture

The architecture of ARMS integrates AI and VR technologies to create a cohesive and interactive learning environment (Fig. 1). The system comprises two main components: the VR metaverse and the AI tutor. These components work together through an RAG pipeline to deliver an immersive, adaptive, and data-driven learning experience.

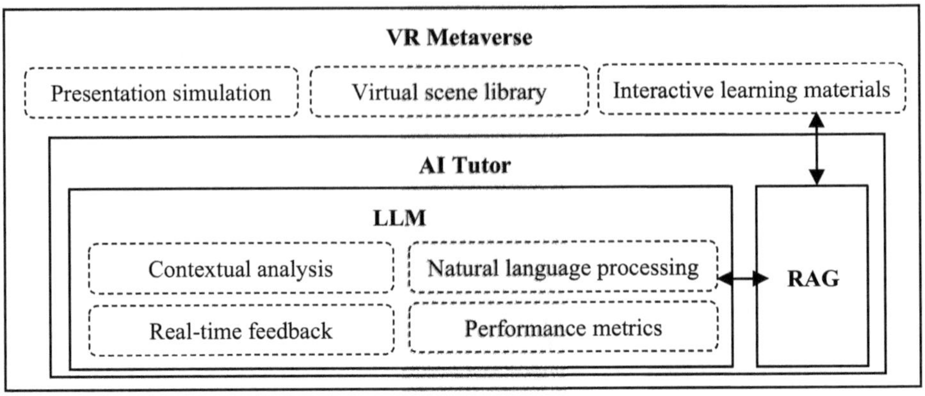

Fig. 1. Overview of ARMS system architecture.

VR Metaverse. The VR metaverse provides a learning space where learners practice and refine their presentation skills. It consists of three core modules:

- *Presentation simulation.* Learners deliver speeches in an immersive virtual environment, such as a classroom, lecture hall, or conference setting. The module captures multimodal input (speech audio, timing, basic head movements) and streams these data to the AI tutor.
- *Virtual scene library.* Learners can select presentation contexts (e.g., academic presentations, business pitches, informal talks) for learning. Scene metadata (audience size, formality, layout) is passed to the AI tutor for generating context-aware feedback.
- *Interactive learning materials.* Learners can access a wide range of learning materials in the VR metaverse. These materials also serve as input for the AI tutor via the RAG mechanism to generate context-specific hints, example expressions, and feedback for presentation practices.

AI Tutor. The AI tutor forms the intelligence layer of ARMS. It is implemented around a large language model (LLM) that is augmented with task-specific retrieval and analytics capabilities. The AI tutor is responsible for understanding learner performance and generating tailored feedback. It supports four key functions:

- *Contextual analysis.* The LLM consumes transcripts and metadata from the VR metaverse (topic, audience type, time constraints, and learner profile) to infer communicative intent and situational requirements. This enables the system to adjust feedback accordingly.
- *Natural language processing.* Speech recognition output from learners' presentation practices is processed to identify features such as lexical choice, grammatical accuracy, and rhetorical structure. The LLM detects issues such as unclear statements, weak transitions, or inappropriate register.
- *Real-time feedback.* After presentation simulations, the AI tutor provides low-latency and personalised guidance, such as highlighting excessive filler words or indicating when key points have not been sufficiently elaborated.

- *Performance metrics.* After each session, the AI tutor computes interpretable metrics based on IELTS speaking assessment criteria, covering fluency and coherence, lexical resource, grammatical range and accuracy, and pronunciation. Qualitative feedback is also generated to highlight areas for improvement.

RAG Integration. RAG serves as the bridge between the VR metaverse and the AI tutor. When a learner engages in a task, the AI tutor accesses the current context (e.g., topic, presentation setting, and proficiency level) and incorporates relevant information into the LLM's prompt, enabling the generation of personalised feedback aligned with established presentation criteria and instructional design principles.

Through this architecture, ARMS combines immersive VR practice with an AI-driven tutoring backend, ensuring learners receive context-sensitive support grounded in curated educational content.

2.3 Key Features

ARMS aims to promote comprehensive skill development, enabling learners to overcome public speaking anxiety, refine their delivery techniques, and build confidence in their abilities.

The platform supports access through VR headsets or web browsers. It accommodates various learning approaches, including ubiquitous, blended, and personalised learning, making it suitable for diverse educational settings. Its features are designed to positively influence learners' attitudes—such as motivation, engagement, and satisfaction—while enhancing their ability to acquire and master presentation skills. Below are the key features of ARMS:

Immersive VR metaverse environment. ARMS provides learners with an immersive VR metaverse environment featuring a variety of interactive learning resources, including instructional videos, textual guides, and quizzes (Fig. 2). These materials are designed to equip learners with foundational knowledge and practical strategies for delivering effective presentations.

Fig. 2. The VR metaverse of ARMS, where learners can access diverse learning resources.

AI tutor. Within the VR environment, learners interact with the AI tutor, which acts as a personalised learning assistant (Fig. 3). The AI tutor offers customised guidance to help learners prepare for presentations, providing feedback and recommendations on content structure, clarity, delivery techniques, and audience engagement. It collaborates with learners to evaluate the context, formality, and audience characteristics of presentations, delivering tailored advice to optimise delivery and impact.

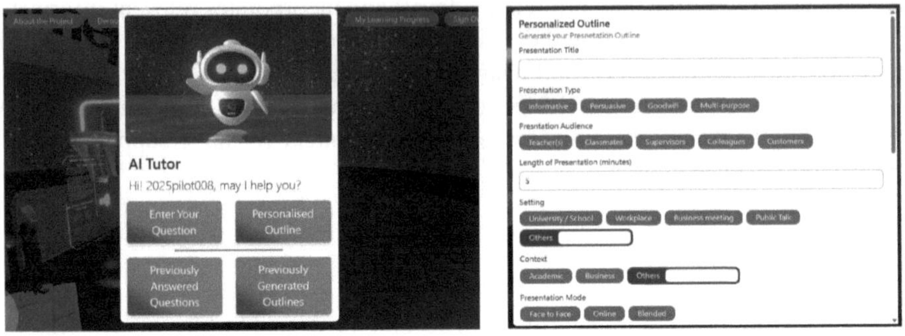

Fig. 3. The AI tutor providing personalised assistance and the customised outline feature for presentation preparation.

Realistic presentation practice scenarios. ARMS includes a VR environment specifically designed for learners to practice their presentations in realistic, immersive settings (Fig. 4, left). Learners can upload their presentation materials, such as slides, and select a virtual scene that matches their preferences or anxiety levels. Options include settings such as classrooms, conference halls, and auditoriums, allowing learners to simulate real-world presentation scenarios. This feature helps learners gradually build confidence, reduce anxiety, and adapt to different audience dynamics.

AI-driven personalised feedback. During each practice session, the AI tutor offers immediate, customised Q&A based on the learner's presentation content and anxiety level. After the session, it generates a comprehensive assessment report that provides personalised feedback on the learner's presentation performance (Fig. 4, right). The feedback covers various dimensions, including content quality, organisational structure, and language use. Specific aspects of language feedback include fluency, coherence, grammatical range and accuracy, and pronunciation. This targeted feedback enables learners to identify areas for improvement and refine their skills.

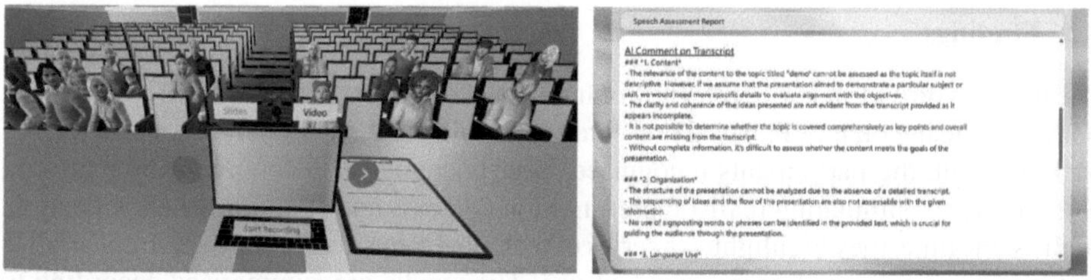

Fig. 4. [Left] The VR environment of ARMS for learners to practice presentations; and [Right] the AI-generated personalised feedback on presentation performance.

3 Evaluation on Learners' Experience and Perception

To assess the effectiveness of ARMS, particularly its immersive VR metaverse and AI-powered personalised feedback capabilities, a qualitative study was conducted to gain insights into learners' experiences and perceptions with the platform and evaluate its potential and limitations for enhancing presentation skills.

3.1 Research Method

The study involved six undergraduate students majoring in language and communication, recruited through convenience sampling. Given the small number of participants, the study adopted a qualitative approach, focusing on insights into their experiences and perceptions with ARMS.

Semi-structured interviews were conducted after participants completed a presentation practice session using ARMS. Each participant utilised a Meta Quest 3 VR headset to interact with the platform and explore its core features, including the immersive VR environment and AI-powered feedback. The interviews aimed to capture participants' perspectives on the platform and its influence on their learning experience.

The interview was developed using a modified version of the Mobile Augmented Reality Acceptance Model [14] to cope with the learning context in ARMS. This framework included seven dimensions to evaluate participants' experiences: perceived relative advantage, VR self-efficacy, perceived enjoyment, perceived ease of use, perceived usefulness, attitude, facilitating conditions, and intention to use.

The interviews were audio-recorded and transcribed for analysis. A thematic analysis approach was employed to identify recurring patterns and themes in participants' responses, offering an in-depth exploration of learners' perceptions, the platform's strengths and areas for improvement.

3.2 Findings

The findings provide an in-depth view of how the participants perceived and experienced ARMS, focusing on its VR-based presentation training and AI-driven personalised feedback. Overall, the participants recognised clear pedagogical potential in the platform, particularly for simulating realistic presentation contexts and supporting self-reflection. At the same time, they highlighted a series of technical, physical, and affective constraints that may limit sustained or independent use. The results are summarised according to the framework dimensions, as outlined in Table 1.

Table 1. Key findings from learner experiences with ARMS.

Dimension	Key findings
Perceived Relative Advantage	- The VR metaverse was commended for its immersive and realistic simulation of environments like classrooms and lecture halls - Participants noted reduced anxiety and increased confidence due to the realistic practice scenarios - The ability to switch between scenarios without physical movement was seen as a significant advantage - AI feedback provided detailed insights into verbal and non-verbal communication, such as tone, pauses, and filler words - Challenges included difficulty reading text in VR, the "uncanny valley effect" with virtual audiences, and the absence of follow-up interaction compared to teacher feedback - Some participants felt VR was not indispensable, as alternatives like practising with peers or using smartphones were available
VR Self-Efficacy	- Confidence levels varied depending on prior exposure to VR or similar technologies - Students with experience in VR gaming or smartphone use reported higher self-efficacy - Technical issues, such as unresponsive controls and difficulties with saving progress, negatively affected confidence
Perceived Enjoyment	- The novelty and realism of VR were appreciated by participants - AI feedback was described as engaging and timely - Technical challenges, such as erratic zoom angles and distance adjustments, detracted from the experience - Some students found the process of presentation practice inherently unenjoyable, and the complexity of the equipment reduced motivation
Perceived Ease of Use	- Experiences varied: while some participants found the controls intuitive after repeated use, others found the VR headset cumbersome and restrictive - Suggestions for improvement included providing a user manual and enhancing focal length adjustments - The need for a suitable location for VR use was identified as a barrier

(continued)

Table 1. *(continued)*

Dimension	Key findings
Perceived Usefulness	- The platform was regarded as beneficial for improving presentation skills - AI feedback was valued for its actionable insights, such as identifying pronunciation issues and structural weaknesses in presentations - The realistic simulation of presenting with PowerPoint slides was seen as helpful for real-world preparation - Some participants felt the platform had limited impact if they were already confident in their abilities
Attitude	- Participants generally expressed positive attitudes, recognising the potential of VR to enhance confidence and communication skills - The immersive environment and AI feedback were particularly appreciated by those with limited public speaking experience - Drawbacks included physical discomfort, such as eye strain and dizziness, as well as the lack of realism in virtual audiences
Facilitating Conditions	- Reliable internet, quiet spaces, and sufficient power supply were identified as essential for effective use - Participants suggested that schools providing VR resources, such as booking systems and lighter equipment, would encourage adoption - Overcoming feelings of awkwardness when using VR in public spaces was noted as important
Intention to Use	- Participants expressed mixed intentions: while some were eager to integrate VR into their learning, others preferred traditional methods but were open to occasional VR use - VR was seen as suitable for short practice sessions but less appealing for extended use due to physical discomfort - The AI feedback feature was highlighted as a motivating factor for improving performance and fostering self-discipline

Perceived relative advantage. Participants recognised clear benefits of ARMS compared with conventional rehearsal. The VR metaverse allowed them to practise in realistic environments without needing an actual venue or live audience. This immersion was seen as helpful preparation for real presentations, and the students reported reduced anxiety and increased confidence after practising in VR. Being able to switch instantly between presentation scenarios was perceived as efficient and convenient. The AI feedback was also considered a major advantage: it offered detailed, immediate analysis of verbal and non-verbal features.

At the same time, the perceived advantage of VR was not absolute. Reading text in VR was often difficult and uncomfortable. The virtual audience, while useful for creating a sense of social presence, sometimes felt unnatural or "uncanny" and could be distracting. Some participants considered VR non-essential, noting that they could still practise effectively with smartphones or peers. They also pointed out that AI feedback lacked the interactive, dialogic element of teacher guidance, reinforcing the view that ARMS should complement, not replace, human feedback.

VR self-efficacy. Learners' confidence in using ARMS was strongly influenced by their prior experience with VR and digital technologies. Those familiar with VR gaming or smartphone use adapted quickly and felt more capable of using the system. In contrast, participants with little VR experience were more hesitant and affected by technical difficulties. Technical issues such as unresponsive controls undermined confidence and disrupted the learning flow.

Perceived enjoyment. The participants generally found ARMS engaging due to the novelty and realism of VR and the interactive nature of the AI feedback. The system made practice feel purposeful, as learners received specific, actionable points to work on, which some linked to increased motivation.

However, enjoyment was not uniform. Some students viewed presentation practice as inherently stressful, and VR did not change this. Technical irritations reduced enjoyment, as did physical discomfort such as eye strain or mild dizziness, particularly during longer sessions. For some, the complexity and setup effort of the VR equipment reduced their motivation to use the system frequently.

Perceived ease of use. Perceptions of ease of use were mixed. Some participants found the controls and navigation reasonably intuitive after an initial familiarisation period and were able to operate ARMS without major difficulty once they understood the core functions (scenario selection, slide control, triggering feedback).

Others experienced the VR headset as heavy or restrictive, with frequent adjustments needed for fit and focal clarity, which distracted from the actual presentation task. The absence of clear onboarding materials (e.g. user manual) was noted as a barrier, particularly for less tech-savvy users. In addition, the need for a quiet, spacious location for VR use was seen as less convenient than portable tools like laptops or smartphones.

Perceived usefulness. Participants valued the system's ability to identify specific weaknesses, especially in pronunciation and presentation structure. The realistic simulation of presenting with slides in a lecture hall format was particularly helpful for practising timing, slide transitions, and coordination between speech and visual aids. Perceived usefulness was shown to be moderated by prior confidence. More confident speakers tended to view ARMS as a refinement tool rather than essential, while less experienced speakers saw stronger benefits in building confidence.

Attitude. Participants recognised the potential of VR and AI feedback to enhance confidence and communication skills and were generally open to using such technologies in their learning. The combination of a safe, private practice space with a realistic environment and rich feedback was especially attractive to those anxious about public speaking.

Yet, physical discomfort and the imperfect realism of the virtual audience limited enthusiasm for extended use. Most participants framed ARMS as a helpful addition to, rather than a replacement for, traditional face-to-face practice and teacher feedback.

Facilitating conditions. Effective use of ARMS was seen as dependent on several external conditions: reliable internet connection, quiet surroundings, and sufficient physical space. Participants suggested that institutions could support adoption by providing VR equipment or dedicated labs, offering lighter headsets, and ensuring technical support. Some also mentioned feeling self-conscious about using VR in shared spaces, suggesting that dedicated practice areas of VR-based learning would help.

Intention to use. Intentions to use ARMS in the future were mixed but generally cautious. Some participants were keen to use VR for short, targeted practice sessions before important presentations. Others preferred familiar methods (practising with peers, using smartphones, rehearsing in actual rooms) and were reluctant to rely heavily on VR, mainly due to comfort and convenience issues. Even so, most were open to occasional use, especially when ARMS is integrated into course activities.

4 Discussion and Conclusion

This study highlights the potential of integrating AI-driven personalised feedback within a VR metaverse platform to enhance English presentation training. By combining immersive virtual environments with AI capabilities, the platform offers a novel approach to skill development, with implications for broader educational applications. Participants highlighted the immersive nature of the VR environment, which effectively simulated realistic presentation scenarios. This aligns with prior research suggesting that VR can alleviate public speaking anxiety and foster confidence by providing a safe, controlled space for practice [5, 15]. However, challenges such as the "uncanny valley effect," blurry visuals, technical glitches, and connectivity issues detracted from the overall experience [16]. These findings indicate the need to refine both hardware and software to enhance usability and engagement.

The AI-powered feedback feature was a key strength of the platform, offering detailed, actionable insights into various aspects of presentation performance. This supports existing research on the value of AI in delivering immediate, data-driven feedback for skill acquisition [1, 4, 17]. However, participants noted that the AI lacked the nuanced, adaptive qualities of human feedback, such as the ability to address follow-up questions or provide context-specific advice. This limitation points to the need for enhancing human-AI synergy in augmented learning environments. Future improvements to the platform should incorporate additional interactive AI features, enabling learners to engage in dynamic, conversational exchanges that simulate human tutoring.

Participants expressed mixed views on the platform's effectiveness. While some appreciated the novelty and interactivity of the VR experience, others were discouraged by the physical discomfort of the headset, technical difficulties, and the steep learning curve associated with the technology. Additionally, the perceived value of the platform varied based on individual confidence levels and prior experience with public speaking. Learners with higher proficiency in presentation skills reported fewer benefits, suggesting that the platform may be more impactful for beginners or those with higher levels of anxiety. Addressing these challenges through ergonomic improvements, simplified interfaces, and greater customisation options could make the platform more accessible and appealing to a wider range of users [18].

Given the qualitative nature of this study and its small sample size, the findings should be interpreted with caution. Future research involving larger, more diverse participant groups is needed to validate these results and explore the long-term impact of the platform on presentation skill development. Comparative studies examining the effectiveness of this platform against traditional and other technology-enhanced methods would provide more insights into its advantages and limitations.

Acknowledgments. The work described in this paper was supported by grants from Hong Kong Metropolitan University (TLRF-2024/11 and CP/2022/04).

Disclosure of Interests. The authors have no competing interests to declare that are relevant to the content of this article.

References

1. Li, K.C., Wong, B.T.M.: Artificial intelligence in personalised learning: a bibliometric analysis. Interact. Technol. Smart Educ. **30**(3), 422–445 (2023)
2. Chan, V.: Using a virtual reality mobile application for interpreting learning: listening to the student's voice. Interact. Learn. Environ. **32**(6), 2438–2451 (2024)
3. Tang, K.W.W., Chan, V., Zhang, X.Y.: Agile-blended learning for metropolitan learners: Insights and trends. Asian Assoc. Open Univ. J. **20**(3), 215–227 (2025)
4. Chan, V.: A qualitative study of an XR-enhanced and AI-powered mobile app for public speaking training: student perceptions and experiences. SN Comput. Sci. **6**, 796 (2025)
5. Li, K.C., Wong, B.T.M.: A literature review of augmented reality, virtual reality, and mixed reality in language learning. Int. J. Mobile Learn. Organ. **15**(2), 164–178 (2021)
6. Chan, V.W.M., Wong, B.T.M.: A theoretical framework for integrating artificial intelligence, virtual reality, and metaverse in speaking skills enhancement. Proceedings of the 11th International Conference on Frontiers of Educational Technologies 2025, Lecture Notes in Educational Technology, pp. 99–111 (2026)
7. Fadhel, M.A., et al.: Navigating the metaverse: Unraveling the impact of artificial intelligence—A comprehensive review and gap analysis. Artif. Intell. Rev. **57**, 264 (2024)
8. Soliman, M.M., Ahmed, E., Darwish, A., Hassanien, A.E.: Artificial intelligence powered Metaverse: analysis, challenges and future perspectives. Artif. Intell. Rev. **57**, 36 (2024)
9. Lee, S., Jeon, J., Choe, H.: Enhancing pre-service teachers' global Englishes awareness with technology: a focus on AI Chatbots in 3D Metaverse environments. TESOL Q. **59**(1), 49–74 (2025)
10. Hwang, Y., Lee, S., Jeon, J.: Integrating AI chatbots into the metaverse: pre-service English teachers' design works and perceptions. Educ. Inf. Technol. **30**, 4099–4130 (2025)
11. Poeschl, S.: Virtual reality training for public speaking—a QUEST-VR framework validation. Frontiers in ICT **4**, 1–13 (2017)
12. Chan, V.: Investigating the impact of a virtual reality mobile application on learners' interpreting competence. J. Comput. Assist. Learn. **39**(4), 1242–1258 (2023)
13. Kim, W.H., Kim, J.H.: Individualised AI tutor based on developmental learning networks. IEEE Access **8**, 27927–27937 (2020)
14. Koutromanos, G., Mikropoulos, A.T., Mavridis, D., Christogiannis, C.: The mobile augmented reality acceptance model for teachers and future teachers. Educ. Inf. Technol. **29**, 7855–7893 (2024)
15. Chen, Z.: Exploring the application scenarios and issues facing Metaverse technology in education. Interact. Learn. Environ. **32**(5), 1975–1987 (2024)

16. Diekhof, E.K., Kastner, S., Deinert, D., Foerster, M., Steinicke, F.: The uncanny valley effect and immune activation in virtual reality. Sci. Rep. **15**, 30473 (2025)
17. Zou, B., Du, Y., Wang, Z., Chen, J., Zhang, W.: An investigation into artificial intelligence speech evaluation programs with automatic feedback for developing EFL learners' speaking skills. Sage Open **13**(3) (2023)
18. Souchet, A.D., Lourdeaux, D., Pagani, A., Rebenitsch, L.: A narrative review of immersive virtual reality's ergonomics and risks at the workplace: cybersickness, visual fatigue, muscular fatigue, acute stress, and mental overload. Virtual Reality **27**, 19–50 (2023)

DSCAM: A Three-Dimensional Evaluation Framework for Synthetic Corpus Quality in Online Education

Nan Zhou[1] and Jiazheng Yuan[2](✉)

[1] Capital Research Base for Lifelong Education, Beijing Open University, Beijing, China
[2] School of Literature/Research Center for Language Intelligence of China, Capital Normal University, Beijing, China
1075732515@qq.com

Abstract. The construction of online educational resources is constrained by the scarcity of high-quality Chinese corpora. While the application of synthetic corpora can alleviate data shortage, its quality, ethical norms, and accuracy still face significant challenges. Focusing on online education scenarios, this study aims to optimize teaching processes by constructing a high-quality synthetic corpus and proposes, for the first time, the Deep Synthetic Corpus Assessment Method Based on DeepSeek Model (DSCAM)—a three-dimensional synthetic corpus quality evaluation system encompassing "Authenticity-Diversity-Ethical Safety". Integrating Chain-of-Thought (CoT) prompt engineering and knowledge graph technology, this method provides systematic guarantees for generating safe, reliable, target-adaptive, and regulatory-compliant synthetic corpora in the education sector. Experimental results demonstrate that the synthetic corpus constructed based on the DSCAM framework can effectively support the development of teaching resource repositories, intelligent courseware generation, and question bank construction, while significantly enhancing teaching application effectiveness. Specifically: 1) In terms of courseware development efficiency, the average total development time and teachers' subjective cognitive load were both significantly reduced; 2) Regarding courseware quality, key dimensions such as knowledge comprehensiveness, systematicity, and balanceability scored significantly higher, with no disadvantage observed in knowledge accuracy and ethical safety; 3) In learning outcomes, students who used the courseware showed significantly improved post-test standardized scores, indicating better knowledge mastery. This study not only lays a theoretical foundation and provides a technical paradigm for AI-empowered high-quality educational development, but also offers important references for formulating ethical guidelines and quality standards for synthetic data in educational AI applications.

Keywords: Chinese Large Language Models · Synthetic Corpora · Intelligent Evaluation · Online Education · Ethical Risks

K. T. Chui et al. (Eds.): ICBL 2026, LNCS 16778, pp. 394–412, 2027.
https://doi.org/10.1007/978-981-92-3761-6_28

1 Introduction

The rapid development of technology is reshaping the ecological landscape of global linguistic resources. The innovative breakthrough of the Transformer architecture has propelled the rise of Large Language Models (LLMs). Endowed with powerful semantic understanding and generation capabilities, LLMs have become the core engine driving the evolution of digital civilization. However, in the field of education, Chinese LLMs face more complex challenges: they not only suffer from relatively scarce corpus resources but also need to meet the strict requirements of educational resources for quality and ethics.

In current global general datasets, Chinese corpora account for only about 1.3% [1], with both quantity and quality significantly lagging behind English corpora. This directly hinders the training of Chinese LLMs. Meanwhile, Chinese content on the internet constitutes less than 2% of the global total. The weak foundation of basic corpora further restricts the models' generalization and reasoning abilities. As a potential solution to data scarcity [2], synthetic corpora have demonstrated application potential in education—for instance, they can rapidly generate diverse teaching materials to support personalized learning [3]. Their widespread application, however, must be premised on ensuring the rigor of knowledge, the correctness of value orientation, and cultural inclusiveness.

Synthetic corpora refer to virtual corpora generated by algorithms that retain the characteristics of real data and achieve scale expansion. They have been widely used in fields such as speech synthesis but still face numerous challenges in educational scenarios. Gartner's forecast data indicates that by 2030, most model training data will come from synthetic data [4, 5]. Against this backdrop, Chinese synthetic corpora are regarded as a key resource for breakthroughs in local LLMs [6]. Nevertheless, synthetic corpora exhibit "dual effects": on the one hand, they can fill data gaps at low cost and high efficiency; on the other hand, their potential problems such as uneven quality, cultural fragmentation, and ethical risks may lead to model performance degradation and value biases. Particularly in education, these issues may cause distortions in teaching content and exacerbate cognitive biases among students [7].

To address the aforementioned challenges, there is an urgent need to construct a targeted synthetic corpus evaluation system. However, existing evaluation systems have obvious shortcomings: they generally ignore key dimensions such as right cleanliness, cultural appropriateness, and value orientation, and the evaluation process is often inefficient and costly. The DeepSeek model, by adopting the Mixture of Experts (MoE) sparse structure and multi-layer attention architecture, has effectively reduced inference costs and hardware requirements. It has also demonstrated excellent performance in Chinese context processing, and its outstanding long-context handling capability provides new possibilities for solving evaluation dilemmas [8, 9].

Focusing on the issue of synthetic corpus evaluation in online education scenarios, this paper, grounded in an artificial intelligence ethics framework and leveraging the DeepSeek model, proposes Deep Synthetic Corpus Assessment Method Based on DeepSeek Model (DSCAM) that integrates Chain-of-Thought Prompting (CoTP) and knowledge graphs. This method comprises a three-dimensional framework for synthetic corpus quality assessment—authenticity, diversity, and ethical safety—with a particular emphasis on knowledge accuracy, cultural inclusiveness, and value orientation. It enables the quantitative evaluation of synthetic corpus quality and the effective verification of ethical safety. Empirical research demonstrates that this method can effectively support application scenarios such as the construction of teaching resource libraries, courseware generation, and question bank development, thereby promoting the responsible application of artificial intelligence technology in the field of education. The primary contributions of this paper lie in addressing the current gap of insufficient AI ethical considerations in synthetic corpus evaluation within online education, providing theoretical support for building "Trustworthy AI in Education", proposing a highly operational DSCAM assessment method, demonstrating its application potential using the Computer Networks course as a real teaching scenario, and offering methodological guidance for the safe, effective, and ethical implementation of large models in specialized online education.

2 Related Work

Synthetic corpora are not an entirely new concept; the idea of synthetic corpora (synthetic data) was first proposed by the renowned statistician Donald Rubin in his 1993 paper [10]. In recent years, with LLMs, the concept of synthetic corpora has gained increasing attention. In June 2024, NVIDIA released its new-generation open-source large model, Nemotron-4 340B, whose instruction tuning was accomplished using 98% synthetic corpora [11]. In July 2024, Apple also unveiled its self-developed artificial intelligence system, Apple Intelligence, which extensively utilized synthetic corpora during its pre-training phase [12]. Many studies suggest that the high-quality corpora required for LLMs will soon be depleted, and synthetic corpora offer an effective solution to this challenge [13, 14]. Therefore, conducting research on synthetic corpora—particularly focusing on their generation methods, risk assessment, and related aspects—warrants in-depth consideration.

2.1 Generation Methods of Synthetic Corpora

The technical routes for generating synthetic corpora exhibit diverse characteristics, with three mainstream categories of methods: synthetic corpus generation based on LLMs [15]; synthetic corpus generation based on Generative Adversarial Networks (GANs) or diffusion models (see Fig. 1) [16]; and synthetic corpus generation based on statistical modeling and simulation [17]. In practical application scenarios, these methods are often used in a collaborative and complementary manner to effectively improve the quality of synthetic corpora [18, 19].

Constrained by the generation mechanisms and technical characteristics of synthetic corpora, model training using such corpora tends to overlook outliers and distribution biases in the original data. This leads to the attenuation of the long-tail characteristics of the original data, while high-frequency content is overly emphasized, resulting in the model deviating significantly from the original data distribution. Studies have shown that after 9 iterations of training with synthetic data, large language models will inevitably experience performance degradation [20]. Therefore, to specifically address the defects of synthetic corpora in terms of fidelity, bias, credibility, and ethical compliance, establishing a scientific evaluation system is crucial.

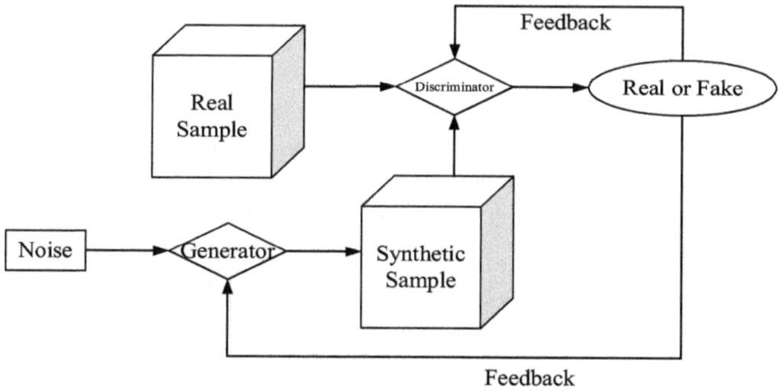

Fig. 1. Schematic Diagram of the Technical Principle of GANs.

2.2 Evaluation Methods and Comparisons of Synthetic Corpora

Traditional corpus evaluation methods mainly focus on the optimization of technical indicators, and have significant limitations in addressing the complexity of synthetic corpora. As shown in Table 1, lexical overlap-based evaluation metrics—such as Recall-Oriented Understudy for Gisting Evaluation (ROUGE) for summary recall and Bilingual Evaluation Understudy(BLEU)—assess similarity by calculating the lexical overlap rate between generated texts and reference texts [21, 22]. However, these metrics only focus on the surface structural features of texts and fail to fully incorporate semantic understanding and contextual analysis. For texts with equivalent semantics but different lexical expressions, lexical overlap-based metrics may underestimate their similarity, making it difficult to accurately characterize the quality of synthetic corpora. For example, when the reference text is "He likes reading books very much" and the generated text is "He is extremely fond of reading books", although the semantics of the two are highly consistent, the ROUGE and BLEU metrics may give low similarity scores due to incomplete lexical overlap.

In the research on language model evaluation methods, existing semantic similarity-based metrics,such as BERTScore and BARTScore, can capture partial semantic information and enhance the depth of semantic understanding, but they cannot effectively detect the cultural adaptability and value stance of synthetic corpora, posing significant potential risks.

Current ethical review mechanisms generally adopt a "post-hoc correction" model rather than integrating "priori constraint"-based ethical reviews into the entire process of corpus generation. The flaws of this mechanism lead to systematic dilemmas in the traceability and governance of value biases: the ethical review link lags behind the corpus generation process, making it difficult to achieve source tracing for risk identification and handling, which essentially weakens the effectiveness of ethical norms [25]. A typical example is that when embedded ethical review mechanisms are lacking in the synthetic corpus generation stage, ethical issues such as privacy leakage and copyright infringement are often identified only after generation is completed. At this point, the negative impacts are already difficult to eliminate, and the post-event tracing mechanism cannot realize dynamic adjustments to the generation process [26, 27].

Table 1. Comparison of traditional corpus evaluation methods.

Name of Method	Technical Focus	Problem
ROUGE	Compute precision based on n-grams to reflect the frequency of n-grams in the generated text appearing in the reference text	The two methods primarily focus on the surface form of the text, with limited consideration for semantic meaning and contextual understanding
BLEU	Compute precision based on n-grams to reflect the frequency of n-grams in the generated text appearing in the reference text	
BERTScore [23]	Compute semantic similarity between generated text and reference text based on the BERT pre-trained model, taking into account contextual information of words	They cannot detect the cultural adaptation and value stance within synthetic corpora
BARTScore [24]	Assess the similarity between generated text and reference text by computing the generation probability between them using the BART model	

Although LLMs have been widely used in synthetic corpus quality evaluation and have shown good results [28, 29], studies have indicated that LLM-based evaluation methods still have fairness and reliability issues, such as order bias and verbosity bias. Notably, LLMs constructed with Retrieval-augmented Generation (RAG) architectures by introducing prior knowledge can significantly reduce hallucinations and enhance domain-specific professional evaluation capabilities, thereby optimizing their evaluation performance in specific professional fields [30–32].

3 Construction of the Three-Layer Evaluation Framework DSCAM for Synthetic Corpora

In response to the current technical challenges in the field of synthetic corpus evaluation, this study constructs DSCAM of "Authenticity-Diversity-Ethical Adaptability", providing a systematic paradigm for synthetic corpus quality assessment. The system includes: the authenticity evaluation dimension covers semantic similarity monitoring and logical consistency verification; the diversity evaluation dimension involves analysis of regional dialect and professional terminology coverage, as well as detection of stylistic diversity; the ethical adaptability evaluation dimension comprises rights compliance review, value stance analysis, and bias propagation monitoring.

Among these, the analysis of dialects and specialized terminology within synthetic corpora is key to assessing linguistic richness. If synthetic corpora can extensively encompass the characteristic vocabulary and expressions of different regional dialects, it indicates a certain advantage in linguistic diversity, enabling a better reflection of the richness of the Chinese language. If synthetic corpora can include abundant specialized terminology across multiple fields such as medicine, law, finance, and technology, and if the usage of these terms is accurate and appropriate, it demonstrates a high level of proficiency in professional language expression, providing strong support for applications in related fields. Furthermore, analyzing synthetic corpora from perspectives such as vocabulary, sentence structures, and rhetoric allows for a comprehensive evaluation of the diversity of their stylistic features. To effectively analyze the diversity of regional dialects, specialized terminology, and stylistic features, this study constructs a specialized domain knowledge base for LLMs to facilitate the analysis of stylistic diversity.

To achieve the goal of systematic evaluation, this research constructs an ethical adaptability-oriented three-layer evaluation framework by optimizing the triple content filtering mechanism and value alignment module of the DeepSeek model.

As elaborated earlier, the "Authenticity-Diversity-Ethical Adaptability" three-dimensional evaluation system established in this study encompasses a three-layer evaluation framework, which includes 3 first-level indicators and 7 s-level indicators (see Fig. 2). The weight of each indicator is calculated using Principal Component Analysis (PCA) based on the objective weighting method, aiming to provide fundamental support for the subsequent establishment of a computer-aided judgment model and the realization of comprehensive evaluation of synthetic corpora. The specific research process is as follows:

(1) Selection of evaluation indicators. As shown in Fig. 2, based on the three-layer evaluation framework (including 3 first-level indicators and 7 s-level indicators), five rounds of expert consultation are conducted using the Delphi Method to ultimately determine the constituent elements of the indicator system.
(2) Weight assignment of evaluation indicators. After confirming the indicator system, domain experts are selected to score the importance of each indicator using a 5-point Likert Scale, with evaluation levels classified into five categories: Very Important, Important, Moderately Important, Slightly Important, and Unimportant.

(3) Principal Component Analysis modeling. Through orthogonal linear transformation of the first-level and second-level indicator variables, a linear combination model equation of principal components is constructed(1).Where denotes the i-th principal component, represents the eigenvector coefficient, and denotes the standardized original variable.

$$f(i) = a(i, 1)x_1 + a(i, 2)x_2 + \dots + a(i, p)x_p \tag{1}$$

(4) Calculation of the weight of each evaluation indicator. The weight of principal components is determined based on the variance contribution rate, and the weight value of each indicator factor is obtained through normalization processing of eigenvector coefficients.

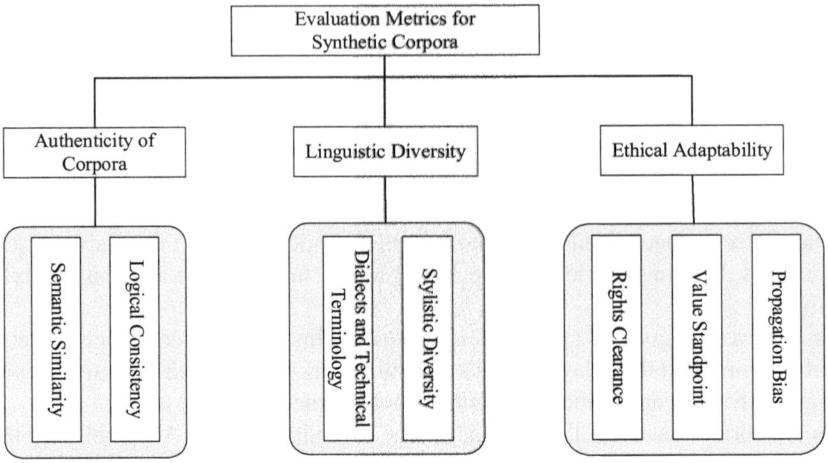

Fig. 2. Indicators and Factors of the Three-Tiered Evaluation Framework for Synthetic Corpora.

4 Experimental Data Analysis

4.1 Experimental Dataset

To ensure the reliability and representativeness of experimental results, this study adopts both a real corpus and a self-constructed synthetic corpus as the experimental dataset. The dataset contains 161,268 real corpora, along with the same number of synthetic corpora and their corresponding scores. The synthetic corpora are built based on the DeepSeek large model, focusing on the field of online education and generated using specific prompts. Scoring is completed by interdisciplinary experts in online education and linguistics based on a three-dimensional measurement scale: authenticity (50 points), diversity (20 points), and ethical adaptability (30 points). In the experiment, LLMs are used for automatic scoring of 161,268 synthetic corpora. By comparing the scoring results with the benchmark scores of the dataset, the Pearson correlation coefficient and classification accuracy indicators are calculated.

4.2 Evaluation Metrics

In this experiment, the manual scores in the dataset are taken as the benchmark. The scores output by the model are compared with these benchmark scores, and Spearman's rank correlation coefficient ρ and Kendall's Tau correlation coefficient τ are calculated as evaluation metrics. The specific calculation formulas are as follows:

$$\rho = 1 - \frac{6\sum d_i^2}{n(n^2 - 1)} \tag{2}$$

$$\tau = \frac{6\sum d_i^2}{n(n^2 - 1)} - 1 \tag{3}$$

In the formula for Spearman's ρ, n denotes the sample size, and d represents the differences in ranks after sorting the two sets of data. In the formula for Kendall's Tau τ, n is the sample size, and P is the sum of the number of data points that are ranked after the given data in both sets of data. The experiment uses Spearman's ρ and Kendall's Tau τ correlation scores to obtain the monotonic relationship and ranking consistency metrics between the model's output scores and the dataset's benchmark scores, thereby measuring the accuracy of the model in evaluating the quality of synthetic corpora.

4.3 Evaluation Results and Analysis

This experiment uses small-parameter LLMs such as Baichuan2-13B-base, Baichuan2-13B-cha, and DeepSeek-R1 14b as comparison models. The DSCAM method is adopted without manual review, and experiments are conducted on the self-constructed synthetic corpus dataset, ultimately obtaining the experimental results. Table 2 shows that the DSCAM method comprehensively outperforms the baseline models in terms of authenticity evaluation, diversity evaluation, ethical adaptability evaluation, and overall evaluation.

Table 2. Comparison between the DSCAM method and Baseline Models

Model	Authenticity of Corpora	Linguistic Diversity	Ethical Adaptability Evaluation	Overall Assessment
Baichuan2-13B-base	0.4013	0.6777	0.3311	0.4522
Baichuan2-13B-chat	0.4211	0.6783	0.3335	0.5521
DeepSeek-R1 14b	0.5421	0.7012	0.4232	0.6785
DSCAM	0.7231	0.7221	0.6221	0.7112

Using the DSCAM method, 50, 100, 200, 500, and 1000 corpora are randomly selected from the self-constructed Chinese synthetic corpus for evaluation and scoring. Assessments are conducted from 7 important indicators of the synthetic corpora, with relevant examples shown in Table 3.

According to the results in Table 3, among the 7 evaluation indicators: semantic similarity quantifies the degree of semantic matching between generated content and real content, where manual scores are close to those of the DSCAM method, and both increase with the increase in sample size; logical consistency evaluates the coherence of the internal logic of the content, with manual scores slightly higher than those of the DSCAM method but without significant differences; right compliance reflects the copyright compliance status of the content, where both methods perform excellently with the smallest difference, and the right compliance indicator exhibits the highest stability. As the sample size increases, the scores of all indicators show a significant upward trend. Notably, the DSCAM method performs slightly better than manual scoring in the diversity dimension (dialects and professional terms, stylistic diversity). The bias

Table 3. Sampling Comparison between the DSCAM method and Human Scoring

Sample Size	Category of Methods	Authenticity of Corpora		Linguistic Diversity		Ethical Adaptability Evaluation		
		Semantic Similarity	Logical Consistency	Dialects and Technical Terminology	Stylistic Diversity	Rights Clearance	Value Standpoint	Propagation Bias
50	Human Scoring	42	47	12	8	49	32	6
	DSCAM	45	43	13	8	48	30	7
100	Human Scoring	92	94	28	26	93	65	21
	DSCAM	90	93	31	28	92	67	23
200	Human Scoring	182	197	63	57	190	142	47
	DSCAM	178	193	61	55	185	136	43
500	Human Scoring	410	437	287	192	491	311	62
	DSCAM	406	443	278	205	487	307	65
1000	Human Scoring	903	943	293	275	941	632	231
	DSCAM	912	925	289	283	947	641	239

propagation indicator has the lowest score and the most significant volatility, becoming a common weakness of both methods. When the sample size is ≥ 200, the DSCAM method approaches the level of manual scoring in most indicators. The line chart of key indicators (semantic similarity, logical consistency, stylistic diversity, and bias propagation) shown in Fig. 3 further indicates that the results of the DSCAM method are highly consistent with manual scoring. Comprehensive evaluation results show that the DSCAM method is basically consistent with manual scoring results, and its processing efficiency is significantly superior to traditional methods, verifying the effectiveness of this method.

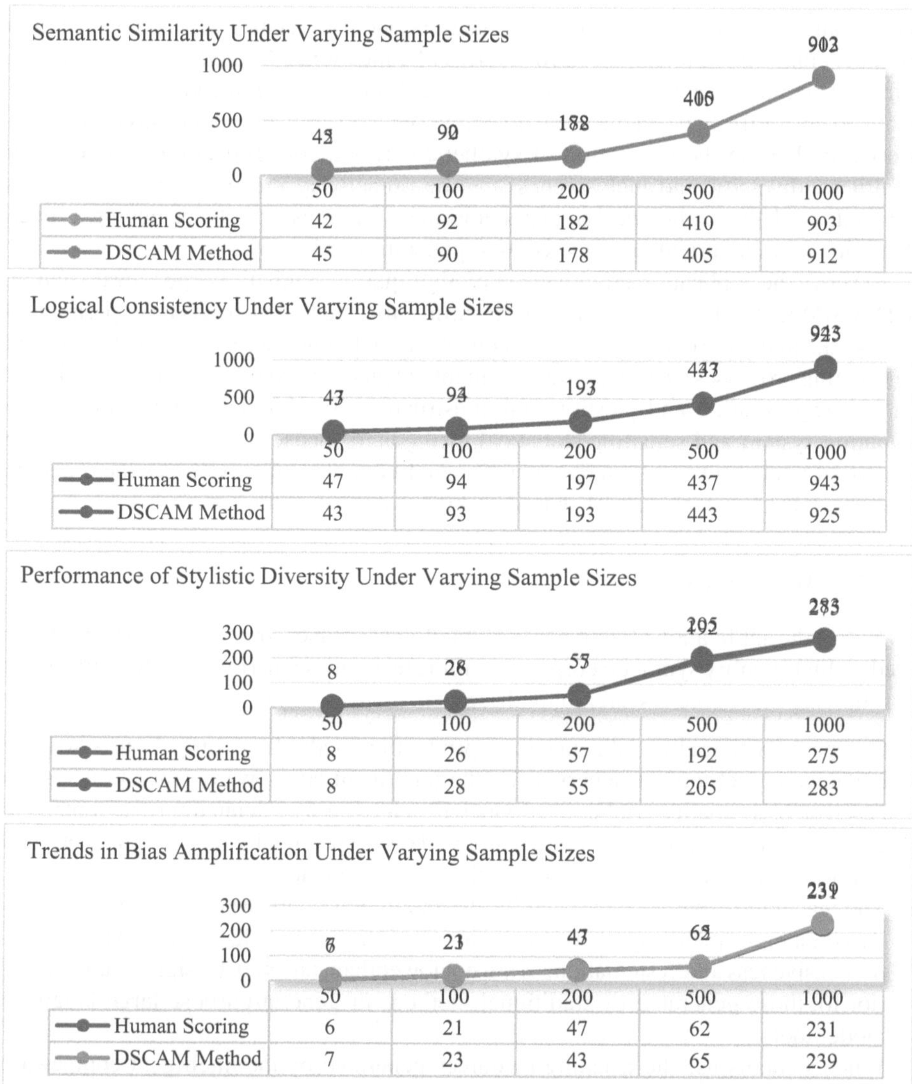

Fig. 3. Sampling Comparison Between the DSCAM Method and Human Scoring.

5 Teaching Scenarios and Applications

In the field of education, high-quality synthetic corpora hold significant application value. First, they help strengthen the bottom line of privacy protection and data security. Synthetic corpora can effectively mitigate the risk of privacy leakage that may arise during the sharing and use of real data, thereby providing stable and secure data support for the development, training, and related academic research of educational AI models while fully safeguarding students' legitimate rights and interests. Second, they enable data augmentation and the simulation of special education scenarios. Synthetic corpora can not only expand the overall scale of datasets but also balance the data distribution structure, contributing to enhanced robustness of educational AI models and promoting their more equitable application. Third, they facilitate value embedding and the personalized customization of educational content, which is the core dimension this study focuses on. During the generation of synthetic corpora, core educational values such as fairness, diversity, and inclusiveness can be proactively integrated into the corpus content through the explicit design of generation instructions, thereby achieving a "deep integration of value orientation and content generation" [33–35].

To verify the application effectiveness of high-quality synthetic corpora evaluated by the DSCAM method in online teaching scenarios, this study constructs an experimental framework, taking the core professional course Safety Economics as an example, around key teaching processes such as the development of teaching resource libraries, intelligent courseware generation, and question bank construction. By adopting a multi-dimensional evaluation system and scientific statistical methods, it focuses on the core application scenario of intelligent courseware generation and systematically examines the practical value of intelligent teaching tools based on high-quality corpora.

5.1 Core Hypotheses

To validate the application effectiveness of intelligent courseware generation technology based on high-quality synthetic corpora in online teaching scenarios, this study proposes the following three core research hypotheses:

(1) Compared with traditional courseware production methods or general-purpose large language model tools, teachers using the intelligent courseware generation system based on high-quality synthetic corpora will achieve a significant improvement in the efficiency of designing teaching resources. This is specifically reflected in shortened development time and reduced subjective cognitive load.
(2) The teaching resources generated by the intelligent courseware generation system based on high-quality synthetic corpora will have a knowledge system whose comprehensiveness and systematicness are not lower than, and may be significantly superior to, those generated by traditional methods or general-purpose large language model tools.
(3) When students use the teaching resources generated by the intelligent courseware generation system based on high-quality synthetic corpora for learning, their learning effects in terms of knowledge mastery and cognitive development will not be lower than, and may be significantly superior to, those of students using resources generated by traditional methods or general-purpose large language model tools.

5.2 Research Design

This study adopts a quasi-experimental design, with an experimental group and control groups. Given the difficulty of implementing complete random assignment in real educational environments, a pre-test is conducted to ensure that students participating in subsequent learning effect evaluations have no statistically significant differences in their initial academic levels.

Participant Recruitment: 40 teachers with online teaching experience are recruited as core research subjects and randomly assigned to the following three groups:

(1) Experimental Group (EG). 20 teachers, using the intelligent courseware generation system based on high-quality synthetic corpora developed in this study.
(2) Control Group 1 (CG1). 10 teachers, producing courseware through conventional methods (e.g., manual data collection, independent design and production using regular PPT software or similar tools).
(3) Control Group 2 (CG2). 10 teachers, producing courseware using the DeepSeek model. Meanwhile, based on the final courseware content produced by the teachers, students from parallel classes are recruited to participate in subsequent learning effect evaluations.

Experimental Process: First, all participating teachers are required to independently complete the development task of a complete set of courseware for the designated course Safety Economics within two weeks. Subsequently, teachers in the experimental group receive standardized operation training on the intelligent courseware generation system. They need to input structured instructions such as specific teaching objectives and core knowledge point requirements into the system; after the system generates the initial draft of the courseware, teachers can review, revise, and improve it. During the same period, teachers in CG1 independently complete the entire courseware production process relying solely on their conventional methods and tools; teachers in CG2 use the designated general-purpose large language model to generate the initial draft of the courseware, which can be reviewed and revised as needed.

5.3 Design of Evaluation Indicators

This study sets multi-dimensional evaluation indicators to comprehensively test the system's effectiveness and the aforementioned three core hypotheses, specifically including courseware development efficiency indicators, courseware quality indicators, and student learning effect indicators. Courseware quality evaluation adopts a double-blind review method: all completed courseware are anonymized and then submitted to an independent expert review panel for evaluation using a 5-point Likert scale. Finally, the average score of each courseware in each dimension and the comprehensive quality score are calculated for inter-group comparison. Student learning effect evaluation adopts a pre-test and post-test design: the pre-test is conducted before the start of teaching intervention, where a standardized knowledge test is administered to students from parallel classes participating in the study to assess their initial knowledge level of Safety Economics related content. Independent samples t-test/analysis of variance (ANOVA) is used to ensure no significant differences in baseline levels among groups. Subsequently, teaching is implemented in corresponding classes using courseware produced by teachers from Control Group 1 (CG1) and Control Group 2 (CG2) respectively. After the completion of teaching, the post-test uses a standardized knowledge test equivalent to the pre-test to assess students' knowledge mastery, and learning gains are calculated. Details of the specific evaluation indicator design are shown in Table 4.

Table 4. Evaluation Metrics

Total Indicator	Sub-indicator	Indicator Description
Evaluation of Courseware Development Efficiency	Objective Efficiency Metrics	Use timing software to accurately record the total duration each teacher spends on developing the complete set of "Safety Economics" courseware. Calculate and compare the average development time across groups of teachers
	Subjective Workload Indicators	After completing the task, teachers fill out the NASA Task Load Index (TLX) questionnaire. This well-established scale assesses subjective cognitive load perceived by teachers during the task across six dimensions: mental demand, physical demand, temporal demand, effort, frustration, and performance
Courseware Quality Assessment	Knowledge Accuracy	Scientifically rigorous with no factual errors
	Instructional Design Rationality	Clear logical structure, well-defined teaching objectives, focused content highlights, appropriately graded difficulty levels, and alignment with pedagogical principles
	Comprehensiveness, Systematicity, and Balance of Knowledge	Covers broad and comprehensive knowledge, organized systematically and coherently, with reasonable and balanced content distribution
	Content Diversity	Diverse use of case studies, scenarios, charts, multimedia elements, etc

(*continued*)

Table 4. *(continued)*

Total Indicator	Sub-indicator	Indicator Description
	Inspirational and Interactive Qualities	Effectively stimulates student thinking and includes interactive components such as questions, discussions, and exercises
	Ethical Safety and Appropriateness	Content aligns with socialist core values, free from bias, discrimination, or safety risks, and suitable for target learners
Student Learning Outcome Evaluation	Learning Gain	Uses standardized knowledge standardized knowledge tests equivalent or parallel to pre-tests to assess students' knowledge mastery, calculating learning gains (post-test scores – pre-test scores)
	Learning Interest	After instruction, students complete anonymous questionnaires measuring their learning interest, engagement levels, and perceived usefulness of the courseware

5.4 Result Analysis

Efficiency Comparison: The experiment selected the development of a 2-lesson courseware package for comparison between the two groups CG1 and CG2. The average total time spent on courseware development by teachers in CG1 was significantly lower than that of teachers in CG2 ($p < 0.05$). Meanwhile, the NASA Task Load Index (NASA-TLX) reported by the teachers was analyzed across six dimensions: total duration, mental demand, physical demand, temporal demand, performance, effort, and frustration level. Histograms and radar charts were plotted as shown in Fig. 4. The figures indicate that the total subjective cognitive load score for group CG2 was also significantly lower than that for group CG1 ($p < 0.05$), with particularly significant differences in the dimensions of temporal demand and effort.

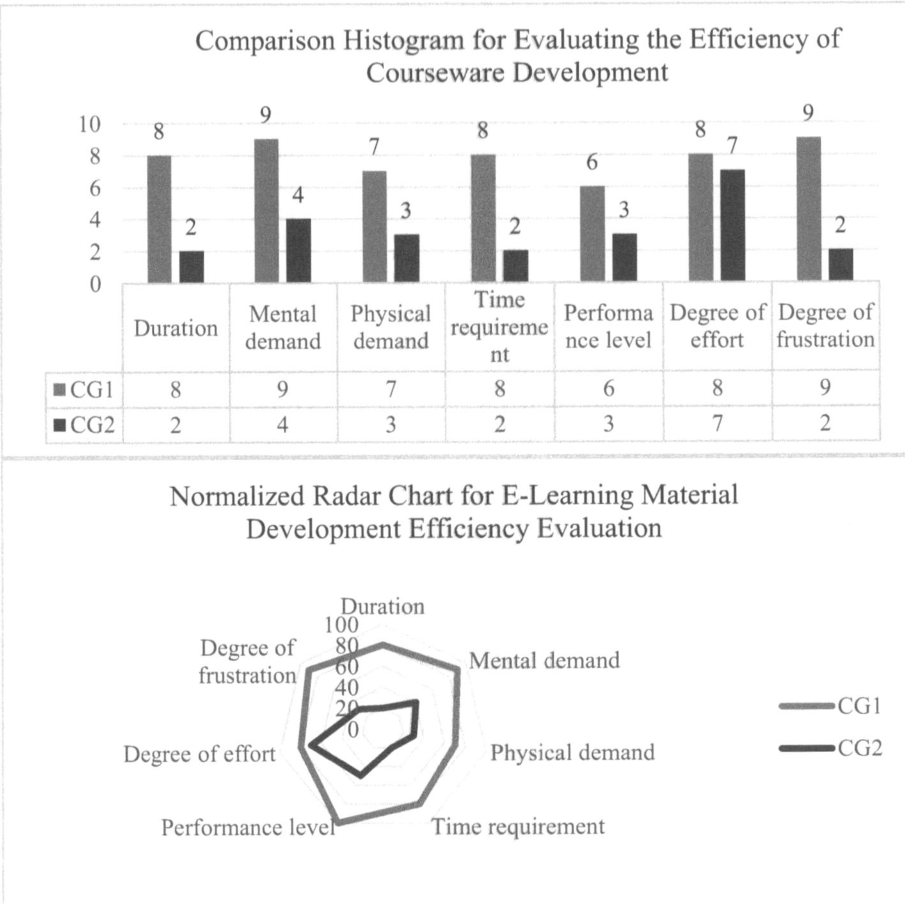

Fig. 4. Comparison of Evaluation Methods for Courseware Development Efficiency.

Quality Comparison: Among the teachers in the Experimental Group (EG), the courseware developed by CG2 scored significantly higher than those developed by the control group CG1 in terms of comprehensive quality score, knowledge comprehensiveness and systematicness, balance, and scores in key dimensions ($p < 0.05$), and showed no significant disadvantages in the dimensions of knowledge accuracy and ethical safety ($p > 0.05$), as shown in Fig. 5.

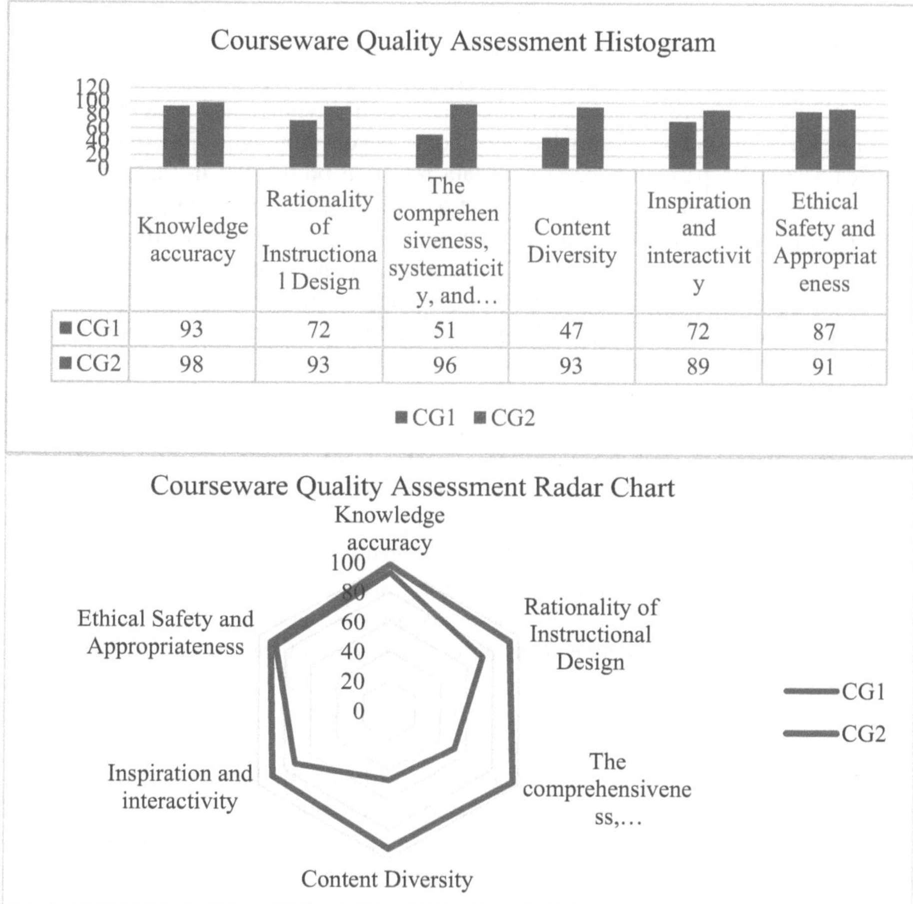

Fig. 5. Comparison of Courseware Quality Assessment Methods.

Learning Effect Comparison: After controlling for pre-test scores, students who learned using courseware from the experimental group CG2—due to the synthetic corpus being more diverse and balanced—achieved significantly higher standardized post-test scores than students who used courseware generated by the control group CG1 ($p < 0.05$), indicating better knowledge mastery.

6 Conclusion

Based on artificial intelligence ethical norms and the technical characteristics of Chinese large language models, this study takes cutting-edge models such as DeepSeek as the research foundation, and constructs a three-dimensional synthetic corpus quality evaluation system DSCAM with the dimensions of "Authenticity-Diversity-Ethical Safety". It realizes multi-dimensional quantitative analysis of synthetic corpus quality and ethical compliance verification. Experimental results show that the conclusions of this method in core indicators such as knowledge accuracy evaluation and value orientation detection are highly consistent with expert review results, with significantly improved processing efficiency. It has demonstrated remarkable application value in practical teaching scenarios, effectively verifying the positive role of high-quality synthetic corpora in improving teaching efficiency and promoting learners' cognitive development. This study not only provides a specific path to address the data resource bottleneck in the construction of Chinese educational resources, but more importantly, by integrating a strict ethical constraint mechanism into the evaluation system, it effectively ensures the ideological security and cultural appropriateness of generated content. It offers important practical reference for the safe, reliable, and high-quality application of large language models in the educational field, as well as for promoting the comprehensive, systematic, and balanced development of the organization of teaching knowledge systems.

Although this study has achieved phased results, it still has certain limitations. In terms of the evaluation system, the index coverage of the three-dimensional framework is not comprehensive, and the quantitative accuracy of some indicators needs to be improved. The self-built synthetic corpus constructed in the experimental link covers various types of corpora, but the data scale is relatively limited and the types are not sufficiently rich, failing to fully reflect the actual distribution characteristics of synthetic corpora. In terms of the verification scope, the empirical analysis of this study is mainly focused on online education scenarios and has achieved good results. However, there are significant differences between different disciplines in the educational field, and educational scenarios are vastly different from other fields such as medical care, finance, and law. The cross-domain and cross-scenario universality of the evaluation system and methods still needs extensive verification.

With the continuous evolution of generative artificial intelligence, the training corpora of large language models have expanded from single text to multi-modal forms such as text, audio, and video. Multi-modal synthetic corpora have become increasingly important in model training, and the evaluation of their credibility and ethical value is crucial for improving the practical application capabilities of large models. Relevant research has significant scientific value and application prospects. Future research should focus on the challenges and opportunities derived from new technologies and applications, and continuously optimize the evaluation system to adapt to the rapid development of synthetic multi-modal corpora.

Acknowledgments. This study was funded by the R&D Program of the Beijing Municipal Education Commission (Grant No. KM202451160001).

References

1. Duncombe, J.U.: Infrared navigation—Part I: an assessment of feasibility. IEEE Trans. Electron. Devices **11**(1), 34–39 (1959)
2. Alibaba Research: The State of AI Large Model Training Data White Paper. Alibaba Group, Hangzhou, China (2024)
3. Zhang, R., Zhang, Y.: DeepSeek V3/R1 in international Chinese language education: opportunities, challenges, and solutions. NJHSS **24**(1), 1–10 (2025)

4. Li, C.H., Botelho, A.F.: Balancing the imbalance: enhancing MOOC discussion forum urgency prediction with LLM-Generated data augmentation. In: Proceedings of the 15th International Conference on Computer-Supported Collaborative Learning, pp. 455–459. International Society of the Learning Sciences (2025)
5. Gartner: The Gartner 100+ Data, Analytics & AI Predictions Through 2030. Gartner (2024)
6. Wang, M., Chandra, J., Algazinov, A.: Mimicking humanity: a synthetic data-based approach to voice cloning in text-to-speech systems. EasyChair Preprint (2025)
7. Zhang, Y., et al.: A series of high-quality chinese datasets for LLM training: OpenCSG Chinese corpus (2025). arXiv preprint arXiv:2501.08197
8. Liu, X., et al.: Ensuring privacy through synthetic data generation in education. Br. J. Edu. Technol. **55**(3), 1125–1140 (2024)
9. Dai, D., et al.: DeepSeekMoE: towards ultimate expert specialization in mixture-of-experts language models (2024). arXiv preprint arXiv:2401.06066
10. DeepSeek-AI: DeepSeek-V3 technical report (2024). arXiv preprint arXiv:2412.19437
11. Rubin, D.B.: Discussion: statistical disclosure limitation. J. Official Stat. **9**(2), 461–468 (1993)
12. NVIDIA: Nemotron-4 340B: open models for generating synthetic data for large language models. NVIDIA Blog (2024)
13. Apple Inc.: Foundation language models for apple intelligence (2024). arXiv preprint arXiv: 2407.1075
14. Villalobos, P., et al.: Will we run out of data? Limits of LLM scaling based on human-generated data. Epoch AI (2024)
15. Long, L., et al.: On LLMs-Driven synthetic data generation, curation, and evaluation: a survey. In: Findings of the Association for Computational Linguistics: ACL 2024, pp. 11065–11082. Association for Computational Linguistics (2024)
16. Wang, Y., et al.: Self-Instruct: aligning language model with self generated instructions (2022). arXiv preprint arXiv:2212.10560
17. Ashrafi, N., et al.: Protect and Extend—Using GANs for synthetic data generation of time-series medical records (2024). arXiv preprint arXiv:2402.14042
18. McKinsey & Company: Technology Trends Outlook 2024. McKinsey Global Institute (2024)
19. Shi, R., et al.: A comprehensive survey of synthetic tabular data generation (2025). arXiv preprint arXiv:2504.16506
20. Chapman-Smith, R.: OpenAI's text-to-video AI, Sora, is futurism come to life. Freethink (2024)
21. Shumailov, I., et al.: AI models collapse when trained on recursively generated data. Nature **631**(8022), 755–759 (2024)
22. Lin, C.-Y.: ROUGE: a package for automatic evaluation of summaries. In: Text Summarization Branches Out, pp. 74–81. Association for Computational Linguistics (2004)
23. Papineni, K., et al.: BLEU: a method for automatic evaluation of machine translation. In: Proceedings of the 40th Annual Meeting on Association for Computational Linguistics, pp. 311–318. Association for Computational Linguistics (2002)
24. Zhang, T., et al.: BERTScore: evaluating text generation with BERT. In: Proceedings of the International Conference on Learning Representations (2019)
25. Yuan, W., et al.: Bartscore: evaluating generated text as text generation. In: Proceedings of the 34th International Conference on Neural Information Processing Systems (2021)
26. Pistilli, G.: For an ethics of conversational artificial intelligence. Sorbonne Université (2024)
27. Wang, T., et al.: Security and privacy on generative data in AIGC: a survey. ACM Comput. Surv. **57**(4), 1–25 (2024)
28. Deng, J., Zhao, Z.: The breakthrough and transformation of DeepSeek: the New rules for AIGC regulation. J. Xinjiang Norm. Univ. (Philos. Soc. Sci. Ed.) **46**(4), 99–108 (2025)

29. Mathur, N., et al.: Putting evaluation in context: contextual embeddings improve machine translation evaluation. In: Proceedings of the 57th Annual Meeting of the Association for Computational Linguistics (2019)
30. Zhao, W., et al.: MoverScore: text generation evaluating with contextualized embeddings and earth mover distance. In: Proceedings of the Conference on Empirical Methods in Natural Language Processing (2019)
31. Luo, W., Wang, H.: Evaluating large language models: a survey of research progress. J. Chin. Inf. Process. **38**(1) (2024)
32. Liu, Z., et al.: Survey on hallucinations in large language models. J. Softw. **36**(3), 1152–1185 (2025)
33. Houghtaling, M.A., et al.: Standardizing an ontology for ethically aligned robotic and autonomous systems. IEEE Trans. Syst. Man Cybern.: Syst. **54**(3), 1791–1804 (2024)
34. Huang, L., et al.: A survey on hallucination in large language models: principles, taxonomy, challenges, and open questions. ACM Trans. Inf. Syst. **43**(2), 1–55 (2025)
35. Sallam, M.: ChatGPT utility in healthcare education, research, and practice: systematic review on the promising perspectives and valid concerns. Healthcar **11**(22), 887 (2023)

Factors Influencing Educational Management Performance Results Under the EdPEx Framework

Anan Mungwattana and Naraphorn Paoprasert(✉)

Department of Industrial Engineering, Faculty of Engineering, Kasetsart University, Bangkok, Thailand
naraphorn.p@ku.th

Abstract. This study examines the relationships between Education Criteria for Performance Excellence (EdPEx) categories and institutional performance outcomes using assessment data collected from faculties within a higher education institution over a five-year period. The EdPEx framework consists of seven categories: leadership, strategy, customers, measurement, analysis and knowledge management, workforce, operations, and results. In this study, the first six categories were treated as explanatory variables, and the results category as the performance outcome. Analysis of covariance (ANCOVA) was applied to identify the factors associated with different result categories. The findings show that the influence of EdPEx categories varies across performance outcomes. Leadership and governance were associated with student learning and service outcomes. Measurement, analysis, and knowledge management contributed to several result categories, highlighting the importance of effective use of organizational information. Customer-related and operational factors were also significant predictors in several models. In contrast, some categories were significant only for specific outcomes. The results suggest that higher education institutions should focus improvement efforts on the factors most closely related to their desired outcomes rather than allocating resources equally across all categories. The study provides empirical evidence on the effectiveness of EdPEx, using actual assessment scores, and offers practical guidance for institutions seeking to improve educational management and organizational performance.

Keywords: Baldrige Framework · EdPEx · ANCOVA · Statistical Analysis · Quality Improvement

1 Introduction

Higher education institutions face increasing pressure to improve the quality of their management systems and achieve performance excellence. Expectations from students, parents, employers, and accreditation bodies continue to increase. At the same time, institutions compete domestically and internationally. Consequently, higher education institutions require systematic management frameworks that support continuous improvement and organizational excellence.

K. T. Chui et al. (Eds.): ICBL 2026, LNCS 16778, pp. 413–425, 2027.
https://doi.org/10.1007/978-981-92-3761-6_29

In Thailand, one of the most widely adopted frameworks is the Education Criteria for Performance Excellence (EdPEx). EdPEx was adapted from the Malcolm Baldrige Criteria for Performance Excellence and has been promoted as a comprehensive framework for institutional quality improvement and performance management [1]. Similar to the Baldrige framework, EdPEx adopts a systems perspective that emphasizes alignment among leadership, strategy, customers, workforce, operations, measurement, knowledge management, and organizational results. The first six categories represent organizational management processes and enabling factors, while the results category captures institutional performance outcomes. Institutions adopting EdPEx are expected to improve organizational effectiveness through systematic planning, execution, evaluation, and continuous learning.

Although many institutions have adopted EdPEx as a framework for organizational improvement, empirical evidence regarding its effectiveness remains limited. Existing studies primarily focus on implementation guidelines, self-assessment processes, or stakeholders' perceptions. Few studies have quantitatively examined how different EdPEx categories influence institutional performance using actual assessment data. Understanding these relationships is important because it allows institutions to identify which management factors contribute most strongly to organizational results.

This study used actual EdPEx assessment scores collected from a higher education institution with 18 faculties that have implemented the framework continuously for 5 years. A multivariate statistical approach was applied to investigate the relationships between EdPEx input categories and performance results at both category and subcategory levels. The findings provide empirical evidence on the effectiveness of EdPEx and offer insights to help higher education institutions prioritize improvement efforts.

2 Literature Review

2.1 Malcolm Baldrige Framework and Performance Excellence in Higher Education

The Malcolm Baldrige Criteria for Performance Excellence have served as the foundation for performance excellence initiatives across various sectors, including education [1]. The framework has been recognized as a comprehensive model for organizational assessment and continuous improvement. Several studies have examined the application of the Baldrige framework in higher education. Ilić and Ilić-Kosanović [2] examined how principles of performance excellence can support strategic management in higher education. Their study integrated the Baldrige framework with Hoshin Kanri concepts [3] and applied the approach at the School of Engineering Management in Serbia. The results showed that the framework can help institutions develop their mission, vision, and strategic direction more systematically.

Taraza et al. [4] reviewed studies on the implementation of the Baldrige framework in education. They observed that empirical research in this area remains limited. Despite the small number of studies, the available evidence suggests that institutions can benefit from adopting performance excellence principles.

Several studies have also investigated factors that influence successful implementation. Blouin and Smith [5] surveyed 491 leaders and teachers from 16 Canadian medical schools. Their findings provided evidence that the framework can support institutional quality improvement. Ibrahim [6] examined vocational education institutions and identified senior management commitment as the most important factor for successful quality management implementation. Together, these studies highlight the importance of leadership support in achieving performance excellence.

Several studies have reported successful applications of Baldrige-based frameworks in higher education. Ilić and Ilić-Kosanović [2] demonstrated the use of Baldrige principles and Hoshin Kanri to support mission development and strategic planning at the School of Engineering Management in Serbia. The framework helped align institutional goals with strategic priorities and provided a structured approach for organizational development. Ruben and Gigliotti [7] described the implementation of the Excellence in Higher Education model, a Baldrige-based framework applied in more than 100 educational organizations. The framework was used to conduct systematic self-assessments, identify organizational strengths and weaknesses, establish improvement priorities, and develop action plans. Reported benefits included stronger stakeholder engagement, better communication of institutional goals, and a greater focus on continuous improvement. These examples illustrate how performance excellence frameworks can be translated into practical management tools that support institutional effectiveness.

2.2 EdPEx and Higher Education Management in Thailand

In Thailand, the Baldrige framework has been adapted as the Education Criteria for Performance Excellence (EdPEx) [9]. The framework retains the core philosophy of performance excellence while adapting its criteria to reflect the context of higher education institutions. EdPEx has become an important mechanism for institutional quality development and internal quality assurance.

Previous studies have discussed the role of EdPEx in transforming educational quality management. Shawyun [10] argued that EdPEx represents a shift away from documentation-driven quality assurance systems toward a more integrated approach that emphasizes organizational performance and continuous improvement. The study highlighted the importance of viewing quality assurance as a long-term institutional development process rather than a compliance exercise. More recently, Phuangsuwan et al. [11] reviewed the implementation of EdPEx in Thai higher education institutions and reported increasing adoption of the framework. The authors noted that EdPEx helps institutions identify development opportunities through an integrated assessment of leadership, strategy, customer focus, workforce development, operations, measurement systems, and results. Their review further emphasized the growing importance of EdPEx as a management tool rather than merely an evaluation framework.

A limited number of empirical studies have investigated factors influencing EdPEx implementation. Mungwattana et al. [12] proposed a seven-step process known as the EdPEx Improvement Cycle to guide institutional development. How-ever, the study did not quantitatively evaluate the effectiveness of the proposed approach. Pangkasa and Armartpon [13] examined factors influencing EdPEx implementation through questionnaire-based analysis and found that management support, communication effectiveness, process clarity, and stakeholder involvement significantly contributed to successful implementation.

Despite the increasing adoption of EdPEx, empirical evidence regarding its effectiveness remains limited. Most existing studies focus on implementation guidelines, organizational readiness, or stakeholder perceptions. Few studies have quantitatively examined how the different EdPEx categories contribute to institutional performance outcomes using actual assessment score data. As a result, there is still limited evidence regarding which management factors have the strongest influence on performance results. This gap motivates the present study, which applies statistical analysis to actual EdPEx assessment data to investigate the relationships between management factors and institutional performance outcomes.

3 Methodology

To begin the statistical analysis, the seven criteria, along with the subcategory level, were carefully reviewed (Table 1). The authors then collected data by contacting all educational institutions in Thailand that had adopted EdPEx as part of their management strategy. EdPEx scoring data from 18 faculties of an institution for 2020–2024 were collected from official EdPEx assessment reports conducted by certified EdPEx assessors using standardized evaluation criteria and scoring guidelines. The assessors reviewed institutional evidence and assigned scores according to the seven-category EdPEx framework. As a result, the data represent expert evaluations of organizational performance rather than self-reported perceptions. Reliability was supported by a common assessment framework, standardized scoring procedures, and certified assessors. Validity was supported by the assessment criteria being derived from the Education Criteria for Performance Excellence framework, which was adapted from the Malcolm Baldrige Criteria for Performance Excellence and is widely adopted in higher education quality management. Therefore, the scores provide direct measures of the organizational dimensions examined in this study.

Criteria presented in Table 1 were adopted directly from the official EdPEx assessment framework [9]. Each criterion represents a specific management practice or organizational capability evaluated during the EdPEx assessment process. The use of these criteria ensures consistency with nationally recognized assessment standards and allows the analysis to reflect the actual structure of institutional performance evaluation. In Table 1, categories A to F were treated as input factors, while category X was treated as a result. Full score information was also provided for all criteria. Figure 1 plots the average scores for all input factors for all organizations. It is interesting to see that the actual scores for all 18 organizations (faculties) remain well below the full scores shown in Table 1, indicating there is definitely room for improvement and making the results of our analysis even more valuable. Figure 1 presents a heatmap of the average scores across all result categories and organizations. The heatmap provides a visual comparison of organizational performance and makes it easy to identify patterns across result categories. Darker shades indicate higher scores, while lighter shades indicate lower scores.

To identify significant factors influencing performance results while controlling for other variables, Analysis of Covariance (ANCOVA) was employed. ANCOVA combines features of analysis of variance (ANOVA) and multiple linear regression, enabling the

Table 1. EdPEx criteria and the full score for each criterion.

Category	Criteria	Full Score
A: Leadership	A1: Senior leadership A2: Governance and societal contributions	65 50
B: Strategy	B1: Strategy development	45
	B2: Strategy implementation	45
C: Customers	C1: Customer expectations	40
	C2: Customer engagement	45
D: Measurement, Analysis, and Knowledge Management	D1: Measurement, analysis, review, and improvement of organizational performance	45
	D2: Information and knowledge management	45
E: Workforce	E1: Workforce environment	40
	E2: Workforce engagement	45
F: Operations	F1: Work processes	45
	F2: Operational effectiveness	40
X: Results	X1: Student learning and processes results	120
	X2: Customer results	80
	X3: Workforce results	80
	X4: Leadership and governance results	80
	X5: Budgetary, financial, marketplace, and strategy results	90

examination of the adjusted effects of explanatory variables on a continuous result variable. ANCOVA is particularly suitable for this study because the EdPEx framework is grounded in a systems perspective, in which multiple interrelated factors jointly influence organizational outcomes. By incorporating covariates into the analysis, ANCOVA allows the estimation of each factor's unique contribution while accounting for shared variance among predictors. A backward elimination procedure was applied. All candidate explanatory variables were initially included in the model, and non-significant variables were sequentially removed based on statistical significance criteria. The Bonferroni correction was applied to adjust the significance threshold to avoid Type I error. Model significance was assessed using partial F-tests from Type II sums of squares, which evaluate the contribution of each explanatory variable while accounting for other predictors. Model fit was evaluated using the coefficient of determination (R^2) and the adjusted R^2, with the latter accounting for model complexity. Variance Inflation Factors (VIFs) were also calculated to assess potential multicollinearity among explanatory variables. VIF values below commonly accepted thresholds indicated that multicollinearity was not a major concern.

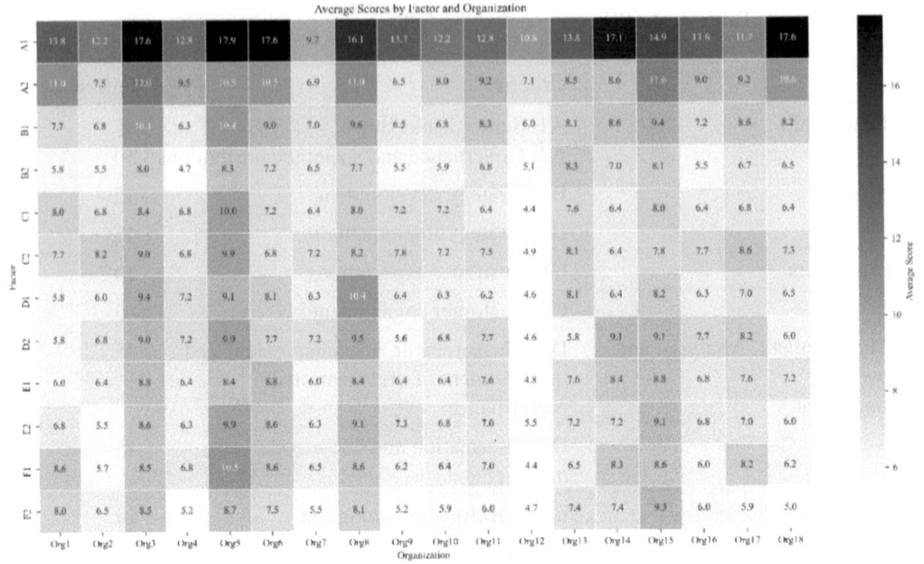

Fig. 1. Heatmap of average EdPEx result scores by organization. Darker shades represent higher average scores.

4 Results and Discussion

The heatmap in Fig. 1 shows variations in scores across organizations and EdPEx categories. Organization 5 achieved consistently high scores across most input and result categories. Organizations 3 and 8 also demonstrated strong performance in several categories. Among the result categories, Organization 5 obtained the highest overall scores, while Organizations 8, 3, and 15 also performed well. The heatmap further indicates that Organization 6 achieved relatively strong scores in leadership and governance (X4).

Table 2 presents the model evaluation results and the statistically significant factors identified through the backward elimination procedure. The selected factors were subsequently used to examine the relationships between EdPEx input categories and performance results. In Table 2, all key indicators, including the Bonferroni values, R^2 values, adjusted R^2 values, and VIF values, remain within acceptable ranges.

Table 2. Model validation measures, significant factors, and p-values for all results.

Result factor	R^2	Adjusted R^2	Bonferroni alpha	Significant factor	VIF	p-value
X1: Student learning and processes results	0.6251	0.6120	0.0167	**A2**	1.8515	0.0045
				C1	2.0253	0.0008
				D2	2.0535	0.0011
X2: Customer results	0.5849	0.5753	0.0250	**C2**	1.6441	0.0000

(continued)

Table 2. (*continued*)

Result factor	R^2	Adjusted R^2	Bonferroni alpha	Significant factor	VIF	p-value
				F2	1.6441	0.0000
X3: Workforce results	0.5723	0.5625	0.0250	**C1**	2.1312	0.0002
				F2	2.1312	0.0001
X4: Leadership and governance results	0.6477	0.6354	0.0167	**A2**	1.8515	0.0014
				C1	2.0253	0.0022
				D2	2.0535	0.0003
X5: Budgetary, financial, marketplace, and strategy results	0.5980	0.5887	0.0250	**B1**	2.0951	0.0000
				C1	2.0951	0.0003

The results show that each result dimension is influenced by a different group of factors. This suggests that institutional improvement should focus on specific results rather than applying the same management approach to all areas. Customer expectations are found to be significant in almost all of the results models. This indicates that understanding students' and other stakeholders' needs is a key driver of institutional performance. Other factors, such as operational effectiveness, governance and contribution to society, information and knowledge management, and strategy development, show significance only in certain result areas. The discussion of factors influencing each individual result is presented as follows.

4.1 Factors Influencing Student Learning and Process Results

From Table 2, the results show that student learning results are significantly affected by customer expectations, continuous governance and societal contribution, and measurement, analysis, and knowledge management. This relationship can be explained by the way learning systems operate in educational institutions. Customer expectations directly affect student learning results. When an institution makes strong efforts to understand expectations, learning goals become clearer for both students and instructors. Students understand what they are expected to achieve at the end of each program. This clarity helps students align their efforts with program goals. Understanding expectations also guides curriculum design, learning results, course content, and assessment. In addition, awareness of expectations increases student motivation. Students are more likely to engage in learning when they see clear links between learning results and future opportunities. Therefore, understanding customer expectations is a driving force for more effective learning results.

Beyond understanding customer expectations, continuous governance supports learning results by providing stability and consistency in academic systems. Moreover, contributions to society reinforce the relevance of learning results. When institutions connect education with societal needs, learning results become meaningful and applied.

Students develop competencies that benefit the community. This relevance strengthens learning effectiveness. Governance also ensures ethical conduct and fairness in teaching and assessment. Clear rules and transparent decision-making create trust in the learning system. This trust supports student engagement and commitment to learning goals.

The last significant factor influencing student learning and process results is measurement, analysis, and knowledge management, which can enable institutions to monitor and improve learning results. Data from student assessments, course evaluations, and graduate performance provide evidence of learning effectiveness. Institutions can identify gaps and weaknesses in learning processes. Knowledge management enables the sharing of best practices across programs and departments.

The results are generally consistent with previous studies. Ibrahim [6] reported that management commitment is a key factor in the successful implementation of quality management. Similarly, leadership and governance were significant predictors of student learning and service outcomes in this study. The importance of measurement and knowledge management also supports the findings of Iqbal et al. [8], who emphasized the role of organizational information and management practices in improving institutional performance. A difference from previous studies is that the present analysis was based on actual EdPEx assessment scores rather than questionnaire responses. Therefore, the findings provide empirical evidence based on institutional performance assessments rather than stakeholder perceptions.

4.2 Factors Influencing Customer Results

Customer results are significantly influenced by customer engagement and operational effectiveness. Customer expectations are not significant in this result group. This pattern reflects the nature of customer results and how they are formed in educational institutions. Customer results are strongly linked to direct experiences. Customer engagement represents how institutions interact with students and other stakeholders during service delivery. This includes communication, responsiveness, feedback handling, and relationship management. These interactions shape customer results such as satisfaction, trust, and perceived value. Even if expectations are clearly identified, customers evaluate institutions based on what they actually experience. Regular communication, timely support, and effective problem-solving therefore strongly influence customer results. This result is consistent with Pangkasa and Armartpon [13].

For a Thai institution, unmet or exceeded expectations are revealed through engagement and operations. Expectations influence results indirectly through how institutions engage customers and operate processes. When engagement and operations are included in the model, the direct effect of expectations becomes weaker.

Operational effectiveness is the second significant factor to determine how smoothly services are delivered. Efficient processes reduce delays, errors, and confusion. This directly improves customer experience. When operations are effective, customers receive services on time and with fewer problems. This leads to higher satisfaction and better customer results. Operational effectiveness also supports consistent service quality across departments. Consistency is important for customers when evaluating institutional performance. This explains the strong relationship between operational effectiveness and customer results. Unlike previous studies that focused on implementation success, this study examines performance outcomes using assessment data. The results therefore provide additional evidence regarding the contribution of customer-focused practices to organizational performance.

4.3 Factors Influencing Workforce Results

Customer expectations and operational effectiveness significantly influence workforce results. At the same time, customer expectations do not have a significant direct effect on customer results. This does not represent a contradiction. The difference lies in how expectations operate inside the institution. Customer expectations primarily influence workforce outcomes through internal mechanisms. When institutions clearly understand what students and stakeholders expect, those expectations translate into workload requirements for staff. From a Baldrige perspective, customer expectations belong to Customer Focus. Workforce results belong to the Workforce category. Baldrige theory suggests that customer requirements shape workforce systems and work design. These systems then influence customer experience through operational processes. Therefore, expectations act as upstream drivers of workforce results. Engagement and operations act as downstream drivers for customer results. Furthermore, operational effectiveness is significant for both workforce and customer results. This is because efficient processes support both staff and customers.

The significance of workforce-related factors is consistent with the findings of Iqbal et al. [8], who reported that staff development contributes to institutional performance. The results also support earlier studies that highlight the importance of employee engagement and organizational support in quality management initiatives. However, the present study identifies specific relationships between workforce factors and categories of EdPEx results. This level of analysis was not explored in most previous studies, which focused primarily on implementation factors and stakeholder perceptions.

4.4 Factors Influencing Leadership and Governance Results

Leadership and governance outcomes are significantly affected by continuous governance, contributions to society, customer expectations, and information and knowledge management. Senior leadership does not show a significant effect. These results are reasonable when considering how leadership results are evaluated in educational institutions. Leadership and governance results reflect institutional credibility, transparency, and trust. These results are strongly shaped by how well leaders respond to stakeholder expectations.

The findings are consistent with the work of Ilić and Ilić-Kosanović [2], who demonstrated the importance of leadership and strategic planning in higher education management. The significance of strategy-related factors in this study suggests that institutional performance is strongly influenced by the ability to translate organizational goals into operational activities. While previous studies mainly discussed implementation practices, the present study provides quantitative evidence linking leadership and strategy scores to performance outcomes measured through the EdPEx framework.

When leaders understand and respond to customer expectations, governance practices become more aligned with external accountability. This strengthens trust in leadership systems. Unlike customer results, leadership results are not based on service experience. They are based on perceived alignment between institutional direction and stakeholder expectations. This explains why customer expectations are significant.

Besides, continuous governance involves institutions monitoring, evaluating, and improving governance practices over time. Leadership and governance results directly depend on these mechanisms. Contribution to society is a key expectation of public and autonomous universities in Thailand—strong performance in this area signals effective governance.

Leadership and governance results are at the institutional level. These results reflect the entire system rather than personal leadership style. In many Thai educational institutions, leadership authority is formalized. Regulations and policies clearly define roles and responsibilities. As a result, variations in individual leadership behavior may not strongly influence governance results. Hence, continuous governance mechanisms better capture the drivers of governance results. This reduces the apparent impact of senior leadership. Finally, effective governance depends on information and knowledge management. Hence, it is the factor that supports leadership and governance results.

4.5 Factors Influencing Budgetary, Financial, Marketplace, and Strategy Results

Budgetary, financial, marketplace, and strategy results are significantly influenced by strategy development and customer expectations. Strategy implementation does not show a significant effect. Customer engagement, measurement, analysis, and knowledge management are also not significant. These findings reflect the nature of strategic and financial results in educational institutions. Strategy development defines institutional priorities, allocates resources, and sets long-term direction. Budget and financial results depend strongly on how strategies are formulated. When strategies are clearly developed, institutions can align budgets with strategic goals. In Thai educational institutions, strategic plans are closely linked to government funding, accreditation requirements, and performance agreements. Therefore, strategy development directly affects financial and market results. On the other hand, Strategy implementation focuses on execution at the operational level. However, budget and financial results are often determined earlier in the planning cycle. Once budgets are approved and funding is allocated, short-term variations in implementation are unlikely to significantly affect financial results. Implementation affects operational efficiency rather than strategic financial indicators. In addition, implementation activities are often constrained by regulations and fixed budget structures. This limits the visible impact of implementation on financial results in the analysis.

The second significant factor is customer expectations, which seem to directly influence market demand. Understanding expectations helps institutions design strategies that attract students and meet labor market needs.

This finding is consistent with the work of Ilić and Ilić-Kosanović [2], who emphasized the role of strategic planning in guiding institutional development and performance improvement. Their study demonstrated that clear strategic direction helps align institutional activities with long-term objectives. The present findings suggest that this alignment is also reflected in measurable organizational results.

Customer-related factors were also associated with marketplace and strategy outcomes. This observation is consistent with the EdPEx and Baldrige frameworks, which emphasize understanding stakeholder needs and translating those needs into organizational plans and services. Similar conclusions were reported by Pangkasa and Armartpon [13], who found that stakeholder involvement and communication contribute to successful EdPEx implementation. The current study extends these findings by showing that customer-related factors are associated not only with implementation success but also with organizational performance outcomes.

The significance of leadership and governance factors is also consistent with previous studies. Ibrahim [6] identified management commitment as a critical success factor in quality management initiatives. Strong leadership can influence resource allocation, policy development, and institutional priorities, all of which affect financial and strategic performance. The present results support this argument and suggest that leadership continues to play an important role even after EdPEx has been implemented.

However, similar to the previous discussion, earlier studies primarily relied on surveys, implementation reviews, or conceptual discussions. As a result, they focused on factors that support adoption of quality management frameworks. In contrast, this study evaluates the relationships between EdPEx categories and performance results using assessment data collected over multiple years. The findings therefore provide direct empirical evidence regarding which management factors are associated with financial, marketplace, and strategic outcomes.

5 Conclusions, Limitations, and Future Directions

This study examined the relationships between EdPEx input categories and institutional performance results using five years of assessment data. The findings showed that not all EdPEx categories contribute equally to performance outcomes. Leadership, strategy, customer-related factors, measurement and knowledge management, workforce factors, and operations influenced different result categories to varying degrees.

Several factors appeared repeatedly across multiple analyses. Leadership and governance were associated with student learning and service outcomes. Measurement, analysis, and knowledge management were significant for several result categories, suggesting that institutions benefit from effective use of information when making decisions and monitoring performance. Customer-related factors and operational effectiveness also contributed to several organizational outcomes.

The results provide practical implications for higher education institutions. To improve student learning and service quality, institutions should strengthen leadership practices, governance processes, and the use of performance information. Customer results can be improved by understanding students' and stakeholders' needs and by optimizing operational processes. Workforce results may benefit from clearer communication of expectations and stronger support for staff engagement. Financial and strategic outcomes require effective strategic planning and regular monitoring of performance indicators.

The findings also suggest that institutions should focus their improvement efforts on factors most closely related to their desired outcomes. Improving every category simultaneously may not be the most effective use of limited resources. Instead, institutions should identify priority areas of results and allocate resources accordingly. Several factors were not statistically significant in some models. This does not imply that these factors are unimportant. They may support organizational performance indirectly or influence results over a longer period. They may also become more important under different institutional conditions.

This study has several limitations. First, the analysis was based on data from a single higher education institution. Although the institution had implemented EdPEx continuously for five years, the findings may not fully represent other universities with different missions, governance structures, or resource levels. Second, the study was conducted within the Thai higher education system. Institutional management practices, regulatory requirements, and quality assurance expectations may differ across countries. Therefore, caution should be exercised when generalizing the results beyond the Thai context. Third, the analysis was based on assessment scores and statistical relationships among EdPEx categories. While the results identify significant associations, they do not establish direct causal relationships. Some factors may influence performance indirectly or through mechanisms that were not captured in the present study.

Future research should examine multiple institutions to determine whether similar relationships are observed across different organizational settings. Comparative studies between public and private universities may also provide additional insights. Furthermore, advanced analytical approaches such as structural equation modeling may be used to examine indirect relationships among EdPEx categories. International comparative studies would also help assess the generalizability of the findings and strengthen the evidence supporting the use of EdPEx in higher education management.

Disclosure of Interests. The authors have no competing interests to declare that are relevant to the content of this article.

References

1. Baldrige Performance Excellence Program. 2023–2024 Baldrige Excellence Framework: Proven Leadership and Management Practices for High Performance (Education). US Department of Commerce, National Institute of Standards and Technology, Gaithersburg, MD (2023)
2. Ilić, D., Ilić-Kosanović, T.: Engineering an excellence model in higher education based on Baldrige criteria and Hoshin Kanri principles. Serb. J. Eng. Manage. **4**(1), 35–44 (2019)
3. Ennals, R., Hoshin, K.: The strategic approach to continuous improvement. AI & Soc. **25**, 371–372 (2010)
4. Taraza, E., Anastasiadou, S., Masouras, A.: Malcolm Baldrige National Quality Award (MBNQA) quality tool in education. A systematic literature review. Eur. Conf. Innovation Entrepreneurship **18**(1), 29–38 (2023)
5. Bluin, D., Smith, E.: Measuring the continuous quality improvement orientation of medical education programs. A validity study of the Baldrige "are we making progress" questionnaire. Int. J. Health Care Qual. Assur. **33**(2), 158–171 (2020)

6. Ibrahim, A.: Selection of total quality management implementation success factors for vocational education institutes using analytic hierarchy process. In: Maurya, A., Srivastava, A.K., Jha, P.K., Pandey, S.M. (eds.) Recent Trends in Mechanical Engineering. Lecture Notes in Mechanical Engineering. Springer, Singapore (2023)
7. Ruben, B.D., Gigliotti, R.A.: The excellence in higher education model: a Baldrige-based tool for organizational assessment and improvement for colleges and universities. GBOE **38**(4), 26–37 (2019)
8. Iqbal, T., Ahmad, S., Aftab, F., Mahmood, C.K.: Enhancing higher education institutions' performance: the mediating role of academic accreditation in quality management initiatives in UAE. SAGE Open **15**(3) (2025)
9. Office of the Permanent Secretary, Ministry of Higher Education, Science, Research and Innovation. Ket Khunnaphap Kan Sueksapuea Kan Damnoen Ngan Thi Pen Loet Chabap Pi 2567–2570 [Education criteria for performance excellence (EdPEx) 2024–2027], (2024). http://www.edpex.org
10. Shawyun, T.: Thai EdPEX: fad or sustainable education performance excellence. J. Suvarnabhumi Inst. Technol. (Hum. Soc. Sci.) **3**(2), 52–84 (2017)
11. Phuangsuwan, P., Siripipatthanakul, S., Suttipong, R., Praesri, S., Wadpong, S.: Development of higher education institutions based on education criteria for performance excellence (EdPEx) in Thailand. Adv. Knowl. Executives **3**(1), 1–14 (2024)
12. Mungwattana, A., Paoprasert, N., Prayadsab, P., Yousuk, R.: An improvement cycle framework of Education Criteria for Performance Excellence (EdPEx) for Thai higher education. In: 2025 International Symposium on Educational Technology (ISET), pp. 1–5. Bangkok, Thailand (2025)
13. Pangkasa, T., Armartpon, T.: Factors affecting the operation of the internal education quality assurance system according to the criteria for developing educational quality towards excellences (EdPEx) Udon Thani Educational Center Suan Sunandha Rajabhat University. In: 18th National and International Conference "Advancing Knowledge for Societal and Economic Development," Osaka, Japan (2025)

Identifying Multi-Level Interaction Patterns Based on Learner Avatar in the Educational Metaverse

Zhongmei Han[1], Xuan Xue[1], Ziwei Dang[1], and Siyi Wu[1,2](✉)

[1] Zhejiang Key Laboratory of Intelligent Education Technology and Application, Zhejiang Normal University, Jinhua 321004, Zhejiang, China
siyiw2002@163.com

[2] Zhenhai High School, Ningbo 315200, Zhejiang, China

Abstract. The Educational Metaverse offers new opportunities for immersive and personalized learning, with virtual avatars serving as the primary interface for interaction. However, existing designs overlook pedagogical requirements and interaction logic, resulting in interaction blind spots and limited cognitive engagement. Therefore, this study develops a learner avatar for Educational Metaverse environments, examines avatar-based interaction model, and constructs a multi-level interaction pattern, which is validated through experiments on the VRChat platform. Specifically, a multi-dimensional learner avatar model is proposed based on perspectivity, embodiment, and situatedness. Interaction behaviors are further operationalized into three levels (operational, informational, and conceptual), enabling the identification of four learner types (exploratory, reflective, practical, and focused learners) based on interaction frequency and depth. The effects of the multi-level interaction pattern on academic performance are then examined. The results indicate that lower interaction frequency within high-level interaction is associated with deeper engagement. Group interaction demonstrates intra-group homogeneity and inter-group heterogeneity, with high-level exploratory learners unaffected by low-level learners. Exploratory learners achieve the highest academic performance, and interaction types are significantly associated with learning outcomes. These findings offer theoretical and practical implications for the application of the Educational Metaverse in blended learning.

Keywords: Educational Metaverse · Learner Avatar · Multi-Level Interaction · Blended Learning

1 Introduction

With the maturation of technologies such as 5G, Virtual Reality (VR), Artificial Intelligence (AI), the concept of the "Metaverse" has emerged and is viewed as a key direction for the digital economy and the digital transformation of education [1]. By employing innovative teaching methods, providing diverse learning resources, facilitating rich learning activities, and implementing multidimensional learning assessments, the Educational Metaverse aims to foster the intellectual development of learners. In this study,

K. T. Chui et al. (Eds.): ICBL 2026, LNCS 16778, pp. 426–443, 2027.
https://doi.org/10.1007/978-981-92-3761-6_30

the Educational Metaverse is defined as an intelligent blended learning environment that integrates the virtual and real worlds, enabling students to engage in free and efficient learning within a more vivid, engaging, and authentic classroom setting [2].

Compared with traditional online learning environments, the Educational Metaverse provides stronger immersive experiences and richer interactive support, which helps address the limitations of existing educational software and hardware in sustaining authentic learning interaction. In the Educational Metaverse, avatars serve as the learners' entry points into digital teaching environments, guiding them to participate in interactive activities, facilitating engagement, and thereby shaping the learning space [3]. Furthermore, avatars represent learners' virtual selves and establish a close connection with them. The information perceived by learners in the Educational Metaverse is translated into avatar behavior, and avatars interact with real-world learners in the virtual space through various learning activities [4]. More importantly, to achieve the symbiosis of virtual and real educational elements in the Educational Metaverse, teachers and students, as well as students among themselves, must be able to establish diverse forms of interaction through their virtual avatars. For example, by utilizing terminal devices to simulate interactive effects such as visual, auditory, and tactile sensations, learners can facilitate interactive communication in the learning process.

Learning interaction is a central component of the Educational Metaverse, directly influencing instructional effectiveness and the quality of knowledge construction [5]. However, there are still shortcomings in the current design of learner avatars and interaction patterns. Existing studies predominantly focus on the technical implementation and ethical considerations of avatars, while overlooking pedagogically grounded interactions both between avatars and learners and among avatars themselves, thereby limiting the adaptability of avatar design to instructional contexts [6]. For example, current avatar designs rarely support differentiated instructional needs such as collaborative inquiry, reflective learning, embodied practice, or adaptive interaction guidance across different learning scenarios. Moreover, interaction patterns exhibit "blind spots", as learners lack clearly defined boundaries for interaction behaviors and explicit guidance for interaction pathways [7]. This deficiency reflects a deeper absence of a structured interaction framework. Therefore, it is essential to conceptualize interaction as a multi-level process and construct a learner-avatar interaction pattern that systematically supports different levels of engagement in Educational Metaverse environments. To address this issue, this study constructs a multi-level interaction framework for learner avatars in the Educational Metaverse, classifies different learner interaction patterns, and further explores the relationship between interaction behaviors and learning performance.

2 Literature Review

2.1 Educational Metaverse

The Educational Metaverse is a blended learning environment integrating virtual and physical worlds, supported by technologies such as virtual reality, augmented reality, and blockchain [8]. Researchers have primarily focused on its conceptualization, technical frameworks, and macro-level characteristics, with particular emphasis on system architecture, user experience, and collaborative functions [9]. Nevertheless, limited attention has been paid to the internal interaction patterns that shape learner engagement and knowledge construction in educational contexts. Meanwhile, concerns regarding social order and ethical governance have been widely discussed. The extensive tracking of user data in the metaverse raises risks related to privacy, virtual identity, and behavioral regulation [10, 11]. Although immersive environments offer new opportunities for educational innovation, they may also lead to reduced real-world engagement and excessive use. From an application perspective, the metaverse has been explored across domains such as education, e-commerce, healthcare, and logistics, demonstrating its potential to enhance interaction and address limitations of traditional online environments [12]. However, these studies remain largely exploratory and lack in-depth empirical evidence. Overall, existing research pays insufficient attention to structured interaction design in educational contexts, particularly patterns that support multi-level learning engagement. In this regard, the learner avatar, as the primary interface for interaction in the Educational Metaverse, provides a critical entry point for addressing these limitations.

2.2 Learner Avatar

Virtual avatars serve as the primary medium through which users interact with the metaverse environment. Existing theoretical research has conceptualized avatar characteristics from multiple dimensions, including similarity, familiarity, appeal, interactivity, and customization [13]. These attributes have been shown to play a crucial role in shaping user experience, thereby providing an important theoretical foundation for avatar design. From a technical perspective, significant progress has been made in avatar construction and motion representation [14]. Current approaches include optical motion capture systems that enable real-time tracking of human movement with high precision, as well as sensor-based methods that integrate inertial data to support activity recognition. In addition, model-based techniques have been developed to simulate human motion by incorporating physiological features, facilitating the visualization of dynamic behaviors [15]. Such technologies have also been applied in various simulation and training contexts. Despite these advances, existing research has largely focused on general avatar design and technical implementation [16], with limited attention to learner avatars in educational settings [17]. In particular, further research is needed to explore how avatar characteristics align with instructional objectives and how they support meaningful learning interactions.

2.3 Interaction in Learning

The interactive behaviors and patterns of avatars have a significant impact on the learning outcomes of learners in the Educational Metaverse [16]. A variety of interaction models and strategies have been proposed, including social network-based learning models, hierarchical interaction frameworks, and role-based interaction patterns in virtual learning environments. These approaches emphasize the integration of learner roles, interaction content, and learning environments to facilitate effective knowledge construction [18]. In addition, interaction design has also been increasingly framed as learner-centered, highlighting the importance of user experience and the role of well-structured interaction frameworks in supporting meaningful learning [19]. Recently, research has primarily focused on the relationship between interaction and learning outcomes [20]. Findings suggested that higher levels of interaction are positively associated with improved academic performance, with deep interaction playing a particularly critical role in enhancing learning efficiency [21]. Moreover, learners who occupy central positions within interaction networks tend to achieve better performance, underscoring the importance of interaction structure and social dynamics [22]. Existing research has primarily focused on traditional online and blended learning environments [23]. Scholars are calling for more empirical research on online learning interactions, arguing that traditional static coding is no longer sufficient to meet research needs [24]. Consequently, research on avatar-mediated interaction in metaverse-based learning remains limited, particularly with regard to the systematic development of multi-level interactive behaviors to support the learning process.

2.4 Research Questions

Research on the multi-level interaction patterns of learner avatars in the Educational Metaverse is an emerging field that integrates metaverse technology, educational theory, and cognitive science. Existing research has gradually evolved from single technological implementation or theoretical discussion to an integrated direction of technology adaptation, theoretical support and practical verification. However, existing studies still lack a systematic understanding of how learner avatars support instructional interaction, how multi-level interaction patterns are formed, and how these interaction patterns influence learning outcomes in Educational Metaverse environments. Therefore, this study investigates learner avatar-based interaction patterns in the Educational Metaverse, taking into account its unique characteristics, with the aim of providing both theoretical insights and practical guidance for pedagogical advancement. Accordingly, the core research questions of this study are as follows:

(1) How can learner avatars be effectively designed in the Educational Metaverse to support instructional goals?
(2) What interaction behavior patterns emerge in learner-avatar interactions, and how can these patterns provide effective guidance for multi-level interactions?
(3) To what extent does the avatar-based multi-level interaction pattern influence learners' academic performance, and how is it associated with learning outcomes?

3 Methodology

3.1 Participants

The participants of this study were 25 undergraduate students (10 males and 15 females; aged 21.2 on average) majoring in Chemistry, Physics, Geography, and Biological Sciences Education at a university in China. All of them reported having no prior knowledge or experience in the Educational Metaverse. Ethical approval for this study was granted by the relevant university committee.

3.2 Learning Design in the Educational Metaverse

In this study, the learning tasks were designed to provide participants with a comprehensive understanding of the Educational Metaverse via hands-on experience.

The instructional design followed a structured workflow comprising four phases: preparation, classroom activity, group task (after class), and data collection and analysis (see Fig. 1).

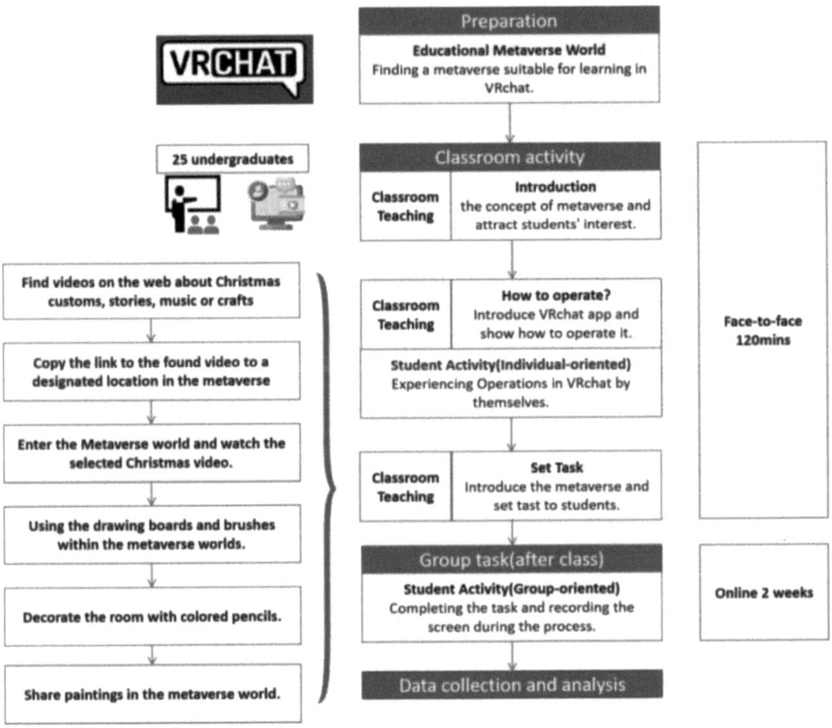

Fig. 1. Workflow of the Educational Metaverse learning experiment.

Prior to the course, this study conducted a systematic exploration of various metaverse platforms. After comprehensively comparing their immersion, interactivity and usability, the VRChat platform was ultimately selected as the metaverse experimental environment for this study. The Christmas-themed scene was selected based on its immersive atmosphere, interactive affordances, and suitability for both individual and collaborative activities. This environment allowed participants to watch instructional videos and engage in creative painting tasks. Integrating the principles of perspectivity, embodiment and situatedness, virtual avatars were designed to enhance the learning outcomes and experiences of learners in the Educational Metaverse (see Fig. 2). Virtual avatars enabled multiple interactive modalities, such as voice, text, motion, visual, and environmental interaction. The two-hour in-class session equipped participants with foundational knowledge and practical skills related to the Educational Metaverse. It began with a lecture on key concepts, followed by step-by-step guidance on operating the VRChat platform. Participants then engaged in hands-on practice to familiarize themselves with navigation, communication tools, and interactive features within the selected scene.

Following the classroom session, participants completed a collaborative group task within two weeks. This open-ended activity required group members to interact within the metaverse scene to discuss, create, and complete their assignments. Participants recorded their interactions throughout the process and submitted video files as final deliverables, capturing both the process and outcomes of their collaborative work. All interaction sessions were recorded, either automatically by the platform or manually by participants during the two-week period. The research team then analyzed and coded the submitted videos to examine patterns of interaction, collaboration, and learning outcomes in the Educational Metaverse environment.

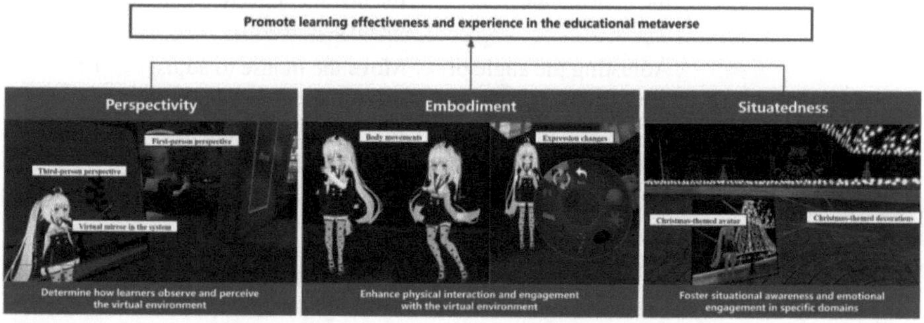

Fig. 2. Virtual avatars in the Educational Metaverse.

3.3 Coding Scheme

According to a learning process model centered on instructional interaction, students engaged in adaptive and dialogic interactions during the learning process [25]. Building on this existing concept, some scholars have developed a modified and expanded model, proposing an instructional interaction model and a hierarchy of instructional interaction specifically tailored to distance learning [26]. They classified instructional interaction into three main domains: operational interaction (OI), informational interaction (II), and conceptual interaction (CI). To explore the multi-level interactive behaviors of learners in metaverse learning environments, the interactive behavior coding framework developed by Chen Li was adopted. This coding scheme was structured around three dimensions (behavior, knowledge, and conceptual interaction) and enabled a comprehensive examination of learners' behavioral engagement and knowledge acquisition within the metaverse. More importantly, different dimensions of avatar interaction, including operational, informational, and conceptual interaction, contribute to learners' behavioral participation, emotional immersion, and cognitive engagement in the Educational Metaverse (see Table 1).

Table 1. The behavior classification table and code numbers.

Domain	Behaviour	Explanation of behaviour	encoding
	Entering/exiting the world	Entering or exiting a metaverse world created by the group	1.1
OI	Setting new worlds in group	New worlds in VRChat for group members to access	1.2
	Shortcut action via "R"	Call up the dials with the shortcut key R for quick actions	1.3
	Operating the buttons in the world to change the appearance	Manipulate preset buttons in the created world to change the layout, appearance in the metaverse worlds	1.4
	Adjusting the angle of view	Move the mouse to adjust the perspective of the avatar	1.5
	Picking up or putting down colour pencils/brushes	Pick up or put down the coloured pencils or brushes in the world of the metaverse	1.6
	Changing colors	Adjust the colour of the brush in avatar's hand	1.7
Avatars II and Avatars	Social Communication	Chilling, discussions unrelated to the content of the task	2.1
	Participatory communication	Task-related queries, clarifications	2.2
	Discussion-based communication	Share reflections and insights on the content of the assignment with group members	2.3
	Exemplary communication	Examples learned from the video	2.4
	Emotional communication	Personal emotional interactions related to the course, including expressions of encouragement, praise, and gratitude	2.5
	Explanatory communication	In-depth analysis and further examples of knowledge	2.6
	Cognitive communication	Expressions based on critical thinking	2.7

(continued)

Table 1. (*continued*)

Domain	Behaviour	Explanation of behaviour	encoding
Avatars and information	Sharing Resource Links	Find videos on the web and paste the link to the video into the link sharing place in the world	3.1
	Watching the video	Watch videos played in the world	3.2
	Watching group members painting/photographing	Viewing paintings and photographs taken by group members or themselves	3.3
	Photographing	Take pictures with the Polaroid in the metaverse world or with VRChat's own camera!	3.4
	Checking out the tasks	Check out the tasks assigned	3.5
CI	Resolving difficult problems	The behavior of seeking solutions when encountering difficulties and completing tasks	4.1
	Gaining consensus	Behaviour of reaching consensus with group members on certain points of knowledge	4.2
	Completing the work	Behaviour of active completion of assigned work	4.3
	Reflection and evaluation	Reflecting on and evaluating the content of the task	4.4

As learners engage with the Educational Metaverse, interactive learning behaviors at different levels were not isolated from one another; rather, they were interconnected and influenced one another. Operational interaction, also known as surface-level interactive behaviour, served as the foundation for deeper interactive behaviour. This deeper behaviour encompassed the immediate response of the student and their initial exploration of the metaverse. Informational interaction at the intermediate level was actively based on lower-level interaction behaviour. The process primarily entailed questioning to complete tasks, reflecting on information, organizing knowledge, and actively constructing knowledge through discourse and interaction between learners and information. Conceptual interaction, which involved high-level interactive learning behaviour, was more challenging and required development after reaching a particular degree of low-level and middle-level interactive behaviour. It entailed the active process of constructing and evaluating knowledge. The learner avatar engaged in high-level conceptual interaction within the Educational Metaverse after the current operations and learner exchanges reached a specific threshold. These three interaction levels form a progressive hierarchy, in which operational interaction provides the foundation for informational interaction, while conceptual interaction represents the highest level of cognitive engagement and knowledge construction.

3.4 Data Analysis

After the 25 students participating in the study submitted their video assignments, each dataset contained interaction behavioral data, including interaction frequency, communication duration, operational behaviors, and collaborative activities coded according to the coding scheme. Moreover, the data analysis consisted of two steps, each with its own analysis method. The analysis process is shown in Fig. 3.

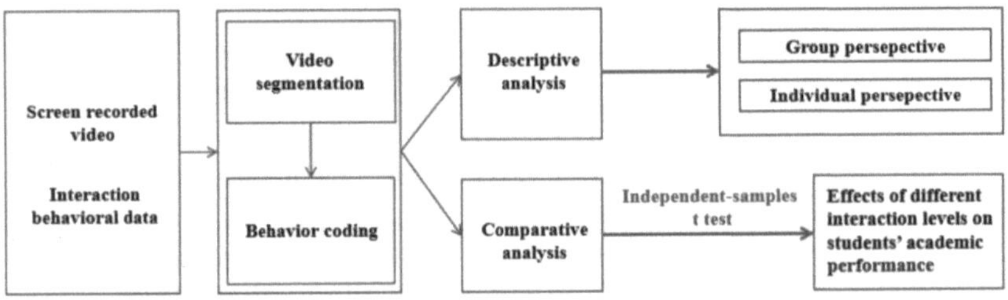

Fig. 3. Workflow of data analysis in the Educational Metaverse.

The video data was encoded by slice according to the encoding table and organized into separate data tables for each learner. The slicing was performed in such a way that one segment of each participant in the interaction had a fully meaningful behaviour. Gaps in the timeline were coded to be supplemented with 1.5 (switching perspectives) to ensure that each learner remained consistently engaged in the timeline. Behaviors were analyzed and categorized based on different levels of avatar engagement within the Educational Metaverse. A two-dimensional framework was then formed based on the number of learner interactions and the level of interaction.The degree of interaction hierarchy was determined by calculating the proportion of time allocated to each level of behaviour relative to the total time spent. A higher percentage indicates a higher level of behavioral interaction. Since learners may exhibit dual behaviors simultaneously, such as completing a task while engaging in conversation with a group member, it is conceivable for the combined percentages of the three levels to exceed 100%. The avatar interactions refer to the cumulative count of all actions performed on a specific video segment. The two axes were established by calculating the mean of the avatar interaction levels and the total number of interactions.

In order to explore the characteristics of learner avatar' interacting in the Educational Metaverse, the data were analyzed using descriptive and correlation analysis. From an individual perspective, the data were analyzed by describing the characteristics of each level of interaction and each type of learner interaction, and exploring the relationship between the level of interaction and the number of interactions. From a group perspective, the analysis described the characteristics of each group's interaction behaviors and explored whether there was a difference in the impact of different levels of interaction on other learners in the same group, and whether it affected the tendency and willingness of other learners in the group to interact.

Next step was to explore whether the different levels of interactive behaviour had an effect on students' academic performance. Firstly set up an evaluation system and made a scoring sheet for the scoring criteria of the task. A total of four dimensions were summarized for use in the scoring sheet: task completion, relevance of the work to the video, creativity of the work, and aesthetics of the work. The percentages were 30%, 30%, 20% and 20% respectively. The two dimensions of task completion and relevance of the task to the video were more objective, so the first two dimensions were scored by the author. The last two dimensions were creativity and aesthetics, which were more subjective, so three volunteers were invited to score them at the same time, and the average of the scores was taken as the final score obtained by the learner. The relationship between students' academic performance and the level of student interaction was analyzed using an independent samples t-test based on the scores obtained by the students.

4 Results

4.1 Classification of Learners

Based on the two-dimensional framework analyzing interaction frequency and depth, 25 learners were categorized into four distinct groups with significant differences in both numerical distribution and behavioral characteristics. From Fig. 4, The first quadrant (Q1) comprised three exploratory learners who demonstrated high-level interactions with frequent engagement. These learners actively participated in group discussions, thoroughly explored virtual space functionalities, and produced high-quality task outputs through deep and comprehensive interactions. The second quadrant (Q2) included seven reflective learners characterized by high-level interactions with low frequency. They prioritized independent thinking and creative expression, maintaining minimal interaction with peers while delivering high-quality outputs through deep cognitive engagement. The fourth quadrant (Q4) consisted of seven practical learners who exhibited low-level interactions with frequent but superficial operations, focusing on basic virtual space experiences without deep cognitive participation or creative output. The largest group (Q3) comprised eight focused learners who maintained low-level interactions with minimal peer engagement. Their interactions primarily involved basic operational behaviors, resulting in lower task completion rates and innovation in their outputs.

Additionally, several outliers were observed in Fig. 4. For example, some exploratory learners demonstrated exceptionally high interaction frequencies while maintaining relatively high conceptual interaction levels. This may be attributed to their strong collaboration willingness and active participation in exploratory activities. In contrast, several reflective learners exhibited extremely low interaction frequencies but high conceptual interaction proportions, indicating that deep cognitive engagement can also emerge through highly focused and independent learning behaviors.

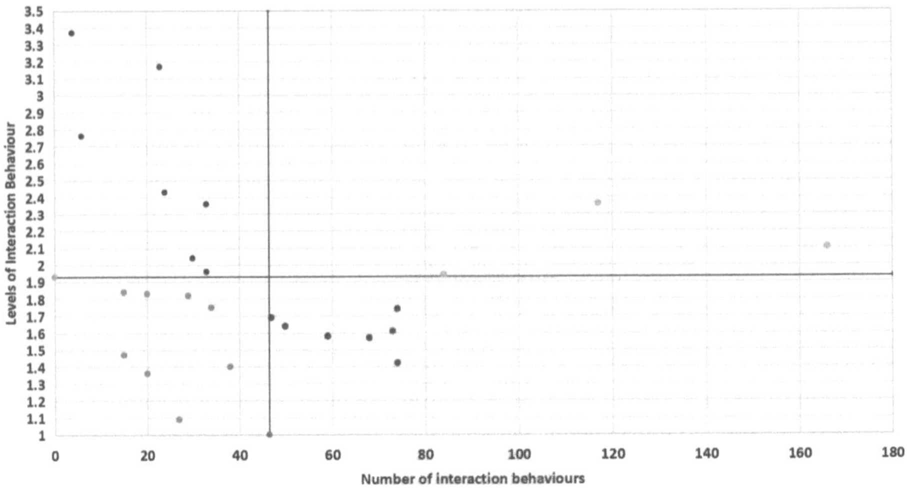

Fig. 4. Scatter plot of learner interaction characteristics.

4.2 Analysis of Interactive Behavior Characteristics

From an overall interaction perspective, the three behavioral tiers (operational, informational, and conceptual interaction) exhibited distinct distribution patterns. Operational interaction accounted for 41.63% on average, with a peak of 74.12% and a low of 1.59%. This primarily included basic actions like entering/leaving virtual worlds, adjusting perspectives, demonstrating its foundational role in all interactions and adaptability to specific scenarios. Informational interaction averaged 30.7%, peaking at 74.15%. Some learners did not engage in informational interaction. This tier further divided into avatar interactions (10.41% average) and avatar-information interactions (20.39% average). The behavioral types within avatar interactions (such as, social, participatory, and discussion-based) showed balanced time distribution, reflecting diverse interaction content. Conceptual interaction averaged 30.03%, encompassing deep-level behaviors like completing projects, resolving issues, reaching consensus, and reflective evaluations, highlighting learners' emphasis on core tasks.

Table 2 showed the differences in interaction among different types of learners. Exploratory learners exhibited 27.94% operational interactions, 40.04% avatar-to-avatar interactions, 9.76% avatar-to-information interactions, and 28.59% conceptual interactions, averaging 122.33 interactions per session. This demonstrated their deep collaboration and cognitive engagement through intensive information and conceptual exchanges. Reflective learners showed 24.01% operational interactions, 5.86% avatar-to-avatar interactions, 24.94% avatar-to-information interactions, and 57.36% conceptual interactions, averaging 21.86 interactions per session. Their significantly higher conceptual interaction rate highlighted their core strengths in independent reflection and deep cognition. Practical learners dominated with 52.52% operational interactions, 9.57% avatar-to-avatar interactions, 19.67% avatar-to-information interactions, and only 16.81% conceptual interactions, averaging 63.57 interactions per session. This reflected their superficial participation and relatively limited engagement in information and conceptual exchanges. Focused learners maintained balanced but generally low interaction levels: 52.66% operational interactions, 4.03% avatar-to-avatar interactions, 21.01% avatar-to-information interactions, and 18.23% conceptual interactions, averaging 24.75 interactions per session. Their overall lack of proactive engagement and motivation for deep participation was evident.

Further analysis of the correlation between interaction frequency and interaction levels revealed distinct patterns. At the individual level, high-level learners (explorers and reflectors) demonstrated that fewer interactions facilitated deeper engagement. For example, reflectors achieved the highest proportion of conceptual interactions with minimal interactions, while explorers, despite frequent interactions, experienced cognitive resource allocation from low-level operational tasks, resulting in slightly lower conceptual interaction rates. For low-level learners (practitioners and focused learners), interaction frequency showed no significant impact on interaction levels. Even with frequent interactions, practitioners struggled to enhance depth, remaining at superficial operational levels. At the group level, significant differences emerged in interaction frequency and levels across groups, while intra-group interactions tended to be homogeneous. Groups 1 and 2, predominantly composed of reflectors, exhibited high interaction levels with fewer interactions, whereas Groups 3 and 5, mainly consisting of explorers and practitioners, demonstrated more frequent interactions with greater level variations. Additionally, high-level explorers maintained their depth of interaction independently, showing strong autonomy and stability, as they were less influenced by low-level peers within the same group.

Table 2. Comparison of interactions across different types of learners.

Indicator	Exploratory learners	Reflective learners	Practical learners	Focused learners
Mean (S.D)				
Proportion of operational interaction time	27.94% (1.43%)	24.01% (16.39%)	52.52% (11.92%)	52.66% (17.47%)
Proportion of avatar–avatar interaction time	40.04% (23.32%)	5.86% (5.94%)	9.57% (8.42%)	4.03% (5.32%)
Proportion of avatar–information interaction time	9.76% (8.24%)	24.94% (12.40%)	19.67% (8.01%)	21.01% (18.35%)
Proportion of conceptual interaction time	28.59% (20.97%)	57.36% (24.77%)	16.81% (5.53%)	18.23% (9.79%)
Total number of interactions	122.33 (41.26)	21.86 (12.19)	63.57 (11.59)	24.75 (8.61)

4.3 The Association Between Multi-Level Interaction Patterns and Academic Performance

The multi-level interaction pattern reflected a progressive cognitive development process from surface-level operational engagement to deep conceptual understanding. As shown in Table 3, the academic performance of different learner types showed distinct correlations with their interactive practice characteristics. Exploratory learners achieved an average score of 81, excelling in task completion and work-video relevance dimensions while demonstrating moderate creativity and aesthetic appeal. Through deep collaboration and cognitive engagement, they accurately grasped core requirements and delivered high-quality results. Reflective learners scored 74.29, showing strong creativity and aesthetics but slightly weaker task completion and work relevance. Their independent reflection and creative expression gave them quality advantages, though insufficient collaboration limited comprehensive task execution. Practical learners scored the lowest at 51.13, performing poorly across all dimensions, particularly in creativity and aesthetics. Superficial interaction patterns hindered deep cognition and creative output, resulting in poor academic performance. Focused learners achieved 73.79, excelling in task completion while maintaining average performance across dimensions. Their lack of interactive experience and creative stimulation led to mediocre overall results without standout features.

The correlation analysis between interaction patterns and academic performance revealed three key relationships: Interaction levels showed positive correlations with task completion rates and project-video relevance. Exploratory and reflective learners demonstrated higher engagement in advanced interactions, achieving deeper task comprehension and precise integration of video core content into creative works, which contributed to their superior performance in these dimensions. Interaction frequency correlated positively with project creativity and visual appeal. Exploratory and hands-on learners frequently collaborated, sparking innovative ideas through frequent exchanges while refining visual presentation through iterative revisions, thereby enhancing their creative and aesthetic scores. Overall, exploratory learners combined high interaction levels with frequent engagement, ensuring thorough task understanding while stimulating creativity through active participation, ultimately achieving optimal academic outcomes. Reflective and focused learners each exhibited distinct strengths but also notable limitations: the former demonstrated creativity but lacked collaboration, while the latter focused on fundamentals but lacked breakthroughs. Hands-on learners, despite frequent interactions, struggled to achieve significant academic improvement due to insufficient interaction levels, highlighting the critical impact of interaction quality on learning effectiveness.

Table 3. Score statistics for each type of learner.

Learner type	Score of task completion	Score of relevance between artwork and video	Score of creativity	Score of aesthetic quality	Total score
	Mean (S.D)				
Exploratory learners	30.00 (0.00)	23.33 (2.89)	13.67 (4.93)	14.00 (3.00)	81.00 (10.58)
Reflective learners	25.71 (7.32)	21.42 (3.78)	13.71 (3.99)	13.43 (4.58)	74.29 (16.67)
Practical learners	20.63 (3.47)	13.50 (5.55)	9.13 (4.61)	7.88 (4.32)	51.13 (15.75)
Focused learners	28.93 (2.83)	19.29 (3.45)	13.43 (4.28)	12.14 (4.63)	73.79 (13.22)

5 Discussion and Implications

This study identifies three key elements for adapting to Educational Metaverse scenarios: the learner avatar's perspective, embodiment, and locality. These three elements synergize and organically integrate to create a unified "perception-body-context" virtual learning experience, laying a solid foundation for effective interaction in virtual environments [27]. Moreover, avatar interactions in Educational Metaverse can be categorized into three progressive levels: operational interaction, informational interaction, and conceptual interaction, demonstrating a clear cognitive development logic (see Fig. 5). Operational interaction serves as the foundation for all interactions, informational interaction bridges surface-level operations with deep cognition, while conceptual interaction is the core of knowledge construction. The organic combination of these three elements fully mobilizes learners' cognitive resources, promoting deep knowledge internalization and application. Furthermore, a two-dimensional classification framework based on interaction frequency and levels accurately distinguishes interaction characteristics among different learner types [28]. Four learner categories (exploratory, reflective, practical, and focused learners) show significant differences in interaction initiative, participation depth, and collaboration willingness, which directly influence their academic performance. The study further reveals that interactive patterns exhibit distinct selectivity in influencing academic performance. Multi-level interaction patterns primarily affect task accuracy and the relevance of student-created works and videos. More importantly, high-level interactions enable learners to thoroughly comprehend task requirements and precisely grasp learning content. Interaction frequency mainly impacts the creativity and aesthetic quality of works. More frequent interactions foster creative exchanges among learners and refine their creations. To a certain extent, only by achieving a synergistic integration of high-level interactions and frequent interactions can learning outcomes be maximized, ultimately leading to optimal academic performance. Specifically, the observed intra-group homogeneity suggests that collaborative learning environments may gradually shape learners' interaction tendencies through shared participation patterns. In contrast, inter-group heterogeneity indicates that different group compositions may produce distinct collaborative dynamics and learning outcomes in Educational Metaverse environments. This finding highlights the importance of group formation strategies and interaction guidance in virtual collaborative learning.

In terms of avatar design optimization, three key functions warrant particular attention. First, improve the camera angle switching feature. It is recommended to implement a one-click perspective switching feature in Educational Metaverse platforms, eliminating the need for indirect methods like mirrors, thereby reducing operational costs and enhancing learners' perspective adaptation efficiency across different learning scenarios [29]. Second, diversify the forms of embodied interaction. This involves improving motion capture technology accuracy to support real-time simulation of complex gestures, body movements, and facial expressions, while optimizing shortcut key systems for learners without VR devices. This ensures more diverse and learner-centric embodied interaction options, guaranteeing optimal experiences across various device conditions. Third, enhance situational adaptability. Platforms should develop diversified scenario templates and avatar material libraries tailored to specific teaching themes and subject characteristics [30]. For example, providing laboratory-dressed avatars and virtual experimental equipment for science experiments, and culturally contextualized avatars with authentic communication scenarios for language learning. This deep integration of avatars with learning environments will significantly enhance situational immersion.

In addition, priority should be given to three core approaches for optimizing teaching strategies. First, design differentiated tasks for different learner types [31]. Provide collaborative inquiry tasks for exploratory learners to leverage their strengths in deep interaction and teamwork; offer creative assignments for reflective learners to foster independent thinking and self-expression; create tiered practice tasks for practical learners to guide them from surface-level operations to deeper engagement; and design guided tasks for focused learners with clear steps and moderate interaction incentives to stimulate proactive participation. Second, cultivate a positive group collaboration atmosphere. When forming study groups, appropriately mix different learner types to maximize the exemplary role of exploratory learners, driving group members to enhance interaction quality. Establish clear collaboration rules and task distribution to prevent negative influences from low-level learners [32], creating a "stronger leading weaker, collaborative progress" group interaction ecosystem. Third, strengthen interaction guidance and feedback. Before virtual teaching begins, define interaction goals, methods, and evaluation criteria for different learning stages to provide clear guidance. During instruction, monitor learners' interactions in real-time, offering timely feedback and encouragement for deep engagement and effective collaboration, while promptly correcting superficial operations and meaningless interactions to guide learners toward high-quality interactions.

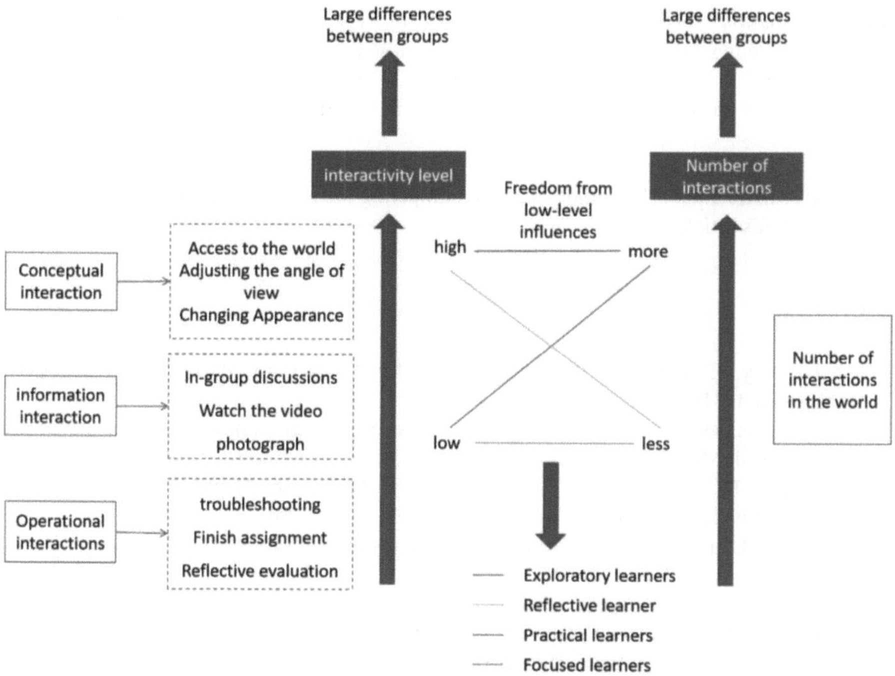

Fig. 5. Diagram of avatar-based learner interaction patterns in the Educational Metaverse.

6 Conclusions

This study examines interaction patterns of learner avatars in the Educational Metaverse and proposes a multidimensional model to guide avatar design, providing a structured framework for Educational Metaverse applications. Moreover, it proposes a three-tiered interaction behavior system, systematically revealing the intrinsic characteristics and logical relationships of multi-level interaction. Furthermore, a learner classification model based on interaction frequency and proficiency level categorizes learners into four groups (exploratory, reflective, practical, and focused learners), clearly defining the interaction characteristics and behavioral preferences of each type. The study verifies the significant correlation between avatar interaction patterns and academic performance, discovering that exploratory learners exhibit an optimal interaction pattern combining high interaction levels and frequent interactions, which most effectively enhances learning outcomes. More importantly, this provides solid empirical evidence for optimizing teaching strategies. The study effectively fills a gap in existing research on the Educational Metaverse regarding interaction patterns, providing solid theoretical support and a feasible path for the design and implementation of virtual teaching scenarios. Meanwhile, this study has certain limitations. For example, the collection of interactive behaviors is not enough, the sample is single and small in scale, and the stability of the experimental platform is insufficient. To address these limitations, future research needs to expand the dimensions of interactive behavior collection, optimize judgment methods, expand the sample scope, and develop a dedicated Educational Metaverse platform to further improve the research conclusions and enhance their universality and practicality.

Acknowledgments. This study was funded by the Zhejiang Provincial Philosophy and Social Science Planning Young Talent Cultivation Project (grant number: 26QNYC011ZD*), the National Natural Science Foundation of China (grant number: 62477042), the Zhejiang Provincial Teaching Reform Project of the 14th Five-Year Plan (grant number: JGBA2024093).

Disclosure of Interests. The authors have no competing interests to declare that are relevant to the content of this article.

References

1. Ashalakshmy.: Exploring trends and prospects of metaverse in emerging economies. Eur. J. Manage. Stud. **31**(1), 3–22 (2026)
2. Mitra, S.: Metaverse: a potential virtual-physical ecosystem for innovative blended education and training. J. Metaverse **3**(1), 66–72 (2023)
3. Buragohain, D., Chaudhary, S.: Learning in the Metaverse: Exploring the Potential of Metaverse Applications in Education. Taylor & Francis (2026)
4. Falloon, G.: Using avatars and virtual environments in learning: what do they have to offer? Br. J. Edu. Technol. **41**(1), 108–122 (2010)
5. Singh, M., Sun, D., Zheng, Z.: Enhancing university students' learning performance in a metaverse-enabled immersive learning environment for STEM education: a community of inquiry approach. Future Educ. Res. **2**(3), 288–309 (2024)
6. Richter, S., Kishore, S., Piven, I., Dodd, P., Bate, G.: Chatbots in tertiary education: exploring the impact of warm and competent avatars on self-directed learning. Br. J. Edu. Technol. **56**(5), 2102–2124 (2025)
7. Lachner, A., Hoogerheide, V., van Gog, T., Renkl, A.: Learning-by-teaching without audience presence or interaction: When and why does it work? Educ. Psychol. Rev. **34**(2), 575–607 (2022)
8. Aloqaily, M., Bouachir, O., Karray, F., Al Ridhawi, I., El Saddik, A.: Integrating digital twin and advanced intelligent technologies to realize the metaverse. IEEE Consum. Electron. Mag. **12**(6), 47–55 (2022)
9. Hadjistassou, S.K.: Culturally afforded tensions in the second life metaverse: from sustainability initiatives in Europe to sustainability practices in the United States. Int. J. Web-Based Learn. Teach. Technol. **11**(2), 14–38 (2016)
10. Falchuk, B., Loeb, S., Neff, R.: The social metaverse: battle for privacy. IEEE Technol. Soc. Mag. **37**(2), 52–61 (2018)
11. Pearson, J., Trinidad, S.: OLES: an instrument for refining the design of e-learning environments. J. Comput. Assist. Learn. **21**(6), 396–404 (2005)
12. Jagatheesaperumal, S.K., Ahmad, K., Al-Fuqaha, A., Qadir, J.: Advancing education through extended reality and internet of everything enabled metaverses: applications, challenges, and open issues. IEEE Trans. Learn. Technol. **17**, 1120–1139 (2024)
13. Wu, S., Xu, L., Dai, Z., Pan, Y.: Factors affecting avatar customization behavior in virtual environments. Electronics **12**(10), 2286 (2023)
14. Caserman, P., Garcia-Agundez, A., Göbel, S.: A survey of full-body motion reconstruction in immersive virtual reality applications. IEEE Trans. Visual Comput. Graphics **26**(10), 3089–3108 (2019)
15. Wren, C.R., Pentland, A.P.: Dynamic models of human motion. In: Proceedings Third IEEE International Conference on Automatic Face and Gesture Recognition, pp. 22–27. IEEE (1998)

16. Petrakou, A.: Interacting through avatars: virtual worlds as a context for online education. Comput. Educ. **54**(4), 1020–1027 (2010)
17. Nasir, S.M., Hashim, M.E.A.H., Chee, K.N., Kamaruddin, N.H., Wibawanto, W., Hanapiah, M.L.H.M.: Enhancing student engagement in learning management systems through exploration of avatars in virtual classrooms: a systematic review. J. Adv. Res. Appl. Sci. Eng. Technol. **61**(4), 187–200 (2024)
18. Wang, Q., Woo, H.L., Zhao, J.: Investigating critical thinking and knowledge construction in an interactive learning environment. Interact. Learn. Environ. **17**(1), 95–104 (2009)
19. Kartal, M., Bıkmaz, F.: Establishing standards for learner-centered education in higher education: a comprehensive framework for Türkiye. e-Kafkas J. Educ. Res. **12**(3), 700–740 (2025)
20. Sunar, A.S., White, S., Abdullah, N.A., Davis, H.C.: How learners' interactions sustain engagement: a MOOC case study. IEEE Trans. Learn. Technol. **10**(4), 475–487 (2016)
21. Gao, F., Wang, C., Xie, H., Hong, J.: Social interaction and online learning efficiency for middle school students: the mediating role of social presence and learning engagement. Behav. Sci. **14**(10), 896 (2024)
22. Joksimović, S., Gašević, D., Loughin, T.M., Kovanović, V., Hatala, M.: Learning at distance: effects of interaction traces on academic achievement. Comput. Educ. **87**, 204–217 (2015)
23. Pan, Y.: Exploring questioning practices in blended synchronous learning: facilitating assessment conversations through linguistic and cultural perspectives in EFL classrooms. Eur. J. Educ. **61**(1), e70432 (2026)
24. Abrami, P.C., Bernard, R.M., Bures, E.M., Borokhovski, E., Tamim, R.M.: Interaction in distance education and online learning: using evidence and theory to improve practice. J. Comput. High. Educ. **23**(2), 82–103 (2011)
25. Passerini, K., Granger, M.J.: A developmental model for distance learning using the Internet. Comput. Educ. **34**(1), 1–15 (2000)
26. Jung, I.: Building a theoretical framework of web-based instruction in the context of distance education. Br. J. Edu. Technol. **32**(5), 525–534 (2001)
27. Huang, C.Q., Han, Z.M., Li, M.X., Jong, M.S.Y., Tsai, C.C.: Investigating students' interaction patterns and dynamic learning sentiments in online discussions. Comput. Educ. **140**, 103589 (2019)
28. Han, Z.M., Huang, C.Q., Yu, J.H., Tsai, C.C.: Identifying patterns of epistemic emotions with respect to interactions in massive online open courses using deep learning and social network analysis. Comput. Hum. Behav. **122**, 106843 (2021)
29. Chamola, V., et al.: Metaverse for education: developments, challenges, and future direction. Comput. Appl. Eng. Educ. **33**(3), e70018 (2025)
30. Oladokun, B.D., Gaitanou, P.: Avatars and their players–art in the libraries. Libr. Hi Tech News **41**(9), 1–6 (2024)
31. Ozdemir, D., Isiksal Bostan, M.: A design based study: characteristics of differentiated tasks for mathematically gifted students. Eur. J. Sci. Math. Educ. **9**(3), 125–144 (2021)
32. Cohen, E.G.: Restructuring the classroom: conditions for productive small groups. Rev. Educ. Res. **64**(1), 1–35 (1994)

A Systematic Review of Empirical Studies on Applying Embodied Agents in Education

Peiyu Yin, Chuan Sin Cheok, Peng Zhang(✉), and Junjie Shang

Lab of Learning Sciences, Graduate School of Education, Peking University, Beijing, China
2401213121@pku.edu.cn

Abstract. Embodied agents, which utilize physical or virtual representations to simulate human-like social cues and multimodal interactions, have gained significant traction in educational settings. However, while empirical studies on embodied agents in education have grown significantly, there remains a lack of systematic reviews to synthesize their application status, technological evolution, and theoretical mechanisms, particularly concerning the paradigm shifts in "embodiment" and "inquiry" brought by large language models. Therefore, this study systematically reviews and analyzes 47 core empirical studies on embodied agents in education, detailing their developmental trajectories, functional characteristics, and outlining future research directions. Our findings indicate that embodied agent applications are primarily concentrated in domains with high cognitive load and strong empathy demands, such as healthcare, social sciences, and STEM. Technologically, these agents have undergone three paradigm shifts: from rule-driven pedagogical agents to adaptive learning companions, and currently to GenAI-driven conversational inquiry agents. Furthermore, the empirical evidence highlights that their intervention mechanisms are deeply rooted in cognitive load theory, social agency theory, and self-regulated learning theory, forming a multidimensional functional system that encompasses emotional engagement, cognitive and inquiry support, empathy cultivation, and social collaboration. Our review also elaborates on essential future directions, emphasizing the need to construct stage-specific cognitive scaffolds for complex inquiry, deepen metacognitive guidance for human-machine shared regulation, explore multi-agent collaborative ecosystems, and mitigate the implicit biases of GenAI. These insights provide valuable guidelines for future empirical research and the design of intelligent educational environments.

Keywords: Embodied Agents · Education · Generative Artificial Intelligence · Human-machine Collaboration

1 Introduction

1.1 A Subsection Sample

As education paradigms increasingly shift toward artificial intelligence (AI) integration and human-machine collaboration, the construction of novel digital learning ecosystems has become a global priority. As an important focus in the evolution of artificial

K. T. Chui et al. (Eds.): ICBL 2026, LNCS 16778, pp. 444–461, 2027.
https://doi.org/10.1007/978-981-92-3761-6_31

intelligence, embodied agents have become one of the core driving forces behind this transformation. An embodied agent is an important concept at the intersection of artificial intelligence and educational technology. It generally refers to an artificial intelligence system that is presented in embodied forms, such as virtual characters, embodied conversational agents, AR/MR avatars, and social robots, within digital or physical learning environments, and that possesses a degree of autonomy, goal orientation, and contextual adaptability. The theoretical foundations are derived from embodied cognition, embodied artificial intelligence, social agency theory, and research on pedagogical agents in educational technology. Embodied cognition emphasizes that cognitive activities are embedded in the dynamic relations among the body, action, and the environment, and are generated through perception, movement, social interaction, and contextual feedback [1–4]. Furthermore, research on ECAs indicates that anthropomorphic characters can facilitate face-to-face-like, multimodal interactions utilizing verbal and nonverbal cues, including speech, facial expressions, gestures, and gaze [5].

In educational contexts, the utility of embodied agents extends far beyond their visible physical appearance; their embodied representations actively mediate learners' perception, attention, emotion, social attribution, and meaning-making processes. Building upon these mechanisms, embodied agents are capable of providing critical cognitive scaffolding, emotional support, social interaction, collaborative regulation, and inquiry guidance [6–8]. Historically driven by predefined rules and adaptive feedback systems, these agents are currently undergoing a profound evolution fueled by the advent of generative artificial intelligence (GenAI) [9]. In particular, the breakthrough progress of large language models (LLMs) has endowed agents with unprecedented capabilities in natural language processing, logical reasoning, and multimodal interaction [9], This technological leap has transformed embodied agents into dynamic learning companions capable of open-ended dialogue, contextual content generation, and sophisticated support for complex inquiry learning.

By simulating human social cues, embodied agents can effectively activate learners' social schemas, enhancing the sense of learning presence while mitigating cognitive load. Consequently, a growing body of empirical literature has explored their efficacy in domains such as scientific inquiry, collaborative learning, and emotional support. For example, Kim et al. [10] developed an agent-guided algebra course and found that the agent helped highly anxious students reduce their anxiety. Wang et al. [11] examined users' perceptions and behaviors when interacting with virtual agents in augmented reality during a hidden-object game, and found that users were more willing to interact with mini embodied agents that had novel body sizes and were perceived as less threatening. Cai et al. [12] designed and developed a virtual scientist, an augmented reality-based embodied conversational agent (ECA), and examined its effects on students' learning outcomes and experiences. Their findings showed that the intervention of the AR-based embodied conversational agent significantly enhanced students' critical thinking, curiosity, and learning motivation. However, existing reviews predominantly concentrate on singular technological trajectories or specific functional domains of these agents. There is a conspicuous lack of discussion regarding the deep paradigmatic shifts in "embodiment" and "inquiry" precipitated by LLMs. Specifically, the literature lacks a systematic synthesis that integrates the current application landscape, technological evolution, and underlying theoretical foundations of embodied agents.

To bridge these research gaps, this study adopts a systematic literature review approach to conduct an in-depth analysis of empirical studies on embodied agents supporting educational learning. By systematically summarizing the theoretical foundations and functional systems within this field, and exploring the evolutionary trends of embodied agents in future learning spaces, this review aims to provide robust theoretical references and practical guidelines for the design and application of human-AI collaborative educational systems.

2 Research Methods

This study adopts a systematic literature review method and follows the PRISMA guidelines. Standardized procedures for retrieval, screening, coding, and analysis were employed to ensure the objectivity and reproducibility of the findings. The Web of Science (WoS) Core Collection database was used as the primary data source, with a focus on the latest developments in embodied agent research from a global perspective. The search was conducted using the keyword "education & embodied agent" and covered publications up to March 30, 2026, yielding 307 relevant records.

The literature screening followed a multi-stage progressive process (Fig. 1). To ensure the empirical nature and relevance of the analytical sample, the following inclusion criteria were established: (1) Core relevance: studies had to address both core dimensions, "embodied agent" and "education," ensuring that the included research focused on the application of embodied agents in various educational contexts. (2) Empirical research: studies had to include a clear experimental design, as well as data collection and analysis procedures. Purely technical studies and review articles that only involved algorithm optimization, model development, or system design, or that lacked an educational context, were excluded. (3) Text accessibility: studies had to be full-text accessible peer-reviewed journal articles or conference papers to support in-depth content coding. Furthermore, to ensure a comprehensive global perspective, no language restrictions were applied during the screening process; relevant peer-reviewed empirical studies published in non-English languages were also included and analyzed. During the screening process, each study was examined based on its abstract or full text. After excluding studies that were thematically irrelevant, non-empirical, or lacked full-text availability, 47 core studies were ultimately included for analysis.

To ensure the scientific rigor and structural clarity of the literature content analysis, this study drew on the classic PICOS (Population, Intervention, Comparison, Outcomes, Study Design) framework in evidence-based research [13], It further adapted and expanded this framework by incorporating theories from educational technology and multimodal human-computer interaction, thereby constructing a four-dimensional coding matrix suitable for the educational applications of embodied agents. The 47 core studies included in the review were read in full, followed by in-depth data extraction.

(1) Research population and design (corresponding to P and S): This dimension extracts the experimental subjects and methodological frameworks from the literature, including the characteristics of target learners, research domains, as well as sample size

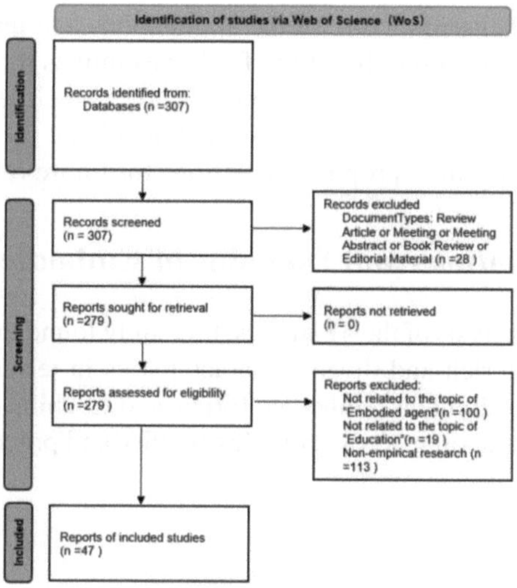

Fig. 1. Literature Selection Process.

and intervention duration. It aims to assess the ecological validity and generalizability of existing empirical studies.

(2) Agent feature design (corresponding to I): Beyond the basic instrumental functions of embodied agents, this dimension provides an in-depth analysis of the dual attributes of embodiment and intelligence. It focuses on three aspects: (i) representational form, such as fixed on-screen virtual characters, immersive AR/MR agents, and physical robots; (ii) technical mechanisms, examining technological evolution by distinguishing among traditional script-based systems, adaptive systems, and dynamic systems based on generative artificial intelligence such as large language models (LLMs); and (iii) role design, identifying the specific roles that embodied agents play in complex learning environments.

(3) Intervention mechanism design (corresponding to C): This dimension focuses on analyzing the different educational contexts in which embodied agents operate and the specific support strategies they provide in these contexts.

(4) Multidimensional learning outcomes (corresponding to O): In coding the literature, this study draws on Bloom's taxonomy of educational objectives [14], and divides learning outcomes into two dimensions: cognitive and inquiry abilities, and affective and motivational levels, in order to systematically examine the effects of embodied agents on users in educational contexts. At the level of cognitive and inquiry outcomes, attention is given to their impact on knowledge acquisition, conceptual understanding, behavioral development, and higher-order thinking. At the level of affective and motivational outcomes, the focus is on users' experience and learning motivation.

Through the above structured coding based on the adapted PICOS framework, this study not only systematically organizes the evolutionary logic and application outcomes of embodied agents, but also provides a solid data foundation for subsequent comparisons of how different underlying technologies support complex inquiry learning. To present a more comprehensive picture of the applications and underlying mechanisms of embodied agents in education, this study further examines their current distribution across educational stages and disciplinary domains, traces their technological evolution and functional application systems, explores the educational theories underlying their development, and, on this basis, proposes directions for future research.

3 Research Populations and Domains of Embodied Agents

Through a systematic analysis of the 47 studies, this study found that research on embodied agents demonstrates rich and diverse characteristics in terms of educational stage distribution, disciplinary domains, embodied forms, and teaching functions. Their applications are gradually expanding across complex inquiry and practice-based contexts for different learner groups.

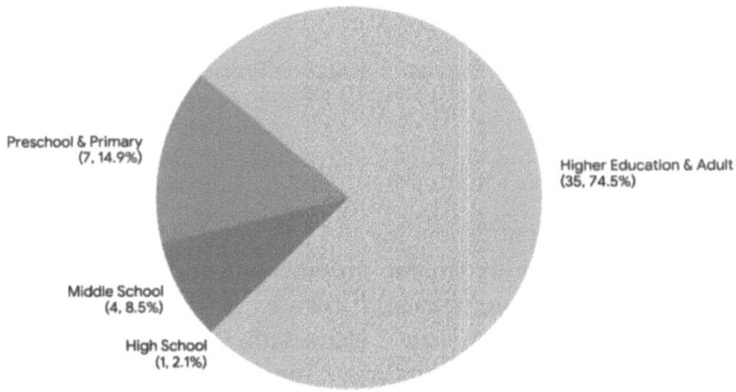

Fig. 2. Educational Stage Distribution.

In terms of educational stage distribution, as shown in Fig. 2, current research on embodied agents is mainly concentrated in higher education and adult learner groups, while basic education (K–12) is rapidly following up. Among the 47 empirical studies, 35 focused on university students and adult learners, accounting for 74.5%. In these groups, embodied agents are mainly used to create active learning environments or conduct professional skills training. For example, medical students used virtual standardized patients to practice psychiatric history-taking and interview skills [15, 16];Embodied agents have also been applied to active learning environments, where large model-driven agents support students' self-regulated and shared regulation learning [17], as well as to nanoscale science education [18]. This type of research focuses on evaluating the technological acceptance of embodied agents in complex cognitive tasks and their effects on cultivating higher-order thinking.

By comparison, studies in basic education (K–12) and preschool education account for approximately 26.5%. In these studies, embodied agents are often designed as interactive story characters or scientific inquiry companions, aiming to stimulate children's learning interest and curiosity through multimodal embodied interaction. For example, one study designed an embodied agent named Chris as both a learning companion and tutor in a middle-school introductory algebra classroom, and found that Latina students and White female students reported more positive user experiences than White male students [19]. Other studies used the physical robot Ozobot to help children master abstract concepts and behavioral principles [20], or used Lhamo, an embodied agent developed based on the Coze platform, to support Tibetan students'Mandarin oral learning, thereby improving their accuracy, fluency, and positive engagement [21]. This difference in proportion is partly due to the fact that embodied agents require learners to possess relatively high self-regulated learning abilities [22]. University students are able to conduct metacognitive monitoring in low-supervision environments. For example, Rawson and Dunlosky [23] found that university students could improve the accuracy of metacognitive monitoring through retrieval practice, which is particularly important in low-supervision environments. However, the application of embodied agents in K–12 contexts has progressed relatively slowly. On the one hand, children have lower cognitive load thresholds, and complex agent interfaces can easily lead to high cognitive load and attention distraction. On the other hand, such applications are constrained by strict data privacy and ethical requirements in basic education, as well as the difficulty of integrating embodied agents into classroom settings. Therefore, future applications in K–12 education should move toward high interest and low cognitive burden, so as to provide learners with positive embodied interaction experiences.

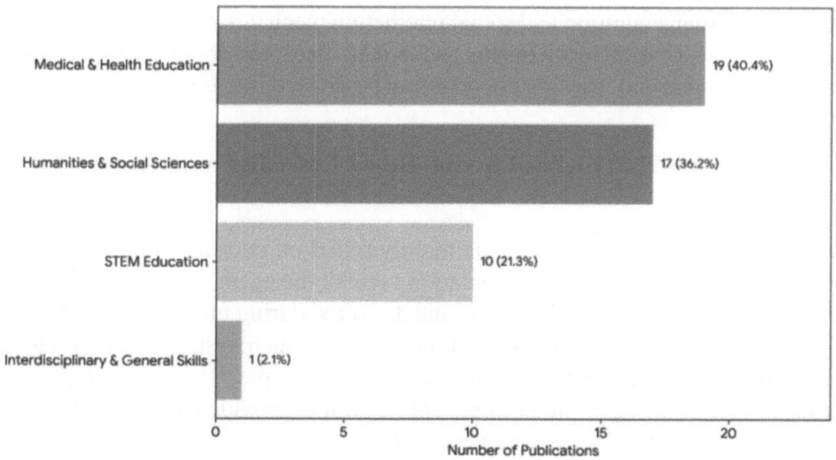

Fig. 3. Distribution of Disciplinary Domains.

In terms of disciplinary domains, as shown in Fig. 3, research on embodied agents is mainly concentrated in healthcare, social sciences, STEM, and related fields. Applications in healthcare and psychology include the use of embodied agents to support self-management among patients with diabetes [24, 25], daily care coaching for patients with spinal cord injury [26], and health literacy education for vulnerable groups such as patients with depression and African American men [27, 28]. These studies show that, when communicating with users in areas such as health and disease treatment, embodied agents can provide users with a stronger sense of trust and safety than human teachers or doctors. They can help users deepen their health-related knowledge systems and improve their physical and mental health more effectively. Learning, communication, and dissemination in these fields are often constrained by users' psychological barriers and low psychological acceptance. Embodied agents provide an objective, low-pressure, and confidential space in which medical students can make mistakes without harming real patients, and patients with depression can safely disclose sensitive information. This is an important reason why embodied agents have been widely applied in fields with high demands for empathy.

In addition, in the social sciences, embodied agents can be innovatively used for role-playing and perspective transformation, thereby cultivating higher-order thinking abilities. For example, a VR historical scene of the Boston Massacre containing as many as 486 virtual humans was constructed for students to explore historical events and acquire historical knowledge [29]. These studies demonstrate the adaptability and great development potential of embodied agents across different disciplinary domains.

4 Technological Evolution of Embodied Agents

Through an in-depth analysis of the underlying technologies of the agents in the 47 core studies included in this review, it can be found that the development of embodied agents is not merely an upgrade of interactive interfaces, but a deeper paradigm shift in how they participate in human cognition and social interaction mechanisms. Taking technological evolution and intervention mechanisms as the main axes, the applications of embodied agents in educational and learning contexts can be divided into three progressive stages.

4.1 Rule-Driven and Predefined Script–Based Embodied Pedagogical Agent Stage

In early applications, embodied agents mainly relied on decision tree algorithms and predefined dialogue scripts. The presentation logic of the agent's language, actions, and expressions was predefined by designers and delivered during interactions with learners.

From the perspective of intervention mechanisms, such systems were grounded in behaviorism and information processing theory. For example, Baptista et al. [25] used a script-based embodied agent in a mobile application to provide daily self-management and educational support for patients with diabetes. Guo et al. [30] and Guo et al. [31] conducted two studies using script-based virtual instructors and student assistants to support information literacy education among university students in Illinois. These studies demonstrate that agents driven by predefined scripts can effectively support the large-scale dissemination of structured knowledge with relatively low technical deployment requirements, thereby promoting more effective learning. However, the outputs of script-based agents tend to be fixed and mechanical, making it difficult to handle open-ended questions beyond the predefined scope, and thus limiting their ability to support complex inquiry-based learning.

4.2 Embodied Learning Companion System Stage Centered on Multimodal Perception and Adaptive Regulation

To overcome the limitation of script-based agents, researchers began to deeply integrate technologies such as intelligent tutoring systems (ITS) and affective computing into the design and development of embodied agents, In such systems, the design logic of embodied agents has gradually shifted toward constructivist and social cognitive theories. These agents are able to assess learners' knowledge mastery, level of acceptance, and degree of understanding in real time. For example, Zhou and Bickmore [32] integrated ITS into a virtual genetic counselor, enabling real-time adjustment of counseling strategies based on patients' dynamically assessed understanding, which significantly improved patients' knowledge of breast cancer genetics. Milne et al.[33] developed an embodied agent that adapts content and instructional sequences according to individual learners' progress and difficulty levels, helping children with autism improve their social skills. Moridis and Economides [34] designed agents capable of responding to students' fear, sadness, and happiness through parallel empathy and reactive empathy, thereby helping to alleviate negative emotions.

These studies indicate that adaptive agents can influence learners' knowledge acquisition and emotional regulation, and, compared with script-based agents, can play a more active role in enhancing learning outcomes and guiding emotions. However, despite the substantial improvement in adaptive capabilities, the feedback generated by agents at this stage still relies on intelligent retrieval from predefined question banks or dialogue repositories, and does not yet demonstrate a deep understanding of natural language semantics or the ability to generate open-ended content.

4.3 Generative Artificial Intelligence-Driven Conversational Inquiry Agent Stage

In recent years, with the rapid development of generative artificial intelligence technologies such as large language models (LLMs), the design and development of embodied agents have entered a transformative stage. In supporting learning, embodied agents can also foster the development of higher-order thinking by providing cognitive scaffolding or engaging learners in Socratic questioning.

For example, Dang et al. [35] introduced GPT-4o–driven agents into a mixed reality (MR) environment and found that, when acting as guiding partners, generative AI can promote students' structured cognitive engagement, while, when acting as instructors, it can serve as a springboard for deeper exploration and the development of critical thinking. Cai et al. [12] developed an augmented reality application called "Virtual Scientist" using Unity, integrating the Xunfei Spark large model, Baidu Intelligent Cloud speech technologies, and ChatGPT. In authentic interactive contexts, this application significantly enhanced primary school students' critical thinking, curiosity, and learning motivation. Haider et al. [36] created an interactive AI physician digital twin using the HeyGen IV video generation model, Google's speech-to-text API, and the Gemini 2.0 large model, which was well received by patients in postoperative education. However, the application of embodied educational agents powered by generative AI also introduces new risks and boundaries. For instance, some studies have pointed out that large models may exhibit biases related to race, political orientation, sexual orientation, or socioeconomic status, which may lead to the dissemination of incorrect information in high-risk fields such as medicine. Therefore, it is necessary to use domain-specific large models trained on controlled datasets as much as possible [37].

5 Theoretical Foundations of Embodied Agent Applications

The wide application of embodied agents in education is underpinned by profound mechanisms from the learning sciences and educational psychology. Through a systematic review of existing studies, current research and design of embodied agents can be summarized into the following three theoretical dimensions. These theories not only guide the system design, instructional application, and evaluation of educational agents, but also shape the future evolution of embodied agents within the educational ecosystem.

First, at the cognitive level, the design of embodied agents is mainly guided by cognitive load theory and embodied cognition theory. Cognitive load theory holds that learners' working memory capacity is limited [38]. As a form of cognitive scaffolding, embodied agents can help learners undertake part of the information-processing and procedural guidance tasks, thereby supporting effective learning. However, inappropriate design or excessive accumulation of multimodal elements may also induce cognitive load [39], leading to learners' distraction and increased learning pressure. In addition, embodied cognition theory [3] emphasizes the coordination among mind, body, and environment. In immersive environments based on large models and multimodal technologies, agents can not only deliver symbolic knowledge, but also provide shifts in spatial perspective and support learners' embodied reasoning. For example, Lai's [18] study showed that embodied agents can effectively guide learners in transforming abstract nanoscale science into perceptible physical logic, thereby enabling more efficient construction of explanatory knowledge.

At the socio-emotional theoretical level, the strong performance of embodied agents in emotional intervention and motivation stimulation is deeply rooted in social agency theory. This theory holds that social cues in multimedia information can activate learners' social schemas, prompting them to interpret human–computer interaction as closer to real interpersonal dialogue [7]. Based on this mechanism, embodied agents can establish psychological connections with learners and gain their trust and positive evaluations.

At the cognitive theoretical level, with the deepening of interaction, the theoretical foundations of embodied agents are gradually extending toward self-regulated learning theory. Self-regulated learning theory emphasizes learners' planning, monitoring, and reflection on their own cognitive processes [40]. Traditional embodied agents in educational contexts mostly played the role of objects that directly transmit knowledge. However, current research increasingly highlights the role of agents in providing cognitive scaffolding at the metacognitive level. For example, GenAI-powered embodied agents can promote deep metacognitive monitoring among learners through dynamic Socratic questioning, progress feedback, and goal alignment. Studies by Dang et al. [35] and Nguyen et al. [17] show that when GenAI agents are introduced into mixed-reality team collaboration environments, they can trigger cognitive conflict or sustain motivation, thereby promoting learners' transition from individual self-regulation to higher-level regulation supported by human-AI collaboration.In this process, the agent itself also transforms into a"coach"that cultivates students'metacognitive abilities during inquiry.

6 Functions and Applications of Embodied Agents

From the perspective of teaching functions, as shown in Fig. 4, the application of embodied agents presents a diversified development trend. Overall, these functions can be categorized into four types: emotional support and motivation, cognitive and inquiry support, empathy and perspective-taking, and social interaction and collaboration. These functions cover the mastery of basic knowledge, the regulation of individual emotions, the construction of complex cognitive abilities, and the cultivation of deep social empathy. This reflects the broad adaptability of embodied agents across different educational contexts, where they can serve multiple roles such as learning companions, instructional guides, and objects of inquiry.

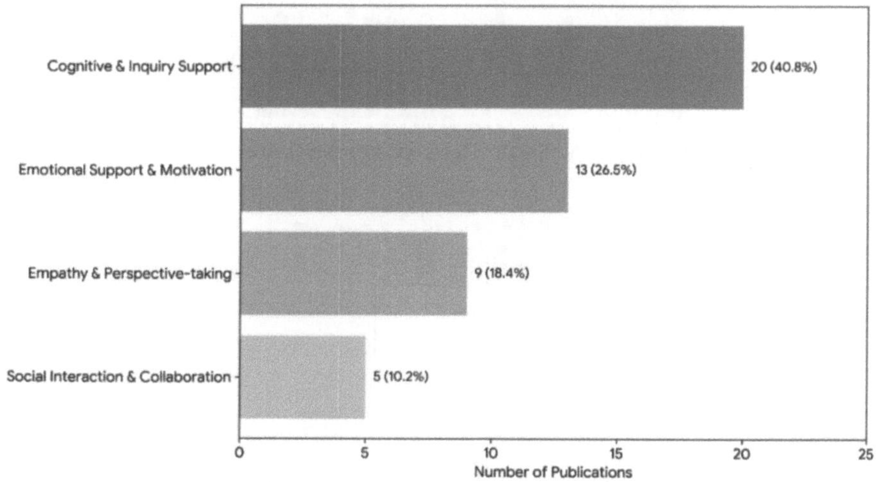

Fig. 4. Distribution of Teaching Functions.

6.1 Emotional Support and Motivation

Emotional support and motivation is a key focus in current research on the application of embodied agents [41]. This line of research generally emphasizes that learners can obtain a sense of comfort and satisfaction through interaction with embodied agents, thereby enhancing learning motivation and adherence to interventions. For example, in interventions targeting academic stress among university students [42], embodied agents can provide explanatory learning suggestions based on students' beliefs and goals, effectively alleviating learners' social anxiety. In addition, in healthcare education, for patients with severe depressive symptoms [27] or diabetes [25], embodied agents can gain users' trust through their high level of affinity and demonstrate emotional support value beyond that of traditional media. However, some studies have also pointed out that, in the absence of appropriate task design, emotional and motivational support may not directly translate into substantive improvements in academic performance [43]. From the perspective of social agency theory [7], the facial expressions, tone, and actions of embodied agents can simulate authentic problem situations, allowing learners to experience interactions similar to those with real people, thereby fostering psychological identification or reducing social anxiety. On the other hand, if embodied agents introduce excessive or redundant cognitive activities, the initial sense of emotional novelty may quickly diminish, and learners may experience increased cognitive load, making it difficult for interaction with the agent to translate into actual academic achievement (Figs. 5 and 6).

Fig. 5. The ECA "Sarah" Developed by Nelekar et al. [42].

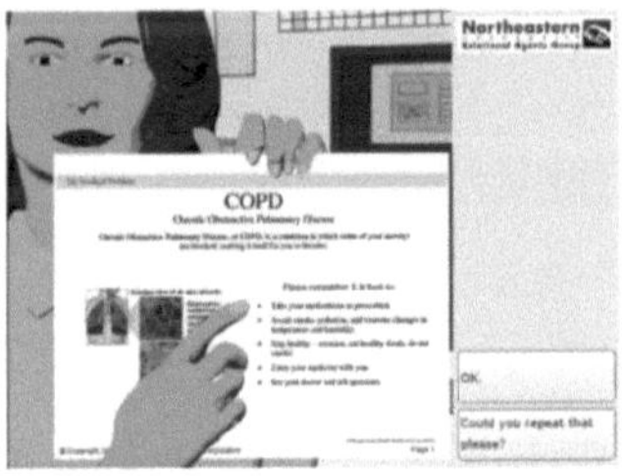

Fig. 6. The Virtual Nurse Developed by Bickmore et al.[27].

6.2 Cognitive and Inquiry Support

Cognitive and Inquiry Support focuses on helping learners understand complex concepts, acquire specialized skills, and develop higher-order reasoning. In basic science education, agents often function as inquiry scaffolds. For example, Lai [18] used AI-based embodied agents to provide university students with scaffolding for interactive simulations, which significantly enhanced learners' mastery and understanding of nanoscale science compared with video-based learning. Cai et al. [12] designed a "virtual scientist" using AR to guide primary school students in interactive science learning, effectively improving their critical thinking. In the context of operational skill training, agents often take on the roles of"virtual coaches"or "standardized patients".For instance, medical students can engage in natural language interaction with virtual patient characters that exhibit emotional responses, thereby developing both knowledge acquisition and empathy toward patients [16], and can also practice history-taking skills [15], effectively reducing the time and resource costs of clinical training. From the perspective of cognitive load theory [38], embodied agents, as cognitive scaffolds for learners, can alleviate part of the information-processing burden and facilitate more effective knowledge acquisition. The introduction of large models further upgrades such scaffolding from providing static prompts to dynamically generated guidance and responses, enabling Socratic questioning and supporting the development of learners' cognitive and inquiry abilities (Figs. 7 and 8).

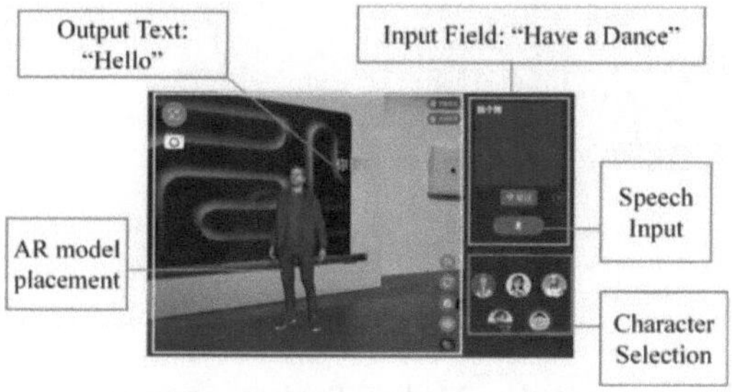

Fig. 7. The "Virtual Scientist" AR Application Developed by Cai et al. [12].

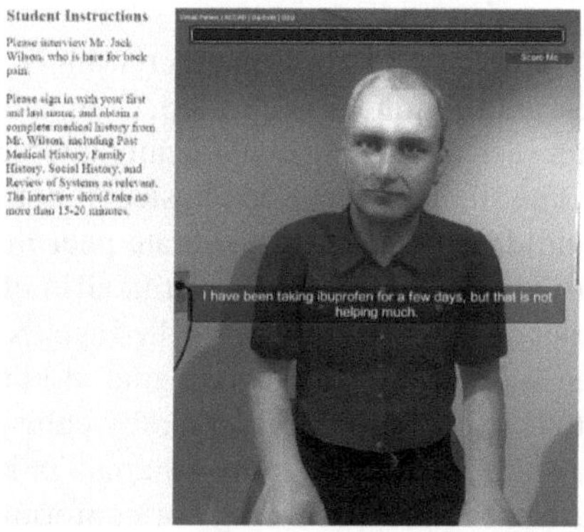

Fig. 8. The Virtual Standardized Patients (VSPs) Developed by Maicher et al. [15].

6.3 Empathy and Perspective-Taking

Empathy and perspective-taking has become a rapidly developing functional direction of embodied agents in recent years. Unlike the traditional positioning of agents as "knowledge authorities", agents in such applications are often used as objects and representations of social construction. For example, automated virtual characters have been used to develop the social and conversational skills of children with autism [33] and to examine students' emotional experiences when using self-assessment systems [34].Some studies have further extended conventional interaction boundaries. For instance, Halan et al. [44] supported medical students in creating virtual patients of specific racial backgrounds, enabling them to experience situations from the perspectives of those patients, thereby enhancing empathy and understanding in subsequent interactions with patients from the same groups. Such practices of deep perspective-taking supported by embodied agents significantly deepen learners' cross-cultural understanding and empathy, and help them internalize and perform future professional and social roles more effectively (Fig. 9).

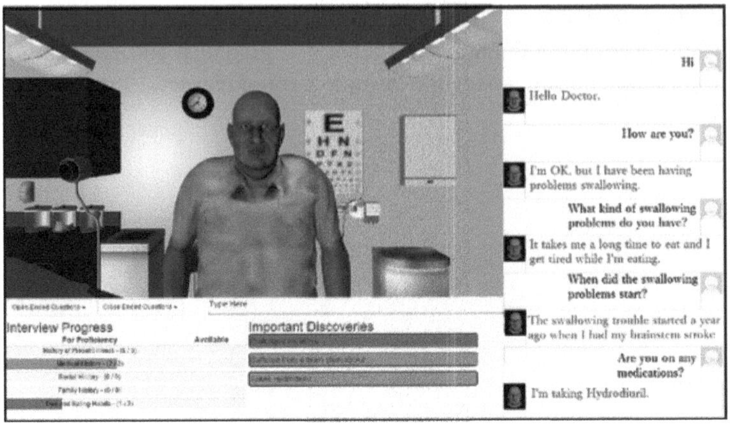

Fig. 9. Virtual Patients Created by Medical Students Supported by Halan et al. [44].

6.4 Social Interaction and Collaboration

Social Interaction and Collaboration has become increasingly prominent as computer-supported collaborative learning continues to develop. Compared with systems that only support individual learning, such agents can dynamically intervene in peer collaboration processes. For example, some studies have used physical robots to promote social interaction among preschool children [45] and to facilitate peer instruction in high school science classrooms[46]. In recent years, generative artificial intelligence (GenAI) has further expanded the boundaries of collaboration. Embodied agents driven by large language models (e.g., GPT-4o) can support learners in engaging in human-machine collaboration within immersive interactive environments, thereby enhancing both cognitive and socio-emotional abilities [35]. In traditional human-human or human-machine collaborative learning, learners are prone to "free-riding" or conformity in thinking [47]. The intervention mechanism of embodied agents lies in addressing these issues by, for example, introducing counterpoints at appropriate moments or creating immersive collaborative inquiry environments, thereby promoting group collaboration and communication (Fig. 10).

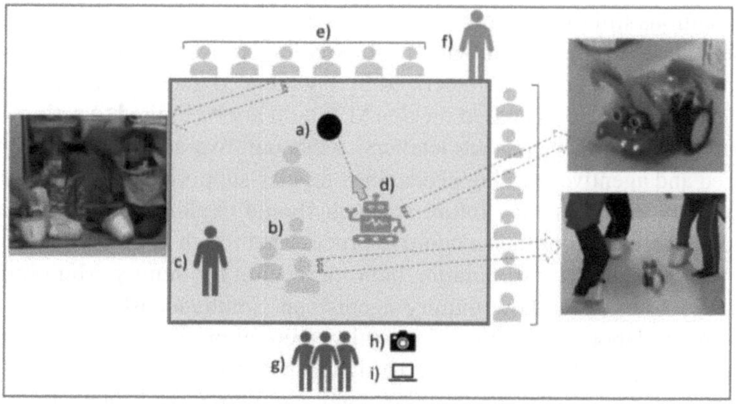

Fig. 10. Workshop built by Caceffo et al. [45] using the mBot Robot.

7 Implications and Future Research

Although the application of embodied agents in education has achieved significant progress, challenges remain in the face of the rapid iteration of generative artificial intelligence technologies and the complexity of real-world teaching contexts. Existing research still has limitations in the precision of intervention strategies, the construction of collaborative ecosystems, and the ethical and normative aspects of generative models. Therefore, future research on embodied agents can be further developed along the following four dimensions.

7.1 Reducing Cognitive Load and Constructing Controllable Inquiry Scaffolds

Some studies have found a positive correlation between the depth of interaction with embodied agents and cognitive load. If multimodal interaction cannot be effectively integrated with the depth of cognitive tasks, it may lead to increased cognitive load for learners [39]. In addition, the open-ended outputs of GenAI-supported agents may sometimes deviate from the task focus and hinder learning [12]. Therefore, future research should shift from providing general knowledge-based question–answer support to constructing precise and controllable cognitive scaffolds. In particular, in complex inquiry-based learning, agents should be able to dynamically perceive the learner's current stage of inquiry and provide differentiated cognitive offloading and guidance at different stages. At the same time, future embodied agents should aim to enhance the controllability of generated content, for example by optimizing prompts and implementing monitoring and filtering mechanisms, so as to provide precise support without increasing learners' visual and working memory load.

7.2 Deepening Metacognitive Guidance and Reshaping Higher-Order Thinking in Complex Learning Ecosystems

Although recent studies have begun to explore the use of GenAI to simultaneously foster learners' knowledge acquisition and higher-order abilities such as critical thinking, most interventions still focus on providing cognitive scaffolds at the individual level, and deeper applications in complex human–machine collaborative learning remain at an early stage. In real-world contexts characterized by open-ended and ill-structured problems, multimodal embodied agents based on GenAI should not be limited to acting as inquiry guides, but should further enhance learners' metacognitive abilities and support their personalized and agentive learning needs. In computer-supported collaborative learning or mixed reality environments, future research should explore how agents can guide learners to actively monitor their cognitive processes through Socratic questioning and reflective feedback, thereby stimulating their motivation for inquiry. More importantly, it is necessary to examine how inquiry agents can simultaneously act as scaffolding assistants and collaborative partners in inquiry, thereby promoting learners' transition from individual knowledge construction to higher-level regulation supported by human–AI collaboration, and deepening cognitive and socio-emotional interactions between learners and GenAI [35].

7.3 Expanding the Boundaries of Social Interaction and Exploring Multi-Agent Collaborative Educational Ecosystems

At the level of socio-emotional intervention, highly anthropomorphic embodied agents have demonstrated clear advantages in establishing trust and providing a psychologically safe space for users. Future development is expected to move beyond the traditional one-to-one human–machine teacher–student model toward more complex multi-agent ecosystems. On the one hand, researchers can design multi-agent systems with heterogeneous perspectives to introduce appropriate cognitive conflict, thereby promoting learners' evaluation and integration of different viewpoints in collaborative learning and fostering critical and multi-perspective thinking [29]. On the other hand, it is necessary to reconsider the traditional teacher–student relationship of "teaching and learning" and explore the reversal of roles and power in human–machine interaction. For example, extending the approach of Halan et al. [44], learners could be allowed to "create" embodied agents representing specific social groups (such as different racial groups or individuals with particular cognitive characteristics) and interact with them. Such designs, which treat agents as objects of social construction, can play an important role in fostering learners' cross-cultural understanding and social empathy.

7.4 Enhancing Model Interpretability and Value Alignment to Mitigate Implicit Biases in GenAI

With the increasing application of embodied agents in areas such as clinical training and psychological crisis intervention, the transparency and ethical safety of their intervention logic have become key concerns. The inherent "hallucination" phenomenon of generative large language models, as well as biases related to race, gender, or culture embedded in training data, may inadvertently mislead learners. Future research should focus on deeply integrating classical educational theories with algorithmic models to construct explainable artificial intelligence (XAI) frameworks for the education domain, thereby addressing the ethical risks associated with AI. In practice, techniques such as retrieval-augmented generation (RAG) [37] and strict value-alignment mechanisms can be introduced to ensure that embodied agents are not only "human-like" in interaction, but also scientifically grounded, traceable, and ethically compliant in their instructional decision-making.

In summary, embodied agents are evolving from rule-based instructional tools to generative, interactive partners that support complex learning processes. Future progress in this field will depend on aligning technological capabilities with pedagogical needs and ethical considerations in real-world educational contexts.

Acknowledgments. 2025 Doctoral Student Program of National Education Sciences Planning, National Office of the National Education Sciences Planning Leading Group "Research on the Effectiveness and Support Mechanisms of Agent-Based Virtual Scientific Inquiry Learning" (Grant No: FCA250470).

References

1. Clark, A.: Being There: Putting Brain, Body, and World Together Again. MIT Press, Cambridge, MA (1998)
2. Pfeifer, R., Scheier, C.: Understanding Intelligence. MIT Press, Cambridge, MA (2001)
3. Wilson, M.: Six views of embodied cognition. Psychon. Bull. Rev. **9**(4), 625–636 (2022)
4. Barsalou, L.W.: Grounded cognition. Annu. Rev. Psychol. **59**, 617–645 (2008)
5. Cassell, J., Sullivan, J., Prevost, S., et al.: Embodied Conversational Agents. MIT Press, Cambridge, MA (2000)
6. Moreno, R., Mayer, R.E., Spires, H.A., et al.: The case for social agency in computer-based teaching: Do students learn more deeply when they interact with animated pedagogical agents? Cogn. Instr. **19**(2), 177–213 (2001)
7. Mayer, R.E., Sobko, K., Mautone, P.D.: Social cues in multimedia learning: Role of speaker's voice. J. Educ. Psychol. **95**(2), 419–425 (2003)
8. Mayer, R.E., Dapra, C.S.: An embodiment effect in computer-based learning with animated pedagogical agents. J. Exp. Psychol. Appl. **18**(3), 239–252 (2012)
9. Xi, Z., Chen, W., Guo, X., et al.: The rise and potential of large language model based agents: a survey. SCIENCE CHINA Inf. Sci. **68**(2), 121101 (2025)
10. Kim, Y., Thayne, J., Wei, Q.: An embodied agent helps anxious students in mathematics learning. Education Tech. Research Dev. **65**(1), 219–235 (2017)
11. Wang, I., Smith, J., Ruiz, J.: Exploring virtual agents for augmented reality. In: Proceedings of the 2019 CHI Conference on Human Factors in Computing Systems, pp. 1–12 (2019)
12. Cai, S., Huang, H., Jiao, X. et al.: Generative AI+ AR: a novel embodied conversational agent in an interactive learning environment. Interactive Learning Environment, (Early Access)
13. Richardson, W.S., Wilson, M.C., Nishikawa, J., et al.: The well-built clinical question: a key to evidence-based decisions. ACP J. Club **123**(3), A12–A13 (1995)
14. Bloom, B.S., Engelhart, M.D., Furst, E.J. et al.: Taxonomy of educational objectives: The classification of educational goals. Handbook 1: Cognitive domain. Longman, New York (1956)
15. Maicher, K., Danforth, D., Price, A., et al.: Developing a conversational virtual standardized patient to enable students to practice history-taking skills. Simulation in Healthcare **12**(2), 124–131 (2017)
16. Dupuy, L., de Sevin, E., Cassoudesalle, H., et al.: Guidelines for the design of a virtual patient for psychiatric interview training. J. Multimodal User Interfaces **15**(2), 99–107 (2021)

17. Nguyen, A., Gul, F., Dang, B., et al.: Designing embodied generative artificial intelligence in mixed reality for active learning in higher education. Innov. Educ. Teach. Int. **62**(5), 1632–1647 (2025)
18. Lai, P.K.: Enhancing learning of nanoscale phenomena: the role of agent-based models and embodied reasoning. Instr. Sci. **54**(1), 22 (2026)
19. Kim, Y., Lim, J.H.: Gendered socialization with an embodied agent: Creating a social and affable mathematics learning environment for middle-grade females. J. Educ. Psychol. **105**(4), 1164 (2013)
20. Leostel, J., Pastor, L., López, J.S.M., et al.: Using Robots for Digital Storytelling. A Game. Robotics in Education: Methodologies and Technologies **26** (2021)
21. Wu, Y.: The impact of AI-and peer-assisted interaction modes on oral ability, interactive experiences, and perceptions among adolescent Chinese Tibetan students. Journal of Multilingual and Multicultural Development, (Early Access)
22. Wiedbusch, M., Lester, J., Azevedo, R.: A multi-level growth modeling approach to measuring learner attention with metacognitive pedagogical agents. Metacogn. Learn. **18**(2), 465–494 (2023)
23. Dunlosky, J., Hartwig, M.K., Rawson, K.A., et al.: Improving college students' evaluation of text learning using idea-unit standards. Q. J. Experim. Psychol. **64**(3), 467–484 (2011)
24. Sinoo, C., van Der Pal, S., Henkemans, O.A.B., et al.: Friendship with a robot: children's perception of similarity between a robot's physical and virtual embodiment that supports diabetes self-management. Patient Educ. Couns. **101**(7), 1248–1255 (2018)
25. Baptista, S., Wadley, G., Bird, D., et al.: Acceptability of an embodied conversational agent for type 2 diabetes self-management education and support via a smartphone app: mixed methods study. JMIR Mhealth Uhealth **8**(7), e17038 (2020)
26. Shamekhi, A., Trinh, H., Bickmore, T.W., et al.: A virtual self-care coach for individuals with spinal cord injury. In: Proceedings of the 18th International ACM SIGACCESS Conference on Computers and Accessibility, pp. 327–328 (2016)
27. Bickmore, T.W., Mitchell, S.E., Jack, B.W., et al.: Response to a relational agent by hospital patients with depressive symptoms. Interact. Comput. **22**(4), 289–298 (2010)
28. Owens, O.L., Felder, T., Tavakoli, A.S., et al.: Evaluation of a computer-based decision aid for promoting informed prostate cancer screening decisions among African American men: iDecide. Am. J. Health Promot. **33**(2), 267–278 (2019)
29. Novick, D., Rodriguez, L., Pacheco, A., et al.: The Boston massacre history experience. In: Proceedings of the 19th ACM International Conference on Multimodal Interaction, pp. 499–500 (2017)
30. Guo, Y.R., Goh, D.H.L., Luyt, B., et al.: The effectiveness and acceptance of an affective information literacy tutorial. Comput. Educ. **87**, 368–384 (2015)
31. Guo, Y.R., Goh, D.H.L.: Evaluation of affective embodied agents in an information literacy game. Comput. Educ. **103**, 59–75 (2016)
32. Zhou, S., Bickmore, T.: A Virtual Counselor for Breast Cancer Genetic Counseling: Adaptive Pedagogy Leads to Greater Knowledge Gain (CHI'22). Association for Computing Machinery, New York, NY, USA, 436 (2022)
33. Milne, M., Raghavendra, P., Leibbrandt, R., et al.: Personalisation and automation in a virtual conversation skills tutor for children with autism. J. Multimodal User Interfaces **12**(3), 257–269 (2018)
34. Moridis, C.N., Economides, A.A.: Affective learning: Empathetic agents with emotional facial and tone of voice expressions. IEEE Trans. Affect. Comput. **3**(3), 260–272 (2012)
35. Dang, B., Huynh, L., Gul, F., et al.: Human–AI collaborative learning in mixed reality: Examining the cognitive and socio-emotional interactions. Br. J. Edu. Technol. **56**(5), 2078–2101 (2025)

36. Haider, S.A., Prabha, S., Gomez-Cabello, C.A., et al.: Artificial Intelligence Physician Avatars for Patient Education: A Pilot Study. J. Clin. Med. **14**(23), 8595 (2025)
37. Choo, S., Yoo, S., Endo, K., et al.: Advancing clinical chatbot validation using AI-powered evaluation with a new 3-bot evaluation system: instrument validation study. JMIR Nursing **8**(1), e63058 (2025)
38. Sweller, J.: Cognitive load theory. Psychology of learning and motivation. Academic Press **55**, 37–76 (2011)
39. Vankit, S.A., Zamanifard, S., Diaz, D., et al.: Exploring the Impact of Multimodal Long Conversations in VR on Attitudes Toward Behavior Change, Memory Retention, and Cognitive Load. Computer Animation and Virtual Worlds **36**(3), e70023 (2025)
40. Zimmerman, B.J.: Becoming a self-regulated learner: Which are the key subprocesses? Contemp. Educ. Psychol. **11**(4), 307–313 (1986)
41. Zall, R., Kheyrkhah, A., Cambria, E., et al.: Intelligent Agents with Emotional Intelligence: Current Trends, Challenges, and Future Prospects. arXiv preprint arXiv:2511.20657 (2025)
42. Nelekar, S., Abdulrahman, A., Gupta, M., et al.: Effectiveness of embodied conversational agents for managing academic stress at an Indian University (ARU) during COVID-19. Br. J. Edu. Technol. **53**(3), 491–511 (2022)
43. Guo, Y.R., Goh, D.H.L., Luyt, B.: Using affective embodied agents in information literacy education. IEEE/ACM Joint Conference on Digital Libraries, pp. 389–398 (2014)
44. Halan, S., Sia, I., Crary, M., et al.: Exploring the effects of healthcare students creating virtual patients for empathy training. In: International Conference on Intelligent Virtual Agents. Cham: Springer International Publishing, pp. 239–249 (2015)
45. Caceffo, R., Gonçalves, D.A., Bonacin, R., et al.: Children's social interactions within a socioenactive scenario. Comput. Educ. **176**, 104324 (2022)
46. Edwards, B.I., Muniru, I.O., Khougali, N., et al.: A physically embodied robot teacher (PERT) as a facilitator for peer learning. In: 2018 IEEE frontiers in education conference (FIE). IEEE, pp. 1–9 (2018)
47. Bazazi, S., Von Zimmermann, J., Bahrami, B., et al.: Self-serving incentives impair collective decisions by increasing conformity. PLoS ONE **14**(11), e0224725 (2019)

Advanced Training and Curriculum Designs

Research on the Construction of the DC-OPPP Model for Digital Curriculum Empowered Project-Based Learning Among Undergraduates

Youru Xie(✉), Tingyun Lu, Jinlin Lou, and Chengjun Li

School of Educational Information Technology, South China Normal University, Guangzhou, China

xieyouru@aliyun.com

Abstract. The intelligent era urgently demands new-quality talent. PBL is crucial for developing undergraduates' innovative thinking and complex problem-solving skills. However, it faces practical challenges: heavy teaching workloads, lack of formative assessment data, and delayed personalized support. Leveraging the digital curriculum to break through these bottlenecks has become a core issue for higher education reform. Drawing on theories of PBL, human-machine collaborative learning, and distributed cognition, and utilizing methods such as literature review and theoretical deduction, this study revealed the mechanisms through which the digital curriculum empowers undergraduates' PBL. It formed a Plan-Path-Product (PPP) framework and constructed the DC-OPPP model. Next, addressing the needs of the *Research on Educational Technology Empowered by Digital Intelligence* project, this study applied the DC-OPPP model to a teacher-student-AI tripartite collaborative teaching innovation. Finally, this study analyzed and validated the model's application effectiveness based on overall course grades, project outcomes, and learning experiences. The results indicate that the DC-OPPP model helps students generate high-quality project outcomes, enhance their learning experience in the intelligent learning environment, and achieve higher overall course grades. This study provides theoretical and practical guidance for the deep empowerment of PBL through the digital curriculum, aiming to drive new-quality talent cultivation in the intelligent era.

Keywords: Project-based learning · Digital Curriculum · DC-OPPP Model · Construction

1 Problem Statement

Project-Based Learning (PBL) emphasizes collaborative inquiry in authentic problem contexts to form creative solutions. It is crucial for developing undergraduates' innovative thinking and complex problem-solving skills [1, 2]. However, in traditional higher education, the implementation of PBL faces heavy teaching workloads, a lack of formative assessment data, and delayed personalized support. Consequently, some projects become superficial exercises [3]. With the deepening of the digital transformation in

K. T. Chui et al. (Eds.): ICBL 2026, LNCS 16778, pp. 465–479, 2027.
https://doi.org/10.1007/978-981-92-3761-6_32

education, the digital curriculum, integrating big data, AI, and knowledge graphs have emerged. The algorithm-driven digital curriculum enables adaptive learning paths, real-time state tracking, and intelligent feedback. These capabilities provide a key opportunity to overcome the bottlenecks of traditional PBL [4, 5]. Although existing research has yielded substantial findings, there is still a lack of systematic theoretical models for deeply embedding the digital curriculum into PBL. Therefore, this study proposes the following research questions to drive the research forward, strictly adhering to the logical progression of revealing mechanisms, constructing a model, and validating effectiveness. The aim is to provide theoretical and practical references for empowering PBL through the digital curriculum.

RQ1: What are the underlying mechanisms through which the digital curriculum empowers undergraduates' PBL?

RQ2: How can a model be constructed for the digital curriculum to empower undergraduates' PBL?

RQ3: How effective is this model in practice?

2 Literature Review

2.1 Construction and Application of Digital Curriculum

The digital curriculum is the core driver for teaching reform in higher education in the intelligent era. Existing research primarily focuses on three dimensions: structural features, design and development, and innovative applications. Regarding structural features, Xie et al. regarded digital, networked, and intelligent technology and data as the fifth element of the curriculum. They clarified its collaborative innovation and relationship mapping with objectives, content, activities, and evaluation, thereby proposing the D-OCAE structural features framework for the higher education digital curriculum [6]. Khodabandelou et al. pointed out that successful digital curriculum design is characterized by a structured learning environment, active learning and engagement, and learner-centered design [7]. In terms of design and development, Liu et al. proposed curriculum development principles that are competency-oriented, student-centered, and data-driven [8]. Tian et al. applied knowledge graphs to construct three development models: an information extraction layer, a knowledge fusion layer, and a service application layer. This approach drives the structuring of curriculum knowledge [9]. Chen et al. developed an intelligent teaching assistant system to address the lack of personalized support in the curriculum [10]. Liang et al. constructed virtual simulation laboratories using digital twin technology to facilitate the visualization of abstract knowledge [11]. Regarding innovative applications, Lan and Ren proposed a SPOC + KG + AI blended teaching model to address the significant foundational differences among vocational students [12]. Zou et al. constructed a curriculum framework aimed at cultivating the research capabilities of graduate students. This framework features a knowledge graph-competency matrix-intelligent companion structure [13]. Focusing on experimental and practical training scenarios, Wei et al. constructed a curriculum system. This system features digitalized curriculum resources, standardized evaluation processes, intelligent curriculum platforms, and collaborative resource sharing [14]. In summary, existing research has established the technical foundation of the digital curriculum. Furthermore, it has explored its innovative applications across multiple scenarios. However, the intelligent era has shifted the logic of talent cultivation from a knowledge-based to a capability-oriented approach. Amid this transition, there remains a lack of systematic mechanism construction and empirical exploration. Specifically, it is unclear how to deeply embed the core functions of the digital curriculum into PBL to maximize the educational role of projects. This integration is essential to support students in iteratively generating high-quality inquiry projects. Ultimately, it facilitates a paradigm shift in talent cultivation toward a human-centered and competency-first approach.

2.2 Current Status and Development of Undergraduates' PBL in the Intelligent Era

The intelligent era is driving college PBL to shift from simple knowledge construction to deep inquiry through human-AI co-creation. Current research has addressed this transition across three areas: theoretical logic reconstruction, instructional structure transformation, and practical model innovation. In theoretical logic reconstruction, Dong and He asserted that deep learning in PBL relies on the synergy of active construction, situated learning, social interaction, and cognitive tools [15]. Furthermore, Liu et al. merged PBL and phenomenon-based learning into PBL2 [16]. For instructional structure transformation, Wu and Gao established a teacher-student-AI tripartite classroom structure [17], while Yu et al. revealed the core concepts of human-machine collaborative learning within blended environments [18]. In terms of practical model innovation, Dai and Xia constructed an online-offline blended teaching model based on PBL. This model aims to enhance the disciplinary knowledge and deep learning capabilities of preservice teachers [19]. Omeh et al. validated the effectiveness of AI-assisted PBL in improving students' programming skills [20]. Similarly, Pasmala et al. developed a digital PBL model, using AI to facilitate students' digital content creation and personalized learning paths [21]. However, these studies have predominantly focused on macroscopic paradigms or isolated AI tool applications. As the digital curriculum serves as the core vehicle for higher education reform, further exploration is needed on how to deeply integrate its inherent elements into the PBL process.

3 Model Construction

To construct a digital curriculum-empowered PBL model for undergraduates, this study first systematically reviews relevant theories, including the theories of PBL, human-machine collaborative learning, and distributed cognition. This review provides a solid theoretical foundation for model construction. Second, it conducts an in-depth analysis of the empowerment mechanisms of the digital curriculum for PBL. This analysis covers four dimensions: theme determination, content reconstruction, activity implementation, and evaluation. Finally, this study distills the general process of PBL in higher education. Based on this process, it deduces the PPP framework, which comprises overall planning (Plan), implementation paths (Path), and product evaluation (Product). Ultimately, it constructs the DC-OPPP model of digital curriculum-empowered PBL for undergraduates.

3.1 Theoretical Basis

Project-Based Learning Theory. PBL is a problem-driven learning paradigm situated in authentic contexts, presenting learning content as project activities. Empowered by digital intelligence, it uses teacher-student-AI tripartite collaboration to facilitate inquiry, problem-solving, and outcome generation. This collaborative process cultivates students' cross-disciplinary knowledge, higher-order thinking, and comprehensive literacy. Driven by digital transformation, it reconstructs classroom formats and evaluation methods by evolving teaching from binary teacher-student interaction to teacher-student-AI tripartite collaboration.

Human-Machine Collaborative Learning Theory. Human-machine collaborative learning theory reveals the transformation of teaching subjects within intelligent environments, emphasizing the deep integration of human wisdom and machine intelligence. It posits that intelligent agents are not mere tools in teaching, rather, they act as digital companions or intelligent tutors, undertaking tasks such as data retrieval and logical deduction. In PBL, the teacher-student-AI tripartite collaboration facilitates efficient execution and deep innovation in complex problem-solving.

Distributed Cognition Theory. Distributed cognition theory posits that cognition is distributed across individuals, others, and the environment. Learning is the flow and integration of cognitive resources across various mediums. This theory explains cognition in intelligent environments. It supports designing assessments and task chains. In PBL empowered by the digital curriculum, knowledge transcends the individual's brain. It is distributed across digital spaces via knowledge graphs and digital profiles. Consequently, project outcomes result from learners mobilizing these resources and tools for distributed processing.

3.2 Analysis of How the Digital Curriculum Empowers Undergraduates' PBL

The digital curriculum cultivates higher-order skills, reconstructs teacher-student relations, and innovates instructional models. This perfectly aligns with the focus of modern PBL on critical thinking and innovation. This study integrates the characteristics of the digital curriculum with the elements of PBL. Based on the teacher-student-AI tripartite structure, it deeply analyzes how the digital curriculum empowers PBL across four areas: theme determination, content reconstruction, activity implementation, and diagnostic evaluation.

Empowering Project Theme Determination Through Digital Profiles. Reflecting societal talent demands and educational value is an intrinsic requirement for project themes. Data profiling within the digital curriculum enables the creation of talent demand and teaching objective profiles based on "person-job" matching. Large language models then integrate these profiles with dynamic knowledge graphs. They mine capability requirements from cases to generate project themes, thereby guiding the design of driving questions. Ultimately, this integration ensures unified value guidance, knowledge transfer, and capability cultivation throughout learning.

Empowering Project Content Reconstruction Through Multi-Dimensional Graphs. Supporting talent cultivation goals is the core requirement of project content. In cultivating new-quality productive forces, traditional linear knowledge systems cannot support complex problem-solving. Thus, content must be reconstructed around project themes. The digital curriculum utilizes multi-dimensional graphs of knowledge, competencies, and problems. They dismantle disciplinary barriers through dynamic evolution and logical reasoning. Furthermore, the curriculum provides knowledge maps for rapid problem pinpointing. Supported by digital profiles, it enables personalized learning, ensuring each student enhances higher-order skills via optimal paths.

Empowering Human-AI Collaborative Activities Through Multi-Agents. Activities are central to the educational value of PBL. As human-AI collaboration becomes the fundamental paradigm of future society, traditional teacher-student interaction is shifting to a teacher-student-AI tripartite structure. The digital curriculum introduces multi-agent systems with diverse functions to support scenario-based teaching. They push personalized resources to promote human-AI collaborative learning. Concurrently, retrospective analysis of teacher-student-AI interactions extracts course essentials and identifies teaching gaps. This improves overall teaching quality.

Empowering Evidence-Based Evaluation Through Multi-Dimensional Data. Evidence-based evaluation enables learners to diagnose issues and achieve continuous development [22]. The digital curriculum achieves this through digital intelligence, following the human-AI collaborative pathway of co-constructing standards, implementing process evaluations, and conducting retrospective analysis [23]. This process seamlessly collects scenario-based learning data. It builds multi-dimensional inferential models covering knowledge mastery and interaction frequency for personalized intervention. Applying the longitudinal analysis within the digital curriculum and horizontal evaluation of students' *ideology-knowledge-capability-quality* enables agile teaching strategies [24]. This achieves aligned diagnosis and improvement across teaching, learning, and evaluation.

3.3 Model Construction of the Digital Curriculum Empowering Undergraduates' PBL

The General Process of Undergraduates' PBL. Undergraduates' PBL provides a new activity model for classroom teaching. It shifts teaching from one-way lecturing to two-way, teacher-guided exploration. Based on the core elements of PBL, integrating contemporary needs, and guided by PBL and instructional theories, this study proposes a general process for PBL in higher education (Fig. 1).

The PBL process adopts the framework of *Project Initiation—Project Execution—Project Evaluation.* It links five stages: Problem Identification, Plan Formulation, Plan Implementation, Outcome Presentation, and Evaluation. This forms a complete loop from context introduction to problem-solving and outcome conversion. It also embeds interactive mechanisms empowered by digital technology.

Project initiation is the starting point of undergraduates' PBL. This stage transforms real-world problems into perceptible learning contexts. It guides students to clarify the

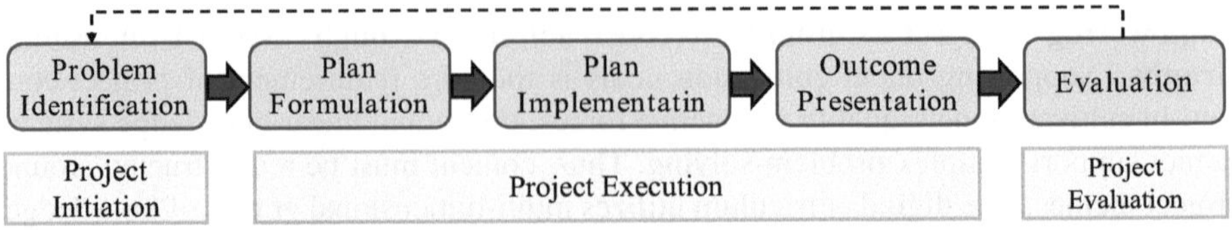

Fig. 1. The General Process of PBL for University Students

core tasks and driving questions, thereby activating motivation, defining the direction for meaning construction, and propelling the project forward.

Project execution is the core of undergraduates' PBL. It comprises plan formulation, plan implementation, and outcome presentation. Students conduct practices such as data collection, scheme design, and prototype development through group collaboration, interdisciplinary integration, and teacher-student-AI tripartite collaboration. This stage builds an inquiry-outcome loop ensuring the achievement of PBL objectives.

Project evaluation is the endpoint of undergraduates' PBL. It focuses on outcome generation and capability transfer. Here, students and teachers utilize digital tools for simulation, AI-assisted optimization, and experimental verification. This deeply integrates theory and practice. Simultaneously, evidence-based feedback from a multi-dimensional evaluation system promotes outcome transformation, enhancing students' capacity to solve ill-structured problems.

The PPP Framework of the Digital Curriculum Empowering PBL for Undergraduates. Based on the empowering mechanisms of the digital curriculum, university PBL processes, and instructional theories, this study proposes a PPP framework. It comprises Plan, Path, and Product for the digital curriculum empowering undergraduates' PBL (Fig. 2).

Plan: integrating Industry and Academia to Define Themes and Driving Questions. Driven by the core logic of industry-academia integration, the Plan stage synergizes industry demands with academic frontiers. By analyzing elements such as disciplinary difficulties, competency gaps, contemporary social issues, and pedagogical challenges, this stage extracts driving questions that are both authentic and challenging. These questions serve as the foundation for defining the project theme, thereby ensuring that the project design aligns with talent cultivation goals and provides a clear direction for subsequent implementation.

Path: defining Constraints, Deconstructing Tasks, and human-AI Collaboration. The Path stage follows the core logic of defining constraints, deconstructing tasks, providing scaffolding, and embedding feedback. It breaks down complex projects into executable task chains. During the project execution process, teacher-student-AI tripartite collaborative activities are conducted. These activities deepen learning through task-driven approaches, problem-solving, and collaborative inquiry. This process ensures orderly progression and provides a practical basis for subsequent evaluation.

Product: generating Diverse Outcomes and evidence-based Evaluation. Centering on evidence-based evaluation, the Product stage generates diverse outcomes, such as solutions, actual products, and conceptual prototypes, to meet talent cultivation goals,

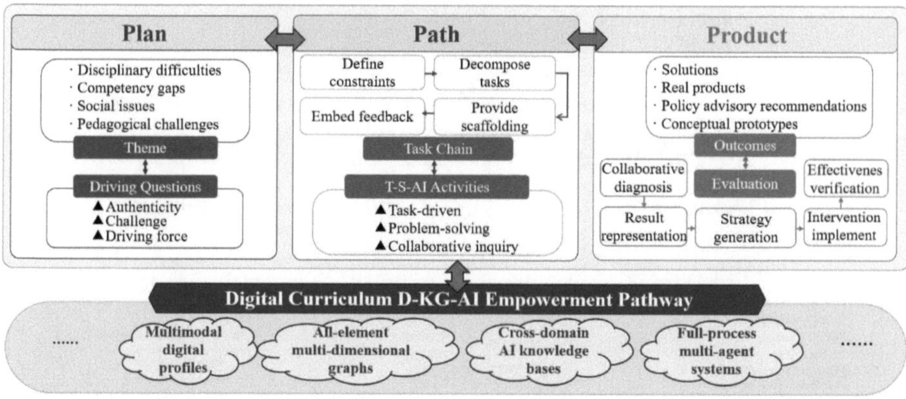

Fig. 2. The PPP Framework of the Digital Curriculum Empowering PBL for Undergraduates

thereby ensuring high outcome-goal alignment. Through collaborative diagnosis, strategy generation, intervention implementation, and effectiveness validation, this stage dynamically monitors and improves project implementation. Ultimately, it forms a goal-outcome-evaluation-improvement closed-loop feedback mechanism that sustains the continuous enhancement of talent cultivation quality.

The DC-OPPP Model of the Digital Curriculum Empowering Undergraduates' PBL. Guided by PBL, human-machine collaborative learning, and distributed cognition theory, this study clarifies how the digital curriculum empowers university PBL. Building upon the general PBL process, it constructs the DC-OPPP model (Fig. 3).

This model uses the Digital Curriculum (DC) as an intelligent foundation. The DC features multi-modal profiles, multi-dimensional graphs, cross-domain AI knowledge bases, and multi-agent systems. The model deeply integrates the PPP mechanism—Plan, Path, and Product—with general PBL stages to achieve the core Objective (O) of cultivating new-quality talent.

The Plan stage starts by addressing talent goals. It uses the multi-modal profiles of the digital curriculum to match talent demand with students' capabilities. This process extracts project themes and authentic, challenging driving questions. The Path stage uses the dynamically updated multi-dimensional graphs of the digital curriculum to break disciplinary boundaries. This provides students with cross-domain knowledge navigation for solving complex problems. Meanwhile, embedded agents play multiple roles. This realizes teacher-student-AI tripartite collaboration and promotes in-depth project inquiry. The Product stage uses the digital curriculum for unobtrusive data collection and comprehensive evaluation. Then, agents generate diagnostic reports that support teachers' evidence-based guidance and provide personalized feedback to promote students' reflection. This comprehensively enhances knowledge and competencies.

This model empowers the entire PBL process with digital technology. It overcomes traditional PBL bottlenecks, thereby providing theoretical support for PBL-oriented digital curriculum design.

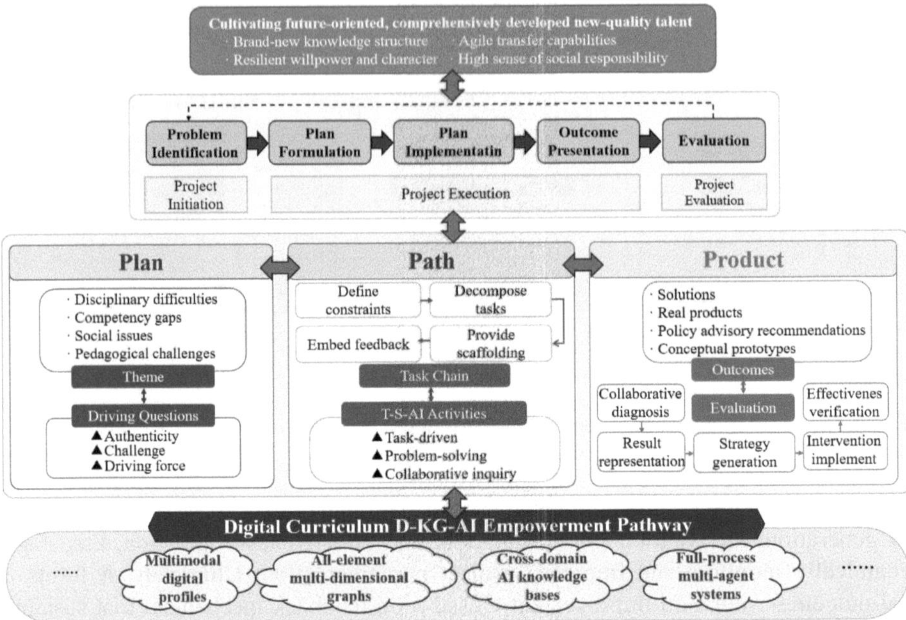

Fig. 3. The DC-OPPP Model of the Digital Curriculum Empowering Undergraduates' PBL

4 Application Effectiveness

4.1 Experimental Design

This empirical study centers on the project Research on Educational Technology Empowered by Digital Intelligence. Participants were undergraduates from the 2023 cohort majoring in Educational Technology at H University. The digital curriculum *Research Methods in Educational Technology* on the MOOC platform served as the PBL environment.

Targeting the core content and key competencies of the curriculum, students followed a progressive task chain of understanding frontiers, mastering research design, conducting digital-intelligence educational reform, and generating research outcomes. This 15-h project spanned four modules: *New Developments in EdTech Research in the Intelligent Era*, *EdTech Research Design*, *Knowledge Graph-Empowered Teaching Reform Research*, and *AI-Empowered Teaching Reform and Paper Writing*. Ultimately, students produced two outcomes: a Research Proposal and a Research Report.

To verify the effectiveness of the DC-OPPP model, this study first organized conventional PBL for the Knowledge Graph-Empowered Teaching Reform Research module, followed by a learning experience pre-test. Next, it applied the DC-OPPP model to the AI-Empowered Teaching Reform and Paper Writing module, concluding with a post-test to assess changes in learning experiences (Fig. 4).

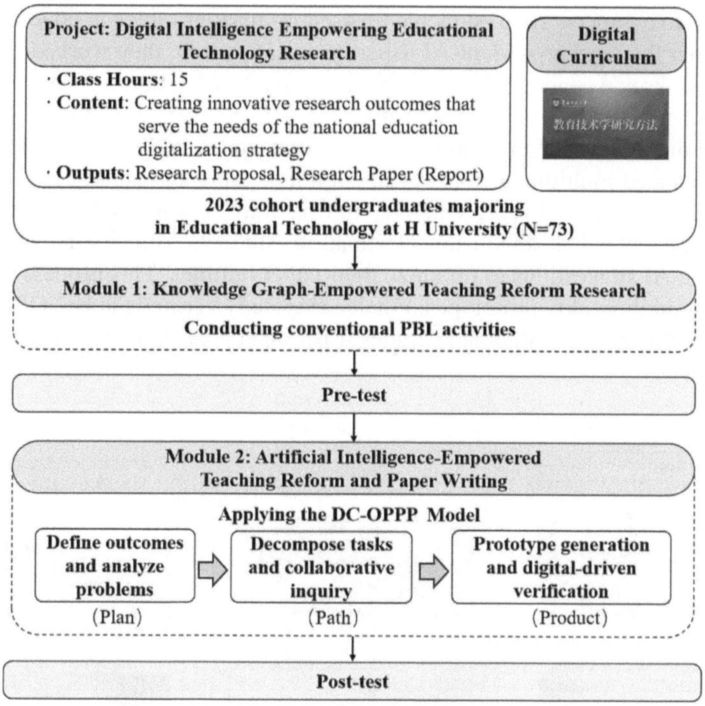

Fig. 4. Empirical Research Design

4.2 Experimental Process

During the experimental intervention phase, this study focused on the module AI-Empowered Teaching Reform and Paper Writing. The driving question was: *How to design a research plan and write a research paper?* Following the DC-OPPP model, the study implemented a teacher-student-AI tripartite collaborative teaching practice. This practice comprised three core stages: overall planning, implementation path, and product evaluation (Fig. 5).

The Plan focused on clarifying outcomes and analyzing problems. Starting by addressing the Education Digitalization Strategy 2.0 and students' actual developmental needs, the teacher established the project theme as *Digital Intelligence Empowering Educational Technology Research* and posed the driving question: How to design a research plan and write a research paper? Next, the teacher analyzed representative cases and guided students to examine the structure of high-quality papers. Through this activity, students developed an intuitive judgment of paper quality, thereby clarifying the direction for advancing research design tasks through subsequent human-machine collaboration.

The Path focused on decomposing tasks and collaborative inquiry. First, the teacher divided the complex research design task into a progressive chain of subtasks. Subsequently, the teacher organized group discussions, provided targeted feedback, and summarized key points. This process deepened students' understanding of the paper's structure. Students acted as active explorers in the learning process. They leveraged the digital curriculum's knowledge graph and the Addie AI agent to complete the analysis of representative papers. Then, students focused on frontier topics in educational technology. Under the teacher-student-AI tripartite collaboration, they worked in groups to decompose tasks and conducted collaborative inquiry. Finally, they determined the paper topic and constructed the preliminary outline.

The Product focused on prototype generation and data-driven verification. The teacher introduced multidimensional evaluation indicators and an AI evaluation agent. Next, the teacher selected representative student draft outlines and collaborated with AI tools to conduct a dual-dimensional evaluation. Students critically integrated teacher feedback and AI suggestions to optimize their paper outlines. This process enabled the generation of high-quality prototypes. Finally, this study verified the DC-OPPP model's effectiveness through overall course grades, PBL outcomes, and learning experiences.

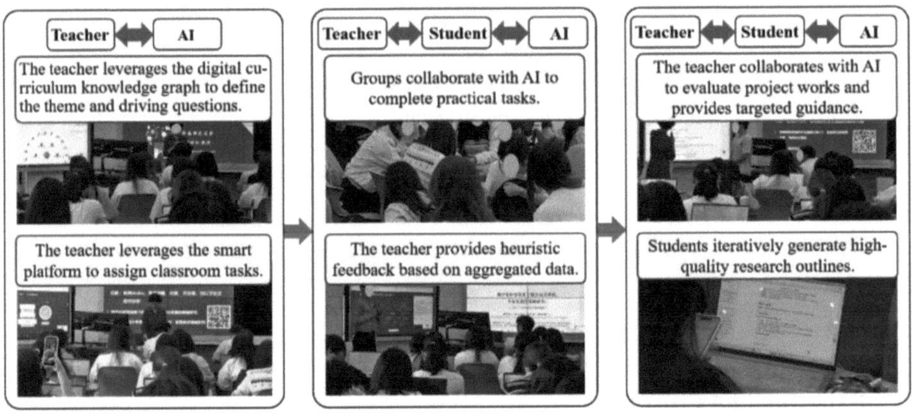

Fig. 5. Instructional Practice

4.3 Effectiveness Analysis

Overall Course Grades. Overall course grades provide the most direct objective evidence of teaching reform effectiveness. They assess students' theoretical knowledge and project-based performance. To evaluate the model's impact on overall learning outcomes, this study conducted descriptive statistical analysis on course grades (Table 1).

Table 1. Descriptive Statistical Analysis of Students' Overall Course Grades

Indicators	Sample Size (N)	Mean (M)	Median	Standard Deviation (SD)	Min. Score	Max. Score	Excellent/Good Rate
Final Comprehensive Grade	73	78.85	80	8.06	54	94	56.16%

Based on the course teaching objectives and evaluation rubrics, this study defined Overall Course Grades of 80 or above as the excellent/good level. This criterion was used to calculate the excellent/good rate. As shown, the class (N = 73) mean score was 78.85. The data exhibits typical negative skewness (median = 80.00, excellence/good rate = 56.16%). This indicates that, under the DC-OPPP model, the vast majority of students can overcome implementation obstacles inherent in PBL to successfully complete learning tasks and generate substantial project outcomes, thereby reaching a high level of proficiency in solving ill-structured problems and realizing innovative outcomes.

Project Outcomes. Project outcomes comprehensively assess students' knowledge, abilities, and competencies. Guided by evaluation theory and instructional design theory, this study developed an evaluation index system for Research on Educational Technology Empowered by Digital Intelligence. It comprises five dimensions: research topic, content, design, innovation, and writing standards (Table 2).

Table 2. Evaluation Index System for Undergraduates' Project Outcomes

Indicator	Evaluation Criteria
Research Topic Selection (30%)	Aligns with national education digitalization strategies, targeting foundational disciplinary issues or industry problems with a forward-looking, leading-edge formulation
Research Content (25%)	Clearly defines specific research content centered on a distinct problem within a targeted field
Research Design (15%)	Features rational design, strong logic, reliable data, and comprehensive literature citations
Research Innovation (20%)	Demonstrates broad application prospects and potential for large-scale disciplinary promotion
Writing Standards (10%)	Exhibits clear articulation, complete structure, and standardized use of terminology and references

Three teachers independently evaluated the outcomes using the index. Their average formed the final teacher score. Concurrently, the AI evaluation agent generated machine scores (Table 3). The teachers' evaluations demonstrated high consistency and reliability (Kendall's $W = 0.734$; average pairwise Pearson's $r = 0.632$).

However, agent scores and average teacher scores lacked a significant positive correlation ($r = -0.468$, $p = .067$). The agent likely favored textual formatting and structural completeness. Conversely, human teachers prioritized project outcomes' innovation and logical soundness in real-world contexts. This discrepancy substantiates the necessity of human-AI collaborative evaluation. In the evaluation of complex problems, while agents offer preliminary assessments, human teachers' expert oversight remains irreplaceable.

Table 3. Human-AI Collaborative Scores for Project Outcomes

Group	Project Titles	T1	T2	T3	Avg	AI
1	Effects of GAI-Assisted Instructional Design on Pre-Service Teachers' Teaching Efficacy	80	76	83	80	91
2	Design and Practice of GAI-Based Personalized Training Paths for Pre-Service Teachers' Teaching Competencies	90	80	87	86	92
3	Components, Status, and Enhancement Strategies of Undergraduates' AI Literacy	85	92	89	87	79
4	Iterative Design and Practice of GAI-Empowered Interdisciplinary PBL	81	76	75	77	93
5	Effectiveness of AI Adaptive Learning Systems in Personalized Tutoring for Middle School Math Underachievers	83	79	80	81	91
6	Effects of GAI-Generated Assignments on Undergraduates' Learning Autonomy	85	88	85	86	92
7	Mechanisms of Human-Machine Collaborative Problem-Solving in Fostering Undergraduates' Critical Thinking	86	91	90	89	81
8	Scenario-Based Investigation of Core Bottlenecks and Implementation Pathways for Educational Digitalization in Border Ethnic Regions	87	91	86	88	92

In terms of content, the students' research outcomes exhibited high academic quality and foresight. Topics covered field hotspots like *AI-assisted instructional design* and *AI adaptive learning systems*. Both teacher scores ($M = 83.06$, $SD = 4.63$) and agent scores ($M = 90.13$, $SD = 4.10$) reached excellent/good levels. This achievement demonstrates that under the DC-OPPP model, students mastered the research methods. Furthermore, they developed agile transfer skills and innovative competencies to solve complex problems in real-world contexts.

Learning Experience. This study used a scale to assess students' experiences after each module. Data from 30 randomly selected students per module were analyzed via an independent samples t-test (Table 4).

Table 4. Independent Samples t-Test Results of Student Learning Experience

Group	N	M	SD	t	df	p	Cohen's d	95% CI
Knowledge Graph-Empowered Teaching Reform Research	30	4.03	0.36					

(continued)

Table 4. (*continued*)

Group	N	M	SD	t	df	p	Cohen's d	95% CI
AI-Empowered Teaching Reform and Paper Writing	30	4.27	0.45	-2.27	58	.027*	0.59	[0.03, 0.45]

Note: $p < .05$; CI represents the confidence interval of the mean difference

Results showed students' learning experience scores were significantly higher in the DC-OPPP module ($M = 4.27$, $SD = 0.45$) than in conventional PBL ($M = 4.03$, $SD = 0.36$). This difference was statistically significant ($t\ (58) = -2.27, p = .027 < 0.05$). The moderate effect size (Cohen's d = 0.59) indicates that the DC-OPPP model effectively enhanced students' learning experiences.

5 Discussion and Conclusion

Due to constraints in the research timeframe and conditions, this study has certain limitations. Currently, the effectiveness evaluation relies solely on short-term intervention data from a single course. Therefore, future studies should conduct longitudinal experiments across other disciplines. Furthermore, researchers must optimize the AI agent's ability to evaluate complex, higher-order projects. These efforts will comprehensively verify and enhance the model's generalizability and long-term educational value. This study also identifies the practical challenges encountered during implementation. First, conducting teacher-student-AI tripartite collaborative activities places high demands on students' digital literacy. Therefore, teachers must provide appropriate guidance during actual instruction to prevent students from over-relying on content generated by the intelligent agent. Second, current AI agents have algorithmic limitations when evaluating students' higher-order innovative thinking. Consequently, teachers and students must critically evaluate and adopt the agent's evaluation suggestions during human-machine collaborative assessments. Furthermore, continuous training and related activities are necessary to enhance the critical thinking skills of both teachers and students.

The findings of this study align with similar domestic and international research. Furthermore, this study builds upon and advances existing research. Specifically, it echoes the consensus that the digital curriculum provides effective resource support and process management tools for PBL. The advancement is that, by following the logic of revealing mechanisms, constructing a model, and validating effectiveness, this study elucidates the underlying mechanisms of how the digital curriculum empowers PBL. Moreover, it proposes the practically applicable and empirically validated DC-OPPP model. This model provides clear guidance and pathways for deeply integrating the digital curriculum with PBL. Further, it offers a valuable reference for scaling up the cultivation of new-quality talent.

This study focuses on the demands of cultivating new-quality talent in the intelligent era. It analyzes how the digital curriculum functionally empowers undergraduates' PBL. Additionally, it constructs and validates the DC-OPPP model to facilitate this empowerment. The research results indicate that this model helps students generate high-quality project outcomes, enhance their learning experience in the intelligent learning environment, and achieve higher overall course grades.

Acknowledgements. This study was supported by the 2023 Guangdong Province Undergraduate University Teaching Quality and Teaching Reform Engineering Construction Project, titled "Research on Knowledge Graph-Enabled Curriculum Digitalization and Scenario-Based Application."

References

1. Thomas, J.W.: A review of research on project-based learning (2000)
2. Liu, J., Zhong, Z.: Research on the project-based learning (PBL) model. Studies in Foreign Education **11**, 18–22 (2002)
3. Barron, B.: When smart groups fail. J. Learn. Sci. **12**(3), 307–359 (2003)
4. Zhu, Z.: New development of smart education: From flipped classroom to smart classroom and smart learning space. Open Educ. Res. **22**(01), 18–26 (2016)
5. Wu, D., Guo, Q., Wu, L., Cheng, H.: Educational evaluation reform empowered by intelligent technology. Open Educ. Res. **29**(04), 4–10 (2023)
6. Xie, Y., Li, C., Li, C., Qiu, Y.: Digital curriculum in universities in the intelligent era: Connotation, structural features, and construction. e-Education Research **45**(11), 5–12 (2024)
7. Khodabandelou, R., Yousef, A.M.F., Elhaj, A.: Affordances and core features of successful digital courses design in higher education. Open Praxis **17**(3), 544–560 (2025)
8. Liu, C., Lu, F., Hu, J.: Strategies and reflections on the smart upgrade of national first-class online courses empowered by AI: A case study of the Basic Immunology and Pathogenic Biology course. Chinese J. Immunol. 1–11
9. Tian, W., Wu, Z., Sui, P.: Innovative practice of in-depth development of professional courses empowered by knowledge graphs. China University Teaching **05**, 16–25 (2025)
10. Chen, L., Yang, Y., Chen, M., Chen, W., Zhao, Y.: GenAI-driven online learning: Construction and pedagogical exploration of intelligent teaching assistants. Mod. Educ. Technol. **35**(06), 86–96 (2025)
11. Liang, G., Pang, X., Li, S., Shi, B., Liu, D.: Application of digital twins in virtual simulation experimental teaching of control courses. Experim. Technol. Manage. **41**(03), 175–183 (2024)
12. Lan, C., Ren, J.: Model innovation and effectiveness enhancement of curriculum teaching empowered by knowledge graphs from the perspective of smart education. Vocational Education Forum **42**(04), 73–80 (2026)
13. Zou, Q., et al.: Construction and teaching practice of the "Genetic Engineering" smart curriculum integrating artificial intelligence and outcome-based education. Chin. J. Biotechnol. **42**(03), 1413–1423 (2026)
14. Wei, M., Lu, Z., Fu, Y., Jiang, H., Li, W.: Experimental curriculum reform empowered by digital teaching: A case study of the construction of a smart microbiology experiment curriculum for new agricultural sciences. Microbiology China **53**(04), 1969–1980 (2026)
15. Dong, Y., He, J.: Application of project-based learning (PBL) in university teaching. Mod. Educ. Technol. **29**(09), 53–58 (2019)
16. Liu, J., Zhang, Q., Zhao, Z., Wu, Z., Zhang, D.: Innovative pathways for psychology education in the artificial intelligence era: Construction and practice of the PBL2 pedagogy. Research in Teaching **48**(03), 56–67 (2025)

17. Wu, F., Gao, S.: Paradigm shift in classroom teaching in the intelligent era: The structure and form of human-AI integration. e-Education Research **47**(01), 75–83 (2026)
18. Yu, L., Zhang, X., Deng, S.: Human-AI collaborative learning in blended teaching: Essential characteristics and practical forms. Journal of Southwest University (Social Sciences Edition) **51**(05), 189–201 (2025)
19. Dai, G., Xia, X.: Application of online and offline blended teaching model based on project-based learning in university biological science courses: A case study of the Biology Teaching Design and Case Analysis course. Life Science Research **29**(03), 265–271 (2025)
20. Omeh, C.B., Ayanwale, M.A., Mnguni, L.E., Olelewe, C.J.: Fostering programming skill and critical thinking through AI-assisted PBL integration. J. New Approach. Educat. Res. **14**(1), 22 (2025)
21. Pasmala, R., Chatwattana, P.: Adaptive Digital Project-Based Learning Model with Artificial Intelligence Technology to Promote Digital Creations. High. Educ. Stud. **15**(4), 75–84 (2025)
22. Xie, Y., Gao, L., Qiu, Y., Peng, Z., Li, C.: Evaluation innovation of high-quality classrooms empowered by intelligent technology. e-Education Research **44**(12), 73–79 (2023)
23. Xie, Y., Li, C., Wu, B., Pan, D.: How generative artificial intelligence empowers project-based learning in primary and secondary schools. Modern Distan. Educ. Res. **37**(05), 97–104 (2025)
24. Xie, Y., Qiu, Y., Zhang, R., Luo, W.: Implementation pathways and evaluation innovation of ideological and political education in university courses empowered by digital transformation. China Educ. Technol. **09**, 7–15 (2022)

A Scenario-Based Experimental Design for Cybersecurity Curriculum Implementation

Wei Wang, Chen Yi, Chun-Wah Ho, and Lam-For Kwok(✉)

Institute of Cyberspace Technology, HKCT Institute of Higher Education, Ma On Shan, Hong Kong
{waynewang,alexyi,cwho,lfkwok}@ctihe.edu.hk

Abstract. Secondary-level cybersecurity education often faces difficulties in linking abstract concepts with meaningful practical experience. To address this challenge, applied learning courses are increasingly used to support students' career exploration and early skill development. This paper presents a scenario-based experimental design that supports the implementation of an existing secondary-level cybersecurity curriculum. The design organizes cyber range activities into a sequence of connected security scenarios that reflect common cybersecurity workflows. Scenarios progress from routine system operation and risk exposure to vulnerability identification, attack analysis, and remediation. Course activities are used to illustrate how scenario progression is implemented in practice. Assessment results from an early stage of the course provide initial evidence of student learning. The results indicate that the proposed design supports students' understanding of fundamental cybersecurity concepts and basic security practices. This study shows how scenario-based experiments can better align curriculum objectives with hands-on learning in secondary-level cybersecurity education.

Keywords: Scenario-Based Learning · Cybersecurity Curriculum · Cyber Range

1 Introduction

Cybersecurity education at the secondary level faces several challenges, especially in applied learning courses. These courses aim to provide practice-oriented learning and support students' career exploration. Cybersecurity education is essential to prepare students to use the Internet safely [1]. However, many secondary students have limited technical backgrounds. They often find cybersecurity concepts abstract and difficult to understand. Their exposure to computer systems, networks, and security practices is usually minimal. Spencer [2] revealed the challenges and successes of developing and implementing a cybersecurity curriculum in STEM. In addition, most secondary schools lack dedicated cybersecurity infrastructure, such as secure laboratories or specialized training platforms. Alotaibi, et al. [3] highlighted the practical challenges teachers face incorporating cyber security into other subjects. This study was motivated by the need to design practical learning activities for applied cybersecurity courses that are both accessible and engaging for secondary students.

K. T. Chui et al. (Eds.): ICBL 2026, LNCS 16778, pp. 480–490, 2027.
https://doi.org/10.1007/978-981-92-3761-6_33

Scenario-based learning offers a practical way to support applied cybersecurity education. Domínguez-Dorado, et al. [4] suggested that an interactive, scenario-based approach could significantly improve situational awareness in cybersecurity. So [5] proposed a scenario-based web security education model to increase the effectiveness of teaching web application security. In this study, the term scenario-based learning refers to structured learning activities designed to represent typical working contexts in the field of cybersecurity. It places students in concrete situations rather than abstract descriptions. Each scenario represents a specific working context in cybersecurity practice, such as system operation, vulnerability identification, or attack analysis. Cyber range environments provide suitable technical support for this approach. They allow security scenarios to be simulated in a controlled and repeatable environment. This makes hands-on cybersecurity learning possible even in secondary schools with limited physical infrastructure [6].

Existing studies have explored the use of cyber ranges and scenario-based activities in cybersecurity education, particularly in higher education and professional training contexts [7–9]. Much of this work focuses on technical skill development, tool usage, or competition-oriented tasks [10]. In short, existing studies provide useful references for cybersecurity education through cyber ranges, scenario-based learning, and hands-on technical exercises. However, they mainly focus on higher education, professional training, or competition-oriented skill development. Less attention has been paid to how scenario-based experimental activities can be organized to support curriculum implementation for secondary-level applied cybersecurity education. A recent systematic literature review also reports that cybersecurity education content varies widely across countries and still contains significant gaps[11]. In the classroom, students often find cybersecurity learning dull when it is dominated by abstract explanations and isolated technical exercises. It is also hard for middle school students to understand the actual work scenarios of this profession from a professional standpoint. To address this issue, a scenario-based approach is introduced to connect learning activities with realistic security situations and professional contexts. In addition, the alignment between curriculum content, professional cybersecurity workflows, and experimental activities is often not explicitly discussed. This study addresses this gap by proposing a scenario-based experimental design tailored to secondary-level applied cybersecurity education. This study explores how scenario-based experiments can support the implementation of a secondary-level cybersecurity curriculum and how these scenarios can be aligned with curriculum learning objectives and professional cybersecurity workflows. The study focuses on two research questions: RQ1: How can scenario-based experiments be designed to support cybersecurity curriculum implementation at the secondary level? RQ2: How can cybersecurity scenarios be aligned with curriculum objectives and professional cybersecurity workflows?

In this design, course topics are organized around corresponding cybersecurity practice scenarios. This design follows the VPET approach [12]. This approach groups knowledge elements and required skill sets into learning units, supporting them with hands-on exercises in cyber range environments. In this study, the scenarios link cybersecurity knowledge with practical security skills. The experimental activities and course design in this study follow the same principle. Different course topics are matched with different security scenarios. The paper is organized into four sections. Section 2 introduces the cybersecurity curriculum and learning outcomes. Section 3 presents the scenario-based experimental design. Section 4 reports the observed learning outcomes, followed by the conclusion in Sect. 5.

2 Cybersecurity Curriculum Overview and Learning Outcomes

2.1 Curriculum Overview

This study discusses a secondary-level applied cybersecurity course designed to introduce students to the subject through practice-oriented learning. The curriculum is structured to support gradual learning progression, moving from general understanding to applied practice (Fig. 1). Foundational topics introduce students to cybersecurity concepts, risks, and industry context, while later learning activities emphasize practical engagement and contextual understanding. Modules 2 and 3 are designed as parallel components that provide complementary operational and defensive perspectives, both of which support the scenario-based practice in Module 4. This structure reflects the VPET principle of combining knowledge elements and skill development through hands-on learning units. At the secondary level, the course builds foundational cybersecurity competence, helps students make informed learning choices, and raises awareness of possible cybersecurity career pathways.

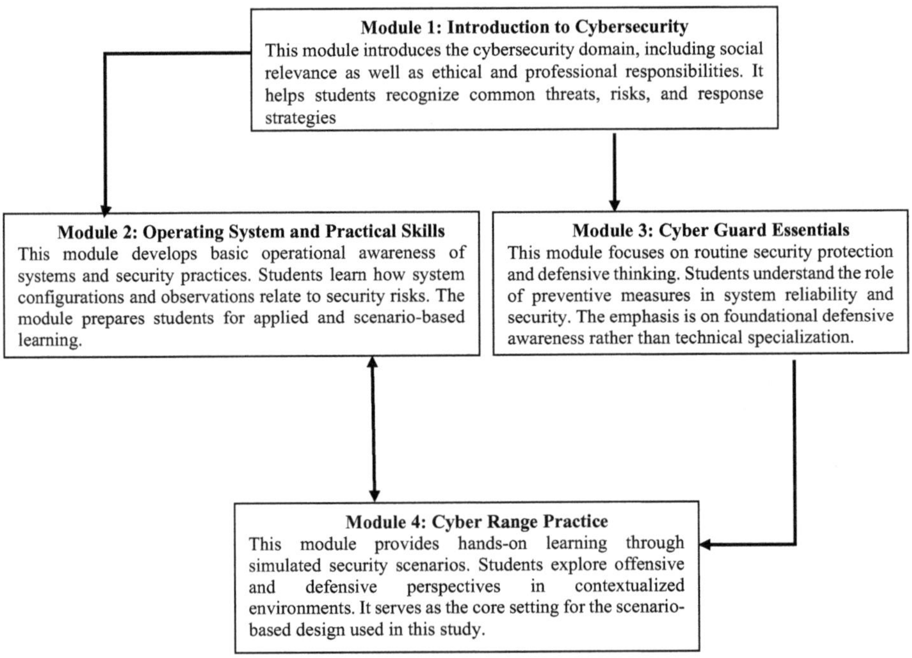

Fig. 1. Curriculum Map.

2.2 Learning Outcomes and Career Orientation

Modern cybersecurity education increasingly adopts learner centered and competency-based methodologies [13]. Upon completion of the course, students are expected to achieve learning outcomes across several complementary dimensions. At the knowledge level, students develop an understanding of common cybersecurity threats, risks, and response strategies, as well as basic concepts and principles underlying cybersecurity practices. This knowledge helps students recognize security issues when they appear in simple system situations. At the skills level, students gain familiarity with introductory professional tools, operating environments, and simple security tasks, enabling them to engage with cybersecurity activities at an entry level. Students use these skills to handle routine security tasks in structured practice.

Beyond technical knowledge, the course emphasizes professional awareness and ethical responsibility. Students are guided to recognize the importance of work ethics, legal considerations, and social responsibility in cybersecurity-related contexts. These outcomes support students in making informed and responsible judgments when engaging with security issues. Overall, these learning outcomes support career exploration rather than immediate professional qualification. The course focuses on raising awareness, encouraging early readiness and facilitating informed progression towards further study.

2.3 Conditions Supporting Scenario-Based Experimental Design

Within the existing applied cybersecurity curriculum, the learning objectives require students to engage with cybersecurity concepts in practical and contextualized ways. While the curriculum defines what students are expected to learn, how these expectations are realized depends largely on the design and organization of experimental activities.

The increasing sophistication of cybersecurity threats necessitates an educational approach that blends theoretical knowledge with practical experience [14]. In this study, the required conditions focus on structuring practical experiences that allow students to observe and reason about cybersecurity work in context. Rather than redesigning course content, the emphasis is placed on organizing experimental activities so that students can understand how security issues emerge, how risks are interpreted, and how responses are formed in realistic situations. Prior studies on scenario-based learning have shown that interactive scenario approaches can enhance situational awareness and support the development of practical decision-making skills in cybersecurity contexts [4]. Scenario-based training frameworks have also been used to strengthen team competencies and prepare learners for real-world challenges in professional settings [15, 16]. These conditions enable students to experience cybersecurity as a process, without exceeding the technical scope of the existing curriculum.

By aligning experimental activities with professional working contexts and task sequences, the course establishes suitable conditions for scenario progression. This approach forms the basis for the scenario-based experimental design presented in the next section, which aims to support the effective implementation of the existing cybersecurity curriculum.

3 Scenario-Based Experimental Design

3.1 Design Rationale and Scenario Progression Logic

This study uses a workflow-oriented reference framework to model defensive cybersecurity work scenarios, based on common industry security operations workflows (Fig. 2). This framework summarizes the common stages of authorized cybersecurity work, including system operation, risk exposure, vulnerability identification, threat and attack analysis, and response and remediation. It provides the design logic for scenarios in which learning activities follow the defensive cybersecurity workflow, from system operation to security response.

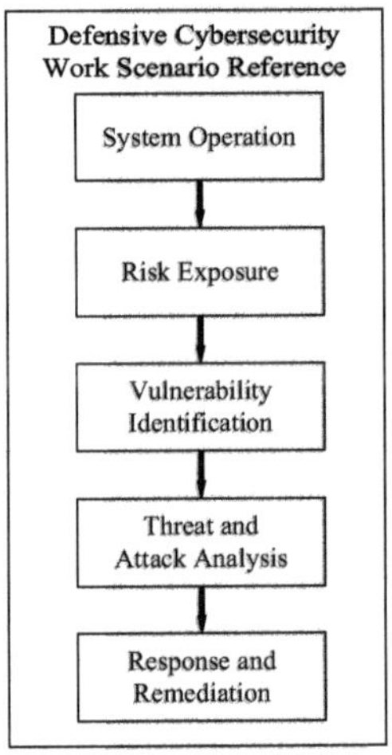

Fig. 2. Defensive Cybersecurity Work Scenario Progression.

The reference framework is introduced to ensure that scenario design reflects how cybersecurity work is normally carried out in practice, while remaining appropriate for secondary-level education. In real-world settings, cybersecurity tasks are commonly defensive and follow a clear process, beginning with system operation and leading to risk identification, analysis, and response. This progression is broadly consistent with task categories described in the NICE Cybersecurity Workforce Framework [17]. In this study, the NICE task categories are used only as a reference and are simplified for secondary-level learning. The scenario-based activities are designed to help students understand basic security risks through observable system situations and simple defensive tasks. Through these activities, students are expected to develop basic threat awareness, simple analytical skills, and an initial understanding of how defensive cybersecurity work is carried out.

Based on the reference framework, scenario progression in this study follows a structured path from routine system operation to security response. Students first engage with basic system configuration and observation tasks, which naturally reveal potential risk exposure. These risks lead to the identification of vulnerabilities, followed by the analysis of possible threat behaviors and their impacts. The final stage focuses on response actions, remediation measures, and reflection on security decisions. Each stage builds upon the previous one, allowing students to develop understanding incrementally without exceeding the technical scope of the existing curriculum.

3.2 Mapping Curriculum Content to Scenario-Based Experiments

In this study, Module 2 is used as the design example to show how curriculum content is mapped to scenario-based experiments. This module focuses on operating systems and foundational cybersecurity skills. Its core content includes system operation, security configuration, vulnerability scanning, and network observation. In this mapping, curriculum topics represent the knowledge to be learned, while cybersecurity tasks represent the skills they need to perform. Experimental activities connect these knowledge topics and skills within defensive security scenarios. The relationship between curriculum content, defensive work scenarios, and experimental activities is summarized in Table 1.

Table 1. Curriculum-Scenario-Experiment Mapping.

Mapping Curriculum Content to Defensive Work Scenarios			
Curriculum Content	Defensive Work Scenario Stage	Experimental Focus	Practical Skills Supporting Scenario Progression
Operating System Basics	System Operation	System setup and command-line interaction	Configure system settings and observe normal system behavior
Security Configuration	Risk Exposure	Security setting and configuration tasks	Adjust security settings and recognize configuration-related exposure
Vulnerability Scanning	Vulnerability Identification	Vulnerability scanning and assessment	Run vulnerability scans and identify configuration weaknesses
Network Observation	Threat and Attack Analysis	Network traffic observation and packet analysis	Monitor network traffic and interpret potential threat patterns
System Review and Reporting	Response and Remediation	Mitigation planning and structured reporting	Document findings and apply basic mitigation actions

Based on this mapping, each major curriculum topic is aligned with a specific stage of defensive cybersecurity task. Content related to operating systems establishes the system operation stage, where normal system behavior is observed. Security configuration topics correspond to risk exposure, as routine configuration choices directly affect system security. Vulnerability scanning content aligns with vulnerability identification, while network observation and traffic analysis support threat and attack analysis. Topics related to system review and reporting are associated with response and remediation. This alignment reflects the structure of defensive cybersecurity work in practice.

Experimental activities link curriculum topics with their corresponding work scenarios and take place in a cyber range environment. The cyber range provides system and network settings that enable realistic security scenarios to be constructed without introducing unauthorized or unsafe activities. Experiments place students in controlled system environments derived from course content, where security conditions emerge through normal system use.

System setup experiments allow students to observe baseline system behavior before security issues are considered. For example, students may configure a simple web server and then use Nmap to scan the system. They can observe open ports or services and understand how configuration choices affect system security. In another activity, students capture network traffic with Wireshark and identify unusual connection attempts or repeated login requests. Configuration experiments show how routine administrative decisions can increase or reduce system exposure within the simulated environment. Vulnerability scanning experiments then guide students to identify weaknesses in systems they have already configured, maintaining continuity across activities. These experiments support a coherent progression from normal operation to security analysis while remaining aligned with the scope of secondary-level instruction. Network observation experiments enable students to analyze system behavior and identify potential threat patterns without carrying out attacks. Response-oriented activities focus on mitigation and security decision-making and represent the final stage of the defensive cybersecurity workflow in the course.

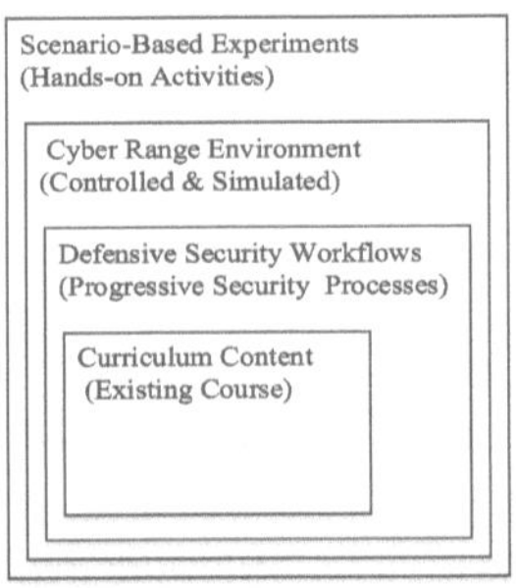

Fig. 3. Structural Framework of the Scenario-Based Experimental Design

Figure 3 summarizes the structural relationship among curriculum content, defensive security workflows, the cyber range environment, and experimental activities in this study. The figure shows that progression is realized through the organization of experiments according to defensive cybersecurity work workflows. Experimental activities are arranged so that security issues emerge and are addressed in a sequence consistent with professional practice. This structure forms the basis of the proposed scenario-based experimental design. The next section presents a representative experimental case.

3.3 A Representative Scenario-Based Experimental Case

The case examined in this study involves vulnerability scanning and network traffic observation conducted within a cyber range environment. The experiment is designed around normal system operation, where students observe system communication behavior and identify potential security risks through scanning results and traffic patterns. This setting reflects a common defensive cybersecurity task in which security issues are examined through observation and analysis.

The experimental scenario follows a defensive workflow in which system behavior is first observed under normal conditions, followed by the identification and interpretation of vulnerabilities and traffic characteristics. In this way, progression is achieved by moving from routine system use to security analysis within the same scenario context. The main elements of this experimental case, including its scenario setting, experimental activities, and assessment focus, are summarized in Table 2.

Table 2. A Scenario-Based Experimental Case.

Aspect	Description
Experiment Focus	Vulnerability scanning and network traffic observation in a cyber range-based environment
Related Defensive Context	Identification and analysis of potential security risks during normal system operation
Scenario Setting	A controlled system environment where vulnerabilities and traffic behavior can be observed
Experimental Activities	Students use AVWS to scan a simulated host with exposed services. They then capture network traffic and identify possible risks from open ports, endpoints, and traffic patterns
Analytical Focus	Interpreting scan results and traffic characteristics to identify potential security issues
Assessment Method	Short analytical report and group-based discussion on observed vulnerabilities and traffic behavior

4 Current Learning Status

This course was implemented for the first time, so no historical cohort data were available for comparison. A total of 43 students participated in the course tests, which include the assessments in both Module 1 and Module 2. The course consists of four modules, each with its own assessment component that includes both theoretical and practical evaluation. The data reported in this section are drawn from the assessment conducted in Module 1 and a formative test conducted during the implementation of Module 2. After Module 1 was completed, Module 2 began. The study assumed that students had completed Module 1 and had gained basic cybersecurity knowledge. However, the participants were secondary students, so their technical background and experience with professional security tools were still limited. Therefore, the Module 2 experiments were designed as introductory and structured activities. This module applies the scenario-based experimental design described earlier in the study. The course and experimental activities are designed based on the integration of knowledge, practical skills, scenarios, and experiments introduced earlier in the study.

The Module 1 assessment provides a baseline for comparison. Table 3 presents the comparison of student assessment scores in Module 1 and the test conducted during Module 2. In Module 1, the average score was 44.7. In the Module 2 test, the average score increased to 54.6. When records with zero scores are excluded, the valid average score increased from 50.6 to 65.2. These results show that many students developed a clearer understanding of the cybersecurity concepts introduced in the course. The test results therefore represent a preliminary indication of student learning rather than the final learning outcome.

Table 3. Module 1 and Module 2 Test Scores.

Comparison of student assessment scores			
Assessment	Students	Average Score	Valid Average Score
Module 1	43	44.7	50.6
Module 2 Test	43	54.6	65.2

*Valid Average Score excludes records with zero scores

Module 2 is still in progress. At the time of writing, no final assessment results are available for this module. However, experimental records from March 2026 provide additional information about students' participation in the scenario-based activities. During this period, a total of 101 experimental log entries were recorded in the cyber range environment. These logs were generated by 29 students participating in the Module 2 experimental activities, representing approximately 67% of the students enrolled in the course. The logs show an average of 3.5 entries per student, and about 41% of these students recorded three or more entries. One student recorded 17 entries, while the next highest record was 12, showing a strong pattern of repeated participation and active engagement in the experiments.

These records include tasks such as system configuration, service security setup, vulnerability scanning, and network observation. These activities correspond to the defensive work scenarios and practical skills described earlier in Table 1. Curriculum-Scenario-Experiment Mapping. Overall, the results of the system logs provide an initial indication that the course design is supporting students in developing foundational cybersecurity awareness and analytical skills, in line with the objectives of the applied curriculum.

5 Conclusion

This paper presents a scenario-based experimental design to support the implementation of a secondary-level cybersecurity curriculum. The design also provides a practical way to transform traditionally structured cybersecurity curricula into more applied learning experiences. Its main benefit is that it provides a clear path from curriculum objectives to executable experimental tasks. The design translates curriculum content into scenario-based experiments aligned with defensive cybersecurity workflows and implemented within a cyber range environment. This helps teachers convert abstract topics into concrete operations that students can observe and complete. Organizing experimental activities around realistic system operation, risk exposure, analysis and response provides a coherent structure for applied learning without increasing technical complexity.

A representative experimental case and current learning observations are used to demonstrate the practical application of the design. The assessment results show that the approach helped students develop foundational cybersecurity awareness and basic analytical skills appropriate for an applied secondary curriculum.

The proposed design offers a practical and adaptable way to integrate scenario-based experiments into secondary-level cybersecurity education. It also shows how a traditionally structured curriculum can support more applied learning in VPET-oriented education. The design links cybersecurity concepts with concrete system scenarios and observable system behavior. This helps students understand how security risks appear and how defensive actions are applied in practice. For secondary students, this reduces the gap between abstract cybersecurity knowledge and real security work situations. Future work will focus on analyzing scenario data generated during experimental activities, including system logs, task completion records, and students' operational actions within the cyber range environment. This analysis will examine how students complete tasks and make security decisions. Further research will compare learning outcomes across modules, refine scenarios based on students' task processes and errors, and examine the adaptability of the design to other cybersecurity topics and secondary-school contexts. Student feedback will also be collected in future studies to evaluate engagement, learning difficulties, and the perceived effectiveness of the scenario-based curriculum.

References

1. Chromiński, K., et al.: New Approach to Learning Cyber-Security in Secondary School. In: Smyrnova-Trybulska, E., Chen, N.-S., Kommers, P., Morze, N. (eds.) E-Learning and Enhancing Soft Skills: Contemporary Models of Education in the Era of Artificial Intelligence, pp. 193–207. Springer Nature Switzerland, Cham (2025)
2. Spencer, R.: The Urgency of Instituting Systemic Cybersecurity Curriculum within STEM at Secondary Educational Levels in Preparation for Postsecondary Institutions. J. Cybersecu. Educ. Res. Practice **2025**, 4 (2025)
3. Alotaibi, M., et al.: Empowering Youth in The Digital Age with Cyber Security Education: Results of the Interviews with Secondary School Teachers in Wales. In: Journal of The Colloquium for Information Systems Security Education, p. 8 (2026)
4. Domínguez-Dorado, M., et al.: Integration of Scenario-Based Learning in CyberTOMP With FLECO Studio: Enhancing Situational Awareness Training in Cybersecurity. IEEE Revista Iberoamericana de Tecnologias del Aprendizaje **20**, 310–320 (2025)
5. So, G.: A Study on Scenario-based Web Application Security Education Method. Int. J. Inter. Broadcast. Comm. **15**, 149–159 (2023)
6. Yi, C., et al.: A Lightweight Method for Process Evaluation in Educational Cyber Range Experiments. In: Technology in Education. Smart and Innovative Learning, pp. 271–282. Springer Nature Singapore (2026)

7. Allison, J.: Cybersecurity Risk Management Scenarios for Teaching Information Security Management. J. Appl. Secur. Res. **20**, 167–188 (2025)
8. Chui, K.T., et al.: A survey of internet of things and cyber-physical systems: Standards, algorithms, applications, security, challenges, and future directions. Information **14**(7), 388 (2023)
9. Yi, C., et al.: From Higher Diploma to Master: A Smart-Tech Vertical Curriculum Framework in Cyber Technology Education. In: Cheung, S.K.S., Liu, X., Xu, G., Kwok, L.F. (eds.) Technology in Education. Smart and Innovative Learning, CCIS, vol. 2752, pp. 340–351. Springer Nature, Singapore (2026)
10. Lazarov, W., et al.: Lessons Learned from Using Cyber Range to Teach Cybersecurity at Different Levels of Education. Technology, Knowledge and Learning (2025)
11. Sağlam, R.B., et al.: A Systematic Literature Review on Cyber Security Education for Children. IEEE Trans. Educ. **66**, 274–286 (2023)
12. Kwok, L.-F., et al.: Technology-Enhanced Cybersecurity Education: A VPET Approach. In: Technology in Education. Innovative Practices for the New Normal, pp. 20–31. Springer Nature Singapore (2024)
13. Sánchez, J., et al.: A framework for designing and certifying ECSF-aligned cybersecurity training through cyber ranges and virtual learning environments. Int. J. Inf. Secur. **25**, 46 (2026)
14. Narain, S., et al.: Practical Cybersecurity Education: A Course Model Using Experiential Learning Theory. Proceedings of the 56th ACM Technical Symposium on Computer Science Education V. 1, pp. 819–825. Association for Computing Machinery, Pittsburgh, PA, USA (2025)
15. Pramon, N., et al.: Conceptual Framework of Artificial Intelligence Strategy with Scenario-Based Training. In: 2025 5th International Conference on Educational Communications and Technology (ICTAECT), pp. 1–8. (2025)
16. Jong, W., Bartolucci, A.: Training future crisis communication advisers in crisis response: Applying scenario-based learning. Commun. Teach. **39**, 284–292 (2025)
17. https://niccs.cisa.gov/tools/nice-framework

An Experimental Online Study on the Impact of Social Media Comments on the Reflective Thinking of the Safe Behaviour of the Learners

Kwan Keung Ng[1(✉)], Yan Wai Chan[2], Simon K. S. Cheung[3], Lap Kei Lee[4], Nga-In Wu[5], Clifford Wong[6], and Miloslava Cerna[7]

[1] Ming-Ai (London) Institute, London, UK
s.ng@ming-ai.org.uk
[2] Department of Science and Environmental Studies, The Education University of Hong Kong, Hong Kong, China
[3] Information Technology Office, Hong Kong Metropolitan University, Hong Kong, China
kscheung@hkmu.edu.hk
[4] School of Science and Technology, Hong Kong Metropolitan University, Hong Kong, China
lklee@hkmu.edu.hk
[5] College of Professional and Continuing Education, The Hong Kong Polytechnic University, Kowloon, Hong Kong, China
ngain.wu@cpce-polyu.edu.hk
[6] Hang Lung Properties Limited, Hong Kong, China
[7] FIM - Department of Applied Linguistics, University of Hradec Králové, Hradec Králové, Czech Republic
miloslava.cerna@uhk.cz

Abstract. This research expands the understanding of social media's influence on adult learning, specifically in the context of safety education. The rapid proliferation of social media platforms in recent years has fundamentally altered the landscape of information dissemination, facilitating immediate access to updates on global events, including industrial accidents and pertinent government policies. These platforms not only provide timely information but also serve as spaces where individuals can articulate their opinions and emotions concerning these incidents. Such comments frequently extend beyond mere personal expressions; they encompass broader perspectives and experiences that resonate with the events being discussed. This study investigates the extent to which exposure to social media comments affects students enrolled in safety courses, particularly their attitudes and behaviours in professional work environments or supervisory roles after their education. Using the Work Safety Scale (WSS), we quantitatively assessed changes in students' reflections on safe behaviours before and after engaging with social media commentary. The findings reveal significant psychological effects stemming from these comments, underscoring the imperative to develop strategies for managing online discourse and promoting critical reflection among learners. Ultimately, this research contributes to the growing body of literature on the intersection of social media and adult education, with particular emphasis on its implications for safety training and the cultivation of informed, responsible practices in professional settings.

K. T. Chui et al. (Eds.): ICBL 2026, LNCS 16778, pp. 491–502, 2027.
https://doi.org/10.1007/978-981-92-3761-6_34

Keywords: Social Media Comments · Reflective Thinking · Work Safety Scale (WSS) · Safety Education · Public Incident Analysis

1 Introduction

Students enrolled in certificate courses often face long periods of study, during which it can be challenging for both lecturers and students to truly understand real-world situations and engage in meaningful reflection. The lack of thoughtful consideration may lead to superficial learning. Classroom practices and exercises can help enhance the learning atmosphere and provide insights into the emotional aspects of safety education.

This paper focuses on the impact of social media comments on learners' reflection. Specifically, after news or information is published on social or electronic media, readers can post their opinions freely. Due to the difficulty in identifying users' real identities [1], these comments tend to be more uninhibited and less constrained. Whether positive or negative, such comments are directly related to the topic and possess certain educational and reflective value.

For example, previous social media challenges have demonstrated unique trends that leverage exponential reach through nomination processes. One landmark case was the "Ice Bucket Challenge," which generated significant public attention and raised awareness about Amyotrophic lateral sclerosis [2]. This event prompted widespread public engagement and discussion about the use and allocation of social resources, as well as public health issues. Therefore, the influence of social media comments on learning and reflection should not be overlooked.

2 Purpose of Research

Educational research has extensively explored how lecturers and students use hashtags and engage with trending topics on social media. Studies have examined how higher education lecturers use social media to communicate with students, demonstrating its potential to strengthen teacher-student interactions. However, research also indicates that integrating social media into classroom activities can pose challenges, as students may need time to learn to interact with social media appropriately and effectively [3]. These findings are consistent with results in the fields of higher education and professional development [4].

Bandura and Walters' [5] earlier social learning theory centres on the concept of triadic reciprocality, a model that highlights the dynamic interplay among personal factors, environmental influences, and behaviour. This approach provides a psychological framework for understanding human behaviour, in which each component both affects and is affected by the other two, illustrating the reciprocal nature of human interaction.

The rapid proliferation of social media has fundamentally changed the way we access information [6], influencing our everyday knowledge, beliefs, and learning processes. Social cognitive theory is now widely applied across various fields, including general studies, education, safety behaviour, and social networks. In this context, it is important to investigate how media information, particularly through reader comments, affects reflective thinking. Therefore, this study aims to explore the impact of social media comments on students' reflection and learning in occupational health and safety-related courses, contributing to a deeper understanding of how online interactions shape educational experiences and outcomes.

Marin, et al. [7] critically examine how affective scaffolding influences critical thinking on social media platforms. Using a conceptual and philosophical approach, the authors review recent literature in social epistemology and the philosophy of emotions to argue that emotions are not inherently detrimental to online critical thinking. Their analysis suggests that the design features of social media platforms, referred to as affective scaffolding, can either facilitate or obstruct epistemically beneficial practices. By synthesising empirical and theoretical studies, the paper demonstrates that certain platform designs tend to amplify divisive emotions such as anger and mistrust, thereby reducing users' openness to alternative viewpoints and hindering critical reflection. In contrast, affective scaffolds that encourage empathy, curiosity, and deliberation can enhance critical thinking online. The authors also note that much of the existing research has focused on the analytic and rational aspects of critical thinking, often overlooking emotional and contextual influences. A main limitation of their study is the conceptual nature of their arguments, as they have not been empirically tested with specific user groups. The authors recommend further empirical research to explore how effective scaffolding can be intentionally designed to promote critical thinking in digital environments.

3 Social Media in Learning

In recent years, educational and psychological research has emphasised the value of social media as a platform for the exchange of social knowledge and networked learning. These studies highlight how social media can improve educational outcomes and enhance students' psychological well-being, particularly by supporting self-regulated learning. Social media enables students to set learning goals, strategically manage information, and monitor their own progress [8]. The strong influence of social media in modern learning environments underscores the need to integrate these tools to maximise their benefits while minimising potential drawbacks. Through focused attention, observation, and reflection on personal experiences, learners can build individualised learning environments that foster organisation, the sharing of learning outcomes, and the development of independent learning skills. Such networked environments can be tailored to individual needs to achieve educational goals, empowering students to consciously address daily challenges and thereby enhancing their chances of academic success. Therefore, promoting reflective engagement in social media-assisted learning is essential for optimising student achievement [9].

4 Changes in Student Needs in Reflective Thinking

A fatal fire incident was used to contextualise the study: the fire tragedy at Wang Fuk Court in Tai Po, Hong Kong, on November 26, 2025. The fire affected seven out of eight buildings in the estate, resulting in 168 deaths, including one firefighter. This tragic event ranks among the deadliest fires in Hong Kong's history. Investigations revealed that materials such as protective nets, waterproof canvases, and plastic sheets on the exterior of the buildings contributed to the unusually rapid spread of the fire. Other issues included the fire burning for more than 43 h and the failure of the alarm and fire suppression systems [10].

This case highlights the need to review current training methods and to incorporate new elements into safety training. It is essential for instructors and students to anticipate and prepare for potential challenges (behavioural intention), think critically and adapt during lessons (reflection in action), and evaluate their practice afterwards to improve future training (reflection on thinking) [11]. Reflective thinking, as suggested by Kember et al. [12], should be added as a core component of safety training (see Fig. 1).

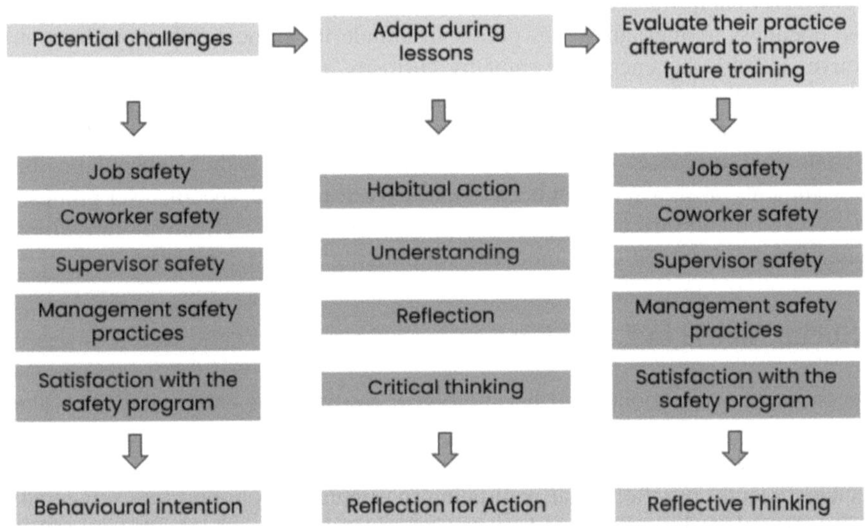

Fig. 1. The Research Model Based on interns' reflective thinking [12] & WSS [13].

Human counterfactual thinking involves considering alternative outcomes, which can significantly influence behavioural intentions. This demonstrates that specific thinking patterns can affect individual attitudes and future actions. According to social cognitive theory, reflective thinking is regarded as a personal element, while career intention is viewed as a behavioural factor. Reflective thinking encompasses habitual action, understanding, reflection, and critical thinking, all of which help shape students' attitudes toward their work and future behaviour [14]. In light of various tragedies, including the recent fire disaster, safety training and education have encouraged students to engage in deeper self-reflection and to learn how to establish a robust safety management system on construction sites. For example, following the fatal fire at Wang Fuk Court, Hong Kong continued to experience several smaller-scale fires, such as domestic fires caused by careless smoking or electrical short circuits in extension cords. These real-life cases not only reinforce the importance of safety awareness among students but also highlight the ongoing need for continuous improvement in workplace safety practices.

5 Research Methodology

The research was structured into three phases. First, a pre-course assessment was conducted using the WSS, in which all students completed a paper-based questionnaire to evaluate their logical reasoning and attitudes towards safety. Second, a social media comment analysis required students to search online news sources and social media platforms, including, but not limited to, Facebook, Instagram, LinkedIn, HK01, and Ming Pao, to collect a total of 30 comments related to the fire incident: ten positive, ten neutral, and ten negative. These comments were selected to reflect public discussions, opinions, and questions regarding the safety of scaffolding and fire protection. Third, a reflection exercise was conducted, in which, after analysing the comments, students recorded their findings and spent 15 min reflecting on what they had learned from the process, identifying five key points about how the activity influenced their understanding of safety. The WSS was also used for the post-assessment evaluation.

The WSS was constructed and validated using three independent samples. It measures five factorially distinct constructs: job safety, coworker safety, supervisor safety, management safety practices, and satisfaction with the safety program. Previous research has demonstrated that supervisor safety and management safety practices are significantly correlated with reported accident rates [13]. The overall methodology of this study was designed to integrate real-world incidents, media analysis, and reflective learning, thereby providing a comprehensive understanding of how social media comments can influence students' attitudes and reflections regarding safety practices. The WSS consists of 20 main statements, each rated on a 5-point Likert scale (e.g., from "Strongly Disagree" to "Strongly Agree"), as is common in safety-climate questionnaires in the construction industry. The scale covers five key categories: (1) Management Commitment and Leadership; (2) Worker Involvement and Communication; (3) Safety Procedures and Training; (4) Co-worker Influence and Behaviour; and (5) Work Pressure versus Safety.

6 Research Results

A total of 39 students participated in the study, and their responses were assessed using the WSS. The following are the relevant results based on this assessment. Regarding education level, 48.7% of participants had completed secondary education, 25.6% had completed matriculation, 20.5% held a bachelor's degree, and 5.2% had completed graduate-level education. This means that over 51.3% of participants received higher education (see Table 1). In terms of age groups, the largest number of participants (30.8%) were in the 18–29 age group (see Table 2).

The post-test group had a higher mean score five key categories (1) Management Commitment and Leadership (+0.16) (see Fig. 2); (2) Worker Involvement and Communication (+0.21) (see Fig. 3); (3) Safety Procedures and Training (+0.07) (see Fig. 4); (4) Co-worker Influence and Behavior (+0.13) (see Fig. 5); and (5) Work Pressure versus Safety (+0.21) (see Fig. 6), indicating an increase following the activities. However, independent sample t-tests showed that this difference was not statistically significant. The observed increase in mean scores suggests a possible positive trend, but the non-significant result indicates that this difference may be attributable to random variation

Table 1. Distribution of participants by educational level.

Education Level	No. of Participate	No. of Percentage
Secondary	19	48.7%
Matriculation	10	25.6%
Bachelor	8	20.5%
Graduate	2	5.2%
Others	0	0%
Total	39	100%

Table 2. Distribution of participants by age group.

Age Group	No. of Participate	No. of Percentage
18–29	12	48.7%
30–39	16	25.6%
40–49	6	20.5%
50–59	4	5.2%
60 or above	1	0%
Total	39	100%

rather than a reliable effect. The effect size was small to moderate (Cohen's d = 0.1161–0.3509), suggesting that the magnitude of the difference between groups was limited. The lack of statistical significance may be due to insufficient statistical power resulting from the small sample size; future studies with larger samples may provide clearer evidence (see Table 3).

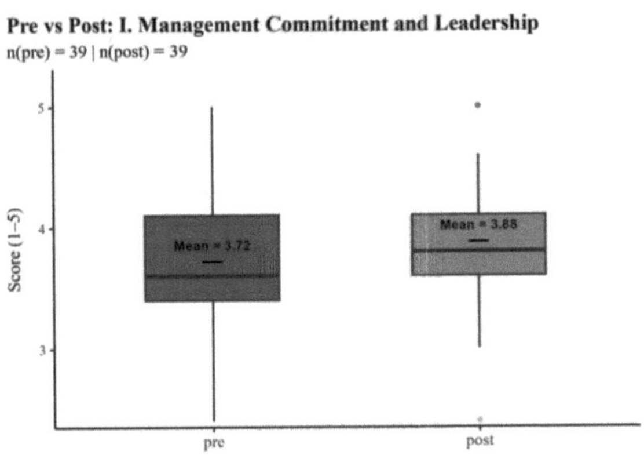

Fig. 2. Pre- and post-intervention analysis on the "Management Commitment and Leadership".

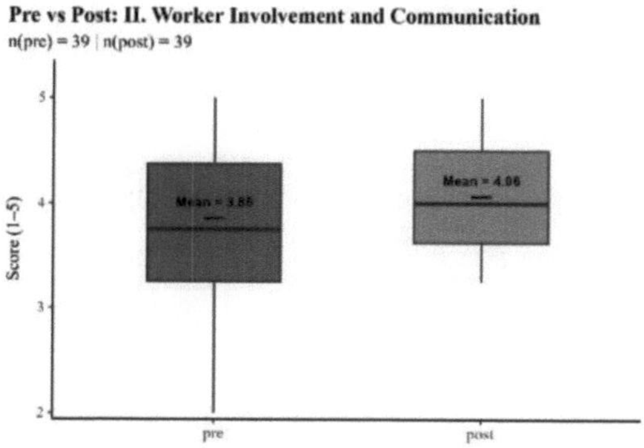

Fig. 3. Pre- and post-intervention analysis on the "Worker Involvement and Communication".

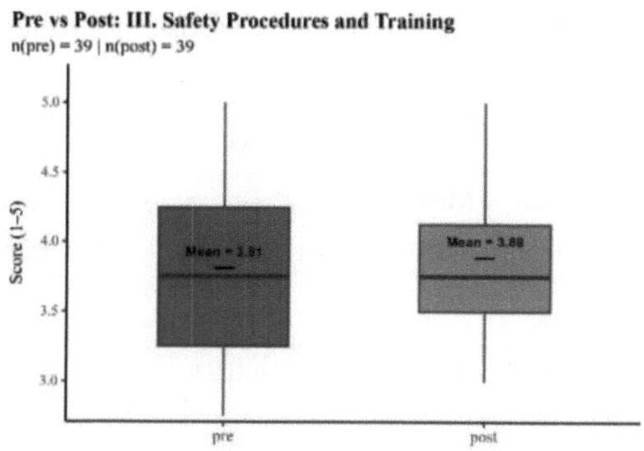

Fig. 4. Pre- and post-intervention analysis on the "Safety Procedures and Training".

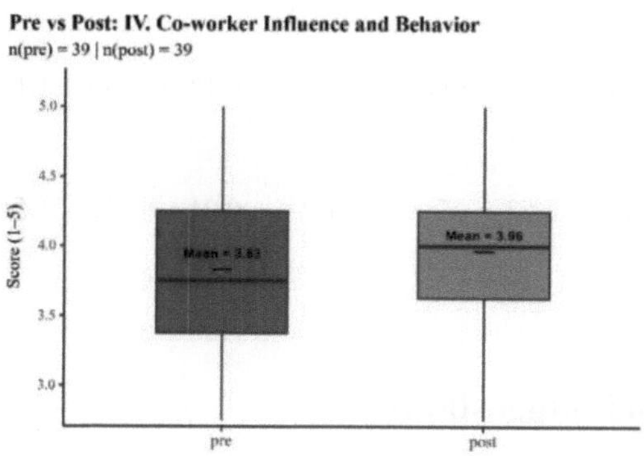

Fig. 5. Pre- and post-intervention analysis on the "Co-worker Influence and Behaviour".

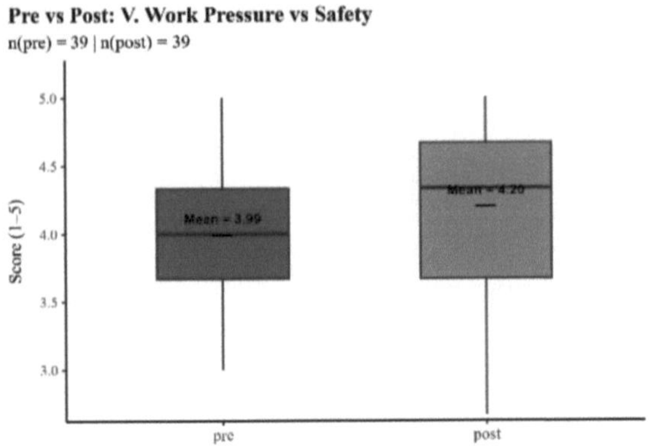

Fig. 6. Pre- and post-intervention analysis on the "Work Pressure vs. Safety".

Table 3. Distribution of participants' pre- and post-intervention analysis.

Items	Pre		Post		Difference in Mean	df	t	P-value	Cohen d
	Mean	SD	Mean	SD					
I. Management Commitment and Leadership	3.72	0.6	3.88	0.54	+ 0.16	75	1.22	0.2246	0.2803
II. Worker Involvement and Communication	3.85	0.75	4.06	0.55	+ 0.21	69	1.42	0.1588	0.3193
III. Safety Procedures and Training	3.81	0.66	3.88	0.54	+ 0.07	43	0.57	0.5734	0.1161
IV. Co-Worker Influence and Behaviour	3.83	0.57	3.96	0.51	+ 0.13	75	1.1	0.275	0.2404
V. Work Pressure vs Safety	3.99	0.53	4.2	0.66	+ 0.21	72	1.51	0.1356	0.3509

7 Discussion and Suggestions

The students' comments regarding the fire incident were categorised into 10 positive, 10 neutral, and 10 negative remarks. After organising these responses, several key themes emerged.

Positive comments highlighted the complete implementation of a smoking ban, the need for the Buildings Department and Labour Department, HKSAR, to establish a more robust management system for scaffolding and safety nets, and suggestions for conducting random inspections. Students recognised the Fire Services Department's timely rescue efforts and noted the buildings' stable structures. There was increased public awareness of fire prevention and safety, with individuals routinely checking fire extinguishers to ensure they were functioning properly. The students also emphasised the need for large-scale reforms in the construction industry and praised the public for promptly reporting fires and assisting residents during evacuations. Effective resource allocation, a focus on disaster prevention through strengthened self-help and community mutual aid, and understanding the inspection process were also identified as important.

Neutral comments included sharing safety information on social media platforms to enhance the sense of security, the government's intervention to strengthen community inspections, and increased public attention to scaffolding safety and shared responsibility. The incident served as a warning to Hong Kong about safety issues and provided an opportunity to investigate the fire's causes and to consider comprehensive, systemic reforms.

Negative comments pointed out that contractors failed to make sufficient efforts to prevent accidents and criticised the lack of effective government supervision. There were concerns that safety nets were not inspected before work commenced and that safety measures could affect work efficiency. Students mentioned that workers often smoked on construction sites without intervention, highlighting severe failures in supervision and the lack of effective safety training. The comments also addressed the breakdown of accountability mechanisms and inadequate oversight of property management.

Based on these findings, it is recommended that safety training programmes incorporate reflective discussions on real-world incidents and actively involve students in analysing public opinions. This approach can enhance students' awareness of safety practices, improve their critical thinking skills, and encourage them to adopt proactive attitudes toward workplace safety. Moreover, regulatory bodies and industry stakeholders should consider these perspectives when designing policies and interventions to address safety challenges more effectively.

The emotional dimension of safety education is a critical yet often underexplored facet that significantly shapes students' attitudes, reflective thinking, and ultimately, their behaviours in real-world settings. Social media, with its immediacy and accessibility, has introduced a new layer of emotional engagement in safety learning by exposing students to authentic, diverse, and sometimes conflicting public opinions on safety incidents. For example, after a high-profile fire disaster, social media platforms become arenas for public debate where users propose solutions such as replacing bamboo scaffolding with metal scaffolding. This suggestion is met with counterarguments regarding the risks of metal deformation under extreme heat, presenting practical dilemmas and complexities rarely covered in textbooks. Engaging with these emotionally charged discussions encourages students to confront the realities of safety decisions and fosters deeper reflection on their own attitudes and responsibilities. The impact of emotionally resonant commentary is further amplified when students encounter direct accounts of loss or blame, which evoke empathy and heighten their sense of accountability. In addition, the recurrence of smaller-scale incidents, such as domestic fires caused by careless smoking or faulty electrical appliances, often discussed on social media, reinforces the importance of vigilance and continuous learning. However, the subjective nature of interpreting social media comments can present challenges. Students may be swayed by misinformation, emotional bias, or polarised viewpoints, which can distort their understanding of safety principles and best practices. This highlights the necessity of structured guidance from educators, who can facilitate critical discussions and help students distinguish between evidence-based insights and emotional rhetoric. By integrating real-world incidents and social media commentary into the safety curriculum, educators can create a dynamic learning environment that enhances cognitive understanding while cultivating emotional intelligence and resilience. Ultimately, harnessing the emotional impact of social media interactions in safety education transforms passive learning into active, reflective practice. This equips students with the critical thinking skills and emotional awareness necessary for effective decision-making and leadership in safety-critical professions.

8 Limitations of the Study

Despite the valuable insights gained from this research, several limitations should be acknowledged. First, interpreting social media comments is inherently subjective and may introduce bias. Different participants may perceive the tone, intent, or credibility of comments differently, influenced by their personal backgrounds, prior experiences, and emotional states. This variation in interpretation can impact the consistency and comparability of reflective responses. Second, the study's sample size was relatively small and drawn from a specific educational context, which may limit the generalisability of the findings to other populations or industries. The influence of educational background was also apparent; participants with higher academic qualifications may already possess established knowledge and critical thinking skills regarding safety practices, potentially reducing the observable effect of the intervention. Moreover, while the use of a recent, high-profile fire incident increased the immediacy and relevance of the reflection exercise, it may have temporarily heightened emotional responses and awareness, rather than reflecting sustained behavioural change. Furthermore, the reflective activities took place in a classroom setting, which may not fully capture the complexities and pressures of real workplace environments. Finally, the evolving nature of social media means that the types of comments and their interpretation may change over time, affecting the reproducibility of the study's results.

9 The Future of Study

Looking forward, future research should address the identified limitations by expanding the sample size and including participants from a wider array of safety-related courses, such as safety officer training and lifting safety supervisor programmes [15]. Engaging individuals with diverse educational and professional backgrounds will enable a more comprehensive understanding of social media's influence on reflective thinking in safety education. Moreover, incorporating additional real-world case studies, including both major and minor incidents, will enrich the learning experience and further enhance students' awareness of workplace safety. Facilitated discussions between instructors and students are essential to mitigate interpretive biases and ensure that theoretical knowledge translates into practical application. Ultimately, these approaches will help establish a robust foundation for ongoing safety training and promote a culture of critical reflection and continuous improvement across the industry.

10 Conclusion

To ensure confidentiality and anonymity, participants in this study were not required to provide names or identifying codes. Although the post-test group exhibited a slightly higher mean score than the pre-test group, an independent-samples t-test revealed that this difference was not statistically significant (t(df = 1.1654), p = 0.273), suggesting that the observed improvement may be due to random variation rather than a robust effect. While the descriptive statistics indicate a positive trend, the effect was not strong enough to achieve statistical significance.

It is noteworthy that the increase in mean scores suggests some potential benefit of the intervention. However, the impact on participants with higher academic backgrounds may have been limited, possibly due to their existing knowledge base and established logical reasoning, which may make them less susceptible to change in their attitudes or behaviours regarding workplace safety. Nevertheless, the upward trend suggests further improvement is possible.

Future studies could address these limitations by increasing the sample size and incorporating participants from diverse educational backgrounds. Additionally, extending the research to include different types of safety training could provide deeper insights into the effectiveness of social media comments in fostering reflective thinking and safe behaviour.

Disclosure of Interests. The authors have no competing interests.

References

1. Ai, Y., von Mühlenen, A.: An experimental online study on the impact of negative social media comments on anxiety and mood. Sci. Rep. **15**(1), 26642 (2025)
2. Ravindra, P., et al.: CPR challenge: Impact of a social media campaign on cardiopulmonary resuscitation awareness and skills among young adults – A quasi experimental study. Resuscitation Plus **19**, 100711 (2024)
3. Gunuc, S., Dogan, A.: The relationships between Turkish adolescents' Internet addiction, their perceived social support and family activities. Comput. Hum. Behav. **29**(6), 2197–2207 (2013)
4. Watson, E.: Education: The Potential Impact of Social Media and Hashtag Ideology on the Classroom. Res. Soc. Sci. Technol. **5**(2), 40–56 (2020)
5. Bandura, A., Walters, R. H.: Social learning theory, Vol. 1, pp. 141–154. Englewood Cliffs, NJ, Prentice hall (1977)
6. Para, A., Batko, B., Ippolito, J., Hanna, G., Edobor-Osula, F.: Developmental Dysplasia of the Hip: How Does Social Media Influence Patients and Caregivers Seeking Information? Children **8**(10), 869 (2021)

7. Steinert, S., Marin, L., Roeser, S.: Feeling and thinking on social media: emotions, affective scaffolding, and critical thinking. Inquiry **68**(1), 114–141 (2025)
8. Findyartini, A., et al.: "How is social media used for learning?": relationships between social media use by medical students with their self-regulated learning skills. BMC Med. Educ. **24**(1), 235 (2024)
9. Abualrob, M.: Mindfulness and Social Media: Impact on Reflective Thinking and Cognitive Engagement in Undergraduate Students. Education Process: International Journal **16**(1) (2025)
10. What the public inquiry into deadly Tai Po blaze has revealed so far South Chian Morning Post. Retrieved on 5 May 2025. https://www.scmp.com/news/hong-kong/society/article/3352423/what-public-inquiry-deadly-tai-po-blaze-has-revealed-so-far (2026)
11. Al-Khamisi, J.H., Al Seyabi, F., Hammad, W.: Exploring the effect of using lesson study approach on Omani EFL teachers' reflective thinking. Reflective Pract. **26**(5), 772–784 (2025)
12. Kember, D., et al.: Development of a Questionnaire to Measure the Level of Reflective Thinking. Assess. Eval. High. Educ. **25**(4), 381–395 (2000)
13. Hayes, B.E., Perander, J., Smecko, T., Trask, J.: Measuring Perceptions of Workplace Safety: Development and Validation of the Work Safety Scale. J. Safety Res. **29**(3), 145–161 (1998)
14. Ng, K.S.P., Rao, Y., Lai, I.K.W., Zhou, Y.Q.: How internship environmental factors affect students' career intentions in the hotel industry through the reflective thinking processes. The J. Hospit. Leisure, Sport & Tourism Educ. **32**, 100421 (2023)
15. Chan, Y.W., Tsang, Y.F., Cheung, S.K., Ng, K.K., Chui, K.T.: A Stakeholder-Focused Strategy for Developing and Executing Smart Safety Systems for Construction Sites. J. Educ. Technol. Develop. Exchan. **18**(4), 20–39 (2025)

Students' Haphazard AI Utilization in Education: Evidence from a Network Cybersecurity SOC Simulation

Gabriel Vitus[1], Tak-Lam Wong[1(✉)], and Simon K. S. Cheung[2]

[1] Department of Computing Studies and Information Systems, Douglas College, 700 Royal Avenue, New Westminster, B.C. V3M 5Z5, Canada
vitusg@douglascollege.ca, tlwong@ieee.org

[2] Hong Kong Metropolitan University, Hong Kong, China
kscheung@hkmu.edu.hk

Abstract. The integration of artificial intelligence into higher education is proceeding under significant institutional pressure, often without the domain-specific methodology required for AI tools to be genuinely reliable. The paper argues that meaningful AI adoption in technically specialized academic programmes requires either the embedding of domain-specific AI model-building methodology within subject courses, or the creation of dedicated AI-for-technical-domains companion courses. Haphazard adoption of general-purpose AI tools in specialized curricula is not a step toward AI literacy, but it is a pedagogical liability This paper presents empirical evidence from a structured assessment in network cybersecurity course at a post-secondary institution in Canada. Students ($N = 22$) were invited to independently analyzed malicious network traffic captured during a live SOC simulation, then repeated the analysis using a general-purpose AI tool of their choice, and compared the two outcomes. The central finding is not that AI tools are inadequate in absolute terms, but that general-purpose AI, which is developed without domain-specific training, structured input pipelines, or environmental context injection, applied haphazardly to a technically specialized domain can produce unreliable, superficial, and in some cases misleading output.

Keywords: Cybersecurity education · AI adoption · Domain-specific AI · SOC simulation · Packet Capture Analysis · Pedagogical AI Integration · LLM Limitations

1 Introduction

Across higher education institutions, the integration of artificial intelligence (AI) into teaching and learning has intensified dramatically in the years following the public release of large language models (LLMs), which are capable of generating fluent, contextually plausible text in response to natural language prompts. Administrators, accreditation bodies, and government agencies have encouraged, and in some cases mandated, rapid AI adoption, often with the implicit assumption that the availability of powerful

K. T. Chui et al. (Eds.): ICBL 2026, LNCS 16778, pp. 503–515, 2027.
https://doi.org/10.1007/978-981-92-3761-6_35

general-purpose AI tools translates directly into educational value across all subject domains [1, 2]. This assumption of the general usefulness of the general-purpose AI tools warrants serious scrutiny, particularly in technically specialized fields such as network cybersecurity, where the domain of knowledge is highly structured, the evidentiary standards are exacting, and the consequences of analytical error are significant.

The contemporary academic environment presents a paradox: institutions are under pressure to adopt AI quickly, while the understanding of what responsible, effective AI adoption requires in specialized disciplines is still being developed. This pressure has produced a characteristic pattern of adoption that might be described as tool availability preceding tool literacy, where students and faculty gain access to powerful AI systems before developing the conceptual framework to use them responsibly in their disciplinary context. In humanities and social sciences, this gap may be manageable: general-purpose LLMs trained on vast corpora of text-based knowledge can produce broadly useful outputs in response to text-based queries [3, 4]. In technically specialized domains, for example, network security, forensic analysis, clinical diagnostics, structural engineering, the gap is qualitatively different. These domains involve rapid changes in technology, and the structured data formats that LLMs were not trained to parse, domain-specific evidentiary standards that general output does not meet, as well as the environmental context that is invisible to a model receiving an isolated file or query. The result is not merely that AI performs less well in these domains, but also it is that practitioners and students without domain-specific AI literacy may not recognize the failure. An LLM that produces seems-to-be fluent, plausible-sounding network forensic analysis that correctly identifying port scanning while misidentifying the attacker, or flagging normal institutional traffic as malicious, is more pedagogically dangerous than an LLM that produces obviously wrong output.

The question this paper addresses is not whether AI has a role in cybersecurity education, but whether general-purpose AI tools, applied without sufficient domain-specific knowledge, training, or contextual grounding, are capable of producing reliable solution in this domain. To address this question, we analyze students' use of AI in an assessment test of a network cybersecurity course in a post-secondary institution. The examination was designed as a live Security Operations Centre (SOC) simulation in which students independently analyzed malicious network traffic, then repeated the analysis using a general-purpose AI tool of their choice, and critically compared the two outcomes. The central argument of this paper is that the gap revealed between student forensic findings and AI output is not primarily evidence of AI inadequacy. It is evidence of a methodological vacuum: students and academics who apply general-purpose AI to technically specialized tasks without understanding what conditions make AI reliable in that domain are not practicing AI-assisted analysis. They are practicing haphazard AI use, and the difference matters enormously for both educational outcomes and professional practice.

2 Literature Review

Since the launch of Large Language Models (LLMs) such as ChatGPT, the integration of into educational environments has been studied extensively, restructuring the pedagogical practices. Existing works largely focus on how to leverage LLMs for personalized learning and task automation [5–8]. Research indicates that generative AI significantly contributes to academic achievement and conceptual understanding, particularly in STEM subjects that require high levels of abstraction [9, 10]. Zhang et al. utilized LLMs in a flipped classroom setting. PromptTutor is designed to provide personalized, immediate feedback to support student learning in flipped classroom by incorporating reflective learning and scaffolding strategies. Wong, Cheung and Zhang demonstrated that LLMs can be used as a conversational resource in Scaffolding, promoting the learning outcomes of students [11]. While LLMs provides substantial opportunities and enhancement to education, they also create various challenges [12]. For example, there is a major concern that students may rely too heavily on AI-generated answers as a "shortcut," which hinders the development of independent critical thinking and problem-solving skills [13]. Standard LLMs tend to provide immediate answers rather than acting like a tutor, making it challenges to align with pedagogy.

The overall workforce shortage in cybersecruity raises the need of professional training in this domain [14, 15]. Kamruzzaman and Sikder revealed the gap between the industrial expectation and the course delivery [16]. They also evaluated different pedagogical approaches such as gamification, interdisciplinary learning, etc. in cybersecurity training. Ramezanian & Niemi identified the shortcomings of the current cybersecurity curricula, and proposed a comprehensive guideline for cybersecurity curriculum development for higher educational institutions [17]. Simulation is a common approach in cybersecurity education to resemble the real cybersecurity threat [18, 19]. Recently, LLMs have been increasingly incorporated in the cybersecurity training [20, 21]. Wang, Zhou and Chen developed CyberMentor, which leverage LLMs and Retrieval-Augmented Generation (RAG), to assist students to accurately retrieve relevant information, and hence to enhance their learning [22]. Agrawal et al. developed a platform called Cyberq for generating questions and answer for cybersecruity education using LLMs and knowledge graph [23]. In this paper, we aim at investigating how students use LLMs in a simulated environment in cybersecurity training.

3 Methodology

Recalling that our research question is: Can general-purpose AI tools be applied without sufficient and adequate domain-specific knowledge, training, or contextual grounding to produce reliable solution in cybersecurity domain. To answer this question, we design a simulation test in a formal assessment in a network cybersecurity course in a post-secondary institution in Canada. Thirty-two students independently analyzed malicious network traffic captured during a live SOC simulation, then repeated the analysis using a general-purpose AI tool of their choice, and compared the two outcomes. Twenty-two complete submissions were retained for analysis across five AI platforms (ChatGPT, Claude, Gemini, DeepSeek, and Copilot). The following presents simulation design.

3.1 Network Environment

The examination was conducted within a controlled, isolated classroom network at Douglas College, configured as a single Class C subnet. Table 1 summarizes the environment parameters.

Table 1. Network environment configuration.

Parameter	Configuration
Network	Class C, institutional address space
Usable hosts	253 IP addresses
Static IP devices	45 Windows desktops with fixed assignments
DHCP pool	Remaining addresses—first-come, first-served
Student VM pair	1 Kali Linux VM + 1 Metasploitable VM per student
Instructor VM pair	1 Kali VM + 1 Metasploitable VM (instructor use only—known baseline traffic)
Malicious VM	1 instructor-controlled VM generating attack traffic—unknown to students
Network topology	Flat Layer 2—all devices on a single broadcast domain (promiscuous capture possible)
Maximum devices	253 (including gateway, static hosts, student VMs, instructor VMs)

The flat Layer 2 topology meant that all network traffic was simultaneously visible to every device on the subnet, replicating the promiscuous capture conditions of a real SOC network tap. The instructor's Kali machine conducted probe activity exclusively against the instructor's own Metasploitable instance, establishing a known baseline of legitimate scanning traffic on the wire. One additional instructor-controlled VM was configured to generate attack traffic whose source and nature were unknown to students, which was tested as the analytical target of the examination.

3.2 Examination Structure

The examination was structured in four parts, progressing from direct forensic identification through first-principles analysis, AI-assisted analysis, and reflective evaluation. This sequencing was deliberate: students were required to form and commit to their own analytical conclusions before consulting AI, ensuring that the AI comparison in Part 3 was conducted against a genuine independent baseline rather than an AI-informed one. Figure 1 shows an overview of the examination.

Part 1—Threat Identification. In this part, students were asked to start with packet capture and were required to identify from the live traffic:

- The IP address of the malicious VM.

- At least three distinct suspicious activities with terminal evidence.
- One username from login attempts, one suspicious destination port, one repeated pattern, and the transport protocol used.

All findings required screenshot evidence inserted directly into the examination document.

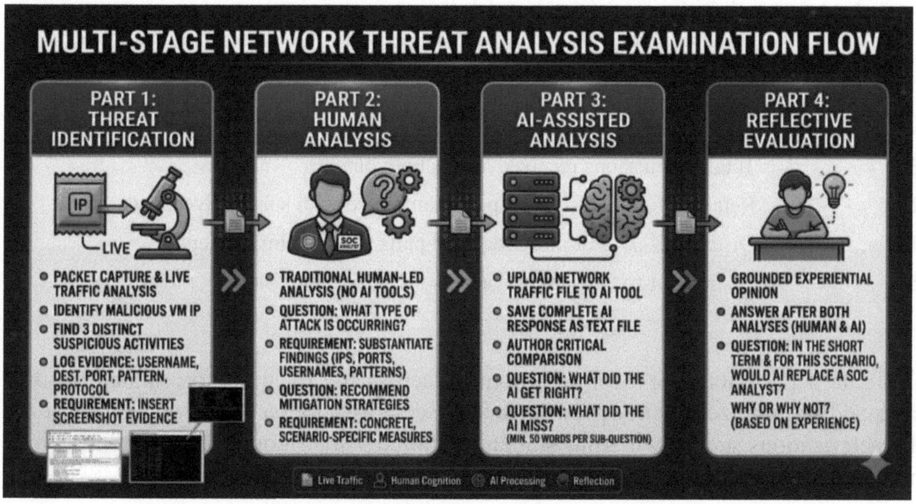

Fig. 1. The overview of the examination

Part 2—Human Analysis. This is a traditional human analysis without the use of any AI-assisted tool. Precisely, students need to answer the following questions:

- What type of attack is occurring? Students were required to identify attack categories and substantiate findings with specific evidence—IP addresses, port numbers, usernames, observable patterns. Generic answers were explicitly disqualified.
- What mitigation strategies would you recommend? Concrete, scenario-specific measures drawn from actual traffic evidence.

Part 3—AI-Assisted Analysis. Students uploaded their prepared network traffic file to a general-purpose AI tool of their choosing. The tool used was declared in their submission. The complete AI response was saved as a text file and submitted as part of the examination bundle. Students then authored a critical comparison (minimum 50 words per sub-question): what did the AI get right, and what did the AI miss?

Part 4—Reflective Evaluation. This question required grounded experiential opinion: students answered after having performed both the human and AI analysis themselves. In essence, they were asked "in the short term and specific to this scenario, considering your experience, would AI replace a SOC analyst as you have been for the duration of this exam? Why or why not?".

4 Results and Discussion

4.1 AI Tool Distribution and Performance

Table 2 summarises the submission statistics in the formal assessment test described in the previous section. Among 32 submissions received, 22 were retained for analysis because these submissions completed all parts of the assessment.

Table 2. Submission statistics.

Count	Description
32	Total submissions received across both batches
22	Retained for analysis—all parts completed with substantive answers
10	Discarded—one or more required parts blank or insufficient
5	Distinct AI tools identified across retained submissions

Table 3 presents the AI tool distribution across the twenty-two retained submissions and summarizes the key performance observations for each tool. All performance characterizations are drawn from student-authored Part 3 comparison responses and cross-referenced against the submitted AI output files.

Table 3. AI tool usage and performance summary across 22 retained submissions. (We use LLM1–5 instead of the actual name of LLMs because the purpose of the paper is not the evaluation of the individual LLMs; *LLM5 submission retained for tool count only as Part 4 was not completed for the student who used LLM5.)

AI Tool	n	%	Performance summary
LLM1	13	59%	Identified primary attack in most cases; false positives on normal LAN traffic; context window limits on large packet captures (pcaps); attacker misidentification without prompting
LLM2	6	27%	Strong on IP identification and SYN scan patterns; surfaced findings students missed; identical context blindness—flagged student Kali as attacker in several cases
LLM3	2	9%	Correct directional findings; shallow evidentiary depth; flagged college-normal protocols (mDNS, HSRP) as malicious without environmental context
LLM4	1	5%	Best reported outcome—student used structured tcpdump text, not binary pcap; surfaced findings beyond student analysis; format advantage cannot be discounted
LLM5*	1	5%	Matched student findings on HSRP reconnaissance; student could not identify AI gaps, suggesting shallow Part 2 baseline; Part 4 not completed

4.2 The Haphazard Use Pattern

Across all five tools, a consistent pattern emerged that is best characterised not as AI failure but as haphazard use producing predictably unreliable results. Students uploaded their capture files—binary, text, or chunked—to general-purpose AI tools without domain-specific prompting, without injecting environmental context (network topology, trusted IP list, expected protocols), and without pre-processing data into formats that AI tools can parse reliably. The resulting outputs were, in the majority of cases, directionally plausible but evidentially inadequate.

This pattern is precisely what should be expected when a general-purpose tool is applied to a specialised domain without the methodology that domain requires. The AI tools performed as general-purpose pattern matchers operating on partially interpretable input without baseline knowledge. They produced general-purpose outputs: correct at the level of attack category, unreliable at the level of specific evidence, and uninformed at the level of environmental context.

Notably, the single submission that approached AI-assisted analysis with greater methodological care, which uses structured tcpdump text output rather than raw binary packet capture (pcap), produced the strongest reported outcome across the entire dataset. This is not a function of the AI tool used; it is a function of input methodology. It suggests that even without domain-specific model training, structured input pre-processing can substantially improve AI output quality. This finding has direct implications for curriculum design.

4.3 Failure Modes as Methodological Indicators

Table 4 presents the six recurring failure modes observed across all tools and submissions. Each is characterized not as a technical deficiency of the AI tool, but as a predictable consequence of a specific methodological gap in how AI was applied. This reframing is important: it shifts responsibility from the tool to the method, and from AI capability to human AI literacy.

4.4 Student Confidence—Part 4 Results

Twenty-two students answered the reflective evaluation question. Their responses are summarised in Table 5. The majority of the students do not agree that AI or LLMs can fully replacement SOC analyst role, after experiencing both analyses first-hand. In particular, the dominant position was that AI cannot replace a skilled analyst in the short term, grounded in specific observations about context blindness, misidentification, and evidentiary inadequacy. 23% of the student who advocated a force-multiplier model were, implicitly, advocating for exactly the structured, informed AI use that the haphazard approach failed to deliver. One student articulated the developmental trajectory most precisely: AI will not replace skilled analysts, but will replace analysts who lack the skill to use AI critically.

It is significant that this distribution emerged from students who had just experienced AI-assisted analysis under conditions of haphazard use. This makes it a particularly robust signal for academic policy: students who learn to use AI haphazardly in technically specialised courses are likely to emerge with lower confidence in AI, not because AI is limited, but because they have never been taught to use it in a way that would make it reliably useful.

Table 4. Recurring failure modes, affected tools, and methodological root causes.

Failure mode	Tools affected	Description	Root cause/remedy
Context blindness	All tools	AI has no knowledge of the network topology, trusted participants, or baseline traffic. Cannot distinguish student Kali activity from attacker activity. Cannot identify normal institutional protocols as benign	Structural—requires domain-specific context injection or dedicated model training
Context window limits	LLM1, LLM2, LLM3	Large pcap files exceed model input limits. Students must curate or chunk data, a process requiring the very analytical skill AI is meant to assist. Truncated input produces truncated or biased output	Partially technical—improving; however, specialised models with streaming pcap parsers are the correct solution
False positives	All tools	Normal LAN protocols (mDNS, NBNS, HSRP) flagged as malicious. Closed-port RST responses flagged as lateral movement. Without a network baseline, AI over-flags noise	Requires model fine-tuning on domain-specific normal traffic profiles
Attacker misidentification	LLM1, LLM2	Student Kali machine—the most active scanner—identified as primary threat actor. Required human correction before useful analysis could proceed	Requires environmental context: asset inventory, role assignments, trusted IP lists

(continued)

Table 4. (*continued*)

Failure mode	Tools affected	Description	Root cause/remedy
Surface-level output	All tools	Primary attack category correctly identified; specific tool fingerprints (Nmap probes), timeline correlation, and attack lifecycle staging consistently missed. Generic summaries rather than evidentiary chains	Requires models trained on structured incident report formats and forensic reasoning patterns
Input format dependency	All tools	AI performance varied significantly with input format. Structured text (tcpdump log) produced better results than binary pcap or chunked raw text. Model capability and input pre-processing are conflated	Domain-specific pipelines should standardise input (e.g., Zeek logs, tshark JSON) before AI ingestion

Table 5. Student positions on AI as SOC analyst replacement (n = 22).

n	%	Position	Representative reasoning
16	73%	AI cannot replace in short term	AI lacks context, misidentifies actors, produces generic output; human analytical judgment remains irreplaceable
5	23%	AI as force multiplier	Accelerates triage and pattern matching; human oversight required for validation, context, and decisions
1	4%	AI raises the analyst bar	Automates basic tasks; elevates—does not eliminate—the skilled analyst role

5 Discussion

5.1 The Core Argument: Methodology Before Adoption

The findings of this study support a clear and actionable conclusion: the integration of AI into technically specialized academic programmes requires that methodology precede adoption. This is not a counsel of delay. AI tools have genuine and significant potential in network cybersecurity for traffic triage, pattern recognition, anomaly flagging, and report generation. But this potential is only realized under conditions of structured, informed use. Without those conditions, AI becomes a source of plausible-sounding misinformation that students and practitioners lack the training to identify.

The institutional imperative to adopt AI quickly is understandable and, in many respects, legitimate. AI literacy is increasingly a workforce requirement across technical fields. But there is a categorical difference between AI literacy and AI exposure. Requiring students to upload a pcap file to ChatGPT and report the results is AI exposure. Teaching students to understand what inputs a network forensic AI model requires, how to evaluate its outputs against domain-specific evidentiary standards, and how to recognize the conditions under which its conclusions should and should not be trusted, is AI literacy. The two are not interchangeable, and conflating them does students a disservice.

5.2 The Pedagogical Value of Human-First Analysis

One of the most important findings of this study is methodological rather than substantive: the requirement that students perform the forensic analysis independently before consulting AI produced measurably better AI evaluation. Students who had already formed their own conclusions identified AI errors, which include false attacker identification, false protocol flagging, missing timeline correlation, that they would likely have accepted uncritically had they consulted AI first.

This finding has a direct curricular implication. In technically specialized courses that incorporate AI, the sequencing of human analysis before AI consultation should be treated as a pedagogical standard rather than an option. The development of AI-critical literacy depends on domain expertise as its foundation. Students who learn to consult AI before developing their own analytical capability are unlikely to develop independent judgment that would allow them to evaluate AI output reliably.

5.3 The Domain-Specific AI Imperative

The context problem, which refers to the inability of general-purpose AI to reason about a specific network environment, its trusted participants, its normal traffic baseline, and the role of the analyst within it, is not a temporary technical limitation awaiting a larger model or a longer context window. It is a structural feature of general-purpose AI operating on domain-specific data without domain-specific grounding.

The appropriate response is not to wait for AI models to become generally smarter. It is to build, configure, or fine-tune AI tools for the specific domain. In the context of network cybersecurity, this means tools that are: trained on structured network telemetry formats (Zeek logs, tshark JSON, normalized pcap summaries); integrated with asset inventories and network baseline profiles; capable of receiving environmental context as structured input rather than inferring it from unstructured data; and evaluated against domain-specific forensic evidentiary standards rather than general natural language quality metrics.

Building such tools or configuring existing models to approximate them is itself a technical skill that students in network cybersecurity programmes should acquire. This is not a peripheral skill; it is precisely the intersection of AI and cybersecurity that the field will increasingly demand of its practitioners.

6 Conclusions and Future Work

This paper has presented evidence from a live SOC simulation examination that AI tools applied haphazardly to network cybersecurity analysis produce directionally plausible but evidentially inadequate results—not because AI is incapable of contributing to this domain, but because the conditions required for reliable AI performance in technically specialised domains are not met by general-purpose tool use without methodology.

The practical implication for academic institutions is clear and urgent. The pressure to adopt AI quickly is real; the risk of adopting it without the methodological framework that makes it trustworthy is equally real. In technically specialised programmes, the path to genuine AI literacy runs through domain-specific model building, structured input methodology, and human-first analytical sequencing. Shortcuts to this path are not shortcuts, however, they are detours that produce students who have been exposed to AI without learning to use it.

The examination design described in this paper, in which students perform the forensic task independently, consult AI, and critically compare the two outcomes, represents a replicable and scalable pedagogical model for developing genuine AI literacy in technically specialised education. It requires no specialised infrastructure, no institutional AI platform, and no departure from existing course objectives. It requires only the willingness to treat AI as a tool with operating conditions, and to teach students what those conditions are.

The students who participated in this examination understood, from direct experience, that dumping data into a general-purpose AI and accepting the output is not analysis. Teaching them to build the tools, the methods, and the critical frameworks that would make AI genuinely useful in their domain is the next step, and it is a step that academic programmes in network cybersecurity and related fields are now equipped, and obligated, to take.

We intend to extend our work to conduct an empirical evaluation of the examination structure. Specifically, a quantitative research design will be employed alongside a pre-test/post-test framework to systematically measure the growth of student AI-critical literacy and cybersecurity domain expertise. This quantitative baseline will allow us to objectively measure whether the sequence of human analysis prior to AI integration significantly minimizes the adoption of AI-generated misinformation and directly increases objective analytical proficiency in technically specialized domains.

References

1. Al-Momani, A.A.M., Ramayah, T.: Adoption of artificial intelligence in education: a systematic literature review. Current and future trends on intelligent technology adoption. **2**, 117–135 (2024)
2. Chen, T., Gascó-Hernandez, M., Esteve, M.: The adoption and implementation of artificial intelligence chatbots in public organizations: evidence from US state governments. Am. Rev. Public Adm. **54**(3), 255–270 (2024)
3. Lavidas, K., Koskina, E., Pitsili, A., Komis, V., Arvanitis, E.: Humanities and social sciences students' views on the use of AI tools for academic purposes: practices, benefits, challenges, and suggestions. Adv. Mobile Learn. Educ. Res. **6**(1), 1699–1709 (2026)

4. Prasetya, S.P.: Artificial intelligence in social sciences education presents new challenges and opportunities. In: 4th International Conference on Social Sciences and Law (ICSSL 2024, pp. 111–121. Atlantis Press (2024)
5. Shahzad, T., Mazhar, T., Tariq, M.U., Ahmad, W., Ouahada, K., Hamam, H.: A comprehensive review of large language models: issues and solutions in learning environments. Discover Sustain. **6**(1), 27 (2025)
6. Ng, L.: LLMS in education. XRDS: Crossroads, The ACM Magazine for Students **31**(1), 66–70 (2024)
7. Lyu, W., Wang, Y., Chung, T., Sun, Y., Zhang, Y.: Evaluating the effectiveness of LLMs in introductory computer science education: a semester-long field study. In Proceedings of the Eleventh ACM Conference on Learning@ scale, pp. 63–74 (2024)
8. Chu, Z., et al.: LLM agents for education: advances and applications. In: Findings of the Association for Computational Linguistics: EMNLP 2025, pp. 13782–13810 (2025)
9. Gunsaldi, M.S., Guner, E.G., Uckan, M., Bati, K.: The impact of generative AI applications on student learning outcomes in science education: a systematic review. J. Educ. Sci. Environ. Health **11**(3), 196–208 (2025)
10. Zhang, Y., Ouh, E.L., Ho, A., Lo, S.L., Tan, K.W., Lin, F.: Prompttutor: effects of an LLM-based chatbot on learning outcomes and motivation in flipped classrooms. In: Proceedings of the 30th ACM Conference on Innovation and Technology in Computer Science Education, pp. 445–451 (2025)
11. Wong, T.L., Cheung, S.K., Zhang, F.: Scaffolding computer programming learning for novice learners using LLM as a conversational resource. In: International Conference on Technology in Education, pp. 98–107, Singapore: Springer Nature Singapore (2025)
12. Voultsiou, E., Moussiades, L.: A systematic review of AI, VR, and LLM applications in special education: opportunities, challenges, and future directions. Educ. Inf. Technol. **30**(13), 19141–19181 (2025)
13. Razafinirina, M.A., Dimbisoa, W.G., Mahatody, T.: Pedagogical alignment of large language models (llm) for personalized learning: a survey, trends and challenges. J. Intell. Learn. Syst. Appl. **16**(4), 448–480 (2024)
14. Blažič, B.J.: The cybersecurity labour shortage in Europe: moving to a new concept for education and training. Technol. Soc. **67**, 101769 (2021)
15. Rahman, N.A.A., Sairi, I.H., Zizi, N.A.M., Khalid, F.: The importance of cybersecurity education in school. Int. J. Inf. Educ. Technol. **10**(5), 378–382 (2020)
16. Kamruzzaman, S.M., Sikder, I.Z.: Innovative approaches to cybersecurity education: tools and strategies for training the next generation of professionals. In: 2025 IEEE/ACIS 29th International Conference on Software Engineering, Artificial Intelligence, Networking and Parallel/Distributed Computing (SNPD), pp. 893–898 (2025)
17. Ramezanian, S., Niemi, V.: Cybersecurity education in universities: a comprehensive guide to curriculum development. IEEE Access **12**, 61741–61766 (2024)
18. Scherb, C., Heitz, L.B., Grimberg, F., Grieder, H., Maurer, M.: A cyber attack simulation for teaching cybersecurity. EPiC Ser. Comput. **93**, 129–140 (2023)
19. Chui, K.T., Liu, R.W., Zhao, M., Zhang, X.: Bio-inspired algorithms for cybersecurity-a review of the state-of-the-art and challenges. Int. J. Bio-Inspired Comput. **23**(1), 1–15 (2024)
20. Chhetri, C.: Exploring large language model-powered pedagogical approaches to cybersecurity education. In: Proceedings of the 25th Annual Conference on Information Technology Education, pp. 163–166 (2024)
21. Sun, N., Miao, Y., Mo, X., Zhang, J.: Large language models for cybersecurity education: a survey of current practices and future directions. In: Pacific-Asia Conference on Knowledge Discovery and Data Mining, pp. 3–20. Singapore: Springer Nature Singapore (2025)

22. Wang, T., Zhou, N., Chen, Z.: Cybermentor: AI powered learning tool platform to address diverse student needs in cybersecurity education (2025). arXiv preprint arXiv:2501.09709
23. Agrawal, G., Pal, K., Deng, Y., Liu, H., Chen, Y.C.:Cyberq: generating questions and answers for cybersecurity education using knowledge graph-augmented LLMs. In: Proceedings of the AAAI Conference on Artificial Intelligence, pp. 23164–23172 (2024)

Developing Tutors' Perceptions of Critical Thinking in Academic Writing Support: A Blended Training Approach

Xiaohong Zhang[1](✉), Yasushi Michita[2], Yuko Sakamoto[1], Chiaki Iwasaki[1], and Tsutomu Nakazawa[1]

[1] Kansai University, Suita City, Osaka, Japan
x_zhang@kansai-u.ac.jp
[2] University of the Ryukyus, Okinawa, Japan

Abstract. This study focuses on a blended tutor training program collaboratively conducted with an external expert in critical thinking. Using tutors' post-training reflections as data, this study qualitatively analyzes their perceptions and orientations toward improving the quality of tutoring. The results indicate that, in diagnostic writing support, particular emphasis was placed on attending to logic structure, including clarifying issues, claims, and evidence, and ensuring logical consistency, thereby reflecting the reasoning dimension of CT. In addition, when responding to diverse consultation contexts, tutors emphasized relationship building based on psychological safety and the adjustment of feedback according to learners' cognitive and affective conditions. At the same time, tutors recognized the difficulty of adequately addressing CT within limited time constraints.

Keywords: Critical Thinking · Blended Training · Academic Writing · Tutors' perceptions · Logic Structure · Psychological Safety

1 Introduction

In writing center contexts, tutoring is increasingly understood not merely as the correction of surface-level issues in students' texts, but as a dialogic practice that supports learners' thinking. To provide effective support, tutors are expected to engage with students' reasoning processes by attending to argumentative structure—such as the relationships among issues, claims, and evidence—and by facilitating interactions that promote deeper reflection. These demands highlight the importance of tutors' own critical thinking (CT), as the quality of tutoring depends not only on what tutors do, but also on how they interpret writing, evaluate reasoning, and make instructional decisions in interaction.

Previous research has conceptualized tutoring through frameworks such as scaffolding, emphasizing observable interactional behaviors in supporting writing processes [1]. However, relatively little attention has been paid to tutors' perceptions and orientations toward CT, which underlie their tutoring practices. In particular, it remains unclear how

K. T. Chui et al. (Eds.): ICBL 2026, LNCS 16778, pp. 516–525, 2027.
https://doi.org/10.1007/978-981-92-3761-6_36

tutors conceptualize CT and how such conceptions can be developed through training. Therefore, this study aims to explore how a tutor training program designed to enhance tutors' critical thinking shapes their perceptions and orientations toward improving the quality of tutoring.

2 Related Work

2.1 Academic Writing Support and Tutor Training in Higher Education

Developing students' ability to write academic reports and papers is a fundamental goal in higher education. Since the Writing as a Process movement, writing instruction has become increasingly systematic, leading to the widespread implementation of writing courses and writing center consultations [2, 3].

Writing centers aim to support students in becoming autonomous writers. Tutors are not editors who correct texts but facilitators who engage in collaborative dialogue with students. Tutors must scaffold students' thinking to help them identify issues in their own writing, while also diagnosing texts across disciplines and responding to diverse learners [4, 5].

Tutor training plays a crucial role in developing tutors' expertise. While tutors improve through practice, structured training is essential for supporting this development [6]. Tutor training is typically divided into initial and ongoing phases [7]. Initial training introduces writing center philosophy and basic tutoring principles, recently using role-play to develop skills in dialogic tutoring and text diagnosis [4, 7].

Ongoing training aims to further refine tutors' expertise and address challenges emerging in practice. One challenge is the knowledge-telling bias, where tutors tend to provide explanations rather than facilitate students' thinking [6] Continuous training is therefore necessary to promote more effective dialogic support.

2.2 Critical Thinking Perception in Tutor Training

Critical thinking (CT) is commonly defined as "reasonable and reflective thinking focused on deciding what to believe or do" [8]. Because CT is a broad and multi-faceted construct, it is important to clarify how it operates within specific educational contexts. CT, characterized by logical, reflective, and skeptical dimensions [9], aligns closely with tutoring practices, particularly in supporting learners' reasoning processes through attention to argumentative structure and reflective dialogue.

Rather than being treated as a single measurable construct, CT should be understood and assessed through context-specific performance. This perspective emphasizes the importance of designing education based on learners' actual conditions, including tendencies such as uncritical acceptance and answer-oriented thinking [10]. Given that CT varies across contexts and resists simple measurement, it is essential to examine how tutors perceive and interpret CT in practice. From this perspective, focusing on tutors' perceptions provides a theoretically grounded approach to understanding tutoring practices.

However, previous tutor training programs have primarily focused on writing center philosophy, text diagnosis, and reflective practice [4, 7, 11], with limited attention to the explicit development of tutors' perceptions of CT. This gap suggests the need to systematically integrate CT into tutor training, particularly in relation to dialogic tutoring.

2.3 The Need for Blended Tutor Training with External Experts

In writing centers, faculty members often specialize in education or linguistics, and tutor training is typically conducted within these disciplinary frameworks. However, to further enhance tutors' expertise, training programs may benefit from involving external experts, enabling the incorporation of diverse perspectives and specialized knowledge.

At the same time, logistical constraints such as travel and scheduling often make it difficult to conduct such training entirely face-to-face. In response to these limitations, blended learning—defined as the integration of online and face-to-face learning environments [12]—offers a viable approach.

Blended training enables the remote participation of external experts while supporting collaborative learning through online tools for sharing ideas and feedback. This approach allows for the integration of specialized knowledge beyond spatial constraints while maintaining the benefits of face-to-face interaction.

Despite these advantages, there remains a lack of research on the design and implementation of blended tutor training collaboratively conducted by external experts and internal faculty. In particular, how such training can be structured to support tutors' learning processes has not been sufficiently examined. This gap highlights the need for studies that explore such training models in practice.

Based on the above, this study aims to design a blended tutor training program focused on developing tutors' CT in a writing center and to examine its impact on tutors' perceptions and tutoring practices.

3 Method

In this study, a tutor training program designed based on a blended learning environment was examined.

3.1 Participants

This study targeted tutors affiliated with the writing center at University A, a comprehensive university. The writing center emphasizes dialogic support rather than corrective feedback, aiming to foster consultees' ability to be autonomous learners. Tutoring sessions typically lasted 40 min.

A total of 15 tutors participated in the training program, including doctoral students (Ph.D. candidates) and master's students from a range of disciplines such as literature, business administration, psychology, policy studies, and informatics. Prior to the training, participants were informed about the purpose of the study and how their data would be used, and informed consent was obtained on a voluntary basis. Among the participants, 14 tutors provided consent, and only their data were included in the analysis.

3.2 Design of the Training Session

Characteristics of the Training Design in a Blended Learning Environment. The tutor training program in this study was designed as follows within a blended learning environment (Fig. 1).

(1) Integration of Online and Face-to-Face Learning Environments. The training was implemented by integrating online and face-to-face modalities. Specifically, Instructor A participated remotely via Zoom, while Instructor B and the tutors attended in person in a global smart classroom. Instructor A was able to simultaneously monitor both the overall classroom environment and the shared instructional materials via Zoom, enabling coordination between remote instruction and in-class activities.
(2) Promotion of Face-to-Face Collaboration through an Active Learning Environment. The classroom was designed as an active learning space equipped with movable tables and chairs, allowing participants to form groups flexibly and engage in collaborative activities. Groups 1 and 2 consisted of three participants each, while Groups 3 and 4 consisted of four participants each.
(3) Design of a Learning Process Integrating Individual Thinking and Dialogue. The learning activities were structured so that participants first completed a worksheet individually, followed by group discussions. This sequence facilitated the clarification of individual ideas and encouraged deeper thinking through dialogue with others.

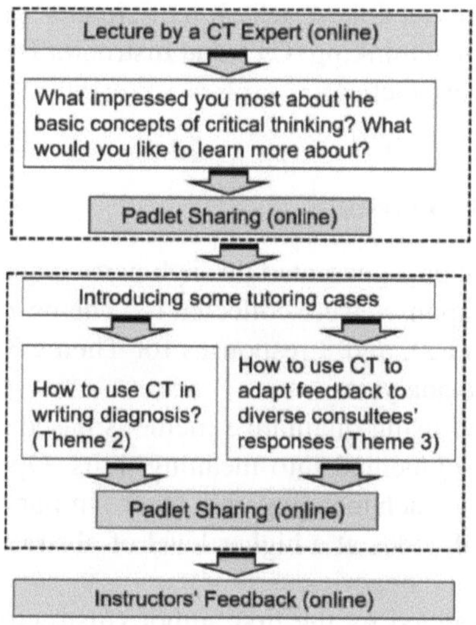

Fig. 1. Design of the blended tutor training program.

(4) Visualization and Sharing of Learning Outcomes through an Online Tool
(5) After the discussions, each group shared their ideas with the entire class. Subsequently, participants individually posted their responses on Padlet, an online collaborative platform. Padlet allows multiple users to post content in real time and

enables the visualization and sharing of ideas across participants. This function connected face-to-face discussions with online information sharing, thereby promoting the externalization and collective sharing of learning outcomes.

Overall, the training was designed as a blended learning environment that integrated face-to-face collaborative activities with online tools for visualization and sharing, thereby structuring the entire learning process in a coherent and integrated manner.

Procedure of the Training. The training was conducted according to the following procedure.

First, Instructor A explained the fundamental concepts of CT. After a question-and-answer session, participants were asked to write about what impressed them most in the lecture and what they wished to learn further (Theme 1). They first recorded their responses on worksheets and then posted them on Padlet.

Next, Instructor B presented case examples of tutoring practices in the writing center. Then, participants engaged in tasks designed to explore how CT could be applied to improve tutoring practices. Participants were divided into four groups. They first completed a worksheet individually, then engaged in group discussions, and finally presented their ideas to the whole class. Theme 2 and 3 were assigned.

Theme 2 focused on exploring how tutors could provide feedback to enhance the logical coherence of students' writing. Theme 3 focused on examining how feedback could be adapted to consultees' reactions and emotions, as well as how CT could be utilized in dialogic support.

Finally, Instructor A provided feedback on participants' presentations and postings from the perspective of critical thinking (CT), and Instructor B encouraged them to apply CT to improve their tutoring practices.

3.3 Data Collection and Analysis

This study collected textual data generated through participants' responses in Activities 1 and 2. Specifically, 14 responses were collected for Theme 1 (Activity 1), 6 responses for Theme 2 (Groups 1 and 2), and 8 responses for Theme 3 (Groups 3 and 4), all of which were included in the analysis.

The data were analyzed using qualitative methods based on grounded theory [13]. First, each response was segmented into meaning units. Open coding was then conducted by assigning codes to each meaning unit. Next, similar codes were compared and integrated to generate axial codes at a higher level of abstraction. Finally, these codes were organized into broader categories.

The analysis was conducted by the first author (Instructor B), who is responsible for managing the writing center. In the Results section, categories are presented in bold, axial codes in italics.

4 Result and Discussion

4.1 Tutors' Perceptions of Critical Thinking in Tutoring: Shared Understanding and Perceived Constraints

An analysis of the Padlet posts related to Theme 1 identified 55 open codes, 7 axial codes, and 5 categories. The extracted categories were **interest in CT**, **understanding of CT components and concepts**, **characteristics of tutoring as writing support through dialogue**, **perceived potential of CT in tutoring**, and **perceived difficulty of implementing CT under time constraints**. These findings reflect tutors' *perceptions and orientations* rather than their actual tutoring practices.

The category of **interest in CT** included axial codes indicating tutors' general curiosity and engagement with CT. The category of **understanding of CT components and concepts** included axial codes representing tutors' recognition of key elements and ways of thinking associated with CT. The category of **characteristics of tutoring as writing support through dialogue** included axial codes describing how tutors perceived tutoring as an interactive process that supports students' writing through dialogue.

In addition, the category of **perceived potential of CT in tutoring** included axial codes indicating tutors' recognition of the possible benefits of incorporating CT into tutoring. The category of **perceived difficulty of implementing CT under time constraints** included axial codes reflecting tutors' concerns about applying CT within limited session time.

4.2 Tutors' Perceptions and Orientations in Text Diagnosis: A Focus on Argumentative structure

An analysis of Padlet posts related to Theme 2 identified 39 open codes, 13 axial codes, and three categories. The content described by tutors as support for improving the logical quality of students' writing was organized into six categories: **support focusing on logic structure**, **dialogic support**, **thinking-promoting support** and **support utilizing CT**. These findings reflect tutors' perceptions and orientations rather than their actual tutoring practices.

Among these categories, support focusing on **logic structure** was the most frequently observed. This category includes axial codes such as *clarifying argumentative structure (issue, claim, and evidence)*, *checking logical consistency*, *supporting the development of logical progression*, *verifying logical connections*, *supporting the use of text structure*, *providing knowledge about logical writing*, and *pointing out logical ambiguity*. These axial codes indicate that tutors perceived the importance of explicitly attending to the structure and organization of arguments in order to enhance the logical quality of writing.

The categories of **dialogic support** and **thinking-promoting support** suggest that tutors oriented themselves toward facilitating students' thinking processes. For example, they emphasized *engaging students in interaction*, *encouraging reflection*, and *making ideas visible to support understanding*. The category of **support utilizing CT** included orientations toward incorporating critical perspectives into the evaluation and development of ideas.

Overall, these findings suggest that tutors conceptualized support for improving logical writing as a combination of attention to logic structure and interactive approaches that promote students' thinking. Rather than simply correcting texts, tutors demonstrated orientations toward engaging students in processes that foster deeper understanding and more coherent argumentation. Furthermore, some participants expressed confusion and difficulty regarding how to incorporate CT in Theme 1, whereas in Theme 2, descriptions emerged on how CT could be applied concretely in diagnostic writing support. This shift suggests that, through worksheet completion and group discussions, participants deepened their understanding of CT from an abstract level to more concrete applications.

4.3 Tutors' Perceptions and Orientations Toward Responding to Diverse Student Reactions and Situations: Emphasis on Psychological Safety

An analysis of the Padlet posts related to Theme 3—"Given that learners show diverse reactions, what should be considered when providing feedback according to their responses and emotions, and what effects can be expected?"—identified 39 open codes, 24 axial codes, and five categories. The extracted categories were **psychological safety–based relationship building, adjustment of feedback based on students' cognitive and affective states, dialogic support to promote awareness, cognitive support based on CT**, and **student growth**. Among these, descriptions related to **psychological safety–based relationship building** and **adjustment of feedback based on students' cognitive and affective states** were most frequently observed.

The category of **psychological safety–based relationship building** includes axial codes such as *aligning with the student's perspective, creating a safe conversational environment, polite communication, showing empathy, adopting an accepting attitude toward the student, respecting the student's intentions*, and *respecting the student's perspectives, views, and ideas*. These codes indicate practices that foster an environment in which students feel comfortable expressing themselves, reduce emotional defensiveness, and promote participation in dialogue.

The category of **adjustment of feedback based on students' cognitive and affective states** includes axial codes such as *setting goals from the student's perspective, attending to the student's individuality, providing advice according to the student's situation, adapting to the student's motivation, exploring topics of interest to the student, thinking together*, and *engaging in constructive discussion*. Psychological safety, defined as a sense of interpersonal trust and being valued within a group, has been shown to be positively influenced by tutor and peer support in educational settings [14]. These codes represent practices in which tutors flexibly adjust their support according to students' levels of understanding and emotional states, and collaboratively engage in problem solving through dialogue.

Furthermore, the category of **dialogic support to promote awareness** includes axial codes such as *asking questions, providing examples*, and *intentionally presenting errors*. The category of **cognitive support based on CT** includes axial codes such as *utilizing knowledge of CT, explicitly sharing knowledge of argumentative structure*, and *encouraging students to articulate claims and reasons*. These practices promote students' thinking and deepen their logical understanding through dialogue and knowledge sharing.

In addition, the category of **student growth** includes axial codes such as *aiming to foster student growth*, *the effect of positive expectations*, and *promoting student autonomy*. These findings indicate that tutors engage in practices intended to facilitate students' developmental transformation.

Overall, the results suggest that tutors do not merely provide feedback; rather, they conceptualize tutoring as a process that fosters growth through dialogic and cognitive engagement, grounded in psychologically safe relationships and adapted to students' cognitive and affective conditions.

5 All Discussion

The finding that tutors placed strong emphasis on attending to argumentative structure in diagnostic writing within this study suggests that support for academic writing is conceptualized not as surface-level correction, but as a process of reconstructing the relationships among issues, claims, and evidence. This indicates that tutors are oriented toward supporting learners' reasoning processes by focusing on the logical dimension of CT. However, an important implication of this study is that such logical support does not operate in isolation. The emphasis on relationship building grounded in psychological safety, as well as the adjustment of feedback in response to learners' cognitive and affective conditions across diverse consultation contexts, suggests that the development of thinking is strongly dependent on the quality of interaction.

The blended training program examined in this study, which integrates theoretical input from an external expert with tutors' reflective practice, can therefore be understood as an effective framework for fostering tutors' tendencies in tutoring.

Furthermore, the challenges associated with time constraints indicate that tutors are required to make immediate judgments and adjustments during sessions. This underscores the importance of reflection-in-action [15], whereby tutors not only apply prior knowledge but also continuously adapt their responses in situ. Such findings highlight the need to reconceptualize tutors not merely as support providers, but as reflective practitioners.

Taken together, these findings call for a reconsideration of tutor training design. Specifically, training programs should aim to develop an integrated set of competencies, including support for argumentative structure, relationship building, adaptive feedback, and real-time reflective practice.

6 Conclusions, Implication and Future Perspective

This study, through a blended training program designed to enhance awareness of CT, revealed that tutors placed particular emphasis on attending to logic structure in academic writing during diagnostic writing support. In addition, when responding to diverse consultation contexts, tutors emphasized relationship building based on psychological safety and the adjustment of feedback according to learners' cognitive and affective conditions. Under time constraints, the need for reflection-in-action, involving immediate judgment and adjustment during tutoring, was also recognized.

The theoretical contribution of this study lies, first, in demonstrating the design and effectiveness of a blended tutor training program collaboratively implemented with an external expert. Traditional tutor training has often been conducted in face-to-face settings led by internal instructors, and limited attention has been paid to training designs that incorporate external expertise. This study contributes theoretically by showing that, within a blended learning environment integrating online and face-to-face modalities, it is possible to reconstruct the learning process by connecting the theoretical knowledge of external experts with the practical experiences of tutors.

Second, this study reconceptualizes tutor expertise from the perspective of critical thinking (CT). While previous tutoring research has primarily focused on analyzing observable behaviors and interactions, this study highlights the importance of tutors' perceptions. By focusing on how tutors interpret and engage with CT, the findings reveal that CT-related aspects—such as attending to argumentative structure and engaging in dialogic interaction—constitute core elements of effective tutoring.

The practical implications of this study are twofold. First, it provides concrete design guidelines for writing centers seeking to implement tutor training programs involving external experts. In particular, the findings demonstrate that a blended learning approach can effectively incorporate specialized knowledge while overcoming temporal and spatial constraints, making it a feasible model for practice.

Second, this study offers a concrete example of positioning critical thinking as a central component of tutor expertise. The process through which tutors moved from an abstract understanding of CT to its practical application—through activities such as worksheet completion and group discussions—provides important insights for the design of future tutor training programs.

Future research should first examine how the tutors' perceptions and orientations identified in this study are enacted in actual tutoring practices. Second, further analysis is needed to clarify how specific components of blended training contribute to the development of these perceptions. Furthermore, in designing AI-supported tutoring for academic writing, it is essential to explore how roles can be effectively distributed between human tutors and AI systems, as well as to develop practical guidebooks to support tutors' professional practice.

Acknowledgements. This work was supported by JSPS KAKENHI Grant Number 26K16831.

References

1. Thompson, I.: Scaffolding in the writing center: a microanalysis of an experienced tutor's verbal and nonverbal tutoring strategies. Writ. Commun. **26**(4), 417–453 (2009)
2. Flower, L., Hayes, J.R.: A cognitive process theory of writing. Coll. Compos. Commun. **32**(4), 365–387 (1981)
3. Hyland, K.: Teaching and researching writing, 3rd edn. Routledge, New York (2015)
4. Sadashima, S., Ota, Y. (eds.): Philosophy and practice of writing tutoring: initiatives at the Waseda University Writing Center. Hituzi Syobo, Tokyo (2013)
5. Nordlof, J.: Vygotsky, scaffolding, and the role of theory in writing center work. Writ. Cent. J. **33**(1), 45–64 (2014)

6. Roscoe, R.D., Chi, M.T.H.: Understanding tutor learning: Knowledge-building and knowledge-telling in peer tutors' explanations and questions. Rev. Educ. Res. **77**(4), 534–574 (2007)
7. Zhang, X., Iwasaki, C., Liang, C., Nakazawa, T., Nishimura, T.: Development and evaluation of a tutor training program for novice tutors in a writing center. Kansai Univ. High. Educ. Res. **17**, 81–89 (2026)
8. Ennis, R.H.: A taxonomy of critical thinking dispositions and abilities. In: Baron, J.B., Sternberg, R.J. (eds.) Teaching Thinking Skills: Theory and Practice, pp. 9–26. W.H. Freeman, New York (1987)
9. Michita, Y.: A review of critical thinking education. Ann. Rep. Educ. Psychol. Jpn **52**, 128–139 (2013)
10. Michita, Y.: Thinking critically about critical thinking: taking IB education as an example. Int. Baccalaureate Educ. Res. **8**, 3–11 (2024)
11. Knorr, D., Edlich, M.G.P.: Toward a systematic approach to developing professional roles: what writing tutors need to know and know how to do. HERMES. J. Lang. Commun. Bus. **64**, 271–285 (2024)
12. Garrison, D.R., Kanuka, H.: Blended learning: uncovering its transformative potential in higher education. Internet High. Educ. **7**(2), 95–105 (2004)
13. Charmaz, K.: Constructing grounded theory, 2nd edn. SAGE Publications, London (2014)
14. Schepers, J., De Jong, A., Wetzels, M., De Ruyter, K.: Psychological safety and social support in groupware adoption: a multi-level assessment in education. Comput. Educ. **51**(2), 757–775 (2008)
15. Schön, D.A.: The reflective practitioner: How professionals think in action. Basic Books, New York (1983)

Author Index

K. T. Chui et al. (Eds.): ICBL 2026, LNCS 16778, pp. 527–528, 2027.
https://doi.org/10.1007/978-981-92-3761-6

MIX
Papier aus verantwortungsvollen Quellen
Paper from responsible sources
FSC® C105338
FSC
www.fsc.org

If you have any concerns about our products,
you can contact us on
ProductSafety@springernature.com

In case Publisher is established outside the EU,
the EU authorized representative is:
Springer Nature Customer Service Center GmbH
Europaplatz 3, 69115 Heidelberg, Germany

Printed by Libri Plureos GmbH
in Hamburg, Germany